Shopping Center DealMaker's Handbook®

(See Order Form at back of this book)

Shopping Center DealMaker's Handbook®

Practical Transaction Guide with 62
Ready-to-Use Electronic Forms on Compact Disc

Bruce G. Zimmerman

Foreword by William A. Reavey, Esq.
Pillsbury, Madison & Sutro

Second Edition

For Real Estate Professionals–
Developers, Owners, Retailers, Brokers, Investors,
Asset Managers, Advisors and Attorneys

Business Source Publishing Co.®
Irvine, California

Dedicated in memory of my wife, Sharron McMullen Zimmerman

Library of Congress Catalog Card Number: 93-90557

Printed in the United States of America on acid-free paper

Cover design: Christine Milnes, Milnes Advertising

ISBN 978-1-881250-00-5 for this text only.
(A separate ISBN number was issued for the first edition of this book and each format of the previously published Forms CD.)

Publisher's Cataloging in Publication Data

Zimmerman, Bruce G.

Shopping center dealmaker's handbook: practical transaction guide with ready-to-use forms on computer CDs. Foreword by William A. Reavey, Esq. Laguna Beach, CA: Business Source Publishing Co., copyrights 1993, 1995, 2014.

Includes "Forms CD" in Microsoft Word®.

"For real estate professionals—developers, owners, retailers, brokers, investors, asset managers, advisors and attorneys."

PARTIAL CONTENTS: Purchasing an unimproved shopping center site. –Ground leasing an unimproved shopping center site. –Acquiring all or a portion of a project still under development. –Project marketing brokerage contract. –Major tenant leases. –Satellite tenant or shop leases. –Joint venturing with a financial partner. –Purchasing the stock of a company to control its real estate. –How to create and maintain a deal-making document form file system. –Index.

1. Shopping center deals. 2. Shopping center deals—Forms. 4. Shopping center deals—Forms—Computer methods—Software. 5. Real estate development—Forms—Computer methods—Software. 6. IBM PC (Computer)—Software. 7. Macintosh (Computer)—Software. 8. Letters of intent. 9. Letters of intent—Computer methods—Software. 10. Shopping centers—Leasing. 11. Shopping centers—Leasing—Forms. 12. Shopping centers—Leasing—Forms—Computer methods—Software. I. Reavey, William A. Foreword. II. Title. III. Business Source Publishing Co.

658.87 or 381.1 or 333.3387

For your convenience, an order form is included in the back of this book.

IMPORTANT NOTICE TO USERS

Please read the following IMPORTANT DISCLAIMER AND ADVISORY before making use of *Shopping Center DealMaker's Handbook*® or any of the forms contained in this book!

IMPORTANT DISCLAIMER AND ADVISORY TO USERS

SHOPPING CENTER DEALMAKER'S HANDBOOK® is a unique sourcebook of letters of intent and other preliminary or informal forms of agreement for the shopping center industry. The book is designed to be used by sophisticated users as a starting point for negotiation, a source of "editable" sample drafts, and a stimulus to creative deal making.

But there are certain important limitations on the uses of *Shopping Center DealMaker's Handbook*®, and the user is strongly cautioned to be mindful of these limitations before using the book or its Forms CD for any purpose.

Who Should Use Shopping Center DealMaker's Handbook®?

Shopping Center DealMaker's Handbook® and the accompanying Forms CD consist of materials designed to be used as a practical resource by the seasoned shopping center developer, owner, tenant, broker, leasing agent, asset manager, equity partner, or other industry professional and their attorneys.

Only a knowledgeable and experienced user should attempt to make use of these materials—and we strongly recommend that even the sophisticated user should always consult an attorney or other professional advisor *before* using these materials.

The goal of *Shopping Center DealMaker's Handbook*® is to stimulate creative deal making, not to take the place of legal or financial advice from a professional advisor.

Please keep all of the following important points in mind when using *Shopping Center DealMaker's Handbook*®!

Do Not Use the Forms in Shopping Center DealMaker's Handbook® in Place of Seeking Legal Advice

The materials contained in *Shopping Center DealMaker's Handbook®* are intended to foster and improve the deal maker's ability to conceive and articulate innovative deal structures that successfully meet the challenges of everyday circumstances. Thus, the forms you will find here are based on hypothetical, factual contexts, and the forms are offered as examples of a variety of conceivable deal structures. Do not use the Forms CD independently of the text; important comments precede each form in the book.

By their very shorthand nature, these forms cannot cover all the issues that may arise in an actual deal, and the forms do not cover each issue in detail. The forms have been edited and shortened to serve as illustrative examples, not as finished legal forms.

The author and the publisher are not engaged in rendering legal or financial advice, and the book is not intended to take the place of the services of a lawyer, accountant, or other professional. If you are looking for legal advice backed by a guarantee, consult a lawyer of your own choosing.

The user should not make use of any of these forms as a binding agreement in actual deals without first seeking appropriate legal and financial advice from a professional advisor!

Special Advisory to Attorneys

If you are an attorney or other professional who wishes to refer to *Shopping Center DealMaker's Handbook®* or the Forms CD in drafting transactional documents, you must carefully review these materials and make necessary revisions and modifications before using them for an actual transaction.

Please bear in mind that this is the second edition of *Shopping Center DealMaker's Handbook®* and the Forms CD. As of this publication the products are *not* routinely updated to take note of changes in cases, statutes, regulations, or other applicable laws. Therefore, an attorney should not rely on *Shopping Center DealMaker's Handbook®* in place of legal research, analysis, and drafting of documents.

Be Mindful of the Limited Function of a Letter of Intent

A letter of intent is, by its very nature, a succinct statement of the deal points of a given transaction. Typically, a letter of intent is used as a proposal or a starting point for negotiation, or as a confirmation of a preliminary agreement.

A letter of intent is not designed as a final binding agreement, and the forms in *Shopping Center DealMaker's Handbook*® should not be used or abstracted for that purpose.

Each of the individual clauses in a letter of intent must be fleshed out and formalized to create a formal legal agreement, and it is not unusual for a short letter of intent to be expanded into a multi-page legal document by attorneys, accountants, and other professional advisors.

The user will note that each of the forms includes a statement of the non-binding nature of the letter of intent. It is very important to speak and behave with this point clearly in mind and to refrain from any words or conduct that may be interpreted otherwise.

Nevertheless, there is a real danger that a letter of intent may be regarded as a binding legal agreement by one or both of the parties, which makes it especially important to seek professional advice before making use of these forms in any manner.

Other Sources of Information and Advice Are Available

The forms and other materials in *Shopping Center DealMaker's Handbook*® are based on information obtained from sources believed to be reliable, but their accuracy and completeness cannot be guaranteed. Despite the best efforts of author and publisher, the book may contain mistakes, and the reader should use the book only as a general guide, not as the ultimate source of information and advice about deal making. Specific prices, percentages or monetary amounts within a given form merely illustrate the form's use and should not be relied upon as evidence of current market conditions.

The book is not intended to reprint all of the information available to the author or publisher on the subject, but rather to simplify, complement, and supplement other available sources. The reader is encouraged to read all available material and to learn as much as possible about the subject.

No Warranties Are Made by Author or Publisher

By purchasing the book, you acquire a right to use the Forms CD solely in accordance with the Software License Agreement accompanying the book. Please read it carefully.

A Note about Unauthorized Copying

This work was produced from a commitment to the shopping center industry at large. This book and its Forms CD took years to produce. We believe this to be a valuable resource at a reasonable price. Please use the materials in accordance with the License and avoid the temptation to violate copyright laws by copying this work for others. Only if this second edition is a commercial success can this resource be improved and updated for the benefit of industry professionals. Thank you for your cooperation.

About the Author

Bruce G. Zimmerman is president and owner of Commercial Devco, Inc., a company formed in 1979 to develop shopping centers on a joint venture basis with financial partners. Commercial Devco, Inc. has been a member of the International Council of Shopping Centers since 1979. Mr. Zimmerman has extensive expertise in shopping center site acquisition, development, leasing, management and construction. He also has a strong background in business, tax, and estate planning. He is licensed as a California real estate broker and a California general contractor.

He received his B.A. degree from Stanford University with Distinction and Departmental Honors in Economics (1969), and his J.D. degree from the U.S.C. Law School (1972). The author practiced law until 1977. Thereafter, until the formation of Commercial Devco, Inc., he was an officer, director and equity partner with a development company engaged in shopping center and other development projects, as well as investment brokerage activities. From July 1987 through July 1989 he was an executive officer and equity partner with a major Denver-based development company, responsible for forming and directing its California Division. Thereafter, he opened a Southern California shopping center development office as an employee/equity partner with Federal Realty Investment Trust, the oldest REIT in America.

Since 1998 he has served as Senior Partner at Clarion Consulting in Irvine, California, where he has worked under contract with America's largest supermarket, drugstore and other anchor retailers. He has been responsible for upgrading and improving client anchor stores and shopping centers throughout the United States, dramatically improving the performance of client stores and creating substantial value for landlords of such shopping centers.

The author is an expert in the dynamic use of letters of intent and other preliminary or informal forms of agreement to enhance deal making competence and productivity. He is available to provide practical instruction to groups in the use of the materials contained in this book.

Bruce's professional education classes, which include strategic and practical instruction on the use of *Shopping Center DealMaker's Handbook*®, have produced dramatic productivity gains for developers, owners, retailers, brokers, asset managers and their attorneys. In fact, most participants have remarked that by using the approach and forms in this resource, transaction time from inception to completion is 30%-40% less than it would be without *Shopping Center DealMaker's Handbook*®.

Deal-Making Productivity Enhancement Seminars

The author of *Shopping Center DealMaker's Handbook*® can teach you or your organization a systematic approach to becoming resourceful, responsive and efficient negotiating and closing shopping center real estate transactions. You will learn to quickly and powerfully make effective proposals and efficiently confirm preliminary agreements covering all major deal points. You will make better, more responsive transactions faster, more professionally and easier. Seminar attendees consistently report that they negotiate much better transactions (also requiring less administrative management and legal costs) with time savings of 30%-40% per transaction. Imagine the productivity gains to your organization after only six months!

Seminar content is customized for your particular industry niche and interest. For example, developer, broker, retailer, or attorney seminars each have a specific perspective and content. Additional follow-up seminars can be designed to monitor results, answer questions that arise following the initial seminars, and focus on follow-up areas unique to your enterprise.

Bruce Zimmerman's seminar contact information:
Email: bzimmerman@ClarionConsultsUSA.com
Instagram: BRUCEZIMMERMAN_
Telephone: (949) 275-5407
FAX: (949) 852-1050

Contents in Brief

Contents

Technical and Special-Purpose Provisions

Foreword

There are three reasons to buy and use *Shopping Center DealMaker's Handbook*®. First, it satisfies a need for preliminary deal making forms. Second, its Forms CD makes it readily useable. Third, it was written by an expert who knows how shopping center deals are put together.

This book satisfies a crucial need in the real estate development industry—the need for comprehensive, easy-to-use, preliminary agreements to facilitate the deal-making process. Experienced real estate professionals know that a lot can happen between the time of the parties' initial agreement on a transaction in principle and the final, formal documentation of their understanding by attorneys. The source of the problem is that the initial understandings are generally oral with little or no supporting documentation.

Unfortunately, good documentation for the preliminary stages of a negotiation is hard to find. Often, preliminary agreements or understandings are put together by individuals with incomplete understanding of the multiple implications of their agreements. This lack of knowledge can result in vague and sometimes inherently self-contradictory term sheets. Of course, sorting out these inconsistencies and smoothing over various misunderstandings are tasks lawyers are trained to do. Lawyers glory in their ability to turn simple deals into complex volumes of paper.

However, times are changing, and so is the practice of law. Emphasis is being placed on preparing complete and comprehensive preliminary documents, not just out of consideration for trees, but also to reduce legal fees and to quicken the pace of transactions. In fact, as preliminary documents become more lucid and coherent, the parties may no longer feel the need to generate the lengthy agreements that have long been the hallmark of American legal practice. *Shopping Center DealMaker's Handbook*® is at the cutting edge of a trend toward efficiency in the management of deal making. This sourcebook provides a series of agreements that will enable the real estate professional to document deals so the parties can move forward and make commitments without incurring expensive legal fees prematurely.

Of course, *Shopping Center DealMaker's Handbook*® is no substitute for good legal advice and tax planning. The forms in this book are not intended to cover every conceivable situation or contingency. Individuals using this book should consult with attorneys and/or accountants before making substantial financial commitments. By using the forms in this book correctly, however, the practitioner will be able to present his advisors with a more thorough and completely thought out transaction, and thus reduce outside legal and accounting fees.

I'm a computer enthusiast and one of the features of *Shopping Center DealMaker's Handbook*® that I especially like is the computer Forms CD. This is an original, valuable feature that will permit the ready use of all the forms contained in the book. I know from personal experience that form books are often not employed because their use requires extensive administrative or secretarial support to put the forms on a computer system. Now, with a copy of *Shopping Center DealMaker's Handbook*®, a deal maker working alone on the road can use the forms to generate helpful, concise documents with a minimum of support.

Over the years I have worked with Bruce Zimmerman on a wide variety of transactions from retail development to corporate acquisitions. Bruce is an able draftsman and a skilled negotiator, extremely knowledgeable in all facets of the shopping center development industry. Users of *Shopping Center DealMaker's Handbook*® are certain to benefit from Bruce's diligence, his creativity, and his diverse experience.

San Diego, California

WILLIAM A. REAVEY, ESQ.

Acknowledgments

My recently-deceased wife, Sharron, and children Juli and Brian, deserve thanks for the grace with which they accepted all the time I had to work outside of normal business hours to create this book. Two individuals should be acknowledged for encouraging me to write this book. Woody Beardsley, a development assistant, and Ann Selbe, my administrative assistant, often encouraged me to make my deal making documents available in book form.

A very special acknowledgment is owed to William A. Reavey, a uniquely talented friend and partner with RSR Law Group in San Diego, California, for his insightful editorial comments and advice. But for Bill's input this work would have stopped far short of its mark. Similarly, a heartfelt thanks goes out to my friend, Mike Bean, retired real estate executive, for his dedicated editorial comments on the manuscript.

The following pre-publication reviewers are gratefully acknowledged for their analysis of and helpful comments on selected portions of the manuscript. They are, in alphabetical order:

Albert J. Auer, past president, International Council of Shopping Centers, and principal, Albert J. Auer and Associates, deceased

Howard S. Biel, principal, Senior Vice President, ECHO Real Estate Services Company

James E. Clarkson, Partner, Strategic Retail Advisors, former Senior Vice President, Retail Properties Division, Grubb & Ellis Commercial Brokerage Company

Jeff A. Dierck, Director of Real Estate, Albertson's LLC

Robert D. Exel, Partner, Center Development

James S. Fassio, President & Chief Development Officer, Ross Stores, Inc.

Harry Newman, past president, International Council of Shopping Centers, and head of Education, deceased

Raymond G. Payne, Esq., Vice President, Real Estate–West, Rite Aid Corporation

William A. Reavey, attorney at law, Partner, RSR Law Group

Malcolm R. Riley, past president, International Council of Shopping Centers, and General Partner, Malcolm Riley & Associates

Donald W.A. Smith, CSM, CPM, principal, D.W.A. Smith & Company, Inc.

A special thanks also to all the developers, tenants, brokers, managers, attorneys, consultants, and others from whom I have learned over the years. Deal making is more an art form than a science; there is no single ideal way to structure all transactions. Over time, however, we improve our skills and become more adept in responding to people's needs, creating specific structures to satisfy them, and accommodating an ever-wider range of transactions.

I also wish to acknowledge those who donate their time to the International Council of Shopping Centers, the Urban Land Institute and other real estate trade organizations and forums intended to enhance our professional skills. Without such sharing of knowledge and experience, our industry would be unable to adapt to the challenges of operating in a business environment that appears to be in a continual state of flux. I hope that this book makes a similar contribution to its readers.

OVERVIEW

Chapter 1 provides a general overview of the organization and use of the text, its deal-making forms, and the Forms CD.

Chapter 1

Introduction

Be not afraid of going slowly,
be only afraid of standing still.
–Chinese proverb

OVERVIEW

Deal making—the conception, negotiation, and closing of successful retail transactions is a demanding profession. Shopping center professionals are tested time and again by the marketplace to devise creative solutions to novel situations. Unfortunately, no one has yet offered an easy-to-use resource specifically designed to facilitate and expedite the deal-making process.

SHOPPING CENTER DEALMAKER'S HANDBOOK® is the first and only deal-making system, on both printed and magnetic media, of letters of intent and other preliminary or informal forms of agreement used in conceptualizing, structuring, and documenting shopping center development and management transactions. These forms address a chronic need among sophisticated shopping center professionals and their attorneys for an editable starting point from which to prepare proposals and confirm preliminary agreements.

Shopping Center DealMaker's Handbook® will improve your ability to be your creative best—to create and reach agreements on business points more comprehensively, more efficiently, and in less time. It will improve your ability to conceptualize appropriate deal structures; to refine, articulate, and reach agreements on major deal points; and to systematically confirm such agreements in letter format.

With this resource, the seasoned shopping center developer, owner, tenant, broker, leasing agent, asset manager, equity partner, or other industry professional and their lawyers will be able to effectively and efficiently use what I shall refer to as "deal-making documents" or "letters of intent." (The terms "deal-making documents" and "letters of intent" are used interchangeably throughout the text, and no particular significance should be attached to one term or the other.) In addition to improving your competence in drafting and using deal-making documents, this book will show you how to organize and maintain a deal-making document form file system.

The forms provided in this book and the accompanying Forms CD are user-friendly. Do not feel intimidated if you are not a skilled writer. This book is designed to help you in your everyday work. At a minimum, you can use it to outline major deal points in longhand to review later with your lawyer and those with whom you are negotiating.

Because no two deals are the same, the deal-making forms in this handbook are not sacrosanct. The forms should stimulate creative thought in an organized manner. They are meant to be changed. If you use a form for a particular transaction without much revision, you should be concerned that you may not have given the deal enough thought. Many of the forms include specific examples to stimulate thinking, which is more conducive to the learning process than a series of plain vanilla forms.[1] Delete what is not applicable and add where necessary. Your goal should be to tailor each proposal to the specific factual issues presented by each project.

The maximum benefit can be achieved by reading *Shopping Center DealMaker's Handbook*® from the beginning. However, after reading the background materials contained in Chapters 1 and 2, each of the remaining chapters stands on its own.

Chapter sequence generally follows the chronological order in which one might use the forms. For example, Chapter 2 broadly discusses the benefits of an enlightened use of deal-making documents. Chapter 3 addresses how the deal maker can share in project equities with an employer or financial partners. Subsequent chapters progress through site acquisition (both fee purchase and ground lease), the site marketing or brokerage contract, a wide array of major and satellite tenant leasing and parcel sale transactions, purchasing the stock of a company to control its real estate, joint venture development with a financial partner, and optional and alternative clauses for purchase and lease proposals.

Read Chapter 19, "How to Create and Maintain a Deal Making Document Form File System," with an open mind. It is one of the most important chapters in this book. The instructions on how to use your computer to organize previously prepared documents for future use can lead to greater efficiency and productivity in many areas of your business.

USER-FRIENDLY LAYOUT AND STRUCTURE

The book's layout is designed for ease of use. Chapter names are concise, yet the table of contents contains detailed descriptions of the sequentially numbered forms within each chapter. A thumb tab in the outside margin of each form page allows quick reference to each of the book's forms. The vertical location of the thumb tab for each form corresponds with a given chapter's

---

[1] As a courtesy to the parties whose transactions generated many of this book's forms, specific rental figures have been excluded, and actual exhibits have been omitted or disguised.

physical location within the one-page "Contents in Brief" at the beginning of the book. For example, Chapter 9, "Major Tenant Leases," is listed in about the middle of the "Contents in Brief" page; thumb tabs for the major tenant lease forms (Forms 9-1 and 9-2) are found in the same horizontal plane as the tab for Chapter 9 in the "Contents in Brief."

The left hand page preceding each chapter contains a brief chapter overview and a list of the forms in the chapter. Distinct type faces differentiate narrative text from form text. To further facilitate form use, each form is printed within a line border incorporating the number of the form and begins at the top of a right-hand page.

To ease editing and subsequent paragraph renumbering from photocopy drafts, margins are wide and optional form paragraphs are preceded by a blank line in which to insert the appropriate paragraph number. Annotations to the text of forms are italicized. (Since annotations are also included on the Forms CD, the annotations must be deleted before printing final output.)

The succinct, bold, underlined paragraph headings in each of the book's forms improve readability and function. Form headings are also boldfaced in this text. Writing deal-making documents with prominent paragraph headings has several advantages. First, specific information needed from a working (or computer) file can be quickly located to recollect key points of a previously prepared document. Second, when considering the suitability of a particular deal-making document as a possible starting point for creating a new document, the specific issues covered in the previous document are readily apparent. This simplifies making a checklist or an outline of any new sections that need to be added or created.

Third, this highlighted "outline" format supports the reader's ability to find, extract, and apply selected provisions from one form to another document. The forms also use a minimum number of consistent party name terms (e.g., "Buyer" and "Seller", "Landlord" and "Tenant"). Limiting such terms reduces the number of required global party name changes when applying selected form provisions to other documents. (The advice of a lawyer is especially important, however, when a deal-making document is prepared from selected sections of various forms.)

An Index and Appendixes are included as handy references. Chapter 17, "Optional and Alternative Clauses For Purchase and Sale Proposals," contains additional and alternative provisions that may be selectively incorporated into the preceding purchase and sale deal-making documents. Chapter 18, "Optional and Alternative Clauses For Lease Proposals," focuses on hotly negotiated issues in shopping center landlord-tenant negotiations and provides a host of clauses for selective insertion into the preceding lease deal-making documents. The book and accompanying Forms CD are designed to complement one another and to be used together, not independently.

Some forms, such as the comprehensive site purchase offer form (Form 4-1) are extremely long; others are very short. Deciding how to satisfy the demands of lawyers for precision and detail and, at the same time, satisfy developers' demands for simplicity and brevity was a constant dilemma in writing this book. The result, like most decisions, is a planned compromise.

In general, issues that are likely to be controversial or problematic are treated with greater detail. The outline format of the forms (with subheading titles leading nearly all paragraphs) allows the reader to rearrange, abbreviate, delete, and add provisions as appropriate. The overriding goal has been to create deal-making documents that foster cooperation and understanding between lawyers and non-lawyer shopping center professionals.

Every attempt has been made to make lawyers aware of key business issues and how developers typically resolve them. At the same time, non-lawyers are provided with sample language that—though far short of legal documentation—will effectively guide lawyers in preparing final transaction documents. Above all, the text and Forms CD serve as a practical starting point from which to prepare customized deal-making documents.

RELATIONSHIP BETWEEN THE BOOK AND THE FORMS CD

The forms on the Forms CD are identical to the forms in the book with the exception of certain notes that are in the book but not on the Forms CD. Although pages of the book are consecutively numbered from beginning to end, each form on the Forms CD starts at page one when printed. The form text within each form paragraph will be the same as in the book, but paragraph and page endings may not be the same in the CD version.

Follow the simple software installation instructions accompanying the Forms CD to save the forms on your computer's hard drive. Ideally, a form should be customized for the user's particular purpose and style before using the particular form for a transaction. For example, provisions rarely used could be deleted, alternative provisions most often used could be inserted, and additional provisions not included in this book could be added. Both the original and custom forms should be stored in your computer, following the directions in Chapter 19, "How to Create and Maintain a Deal Making Document Form File System." This customized prototype can then serve as your starting point for responding to new market opportunities.

YOUR COMMENTS CAN IMPROVE THIS NEW RESOURCE

Although this book is designed primarily for experienced shopping center professionals and their lawyers, it provides valuable, practical information not available elsewhere for those who require a fundamental understanding of how U.S. shopping center development transactions are structured.

The text may serve as an educational tool for consulting firms, investment firms, investors (domestic and foreign), property advisors, redevelopment agencies, city and county planning bodies, university students and others interested in a better understanding of the intricacies and possibilities of the shopping center deal-making process.

This second edition of *Shopping Center DealMaker's Handbook®* is intended to start a dialogue with our readers. We invite your comments, particularly suggestions for additional provisions and forms that would benefit other readers.

If we have erred or overlooked something we should have included, please share your thoughts with the publisher and other "DealMakers." (No; there is no typographical or capitalization error in the title; the book's purpose is to support the reader in becoming a more proficient DealMaker.) Please send your comments and suggestions to:

Bruce G. Zimmerman
Shopping Center DealMaker's Handbook®
c/o Business Source Publishing Co.
18201 Von Karman Ave., Ste. 310
Irvine CA 92612

Depending upon user interest and support, this book may be revised, updated, supplemented, and improved from time to time.

Real estate development is an exciting but difficult business. It is not for the novice or the faint of heart. Success can be ephemeral. What worked in one business cycle may not work in the next. To survive, developers need to be intelligent, flexible, and innovative—intelligent in anticipating changing market conditions, flexible in being willing to adapt to changed market conditions, and innovative in developing new strategies to respond to changed market conditions.

My purpose in writing this book is to help shopping center developers, owners, tenants, brokers, leasing agents, asset managers, equity partners, and other industry professionals and their lawyers work more cooperatively and efficiently with one another and to help *you* be one of the professionals who prospers.

OVERVIEW

Chapter 2 introduces the creative possibilities and benefits of drafting and using letters of intent and other preliminary or informal forms of agreement ("deal-making documents") to conceive, structure, and confirm transactions related to shopping center development, management, and operation. Chapter 2 also includes a brief assessment of legal standards and associated risks.

Chapter 2

The Zen of Using Deal-Making Documents

Three rules of work:
1. *Out of clutter find simplicity.*
2. *From discord make harmony.*
3. *In the middle of difficulty lies opportunity.*

—Albert Einstein

This is a book about the creative possibilities of drafting and using deal-making documents, especially letters of intent. It is not intended to be a dry discussion of legal issues. Rather, it is an attempt to help the reader skillfully frame deal points in a manner that reflects the common interests of the parties.

This resource is a pragmatic tool to help the reader become a more creative communicator in conceiving deal structures and gaining acceptance for them in a competitive marketplace. How much you get out of this book is a direct result of how willing you are to rethink your existing deal-making methods. As told in ancient Zen verse:

If you do not get it from yourself,
Where will you go for it?

This book aims to open new, creative possibilities in using deal-making documents. It's focus is communication. From an existential perspective, the "self" we create and recreate each day is a product of self-expression and dialogue. We *are* our self-expression. Self-expression and dialogue create our union with others and determine how we "show up."

Others consistently make decisions and take actions based on how we manifest ourselves in our conversations and writings. The ability to listen, persuade and attain objectives through dialogue with others is an operative skill. When viewed from this perspective, improving one's skill in creating and using deal-making documents improves one's ability to competently interact with and reach agreements with others, thereby increasing the odds that intended results will be achieved.

Although our ability to communicate determines how we show up in the marketplace, our world of business and commerce is radically changing. Alvin Toffler's influential work, *Powershift:*

Knowledge, Wealth, and Violence at the Edge of the 21st Century,[1] maintains that while current headlines focus on enormous shifts of power on a global level, there are equally significant but largely unnoticed shifts of power in our everyday world—our jobs, supermarkets, banks, the way goods and services are distributed and sold, and on and on.

His work demonstrates that many seemingly unrelated conflicts and changes are the result of a what he calls a "new system of wealth creation": knowledge—and particularly the organization of knowledge itself. "Because knowledge—including art, science, moral values, information (and misinformation)—now provides the key raw material for wealth creation, today's power struggles reach deep into our minds, psyches, and personal lives."[2]

Productive work requires information skills of an increasingly higher order. The worker's core skill is his or her ability to acquire and use information. "The wildfire spread of the computer in recent decades has been called the single most important change in the knowledge system since the invention of moveable type in the 15th century or even the invention of writing."[3]

As time becomes an increasingly valuable resource, our "power" in the marketplace will be determined by the speed with which we are able to organize and productively use an intangible: knowledge. It follows, therefore, that to consider each proposal or letter of intent you prepare an isolated event to be forgotten and ignored if not accepted, is a naive, "smokestack-age" response to the demands of the information age. What is needed is an enlightened approach, which includes, among other innovations, your own custom, computerized system of creating successful deal structures, one that meets the needs of the marketplace with sensitivity and timeliness. This will take thought and effort on your part, but once you have set up a systematic approach and trained yourself and your staff to follow it, the results will be well worth the effort.

To illustrate the benefits of the pragmatic use of deal-making documents, consider the dynamics of a typical proposed shopping center site acquisition. The dialogue usually begins as the developer and the landowner discuss the potential site acquisition. Other than a communication of the asking land price, general site information, and possibly a discussion of terms, there is often little discussion of the landowner's needs. Similarly, the landowner seldom fully understands the developer's needs. The developer makes an offer, which may trigger a counter-offer from the landowner. At some point their lawyers step in—often before all business issues have been fully negotiated.

Expensive legal involvement and documentation begin. Whether the deal falls apart or is ultimately consummated, substantial costs result from excessive

---

1 Alvin Toffler, ***Powershift: Knowledge, Wealth and Violence at the Edge of the 21st Century*** (New York: Bantam Books, 1990) (hereafter cited as *Powershift*). All references herein to *Powershift* are made with the permission of Bantam Books, New York, New York.

2 Toffler, *Powershift*, cover jacket.

3 Toffler, *Powershift*, 426-427.

or wasted attorney involvement. These costs, in some cases, may contribute to the premature death of the transaction. If the deal falls apart, who is responsible? Often the developer and broker point to the attorney as the eternal scapegoat, the "deal killer," or to the landowner who is unable to fully appreciate the proposal.

Similarly, in a lease negotiation the parties may reach an understanding on the rent, lease term, and tenant concessions, but all too often fail to refine all business issues of the deal. The parties give what information they have to the attorney to "make it all legal." The developer's attorney will be obligated to call the developer with numerous necessary questions. The developer, as a result, will be interrupted from work on new transactions. Finally, a lease proposal from the developer's attorney is presented to the tenant. The perplexed tenant says that this proposal is not what he or she had in mind. Heavy negotiation occurs again; drafts and comments go back to the attorneys, ad infinitum.

BENEFITS OF USING DEAL-MAKING DOCUMENTS

Assume, for the benefit of the parties, their attorneys, and the deal, that the developer is committed at the outset to engage in comprehensive, pragmatic dialogue resulting in negotiation of all the deal points. Suppose also that the developer prepares a comprehensive letter of intent (which typically can be accomplished in less than an hour or two) for the landowner's or tenant's review and approval. A practice of comprehensively negotiating agreements and reducing them to a preliminary writing yields the following benefits:

Initiates Movement toward Desired Results

The letter of intent in a typical real estate transaction is normally not meant to be a binding document. It is, however, an attractive means of assuring the parties that enough mutual interest and understanding exists to justify proceeding to the next step, usually binding documentation. The letter of intent provides an important planning function by providing a path to follow to get the deal done. It marks the beginning of serious negotiation and confirms a level of commitment between the parties.

The letter of intent also moves each of the parties—and other individuals within the respective business organizations—toward the desired transaction. In other words, summarizing an entire transaction in a letter creates movement toward the intended result. Also, it helps to refine the specific issues or contingencies that will have to be overcome or satisfied. The parties will begin to incur costs—such as due diligence, legal analysis, site planning, or space planning—not out of obligation to the other party, but as a reasonable business risk that an agreement will ultimately be reached. The letter of intent, therefore, is a tool to bring forth and test the interest, attention, concerns, reservations, and commitment of the other party.

Although letters of intent have traditionally been used merely to confirm a proposed transaction once negotiated, their judicious use need not be so limited. For those skilled in preparing letters of intent and mindful of the power of a request, a "proposed" letter of intent or "term sheet" could be presented for discussion early in negotiation. The response and dialogue relative to specific, proposed deal points will usually be more direct and revealing than another face-to-face discussion without a document or an agenda. This initial letter can then be edited to confirm a revised agreement.

Efficiency: Saves Time for the Deal Maker and the Deal Maker's Lawyer

The disciplined use of a letter of intent will reduce the deal maker's time and the energy required to consummate the transaction. Moreover, the deal maker's legal expense relative to the transaction should be reduced. A lawyer's time is usually more productive when used to legally document negotiated transactions. If a lawyer is instructed to take over before all deal points have been negotiated, the lawyer must first spend time to reach a comprehensive understanding of the intended transaction from the client's perspective. The transaction can be documented only after the deal points are negotiated and understood and reconfirmed through further negotiation. A disciplined letter of intent avoids yields efficiencies for both the deal maker and legal counsel.

This technique does *not* advocate acting without advice from your lawyer during negotiation. Legal counsel can be of critical importance in structuring and refining the transaction. In essence, diligently do your job, and do not "hand off" the deal to your lawyer until you have given it your best effort. And when you do, giving your lawyer a letter containing the deal points—even if the letter is not artfully done—is a big help to your lawyer. Non-lawyers should realize that skilled lawyers generally prefer to bill for legal work and appreciate a relationship where the client champions the business matters.

Adding Current Letters of Intent to Your Computerized Form File Improves Future Efficiency

Each deal-making document you prepare should be filed away in an efficiently organized, computerized form file. The next time you need to create a land purchase proposal, parcel sale, lease proposal, or similar document, you will spend less time because you will have a selection of applicable proposal formats from which to work. (In Chapter 19 you will learn an easy and efficient method of systematically creating and maintaining your own computerized deal-making document form file.)

Future Recurring Administrative Benefits

From a management or administrative perspective, particularly when more than one staff member is involved in consummating the transaction, having a written memorandum of understanding conveniently confirms the intentions of the parties in one concise document. Staff secretaries, construction personnel, leasing agents, and others may refer to this writing while they do their respective jobs. Using this document as a communication aid among staff can result in fewer interruptions, allowing the deal maker to productively concentrate on the next deal. In some cases I have even used the letter of intent as a starting point for summarizing property management standards to a property management department.

Writing a Deal-Making Document Fosters Critical Thinking

Forcing yourself to reduce a deal structure to writing compels you to identify areas of unclear thinking and to clean up and refine incomplete deal points. Addressing the difficult issues and areas where problems are likely to arise saves time and money in the long run. Having in hand a proposal from a previous deal that resembles the proposed transaction makes it much easier to ask yourself, "What haven't I covered? What should be in this proposal that wasn't in the last one?" Having an organized form file of transactions of a similar type helps you to be at your creative best.

Creates a Favorable impression

A well-thought-out, professionally prepared proposal or letter of intent demonstrates that you know what you are doing and instills confidence and credibility even though the reader may be unwilling to accept the proposal as written. For example, an anchor tenant is more likely, upon receipt of such a developer proposal (accompanied, of course, by consistent first-class performance in all other areas of the relationship) to want to deal with the developer now and in the future.

Accelerates Early Focus on Critical Issues

Engaging in full dialogue with the landowner or tenant from the beginning and producing an initial letter of intent early in negotiations accelerate results. Assume, for example, that a particular issue, such as a developer's desire to substantially limit the tenant's assignment rights under the lease, is of critical importance to the developer. The early negotiation of this issue could save the developer and the tenant wasted time and effort, particularly if the issue may be a "deal breaker" for the tenant.

Creates a Competitive Advantage

Especially in situations where a developer is in competition for a specific development opportunity, success may hinge in large part upon the decision-maker's assessment of the developer's written proposal. For example, in redevelopment projects or other competitive-bid situations where numerous developers are competing, a comprehensive, professionally prepared proposal can give a developer a distinct advantage. Often the decision will be based in large part upon the developer's written proposal. However, the best developers are not necessarily the most adept at reducing their proposals to writing. For the smaller, less heavily capitalized developer, excelling in the ability to quickly and professionally prepare such proposals may be a significant advantage leading to increased market share. Similarly, having a comprehensive letter of intent signed with a major tenant (even if not legally binding) may be the key to securing a timely loan.

In summary, cultivating skill in preparing deal-making documents consistent with the approaches outlined in this book will ultimately result in more creative transactions, more comprehensive and professional proposals and letters of intent, speedier consummation of transactions, an improved and more resourceful attorney-client interface, and, ultimately, a substantial reduction in transaction costs.

RISKS IN USING DEAL-MAKING DOCUMENTS

Even though these principles are not easily learned, if you are committed and diligent, you can ultimately master the techniques described in this book. However, blind use of letters of intent will not in any way insure success. In fact, there are times when it is not in your best interests to put together a letter of intent.

Be pragmatic and do not feel compelled to draft a letter of intent for every deal. Producing more paper does not necessarily make you a better developer. An ability to effectively create and use deal-making documents is merely one of an arsenal of tools that will make you a better communicator and, consequently, a more effective real estate professional. The choice of when and whether or not to use the tool is always yours. The purpose of this book is to assist you in mastering your own ability to skillfully prepare and use deal-making documents.

The advantages of using a letter of intent to confirm major deal points and generate commitment should be evident, but caution is in order. There is some risk under current case law that a letter of intent could possibly be considered an enforceable contract (supporting a claim for breach of contract damages or specific performance), even if the parties did not intend to be bound when the letter was signed. Tort liability (and punitive damages) is conceivable in the event of a bad faith denial that a contract existed or for breach of the implied covenant of good faith and fair dealing. Recent case law has articulated a duty to negotiate in good faith (which duty may arise before consummation of a binding contract between the parties). Similar to a condition precedent, where performance under a contract is conditioned upon the satisfaction of one of the parties, the other party is under a good faith duty not to interfere with the occurrence of the condition. Work with your lawyer in understanding how these risks can be avoided through appropriate documentation, supervision, and guidance.

Although you and your lawyer will generally clearly state within the letter of intent that no binding agreement is intended, be absolutely certain that your conduct and communications are consistent with your written intentions. Speak and behave scrupulously consistent with the manifested non-binding intent of the letter. Refrain from comments, such as "the deal's done," or from press releases that could evidence an intent to be bound, notwithstanding language to the contrary in the letter.

Do not treat the letter of intent as the final documentation of the transaction. Insist, instead, on complete documentation. Manage the transaction and see that it is promptly taken through final, binding documentation. Accept money, transfer possession, commence improvements, and the like only pursuant to completed, final, binding documentation.

For example, in a case in which a letter of intent expressly anticipated execution of a formal lease but none was prepared, allowing a tenant to take possession, make leasehold improvements and pay rent under the letter of intent was held to constitute an intention to create a binding contract.[4] Consider also the following cautionary language from the California Supreme Court in reviewing an ambiguous agreement:

> It is well-settled law that, although an agreement may be indefinite or uncertain in its inception, subsequent performance by the parties under the agreement will cure this defect and render it enforceable. When one party performs under the contract and the other party accepts his performance without objection it is assumed that this was the performance contemplated by the agreement.[5]

If a dispute arises, the letter's language, the factual context surrounding its negotiation, and subsequent conduct and communications of the parties will determine whether a court will find a binding agreement. In determining whether a contract exists, the test is whether the parties outwardly manifested an agreement to be mutually bound on definite terms. Internal or subjective thoughts are not determinative. Nevertheless, it is not sufficient to merely state in the letter of intent that it is not intended to be a binding agreement. The parties' conduct, particularly partial performance, can indicate an intent to be bound even if the letter of intent contains contrary language.

If a non-binding agreement is intended:

- make such intention clear in negotiations;
- specifically provide in the letter of intent that it is not intended to be a binding agreement;
- recite that significant additional issues remain to be negotiated (ideally, giving examples of such issues);
- state that any agreement between the parties is conditioned upon execution of formal, final documentation between the parties; and
- give a specific time frame in which to complete final documentation and negate any duty to continue negotiations if negotiations break down or the date is reached without a final agreement.

Provide for a reasonable, specific time period in which to negotiate a binding agreement and stick to it. If that time passes without the consummation of a binding agreement, make clear in any subsequent negotiations that al-

[4] *City of Santa Cruz v. MacGregor*, 178 Cal. App. 2d 45 (1960).

[5] *Bohman v. Berg*, 54 Cal. 2d 787, 794-95 (1960).

though you have elected to continue good faith discussions you are, nevertheless, not bound to any agreement and may unilaterally elect to suspend further negotiations. If, in a particular situation, you believe you are dealing with a potentially litigious party, consider circulating an unsigned "term sheet" labeled "for discussion purposes only" or proceeding directly to a definitive agreement.

If approval from a board of directors is a condition of the deal, always acknowledge the need for any required intermediate officer or committee approvals before any obligation will arise to submit the matter for board approval. Sometimes a transaction may not be submitted for board approval because it was turned down at intermediate approval levels. Where an agreement is conditioned upon obtaining board approval, failure to request board approval has been held to be a breach of an implied covenant of good faith and fair dealing implicit in all contracts.

In summary, although case law provides examples of letters of intent that became binding contracts, risks of unwanted enforceability can be overcome by unambiguous drafting and diligent work to implement the letter of intent. Speak the truth, be consistent, and attempt in good faith to consummate the transaction within the agreed time. Be ever mindful that your writings, speech, and conduct will be judged by what you manifest to the other party—not by what you subjectively think or intend.

Ponder what the other party would reasonably, rationally conclude based upon your communications or conduct. Confirm that the other party's perceptions are consistent with your intent. If your performance is conditioned upon approval of your board of directors, seek board approval. If intermediate approvals will be required, tell the other party, restate the obligation as a contingency in your letter of intent, and seek each such intermediate approval on a timely basis. Most legal problems in this area are the result of inattention, failing to manage the negotiation to completion, and neglect in providing what the other party reasonably expected and relied upon.

NONE OF THE FORMS IN THIS BOOK SHOULD BE USED WITHOUT CAREFUL THOUGHT AND EDITING ON YOUR PART

Although most of the forms will require substantial editing, some may require only modest editing. A few forms are only examples of a specific principle or technique and are not designed for direct reuse. In some cases, land prices, rents, or specific information have been included to make the form more understandable or to illustrate a specific principle. In such cases, it was deemed more beneficial to include those items to make the purpose clear rather than to provide a skeletal form with uncertain application. Again, specific prices, percentages, or monetary amounts within a given form merely illustrate the form's use and should not be relied upon as evidence of current market conditions.

With your computer's delete key, you can easily remove unwanted material and add new language to meet the standards and guidelines established by your legal counsel. Above all, with the aid of Chapter 19, "How To Create and Maintain a Deal-Making Document Form File System," you can create your own systematic approach to retain, organize, and recreate deal-making documents consistent with your company's own practice and style.

Welcome to the enlightened world of deal-making documents. Aware and disciplined to meet the challenge, may the organization be with you.

OVERVIEW

Chapter 3 covers the formation and termination of an employment and partnership arrangement between a substantial developer and an executive retained to establish and manage a division development office. Form 3-1 provides an agreement whereby the executive receives salary, an equity participation in division projects, and a non-recourse draw secured by project equities. The form highlights the complexities and alternative deal structures relative to the allocation of operating expenses and project revenues in a multi-state context. The multi-state format facilitates discussion of many potential problems and potential solutions. However, Form 3-1 can readily be amended to serve the single-office developer.) Form 3-2 addresses the termination and dissolution of the relationship created in Form 3-1.

FORMS

3-1 Employee Equity Participation. Employment and Project Equity Participation Agreement for an Individual Forming and Managing a Local Development Division for a Major Out-Of-State Developer.

3-2 Termination of Employment and Equity Participation. Letter of Resignation Confirming Agreement Terminating Employment and Settling Developer and Employee-Partner's Accrued Project/Partnership Rights.

Chapter 3

Project Equity Participation by Employees of a Developer

Make your bargain before beginning to plough.
—Ancient proverb

Key development executives or "deal makers" responsible for initiating and overseeing the development of company projects are typically compensated in some incentive arrangement designed to compensate them commensurate with the value they create. Although there are substantial differences in the weighting or preferences toward any one item, the components of a deal maker's compensation package usually can be reduced to three major elements:

- salary and bonus;
- equity participation in company projects ("project equity"); and
- a draw secured by project equities.

Usually of significantly lesser importance, except in more institutionalized or public companies, is the deal maker's participation in company profit-sharing plans and company stock-option programs.

Form 3-1 was derived from a letter agreement establishing an executive "deal maker" partnership relationship between an individual developer experienced in a local market and a large out-of-state developer desiring to open a local development division. The form contemplates that a pension fund, real estate investment trust, major life insurance company, or similar entity will be the long-term financial partner of the out-of-state developer. The form also contemplates that the local partner will receive a salary, project equity participation in local projects, and a non-recourse draw (with, it is hoped, tax advantages) secured by the local partner's project equities. The out-of-state developer supplies all working capital to establish and maintain the local operation.

As noted in the text of Form 3-1, formulating an appropriate structure to fairly allocate and pay the overhead burden—particularly in a multi-state operating context—requires careful understanding, planning, and foresight by both the out-of-state developer and the local partner. Both the out-of-state developer and the local employee/partner should seek legal and accounting advice, particularly in the drafting of the revenue-sharing and cost-allocation provisions of such an employer-employee "venture." Both parties should realize at the outset that each may be unaccustomed to the other's customary business practices, operating style, and culture.

Initial and continuing dialogue should focus on refining the operative revenue- and cost-sharing formulas negotiated between the parties. In essence, although the parties must negotiate binding agreements and be committed, each must realize that such a venture is really an "experiment" and be willing to pragmatically adjust operating methods as a result of the parties' joint experience in the market. In the absence of such openness, and if regular accountings are not provided or misunderstandings are not promptly discussed and resolved, the relationship will be in jeopardy.

Paragraph 6 of Form 3-1 contains two separate alternative provisions for the allocation of local administrative overhead, home office administrative expense applicable to local operations and the repayment of the local partner's draw. Neither of these provisions may fit many situations, but they highlight relevant issues and should provoke your independent thought. What revenues are to be shared and how? What are the various anticipated costs to be incurred? How is each to be paid back (out of whose share of which revenues)? How can the developer and local partner implement a rational, systematic, and objective overhead-allocation method that is fair to both parties and appropriately balances the needs of each for control over costs?

Form 3-1 raises some of the most difficult issues addressed in this book. Skilled legal and accounting will be necessary to create an operative agreement. Furthermore, although the form addresses a multi-state operating context, Form 3-1 can readily be amended to provide for employment and project equity participation by an employee of a single-office developer. It can also be amended to fit a wide variety of business relationships and deal structures.

As this is the first of some complex forms contained within this book, a comment on the form's organization is in order. To improve comprehension and facilitate editing, descriptive definitional clauses such as "Direct Project Costs", "Local Administrative Overhead", "Home Office Expense", "Project Payout", and the like, are adopted in the form. Such concepts were created to facilitate an overall logical structure and to support effective editing. For example, by carefully amending such definitions, new deal structures can be created more easily than by starting from scratch. The reader is invited to similarly create appropriate concepts in preparing proposals.

Close attention should be paid to what is and what is not included within each of these definitional categories. By carefully redefining these various categories, adding additional provisions and amending the form for logical consistency, you should be well on your way to negotiating a customized deal structure. Stylistically, the agreement is a letter from the new local partner to the employing developer.

Two alternative versions of Paragraph 6 are included to present the issue of developer reimbursement for administrative and project costs. Many deal makers will have limited experience negotiating such issues. Therefore, first read the notes preceding Alternatives "A" and "B," then read the commentary and example following "Alternative "B." Next, scan the text of both Alternatives "A" and "B." Having a broad familiarity with the issues will help when you proceed to carefully read the texts of these alternatives. This is probably the only material in this book that will require such careful reading.

Form 3-1 is not entirely neutral. A form that favors the development company would be much briefer and avoid the issues and nuances outlined below for which the local partner has great concern. Unfortunately, however admirable such a developer-oriented form might be, it would have limited audience appeal.

Form 3-1

FORM 3-1

Employment and Project Equity Participation Agreement for an Individual Forming and Managing a Local Development Division for a Major Out-of-State Developer

Agreement in Letter Format from New Local Employee-Partner to Employing Multi-State Developer

[Date]

[Officer of multi-state developer "Developer" ________________

____

[Address] ____________________ *]*

Dear ______________:

This letter will confirm our mutual understanding that __*[name of development company]*__("Developer") is forming a real estate development entity in the state of __*[e.g., Texas]*__ (the "Local Division") to develop __*[e.g., neighborhood and community shopping centers in Texas]*__. Developer may also elect to undertake other commercial, industrial, or mixed-use projects through the Local Division. Developer has substantial financial, construction and development capabilities that it will commit to __*[e.g., Texas]*__. This letter will confirm the essential terms by which I will manage, subject to Developer's direction, the Local Division:

> ***Note:** For ease of reference, "Texas" is used throughout this form for readability purposes since accounting distinctions concerning home office vs. local office expense could become confusing if no state name was selected. The state name can be globally changed by your word processing program.*

1. Duties. I will be the __*[specify title, e.g., President]*__ *OR* __*[Vice President of Development]*__ of the Local Division. I will identify potential development sites and opportunities and manage Developer's Texas operations, including the development, marketing, and lease-up of Developer's Projects (defined below) in Texas.

2. Commencement. After __*[describe events or engagements that require completion before start of employment]*__, I anticipate that I will be available for exclusive, full-time work not later than __*[month/year]*__. I will start earlier, however, if possible. For convenience, the actual date I am able to actually commence work for Developer is referred to hereafter as the "Start Date."

3. Developer's Commitment. Developer will supply the working capital required to establish and maintain the Local Division and advance the necessary seed money to option properties and begin marketing and processing potential projects prior to formation of development ventures with third party financial partners. Developer will form an arrangement with an institutional financial joint venture partner (such as __*[e.g., name of the pension fund, real estate investment trust ("REIT"), life insurance company or similar entity]*__ ("Joint Venture Financial Partner") whereby the Joint Venture Financial Partner will contribute its guarantee to secure financing or fund the required equity capital for each project, typically in return for a __*[e.g., 50]*__ % equity interest.

4. Compensation and Partner Loan. Commencing on the Start Date, Developer will pay me $__________ per __*[month/year]*__ as salary. I will also be loaned $___________ per __*[month/year]*__ (the "Partner Loan"). Such Partner Loan shall be non-recourse and repayable only out of the proceeds of a "Project Payout," as described below. The Partner Loan shall accrue interest at the rate of __ % per annum. The Partner Loan shall be repaid as provided in Paragraph __*[6]*__, below. Salary and the Partner Loan shall be payable in equal semi-monthly installments.

5. Partnership Interests. In each escrow, acquisition, investment, development project, partnership, venture, __*[fee for services contract (between Developer, as a provider of services, and a third party),]*__

> *See note preceding Alternative "A" for Paragraph 6 before using the preceding italicized phrase with Alternative "A" for Paragraph 6.*

or any other business activity which Developer undertakes anywhere in Texas during the term of my employment ("Project" or "Projects"), I will receive a __ % carried __*[e.g., limited partnership]*__ interest (hereinafter "Project Sharing Interest") in all Developer's beneficial capital, profits, and losses of each such Project __*[, subject to the provision on "Project Losses" contained in]*__ __*[e.g., Paragraph 6.3.3 (See Alternative "A" to Paragraph 6)* OR *Paragraph 6.5.3 (See Alternative "B" to Paragraph 6), below]*__. My Project Sharing Interest shall be subject to dilution on the same basis the total interest of Developer in the Project is diluted by the Joint Venture Financial Partner's interest, i.e., the Joint Venture Financial Partner typically receiving a __*[e.g., 50]*__ % interest.

Add the following sentence to the end of the preceding paragraph if you select the Alternative "A" version of Paragraph 6:
However, I will not participate in Developer's receipt of any normal and customary Project overhead reimbursement fee which the Joint Venture Financial Partner typically advances to Developer as a joint venture reimbursement for construction management, overhead expense, property management and the like.

I will have no personal obligation or risk of loss as a result of holding any such Project Sharing Interest, except that the equity value of any specific Project Sharing Interest held in partnership could be lost in whole or in part as a result of (i) losses experienced by that particular Project partnership or (ii) dilutions resulting from failure of the Project partnership to meet capital calls. Developer shall cause to be prepared for my signature a specific partnership agreement for each specific Project after major tenant documentation is completed, entitlements appear reasonably certain, or the Project otherwise appears viable.

Two alternative versions of Paragraph 6 are included to present the issue of Developer reimbursement for administrative and Project costs. These two alternative versions of Paragraph 6 highlight the potential diversity and complexity (especially in a multi-state context) of possible operating formats.

Alternative "A"—Paragraph 6
Developer pays or absorbs all Local Administrative Overhead; local partner's Project Sharing Interest is not responsible for operating overhead attributable to local operations. As drafted, this provision is not applicable to transactions for which the Developer will receive development fees without equity participation.

The following Alternative "A" to Paragraph 6 assumes that Developer receives 100% of all Project overhead reimbursement fees advanced by Developer's Joint Venture Financial Partner, pays all office administrative overhead obligations, and has no charge or lien on local Projects other than the right to be reimbursed out of the local partner's specific Project Sharing Interest for the "Partner Loan" [referenced in Paragraph 4], as Local Division revenues are received. Briefly, Developer receives 100% of the Project overhead reimbursement advanced by the Joint Venture Financial Partner in return for paying all Local Division administrative costs (other than the Partner Loan, which is repaid out of the local partner's Project Sharing Interest at "Project Payout").

Alternative "A" is most appropriate for projects in which the Developer has an equity participation. If the Developer is developing a project on a fee basis, thought should be given to modifying the definition of Project Payout in Section 6.3 below in order to define net development fees. Perhaps Alternative "B" below would be better suited for a fees only development project. (Alternative "B" charges the local partner's Project Sharing Interest with a prorata share of the Developer's overhead. Therefore, under Alternative "B", the overhead attributable to a fee project would be charged against the local partner's Project Sharing Interest in the same manner as other Projects.)

To avoid possible confusion, Alternative "A" has been drafted to be applicable only to an equity project. Major revisions would be required to adapt it for a project from which the Developer will receive only fee income.

On a fee project, the project owner would probably pay all Direct Project Costs, and the Developer would pay its Local Administrative Overhead and other overhead expenses such as Home Office Expense (as defined in Alternative "B"). To simplify matters, it is suggested that these other overhead expenses be expressed as a percentage of Local Administrative Overhead, e.g., 10%. The local partner would receive his or her prorata share of the development fees, less a specified percentage [e.g., 110%] of Local Administrative Costs.

6. Calculation of Project Costs and Developer's Cost Reimbursement Right. Only Direct Project Costs (as defined below) may be charged to Texas Projects. Developer shall not charge any Texas Project any Local Administrative Overhead (as defined below).

6.1 Direct Project Costs. "Direct Project Costs" are those out-of-pocket costs payable by Developer to third parties for goods or services provided to a specific Project and shall be charged to Texas Projects as such costs are incurred. Direct Project Costs may be collected only from the subject Project for which such cost was incurred. Direct Project Costs not reimbursed from the subject Project may not be reimbursed from any other Project. I shall pay my prorata share of Direct Project Costs from my prorata share of any Project Payout.

6.2 Local Administrative Overhead. "Local Administrative Overhead" as used herein shall refer to Developer's out-of-pocket cost in maintaining Developer's Texas office. Local Administrative Overhead shall include all salaries, personnel expense, benefits, office rent and related expenses of maintaining the Texas office, including my salary, but shall not include the Partner Loan. I shall not be responsible for paying any Local Administrative Overhead.

FORM 3-1

6.3 Project Payout. "Project Payout" shall mean the difference between a Project's Gross Proceeds (as defined below) and Allocated Costs (as defined below). Project Payout will be determined on a __*[Project-by-Project basis]*__ OR __*[insert some other agreed basis]*__.

> ***Note:*** *Determining Project payout on a project-by-project basis will prevent losses from one project being used to offset profits on successful projects. As used here, Project Payout is assumed to be a single event resulting from a major capital transaction; i.e., a loan or sale. If the parties intend to hold a project and share cash flow from operations on a continuing basis, thought should be given to adding a separate paragraph to deal with that contingency. Such a paragraph could be entitled "Operating Income." This form does not include such a paragraph.*
>
> *The reason for making a distinction regarding operating income is that it is likely to be received at regular intervals over time, not at a single moment in time. Care should be given in defining net operating income. How it is paid out and what expenses are applied to it are very different. However, by the time operating income is received, procedures for distributing net operating income will be more fully described in final transaction documents (e.g., the specific partnership agreement for a given Project).*

6.3.1 Gross Proceeds. "Gross Proceeds" means the total gross proceeds resulting from:

(i) The net proceeds of a Project financing, e.g., a permanent (take-out) loan for each Project's construction loan, or a subsequent refinancing of an existing permanent loan (hereafter, collectively, "Take-Out Financing");

(ii) The proceeds of any sale of a Project, in whole or part, remaining after payment of loans encumbering the subject Project; and

(iii) Any other proceeds or consideration which is capital in nature.

6.3.2 Allocated Costs. "Allocated Costs" means Direct Project Costs, but not Local Administrative Overhead.

> ***Note:*** *Not all projects are profitable. Therefore, thought should be given to the following provision:*

6.3.3 Project Losses. I will not be obligated to contribute cash to any Project. If the determination of Project Payout yields a negative number, Developer shall be solely responsible for contributing all cash or other consideration to cover any shortfalls resulting from a sale or loan transaction.

For benefit of local partner:

6.3.4 Exchanges. In no event shall I be obligated to participate in a tax deferred exchange of real property interests which would delay or defer the receipt of my share of Project Payout. If Developer elects to engage in a tax deferred exchange, provision shall be made to pay me my prorata share of the Project Payout at the time the exchange is consummated.

6.4 Payment of Project Payout. The proceeds of a Project Payout shall be paid on a Project-by-Project basis no later than ___ days after the funding of a Take-Out Financing, the closing of a sale of a Project, in whole or part, or the closing of any other transaction yielding consideration which is capital in nature.

6.5 Repayment of Partner Loan at Project Payout. Out of each Project Payout, prior to any distribution to me, Developer shall have the right to charge my Project Sharing Interest in an amount sufficient to repay the then outstanding accrued balance of the Partner Loan advanced pursuant to Paragraph __*[4]*__. Developer shall be solely responsible for the payment of all Local Administrative Overhead. Other than Developer's right at Project Payout to be paid the then outstanding Partner Loan balance, Developer shall have no other charge or lien against my Project Sharing Interest for Local Administrative Overhead or Direct Project Costs or otherwise. If proceeds of a final Project Payout are not sufficient to pay the Partner Loan, the unpaid balance will be forgiven.

> ***Note:*** *The parties can negotiate whether the Partner Loan is either a project expense to be taken into account in computing Project Payout or an advance payment of the local partner's share of Project Payout. Under Alternative "A", the Partner Loan is treated as the latter.*

Alternative "B"—Paragraph 6
Local partner's Project Sharing Interest charged with prorata share of Local Administrative Overhead and Home Office Expense

Like the preceding Alternative "A" to Paragraph 6, the following Alternative "B" assumes that Developer receives the development overhead reimbursement fees advanced by Developer's Joint Venture Financial Partner and advances all Local Administrative Overhead. In Alternative "B", however, Developer may charge local Projects with a "Net Overhead Charge" consisting of (i) the Local Division's "Local Administrative Overhead", i.e., salaries, office expense and other direct administrative costs of maintaining local operations, (ii) "Home Office Expense"; i.e., Developer's home office administrative overhead attributable to the Local Division's operations; and (iii) the cost of the Partner Loan (Paragraph 4). However, charges (i) through (iii) are offset or reduced by the developer overhead reimbursement fees received by Developer from the Joint Venture Financial Partner. Therefore, unlike the preceding version of this Paragraph 6, there is no separate charge or lien for repayment of the Partner Loan out of the local partner's specific Project Sharing Interest—the Partner Loan is treated, in effect, like any other office administrative expense item.

As noted above, Alternative "B" is better suited to accommodate projects for which the Developer will receive fee income because it more readily permits the parties to account for the expenses needed to compute net fee income.

FORM 3-1

6. Calculation of Project Costs and Developer's Cost Reimbursement Right. Direct Project Costs (as defined below) shall be charged to Texas Projects as such costs are incurred. Developer may charge Texas Projects with a Net Overhead Charge (including Local Administrative Overhead and Home Office Expense) at Project Payout (as defined below).

6.1 Direct Project Costs. "Direct Project Costs" are those out-of-pocket costs payable by Developer to third parties for goods or services provided to a specific Project and shall be charged to Texas Projects as such costs are incurred. Direct Project Costs may be collected only from the subject Project for which such cost was incurred. Direct Project Costs not reimbursed from the subject Project may not be reimbursed from any other Project. I shall pay my prorata share of Direct Project Costs from my prorata share of any

Project Payout.

6.2 Local Administrative Overhead. "Local Administrative Overhead" as used herein shall refer to Developer's out-of-pocket cost in maintaining Developer's Texas office. Local Administrative Overhead shall include all salaries, personnel expense, benefits, office rent and related expenses of maintaining the Texas office, including my salary, but shall not include the Partner Loan.

6.3 Home Office Expense. "Home Office Expense" shall mean a systematic, rational, and consistently applied allocation of fixed and variable costs of Developer's home office expenditures applicable to Texas Projects and investigations of potential Projects. Developer shall account for inter-company charges for salaries, payroll taxes, insurance, other benefits, travel, professional services, building rent and other office operating expenses, such that the Texas division is burdened only by its net fair share of actual overhead expense attributable to administrative and management support of Texas operations.

__*[Within 60 days following each calendar quarter]*__, Developer shall calculate and provide me with an accounting of Home Office Expense for the preceding __*[quarter]*__ together with an accounting of total, accrued to date Home Office Expense. We will review and approve each such accounting within 30 days of my receipt thereof. The specific, initial methodology used to calculate Home Office Expense shall be summarized by Developer's independent accountants prior to execution of this agreement and shall be attached hereto as Exhibit "A" and entitled the "Policy Statement For Allocation of Home Office Expense to Texas Projects" ("Policy Statement"). The Policy Statement shall be subject to review and revision concurrent with each such accounting review period to insure that the Policy Statement continuously and fairly allocates Developer's Home Office Expense to Texas operations. Among other things the Policy Statement shall provide that __*[include any specific provisions the parties agree should be included in the Policy Statement, e.g., in allocating home office personnel charges to Texas operations, Developer shall use home office personnel time allocations actually used in determining Developer's inter-company charges among all Developer's home office departments and multi-state operating units]*__.

> ***Note:*** *Obviously the foregoing procedures for computing Home Office Expense are somewhat complicated. Their implementation could become tedious and time-consuming. Therefore, the parties may elect to express Home Office Expense as a simple percentage of*

Local Administrative Overhead, e.g., 10 or 15%.

6.4 Net Overhead Charge. "Net Overhead Charge" shall mean the accrued, outstanding balance of the Local Administrative Overhead, Home Office Expense and the Partner Loan. In other words, to calculate the "Net Overhead Charge" at any moment in time, the sum of Local Administrative Overhead, Home Office Expense and the Partner Loan shall be reduced by the following offsets: (i) the full amount of Net Overhead Charge previously reimbursed to or otherwise recaptured by Developer from prior Texas Project Payouts, (ii) fees which Developer receives as a development partner or venturer for development services, construction management, overhead reimbursement, property management and the like payable by its Joint Venture Financial Partner or third parties on Texas Projects and (iii) any other revenues or fees which Developer earns on Texas sites or Projects. If the parties develop multiple Projects, Net Overhead Charge will be allocated among the various Projects as follows: __*[describe]*__.

FORM 3-1

Note: *In Alternative "B", the accrued, outstanding balance of the Partner Loan is included within "Net Overhead Charge". The Partner Loan is repaid to Developer, in effect, like an administrative cost of Texas operations (though technically excluded from the definition of "Local Administrative Overhead") rather than as a specific charge repayable in full out of the local partner's Project Sharing Interest (as in the Alternative "A" example). In completing the blank at the end of Paragraph 6.4, the parties need to decide whether each Project will stand alone or whether profits and losses from all Projects will be aggregated.*

6.5 Project Payout. "Project Payout" shall mean the difference between a Project's Gross Proceeds (as defined below) and Allocated Costs (as defined below). Project Payout will be determined on a __*[Project-by-Project basis]*__ OR __*[insert some other agreed basis]*__.

Note: *Determining Project payout on a project-by-project basis will prevent losses from one project being used to offset profits on successful projects. As used here, Project Payout is assumed to be an event resulting in a major capital transaction (i.e., a loan or a sale), the receipt of an overhead reimbursement from Developer's Joint Venture Financial Partner, or the receipt of fee income pursuant to a services contract. If the parties intend to hold a project and share cash flow from operations on a continuing basis, thought should be given to adding a separate paragraph to deal with that* *contingency. Such a paragraph could be entitled "Operating Income." This form does not include such a paragraph.*

The reason for making a distinction regarding operating income is that it is likely to be received at regular intervals over time, not at a single moment in time. Care should be given in defining net operating income. How it is paid out and what expenses are applied to it are very different. However, by the time operating income is received, procedures for distributing net operating income will be more fully described in final transaction documents (e.g., the specific partnership agreement for a given Project).

6.5.1 Gross Proceeds. "Gross Proceeds" means the total gross proceeds resulting from:

(i) Project overhead reimbursement from Developer's Joint Venture Financial Partner for each Texas Project;

(ii) The net proceeds of a Project financing, e.g., a permanent (take-out) loan for each Project's construction loan, or a subsequent refinancing of an existing permanent loan (hereafter, collectively, "Take-Out Financing");

(iii) Development fees earned by the Local Division pursuant to a services contract for development services provided by Developer to third parties on specific Projects ("Fee Projects"); and

(iv) The proceeds of any sale of a Project, in whole or part, remaining after payment of loans encumbering the subject Project; and

(v) Any other proceeds or consideration received with respect to any Texas Projects __*[e.g., other than Project operating income]*__.

Note: *"Gross Proceeds" is defined more broadly in Alternative "B." In particular, items "(i)" and "(iii)" are significant proceeds not included in "Project Payout" in Alternative "A." See preceding note regarding operating income.*

6.5.2 Allocated Costs. "Allocated Costs" means the sum of Direct Project Costs and Net Overhead Charge.

Note: *Compare this version of "Allocated Costs" to the version contained in Alternative "A" as Paragraph 6.3.2.*

Note: *Not all projects are profitable. Therefore, thought should be given to the following provision:*

6.5.3 Project Losses. I will not be obligated to contribute cash to any Project. If the determination of Project Payout yields a negative number, Developer shall be solely responsible for contributing all cash or other consideration to cover any shortfalls resulting from a sale or loan transaction.

FORM 3-1

For benefit of local partner:

6.5.4 Exchanges. In no event shall I be obligated to participate in a tax deferred exchange of real property interests which would delay or defer the receipt of my share of Project Payout. If Developer elects to engage in a tax deferred exchange, provision shall be made to pay me my prorata share of the Project Payout at the time the exchange is consummated.

6.6 Payment of Project Payout. The proceeds of a Project Payout shall be paid on a Project-by-Project basis no later than ___ days after the funding of a Take-Out Financing, the receipt of payment on a Fee Project, the closing of a sale of a Project, in whole or part, or the closing of any other transaction yielding any other proceeds or consideration for the subject Project. Proceeds included within the definition of Project Payout which are received before the Project Payout is actually distributed (e.g., Project overhead reimbursement or development fees), shall be used to reduce the principal balance of any loan against the subject Project.

Commentary regarding application of Alternatives "A" and "B" for Paragraph 6:

Application of the alternative approaches outlined in Alternatives "A" and "B" can result in substantially different results depending upon relative assumed values for the projected or accrued Partner Loan, Local Administrative Overhead, and Home Office Expense. The following hypothetical example, which illustrates the operative financial results of Alternatives "A" and "B" to the local partner, demonstrates the potential effects of the two approaches. Different outcomes would result if the numerical assumptions were changed.

Assume, for example, that the local partner's Project Sharing Interest was 25% and that a Project Payout of $500,000 occurred when the Partner Loan was $50,000. Other assumed figures are set forth in the table below.

	Alternative "A"	*Alternative "B"*
1. GROSS PROCEEDS	*$1,000,000*	*$1,000,000*
Overhead Reimbursement by Financial Partner	*N.A.*	*$250,000*
Subtotal of Item 1	*$1,000,000*	*$1,250,000*
2. LESS ALLOCATED COSTS		
a. Direct Project Costs	*($500,000)*	*($500,000)*
b. Local Administrative Overhead	*N.A.*	*($100,000)*
c. Home Office Expense	*N.A.*	*($25,000)*
d. Partner Loan Repayment	*N.A.*	*($50,000)*
Subtotal of Item 2	*$500,000*	*$675,000*
3. PROJECT PAYOUT	*$500,000*	*$575,000*
4. LOCAL DEVELOPER'S SHARE BASED UPON PROJECT SHARING INTEREST OF 25%	*$125,000*	*$143,750*
5. LESS REPAYMENT OF PARTNER LOAN	*($50,000)*	*N.A.*
6. NET PROCEEDS TO LOCAL PARTNER	*$75,000*	*$143,750*

Under Alternative "A," the local partner's Project Sharing Interest is subject to a $50,000 charge for repayment of the Partner Loan (100% of $50,000), but not subject to any obligation other than the local partner's share of Direct Project Costs.

Under Alternative "B," the local partner's Project Sharing Interest is, in effect, charged with the local partner's proportionate share of Allocated Costs. However, the "Overhead Reimbursement by Financial Partner" is included in Gross Revenues and the Partner Loan is repaid off the top rather than out of the local partner's Project Sharing Interest (as in Alternative "A").

The foregoing example illustrates the importance of fully understanding the financial implications of negotiations between the local partner/employee and the developer/employer. Whether expenses come off the top or the bottom can have a significant effect on each party's bottom line and tax consequences. No one should assume that the foregoing illustration uses realistic numbers or that every relationship between a local partner/employee and developer/employer will result in the various income and expense items being in the illustrated positions above and below the "bottom (profit) line." Obviously, in Alternative "B" as shown above, the local partner/employee is directly repaying only 25% of his or her Partner Loan!

FORM 3-1

Paragraph 6 is intended only to stimulate creative thought in devising an appropriate cost reimbursement mechanism. Get expert legal, tax, and accounting help in developing your own specific structure. It is critical that both parties have a full understanding of how overhead will be charged to projects and when income tax consequences attach to receipt, repayment, or forgiveness of the Partner Loan. It is also unrealistic to assume that the parties' initial agreement will be appropriate over time. This issue should be reviewed frequently by the parties and revised as necessary.

End of Alternatives "A" and "B" to Paragraph 6
—Continue to Paragraph 7

7. Operating Budget. Before signing this letter, the parties shall prepare and agree upon a preliminary budget ("Operating Budget") which includes __*[accrued (if Texas division has an operating history) and]*__ projected Local Division revenues and expenses for the first __*[e.g., two years]*__ of Texas operations following the Start Date. Such revenues and expenses shall be assembled and projected in the following revenue and expense categories:

Add the following if Alternative "A" to Paragraph 6 was selected:
Project Payouts with assumed Gross Proceeds, Direct Project Costs, Local Administrative Overhead and Partner Loan advances (and interest thereon). The Operating Budget shall be attached as Exhibit "A" to this agreement.

OR

Add the following if Alternative "B" to Paragraph 6 was selected:
Project Payouts with assumed Gross Proceeds, Direct Project Costs and Net Overhead Charge. Net Overhead Charge shall include separate projections of Local Administrative Overhead, Home Office Expense, and Partner Loan advances (and interest thereon). The Operating Budget shall be attached as Exhibit "B" to this agreement.

End of Paragraph 7—Continue to Paragraph 8.

Do not use Paragraph 8 if there are no pre-existing projects.

8. Pre-existing Projects. Developer is currently in the process of developing the following projects ("Developer's Pre-existing Projects") in Texas: __*[describe]*__.

I am currently developing the following projects ("My Pre-existing Projects") in Texas: __*[describe]*__.

We hereby agree that my interest in Developer's Pre-existing Projects shall be as follows: (i) I will have a reduced Project Sharing Interest of __ % and (ii) my other rights and obligations with respect thereto shall be as set forth in Paragraph __*[5]*__. With respect to My Pre-existing Projects, Developer shall have the following rights and obligations with respect thereto: __*[Describe in detail Developer's role and participation, if any, in the new local employee-partner's pre-existing projects]*__.

There are no other Pre-existing Projects or other specific sites, agreements or exceptions that modify my partnership participation described in Paragraph __*[5]*__.

9. Profit Sharing and Pension Plan. I will participate in Developer's profit sharing and pension plan on the same basis as other executives of similar status, as such plans may exist from time to time, which is currently at the rate of approximately ___ % of salaried compensation after an initial vesting period of __*[e.g., 24]*__ months.

> ***Note:*** *Profit-sharing or pension-plan participation is a function of salaried income. To the extent salaried income is given up to receive the potentially tax-advantaged "draw" [Paragraph 4 above], such benefits are foregone.*

10. Medical Insurance. Developer will include __*[e.g., my spouse, my children and myself]*__ under Developer's group major medical and life insurance plan on the same basis applicable to Developer's other executive partners. __*[If I elect not to become covered under Developer's group medical plan on a current basis as a result of a pre-existing condition of any of my dependents or myself, during the term of my employment, Developer will directly pay my existing medical insurance carrier that sum which Developer would have paid had I elected to insure my dependents and myself under Developer's group medical plan]*__.

Optional:

__. **Existing Office.** I currently occupy office space at *__[address]__*. Rent is payable $________ monthly under an office lease dated __________, 20__ which terminates *__[________, 20__]__*. The lease contains a *__[e.g., 30]__* -day right by tenant to terminate the lease. The security deposit is $_________. The parties plan to locate and move to a larger office. Developer will pay all costs of the relocation. Developer will make all payments on the existing office lease and all other related office expenses *__[including payment for parking, photocopying and ________]__* effective as of the Start Date and ending on the first to occur of the following events: (i) Developer begins occupancy under a new Texas office space lease, (ii) *__[other applicable event(s)]__*, or (iii) this agreement is terminated. From then on, assuming this agreement is not terminated, Developer will directly provide and pay for all new office expenses required for Developer's Texas operations.

Optional:

__. **Existing Office Supplies, Furniture, Equipment and Insurance.** I will contribute my existing office supply inventory, office furniture, *[specify specific equipment:] __[e.g., dictation equipment, __[e.g., IBM]__ computer/word processor(s), typewriter(s), file cabinets, desks, book shelves, furniture and furnishings]__* pending our anticipated move to expanded space. *[Reference and attach an inventory exhibit if this list is extensive.]* I will also continue to pay for property insurance and unsecured property tax on such items after the Start Date.

Developer will reimburse me for such contribution by paying me an additional $__________ per month for the first __ months of operations at which time we will reconsider and renegotiate the arrangement. In addition, Developer will pay for reasonable maintenance and repair costs of all such items in Developer's use after the Start Date. Developer will separately obtain an endorsement or appropriate insurance to cover potential liability claims arising from its Texas operations or loss or damage to my property or equipment on the premises after the Start Date.

11. Devotion of Entire Time. I will devote all my productive time, ability, and attention to Developer's business with the exception of *__[describe development or other business activities requiring time and attention, e.g., certain pending consulting engagements with __(specify excluded work or projects)]__* which engagements I have fully disclosed to Developer and which will have a relatively nominal impact on my time until such matters are concluded.

12. Automobile Allowance. It will be necessary that I use my existing automobile to carry out the duties of this employment. Accordingly, in addition to the compensation above, I will receive an automobile allowance of $__________ per month. *[Alternatively, negotiate use of company car, payment of existing loan payments plus fixed dollar and/or mileage sum, etc.]*

13. Business Expenses. Developer will directly pay or I will be promptly reimbursed for all reasonable business expenses incurred in promoting Developer's business, including expenditures for entertainment, travel, International Council of Shopping Centers programs and conferences, real estate continuing education courses relating to shopping center development and the like. __*[However, total annual reimbursement for qualified continuing educational programs shall be limited in accordance with Developer's existing continuing education policy statement applicable to senior executives, which provides that...]*__.

14. Title. The following or similar mutually acceptable title shall be used on business cards:

__*[e.g., Vice President–Development*
*Director– __[state]__ Division]*__

15. Termination. Although provisions herein may from time to time be renegotiated in the interests of the parties, both parties intend that this letter agreement will establish the basis for a long term relationship between them. Nevertheless, either party may, without cause, terminate this agreement upon prior written 90-day notice. Any such termination and final accounting as of the final date of employment ("Termination Date") shall be in good faith and neither party shall use the relationship created herein to exploit the business interests created during the term of this agreement. Within __*[e.g., 60 days following the Termination Date]*__, the parties will negotiate an equitable termination agreement providing for purchase or division of shared Project interests. Projects shall be evaluated and settled in an attempt to equitably apportion the respective value created through the Termination Date.

Providing in advance for a mutually acceptable partnership phase-out requires skill and finesse. Such dissolutions are extremely difficult in the shopping center development context where so many relationships are involved and transactions are in process for such a protracted period. If the parties are capable of being objective and fair, usually an acceptable settlement can be negotiated. No advance contractual provision will be a panacea. Consider, however, the following paragraph as a guide to negotiating your own termination arrangement.

16. Vested Rights at Termination. While the value of Projects in process at time of any potential termination may be uncertain, the parties shall follow the following procedure to effectuate any such termination agreement:

16.1 Pending Projects. All Projects __*[e.g., which we are currently working on at time of termination]*__ ("Pending Projects") shall be described and itemized as of the Termination Date. The Pending Projects shall consist of three categories of Projects: (i) Fee Projects,

Note: *The term Fee Projects should be used only if the parties contemplate working on projects for which the Developer will receive fee income in lieu of equity participation.*

(The term "Fee Projects" is defined above.) (ii) those Projects (the "Funded Projects") __*[e.g., for which a financial partner has been obtained and formal agreements have been signed with the financial partner]*__, and (iii) those Projects (the "Unfunded Projects") which are in various stages of development, but which do not qualify as Fee Projects or Funded Projects.

16.2 Rights as to Fee Projects. My rights with respect to any Fee Project shall be vested to the extent by which fees have been earned by Developer through the Termination Date. Regardless of the date Developer receives payment, Developer shall account for and pay me my proportionate share of such revenue earned through the Termination Date (as adjusted by the appropriate costs and charges contained in Paragraph __*[6]*__ of this agreement accrued through the Termination Date). I shall have no right to participate in any Fee Project revenues earned after the Termination Date.

16.3 Rights as to Funded Projects. My rights with respect to any Funded Project shall be governed by the subject Project partnership agreement existing at the Termination Date. The termination of my employment shall not effect or constitute my withdrawal from the subject partnership. With respect to any Funded Project for which Developer and I have not yet signed a formal partnership agreement as of the Termination Date, my interest as a partner in each such Project shall remain vested consistent with my Project Sharing Interest and Developer shall cause any subsequently prepared Project partnership agreement to so reflect my vested interest as a partner.

16.4 Rights as to Unfunded Projects. If Developer secures a financial partner within __*[insert time period, e.g., 18 months]*__ after the Termination Date and elects to acquire any of the Unfunded Projects, I will have a __ % limited partnership interest in each such Unfunded Project __ *[consistent with my Project Sharing Interest while an employee-partner]*__ *[**Note:** Some lesser percentage could be inserted.]* except that (a) any development fees would be shared between Developer and myself in proportion to the work performed by each, (b) each party would bear its own overhead burden, i.e., there would be no Local Administrative Overhead or Home Office Expense charged to the Project, and (c) __*[add any additional refinements]*__.

Developer will have 30 days from the time when economic terms of site acquisition are known in which to communicate to me that Developer has a Joint Venture Financial Partner for the Project. If Developer does obtain such a financial partner, ownership of the subject Project would be structured as set forth above. If, however, Developer fails to have such a financial partner by that date, I may bring in another financial partner and financing, in which case all Developer's equity participation in the subject Unfunded Project would be split __ % – __ % between Developer and myself and Developer would not be entitled to participate in receipt of any development fees. If Developer contracts or opens escrow on such a Project within __*[e.g., 18]*__ months, I would participate; otherwise I would not. However, I may pursue for my own account any Unfunded Project in which Developer fails to communicate, within __*[e.g., 18]*__ months after the Termination Date, that Developer has a financial partner for the Unfunded Project who is prepared to proceed with site acquisition and development.

16.5 Rights as to Abandoned Projects. With regard to any other potential Project or Projects (the "Abandoned Projects") which Developer elects not to pursue during the term of my employment and partnership relationship with Developer, we may each elect to proceed to develop or otherwise exploit such opportunities independent of the other, without any obligation to one another. Like Pending Projects, Abandoned Projects shall also be described and itemized as of the Termination Date.

Alternative "A" for Paragraph 17
—Customary "non-binding" intent

Insert the following paragraph assuming this document is intended to be a non-binding letter of intent.

17. Non-binding Letter of Intent. The parties do not intend this letter to be a contract or to be bound by this letter. A contract between the parties will not exist unless and until the parties have executed a definitive employment agreement, approved by legal counsel for each of the parties, containing all other essential terms of an agreed upon transaction. The parties acknowledge that they have not set forth herein nor agreed upon all essential terms of the employment and Project participation described herein, including without limitation, __*[e.g., specific language to implement the intended cost, revenue and profit sharing arrangement under negotiation between Developer and myself]*__. Upon my receipt of a signed copy of this letter, our respective lawyers will prepare a formal agreement for our signatures. While Developer and I agree to continue to negotiate in good faith, if for any reason we fail to agree upon and execute a final, binding agreement concerning this employment and partnership relationship within _______ days of the signing of this non-binding letter of intent, neither party shall be under any obligation whatsoever to the other.

OR

Alternative "B" for Paragraph 17 —"binding" intent (uncommon)

For use by non-lawyers only with advice of legal counsel: Once all legal and accounting refinements to the agreement have been made, a lawyer could insert the following paragraph when the letter agreement is intended to be a final contract between the parties.

17. Binding Agreement. This letter, having been reviewed and approved by legal counsel for each of the parties, is intended to be a final agreement concerning the terms of my employment and participation with Developer.

Please sign and return a copy of this letter for my files. I look forward to working with you on this exciting new challenge for all of us.

Very truly yours,

[Prospective employee/partner's name]

UNDERSTOOD AND AGREED:
This __ day of ___________, 20__.

[Name of Developer]

By: ______________________
Its: ______________________

If Alternative "A" to Paragraph 6 is selected—
Include the Operating Budget as Exhibit "A":

Exhibit "A"
Operating Budget

OR

If Alternative "B" to Paragraph 6 is selected—
Include the accounting "Policy Statement" as Exhibit "A" and the Operating Budget as Exhibit "B":

Exhibit "A"
Policy Statement For Allocation of Home Office Expense to Texas Projects

Exhibit "B"
Operating Budget

END OF FORM 3-1

Like marriages, development partnerships often do not succeed and divorce may become necessary. Form 3-2 may be used as a guide in terminating the employment and partnership relationship created by Form 3-1. Form 3-2 is intended only to illustrate one approach to the problem and the variety of issues that may need to be covered. Skilled legal, and possibly accounting, advice will be necessary to create a satisfactory termination agreement.

Form 3-2

Letter of Resignation Confirming Agreement Terminating Employment and Settling Developer and Employee-Partner's Accrued Project/Partnership Rights

Letter from Local Partner to Multi-State Developer

FORM 3-2

[Date]

[Insert name and address of officer of multi-state developer

____

____

_______________________]

Dear _____________:

This letter will confirm the terms by which I will terminate my employment and partnership relationship with __*[name of developer]*__ ("Developer"). The terms of my employment with Developer are set forth in my ________, 20__ letter creating our employment/partnership relationship (hereinafter "Employment Agreement"), a copy of which is attached as Exhibit "A". *[**Note:** The document drafted from Form 3.1 is Exhibit "A".]* The defined terms contained in the Employment Agreement shall have the same meaning in this termination agreement. *[The defined terms in the Employment Agreement (Form 3-1) include the definition of "Project" (Paragraph 5) as well as the extensive cost or "accounting" definitions (Paragraph 6).]*

1. Termination Notice. On_________, 20__ I gave you my termination notice and hereby confirm that we agreed that Developer's payments of semi-monthly salary and Partner Loan installments, as well as other employment benefits, as set forth in the Employment Agreement, shall continue until ________, 20__ ("Termination Date").

Paragraph 2—assuming Alternative "A" to Paragraph 6, Form 3-1 was selected:

2. Calculation of Accrued Partner Loan. Within __ days Developer will provide an accounting, subject to my reasonable approval, of the outstanding, accrued balance of the Partner Loan chargeable against my Project Sharing Interest as of the Termination Date. Such outstanding balance shall remain a lien against my Project Sharing Interest in any Projects, repayable to Developer out of first revenues received from any such Project.

__[No interest on such final, outstanding balance of the Partner Loan shall accrue after the Termination Date]__.

OR

Paragraph 2—assuming Alternative "B" to Paragraph 6, Form 3-1 was selected:

2. Calculation of Accrued Proportionate Net Overhead Charge. Within __ days Developer will provide an accounting, subject to my reasonable approval, of the outstanding, accrued balance of my proportionate __ % *[insert Project Sharing Interest or other appropriate percentage]* share of Texas Net Overhead Charge that is chargeable against my Project Sharing Interest as of the Termination Date. Such sum *__[and my share of additional Net Overhead Charge that is incurred after the Termination Date and reasonably allocable to my Profit Sharing Interest]__* shall remain a lien against my Project Sharing Interest in any Projects, repayable to Developer out of first revenues received from any such Project. No interest shall accrue either before or after the Termination Date on Net Overhead Charge charged against my Profit Sharing Interest.

> ***Note:*** *Notwithstanding the local partner's departure, Project overhead expenses will continue. Therefore, in Alternative "B" the local partner's Profit Sharing Interest is subject to allocation of both accrued and future Net Overhead Charge. Alternatively, the parties could agree to charge the local partner's Profit Sharing Interest with a negotiated, liquidated sum in satisfaction of the Net Overhead Charge.*

3. Vested Rights. *[First address, if necessary, any issues regarding any completed Projects to clarify vested rights relative to such interests.]* Because the value of certain ongoing development work in process is dependent upon future events, the value of such Projects created through the Termination Date is uncertain. Nevertheless, we are attempting to apportion the parties' rights to potential current and future Project benefits consistent with the Employment Agreement. Consequently, as of the date of this letter, we agree that we are currently working on various pending Projects (the "Pending Projects"), the status of each of which is as stated in Paragraph *__[4]__* below. The Pending Projects consist of three categories of Projects: (i) Those Projects (the "Fee Projects") *__[e.g., for which a Texas development fee for services contract has been executed between Developer, as a provider of services, and a third party]__*, (ii) those Projects (the "Funded Projects") *__[e.g., for which a financial partner has been obtained and formal agreements have been signed with the financial partner]__*, and (iii) those Projects (the "Unfunded Projects") which are in various stages of development, but which do not qualify as Fee Projects or Funded Projects.

4. <u>Listing of Pending Projects</u>. As of the Termination Date, the Texas division is working on the following Projects: *[Italicized inserts are merely illustrative examples of possible language.]*

FORM 3-2

____**4.1 <u>Fee Projects</u>.**

____**4.1.1 <u>[Insert appropriate descriptive heading describing each specific Fee Project]</u>.** *[E.g., Southeast corner of _______ and ______; __[city]__, __[state]__.] __[E.g., Developer is providing development services to __[name of party]__ pursuant to a development fee for services contract dated _________, 20__]__.*

[Continue listing Fee Projects]

____**4.2 <u>Funded Projects</u>.**

____**4.2.1 <u>[Insert appropriate descriptive heading describing each Funded Project]</u>.** *[E.g., Southeast corner of _______ and ______; __[city]__, __[state]__.] __[E.g., This ______ acre site was put under contract _________, 20__ for development of a __________ supermarket and potentially a drug store. __[Name of supermarket chain]__ has given final approval of the site. The Local Division is attempting to acquire development rights to adjacent acreage encompassing __ acres. __________ and __________ have supplied letters of intent to locate stores on the adjacent acreage. [Give other pertinent facts.]*

[Continue listing Funded Projects in process]

____**4.3 <u>Unfunded Projects</u>.**

____**4.3.1 <u>[Insert descriptive heading, like preceding paragraphs]</u>.** *__[E.g., I have presented and am negotiating on behalf of Developer to ground lease this site which proposes the development of a ____________ supermarket, _________ drug store and a _________ home improvement store. To date the site owner has not accepted or rejected our offer.*

4.3.2 <u>[Insert descriptive heading, like preceding paragraphs]</u>. *__[E.g., I have been negotiating with the owner of this site which, if it were put under contract, would involve __[insurance company partner]__ as a financial partner. This site is clearly feasible for retail development and retail development* *on the site is desired by the City of ________. It appears that the key issue whether there will be a deal is whether the land owner will ultimately agree to our proposal. I made a revised offer ten days ago and plan to meet with the owner again ___________, 20__. __[Name of major tenant]__ will probably commit based upon our proposed economics.]*

[Continue listing Unfunded Projects in process]

____**5. Rights as to Fee Projects.** My rights with respect to any Fee Project shall be vested to the extent by which fees have been earned by Developer through the Termination Date. Regardless of the date Developer receives payment, Developer shall account for and pay me my proportionate share of such revenue earned through the Termination Date (as adjusted by the appropriate costs and charges contained in Paragraph *__[6]__* of the Employment Agreement accrued through the Termination Date). I shall have no right to participate in any Fee Project revenues earned after the Termination Date. *[But consider itemizing any specific Projects in which the partner will receive a specified (perhaps reduced) share of revenues earned after the Termination Date in consideration, for example, of the partner's initiation of the Fee Project. Similarly, consider terms by which the partner will provide specified consulting services to Developer after the Termination Date.]*

____**6. Rights as to Funded Projects.** I am a limited partner in the partnerships formed for the Funded Projects and my rights with respect thereto shall be governed by the subject partnership agreement(s). The termination of my employment agreement shall not alter my economic participation or constitute my withdrawal from any subject partnership.

____**7. Rights as to Unfunded Projects.** If Developer secures a financial partner on or before *__[insert future date, e.g., 18 months in future]__* and elects to acquire any of the Unfunded Projects, I will have a __ % limited partnership interest in each such Unfunded Project *__[consistent with my Project Sharing Interest while an employee-partner]__*, except that (a) any development fees would be shared between Developer and myself in proportion to the work performed by each, (b) each party would bear its own overhead burden, i.e., there would be no *__[e.g., Local Administrative Overhead or Home Office Expense]__* charged to the Project and (c) *__[add any additional refinements]__*.

Developer will have 30 days from the time when economic terms of site acquisition are known in which to communicate to me that Developer has a Joint Venture Financial Partner for the Project. If Developer does obtain such a financial partner, ownership of the subject Project would be structured as set forth above. If, however, Developer fails to have such a financial partner by that date, I may bring in my own financial partner and financing, in which case all Developer's equity participation in the subject Unfunded Project would be split __ % – __ % between Developer and myself and Developer would not be entitled to participate in receipt of any development fees. If Developer contracts or opens escrow on such a Project within __*[e.g., 18]*__ months, I would participate; otherwise I would not. However, I may pursue for my own account any Unfunded Project in which Developer fails to communicate, within __*[e.g., 18]*__ months after the date of this letter, that Developer has a Joint Venture Financial Partner for the Unfunded Project which is prepared to proceed with site acquisition and development.

FORM 3-2

____**8. Rights as to Abandoned Projects.** With regard to any other potential Projects (the "Abandoned Projects") which Developer elected not to pursue during the term of my employment and partnership relationship with Developer, we may each elect to proceed to develop or otherwise exploit such opportunities independent of the other, without any obligation to one another under the Employment Agreement or this letter. To the best of our knowledge the Abandoned Projects consist of the following:

[Insert and describe Abandoned Projects]

____**9. Consulting Services to Developer.** We will remain open to discussion relative to my engagement as a consultant to Developer after the Termination Date.

> ***Note:*** *It may be in best interests of both parties that the partner perform services for Developer as a partner in specific deals, as a consultant, or otherwise. Developer and partner should not foreclose the possibility of future involvement with one another. Consider the following paragraph.*

Optional:

______**. Specific Continuing Duties and Compensation.** *[Provide for services relative to specific Projects and compensation therefor:]* __*[E.g., I agree to take part in the upcoming audit negotiations with the County of _______ regarding completion of off-site improvements for _________ Shopping Center]*__. I will be paid $____ per hour for performing such services with an obligation not to exceed ___ total hours.

Optional:

______. **Office Rent.** *After termination to the extent I wish to stay and Developer has space available, we will negotiate a month-to-month office rent agreement for space occupied by me based upon my prorata share of occupancy costs. [Detail as necessary.]*

____**10. Health/Life Insurance.** I elect to continue Developer's group medical insurance coverage for __*[e.g., me and my family]*__ at the rate of $_____ per month after the Termination Date. To the extent life insurance is included, I __*[wish/do not wish]*__ to continue this coverage. I will begin paying applicable premiums as of _________, 20__.

Optional:

______. **401(k) Plan.** My interest under Developer's 401(k) plan is vested. *[Provide for a rollover into a separate plan.]*

Optional:

______. **Profit Sharing Plan.** My interest under Developer's profit sharing plan is qualified/vested to some extent which will be promptly accounted for by Developer not later than _________, 20__.

Optional:

______. **Specific Agreements Relative to Specific Partnerships.** *[Carefully review all other applicable agreements, resolve any ambiguities, and otherwise make certain that rights, duties, and obligations under such agreements are consistent with this termination agreement, e.g., Developer agrees that neither Developer nor any other partner in __[name of partnership]__ shall have any right to elect to purchase my partnership interest in __[name of partnership]__ by reason of the fact that effective ________, 20__ I shall "cease to be employed" by Developer. [See "Option upon Termination of Employment", Section __, Paragraph __ (page __) of Agreement of Limited Partnership of __ [name of partnership]__ dated _______, 20__.]*

Optional:

______. **Tax Treatment Regarding Sale of XYZ Shopping Center.** *The parties acknowledge that Developer is attempting to sell __[insert name]__ Shopping Center and that I am a partner in such Project. If Developer elects to sell __[insert name]__ Shopping Center and the buyer would be willing to allow me to retain my interest in the center, I would prefer not to sell and to maintain my Project Sharing Interest, assuming Developer's sale of its equity would not trigger a taxable sale for me. If I elect not to sell and to retain my interest as a co-tenant with the buyer, as of the closing date of any such sale, I will reimburse*

Developer in an amount necessary to clear my partnership interest of my __ [Partner Loan (if Alternative "A" of Paragraph 6 in Form 3-1 was selected)]__ OR __[proportionate share of Allocated Costs (if Alternative "B" of Paragraph 6 in Form 3-1 was selected)]__ as such terms are defined in the Employment Agreement. Developer will cooperate with me and my tax counsel with respect to the characterization of such payment by me to Developer, provided (i) such characterization is not disadvantageous to Developer from a tax perspective and (i) I pay the legal and accounting costs incident thereto.

FORM 3-2

Optional:
______. **Equipment Rental.** *Currently Developer is renting certain scheduled business equipment from me at a total cost of $_______ per month and such equipment is insured under Developer's office contents coverage. In the event we continue to share space after the Termination Date, Developer agrees to continue such payments for at least ____ months or until we make other arrangements regarding insurance of such equipment, we terminate our office sharing arrangement, or the office lease is assigned to a third party, whichever first occurs.*

Optional:
______. **[Other issues].** *[Separately list and address all other issues not covered above.]*

Alternative "A" for Paragraph 11
—Customary "non-binding" intent

Insert the following paragraph assuming this document is not intended to be binding:
____**11. Non-binding Letter of Intent.** The parties do not intend this letter to be a binding contract. A contract between the parties will not exist unless and until the parties have executed a definitive termination agreement, approved by legal counsel for each of the parties, containing all other essential terms of a final agreement between us. The parties acknowledge that they have not set forth herein nor agreed upon all essential terms of the termination agreement, including without limitation, __*[e.g., mutually-acceptable provisions concerning my participation in Developer's Pending Projects after termination]*__. Upon my receipt of a signed copy of this letter, our respective lawyers will prepare a formal termination agreement for our signatures.

OR

Alternative "B" for Paragraph 11
—"binding" intent (uncommon)

For use by non-lawyers only with advice of legal counsel: Once all legal and accounting refinements to the agreement have been made, a lawyer could insert the following paragraph when the letter agreement is intended to be a final contract between the parties.

11. Binding Agreement. This letter, having been reviewed and approved by legal counsel for each of the parties, is intended to be a final agreement concerning all terms and conditions of the termination of my employment with Developer.

Please let me know if you feel there are issues I have overlooked. Assuming you feel this is complete, please sign and return a copy for my files.

Very truly yours,

____
Vice President
Director __*[State]*__ Development

UNDERSTOOD AND AGREED:
This __ day of ___________, 20__.

[Developer's name]

By: ______________________
Its: ______________________

[Attach a copy of the Employment Agreement as Exhibit "A"]

Exhibit "A"
Employment Agreement

END OF FORM 3-2

OVERVIEW

Chapter 4 covers the preparation of fee purchase proposals for shopping center sites. Form 4-1 is a basic starting point for the reader's creation of a comprehensive, standard long-form offer. Once a comprehensive format is devised, custom and abbreviated versions can be quickly prepared and used to respond to specific market opportunities. Forms following Form 4-1 are examples of abbreviated proposal formats responsive to factual situations likely to be encountered.

FORMS

4-1 Standard Long-Form Purchase Offer. Comprehensive Letter Proposal to Purchase Shopping Center Site; Periodic Release of Funds to Seller During the Escrow Period.

4-2 Short Offer to Option Site. Proposal to Option Shopping Center Site in Approved Master-Planned Community from Residential Land Developer Inexperienced in Shopping Center Development; Exhibit: "Preliminary Development Schedule."

4-3 Brief Letter of Intent to Option Site. Simple Letter of Intent to Enter into Site Purchase Option Agreement.

4-4 Purchase Money Note and Release Clause. Seller's Purchase Money Note Secured by Site; Partial Release Clause Illustrating Economic Effect.

Chapter 4

Purchasing An Unimproved Shopping Center Site

Sitting still and wishing makes no person great. The good Lord sends the fishing but you have to dig the bait.
—Anonymous

CREATING A STANDARD LONG-FORM OFFER

There are significant advantages to the developer in creating a basic standard, comprehensive, or "long-form" site offer form that meets the particular needs and operating style of the developer, and is in a format comfortable to the developer's legal counsel. Having such a form in hand serves as a convenient reminder of issues to be negotiated. Most important, however, once a comprehensive format has been created, abbreviated proposals responsive to specific factual requirements can be quickly and easily prepared.

Form 4-1 is an example of my comprehensive[1] offer form and includes various alternative clauses and annotations describing alterations to the form that were made in a specific factual context. Once such a comprehensive form is customized by the developer and developer's legal counsel and stored on disk, highly abbreviated proposals that are so often needed can be quickly derived from it as circumstances warrant. Many of the forms that follow are illustrative modifications derived from Form 4-1. Think how you might adopt this form or amend your existing offer format to include selected provisions.

Form 4-1 covers the commonly encountered business issues to be negotiated in a site acquisition. Following an initial feasibility/marketing period, the buyer is obligated to periodically release funds to the seller (in this case through an escrow) as a condition to keeping the transaction or escrow open. Although in this form such initial "option" payments are applicable to the purchase price and later payments are not, the form is designed to easily allow the buyer to

[1] "Comprehensive" in this context does not mean the form covers any and all issues that could arise. The form covers only generally occurring issues with a fair degree of specificity, as distinguished from a short letter that tersely describes or lists the major deal points.

customize the dollar amounts and applicability or non-applicability of such payments to the purchase price. An alternative clause is given allowing the purchase price to be calculated based upon a "net" price per square foot, as distinguished from an absolute, fixed purchase price. Often a developer buyer will be able to reduce or delay the release of funds to the seller in exchange for agreeing to (i) advance funds for specific, agreed development and/or site investigatory tasks and (ii) release the resulting work product to the seller upon the buyers failure to exercise the option or acquire the site.

Technically, Form 4-1 is in a contingent "purchase agreement" format. Since a buyer could conceivably be found by a court to have failed to exercise reasonable diligence or failed to satisfy a contingency in good faith, most lawyers prefer a traditional "option" format. Furthermore, a contingent purchase contract with very extensive contingencies could possibly be found to be illusory under a theory that the buyer is not obligated to perform.

Nevertheless, it is my observation, based upon practical development experience, that sellers generally perceive a purchase agreement format to instill a greater buyer commitment, particularly where no monetary consideration is given at the outset. Under an option contract, the buyer will usually be required to pay for time to investigate the site or undertake preliminary marketing efforts, whereas a developer may be able to negotiate a longer "free look" under a conditional purchase contract. Consequently, except in large transaction or transactions involving highly sophisticated parties, for business reasons, I generally use a contingent purchase agreement format. (Attorney readers, for the reasons noted, may prefer to amend Form 4-1 to provide that the parties will enter into a formal option agreement rather than a purchase agreement.)

Although Form 4-1 should be negotiated in its non-binding format, with attorney's input the form could be amended to create a binding contract when signed by the seller. The resulting contract could then be conveniently incorporated by reference and attached to typical boilerplate title company preprinted escrow instructions.

Form 4-1

Comprehensive Letter Proposal to Purchase Shopping Center Site; Periodic Release of Funds to Seller during the Escrow Period

[Date]

[Insert name and address of seller(s)
____
____
______________*]*

Re: __ -acre shopping center site located at the __*[e.g., southeast]*__ corner of __*[e.g.,* ______ *Street and* ______*Avenue]*__; __*[City]*__, __*[State]*__ [See attached maps, Exhibits "A", "B" and "C"]

Dear __*[name of seller]*__:

Your introduction is important. This is your opportunity to set yourself apart from other developers competing to control the site. Typically, you should manifest the preliminary feasibility work you have undertaken and the major issues that you as a developer will have to overcome. This shows that you know what you are doing and have taken the initiative to investigate/study the particular site in order to make an intelligent offer.

If you are willing to take this approach, you will find that often you will uncover issues with which the seller is unfamiliar and that you will make a contribution to the seller whether or not your proposal is currently accepted. It is my general opinion that the more you are open and willing to assist sellers, the more opportunities will ultimately come your way. For one reason or another, a seller may not accept any of a number of offers at a given time. When the time is right and the seller does make a deal, the seller will be inclined to select the developer that has demonstrated to be knowledgeable, cooperative, and committed to making the transaction work for both buyer and seller.

The following introductory paragraph was addressed to a sophisticated managing partner of a selling partnership. The partner, a civil engineer, knew every detail of the site from an engineering perspective but was not experienced in retail marketing. The paragraph is included merely as a stylistic example. (Note also the alternative, second Illustrative Paragraph 4, which addresses in detail an issue unique to the development of the particular site referenced in the same example.)

[I appreciated meeting you and discussing this site rather extensively with _____________ and yourself. Unfortunately, the new 300,000 square foot _________________ Shopping Center and the substantial supermarket and other major retail competition at and east of _____________ Boulevard and _____________ Avenue impose substantial marketing obstacles. Nevertheless, with a careful and focused marketing effort, I believe there is a strong likelihood that sufficient major retail interest can be generated to make this development possible. As I explained, my company will only proceed provided sufficient major tenant interest is established.

I also appreciate the extensive off-site and revetment planning you have undertaken, which should shorten the overall approval time period once sufficient majors are procured and their specific configurations located within an approved site plan for governmental processing. I look forward to the possibility of working together with you on this Project/ I am pleased to submit the following proposal to you:]

OR

[I am pleased to submit the following proposal to you, which contains the major terms that will be included in a final purchase agreement to be negotiated between Buyer and Seller. These terms are not intended to be a comprehensive list of the terms, conditions and obligations of Buyer and Seller that will be included in the purchase agreement, and during negotiation of the purchase agreement, either Buyer or Seller may raise additional issues and propose additional terms and conditions relating to the purchase and sale of the site.]

1. Parties. Upon satisfaction of the escrow contingencies contained herein, __*[name of buyer]*__, or its nominee or assignee ("Buyer"), as hereinafter provided, will purchase the "site" (defined below) from __*[name of seller]*__ ("Seller").

Continue with the following sentence, assuming, as in most cases, this document is intended to be a non-binding agreement:
If this letter of intent is executed by Seller, Buyer's legal counsel will prepare a Purchase and Sale Agreement and Joint Escrow Instructions (the "Purchase Agreement") consistent with the terms and conditions of this letter of intent.

Assuming the offer is drafted by a lawyer intending that the document be a binding agreement when signed by Seller, the following sentence could be inserted in place of the preceding sentence:
__[Upon execution of this agreement by the parties, the parties will sign __[name of escrow company]__'s standard form escrow instructions incorporating the terms and conditions of this agreement]__.

Alternative "A"—Paragraph 2
All cash

2. <u>Purchase Price</u>. *[Subject to adjustment as provided below,]__* the purchase price for the site shall be __*[price]*__ dollars ($________________) payable all cash at closing.

OR

Alternative "B"—Paragraph 2
Part cash and balance in an unsecured, contingent promissory note. (This provision is intended for use when Buyer is obligated to close before building permits and other necessary entitlements are issued.)

2. <u>Purchase Price</u>. __*[Subject to adjustment as provided below,]*__ the purchase price for the site shall be $__*[insert total purchase price]*__, $__*[insert total cash paid through closing]*__ of which (including the "Initial Deposit" referenced in Paragraph __*[9.2]*__ and any "Extension Deposit" amounts applicable to the purchase price and released through escrow to Seller prior to closing pursuant to Paragraph __*[10]*__, below, shall be paid in cash through closing. The balance of the purchase price, or $__*[insert amount of promissory note]*__, shall be paid by Buyer's delivery to escrow of Buyer's promissory note payable to Seller through escrow, which note shall accrue interest at __*[e.g., 10% per annum]*__ from the date of close of escrow. The note shall be held in escrow and shall be due and payable together with all accrued interest, upon the securing of building permits and other entitlements and governmental permits and permissions necessary in Buyer's judgment ("permits") for the construction by Buyer of the first phase of Buyer's proposed shopping center on the site. If permits are not secured to Buyer's satisfaction on or before the __*[e.g., second]*__ anniversary of the close of escrow, interest shall stop accruing on the note, and all interest theretofore accrued under the note shall be permanently canceled and forgiven. If permits are not secured to Buyer's satisfaction on or before the __*[e.g., fourth]*__ anniversary of the close of escrow, the note shall be canceled (and the purchase price shall be deemed reduced by $__*[insert full note amount]*__), and escrow holder shall return the canceled note to Buyer.

OR

Alternative "C"—Paragraph 2
Part cash and balance of purchase price payable by purchase money promissory note secured by the site

2. Purchase Price. __*[Subject to adjustment as provided below,]*__ the purchase price for the site shall be $__*[insert total purchase price]*__, $__*[insert total cash paid through closing]*__ of which (including the Initial Deposit and any Extension Deposit amounts applicable to the purchase price and released through escrow to Seller prior to closing pursuant to __ *[Paragraph 10, below,]*__) shall be paid in cash through closing. The balance of the purchase price, or $____________, shall be payable in the form of a $___________ promissory note secured by a __*[first]*__ __*[deed of trust]*__ *OR* __*[mortgage]*__ on the site. Interest on the note shall be payable __*[e.g., quarterly]*__ at the rate of __*[e.g., 10]*__ % per annum interest only on the outstanding balance. All remaining principal and interest shall be due __*[e.g., 36]*__ months from close of escrow. *[See Form 4-4 for additional note and partial release clause provisions.]*

AND

Optional California additional clause for Alternative "A", "B", or "C"

In addition, Buyer will be responsible for paying the Mello-Roos bonds allocable to the site for the period after ________, 20__. Payments on such bonds for the period before ________, 20__ shall be paid by Seller.

End of Alternatives "A", "B", and "C" to Paragraph 2 —Continue to next, "optional" paragraph

Optional: Add the following as an additional paragraph (and renumber succeeding paragraphs) to provide for a purchase price based upon a price per square foot of "net" land area.

__. **Possible Upward or Downward Adjustment of Purchase Price.** The final purchase price for the site shall be determined by multiplying $____ per square foot of the total net square footage contained in the site, as determined by a certificate prepared by a licensed surveyor to be obtained by Buyer at Buyer's cost prior to close of escrow. The term "net square footage" as used herein shall mean the total area of the site expressed in square footage, as determined pursuant to the above survey, less any land area presently dedicated or committed or required to be dedicated or granted in fee or by easement for public use as of close of escrow. The "net square footage" is intended to mean the net developable land area within the site.

FORM 4-1

3. Site. The "site" is an unimproved, roughly ___ -acre land parcel located at the __*[e.g., southeast]*__ corner of ____________ and ____________________ in __*[city]*__, __*[state]*__ as shown on the attached __*[assessor's parcel map]*__ *OR* __*[plat map]*__ attached hereto as Exhibit "A". The parties understand the site is currently designated ____________ in __*[name of city]*__ 's General Plan and is zoned _______________. Seller represents that the net developable land area (as conceptually designated on the preliminary site plan attached hereto as Exhibit "B") is not less than _____ acres or _______________ square feet of land area __*[describe any adjustments thereto, e.g., less a city-imposed 12' right-hand turn lane dedication, the length of which is not now known. Continue on with any additional specific details. For example: Buyer tentatively plans to purchase up to 1.1 acres of property adjacent to the site owned by the City of __________ ("city property") and may attempt to vacate and incorporate portions of ___________ Road as a portion of Buyer's proposed shopping center. The city property and ___________ Road are designated on the map attached hereto as Exhibit "C"]*__. __*[Although the city property and ___________ Road are not portions of the site, Seller will cooperate with Buyer, consistent with Paragraph 16, if Buyer elects to attempt to integrate such contiguous land area into the proposed shopping center]*__.

The exact legal description of the site shall be approved by Buyer and Seller in escrow.

> *Unfortunately, many developers overlook the strategic use of exhibits. Marking up maps and preliminary site plans and using them as attachments can make your proposal clearer and further demonstrate your knowledge and thought in preparing the offer. Such materials will assist your attorney in understanding the proposed transaction and save time (and money) when it becomes your attorney's role to prepare final purchase and sale documentation. Caveat to attorneys:*

In the rush to meet deadlines, sometimes agreements are prepared leaving referenced blank pages for the client to attach applicable exhibits. Occasionally, the client forgets to make the attachments or generates exhibits inconsistent with the attorney's narrative. Be certain that all exhibits are reviewed for consistency with narrative terms before the proposal is signed and delivered to the other party.

Use a paragraph or more if necessary to refine any unique aspects of the transaction, specific areas of buyer-seller cooperation during the escrow, or development work in process, prior to addressing title and customary specific contingencies. The following are examples of issues that could be inserted as Paragraph 4:

Example 1: Paragraph 4

4. Adjacent Property Escrow. Not later than ____ days after opening of the site purchase escrow, Buyer and __*[insert name of apparent adjacent owner]*__ OR __*[the owner of record]*__ of the approximately ___ (net) acres immediately __*[describe, e.g., southwest of the site as shown on Exhibit "__"]*__ shall have entered into a mutually acceptable purchase agreement for the purchase by Buyer of such adjacent property ("Adjacent Owner Escrow"). If the Adjacent Owner Escrow is not entered into before _________, 20__, this letter shall terminate and any final Purchase Agreement entered into between Buyer and Seller concerning the site shall also terminate (except for continuing obligations, if any, agreed to by the parties in the final Purchase Agreement).

Example 2: Paragraph 4

4. Revetment and Off-Site Improvement Plans. *Seller represents that it is currently processing revetment and off-site improvement plans with the Army Corps of Engineers and the City of _____________. In undertaking such effort, Seller is attempting to reduce the overall anticipated processing time for ultimate development of the site. During the escrow, Seller will complete the processing of such improvement plans at Seller's cost. However, Seller will cooperate with Buyer in making reasonable changes to such plans based upon input from proposed major tenants or Buyer's engineers and other consultants during the processing of Buyer's anticipated shopping center site plan.*

Seller is attempting to form an assessment district composed of the site and the city property whereby the city will construct certain off-site, revetment and limited on-site work as assessment district improvements. Such improvements as are applicable to the site will be bonded and the owner of the site will ultimately be responsible for payment of bonded indebtedness allocable to the site. Buyer understands that if such bonding is in place at close of escrow that Buyer will accept title subject to such bonded indebtedness. Buyer also understands that if Buyer proceeds to purchase, it will be Buyer's obligation to pay for all remaining governmental permit fees and hard costs not included within the scope of the assessment district improvements to the site.

5. Title Search and Document Delivery. Within __*[e.g., ten business]*__ days after execution of __*[this agreement]*__ *OR* __*[the Purchase Agreement]*__ but not later than __*[e.g., 3 business]*__ days after opening of escrow, Seller will provide Buyer with a preliminary title report __*[prepared as of a date after the date of this letter]*__, and all of the following:

FORM 4-1

5.1 Leases and Agreements. Copies of all leases, rental agreements, licenses or other agreements concerning the site which are presently in effect, whether recorded or not;

5.2 Soils Reports and Investigations. Copies of all soils reports and investigations relating to the site, which are in Seller's possession or the possession of Seller's agents or consultants; __*[and]*__

5.3 Surveys, Studies and Plans. Copies of all surveys, preliminary site plans, grading plans, improvement plans, engineering on- and off-site plans and other engineering studies and maps of the site __*[and adjacent parcels]*__ which are in Seller's possession or the possession of Seller's agents or consultants __*[.]*__ *OR* __*[; and]*__

Optional: A sepia will expedite preliminary site planning.

5.4 Sepias. One architect's or engineer's scaled full-sized sepia of Seller's boundary survey. (Seller will authorize, cooperate with or otherwise assist Buyer in obtaining required additional copies provided Buyer pays any necessary copying expense.)

Optional:

5.__ [Additional Items]. *[To eliminate any uncertainty as to whether the preceding itemization is broad enough, if you are aware of specific work Seller has performed, such work product could be itemized and a copy required to be delivered to Buyer. For example: To date Seller has caused to be conducted various tests and studies concerning the site, including, but not limited to, its archeology, geotechnical and hydrologic aspects relative to wetlands and the river frontage, environmental issues, biological characteristics, and fish and game aspects. An application is now pending with the Army Corps of Engineers for issuance of a "404 Permit" and other permits relating to proposed work in the flood plain. Within __ days from opening of escrow, Seller will provide Buyer with* *copies of such information and all pending permits for approval of the proposed assessment district. If Buyer terminates escrow, Buyer shall promptly return such copies to Seller.]*

6. Contingencies. The following contingencies are conditions precedent to Buyer's obligation to complete the purchase of the site. If any of the contingencies are not satisfied prior to the date set forth herein, Buyer may at its option waive such contingencies or terminate the __*[Purchase Agreement]*__ *OR* __*[this agreement]*__ by delivery of written notice to Seller. If notice of approval of any contingency is not received by Seller on or before the applicable deadline set forth in Paragraph __*[7]*__, such contingency shall be deemed __*[not approved]*__ *OR* __*[approved]*__.

> ***Note:*** *Most developers would want developer failure to deliver notice of approval to constitute disapproval of the contingency.*

6.1 Title. Approval by Buyer of a current preliminary title report and legal description as provided by Seller at Seller's cost. Such preliminary title report shall not be deemed received by Buyer until Buyer has been furnished from __ *[e.g., First American]*__ Title Company a preliminary title report complete with copies of each and every document referenced in said title report together with a map prepared by ____________ Title Company depicting each easement, right of way, license, right, etc. which is capable of being plotted in accordance with normal title company practices. Escrow holder is hereby instructed to order and issue such documents upon opening of escrow.

> ***Note:*** *To avoid time and inconvenience of piecemeal review of title documents, this provision provides that Buyer's duty to review title matters does not commence until all backup copies and plotted easements have been delivered to Buyer.*

6.2 Feasibility. Buyer's preliminary investigation and determination that there are no governmental, physical or economic constraints which would render development of the site as a __*[e.g., community]*__ shopping center unfeasible or uneconomic.

6.3 Major Tenant Commitments. Obtaining major tenant commitments in form and substance acceptable to Buyer.

FORM 4-1

6.4 Entitlements. Obtaining building permits for all proposed improvements. (This assumes obtaining final site plan approval and required approvals from all required agencies for Buyer's proposed shopping center on the site.) __*[Such agency approvals include, but are not limited to,]*__ __*[e.g., the Army Corps of Engineers, U.S. Fish and Wildlife, assessment districts governing portions of on-site and off-site improvements and ____________, acceptable development fee agreements, conditional use permits (if required), and any required utility agreements]*__.

6.5 Soils Tests. Buyer's approval of soils tests provided by Buyer or Buyer's contractor at Buyer's cost.

6.6 Hazardous Materials Investigation. Buyer's approval of a Phase 1 environmental investigation of the site to be performed by Buyer at Buyer's cost. (Buyer may elect to but is under no obligation to conduct physical testing of the site.)

Note: *In the event the site contains hazardous materials, Alternatives "A" and "B" of Paragraph 13 provide two examples of how responsibility for completion of corrective work can be allocated. For another example, see Form 17-3, "Hazardous Materials: Example of Expanded Site Purchase Offer Provisions for Use in Acquiring a Site Where Significant Investigation and Cleanup Is Expected."*

Examples of other contingencies

Think: *Have you carefully considered the specific factual situation and tailored the contingencies to meet the factual context? Add other contingencies as necessary. Examples of other contingencies to consider are set forth below. If additional contingencies are added, be certain to also list the contingency approval period for each under Paragraph 7 .*

__.__ **Access.** Satisfactory ingress and egress to both ________ __*[Street]*__ and __________ __*[Avenue]*__.

__.__ **Zoning and Utilities.** *Approval by Buyer that the site is zoned commercially for development of a ______________ shopping center consisting of __[describe type of center/tenant mix, etc.]__ and that sewer capacity, water service, and all other utilities are available for the development.*

__.__ **Site Survey.** *Buyer's approval of Seller's ALTA survey of the site or, if Seller does not have such a survey, Buyer's approval of Buyer's survey of the site conducted at Buyer's expense.*

__.__ **Termination of Easement.** *Termination or removal __[by close of escrow]__ of the apparent water easement running diagonally across the site, as set forth in __[e.g., the assessor's parcel map attached hereto as Exhibit __]__.*

__.__ **Site Plan Approval.** *Final approval by the __[name]__ __[city planning department/city council]__ of the proposed final site plan prepared by Seller as __[name]__ architectural firm job number ________ and last revised _______, 20__, depicting a shopping center complex of __________ square feet of buildings on ______________ square feet of land with parking for ________ cars __[with any governmentally-imposed changes thereto subject to Buyer's approval]__.*

__.__ **Approval of Seller's Development Documentation.** *Seller's delivery to Buyer and Buyer's approval of copies of all documents in Seller's control relating to the project, including but not limited to: (a) existing and required city and other governmental approvals, (b) the status of a proposed ______________ lease for approximately ___________ square feet of space in the proposed center, and (c) all conceptual and proposed site plans, building plans, topographic maps and engineering work.*

__.__ **Site Not in Flood Plain.** *Confirmation that the site is not located in a flood plain.*

__.__ **No Wetlands.** *That no portion of the site is designated or in the process of being designated or protected as a "wetlands" under any federal or state statute.*

__.__ **No Endangered Species.** *That no portion of the site contains a habitat for an "endangered species" or a "threatened species" as defined by the federal Endangered Species Act or any similar federal or state statute which prohibits or restricts development in order to preserve a habitat for the survival of any animal or plant species.*

__.__ **Cap on Governmental Fees and Permit Costs.** *That the sum of all applicable governmental development fees, assessments and permits leviable against the proposed project __[through construction of its initial phase]__ shall not exceed $_____ per square foot of proposed building area.*

FORM 4-1

__.__ **General Plan, Zoning, Infrastructure Financing and Design and Environmental Approvals In Support of Project.** *Passage of __[name]__ city council resolutions approving a general plan amendment of the site consistent with retail commercial use, a zoning amendment allowing retail commercial uses, [California:] formation of the Mello-Roos financing district for the construction of the freeway off-ramp and _______ Road improvements, [California:] CALTRANS approval for the interchange and off-ramp to the site, and environmental permits permitting the construction and operation of Buyer's proposed development of the site, all of which shall be approved by Buyer in its sole and absolute discretion and none of which shall have any conditions unacceptable to Buyer in Buyer's sole and absolute discretion.*

Consider this optional additional clause:
__[If any of the approvals described in the preceding paragraph are delayed beyond the scheduled closing date by more than ____ days for reasons other than Seller's failure to timely process and cooperate in the processing of such matters and all other contingencies to closing have been satisfied or waived by Buyer, (i) the purchase price shall increase at the rate of __ % annually from the end of said __ day period until the closing, which in no event shall be later than _______, 20__ and (ii) notwithstanding Buyer's escrow extension obligations contained in Paragraph __[e.g., 10]__, Buyer shall, under such circumstances, be under no obligation to make any monthly Extension Deposit for the period beginning from the end of said __ day period until the closing.

__.__ **Bankruptcy Court and Lien Holder Approvals.** *Seller securing on or before __________, 20__, all necessary approvals from __[the bankruptcy court]__ and/or existing lien holders which will permit Seller to deliver marketable title to the site free and clear of all monetary and other liens unacceptable to Buyer and otherwise permit Seller to perform all its obligations under __[the Purchase Agreement]__ OR __[this agreement]__; provided, however, that such approvals shall be in a form and substance satisfactory to Buyer in Buyer's sole and absolute discretion.*

__.__ **Financing [Commitment].** *Developer shall have until _________, 20__ in which to obtain a binding __[e.g., construction and/or permanent]__ loan __[commitment]__ to construct the shopping center. If Developer is unable to obtain financing in form satisfactory to Developer by ________, 20__, Developer shall have the right to terminate __[the Purchase Agreement]__ OR __[this agreement]__ by giving written notice of termination.*

Example of an abbreviated approach:

Some sellers will resist a long list of contingencies. Major tenant and approval issues can be combined, as can other issues, to "shorten" the offer, for example:

__.__ Major Tenant Commitments and Entitlements. *Obtaining major tenant commitments acceptable in form and substance to Buyer and obtaining final site plan approval and issuance of appropriate building permits and all other required entitlements from all required agencies for Buyer's planned __[e.g., community]__ shopping center on the site, including but not limited to, all required environmental clearances, acceptable development fee agreements, off-site permits, conditional use permits (if required), and utility agreements.*

End of examples of other contingencies —Proceed to Paragraph 7

7. Contingency Approval Periods. Each of the contingencies listed above shall be approved, disapproved or waived prior to the dates specified below.

7.1 Title. Buyer will have *__[e.g., 21 working]__* days from the receipt of the title documents described in Paragraph *__[e.g., 6.1]__* to approve such documents.

7.2 Feasibility and Major Tenant Commitments. Buyer will have *__[e.g., 120]__* days from the opening of escrow in which to satisfy the contingencies contained in Paragraphs *__[e.g., 6.2 and 6.3]__*.

7.3 Soils Tests and Hazardous Materials Investigation. Buyer will have *__[e.g., 150]__* days from the opening of escrow in which to satisfy the contingencies contained in Paragraphs *__[e.g., 6.5 and 6.6]__*.

7.__ [List each additional contingency by name]. *[After each, insert:]* Buyer will have __ days from the opening of escrow in which to satisfy the contingency contained in Paragraph __.

7.__ Entitlements. Buyer will have __ months from the opening of escrow *__[but not later than ________, 20__]__* in which to satisfy the contingency contained in Paragraph *__[e.g., 6.4]__*.

FORM 4-1

8. Buyer's Reasonable Diligence. During the contingency period Buyer will exercise reasonable diligence to investigate all aspects of the site and attempt to timely satisfy such contingencies. Upon satisfaction of such contingencies, Buyer will work diligently to develop the proposed center in an expeditious manner. __*[Optional: Once acceptable major tenant commitments are obtained, Buyer will proceed with reasonable diligence to attempt to obtain __ [e.g., "Plot Plan Approval"]__ for the layout of a __[e.g., community]__ shopping center on the site in reasonable conformity to Buyer's and its prospective major tenants' requirements for ingress and egress, parking and building size, location, height and building elevations]__*. During the escrow period __*[name of experienced major leasing firm]*__ or persons of similar commercial retail leasing experience shall conduct a first-class marketing effort for the proposed center. Buyer will regularly advise Seller __*[(not less than monthly)]*__ on the status of marketing efforts and negotiations with major tenants.

9. Escrow. __*[Upon deposit into escrow of a mutually approved and executed final Purchase Agreement between the parties, but not later than ________, 20__,]*__ *OR* __*[Within __ business days after acceptance of this proposal by Seller,]*__ Buyer and Seller will open escrow at __________ Title Company in __*[city]*__, __*[state]*__ ("escrow holder"). Escrow holder shall notify Buyer and Seller of the date on which escrow instructions signed by Buyer and all parties required to sign on behalf of Seller have been deposited into escrow ("opening of escrow"). The escrow instructions shall incorporate all terms and conditions of __*[the Purchase Agreement]*__ *OR* __*[this agreement]*__.

9.1 Escrow Fees and Closing Costs. All escrow charges shall be shared equally by Buyer and Seller and all other closing costs not specifically provided for in other provisions of this agreement shall be shared in the manner customary in ____________ county, __*[state]*__.

> **Note:** *Refer to Form 17-4, "Allocation of Specific Purchase and Sale Transaction Costs," for an alternative, more comprehensive clause.*

9.2 Initial Deposit. Upon opening of escrow, Buyer shall deposit $__ *[$25,000 in this example]*__ cash into escrow as a good faith "Initial Deposit". *[Seller oriented insert:]* __*[Until the Initial Deposit has been made, the __[the Purchase Agreement]__ OR __[this agreement]__ shall not be binding upon Buyer and Seller]*__. At the direction of Buyer, the Initial Deposit shall be deposited into an interest bearing account, with all interest accruing to the benefit of Buyer. The scheduled closing shall occur ___ days after satisfaction of all contingencies, but not later than __*[e.g., 5]*__ months from opening of escrow (as defined above) or __*[insert specific, final closing date]*__, whichever occurs later (the "scheduled closing date"). If any of the escrow contingencies described above are not satisfied during the __*[e.g., 5]*__ -month period following opening of escrow and Buyer elects to terminate, Buyer's Initial Deposit shall be returned in full, less any applicable escrow cancellation charge.

I enjoy a close working relationship with individuals in the national accounts division of a major title insurance company. In one case, when the seller had purchased its site, the seller had used another escrow company and spent significant time and energy resolving some complex secured loan issues. Since these issues would arise again upon the seller's resale of the site, the seller wanted to reopen escrow at the prior escrow company. Continually use the best resources and maintain your working relationships with them. To be able to take advantage of my major title insurance company's service in the subject transaction and yet address the seller's legitimate concern, the following additional paragraph was inserted into the buyer's proposal:

Optional additional clause: Use of a sub-escrow

9.__ Sub-escrow. *Seller represents that it used __[name of other escrow holder and its address]__("X Escrow") as an escrow holder when Seller purchased the site and that four or five complex notes secured by complicated liens must be paid off concurrent with the closing. Seller may elect to open a sub-escrow at X Escrow to facilitate the payoff of such liens and the closing of this transaction if Seller believes that __[name of Buyer's preferred major title company]__ cannot timely or effectively handle such payoffs. Buyer and Seller will share any such sub-escrow fee equally.]*

10. Escrow Extensions. So long as Buyer is actively proceeding to develop the site as a shopping center, Buyer may elect to extend, in monthly increments, the scheduled closing date by up to __*[e.g., eight]*__ monthly periods by authorizing escrow holder to disburse from escrow directly to Seller, a sum payable in advance for each such monthly extension ("Extension Deposit"). Each Extension Deposit so made shall extend by one month the then-scheduled or extended closing date and be applicable or not applicable to the purchase price, as follows:

Monthly Escrow Extension	Extension Deposit Amount	Applicable ("A") or Not Applicable ("N.A.") To Purchase Price
1st	$10,000	A
2nd	10,000	A
3rd	20,000	A
4th	25,000	A
5th	25,000	N.A.
6th	30,000	N.A.
7th	30,000	N.A.
8th	30,000	N.A.
	[and so forth]	

The __*[e.g., $25,000]*__ Initial Deposit shall be released to Seller through escrow as a condition to Buyer's right to elect to extend the scheduled closing date by depositing the first Extension Deposit.

> ***Note:*** *Be mindful that this form provides that if Buyer fails to affirmatively terminate, Escrow holder will disburse the Extension Deposit payments from Buyer's escrow deposit until Buyer either closes or terminates escrow.*

Buyer shall redeposit an additional __*[e.g., $25,000]*__ within 10 days of escrow holder's release of the Initial Deposit to Seller. If Buyer fails either to close escrow or give notice to terminate escrow on the scheduled closing date or any extended escrow closing date, escrow holder shall be deemed to be irrevocably instructed to release from escrow to the account of Seller, from Buyer's escrow deposit, the monthly Extension Deposit payable for the following monthly extension period until Buyer either closes or terminates escrow. Buyer shall deposit sufficient additional funds to provide for such releases.

11. Buyer's Termination Right. Buyer may terminate escrow at any time during the contingency period by providing written notice to escrow holder. If any of the escrow contingencies described above are not satisfied and Buyer terminates during the first __*[e.g., 5]*__ months of the escrow period, Buyer's deposit shall be returned to Buyer, less any escrow cancellation charges. If Buyer terminates after the first monthly escrow Extension Deposit has been released to Seller, Seller may retain the Initial Deposit and each Extension Deposit released to Seller through termination. Upon such termination, Buyer shall promptly assign and deliver to Seller, lien

FORM 4-1

free and without charge, copies of all tentative site plans, engineering, and soils and environmental studies concerning the site that Buyer generated prior to termination. Thereupon, Seller shall have the right to use the work and various studies (limited only by such contract, copyright and other legal limitations placed upon such work product in the normal course of business by the third party consultants or producers of such work product. In other words, Buyer shall assign all Buyer's rights to such work product to Seller but Seller shall have no greater rights to such work product than the rights enjoyed by Buyer.) Receipt of the Initial Deposit and any such Extension Deposits shall constitute liquidated damages pursuant to Paragraph __*[e.g., 23]*__ below, and release Buyer from any further claims of Seller concerning the escrow.

Optional: In today's economic climate of limited equity capital and debt financing, a sophisticated seller may negotiate for the insertion of the following Seller-oriented provision:

12. Seller's Termination Right. Buyer shall have until __*[date certain—ideally before any Extension Deposit is required to be released to Seller]*__, 20__, in which to form a venture with an equity financial partner, obtain a binding financing commitment from an institutional lender, or otherwise show sufficient resources to close the escrow. If by the end of this period Buyer has not presented Seller with the name, net worth, and general financial condition of Buyer's financial partner or other financial resources reasonably demonstrating Buyer's intention and ability to close the subject escrow, Seller may, upon ___ days written notice to Buyer and escrow holder, elect to terminate the escrow. __*[If escrow is terminated pursuant to this paragraph, the Initial Deposit and any Extension Deposit(s) released to Seller shall be concurrently refunded to Buyer]*__.

> ***Note:*** *Should developer's soft costs such as preliminary architectural and engineering fees or marketing costs be reimbursed by Seller?*
>
> *A prudent Buyer should require Seller to complete any hazardous waste or contamination cleanup at Seller's expense prior to closing. This conventional approach is outlined in the following Buyer-oriented Alternative "A" of Paragraph 13. Alternative "B" is a more risky and very unconventional approach to the subject and is an example of a negotiated compromise. If, for example, Seller is a limited partnership in which the general partner is unable to collect cleanup costs from the limited partners, language similar to Alternative "B" could be considered. The developer's lawyer should provide guidance in this area, which because of its complexity and potential liability, is beyond the scope of this material.]*

FORM 4-1

Alternative "A"—Paragraph 13
Buyer investigates and Seller completes any corrective work at Seller's expense before closing

13. Hazardous Materials. Assuming sufficient anchor tenant interest is established and Buyer elects to proceed with the purchase of the site, before closing Buyer may conduct an environmental investigation, inspection and testing of the site by a reputable environmental consultant acceptable to Buyer. The results of such study will be set forth in the consultant's report. Seller shall pay for any corrective work required and complete any such work prior to close of escrow. Seller's obligation to pay for corrective work shall include the cost to obtain environmental clearance certificate(s) satisfactory to all appropriate governmental agencies showing the site free and clear of any toxic waste, contamination or hazardous substance.

OR

Alternative "B"—Paragraph 13
Example of negotiated compromise where cleanup appears minimal; Buyer pays limited cleanup cost and receives like credit as offset to purchase price

13. Hazardous Materials. Seller has disclosed to Buyer that the site is contaminated with __*[specify hazardous substance]*__. Assuming sufficient anchor tenant interest is established and Buyer elects to proceed with the purchase of the site, before closing Buyer may conduct an environmental investigation, inspection and testing of the site by a reputable environmental consultant acceptable to Buyer. The results of such study will be set forth in the consultant's report. Buyer shall pay for any corrective work required in an amount not to exceed $____________ and receive a credit at close of escrow for the full amount of such work up to the $__*[same amount]*___ maximum. The above-described work shall be completed prior to close of escrow and the creditable cost of the work shall include the cost to obtain environmental clearance certificate(s) satisfactory to all appropriate governmental agencies showing the site free and clear of any toxic waste, contamination or hazardous substance. If the projected cost to complete such corrective work is more than $__*[same amount]*__ and Seller is unwilling to credit the increased cost of such corrective work against the purchase price, Buyer may elect to terminate escrow and all funds theretofore released to Seller shall be returned to Buyer and escrow holder shall return any escrow deposit to Buyer. __*[Upon opening of escrow Seller shall sign an agreement securing Seller's obligations under this paragraph]*__.

Important Note: *There are significant risks in relying upon Seller's unsecured obligation to return escrow releases. Consider also the need in such a case for reimbursement of other costs incurred through escrow termination. If Buyer is willing to consider purchasing a contaminated site, the purchase contract should be modified as follows:*

1. There should be no releases of cash to Seller before the close of escrow;

2. Buyer should be able to cancel escrow without penalty if Buyer's lender will not finance the purchase of contaminated property;

3. Buyer's obligation to expend money should be carefully limited to an amount the Buyer is prepared to lose; and

4. Buyer should attempt to have Seller pay for all or a portion of the cleanup costs by delaying closing until work is completed and paid for or requiring a very significant "holdback" of the purchase price to pay for the cleanup costs. The amount of the holdback should be equal to 150% of a written estimate of the cleanup cost prepared by a reputable environmental engineering firm.

For a more comprehensive, alternative format where hazardous materials are contemplated, see Chapter 17, Form 17-3: "Hazardous Materials: Example of Expanded Site Purchase Offer Provisions for Use in Acquiring a Site Where Significant Investigation and Cleanup Is Expected".

Get expert advice at the outset if you are aware of any potential hazardous materials issues. The law is complex and the potential liability risks are so significant that a skilled lawyer's advice is crucial.

End of Alternatives "A" and "B" to Paragraph 13
—Continue to Paragraph 14

14. Entry. Buyer shall have an immediate license to enter upon the site for the purpose of conducting economic feasibility, engineering, soil and other tests at its sole cost and expense. Buyer will indemnify Seller and hold Seller harmless from any and all loss or liability resulting from the acts of Buyer or its agents, employees, or invitees upon the site and from all or any mechanics liens or other liens resulting from Buyer's conduct or the conduct of its agents or employees on the site.

15. Marketing Signs. Seller grants to Buyer, and Buyer's nominee or agent, the right to erect a sign or signs offering retail space for lease during the term of the escrow.

Occasionally, additional signage agreement detail is needed, such as illustrated by the following:
__[However, Seller currently is a party to month-to-month agreements with X Corp and Y Corp ("home builders") which allow each of such home builders to place tract marketing signs on the site. Seller shall use its best efforts to renegotiate such signage agreements so as to allow Buyer premier space for its retail marketing signs on the site within __ days after opening of escrow yet allow such home builders to continue to market their tracts so long as such signs do not interfere with Buyer's marketing signs. Seller may retain any sign right income from such home builders through close of escrow]__.

FORM 4-1

16. Seller Cooperation. *[Start with specifying any specific or unique duties which should be required of Seller relative to the site and its development and then continue:]* Seller will fully cooperate in timely supplying the various documents, maps, plans and studies required to be delivered to Buyer pursuant to Paragraph __*[e.g., 5, above]*__. Seller will continue to furnish copies of any such additional materials generated by Seller or Seller's consultants during the escrow period. *[Continue with following broad language:]* Seller will cooperate fully with and assist Buyer in negotiating with private and public special interest groups, adjacent property owners, federal, state and local governmental and quasi-governmental agencies, as such negotiations relate to timely securing approvals and permits for the site. Seller will also execute any and all instruments necessary or appropriate for the development of the site, including but not limited to, maps, dedications or easements and rights of way to governmental and quasi-governmental authorities and adjacent property owners provided such execution is consistent with normal practices.

Under the following optional provision, Buyer retains one of Seller's partners as a consultant for entitlement assistance. Use of such a provision might arise if the partner had substantial expertise relative to the site or entitling authorities, the Seller lacked the necessary development capital to proceed, or the partner sought continued involvement in the project and the Buyer had the capital necessary to complete the project. (Of course, any partner receiving the benefits of such a consulting arrangement must fully disclose and obtain consent from his or her partners in accepting such a contract.)

Optional:

__. **Entitlement Assistance Consulting services.** Buyer and *__[name of one of Seller's partners (for convenience, "John Slick" in this paragraph]__* shall enter into a mutually acceptable consulting agreement whereby *__[John Slick]__* shall provide processing and entitlement assistance to Buyer for Buyer's proposed shopping center development for a total fee of $__________, $__________ of which shall be deposited into escrow at the opening of escrow and shall be released to *__[John Slick]__* upon Buyer's approval *__[in Buyer's sole and absolute discretion]__* of *__[e.g., the title, feasibility, soils, and environmental contingencies described in Paragraphs 6.1, 6.2, 6.5 and 6.6, above]__. [(Conform language with specific selected purchase contingencies contained in proposal—See Paragraphs 6, "Contingencies".)]* The remaining $__________ shall be paid at the rate of $__________ monthly thereafter. Buyer's obligation to make any such payment shall terminate if *__[the Purchase Agreement]__ OR __[this agreement]__* or the escrow is terminated or canceled by Buyer. *__[Buyer shall approve or disapprove such contingencies within __[e.g., 120]__ days from the opening of escrow]__.*

17. Assignment. Buyer may assign all of Buyer's rights and duties under *__[the Purchase Agreement]__ OR __[this agreement and the escrow]__* or nominate any entity to take title to the site, upon the giving of written notice to Seller, which notice may not be given less than *__[e.g., three]__* days prior to closing. Any such assignment is conditional upon such assignee agreeing to be bound by all consents and approvals theretofore given or deemed to have been given by Buyer, and such assignment or nomination shall not relieve Buyer of any of Buyer's obligations under *__[the Purchase Agreement]__ OR __[this agreement and the escrow]__*.

18. Condemnation Prior to Closing. If prior to the closing the site or any part thereof becomes the subject of a condemnation proceeding, Seller agrees to immediately advise Buyer thereof. *__[In the event of such condemnation,]__ OR __[If such condemnation would make it impractical for Buyer to develop the site as contemplated,]__* Buyer shall have the option to (i) take title in accordance with the terms and conditions of the applicable agreements between the parties and negotiate with the condemning authority for the condemnation award and receive the benefits thereof without affecting the purchase price, or (ii) terminate the agreements between Buyer and Seller and declare Buyer's obligations under the purchase escrow null and void and of no further effect, in which event all sums theretofore paid or released to Seller or to escrow holder shall be returned to Buyer.

19. <u>Title</u>. At the close of escrow, Seller shall convey marketable title to Buyer in compliance with __*[state]*__ law, free of any leasehold interests not approved in writing by Buyer, and subject only to those matters of record which have been disclosed to Buyer in the Preliminary Title Report and approved in writing by Buyer. In addition, Seller shall deliver to Buyer at close of escrow, at Seller's expense, a __*[See Appendix A, Form A-1]*__ policy of title insurance insuring marketable title in Buyer for the full amount of the purchase price, subject only to the title exceptions previously approved in writing by Buyer.

The following additional paragraph was unique to a particular transaction but is consistent with the increasing trend of public-private interplay in infrastructure financing. The bigger problem is that with governmental uncertainties, neither Buyer nor Seller really know what they're getting into, creating drafting dilemmas and stressing the need for buyers to carefully select sellers with whom they will be able to work with cooperatively and renegotiate as circumstances warrant.

As set forth above, Buyer understands that Seller is processing proposed assessment district plans with the City of ____________ to build certain revetment, off-site and on-site improvements through the city's bonding capacity. Seller will continuously provide Buyer with full information concerning the status of the pending assessment district and cost breakdowns and proposed security agreements related thereto. Buyer will have a reasonable right to approve documents affecting title to the site. If the assessment district is formed before closing, Buyer understands that title will be encumbered by an obligation to repay the City of _____________ or the assessment district, as the case may be, for such improvements over a specified period of years. Although Buyer will take title subject to such assessment repayment obligation, interest or bond payments on any such indebtedness shall be prorated as of close of escrow in the same manner as real property taxes.

20. <u>Brokerage Commissions</u>. Buyer and Seller each separately represent and warrant that it did not incur any brokerage commission in connection with this transaction and that no commission or finder's fee is payable to Buyer or any third party upon consummation of this transaction __*[with the exception of _______]*__. *[Give details of parties to whom a brokerage or finder's fee is payable, the amounts thereof, and how such parties are to be paid.]*

FORM 4-1

21. Representations and Warranties. __*[The Purchase Agreement]*__ OR __*[The final documentation of this agreement and the escrow]*__ shall give Buyer customary representations, warranties and indemnities concerning all information provided by Seller, and other matters, such as but not limited to, environmental conditions, title, the absence of undisclosed liabilities or material facts regarding the site or Buyer's intended development, claims, litigation and financial matters.

Consider the judicious use of any representations or warranties necessary to protect Buyer. Typically, the negotiation of representations and warranties is resolved by the lawyers documenting the final agreement between the parties. [See, however, Chapter 17, "Optional and Alternative Clauses for Purchase and Sale Proposals," Form 17-6, "Selected Representations and Warranties for a Developer's Site Purchase Agreement," for a listing of various representations and warranties clauses that could be negotiated and inserted. Reading such clauses and carefully thinking about the specific transaction at hand may encourage refinements to the draft proposal. Two basic representations are listed below.]

21.1 Seller's Authority. Seller represents that the party listed under the heading "Seller" on the signature page herein is the sole owner of the entire right, title and interest in and to the site and has the right to convey it to Buyer.

21.2 Site Protection. Seller represents it will not allow the site to be used as a dump site and that no debris will be left on the site at close of escrow. Other than normal, minor modifications resulting from Buyer's soils, environmental or other consultants investigating the site on behalf of Buyer, Seller will maintain the site in its current condition through close of escrow __ *[e.g., subject to assessment district improvements or other permitted approvals or modifications to the site approved by Buyer and Seller and made during escrow]*__.

22. Tax Deferred Exchange. In the event Seller desires to enter into an IRC Section 1031 tax deferred exchange, Buyer will accommodate Seller provided Buyer is free of any risk, cost, loss, liability or expense relating thereto.

***Note:** Most buyers desire to limit their liability to the seller in the event of a breach of the purchase agreement by agreeing to pay the seller a specified sum as liquidated damages. The amount of liquidated damages can be the subject of extensive negotiations. The requirements for an enforceable liquidated damages provision may differ from state to state.*

Alternative "A"—Paragraph 23
Final agreement(s) to contain a liquidated damages clause limiting damages recoverable by Seller to amounts deposited and released to Buyer through escrow

23. Buyer's Default. __*[The Purchase Agreement]*__ OR __*[This agreement and the escrow instructions]*__ shall contain a liquidated damages provision providing that if Buyer defaults under any Buyer obligation, Seller's exclusive remedy shall be to retain amounts theretofore deposited with or paid to escrow holder and released to Seller.

OR

Alternative "B"—Paragraph 23

The following provision is based on California law and attempts to preserve Buyer's right to specific performance in the event of Seller's breach, yet limits damages recoverable by Seller (upon Buyer's breach) to Buyer's deposit(s) released through escrow to Seller. The large type and separate initialing are required under California law. Before using this form, non-lawyers should consult a real estate attorney in the state in which the real property to be purchased is located to insure that the liquidated damages provision complies with local law.

23. Remedies. __*[The Purchase Agreement shall contain the following provision:]*__ Buyer shall, in addition to all other rights provided herein or as may be provided by law, be entitled to specific performance and injunctive relief to enforce Buyer's rights hereunder in the event of a breach by Seller, it being understood hereby because of the special and unique character of the site and the proposed project thereon, a remedy at law would be inadequate to compensate Buyer for any default of Seller under this agreement.

IN THE EVENT BUYER IS IN MATERIAL DEFAULT IN THE PERFORMANCE OR OBSERVANCE OF ANY COVENANT, CONDITION OR AGREEMENT OF BUYER CONTAINED IN THIS CONTRACT, THE SOLE AND EXCLUSIVE REMEDY OF SELLER AGAINST BUYER SHALL BE SELLER'S RETENTION OF THE INITIAL DEPOSIT AND THE EXTENSION DEPOSITS THERETOFORE DEPOSITED WITH OR PAID TO ESCROW HOLDER AND RELEASED TO SELLER PURSUANT TO THE TERMS AND PROVISIONS HEREOF. BECAUSE IT WOULD BE IMPRACTICAL OR EXTREMELY DIFFICULT TO FIX ACTUAL DAMAGE, SUCH SUM IS

THE AMOUNT OF DAMAGE PRESUMED THAT SELLER WOULD SUSTAIN BY REASON OF ANY SUCH DEFAULT BY BUYER, AND BUYER DESIRES TO LIMIT ITS LIABILITY HEREUNDER TO SUCH SUM. SELLER AGREES TO LOOK SOLELY TO SUCH SUM FOR SATISFACTION OF ANY OF SELLER'S REMEDIES FOR THE COLLECTION OF A JUDGMENT OR OTHER JUDICIAL PROCESS REQUIRING THE PAYMENT OF MONEY BY BUYER TO SELLER IN THE EVENT OF DEFAULT BY BUYER HEREUNDER.

_______________ Seller's Initials   _______________ Buyer's Initials

End of Alternatives "A" and "B" to Paragraph 23 —Continue to Paragraph 24

24. Non-binding. When signed by Buyer and Seller, this agreement shall constitute a non-binding letter of intent subject to mutual approval and execution of __*[a final Purchase Agreement]*__ OR __*[a final version of this agreement and applicable escrow instructions]*__. The parties do not intend this letter to be a binding agreement between them and no contract will exist, based upon this writing or the verbal communications of the parties. No contract between the parties shall exist unless or until such comprehensive formal __*[agreement]*__ OR __*[agreements]*__ covering all terms of the proposed transaction are signed by the parties and approved by legal counsel for each.

The developer's lawyer would typically review this document and prepare a final purchase-and-sale agreement and/or escrow instructions. The developer's objective should be to reach a comprehensive business agreement on all major deal points.

A lawyer could prepare this letter agreement to constitute a binding agreement, and escrow instructions could incorporate the letter agreement by reference (in which case the preceding "non-binding" paragraph would be omitted and other adjustments to the form would be made). (Refer to Chapter 17, Form 17-7, "Letter Is to Be a Binding, Conclusive Agreement," for an example. Form 17-7 should only be used with advice of legal counsel.)

Caveat: *State in each letter of intent and manifest by consistent conduct whether the letter is or is not intended to be a binding contract. Except for readers with legal training and in those cases where the proposal has been reviewed by the user's legal counsel,* *the document should specifically state that it is not intended to be a legally binding agreement. Avoid ambiguous writing and conduct and always act in good faith, whether or not the document is a final agreement. Although the prevailing view may be that letters of intent are not binding, parties' conduct at the time of and after execution of a letter of intent has been introduced to prove a binding contract, even though the parties stated in writing that there was no intention to be bound. Be careful and avoid being misunderstood. Consistently establish and maintain a reasonable but firm deadline for preparation and signing of formal documents.*

25. Miscellaneous.

Note: *Generally, an attorney's fees clause would not be included in a letter of intent.*

25.1 Attorney's Fees. __*[While each party shall be responsible for paying its own legal fees in the negotiation and documentation of the proposed transaction,]*__ if an action is brought by either party to enforce the terms of __ *[the Purchase Agreement]*__ *OR* __*[this agreement]*__ or for damages resulting from a breach of __*[such]*__ *OR* __*[this]*__ agreement, the prevailing party in such action shall be entitled to reasonable attorney's fees, costs and expenses in connection with the prosecution or defense of such action.

25.2 Prorations. Real and personal property taxes and assessments (if any) shall be prorated between the parties as of the close of escrow.

25.3 Counterparts. The parties agree that this proposal and any provision of the escrow instructions relating hereto may be signed in counterparts and that when signed by all parties, such counterparts shall constitute the signed agreement by all the parties.

Alternative "A"—Paragraph 26
Buyer oriented

26. Time Limit. This proposal shall terminate at __*[e.g., 5:00]*__ p.m. on __________, 20__ unless written acceptance is received by Buyer on or before such date __*[and is contingent upon Buyer and Seller executing the final Purchase Agreement* __*[and opening escrow at XYZ Title Company]*__ *not later than __________, 20__]*__.

OR

Alternative "B"—Paragraph 26
Seller oriented

26. Time Limit. This proposal shall terminate at __*[e.g., 5:00]*__ p.m. on __________, 20__ unless written acceptance is received by Buyer on or before such date __*[and is contingent upon Buyer and Seller executing the final Purchase Agreement not later than _________, 20__]*__. In the event the parties do not execute the Purchase Agreement and open escrow for the purchase of the site on or before 5:00 p.m. on ________, 20__, Seller shall have the right to offer the site for sale to other parties without any obligation to Buyer and the right to hold the site off the market, even if the parties are engaged in good faith negotiations for the purchase of the site on __*[insert same, preceding date]*__, 20__.

End of Alternatives "A" and "B" to Paragraph 26
—Continue to Paragraph 27

27. Confidentiality and Good Faith. Beginning with the date this letter is signed by Seller and continuing throughout the period ending _______, 20__, *[insert, for example, second date in preceding paragraph]* Seller and Seller's agents will not disclose the terms of this proposed transaction to any third party (except Seller's legal and accounting advisors, who, Seller warrants, shall be obligated not to communicate such information to others) nor will Seller negotiate with any third party for the sale or lease or joint development of the site.

If the foregoing is acceptable as to the terms and conditions upon which __*[you]*__ OR __*[name of entity]*__ will sell and __*[name of buyer]*__ agrees to purchase the site, please so indicate on the signature line provided below and return a signed copy to me.

Very truly yours,

[Name of Buyer entity]

[name of individual signing]
[capacity]

Attachments (as referenced)
cc: __*[Buyer's broker/others]*__

UNDERSTOOD AND AGREED BY "SELLER":

This __ day of ____________, 20__.

Alternative "A": Corporation

XYZ CORPORATION

By: ______________________
[name]
[capacity]

Date: ____________, 20__

Alternative "B": Partnership

XYZ PARTNERSHIP, a
__*[state]*__*[general/limited]*__ partnership,

By: ______________________
[name]
General Partner

Date: ___________, 20__

By: ______________________
[name]
General Partner

Date: ___________, 20__

Add when lawyer prepares as binding agreement:

Accepted For Escrow Purposes:

__*[Name]*__ Title Insurance Company

By: ______________________
Escrow Officer

Date: ___________, 20__

Carefully review and attach exhibits
—in this example, Exhibits "A", "B", and "C":

FORM 4-1

<u>Exhibit "A"</u>
[Assessor's parcel map or plat map describing the "site", as referenced in Paragraph 3]

<u>Exhibit "B"</u>
[Preliminary site plan referenced in Paragraph 3]

<u>Exhibit "C"</u>
[In this case, the illustrative example in Paragraph 3 referenced certain "city" property and a road sought to be abandoned. An exhibit could also be used to depict adjacent land subject to the "Adjacent Owner Escrow" referenced in Paragraph 4. Make liberal use of exhibits to clarify your proposal.]

END OF FORM 4-1

ABBREVIATED PROPOSALS, PURCHASE MONEY NOTES, AND PARTIAL RELEASES

Often, a residential developer of a master-planned community will offer its shopping center sites for sale. Invariably, there are problems inherent in the seller's "plan." Examples include ill-conceived or non-existent grade planning or design controls unnecessarily restricting visibility and/or access, inadequate street and median planning, unworkable "shared" access with residential traffic, insufficient site depth or frontage, and other similar deficiencies. In virtually every case, the residential developer believes that significant value has been created merely by creating a designated retail site and usually does not understand why retail developers are unwilling to offer a quick close.

In one case in my experience, the master-community developer actually placed a sizeable water pumping station on a portion of a major retail site. The fixed location of the pumping station, coupled with the lack of reasonable grade elevation control over the side street, rendered the site physically unworkable for interested major tenants on what was otherwise a superb, well-located freeway off-ramp site. As a group, land developers and developers of master-planned communities seem to persistently fail to get the retail expertise so critically needed in the initial master-planning and broad-entitlement stages.[2]

[2] For more detail on retail development issues from a home builder perspective, see Zimmerman, Bruce G. "Strategy Update: Is It Time to Acquire Retail Development Capability?" *HBC Newsmagazine* (Home Builders Council of the Building Industry Association of Southern California, Inc.), Spring 1992, p. 12.

Notwithstanding such overriding retail site issues, the residential land developer usually recites recent land prices of "comparable" commercial sites (from sites that did not have these problems) and ceaselessly tries to convince the shopping center developer to accept an immediate close on the basis that the site is "ready to go"—it comes with governmental "approvals," is already graded, or some landscaping, utility, off-site, or other improvements are already in place.

Residential builders are accustomed to buying a site and quickly building, with the sales effort occurring when product is built. The retail developer's up-front major tenant marketing effort and the subsequent site-planning "dance" consumes time frames and begets uncertainties the residential builder usually has not experienced and cannot appreciate. Although by no means a panacea, a proposal that includes the underlying factual reasons supporting the buyer's request for time will usually be a positive step in moderating the seller's "residential mentality" and engendering a more sympathetic perspective from the seller. Of course, the principle of using an offer as a tool to educate the seller is by no means limited to the factual situation herein described.

The following form is an example of a proposal given to a substantial residential land developer following introductory discussions. The offer format is not noteworthy, being very similar although somewhat "looser" than the preceding "long-form" proposal, since in this case it appeared obvious the deal was not going to be struck with an initial document. Although purposely short on details, the offer *educates* the seller; the proposal gives the seller a single writing that outlines the various issues that need to be resolved and the time required to accomplish such tasks. Exhibit "B" to the proposal, in fact, outlines step-by-step the tasks the buyer will need to accomplish in order to close.

In this case, certain grading, utility, off-site improvements and entitlements were in place by virtue of the site being a part of a major master-planned community. Exhibit "B" is reproduced substantially unedited to demonstrate the developer's approach. Consider the benefits of educating the seller in such circumstances as a means of establishing a meaningful dialogue and structuring a transaction that meets the needs of both parties. (Note that although Form 4-2 is a letter of intent to enter into an option, the parties are, nevertheless, referred to as "Buyer" and "Seller". This approach is consistent with this book's attempt to limit the number of defined party names and, thus, facilitate ease of use in interchanging provisions from one form to another. Lawyers, feel free to take the liberty to refer to the parties as "Optionor" and "Optionee".)

Form 4-2

Proposal to Option Shopping Center Site in Approved Master-Planned Community from Residential Land Developer Inexperienced in Shopping Center Development; Exhibit: "Preliminary Development Schedule"

[Developer's Letterhead]

[Date]

*[Seller's name
and address*
____
____
___________*]*

Ref: ___-acre parcel located at the
__*[southwest]*__ corner of ___________
and _________; __*[city]*__, __*[state]*__
[See attached map, Exhibit "A"]

Dear ___________:

As we recently discussed, we have completed a substantial preliminary analysis of your ____________ shopping center site and are pleased to submit this letter of intent to enter into an option agreement to purchase the site on the following general terms and conditions:

1. Purchase Price. $__________ all cash.

2. Parties. Upon exercise of the formal option agreement to be hereafter negotiated and signed between the parties, __*[name of developer]*__, or its nominee or assignee, as optionee ("Buyer"), will have the right to purchase the "site" (defined below), from __________ ("Seller").

3. Site. The "site" is an unimproved land parcel located at the __*[e.g., southwest]*__ corner of ___________ and ___________ in _________, ____________ County, California, being Lot ___ of Tract ______ of the ___ -acre ___________ master-planned community named ___________. The site is zoned "___________" and is otherwise approved for development of a shopping center and contains ____ acres of land (_______ square feet of land area). Assuming a ___ -acre site, the purchase price is $_____ per square foot. The exact legal description of the site shall be approved by Buyer and Seller prior to execution of the option agreement. __*[See attached map of site, Exhibit "A"]*__.

4. Possible Upward or Downward Adjustment of Purchase Price. The final purchase price for the site shall be determined by multiplying $____ per square foot of the total net square footage contained in the site, as determined by a certificate prepared by a licensed surveyor to be prepared at Seller's cost and delivered to Buyer within ___ days of the execution of the option agreement by the parties. The term "net square footage" as used herein shall mean the total area of the site expressed in square footage, as determined pursuant to the above survey, less any land area presently dedicated or committed or required to be dedicated or granted in fee or by easement for public use as of close of escrow. The "net square footage" is intended to mean the net developable land area within the site.

> ***Note:*** *When buying land within a master-planned community, sometimes effective shopping center building coverage is increased where, for example, a landscape buffer surrounding the retail site has been installed by the community developer and the shopping center site parcel line begins on the interior boundary of this landscape buffer. In such a case, the retail developer's site improvement obligation may start with the parking lot or even outparcel building improvements rather than the typical peripheral landscape, resulting in above average site building coverage.*

5. Title. Prior to the release of any option payments from Buyer to Seller, the following contingency shall be satisfied within an acceptable time frame negotiated between the parties:

> Approval by Buyer of a preliminary title report and legal description as provided by Seller at Seller's cost. Such preliminary title report shall not be deemed received by Buyer until Buyer has been furnished from __________ Title Company a preliminary title report, complete with copies of each and every document referenced in said title report, together with a map prepared by said title company depicting each easement, right of way, license, right, etc. which is capable of being plotted in accordance with normal title company practices.

6. Option Period Development Tasks. The parties understand that in order to undertake development of a viable, well-anchored shopping center on the site, considerable investigation, marketing analysis and negotiations with governmental authorities will be required, including but not limited to the following:

6.1 First [2] Months of Option Period. Buyer's investigation and determination that there are no governmental, physical or economic constraints which would render development of the site as a __*[e.g., neighborhood]*__ shopping center not feasible or uneconomic; research, analysis and preparation of a trade area income, population and housing supply and demand study showing sufficient trade area population with demographic qualities at time of buildout to currently attract quality anchor tenants on acceptable economic terms and conditions; title review; retaining architects, engineers and related consultants; preliminary site plan studies; and commencement of major tenant marketing.

6.2 Balance of Option Period. Obtaining and consummating major tenant commitments acceptable to Buyer and satisfying all major tenant imposed conditions; obtaining final site plan approval from all required agencies for Buyer's planned __*[e.g., neighborhood]*__ shopping center on the site, including but not limited to, negotiation of desired building density and layout, acceptable development fee conditions and agreements __*[(including the shopping center developer's non-responsibility for additional off-site costs—except off-site costs that are indirectly paid through Buyer's payment of standard governmentally-imposed development fees in accordance with existing fee schedules applicable to retail centers in the same jurisdictional area as the site)]*__, conditional use permits (if required), utility agreements, and issuance of appropriate building permits.

7. Preliminary Development Schedule. In order to assist Seller in comprehending a reasonable estimate of the time required to accomplish specific tasks (i.e., completing major tenant negotiations and thereafter commencing governmental processing and obtaining required approvals from the ________________ __*[city/county]*__ regulatory authorities), a __*[name of proposed center]*__ Shopping Center Preliminary Development Schedule is attached hereto as Exhibit "B."

8. Option Payment Schedule. After evaluation of the potential risks and rewards of this development opportunity, we have concluded that the following option money release schedule is a reasonable compromise between the parties, particularly in light of the fact that (a) governmental processing cannot commence until major tenant transactions are consummated (tenant requirements result in a final site plan for governmental processing) and (b) any closing within the option period is all cash:

Option Month #	$ Released
1st __[2]__ months	0
2nd __[2]__ months	$_______/month
5th—12th months	$_______/month
13th month	$_______
14th month	$_______
15th month	$_______
Total:	$_______

Such option payments are applicable to the purchase price but forfeited to Seller if Buyer fails to close. Notwithstanding the above schedule, the option will terminate __[30]__ days after receipt of building permits if permits are received within the above option period.

> ***Note:*** *Always negotiate at least some "cushion" in the necessary option period, which in this example is the right to extend the closing for the final three months indicated above.*

9. Seller's Right to Work Product. As additional consideration given Seller under the option, if Buyer elects not to exercise the option, Buyer shall deliver copies of all tentative site plans, engineering, soils and hazardous materials studies and other consultant work product concerning the site which is generated by Buyer during the option period.

10. Entry. Upon execution of the option, Buyer shall have an immediate license to enter upon the site for the purpose of conducting economic feasibility, engineering, soil and other tests at its sole cost and expense. Buyer will indemnify Seller and hold Seller harmless from any and all loss or liability resulting from the acts of Buyer or its agents or employees upon the subject property and from all or any mechanics liens or other liens resulting from Buyer's conduct or the conduct of its agents or employees on the site. Seller will grant Buyer, or Buyer's nominee or agent, the right to erect a sign or signs (consistent with applicable governmental sign codes or regulations) offering retail space for lease.

11. Seller Cooperation. During the __[option]__ period, Seller will provide Buyer with copies of any and all documentation in Seller's possession or control relating to development of the site at no expense to Buyer. This data shall include the use of copies of existing engineering reports, site plans, grading plans, reports, and the like, in the possession of Seller or Seller's agents. Seller will cooperate fully with and assist Buyer in negotiations with private and public special interest groups, adjacent property owners, federal, state and local governmental and quasi-governmental agencies, as such negotiations relate to timely securing approvals and permits for the site. Seller will also execute any and all instruments necessary or appropriate for the development of the site, including but not limited to, maps, dedications or easements and rights of way to governmental and quasi-governmental authorities and adjacent property owners, provided such execution is consistent with normal practices. __*[(Any new work required of Seller's existing engineers or other development consultants which is requested by Buyer shall be paid for by Buyer on terms to be separately negotiated between Buyer and any such engineers or consultants.)]*__

Alternative "A"—Paragraph 12
Broad right to assign

12. Assignment. Buyer shall have the right to assign its rights under the __*[option]*__ without the prior consent of Seller.

OR

Alternative "B"—Paragraph 12
more limited assignment right

12. Assignment. Buyer may (i) assign the __*[option]*__ to any entity in which Buyer or its officers, directors or shareholders have a majority interest, or are managing partners and are directly involved, without Seller's consent, or (ii) nominate any entity to take title to the site, upon the giving of written notice to Seller, which notice may not be given less than three days prior to closing. Any other assignment may not be made without Seller's prior written consent, which shall not be unreasonably withheld. Any such assignment is conditional upon such assignee agreeing to be bound by all consents and approvals theretofore given or deemed to have been given by Buyer, and such assignment or nomination shall not relieve Buyer of its obligations under the option.

13. Condemnation Prior to Closing. If the site or any part thereof becomes the subject of a condemnation proceeding during the __*[option]*__ period, Seller agrees to immediately advise Buyer thereof. In the event of such condemnation, Buyer shall have the option to (i) take title in accordance with the terms and conditions of Buyer's rights under the __*[option]*__ agreement and negotiate with the condemning authority for the condemnation award

FORM 4-2

and receive the benefits thereof without affecting the purchase price, or (ii) terminate the *__[option]__* agreement and declare Buyer's obligations null and void and of no further effect, in which event all sums theretofore paid or released to Seller shall be returned to Buyer.

14. Title Insurance. At the close of escrow, Seller shall convey marketable title to Buyer in compliance with *__[insert applicable state]__* law, subject only to those matters of record which have been disclosed to Buyer in the Preliminary Title Report and approved in writing by Buyer. In addition, Seller shall deliver to Buyer at close of escrow, at Seller's expense, a *__[See Appendix A, Form A-1]__* policy of title insurance insuring marketable title in Buyer for the full amount of the actual purchase price, subject only to the title items previously approved by Buyer.

15. Brokerage Commissions. Buyer and Seller each separately represents and warrants that it did not incur any brokerage commission in connection with this transaction and that no commission or finder's fee is payable to Buyer or any third party upon consummation of this transaction, except with respect to ____________ *__[e.g., who/which acted as a finder in this transaction. The parties agree that upon consummation of the purchase of the site by Buyer, Buyer and Seller will each separately pay such finder $____________ out of Buyer's and Seller's funds distributed through escrow]__*.

16. Action. Upon execution of this non-binding letter of intent, the parties will promptly begin to negotiate *__[an option]__ OR __[a contingent purchase]__* agreement *__[and escrow instructions]__* consistent with the economic terms and conditions of this letter. Kindly sign and return a copy of this letter merely confirming *__[Seller's]__* approval of the general economic terms contained herein.

> ***Note:*** *Although this rather "loose" letter of intent manifests an intent not to be bound, conservative legal counsel may wish to insert a more formal "non-binding" clause, such as the one contained in Form 4-1, Paragraph 24.*

17. Expiration of Offer. This proposal shall expire at *__[5:00]__* p.m ____________, 20__ unless written acceptance is received by Buyer on or before such date *__[and is contingent upon Buyer and Seller negotiating and executing a final __[option]__ OR __[purchase agreement]__ __[and escrow instructions]__ not later than __________, 20__]__*.

We would like very much to develop the _________ Shopping Center with you and assure you of our commitment to build a complimentary, quality project which would be an asset to __*[name of master-planned community]*__. We look forward to working with you and appreciate the considerable time you have spent with us prior to our submittal of this proposal.

Very truly yours,

[Buyer Entity]

[Name]
[Title]

UNDERSTOOD AND AGREED BY "SELLER":
This __ day of ____________, 20__.

[Seller entity]

By: ___________________

Its: ___________________

Exhibit "A"
[Attached map of the site]

Exhibit "B"

[Name] Shopping Center
Preliminary Development Schedule

[Developmental tasks and time requirements will differ significantly from site to site. (The following is a very aggressive schedule.) The schedule is included not for its content but to introduce the concept of attaching a schedule as a persuasive tool when warranted. Such an exhibit can succinctly substantiate the developer's request to control the site for an extended time period. Amend and add headings, as necessary, to conform text with appropriate milestones.]

1. Title. Title to be approved within __*[e.g., 14]*__ days from receipt of preliminary title report and copies of all referenced documents and plotted easements, per Paragraph __*[e.g., 5]*__, above.

2. Engineering Feasibility. Buyer's approval of an engineering feasibility study to be performed at its expense within __*[e.g., 1 month]*__ from receipt of title documents. Buyer will engage its typical consultants to prepare a __*[e.g., "Site Investigation and Engineering Feasibility Report"]*__ for the proposed center, which typically takes __*[1 month]*__ from our civil engineer's receipt of approved title documents. __*[(The requested report will include preliminary analysis of required foundation specifications on the adjoining residential project so as to give likely results of a full soils investigation)]*__.

3. Major Tenant Commitments. Buyer's obtaining from acceptable major tenants satisfactory commitments to purchase or lease a portion of the site within __*[3-4]*__ months from commencement of the option period.

4. Soils. After above major tenant commitments are obtained and engineering feasibility completed, Buyer will within __*[1]*__ month undertake and complete a comprehensive soils investigation and evaluate recommended specifications __*[e.g.,including potential site engineering and grading modifications to improve marketability, site efficiency, visibility and traffic flow]*__.

5. Site Plan Approval. Final site plan approval __*[(including required concurrent approval of conceptual landscape plan and building elevations)]*__ will take approximately __*[3-4]*__ months after securing major tenants and preparing site plan and related submission materials acceptable to major tenants. Assuming __*[1 month]*__ is required to prepare for submittal after __*[3]*__ months securing major tenant transactions, and there is a __*[e.g., 1]*__-month delay in getting on approval calender __*[per ________, planner, such delay is to be expected,]*__ __*[8-9]*__months is the estimated time frame in which to obtain site plan approval from time of commencement of the option period.

6. Permits. Buyer's ability to obtain all necessary applicable governmental approvals and building permits for the construction and operation of the shopping center on terms and conditions acceptable to Buyer should total __*[at least]*__ __*[11-12]*__ months.

END OF FORM 4-2

Form 4-3 is an example of a quick letter outlining the terms of a proposed purchase option. It is a representative follow-up to discussions with a sophisticated seller. Frequently, such a seller will request a brief summary of the economic deal the shopping center developer is willing to make.

Form 4-3

Simple Letter of Intent to Enter into Site Purchase Option Agreement

[Developer's Letterhead]

[Date]

*[Name of seller
and seller's address
____
____
___________________]*

Ref: ___ -acre parcel located at the __*[e.g., southeast]*__
corner of __________ and __________ Street;
__*[city]*__, __*[state]*__

Dear __________:

__*[E.g., I appreciate the progress we made at our recent Atlanta meeting. Based upon our subsequent telephone conversations and the general consensus reached at the meeting]*__, we are prepared to enter into a formal option agreement consistent with the following economic terms and conditions:

1. Site. The "site" is an unimproved land parcel located at __*[e.g., the southeast corner of ____________ Boulevard and _________ Street consisting of approximately ___ acres]*__ net of streets, rights of way, or other required dedications. *We agreed that if you are not committed to your possible 1-acre sale to the _______ bank, then all __________ [more than 15] acres would be subject to the option described herein. On the other hand, if at this time you are legally bound to the one-acre bank sale, then the optioned property would consist of approximately ___ acres.*

2. Deposit. We would agree to make an initial $__________ good faith cash deposit into escrow upon execution of an option agreement consistent with the terms and conditions outlined below.

3. Option Payments. At any time during the option period we may elect to give notice ("notice of closing") to you and escrow holder that we irrevocably elect to exercise the option and will close within __*[21]*__ days of such notice, provided that we are then current with respect to the following option payment schedule:

FORM 4-3

Option Payment	For Next Incremental Time
0	First __*[3]*__ months
$______ per month	__*[4th]*__ through __*[6th]*__ months
$______ per month	next __*[3]*__ months
$______ per month	final __*[6]*__ months

If for any reason during the first __*[3]*__ months of the option period (Buyer's due diligence period) we elect not to proceed, the initial $______ option deposit will be returned to us. However, assuming Buyer does not elect to terminate during the due diligence period, beginning with the __*[4th]*__ month of the option period, the initial deposit and all additional option payments made by Buyer would be forfeited if we fail to close but applicable to the purchase price if we exercise the option.

4. Purchase Price. The purchase price shall be $_____ per square foot net of required dedications, provided we give notice of closing during the first __*[6]*__ months of the option. The purchase price would escalate to $____ per square foot if we give notice of closing during the __*[7th, 8th, 9th or 10th]*__ month of the option period and $____ per square foot if we give notice of closing during the __*[11th, 12th, 13th, 14th or 15th]*__ month of the option period. The purchase will be all cash without regard to the time of the actual closing.

Cover any other aspects unique to the transaction, for example:

5. Commencement of Option. *You have mentioned that a third party has an existing option to acquire the site but that such third party option is terminable at will by you and your partner. Our option would commence and the Initial Deposit concurrently deposited when the third party option rights have terminated and our option agreement has been executed.*

6. Action. Upon approval of the economic terms and conditions contained in this letter, we will promptly prepare and negotiate in good faith, an option agreement and escrow instructions consistent with the economic terms outlined herein.

We continue to be very interested in developing your site and doing business with you and your partner. While we do not intend this letter to bind either you or my company, please sign and return a copy to me confirming our mutual understanding regarding the economic terms of the proposed option.

Very truly yours,

[Optionee-developer]

UNDERSTOOD AND AGREED:

This __ day of ___________, 20__.

[Name of Optionor-Seller]

By: ____________________

Its: ____________________

END OF FORM 4-3

Sometimes the developer buyer will request that the seller carry back a purchase money note as a portion of the site purchase consideration (usually secured by a deed of trust or mortgage on the site). Occasionally, sellers will agree to release certain parcels or a designated land area from the lien of the security instrument upon payment of a negotiated sum (a so-called "release" provision).

Most sellers will not subordinate to construction financing. And with most sellers so adamant that they will not subordinate, I will typically specifically state, in any offer proposing that the seller accept a purchase money note, that seller will not be required to subordinate. This approach may increase the frequency with which sellers agree to accept purchase money notes.

The two clauses selected as Form 4-4 were extracted from an old offer to acquire an unparcelized two-acre site near a much larger site under development by my company. Some specific "spillover" tenants from the larger development were being considered for a portion of the smaller site. In most cases, the 125% partial-release language applying to an entire site will not be found acceptable by the landowner. Of course, negotiating a partial-release structure with a landowner is generally much easier when the site is composed of more than one parcel and, thus, a distinct release valuation can be established for each parcel. Although Form 4-4's application of the release concept is not particularly noteworthy, the use of a mathematical example within the proposal is unique. Such a style may be helpful in conceiving and drafting persuasive offers. Demonstrating within an offer how an economic or legal principle would work in the given context clarifies the proposal. With many sellers inexperienced and confused when release provisions are proposed, including a hypothetical example within the offer may assist in opening a dialogue and reaching an acceptable agreement.

FORM 4-4

Form 4-4

Seller's Purchase Money Note Secured by Site; Partial Release Clause Illustrating Economic Effect

__. **Purchase Money Note and Trust Deed [or Mortgage].** At close of escrow a total of $122,720 cash shall be paid to Seller through escrow. The balance of the purchase price shall be payable in the form of a $400,000 promissory note secured by a __*[trust deed]*__ OR __*[mortgage]*__ recorded against the site. Interest on the note shall be payable quarterly at the rate of 10% per annum interest only on the outstanding balance. All remaining principal and interest shall be due __*[e.g., 36]*__ months from close of escrow. Said __*[trust deed]*__ OR __*[mortgage]*__ shall state that at all times it shall remain a first __*[trust deed]*__ OR __*[mortgage]*__ and may not be subordinated to construction or permanent financing without Seller's express written consent. Buyer reserves the right to pay the note in advance of the due date.

__. **Partial Release of Lien of Deed of Trust Upon Additional 125% Per S.F. Cash Payment to Seller.** Seller agrees that during the term of said purchase money note, upon Buyer's request, Seller shall cause to remove any portion of the site from the lien of the __*[trust deed]*__ OR __*[mortgage]*__ upon Buyer's payment of __*[e.g., 125]*__ % of Buyer's average net per square foot acquisition cost of the site multiplied by the square footage of such portion of the site requested to be so released by Buyer. For example, assuming the net site is 2.0 acres, this equates to 87,120 total net s.f. in the site. At the acquisition price of $522,720, Buyer is paying $6.00 per net s.f. of land area. This acquisition cost multiplied by 125% is $7.50 per s.f. Thus, a Buyer request to remove 20,000 s.f. from the lien of the __*[trust deed]*__ OR __*[mortgage]*__ would require a payment of $150,000 to Seller ($7.50/s.f. x 20,000 s.f. = $150,000). Upon Seller's receipt of said $150,000, the note would thereby be reduced to $250,000 (i.e., $400,000 –$150,000 = $250,000). At that point in time, the __*[trust deed]*__ OR __*[mortgage]*__ would then encumber the remaining 67,120 s.f. of land area (87,120 s.f.–20,000 s.f.).

END OF FORM 4-4

OVERVIEW

Chapter 5 considers the preparation of ground lease proposals for unimproved shopping center sites. The chapter begins with a discussion of amendments required to convert the comprehensive long-form fee purchase Form 4-1 into a ground lease proposal format (Form 5-1). Form 5-2 addresses the purchase of an existing leasehold. Subsequent forms illustrate creative uses of the ground lease to make workable deals in a variety of contexts. (A complete "Long-Form Letter of Intent to Enter into Site Ground Lease" is located in Appendix B as Form B-1.)

FORMS

5-1 Amendments to Long-Form Purchase Offer to Make Ground Lease Proposal. Selected Amendments to Standard Long-Form Purchase Offer to Create a Letter of Intent to Enter into Site Ground Lease; Extensive Exhibit: "Summary of Ground Lease Terms."

5-2 Ground Lessee Buyout. Selected Amendments to Standard Long-Form Purchase Offer to Provide for Buyout of a Ground Lessee's Rights under an Existing Ground Lease.

5-3 Converting an Unaccepted Purchase Offer to a Ground Lease Proposal to Improve Likelihood of Acceptance. Revision of Unaccepted Purchase Offer to Provide for Ground Lease of Site; Site Owner's Right to Purchase Developer's Improvements at Fair Market Value.

5-4 Persuasive Financial Analysis of Developer's Proposed Subtenant Income Stream to Favorably Distinguish Developer's Proposal from Competing Proposals. Site Ground Lease Proposal to Landowner with Developer Disclosing Proposed Financial Partner and Major Tenants; Landowner Granted Participation in Subtenant Rental Increases and Option to Purchase Developer's Improvements (Exhibit Compares Financial Attributes of Developer's Key Major Tenant Relative to Competition to Improve Likelihood of Landowner's Selection of Developer over Potential Competing Developers).

5-5 Combining Elements of Fee Purchase, Ground Lease, Option and Land Loan to Meet the Landowner's Needs. Proposal to Enter into Option to Purchase or Ground Lease Major Site: A Defined Portion Is Developed Now and Balance of Property is Optioned for Future Development (Developer's Financial Partner Makes Land Loan Pending Entitlement and Closing to Accommodate Landowner).

Chapter 5

Ground Leasing an Unimproved Shopping Center Site

If you want your dreams to come true, don't sleep.
—Yiddish proverb

To avoid the potential tax burden, a landowner with a low tax basis in his or her property often is not willing to sell but, nevertheless, would like to receive a market return on the land's current value. Often, such a landowner—averse to the risks of becoming directly involved in the development process or forming a venture with a shopping center developer—perceives the ground lease to be the best of available alternatives.

From the developer's perspective, a ground lease will lower the developer's overall capital investment in the project since the developer does not have to make an equity investment in "land." Moreover, because the ground lease payment constant is typically lower than the debt constant obtainable from an institutional lender, the developer's cash flow may be greater than if the site were purchased. If the developer can negotiate (i) an attractive option to purchase the fee in the future and (ii) a rental escalation formula which (in lieu of cost-of-living or onerous fixed increases) gives the landowner a reasonable percentage of developer's revenues or net cash flow above an agreed baseline in return for a relatively fixed minimum rent, ground leasing a site can be quite attractive.

Nevertheless, the developer must be willing to accept the increased complexity in documenting the ground lease (and leases to subtenants) and have sympathetic and understanding equity and debt sources. (The developer will routinely be able to encumber the leasehold estate, but many ground lessors are unwilling to give the ground lessee the right to encumber the ground lessor's fee interest in the site.) Yet, in a difficult financing climate, the economic terms obtainable from the ground lessor must be exceptional for many developers to be willing to assume the legal complexities and financing hurdles incident to developing a ground-leased site.

The purpose of this section is not to make you a technical expert in the use of ground leases and leasehold mortgages. Its goal is to demonstrate how the ground lease, particularly when combined with fee options, land loans, and imaginative problem solving, can be used as a creative tool in your deal-making arsenal. Some very viable transactions can only be accomplished using a ground lease. For example, it is not unusual for a major tenant, with whom a developer has a continuous business relationship, to desperately want to locate on a site owned by a party unwilling or unable to sell. Improvement of one's capabilities in this area improves one's productivity and competitive competence.

The approach advocated in this chapter is designed to make the developer's job easier. Rather than creating an entirely new "ground lease" offer form, it is generally simpler and more efficient to merely make required modifications to the standard long-form fee purchase offer (Form 4-1) and outline the specific ground lease terms in an attached exhibit. Following this logic, Form 5-1 illustrates how certain paragraphs in the standard long-form purchase offer introduced in Chapter 4 as Form 4-1 can be modified to provide for the creation of a ground lease rather than a fee purchase of the site. Essentially, by amending certain key clauses, editing the remaining text and adding an exhibit entitled "Summary of Ground Lease Terms" describing the specific terms of the ground lease, the essential conceptual format of Form 4-1 can be maintained. In short, the amended "ground lease" version of Form 4-1 provides the general escrow terms that take the parties through an escrow closing, at which time the ground lease commences in accordance with the terms of the proposed ground lease described in the exhibit.

To conserve space and to create presentational balance within Chapter 5, Form 5-1 includes only examples of certain key amendments to Form 4-1 together with the vital "Summary of Ground Lease Terms" exhibit. The full-text version of an amended Form 4-1 to provide for ground leasing a shopping center site is in Appendix B as Form B-1, "Long-Form Letter of Intent to Enter into Site Ground Lease."

Be aware that Form 5-1 is designed to serve as a proposal confirming a developer's intention to ground lease a site from a landowner for development of a shopping center. It is *not* intended to serve as a deal-making document between a developer and one of the developer's tenants in the center. Observe, also, that in this form the developer is referred to as "Tenant" (i.e., "tenant" under the long-term ground lease) and the landowner is referred to as "Landlord" (i.e., "landlord" under the ground lease). (The terms selected are consistent with this book's attempt to use the fewest possible party names and thereby facilitate incorporation of selected form language from one deal-making document to another.) The reader can easily change the names of the parties to "Developer" and "Landowner."

This chapter's second form, Form 5-2, demonstrates how various paragraphs from Form 5-1 could be abstracted and amended to create a leasehold buyout proposal. In this example, to acquire an existing ground lease the developer makes a cash payment to a speculative ground lessee willing to sell his or her ground lease position. Mechanics aside, the next three forms, Forms 5-3, 5-4, and 5-5, are specific examples wherein the use of a ground lease meets the unique needs of a landowner, each in different ways.

ALTERING THE STANDARD FEE PURCHASE OFFER TO PROVIDE FOR GROUND LEASING THE SITE

The following form, 5-1, demonstrates that chiefly by modifying introductory paragraphs; i.e., Paragraph "1" ("Parties"), Paragraph "2" ("Purchase Price") and Paragraph "19" ("Title") in the standard long-form fee purchase offer example (Form 4-1) and attaching an exhibit, "Summary of Ground Lease Terms" (Exhibit "D" if following the exhibit sequence of Form 4-1), as outlined below, the deal maker can begin to create a sophisticated ground lease proposal. (Be especially careful to read and appropriately edit each and every other paragraph of any draft ground lease proposal derived from Form 4-1 for logical and internal consistency with the proposed ground lease transaction.)

As mentioned above, the full-text version of a site acquisition ground lease proposal is set forth in Appendix B as Form B-1, "Long-Form Letter of Intent to Enter Into Site Ground Lease." After review, modification, and approval by your legal counsel, your full-text version should be saved in a computer form file system for future use as a basic ground lease proposal format. (See Chapter 19, "How to Create and Maintain a Deal Making Document Form File System," for applicable benefits and technical recommendations.)

Note: *Many states in the U.S. have regulations providing that the creation of a long term ground lease of a certain number of years or more (for example, 30 years) will result in a re-assessment of property taxes. Plan accordingly and negotiate who will be responsible for the payment of such anticipated increase in property taxes.*

Form 5-1

Selected Amendments to Standard Long-Form Purchase Offer to Create a Letter of Intent to Enter into Site Ground Lease; Extensive Exhibit: "Summary of Ground Lease Terms"

[Date]

[Insert Name and
address of landowner
____
____
____________________*]*

Re: ___ -Acre Shopping Center Site located at the
__*[e.g., southeast]*__ corner of _____ __*[Street]* and
_________ __*[Avenue]*; __*[City]*__, __*[State]*__
(See attached maps, Exhibits "A", "B" and "C", and
"Summary of Ground Lease Terms", Exhibit "D")

Dear __*[Name of landowner]*__:

Using initial commentary in Form 4-1 as an illustration, insert appropriate introductory comments regarding status of parties, background and developer's initiative to date.

Replaces Paragraph 1 of Form 4-1:

1. Parties. Upon satisfaction of the escrow contingencies described herein, __*[name of shopping center developer or the developer's entity]*__, or its nominee or assignee ("Tenant"), will ground lease the "site" (defined below), from the site's present owner, __*[name of landowner]*__ ("Landlord").

Replaces Paragraph 2 of Form 4-1:

2. Consideration. Tenant will pay Landlord, as and for the use of the site, the ground rent stated in the attached Exhibit "__*[D]*__", "Summary of Ground Lease Terms", on the terms and conditions stated therein.

Proposing a ground lease (as distinguished from a fee purchase) requires that the word "Buyer" be globally changed to "Tenant" and that "Seller" be changed to "Landlord" throughout the document. Other form paragraphs must be edited for consistency with the ground lease concept. To be consistent with the creation of a lease-

FORM 5-1

hold, amend Paragraph 19 "Title" to provide for a leasehold title policy and recordation of a lease abstract at closing. For example, the following paragraph replaces Paragraph 19 of Form 4-1:

19. Title. At the close of escrow, the parties shall cause to be recorded an abstract confirming Tenant's right, title and interest as ground lessee under the ground lease, which shall be deposited into escrow by Tenant and approved by Landlord on or before __________, 20__. Tenant's title, as ground lessee, shall be a marketable leasehold interest subject only to those matters of record which have been disclosed to Tenant in the preliminary title report and approved in writing by Tenant. In addition, Landlord shall deliver to Tenant at close of escrow, at Landlord's expense, a __*[See Appendix A, Form A-1]*__ policy of title insurance insuring marketable title in Tenant's leasehold interest for $___________, subject only to the reversionary interest of Landlord and the title items previously approved by Tenant.

The core of the proposed ground lease, the following exhibit is designed for attachment to the proposal:

Exhibit "__"
[In this example, Exhibit "D"]

Summary of Ground Lease Terms

1. Parties. __*[Name of landowner]*__ ("Landlord") and __*[name of shopping center developer or the developer's entity]*__, or its nominee or assignee ("Tenant").

2. Site. The leased land (the "site") is __*[specifically describe the site]*__.

3. Term. The lease term shall be __*[e.g., 65 years]*__, for convenience described in the following components:

The following described components of the term are merely possibilities. Change the elements of the term to meet the needs of the transaction.

3.1 Construction Term. The first portion of the term (the "Construction Term") shall commence upon close of escrow and shall continue until the earlier of _________, 20__, or the date that __ % of the building space in __*[e.g., Tenant's first construction phase]*__ is completed and occupied by subtenants open for business to the general public on the premises.

3.2 Completion Term. The second portion of the term (the "Completion Term") shall commence upon expiration of the Construction Term and shall continue until the earlier of ____________, 20__, or the date that __ % of __*[e.g., that amount of total building space shown on Tenant's initial, final governmentally-approved site plan for the entire site]*__ is completed and occupied by subtenants open for business to the general public on the premises.

3.3 Remainder Term. The final portion of the term (the "Remainder Term") shall commence upon expiration of the Completion Term and shall continue until that date which is __*[e.g., 65 years]*__ after the lease commencement date.

FORM 5-1

4. Term Commencement. The Construction Term shall commence upon close of escrow consistent with the escrow instructions to be signed by Landlord and Tenant.

5. Minimum Annual Rent. Minimum annual ground rent shall be due in accordance with the following annual ground rent schedule, payable quarterly, in advance:

Construction Term	$______________
Completion Term	$______________
Remainder Term	
Years __*[e.g., 1-10]*__	$______________
Years __*[e.g., 11-25]*__	$______________
Years __*[e.g., 26-40]*__	$______________
Years __*[e.g., 41—]*__	$______________

[and thereafter—add as necessary]

The developer may elect not to present an initial proposal showing any fixed increases in rent. It may be sufficient to propose merely the initial minimum rent and the concept and general magnitude of potential bonus rents (see next numbered paragraph). Refinements and a specific rent escalation mechanism will evolve out of negotiations with the potential Landlord and Landlord's advisors. The reader may also want to substantially shorten the "Alternative B" provision within Paragraph 6 (below) in preparing an initial offer.

The Alternative "A" and "B" provisions are designed merely to highlight differences in gross rent and net income concepts. These provi-

sions, as shown here, are entirely inadequate for final documentation of the transaction. The final ground lease would cover these provisions with much greater detail and precision.

Optional: Add the following as an additional paragraph (and renumber succeeding paragraphs) to provide for minimum annual ground rent based upon a value per square foot of "net" land area:

__. Possible Upward or Downward Adjustment of Minimum Annual Rent. The final Construction Term annual ground rent shall be determined by multiplying $____ per square foot times the total net land square footage of the site, as determined by a certificate prepared by a licensed surveyor to be obtained by Tenant at Tenant's sole cost prior to close of escrow, and then multiplying such amount by a rent factor of __*[e.g., 9]*__ % (the "rent formula"). The term "net square footage" as used herein shall mean the total area of the site expressed in square footage, as determined pursuant to the above survey, less any land area presently dedicated or committed or required to be dedicated or granted in fee or by easement for public use as of close of escrow. The "net square footage" is intended to mean the net developable land area within the site.

The Construction Term minimum annual rent set forth in Paragraph __*[5]*__ was prepared assuming the net land square footage of the site is _________ square feet. If the net square footage of the site is more than or less than this assumed figure, the Construction Term rent shall be adjusted using the actual net square footage in accordance with the rent formula. If the Construction Term rent is so adjusted, the scheduled rent for the Completion Term and the Remainder Term shown above shall be adjusted upward or downward by the same percentage by which the final, adjusted Construction Term rent bears to the scheduled Construction Term rent.

Where Landlord participation is to be granted, Landlord and Tenant will in all but the most unusual circumstances select a gross rental receipts formula rather than a net cash flow formula.

6. Bonus Rent. Tenant intends to proceed to immediately develop a major __*[e.g., community]*__ shopping center on the site. Tenant estimates that it will achieve a stabilized __ % occupancy level __*[on Developer's initial construction phase or upon total buildout?]*__ consistent with its preliminary development pro forma within __*[____years/months]*__(the "target date") following the term commencement. Based upon such preliminary pro forma, Tenant's __*[gross rental income]*__ OR __*[net cash flow]*__, as defined below, as of the target date is projected to be approximately $_________ per year on a stabilized basis.

The ground lease shall provide that Landlord shall receive, as additional "bonus" rent, __*[insert Alternative "A" OR Alternative "B"]*__

Alternative "A"
Participation in Tenant's gross rental stream above a floor

__*[e.g., 15]*__ % of the amount by which Tenant's actual annual gross rental receipts from the center (excluding reimbursements for common area expense) during each full calendar year following the target date exceeds the above-projected target date stabilized gross rental income of $____________ __*[, as adjusted to reflect the center's actual gross rental receipts as of the target date]*__. __*[However, the gross income base against which bonus rent is calculated shall in no event be less than $__________ nor greater than $___________]*__.

FORM 5-1

OR

Alternative "B"
Participation in Tenant's "net cash flow" (a more complex concept used much less frequently than gross rent participation)

__*[e.g., 15]*__ % of the amount by which Tenant's actual annual "net cash flow" from the center during each full calendar year following the target date exceeds the above-projected target date stabilized net cash flow of $___________ __*[, as adjusted to reflect the center's actual net cash flow as of the target date]*__. __*[However, the net cash flow base against which bonus rent is calculated shall in no event be less than $___________ nor greater than $___________]*__.

Continue, if desired, to refine Alternative "B" concept:

The term "net cash flow" as used in the lease shall include all gross receipts from Tenant's subleases, parking receipts, and any receipts paid on account of business or rental interruption insurance carried by Tenant. However, there shall be deducted therefrom (i) any rebates and/or refunds to Tenant's subtenants, (ii) any specific ad valorem or other tax levied against rental proceeds or sales tax which must be accounted for by Tenant to any government or governmental agency, (iii) all shopping center operating expenses, including real property taxes, insurance, common area maintenance, management fees, and other usual and customary expenses, including depreciation of Tenant's improvements, (iv) imputed debt service on Tenant's initial financing of improvements in an amount stipulated to be

$__________ per calendar year, and (v) debt service on subsequent loans utilized to pay for major capital additions to the center. (To the extent funds used to pay for such capital additions are not borrowed but are derived from Tenant's or Tenant's partner(s') equity or capital contributions, imputed interest thereon shall be deducted from gross receipts at the stipulated rate of __*[e.g., 13]*__ % per calendar year.)

Additional thought should be given to adjustments relative to future substantial capital advances by the developer. What if Landlord constructs a large office building on the site in the future for which it receives substantial rent? Should Landlord's participation in this new rental revenue remain unaltered? Is such a contingency significant enough to address in the initial proposal or should it wait? Make any other refinements to the proposed rental structure based upon specific facts and possible future events relative to the proposed site.

Any rental adjustment formula should bear a continuing relationship with the rental value of the specific site. Although starting with an agreed initial or base ground rent, rental adjustment formulas may escalate ground rent when a specified percentage of Tenant's gross rental stream or net cash flow exceeds a prescribed base, similar to the preceding clause. Similarly, limited periodical adjustments set by MAI appraisal are also common. However, use of a consumer price index formula should be avoided, as over time it may have no relationship with achievable subtenant rents for the specific site. In particular, when leasehold mortgage financing is contemplated, the lender must take into account the total rent payable under the ground lease. If the rent cannot be fixed in an amount certain for the entire leasehold period (at least relative to subtenant income), the mortgagee may be unwilling to make a leasehold mortgage.

Caveat: *Again, the language above is intended merely to assist the developer in creating an acceptable economic structure from a business perspective—DO NOT use the above terminology in your ground lease. A ground lease is an extraordinarily technical, long-term document that should be prepared by an attorney especially skilled in ground lease law and finance. It must be fashioned to meet the present and anticipated needs of the specific parties over an extended time period.*

7. Purchase Option. Tenant or Tenant's nominee or assignee shall have the option to purchase the site during each of the __*[3rd, 6th, etc.]*__ lease years. The purchase price of the site during each such lease year shall be as follows:

Lease Year	Purchase Price
__*[e.g., 3rd]*__	$____________
__*[e.g., 6th]*__	$____________
__*[and so forth]*__	$____________

As an alternative to fixed pricing, consider an escalation adjustment to a fixed price, an economic formula, an appraisal valuation methodology or a combination of such approaches. An appraisal valuation should assume the site is unimproved, with use and zoning consistent with the Tenant's use of the site as of the appraisal date.

The purchase price for the site shall be payable __*[in cash]*__ OR __*[on installment terms]*__ as follows: __*[complete]*__.

Optional: Carefully consider the following concept if Landlord is elderly, has a low tax basis and most likely will retain the site until time of death:

__. [Additional] Purchase Option Exercisable Upon Death of Landlord. __*[In addition to Tenant's right to purchase the site during the lease years at the purchase prices set forth above,]*__ [I]f the site __*[or any fractional, undivided or residual interest therein]*__ is owned by Landlord or a trust controlled by Landlord or is otherwise included within Landlord's taxable estate at the time of Landlord's death, Tenant shall, for the __*[e.g., 18]*__ month period following Landlord's death, have an additional option right to purchase the site __*[or any fractional, undivided or residual interest therein]*__ so included within Landlord's taxable estate. The option purchase price payable by Tenant for such interest in such event shall be determined by __*[e.g., an agreed M.A.I. fair market appraisal clause to be negotiated and included within the ground lease. Such valuation will assume the site is unimproved and subject to both use and zoning consistent with the existing use of the site as of the date of such appraisal]*__.

Explanation of preceding clause: *Deferring the exercise of a purchase option until the landowner's death may provide a unique, yet infrequently considered, advantage to the landowner's estate or beneficiaries. Under I.R.C. Section 1014, the basis of a dece-*

FORM 5-1

dent's interest in property included in the decedent's gross estate gets "stepped-up" to fair market value as of the date of death (or the alternative estate tax valuation date). Like other valuable assets, a landowner's retained ownership interest in a site would be includable in the landowner's taxable estate for estate tax purposes. However, the landowner's estate or beneficiaries enjoy the income tax benefit of the site's "stepped-up" basis to the date of death fair market value. (If the property is "community property," both halves of the property enjoy the step-up to fair market value when the first spouse dies.) In other words, if the property is included in the decedent's taxable estate, from an income *tax perspective, an incremental gain is never taxed—the difference between the decedent's basis and the fair market value for estate tax purposes.*

To illustrate, assume (i) the landowner's adjusted tax basis for the site is $10, (ii) the site is included in the landowner's taxable estate, (iii) the fair market value at date of death for estate tax purposes is $100 and (iv) the developer exercises a post-death purchase option from the estate based upon an agreed fair market value of $100. Whether or not an estate tax would be payable would depend upon the total net value of the estate. From an income *tax perspective, however, the estate's basis would be "stepped-up" from $10 to $100 and, thus, no income tax would be payable upon the estate's sale to the developer at $100. Had the the landowner sold for $100 during the landowner's lifetime (i) a capital gain of $90 ($100 minus $10 basis) would have been realized and (ii) any such sale proceeds retained through date of death would be subject to estate taxation.*

In summary, triggering a purchase option to a date following the landowner's death in such a case could result in a dramatically reduced or non-existent income tax capital gain on the sale, since any gain on sale would be limited to the difference between the exercised purchase option price and the date of death fair market value as determined for estate tax purposes. Although this technical area requires skilled legal input, I'm surprised not to have observed this strategy applied by real estate developers negotiating land purchase options in ground leases.

Of course, a major negotiating hurdle in negotiating any ground lease is obtaining an acceptable purchase option. One of the most common landowner objections to granting an option is the desire to avoid substantial income tax liability arising upon a sale—often the very reason the landowner has elected to ground lease the site in the first place. However, if site ownership is retained through the landowner's death—while the estate tax consequences may remain the same as if the landowner's estate were holding the cash equivalent of the property—the landowner's estate or beneficiaries may be able to escape substantial income tax liability by deferring the sale until after the "step-up" in basis has occurred.

Before using this optional provision, consult with an experienced attorney well versed in income and estate taxation. Be absolutely certain that this concept is valid and appropriate under the user's particular circumstances. (This comment is not a fully balanced discussion of the many tax and estate-planning issues involved and, indeed, in many estate-planning contexts, prudent tax and estate planning advisors would attempt to remove the site from inclusion in the landowner's taxable estate.) Although there are numerous practical, administrative, and political problems in amending U.S. tax law in this area, President Clinton is considering ending or tinkering with the exemption of accrued capital gains from income taxation when a person dies.

8. Right of First Refusal. If during the escrow or the lease term Landlord elects to sell the site or any part or interest therein, Landlord shall in each such instance notify Tenant of the specific property interest and terms upon which Landlord is willing to sell and Tenant shall have the right of first refusal, prior in right to any third party, to purchase such interest on such terms. While the lease will terminate if all of the site is so purchased by Tenant, if Tenant purchases a part of or undivided interest in the site, the lease shall terminate with respect to the interest so purchased and rent shall be reduced __*[e.g., by the percentage by which the value of the interest so purchased bears to the value of the site prior to such purchase]*__.

9. Real Estate Taxes and Insurance. All real property taxes and assessments and insurance shall be paid by Tenant during the lease term such that the lease shall be NNN[1] to Landlord.

AND

1 A "net" lease provides that the tenant pays the expenses typically incurred in ownership of real property. Specifically, under a net lease, the tenant would pay real property taxes, hazard insurance premiums, and common area maintenance costs and other costs to maintain the property. In commercial leasing parlance, a "NNN" lease is one in which all such charges are paid in full by the tenant and thus the lease and rent payable under it is fully "net" to the landlord.

Optional California additional clause:
In addition, Tenant will be responsible for paying the Mello-Roos bonds allocable to the site for the period after ________. Payments on such bonds for the period before _______ shall be paid by Landlord.

10. Use. Tenant shall have the right to use the leased land for any lawful purposes.

11. Mortgage by Lessee. Tenant may, from time to time, hypothecate, mortgage, pledge or alienate Tenant's leasehold estate and rights under the ground lease.

This clause does not request the right to mortgage Landlord's fee interest. Ground rent is negotiated based upon the value of the site, but a ground lease that allows the tenant to mortgage the fee is substantially more valuable than a ground lease which limits the tenant to leasehold mortgage financing. On the one hand, if the landowner allows his or her fee to be mortgaged, he or she stands to lose it all if the tenant defaults. On the other hand, by allowing the fee to be mortgaged, the landowner contributes additional security and thus facilitates a larger loan than the leasehold alone could have supported. A developer requesting that the landowner allow a fee mortgage in support of the project should be prepared to show justifiable reasons and an appropriate risk-adjusted return to the landowner.

12. Cooperation. Landlord shall join with Tenant in signing such documents as may be necessary or appropriate in obtaining entitlements and financing for Tenant's development of the site. Landlord will make such reasonable modifications to the ground lease as Tenant's lender may request, provided such provisions do not materially affect Landlord's rights under the ground lease or reduce Landlord's potential rental income.

13. Assignment. Tenant anticipates that, in order to develop the site, it will contribute its leasehold interest to a partnership or joint venture. Accordingly, the ground lease will contain a clause allowing assignment of Tenant's leasehold interest.

14. Non-recourse Provision. The parties are aware that Tenant will make a major capital investment developing and constructing the proposed buildings and on- and off-site improvements to the site. The lease shall provide that __*[when the first phase of shell building improvements comprising the shopping center have been substantially completed by Tenant,]*__ any money judgment secured by Landlord against Tenant (including any partner, joint venturer, or any other interested party of Tenant) shall be limited to Tenant's (including such affiliated parties') interest in the site, Tenant's buildings and on- and off-site improvements to the site and Tenant's interest in insurance required to be carried under the lease. Tenant shall not have recourse against any other assets of Tenant (and/or any partner, joint venturer, or any other interested party of Tenant).

15. Other Terms. It is anticipated that other essential terms of the ground lease will be promptly negotiated *[assuming escrow is opened when lease is signed:] __[prior to]__ OR [assuming deal structure wherein lease is negotiated after opening of escrow:] __[after]__* the opening of escrow. *[For consideration of alternative approaches, see Appendix B, introduction to Form B-1, "Long Form Letter of Intent to Enter Into Site Ground Lease".]*

> ***Note:*** *In certain cases it may be advisable to negotiate the right to segregate the ground lease into various separate ground leases having similar terms, but that when aggregated together encompass the entire site. Such increased flexibility would allow, for example, the separate sale or disposition of a major tenant store on its "own" separate ground lease on terms that might be more attractive than retaining such revenue stream for the term of the ground lease.*

END OF FORM 5-1

PURCHASING THE GROUND LESSEE'S POSITION UNDER AN EXISTING GROUND LEASE

The preceding section discussed the creation of a ground lease between a landowner as ground lessor and a developer as ground lessee. Occasionally, however, an original ground lessee or an assignee of the original ground lessee is willing to sell a leasehold. Such an opportunity to acquire a project should not be overlooked. Form 5-2 illustrates selected key clauses providing for payment of assignment consideration to a speculative ground lessee willing to sell a leasehold for a negotiated sum.

Because it is an infrequently encountered site acquisition technique, only key selected clauses are shown here to demonstrate the principle. Since extensive modification to either Form 4-1 or Form B-1 ("Long-Form Letter of Intent to Enter into Site Ground Lease" in Appendix B) will be required to complete such a proposal, non-lawyers may need legal assistance in preparing even the initial non-binding draft proposal.

Note the "title" clause providing for the recordation of an abstract assigning "Seller's" leasehold rights to the developer "Buyer" at close of escrow. (Use of the terms "Buyer" and "Seller" avoids globally changing the names of the parties in other applicable paragraphs of the standard fee purchase offer Form 4-1. Recall that "Buyer" and "Seller" were changed to "Tenant" and "Landlord" in Form 5-1 and in Form B-1. Many lawyers would refer to the parties in such context as "Assignor" and "Assignee".)

Form 5-2

Selected Amendments to Standard Long-Form Purchase Offer to Provide for Buyout of a Ground Lessee's Rights under an Existing Ground Lease

FORM 5-2

Replaces Paragraph "1" in Form 4-1, Chapter 4, and in Form B-1, Appendix B:

1. <u>Parties</u>. Upon satisfaction of the escrow contingencies described herein, __*[name of shopping center developer or the developer's entity]*__, or its nominee or assignee ("Buyer") shall purchase and obtain from Seller (defined below) an assignment of all ground lessee's rights under that certain ground lease dated ____________, 20__ by and between ____________ as ground lessor ("Landowner") and __*[insert name of initial ground lessee]*__as the initial ground lessee (the "Lease"). __*[Name of current ground lessee]*__, the successor and current ground lessee under the Lease ("Seller") represents that a true copy of the Lease and all amendments thereto have been delivered to Buyer and that Seller shall effectively assign all rights of ground lessee under the Lease to Buyer, as and for the use of the site pursuant to the Lease for its term, in accordance with the following terms and conditions.

Replaces Paragraph "2" in Form 4-1, Chapter 4, and in Form B-1, Appendix B:

2. <u>Consideration For Leasehold Assignment</u>. In consideration for Seller's leasehold assignment to Buyer, Buyer shall make the following payments to Seller:

2.1 <u>Rent Payable Landowner</u>. Buyer shall, through escrow, cause __*[Landowner to be paid]*__ *<u>OR</u>* __*[Seller to be reimbursed]*__ $____________ for all ground rent payable or accrued under the Lease __*[e.g., for the first full year of the Lease term]*__ *<u>OR</u>* __*[e.g., through close of escrow]*__. Such sum shall be deposited by Buyer into escrow prior to the closing. *[If Landowner is to be paid:]* __*[Escrow holder shall release such sum to Landowner (and not to Seller) at close of escrow]*__; and

2.2 <u>Assignment Fee</u>. An additional sum (the "Assignment Fee") totaling $___________ shall be paid to Seller. *[Describe terms of payment—inside or outside escrow, in one lump sum or installments, etc. For example:]* __ *[A $ _________ portion of the Assignment Fee shall be paid through escrow. The balance of the Assignment Fee shall be paid to Seller in cash outside of escrow in the following installments, upon the occurrence of the following events:*

(i) $ ____________ shall be payable at such time as Buyer obtains a binding construction loan commitment from an institutional lender; and

(ii) $ __[Remaining balance of Assignment Fee]__ shall be payable upon the first to occur of the following: (a) such institutional lender's recordation of its construction loan deed of trust, mortgage, or other security agreement(s) against the site or (b) Buyer's re-assignment of Buyer's rights under the Lease to a third party]__.

Seller represents that the ground rent and other material terms of the subject ground lease are as stated in the Lease and all amendments thereto, all of which are copied and collectively attached hereto as Exhibit "D". *["D" is designated in this example assuming map Exhibits "A", "B", and "C" are attached (as in Form 4-1).]* Seller represents that Buyer shall be entitled to assume all such rights of set off, abatement or refund of rent monies as are contained in the Lease, as modified by any amendments thereto, as if Buyer were the original ground lessee.

If the shopping center developer is acquiring an assignment of a leasehold interest under a ground lease originally entered into between a third-party ground lessee and the landowner, Paragraph "19" in Form 4-1, Chapter 4, and Form B-1, Appendix B, can be revised, consistent with the preceding Paragraphs "1" and "2", as follows:

19. Title. At the close of escrow, Seller shall cause to be recorded an abstract of assignment assigning to Buyer all ground lessee's rights under the Lease. The abstract shall be deposited into escrow by Seller and approved by Buyer concurrent with Buyer's approval of the preliminary title report and copies of referenced title exceptions. Buyer's title, as ground lessee, shall be a marketable leasehold interest subject only to those matters of record which have been disclosed to Buyer in the preliminary title report and approved in writing by Buyer. In addition, Seller shall deliver to Buyer at close of escrow, at Seller's expense, a __*[See Appendix A, Form A-1]*__ policy of title insurance insuring marketable title in Buyer's leasehold interest for $____________, subject only to the reversionary interest of ground lessor and the title items previously approved by Buyer.

END OF FORM 5-2

CASE STUDIES IN CREATIVE USES OF THE GROUND LEASE: A POWERFUL MARKETING TOOL USED TO MEET THE LANDOWNER'S NEEDS

The preceding sections in this chapter addressed the preparation and refinement of ground-lease proposals from basic, reusable forms. This section provides examples of specific proposals designed to demonstrate the creative use of a ground lease format in response to the landowner's specific needs and objectives. Unlike most other forms in this book, the forms in this section are included not as reusable forms but as examples of a technique or style responsive to specific situations. Consider how you might adapt some of the ideas from this section in future proposals—including proposals not limited to ground leases.

Examples of such ideas might include:

- Amending a purchase offer to a ground lease proposal when competing developers are all submitting purchase offers and a ground lease may be more responsive to the landowner's needs and thus improve the likelihood of acceptance (Form 5-3);
- Setting yourself apart from competing developers by demonstrating the superior operating skill and financial attributes of your proposed major tenant(s) relative to major tenant(s) allied with competing developers (Form 5-4); or
- Combining a proposed ground lease with a land loan to the landowner from your financial partner to obtain development rights to a large parcel, a portion of which is developable now and the balance secured for future development (Form 5-5).

Example 1: Although the School District Offered to Sell, It Really Needed to Ground Lease

Many of the best in-fill sites are owned by individuals or institutions unwilling to sell. Occasionally, a governmental body such as a school district will offer a site for sale. Carefully research the opportunity and determine the underlying reasons for the proposed sale before making an offer. When developer competition is keen, having the best possible information about the site and the seller's motivation is particularly important.

For example, in one recent instance, it was discovered that if the proposed sale were to take place, the sale proceeds could not legally be used by the school district to meet its projected budgetary shortfalls; the sale proceeds would actually be transferred to another agency. What the district really needed was a recurring income stream to provide future, continuing revenues to the district. After confirmation of such facts (which began through informal contacts within the district's accounting department), the original purchase offer was amended to provide for a ground lease of the site.

Note in reading the amended offer (Form 5-3) that the underlying reasons for the revised economic and legal structure are woven into the proposal and are intended to meet the needs of the district. Always try to meet the landowner's needs—if you are skilled in gathering data and creative enough, sometimes you can even provide the landowner with an opportunity or an array of benefits previously unconsidered.

Form 5-3

Revision of Unaccepted Purchase Offer to Provide for Ground Lease of Site; Site Owner's Right to Purchase Developer's Improvements at Fair Market Value

[Date]

[Name and address
of proposed ground
lessor's representative
____
____
___________________*]*

Re: ___ -acre parcel located at the __*[e.g., southeast]*__
corner of __*[Avenue]*__ and __*[Street]*__,
__*[city]*__, __*[state]*__
(See attached map, Exhibit "A")

Dear __*[e.g., attorney representing school district]*__:

As a result of our recent discussion and further analysis of the site, we wish to make the following changes to our offer dated _____________, 20__ (the "original offer"):

1. Land Value. The total land value of the assumed __ -acre site shall be $_________, which total sum is based upon a net value of $_____ per square foot. This revised per square foot value should replace the $________ value used in the original offer.

2. Ground Lease. While you have been authorized to accept purchase bids, it appears that the school district's prevailing policy is to enhance its revenue base through improved utilization of under-utilized land. Essentially the district wishes to establish an endowment and guaranteed income stream, ideally with future upside potential. While we prefer to purchase sites, we believe the district's policy may be best implemented by utilizing an unsubordinated ground lease transaction in lieu of a purchase contract on this particular site.

Note: *In such a situation where numerous competing fee purchase offers are contemplated, one's chances of securing the site at a reasonable land value may be improved by differentiating oneself from*

FORM 5-3

the competition by offering to ground lease.

Upon satisfaction of contingencies in our original offer, __*[e.g., name of the pension fund, real estate investment trust ("REIT"), life insurance company, or similar entity]*__("_____________") would serve as developer's financial partner and would sign the ground lease as a general partner with developer. *[Describe in detail the financial partner's net worth and credit strength, relationship and past dealings with developer, and enclose annual reports, brochures, and the like. If possible within the required time frame, also enclose a letter from the financial partner confirming the financial partner's interest in proceeding with the specific transaction. The credit of such a financial partner and the ability to build for cash, if appropriate, should be a major advantage relative to competing developers. Demonstrate that you know how to put the deal together and have the financial relationships to accomplish your objective.]*

Assuming a ___ -acre site at a land value of $_____ per square foot, at a __*[e.g., 9]*__ % annual return, the proposed annual ground rent payable to the school district would be $__________ NNN. The term would be __*[e.g., 65]*__ years with no fixed escalations in minimum ground rent; rental increases would result by virtue of the school district receiving __*[e.g., 15]*__ % of all gross rental income in excess of an agreed pro forma or actual sublease base at initial center leaseup.

To accommodate developer's lack of sublease rental income during the development and construction period, annual ground rent for the __*[e.g., first ____ months/years following close of escrow]*__ *OR* __*[e.g., period ending with completion of construction of the first phase of shops]*__ would be $__*[low amount]*__, payable $________ per month. However, the Initial Deposit and any escrow Extension Deposit amounts released from escrow to the district pursuant to Paragraph __ of the original offer would proportionately offset or reduce such initial ground rent payable.

3. Option by School District to Purchase Developer's Improvements. During a negotiated time frame the school district would have an option to purchase developer's improvements on the site at an appraised fair market value. This option right would allow the school district to acquire all rights to the shopping center and achieve additional cash flow, which probably could be accomplished merely by obtaining an institutional third party loan secured by the land and improvements (i.e., no additional cash outflow required to exercise the option). If the school district did not exercise the option within a certain time frame, the developer partnership would have a "put" option in which it could purchase the underlying land __*[e.g., at an* *appraised fair market value]*__ in a transaction in which the school district could receive equivalent value under an I.R.C. Section 1031 tax deferred exchange. Essentially, we would attempt to maximize the combined future value of the land and improvements by either (i) allowing the completed improvements to be acquired by the school district or (ii) structuring a beneficial land exchange and sale of the improvements so that the land and improvements could be acquired by an independent third party.

Example of commitment to assist the district (but do not make a promise you are not committed to keep):

4. Warehouse and Bus Maintenance Site. As a part of the overall transaction, developer would assist the school district in selecting a new __ -acre industrial site (the "new industrial site") within __*[name of subject city]*__ to accommodate the need for the existing warehouse and bus maintenance facility now located on the site. Notwithstanding the fact that we would endeavor to locate the best available site in the district, the actual funds to purchase the new industrial site would come from other school district parcel sales or the cash flow generated from other district-owned exchanged income producing properties which, unlike the proposed ground lease, would yield substantial immediate cash proceeds.

5. Other Terms. Other terms of the original offer would remain unchanged. Like the original offer, this revision to the original offer is intended to be a non-binding agreement and is subject to negotiation and execution of definitive, final documentation within the time period provided in the original offer.

6. Conclusion. In summary, we suggest the foregoing transaction achieves a very substantial, secure, and permanent income for the school district with a low level of risk. In addition, it creates an increased upside potential for the district under the option to purchase developer's improvements. Perhaps most of all, it is a substantial step in creating an endowment and guaranteed income stream for the district.

Very truly yours,

[Development Company]

[Name]
[Title]

FORM 5-3

UNDERSTOOD AND AGREED:
This __ day of ___________, 20__.

[Name of school district]

By: ____________________

Its: ____________________

END OF FORM 5-3

Example 2: The "Full-Blown" Proposal to a Trust Where Intense Competition is Expected from Other Developers and Negotiating with Individual Trust Beneficiaries Is Not Possible

Form 5-4 is an example of a proposal technique and style responsive to yet another recurring fact pattern. In this example, wealthy beneficiaries of a very long-term landowner family group inexperienced in shopping center development were represented by a sophisticated real estate advisor. The site, held in trust, consisted of approximately 15 acres with extraordinary present and projected demographics. Potential future retail competition was very limited due to the magnitude of existing residential development, restrictive zoning policies, and geography.

A number of other developers had established a relationship with the owner's advisor for many years but the site had never been offered for sale. Although the advisor and the beneficiaries finally concluded that "something" should be done with the property, it was decided that the property would not be offered for sale. Instead, the trust wanted to enter into a long-term, unsubordinated ground lease. A precise plan and other work was needed to process a zoning application and the beneficiaries and the advisor realized substantial developer advice was needed. As a practical matter, the zoning application would require that specific tenants be identified and a qualified developer selected.

In this case, I knew the logical competing developers and their relationships with local supermarket anchors, was comfortable in a relationship with a national supermarket chain and other anchor tenants that strongly desired to locate on the site, and had past estate and trust tax planning experience. Therefore, the development partners proceeded, after further discussions with the trust's advisor, to meet all perceived needs of the trust and to present a comprehensive offer to secure the development rights before the site was put out to "bid." The following proposal was the first formal offer received by the trust and was accompanied by attached letters of intent from three anchor tenants and a major oil company.

Note the unsubordinated ground lease structure. The credit of a major financial partner in the ground lessee development partnership further reduces risk to the landowner trust in its position as ground lessor. Regard also the rather detailed analysis and presentation of the proposed supermarket tenant's credit relative to its competitors. This was done for two reasons: First, the then-recent flurry of mergers, leveraged buyouts, and heavy debt had created substantial differences in the credit- worthiness among likely food chain subtenants. Such issues were material to the trust advisor's evaluation of risk and the stability of the developer's proposed income stream. Second, by focusing on the superior creditworthiness of the developer's proposed supermarket operator vis-a-vis other possible food store anchor subtenants, all other factors being equal, the subject proposal should be found superior to proposals advanced by potential competing developers aligned with alternative anchor tenants. (Refer to the attachment to the proposal entitled "Comparison of Key Financial Attributes For Major Potential Supermarket Tenants at [site] (Based on latest publicly available financial information) dated 4/15/89."[2]

In an economic environment characterized by so many major tenants experiencing financial difficulties, developers working with a quality, high-credit tenant can capitalize on the tenant's enviable financial position in negotiations with landowners, redevelopment agencies, and other decision makers. Put your tenant in the best possible light. When appropriate, consider selectively compiling a financial analysis that persuasively demonstrates your proposed tenant's financial superiority relative to other tenants competing for the site in question.

Depending upon your goals and objectives, you might select from and compare typical "Wall Street" criteria such as stockholder's equity, return on equity, total debt, total debt as a percentage of equity, bond ratings, gross revenues, or number of consecutive years of increased sales and profits, etc., in a manner similar to the financial comparison exhibit attached to Form 5-4. Available data should drive your thinking. Alternatively, average sales volume per store and increases in average store volume over a recent selected period (if you can obtain or abstract such information) could be presented to show that your tenant is more likely than its competitors to create percentage rent revenues over a given period or, similarly, more likely to maximize growth in sales tax revenue notwithstanding a less substantial balance sheet or income statement.

Reflect upon an appropriate advocacy strategy for the case in which, for example, your tenant's overall credit strength is superior but average store volumes and penetration in the given local market are inferior to one or more of its competitors. Although a developer must be an ethical advocate, it is my opinion that too few developers champion their tenants by emphasizing their financial and operating strengths in a quantifiable manner to put them in the best possible light.

Be creative—in an uncertain economic climate it is more appropriate than ever to start considering such an approach.

[2] Although the attachment was based on the best public information available at the time, the information was limited. Therefore it may not be entirely accurate, and it is now outdated. It is not the data itself, however, but the opportunity and potential for tenant advocacy that I wish to convey. No reference to any existing retailer is intended.

Form 5-4

Site Ground Lease Proposal to Landowner with Developer Disclosing Proposed Financial Partner and Major Tenants; Landowner Granted Participation in Subtenant Rental Increases and Option to Purchase Developer's Improvements (Exhibit Compares Financial Attributes of Developer's Key Major Tenant Relative to Competition to Improve Likelihood of Landowner's Selection of Developer over Potential Competing Developers)

[Developer Letterhead]

[Date]

Note: *Although the approach remains powerful, this proposal was prepared in April 1989 and, therefore, the referenced supermarket financial information is outdated. Developer's selected national supermarket chain is referred to herein as "ABC Supermarket" and developer's proposed drugstore tenant is referred to as "XYZ Drugstore."*

[Name and address of proposed ground lessor's advisor ______________
____
______________________*]*

Re: __*[e.g., Southeast]*__ Corner of ____________ *Street]*__ and __*[Avenue]*__, __*[city]*__, __*[state]*__
(Potential shopping center site estimated to be 15 acres.)

Dear __________:

I am writing to you in your capacity as real estate advisor to the __*[XYZ permanent trust]*__ and other family members beneficially involved in the above-referenced site ("beneficiaries"). I understand that you have guided the beneficiaries through a review of various potential development, joint venture and ground lease alternatives and that there is a consensus favoring a low-risk approach which would yield a long term up-side potential.

This letter outlines the general terms by which __________ ("Developer") and its institutional financial partner would enter into a long term unsubordinated ground lease and develop a shopping center on the site. Once the center is completed and income fully stabilized, the beneficiaries could exercise an option to purchase all shopping center building improvements for long term appreciation.

Because you wish to appear before the __*[name]*__ City Council by ________, 20__ on the rezoning application and because it appears that final retail zoning cannot be granted until a specific site plan is submitted and approved, a developer should be selected to work with you and the beneficiaries to formulate a precise site plan and an overall work plan in order to consummate the rezoning and commence development of the site. We hope that after review of this proposal and further discussions with us that you will conclude that working with Developer and our proposed tenants, ABC Supermarket, XYZ Drugstore, ____________, and ______________ *[other specific tenants were named]* is in the best interest of the beneficiaries.

1. Unsubordinated Ground Lease. A general partnership of Developer and Financial Partner *[defined below]* ("ground lessee") would enter into a long term unsubordinated ground lease with the beneficiaries. Although you have hesitated to set a land value until commercial zoning is imminent or in place, we are assuming an appraised value of $______ per square foot multiplied by __ net acres at a 9% return, which would yield an annual ground rent of $_________ NNN. The proposed term would be 75 years with no fixed escalations in ground rent; rental increases would result by virtue of the ground lessor receiving 15% of gross rental income in excess of an agreed initial pro forma or sublease base. In other words, the beneficiaries would receive 15 cents of every $1.00 increase in sublease rents in excess of an agreed initial pro forma. Developer and our financial partner's commitment to lease is subject to satisfactory due diligence, such as availability of utilities and absence of hazardous materials, and final approval of all deal points, consummation of rezoning, finalizing major tenant leases, and issuance of entitlements.

2. Financial Partner. An affiliate of __*[e.g., name of a pension fund, real estate investment trust ("REIT"), life insurance company, or similar entity]*__ ("Financial Partner") would serve as Developer's financial partner and would sign the ground lease as a general partner with Developer. Financial Partner invests approximately $________ annually in real estate joint ventures and has roughly $___________ in real estate assets. According to *Pensions & Investment Age*, Financial Partner is the _____ largest manager of real estate equity in the United States. Financial Partner's specialty is funding development stage projects. A Financial Partner brochure is enclosed together with reprints of Financial Partner articles contained in periodicals such as

Business Week, Institutional Investor, Pensions and Investment Age, and other periodicals and major newspapers.

Depending upon the size and nature of any particular development, Financial Partner will bring in one of its affiliated partnerships as the actual financial partner in any given project. In a project of this type it is possible that Financial Partner's involvement would allow all construction and development to be accomplished for cash, i.e., without third party loans. (For example, our ABC Supermarket project in ______________ is being financed by equity advances from one of Financial Partner's affiliated partnerships without third party debt.)

FORM 5-4

3. Market Position and Financial Strength of Proposed Major Subtenants. Attached hereto you will find letters of intent from ABC Supermarket, XYZ Drugstore, ________________ and ____________, indicating that they are prepared to proceed to enter into ground sublease or build-to-suit transactions with Developer. Although we do not wish to commit ourselves to this entire group as our ultimate major tenant mix, we would commit to develop for ABC Supermarket, XYZ Drugstore and _________ (assuming an appropriate pad can be made available).

According to the attached April 17, 1989 "Food For Thought" article in _________ *Magazine*, ABC Supermarket has posted ___ consecutive years of increased sales and profits. The company's net earnings as a percentage of 1988 gross revenues (2.4%) were almost twice the industry average, and its return on equity was 22.3%. ABC Supermarket's competitors have been adversely affected by LBO's and mergers. For example, __*[second chain]*__'s $___ billion purchase of _______ has produced uncertainty in the proposed merger of _____ and _______. Meanwhile, __*[third chain]*__'s total debt of $800 million—79% of total capital—appears to put severe restrictions on potential expansion and remodeling for the chain. Similarly, __*[fourth chain]*__'s $__ billion debt load with an annual debt cost of $125 million reportedly caused __*[fourth chain]*__ to project a loss for this year. *[See attached article, "_________: Is There Life After Debt?" appearing in the April, 1989 issue of _________. Also, the enclosed _________ article, "Debtor's Prison", addresses the potential consequences of supermarket chain heavy debt loads resulting from LBO's and merger and restructuring schemes.]*

While ABC Supermarket ranks as the ______ largest U.S. retail food-drug chain in terms of sales, it is has been reported to be the most profitable of all supermarket chains. In December of 1988, ABC Supermarket's Board of Directors adopted a five-year plan for 1989 through 2014 which includes a new store capital budget of $___ billion for the opening of ____ new stores. During 1989, __ new stores will be opened and __ stores will be remodeled. (In 1988, __ stores, including __ acquired from other companies, were opened.) Ninety-five per cent (95%) of these budgeted capital expenditures will be funded from internally generated funds and the balance in new borrowings which are projected to be repaid by the end of the five-year period. On ________, 1989, _________, Chairman and CEO, was named the _______ winner in the supermarket industry by the _____________. *(See attached reprint.)*

XYZ Drugstore is a wholly owned subsidiary of __________ *[major identified publicly held chain]*, which does not separately publish financial information on XYZ Drugstore.

> ***Note:*** *Although XYZ Drugstore was financially strong, the inability to obtain detailed financial information on XYZ Drugstore precluded further refinement of developer's proposal along the lines compiled for ABC Supermarket.*

In summary, when evaluating risk to the beneficiaries it is important to look to both the credit behind the ground lessee as well as the credit of its subtenants. To further assist you in your evaluation of ABC Supermarket as our major proposed subtenant, I have attached a "Comparison of Key Financial Attributes For Major Potential Supermarket Tenants at __*[Corner of]*__ __*[street]*__ and __*[street]*__, __*[city]*__, __*[state]*__." Although all salient current financial information is not readily available on all companies, a review of this chart substantiates that ABC Supermarket's credit strength, profitability and future market outlook are superior to such attributes of its competitors. ABC Supermarket's 1989 Annual Report released a few days ago is also enclosed.

4. Developer Background. *[Extensive discussion of Developer's retail experience and results, development experience with proposed major tenants, past development achievements with Financial Partner, and Developer's company brochure.]*

5. Zoning. We are prepared to work with you and the beneficiaries to formulate a precise site plan in order to consummate the rezoning. As you explained, to obtain the required rezoning, the City Council will need a specific site plan delineating the proposed project and must also be convinced that the proposed project developed under the revised zoning would be "economically viable." We feel that the strong major tenant interest which we have generated, as indicated by the attached letters of intent, should substantiate the economic viability of the project. We are prepared to immediately negotiate an acceptable site plan. We are also prepared to undertake the obligation to process a General Plan Amendment and Specific Site Development Plan concurrently with finalizing the site rezoning application. (In addition, we should jointly thoroughly investigate the potential for any new or revised substantial development fees, traffic impact fees, public facility assessments and the like.)

6. References: List of Landowners Who leased or Sold Land to Developer and Retained Development Approvals, Architectural Control or Other Development Restrictions. Obviously this transaction will require a cooperative working relationship among all of us. Accordingly, I have provided a list of ground lessors and land sellers where continuing involvement was required during the development process for one reason or another.

FORM 5-4

List specific ground lessors and land sellers. Give address and telephone numbers in chart format. Consider adding a brief comparison, in each case, showing experience in prior transactions similar to the proposed transaction.

7. Risk Analysis. The proposed development structure and the financial strength of the proposed major tenants create a low level of risk to the beneficiaries.

7.1 Development Structure. Based upon current discussions of the beneficiaries' objective, we believe that the Financial Partner/Developer unsubordinated leasehold as described will provide the greatest opportunity with the lowest risk level to the beneficiaries. The beneficiaries would be able to immediately achieve a market return on their low basis land. As discussed, we would be willing to grant the beneficiaries an option to purchase completed improvements at market terms during an agreed time frame. This option will allow the beneficiaries to hold the shopping center for long term appreciation without being subject to substantial out-of-pocket pre-development costs and risks typically associated with a development venture.

7.2 Financial Attributes of ABC Supermarket and XYZ Drugstore Compared to Potential Competing Anchor Tenants. Based upon the discussion contained in Paragraph 3, above, we believe that the credit strength and long term viability of ABC Supermarket and XYZ Drugstore as subtenants is probably substantially superior to that of other logical major tenants for the site. In particular, we feel that the combined credit strength and outlook for ABC Supermarket is substantially superior to that of other potential supermarket chains and suggest such financial strength should be given great weight in today's market conditions.

8. Marketing Team. We have reached a general understanding with a major brokerage firm which would act as a marketing team in leasing the project. This will consist of a senior marketing consultant with whom I have worked in the past and will include an experienced marketing representative who focuses upon retail leasing in __*[name of city where site is located]*__.

9. Developer Financial References. Developer's banks, construction and permanent lenders and financial partners are listed on Exhibit "__" attached hereto.

List banks and financial partners; give contact name, title, address, and telephone number in chart format.

10. Conclusion. In summary, we submit that the foregoing proposal presents a prudent investment opportunity. The proposal (i) achieves a very substantial, secure, permanent income stream for the beneficiaries, (ii) insulates them from liability and substantial cash outlays, and (iii) considering the option to purchase developer's improvements, creates a unique long term investment vehicle with substantial up-side potential. As we discussed, given the beneficiaries' free and clear interest in the site, the purchase option could probably be exercised without any additional infusion of cash. We are confident that we can form a close working relationship with you and the beneficiaries and enthusiastically seek your commitment to work with us.

After you have had time to review these materials, I would like to discuss and refine the transaction with you and the beneficiaries so that we can promptly reach acceptable agreements and jointly proceed to effectuate the rezoning. As we have discussed, this conceptual proposal is not intended to be a binding agreement. However, if the general economics are found acceptable, we would appreciate an appropriate signature confirming such approval by the beneficiaries. Thank you for your time and consideration to date.

Very truly yours,

[Development Company]

[Name]
[Title]

Enclosures:

(1) Comparison of Key Financial Attributes For Major Potential Supermarket Tenants at __*[Corner of* __*[street]*__ and __*[street]*__ *[city]*__, __*[state]*__;
(2) Financial Partner Brochure and Referenced Published Financial Partner Articles;
(3) __*[Developer]*__ Brochure and Company Profile;
(4) ABC Supermarket Letter of Intent;
(5) XYZ Drugstore Letter of Intent;
(6) ____________________ Letter of Intent;
(7) ____________________ Letter of Intent;
(8) Article: "Food For Thought";
(9) Article: "_______: Is There Life After Debt?";
(10) Article: "Debtor's Prison";
(11) ABC Supermarket 1988 Annual Report;
(12) __*[Other major tenant]*__ Brochure;
(13) References: List of Landowners Who Leased or Sold Land to Developer with Retained Approval Rights; and
(14) Developer Financial References

UNDERSTOOD AND AGREED:
This __ day of ____________, 20__.

[Name of Trust]

By: ____________________

Its: ____________________

__*[Referenced major tenant financial analysis is on next page]*__

FORM 5-4

Comparison of Key Financial Attributes
For Major Supermarket Tenants at NWC street name and street name, city name, state
(Based upon latest publicly available financial information as of 4/15/89)

	A **Standard & Poor's Bond Rating**	B **1988 Gross Revenue**	C **Total Number of Stores**	D **Net Earnings and (Net Earnings as a % of Gross Revenue)**	E **Stockholders' Equity**	F **Return on Equity**	G **Total Debt**	H **Total Debt as a % of Equity**	I **No. of Consecutive Years Increased Sales and Profits**
ABC Supermarket	A+	$6.8 billion	500 as of 3/1/89	$162.6 million (2.4%)	$801 million	22.3%	$177 million ($113 million in capital leases, $44 million mtg. debt, and $20 million all other debt)	22%	19
Supermarket Competitor #1	BB? (not certain)		1,900 approx (Competitors #1 and #2 combined)	[Awaiting annual reports] (Competitors #1 and #2 combined)			In excess of $3 billion (Competitors #1 and #2 combined)		
Supermarket Competitor #2									
Supermarket Competitor #3	B-		325 approx.	[Awaiting annual reports. $100 million additional borrowing in process]			Range: $0.8 billion to $1.0 billion		
Supermarket Competitor #4	B or B- (not certain)	$2.5 billion	134 (includes *x name* stores)	$150 million est. (insufficient info: 10K not to be filed until May with *parent company* filing)			$1.0 billion		

Information contained herein was obtained and provided by sources deemed reliable but may not necessarily be correct. It is now out of date. However, the concept of presenting and comparing financial attributes of major tenants is the purpose of this table.

END OF FORM 5-4

Example 3: Controlling an Entire Site Too Large for Comprehensive Immediate Development: Ground Leasing or Purchasing a Portion and Optioning the Balance by Providing Landowner with an Attractive Tax-Advantaged Income Stream and a Land Loan to Finance Landowner's Fee

The following illustrative proposal combines many of the principles addressed in preceding examples. A 68-acre commercial site within an area of high residential growth was owned by several individuals. Although the landowner partners had owned the most desirable 15 acres at a major intersection for many years, they had only recently acquired an additional 53 continguous acres. The landowners were interested only in a transaction that disposed of all 68 acres. Although highly positive with respect to the property long term, the developer believed that not more than one-half the total acreage was immediately developable.

The landowners' financial advisor preferred a deal that would defer taxes and wanted to consider both a ground lease and a sale proposal. The landowners' land loan was coming due and the landowners had made a substantial cash investment in the recently acquired portion of the property. In evaluating this development opportunity, the development entity assumed that if the developer could assist in recapitalizing the land loan, the landowners might be willing to accept a purchase or ground lease proposal with only nominal developer risk money required prior to issuance of entitlements.

For convenience, Form 5-5 divides the entire 68 acres—referred to as the "Property"—into the "Site" (approximately 35 acres upon which the initial development phase would be commenced) and the "Option Property" (the balance of the Property). The offer gives the landowners a choice whether to sell or ground lease and the respective economic terms of each. If they elect to ground lease the Site, the developer's joint venture financial partner (an affiliate of a pension fund, real estate investment trust ("REIT"), or life insurance company) will fund a major land loan secured by the Property. The proposal provides that two-thirds of each payment of fixed minimum ground rent will be used to amortize the land loan. Conceptually, the land loan is due on (or shortly after) the date developer's option to acquire the "Option Property" is exercised or expires.

Although option payments released to the landowners during the escrow for the initial phase development period are applicable to preliminary ground rent, permanent ground rent does not commence until completion of the initial shops phase on the Site. In essence, from the landowners' perspective, the structure yields ground-lease revenue and defers or avoids the income tax associated with a land sale. The land loan at least temporarily cures the landowners' liquidity needs and provides some additional cash the receipt of which may not be currently taxable. Finally, the landowners receive a future upside given the fixed monthly escalation in the option purchase price or ground lease value of the Option Property.

From the developer's perspective, the structure does not compel the developer to acquire all of the Property initially, yet provides for control of all of the Property for an acceptable time period. The developer assumed that if the initial development on the Site were successful, sufficient tenant demand for the Option Property could be generated such that the developer's financial partner would be willing to purchase the Option Property within the specified option period.

Although quite complex, the drafting of this proposal actually was not time consuming. First, you will find that if you get into the habit of placing a heading on each of the various sections of your proposals, you can very quickly review the contents of your own standard proposal (such as one similar to the comprehensive site offer Form 4-1 in Chapter 4 or the "Long-Form Letter of Intent to Enter Into Site Ground Lease" included as Form B-1 in Appendix B), use such headings to prepare a skeleton outline, amend sections as necessary, add needed additional sections, and then renumber the various provisions. In essence, the various topical components in the standard proposal can be amended or reassembled as sort of "building blocks." With practice, once you have mastered your own basic offer format, you may learn to amend and add to your own "building blocks" consistent with the transaction's needs. Equally as important, once you have organized your own deal-making document form file system comparable to the resource suggested in Chapter 19, a virtual library of additional provisions will be readily available from which to extract ideas and language structure.

To illustrate, rather than merely describing the "Site" (the heading of Paragraph 3 of Form 4-1), Paragraph 2 of Form 5-5 defines the total land area as the "Property" and further divides the Property into two components—the "Site" and the "Option Property"—consistent with the conceived deal structure. Logically, Form 5-5 then proceeds to provide, in effect, an "integrated" proposal that describes the proposed transaction relative to each of these defined land areas. (Stylistically, there is an alternative approach that may reduce the extensive modification to the body of Form 4-1 necessary to produce a proposal similar to Form 5-5: You could reference, edit, and attach the "Summary of Ground Lease Terms" exhibit [attached to Form 5-1] to describe the terms of the proposed ground lease and amend the body of Form 4-1 to cover only the deal points not addressed in the "Summary of Ground Lease Terms" exhibit.)

Finally, to demonstrate the required development milestones and thus substantiate the specific preliminary ground rent or escrow release schedule proposed, a specific "Preliminary Development Schedule" of sequential steps and the estimated time required for each is attached as an exhibit. (Disregard and do not reuse the specific time frames given as an example in the attached "Preliminary Development Schedule"—the required steps and the time required for each will differ substantially from site to site.) As covered previously, educating the landowner (and yourself) with respect to the specific development steps applicable to the site may result in the landowner being more lenient in allowing "free" time or delaying cash installments from the developer.

As a general rule, you should not make a proposal until you have a very good idea of the entitlement issues involved. Once such a preliminary investigation has been made, it takes very little time to outline the marketing and entitlement milestones as an exhibit to your offer. Not only does it manifest professionalism, but forcing yourself to write such a schedule helps to clarify your own thinking and creates a record in both your computer and your paper files for easy future reference. And if you are unsuccessful in acquiring the opportunity the first time, all this information will be readily accessible if the site once again becomes available.

Form 5-5

Proposal to Enter into Option to Purchase or Ground Lease Major Site: A Defined Portion Is Developed Now and Balance of Property Is Optioned for Future Development (Developer's Financial Partner Makes Land Loan Pending Entitlement and Closing to Accommodate Landowner)

[Developer Letterhead]

[Date]

[Name and address of landowner ______
____
_______________]

Re: __*[e.g., 68]*__ -acre land parcel at the
_____ corner of ____ and ______;
__*[city]*__, __*[state]*__
(See Attached Tentative Site Plan, Exhibit "A")

Dear ____________:

__*[Insert introduction—e.g., I enjoyed meeting you and your advisor, __[name]__, on _______, 20__. After discussions among our development partners and our financial partner and preliminary feasibility analysis of your __[name]__ Shopping Center site,]*__ [w]e are pleased to submit this letter of intent to enter into an option agreement to purchase or ground lease your property on the following fundamental terms and conditions:

1. <u>Parties</u>. Upon exercise of a formal option agreement to be hereafter negotiated and signed between the parties, __*[name of developer]*__ or its nominee or assignee, as hereafter provided ("Buyer"), will purchase or ground lease the "Property" and/or the "Site" (as defined below), from __*[name]*__ ("Seller").

2. <u>Property</u>. The "Property" is an unimproved land area located at the _____ corner of _____________ and ____________ in __*[city]*__, __*[state]*__ consisting of approximately __*[e.g., 68]*__ acres as shown on the attached tentative site plan (Exhibit "A"). For purposes of this letter, the westerly 35 acres of the Property is hereinafter referred to as the "Site". The balance of the Property not included within the Site is hereinafter referred to as the "Option Property". The Site and the Option Property are outlined on Exhibit "A".

3. Total Purchase Price/Land Value. The total purchase price or land value for the Property, which Buyer agrees to pay (or, alternatively, upon which ground rent will be calculated) is the product of _______ square feet, the total net square footage of the Property, multiplied by $_______ per square foot value, or $__*[insert product]*__(the "purchase price"). (This figure excludes escalations to the purchase price which apply only to the Option Property, as described below.)

4. Possible Upward or Downward Adjustment of Purchase Price Based Upon Survey. The final purchase price or ground lease land value shall be determined by multiplying $__*[insert per square foot land value from preceding paragraph]*__ per square foot times the actual net square footage contained in the Property, Site or Option Property (as the case may be), as determined by a certificate prepared by a licensed surveyor to be prepared at Buyer's cost and delivered to Seller within __*[e.g., 14]*__ days prior to the closing of any transaction with reference to the Property, Site or Option Property. The term "net square footage" as used herein shall mean the total area of the applicable Property, Site or Option Property expressed in square footage, as determined pursuant to the above survey, less any land presently dedicated or committed or required to be dedicated or granted in fee or by easement for public use __*[(including the proposed flood channel)]*__ as of the closing. This "purchase price" formula shall be used as the land value in the event Seller elects the ground lease acquisition by Buyer.

5. Property Elections, Option and Development Concept. Buyer will either purchase or ground lease the Site, at Seller's election. Similarly, Buyer shall have the option to purchase or ground lease the Option Property (the choice being consistent with Seller's initial election relative to the Site) for the __*[e.g., two-year]*__ period following completion of the first phase of shop buildings on the Site. The purchase price or ground lease land value for the Option Property under such option shall escalate at the rate of __*[e.g., 1]*__ % per month computed from Buyer's closing on the Site through exercise of Buyer's option to purchase or ground lease the Option Property. Buyer will covenant to attempt to consummate anchor tenant transactions with _________, __________, and ____________ as quickly as possible upon opening of escrow with Seller.

6. Ground Lease. If Seller elects to accept the ground lease concept, monthly payments of fixed term base rent under the ground lease will commence __*[e.g., upon Buyer's completion of the first phase of retail shop buildings on the Site]*__.

> ***Note:*** *Particularly in cases where more detail is required to describe the terms of the proposed ground lease, the reader could edit and attach the "Summary of Ground Lease Terms" exhibit attached to Form 5-1 instead of summarizing the ground lease in this Paragraph 6.*

6.1 Rent and Term. Such fixed term ground rent shall be in an annual amount equal to __*[e.g., 9]*__ % of the purchase price of the Site and/ or the Option Property, as the case may be. The term of the ground lease(s) shall be __*[e.g., 65]*__ years. The ground lease(s) shall have a provision allowing Buyer to segregate the Property into separate ground leases based upon revised parcelization within the Property. Additional "bonus" ground rent over and above the fixed minimum base rent shall be payable at the rate of __*[e.g., 15]*__ % of any increases in gross receipts in excess of Buyer's initial gross receipts from the shopping center. Negotiated adjustments to fixed term base rent and percentage rent shall be made to provide for any delayed development phasing within the Site and the Property.

> *Consider potential adjustment to ground rent in the event of extraordinary future capital expenditure by the developer, i.e., upon a change to a more intense development use such as an enclosed mall or high-rise office building. Avoid any adjustments during the initial term. Of course, try to avoid fixed increases to base rent, but if periodic rental increases are required, negotiate acceptable fixed increases or adjustments made by appraisal subject to existing leases at time of the appraisal. Also, try to secure the right to obtain a subordinated fee mortgage—mortgagability provisions become less important and a subordinated fee mortgage will give the developer greater access to financing at better rates. Do not accept a CPI adjustment or its equivalent, since changes in the CPI may not have a direct relationship with achievable rents.*

6.2 Preliminary Ground Rent. Prior to completion of the first phase of shop buildings on the Site, preliminary ground rent shall be paid. Preliminary ground rent shall consist of the escrow option payments referenced in Paragraph __*[10]*__ (below) plus real property taxes accruing against the Site from the period beginning with the close of Buyer's escrow election to ground lease the Site and ending with completion of the first phase of shop buildings on the Site (at which time fixed term base rent shall commence).

Although the developer's escrow option payments are applicable to preliminary rent, this form is somewhat unusual because the developer's only cash obligation payable from time of escrow closing through completion of the first phase of shops is the real property taxes accruing against the Site. In many cases, monthly or quarterly payments of additional preliminary ground rent would be negotiated for the period following close of escrow through completion of the first phase of building improvements. Under a typical ground lease, real property taxes are payable by the ground lessee for the entire term of the ground lease.

6.3 Option to Purchase Fee; Exchange by Seller. The ground lease will give Buyer the option to purchase the underlying fee commencing __*[e.g., three years after completion of the first phase of shop buildings]*__ at the then-appraised fair market land value subject to existing leases. *[**Note:** If you are unable to negotiate a lengthy purchase option period, attempt to obtain a right of first refusal for a longer period.]* If Seller desires to enter into an I.R.C. Section 1031 tax deferred exchange of the underlying fee, Buyer will accommodate Seller provided Buyer is free of any risk, cost, loss, liability or expense relating thereto.

6.4 Financeability. Any ground lease referenced herein shall be NNN to Seller and shall be financeable from Buyer's perspective.

Consider addressing whether unsubordinated leasehold financing is contemplated or whether—since it may be critical to developer—developer must have the right to secure a subordinated fee mortgage. If a subordinated fee mortgage will be required, and the developer believes it appropriate to cover the issue at the initial proposal stage, the developer would also probably want to state that any such mortgage will be structured to protect the ground lessee's interests, i.e., (i) the mortgage will be advanced from an institutional lender and loan proceeds shall be used solely for the project, (ii) the mortgage will be self-liquidating and all payments will be made direct to the mortgagee, (iii) default under the mortgage will constitute a default under the ground lease, and (iv) ground lessor will have no personal liability and lender will look only to the property and improvements, and the like. However, since the entire "financability" issue is so complex—and yet the ground lessor must understand that the deal ultimately will have to be financeable from the ground lessee's perspective—in most cases it is probably not productive to attempt to start negotiating the issue in developer's initial proposal other than a simple statement that the ground lease must be financeable. If the parties have an interest in pursuing the deal, the parties and their respective attorneys should meet to reach a full understanding of the issues and to work out an acceptable solution.

7. Land Loan. If Seller elects the ground lease approach, __*[upon commencement of fixed minimum rent under the ground lease,]*__ Buyer's financial partner will make a __*[e.g., $6.0 million]*__ interest only first trust deed loan secured by the Property in favor of Seller, provided Seller continues to retain fee title to the Property. The interest rate and other loan provisions shall be at market rate and terms. During the loan term, __*[two-thirds]*__ of each payment of fixed minimum rent under the ground lease shall be used to amortize the outstanding loan balance. The loan due date shall be the date __*[e.g., upon which]*__ *OR* __*[e.g., which is 6 months after]*__ Buyer's option rights expire with reference to the Option Property. However, the outstanding loan proceeds shall be converted to Buyer's equity upon Buyer's timely exercise of the option and payment of the option price. *[Insertion of a land loan due date later than the option expiration date gives Seller an opportunity to refinance the land loan if the option is not exercised.] [Seller-oriented optional clause:] If Buyer fails to exercise the option, Seller may concurrently elect to extend the loan due date for an additional __[one]__ year period, upon payment of a fee equal to __ % of the then outstanding principal balance of the loan]__.* This proposal is made subject to Buyer obtaining formal approval from its joint venture partner to make Seller such loan on the preceding terms.

8. Option Period Development Tasks. Buyer and Seller understand that in order to undertake development of a viable, well-anchored shopping center on the Property, considerable investigation, marketing research and analysis, and negotiations with anchor tenants and governmental authorities will be required, including but not limited to the following: *[Demonstrate that you have already conducted a preliminary investigation of development issues by being specific in the tasks you need to accomplish.]*

8.1 First [90] Days of Option Period. During the first __*[e.g., 90]*__ days of the option period Buyer shall undertake the following work: Buyer's initial investigation and determination that there are no governmental, physical or economic constraints which would render development of the Property as a __*[e.g., large "box" anchored "power"]*__ *OR* __*[e.g., community]*__ shopping center not feasible or uneconomic; research, analysis and preparation of a trade area housing supply and demand study showing adequate trade area population at time of first phase buildout to currently attract sufficient quality anchor tenants on acceptable economic terms and

FORM 5-5

conditions; title review; __*[review of Seller's preliminary soils investigation report;]*__ investigation of requirements and cost of __*[e.g., specific off-site or other problem concerning the Property]*__; retaining architects, engineers, traffic and related consultants; preparation of tentative site plans; commencement of final anchor tenant documentation with __________, __________ and __________ *[known tenants];* and pursuing marketing efforts to secure other major tenants. *[Consider specific initial steps to begin resolving particular problems unique to the Property, such as soils or geologic issues, toxic problems, environmental habitat or wetlands issues and specific issues presented by regulatory issues unique to the site, such as the California Coastal Commission, specialized city and county agencies, and the like.]*

8.2 Balance of Option Period. During the balance of the option period Buyer shall undertake the following work: Identifying and consummating major tenant commitments acceptable to Buyer and satisfying all major tenant imposed conditions; obtaining final site plan approval and required permits from all required agencies for Buyer's construction of a __*[large "box" anchored "power"]*__ *OR* __*[community]*__ shopping center, including but not limited to, negotiation of desired building density and layout, acceptable development fee conditions and agreements *[in California this could include Mello-Roos financing for certain off-site improvements],* conditional use permits (if required), utility agreements, and state and local transportation and environmental approvals.

9. Preliminary Development Schedule. In order to assist Seller in understanding a reasonable estimate of the time required to accomplish specific tasks (i.e., completing major tenant negotiations and *thereafter* commencing governmental processing and obtaining required approvals from the __*[city/county]*__ regulatory authorities), a "__*[Name of Shopping Center]*__ Preliminary Development Schedule" is attached hereto as Exhibit "__*[B]*__".

10. Option Payment Schedule. After preliminary evaluation of the potential risks and rewards of this development opportunity, we have concluded that the following option money release schedule is a reasonable compromise between the parties, particularly since (i) governmental processing cannot commence until major tenant transactions are consummated (tenant requirements result in a final site plan for governmental processing) and (ii) any purchase within the option period will be on an all-cash basis:

<u>Option Month #</u>	<u>$ Release</u>
1st __[e.g., 90]__ days	-0-
2nd __[e.g., 60]__ days	$_______
6th through 15th months	$_______/month
Total:	$_______

Such option payments are applicable to the purchase price (or preliminary ground rent) but forfeited to Seller if Buyer fails to close. Notwithstanding the above schedule, the option to purchase or ground lease the Site will terminate __*[e.g., 30]*__ days after receipt of building permits if building permits are received within the above option period.

11. <u>Seller's Rights to Work Product</u>. As additional consideration given Seller under the escrow, if Buyer elects not to exercise the option to purchase or ground lease, Buyer shall assign (lien free) all Buyer's rights to and deliver to Seller copies of all tentative site plans, engineering, and soils studies __*[and other consultant work product]*__ that Buyer generates concerning the Property.

12. <u>Entry</u>. Upon execution of option escrow instructions, Buyer shall have an immediate license to enter upon the Property for the purpose of conducting economic feasibility, engineering, soil and other tests at its sole cost and expense. Buyer will indemnify Seller and hold Seller harmless from any and all loss or liability resulting from the acts of Buyer or its agents or employees upon the Property and from all or any mechanics liens or other liens resulting from Buyer's conduct or the conduct of its agents or employees on the Property.

13. <u>Marketing Signs</u>. Seller will grant Buyer, or Buyer's nominee or agent, the right to erect signs (consistent with applicable sign codes) offering retail space for lease during the escrow.

14. <u>Seller Cooperation</u>. During the escrow option period, at no expense to Buyer, Seller will provide Buyer with copies of any and all documentation in Seller's possession or control relating to development of the Property. This data shall include the use of copies of existing engineering studies and reports, site plans, grading plans, studies and reports and the like, in the possession of Seller or Seller's agents or consultants.

Seller will cooperate fully with and assist Buyer in negotiations with private and public special interest groups, adjacent property owners, federal, state and local governmental and quasi-governmental agencies, as such negotiations relate to timely securing approvals and permits for the Property. Seller will also execute any and all instruments necessary or appropriate for the development of the Property, including but not limited to maps, dedications or easements and rights of way to governmental an quasi-governmental authorities and adjacent property owners, provided such execution is consistent with normal practices.

Alternative "A"—Paragraph 15
Broad right to assign

15. Assignment. Buyer shall have the right to assign its rights under the __*[option]*__ without the prior consent of Seller.

OR

Alternative "B"—Paragraph 15
more limited assignment right

15. Assignment. Buyer may (i) assign the __*[option]*__ to any entity in which Buyer or its officers, directors or shareholders have a majority interest, or are managing partners and are directly involved, without Seller's consent, or (ii) nominate any entity to take title to the site, upon the giving of written notice to Seller, which notice may not be given less than three days prior to closing. Any other assignment may not be made without Seller's prior written consent, which shall not be unreasonably withheld. Any such assignment is conditional upon such assignee agreeing to be bound by all consents and approvals theretofore given or deemed to have been given by Buyer, and such assignment or nomination shall not relieve Buyer of its obligations under the option.

16. Condemnation Prior to Closing. If the Property or any part thereof becomes the subject of a condemnation proceeding during the escrow option period, Seller agrees to immediately advise Buyer thereof. In the event of such condemnation, Buyer shall have the option to (i) take title or become ground lessee on the terms and conditions herein and negotiate with the condemning authority for the condemnation award and receive the benefits thereof without affecting the purchase price or ground rent, or (ii) terminate the option and purchase agreement (or ground lease) and declare Buyer's obligation hereunder null and void and of no further effect, in which event all sums theretofore paid or released to Seller shall be returned to Buyer.

17. Title Insurance. At the close of escrow, Seller shall convey marketable title to Buyer in compliance with __*[name of state]*__ law, subject only to those matters of record which have been disclosed to Buyer in the Preliminary Title Report and approved in writing by Buyer. In addition, Seller shall deliver to Buyer at close of escrow, at Seller's expense, a __*[See Appendix A, Form A-1]*__ policy of title insurance insuring marketable title in Buyer for the full amount of the actual purchase price or the leasehold value, subject only to title exceptions previously approved in writing by Buyer.

18. Brokerage Commissions. Buyer and Seller each separately represent and warrant that it did not incur any brokerage commission in connection with this transaction and that no commission or finder's fee is payable to Buyer or any third party upon consummation of this transaction, except with respect to __*[name and address of broker/ finder]*__ __*[who/which]*__ introduced Buyer to Seller and __*[who/which]*__ is being compensated under separate agreement with Seller. *[Or whatever commissionable or non-commissionable event(s) are appropriate.]*

19. Action. Upon execution of this non-binding letter of intent, the parties will promptly prepare, negotiate in good faith, and execute option escrow instructions and purchase and ground lease documents consistent with the terms outlined herein. While this proposal shall not legally bind either party, would you kindly sign and return a copy of this letter confirming Seller's approval of the general economic terms contained herein.

20. Expiration of Proposal. This proposal shall expire at 5:00 p.m. on __________, 20__ unless written acceptance is received by Buyer on or before such date.

We would like very much to develop the __*[name]*__ Center, assure you of our commitment to build a quality project and would be pleased to provide major tenant, financial, consultant, and governmental agency references, as you may request. We look forward to working with you and appreciate the time you and your advisor spent with __________, for the information gained thereby formed the basis of this proposal.

Very truly yours,

[Developer Entity]

[Name]
[Title]

UNDERSTOOD AND AGREED BY "SELLER":
This __ day of ___________, 20__.
[Name of Seller]

By: ____________________

By: ____________________

Exhibit "A"
[Attach Tentative Site Plan—in this example graphically depicting the "Site" and the "Option Property" (See Paragraph 2)]

Exhibit "B"

[Name] Shopping Center
Preliminary Development Schedule

Note: *Developmental tasks and time requirements will differ significantly from site to site. This particular schedule is attached not for its content, but rather, to demonstrate the concept of attaching a schedule as a persuasive tool when warranted. Such an exhibit can succinctly substantiate the developer's request to control a site for an extended time period. Amend and add headings, as necessary, to conform with text milestones.*

1. Title. Title to be approved within __*[e.g., 14]*__ days from receipt of preliminary title report and copies of all referenced exceptions and plotted easements.

2. Engineering Feasibility (1 month). Buyer's approval of an engineering feasibility study to be performed at its expense. Buyer will engage its typical consultants to prepare a "Site Investigation and Engineering Feasibility Report" for the proposed center. Preparation typically takes __*[e.g., one]*__ month from Buyer's civil engineer's receipt of approved title documents.

3. Major Tenant Commitments (3-4 Months from Commencement of Option Period). Buyer's obtaining satisfactory purchase or lease commitments from sufficient major anchor tenants.

4. Commercial Site Plan Approval (9-10 months from Commencement of Option Period). Final commercial site plan approval (including required concurrent approval of a conceptual landscape plan, building elevations and conformity with the pending __*[e.g., name of jurisdiction]*__ __*[e.g., Specific Plan]*__) to take approximately __*[e.g., 6]*__ months <u>after</u> securing major tenants and negotiating acceptance of final site plan and related submission materials with major tenants.

5. Permits (15 months from Commencement of Option Period). Because the time required to complete working drawings will not commence until issuance of final commercial site plan approval and because plan check of completed working drawings will take an additional __*[e.g., 5 months]*__, obtaining all necessary applicable governmental approvals and building permits for construction of the first phase of the shopping center should take not less than __*[e.g., 15]*__ months.

FORM 5-5

END OF FORM 5-5

OVERVIEW

Chapter 6 provides examples of opportunities in which a developer can acquire development rights to a project where development work has already begun. Narrative and forms in this chapter address site purchase and joint venture relationships with residential developers, acquisition of another retail developer's purchase escrow rights relative to a pending project, purchase of specific land parcels within an entitled project prior to groundbreaking, and the purchase of "residual" land for expanded development within a partially-completed shopping center.

FORMS

6-1 Acquiring Home Builder's Retail Site(s). Letter to Major Home Builder Proposing Continuing Venture Relationship and/or Sale of Home Builder's Shopping Center Project Currently under Development.

6-2 Purchasing Another Developer's Site Purchase Escrow Rights. Letter Agreement, Escrow Assignment and Promissory Note Confirming Short-Term Option to Purchase Another Developer's Purchase Escrow for a Shopping Center Site Still under Development.

6-3 Purchasing All But Anchor Tenant Parcels. Short-Form Offer to Purchase the Shops and Pads Portion of an Entitled, Supermarket-Anchored Neighborhood Center before Groundbreaking.

6-4 Purchasing Undeveloped Portion of Partially Completed Center. Proposal to an Anchor Retailer That Has Constructed an Initial "Free-Standing" Store and Limited Shops on a Portion of a Land Parcel Owned by the Retailer. Developer Proposes to Purchase the Entire Parcel, Less the Land Area Attributable to the Anchor's Retail Operations, Subject to Developer's Ability to (i) Add a Second Anchor Tenant and (ii) Build Additional Shops and Pads, Consistent with Specified Amendments to an Existing, Approved Site Plan.

Chapter 6

Acquiring All or a Portion of a Project Still under Development

Go asking a lot of damfool questions and taking chances. Only through curiosity can we discover opportunities, and only by gambling can we take advantage of them.

—Clarence Birdseye

Site-acquisition strategy and planning should not overlook the extraordinary opportunities that exist in projects already under development. Sources of such opportunities include home builders attempting a retail project but who often lack the skill, experience, determination, and long-term commitment to complete a shopping center project.

Occasionally, a long-term landowner with no development partner will commence processing a site, become stymied, and decide to form a venture or sell the site. Inexperienced or undercapitalized investors, retail operators, and, not infrequently, other shopping center developers may from time to time run short of capital because of overexpansion, market contraction, or an otherwise imprudent land-acquisition program.

Obviously, the longer the project has been under development, the more wary one should become since, as time passes, more of the developer's potential mistakes may become irreversible or compounded.

A real estate representative for a major tenant, obligated to satisfy the major's expansion objectives, is often an excellent lead in finding such potential projects. Tenant real estate representatives naturally want to avoid or extricate themselves from the time-consuming "hand holding," frustration, and delay that can result from having to work with an inexperienced or undercapitalized developer.

Form 6-1 is a letter to a residential builder proposing to create a venture relationship and/or acquire development rights to an initial retail project already under development by the home builder. The second example (Form 6-2) is a letter agreement providing for a short-term option to purchase another shopping center developer's site purchase escrow position relative to a project under development. Form 6-3 is a short letter offer to acquire the "shops" and "pads" portion of an approved retail project nearing groundbreaking. Finally, Form 6-4 is a proposal to purchase a site wherein a major tenant has already constructed a "free-standing" store and some shops pursuant to an approved site plan. The proposal is contingent upon the buyer's ability to initiate a transaction with a second "major" and complete development of the center conditioned upon effectuating specified, proposed amendments to the site plan.

PRE-CONSTRUCTION PURCHASE OF LAND OR ESCROW RIGHTS

Form 6-1 is an example of a brief proposal made to a home builder during the home builder's first in-house attempt to develop a shopping center project. Not knowing the home builder's precise income, expense, and cost structure, usually a short, brief general proposal is appropriate to determine whether there is any possibility of a deal.

Since you are typically working with "guesstimates," take care not to overstate your capabilities in your initial letter. If a transaction appears possible, meet immediately with the potential venture partner or seller. After gathering the necessary financial, legal, and governmental information you need, you should promptly follow up your initial letter with a formal proposal.

Be willing and capable of moving quickly. If you cannot, in most cases you are wasting your time. Residential builders usually move more quickly in land acquisitions and dispositions than shopping center developers and often cannot tolerate the long, complex due diligence, marketing, and entitlement contingencies customarily required by retail developers. Devise a way to move quickly, communicate your capabilities truthfully, then keep your word.

Form 6-1

Letter to Major Home Builder Proposing Continuing Venture Relationship and/or Sale of Home Builder's Shopping Center Project Currently under Development

[Date]

[Name and Address
of potential venture
partner/seller
____
____
_______________*]*

Re: Involvement in future shopping center sites and __*[Name of home builder's center under development]*__ __*[describe location]*__

Dear __________:

__*[Name of developer's company]*__ is actively pursuing shopping center development opportunities in __*[describe region, e.g., Southern Florida]*__. In particular, I am presently focusing upon acquisition of suitable sites in __*[city/county]*__ and have been monitoring progress on your ___ -acre __*[describe/identify]*__ shopping center site in __*[city]*__. Based upon our preliminary estimates of development costs, we are prepared to negotiate purchase of the site for $_______ million cash plus reimbursement of agreed upon development soft costs incurred by your company to date. The major contingency would be our ability to consummate a build-to-suit lease or parcel sale with __*[name of major tenant]*__ and confirm that jurisdictional approvals are in place. I would expect that routine due diligence issues could be accomplished within _____ days by the end of which time you would be assured that we and our financial partner were fully committed and capable of performing. We have assumed in this value estimate that the __*[seller]*__ would complete rough grading of the site consistent with the approved site plan and that we could confirm that projected on- and off-site improvements would not exceed $______ per square foot.

Assuming we could negotiate a purchase agreement acceptable to your company, we would consider retaining __*[name of seller-general contractor]*__ as the site contractor if this would be of interest to your company (subject to typical bidding constraints which may be imposed by __*[name of major tenant]*__). Although purchasing the site is our preference, we would also be willing to discuss a joint venture or possibly a ground lease of the site.

We realize that this project is not now available for sale but wish to convey to you our continuing interest in the __________ area and this particular project. We are sincerely interested in this project and capable of expediting its completion. Additionally, we are very interested in developing future __*[name of seller's home building company]*__ shopping center sites within your master planned communities.

Insert a summary of your company's retail background, experience, and accomplishments in an ethically persuasive manner to demonstrates the potential for a beneficial relationship between your company and the home builder.

We look forward to expanding our position in __*[region]*__ with the development of shopping centers __*[and other commercial properties]*__ and would like to form a continuing relationship with your company in the development of shopping center sites within your planned communities. We have a long track record of successful retail development within guidelines imposed by adjacent residential developments and sensitive governmental and community standards.

We are pleased to share with you our __*[Company Brochure]*__ and __*[Company Profile]*__ and look forward to having an opportunity to discuss possible involvement with your company generally as well as the specific opportunity presented in your __*[name of above-referenced pending project]*__ shopping center development. Please telephone me at _________ to schedule a meeting to discuss this in greater detail.

Very truly yours,

[Name of Buyer entity]

[Name]
[Title]

END OF FORM 6-1

After returning from a relaxing vacation late on a Monday night, I was awakened by a call from an officer of a corporate financial partner. I was shocked to learn that the financial partner would be unable to make our partnership's option payment due a landowner that Friday. Notwithstanding the financial partner's partnership obligation to make the payment, the corporate financial partner's shareholders had suddenly become enmeshed in a hotly contested corporate dissolution and, based upon an overall project-by-project accounting, the assets and liabilities of the corporation were to be divided among its shareholders. The landowner was unwilling to give additional time.

After three days of day-and-night negotiations and document preparation, I purchased control of the particular land purchase escrow that was the subject of our partnership. No solution or plan was evident, but I believed I was better off controlling the escrow than in spending more legal expense and time pursuing legal remedies against the financial partner and its feuding shareholders. The project, however, was unentitled and not in a position to be financed.

Within a couple of weeks, I contacted and struck a deal with another developer who had unsuccessfully attempted to acquire the site at about the same time my partnership had put the site under contract. Because the other developer and I knew and trusted one another, I was willing to spend time to assist him. Since the monthly option payments would soon escalate very substantially, we agreed upon a unique option arrangement.

My company ("Optionor") gave the developer-buyer ("Optionee") a three- or four-day "free look" to review all title, governmental, leasing, and other materials, which were immediately supplied to Optionee. Thereafter, once each week for up to four weeks, an option extension fee was payable to extend Optionee's closing with Optionor to the next week. Substantial increases in each weekly payment were payable—particularly in the last two extensions. If any payment were missed, Optionor could quickly make an alternative disposition of the escrow and retain extension fees paid to date. The option closed on the fourth week, when Optionee was assigned Optionor's purchase escrow rights, the consideration being the sum of the extension fees paid to date plus a final sum due at the closing. To recap, my development company sold its purchase escrow rights to another developer and this new developer stepped into the buyer's shoes in the long-term option escrow with the landowner.

Ultimately, a portion of the assignment consideration payable to Optionor by Optionee was paid in the form of a short-term promissory note from Optionee. (If you are selling an escrow position for which you receive a note, consider securing the note by taking a security interest in the escrow rights that you are selling. This can give you the right to step back into the optionee's position in the escrow if the optionee defaults in payment of the note or the optionee fails to make specified option payments to escrow on a timely basis.)

This transaction exemplifies the need to be able to quickly and creatively invent pragmatic solutions to problems as they arise. Furthermore, but for a developer–seller's sound reputation earned for ethical conduct in past transactions, it is doubtful that another developer would be willing to acquire a land purchase escrow on such terms. In such a case, in the event of Optionor's breach or misrepresentation, Optionee merely has a claim against Optionor, with no right of offset (other then the short-term note ultimately negotiated). Most of all, however, the deal was created and consummated because it met and satisfied the overall interests of both parties. Fortunately, I was known and trusted by Optionee and Optionee had previous knowledge of the site; otherwise, the Optionee could not have responded with such speed.

Actually, an entire section could be devoted to the numerous structures and variations of such sales of escrow rights. One note of caution is warranted, however. If you open a second new escrow whereby you are planning to concurrently sell a site that you will be concurrently buying—a classic so-called "double-escrow"—make certain that the second escrow is drawn by a skilled attorney to avoid inadvertent breaches or misrepresentations caused by your seller's failure to perform or your seller's breach of warranty.

Don't get caught in the middle promising to give your buyer something you cannot get from your seller. Never cavalierly allow a resale escrow to be opened without having every word of both escrows drafted or reviewed by your attorney. Get the protection you need from an experienced attorney before you proceed to "double-escrow" a site. Use the following rather technical letter agreement to reach an understanding of the issues involved, rather than as documentation for your particular transaction.

Form 6-2

Letter Agreement, Escrow Assignment and Promissory Note Confirming Short-Term Option to Purchase Another Developer's Purchase Escrow for a Shopping Center Site Still under Development

[Date]

[Name and Address
of developer purchaser
____
____
___________________*]*

Dear ________:

This letter will confirm that __*[insert name of development company that is selling its position as buyer in the existing escrow, referred to below as "X Co."]*__ has been assigned all rights of buyer with respect to a purchase escrow (the "escrow") to acquire an approximately __ -acre parcel of unimproved land (the "site") as described on the map attached hereto as Exhibit "A". A copy of the assignment from __________ (original buyer in the escrow) to __*[X Co.]*__ is attached hereto as Exhibit "B".

Summarize terms of the existing purchase "escrow", for example:

__[The terms of the escrow provide for a purchase price of $________ in cash on or before a scheduled escrow closing date of _______, 20__. As a condition to extending the scheduled escrow closing date in monthly increments, monthly escrow releases of $_______ per month are payable through ________, 20__ and are fully applicable to the purchase price. Beginning with the escrow release due _______, 20__, monthly escrow releases __[increase]__ to $________ per month and are __[not]__ applicable to the purchase price. In addition, buyer is responsible for all escrow, title, property tax and all related closing costs, which escrow estimates should not exceed about $_________, as itemized and set forth in Exhibit "C". An initial deposit of $_________ made by __[name of partnership comprised of X Co. and assignor]__ applies to the purchase price]__.

Disclose any key material issues—positive or negative—to create an informed consensus to proceed, for example:

__[The city has requested and seller has agreed to allow only one curb cut on __[X Boulevard]__, in return for which the city is paying for the construction *of __[Y Road]__ and certain other off-site improvements now under construction. In addition, the project is in the city's redevelopment area which allows but does not require developer to comply with the "Spanish Colonial" theme outlined in the __[X Boulevard Guidelines]__ established by the city's redevelopment agency. If such guidelines are followed, certain "developer incentives" are offered by the city, including but not limited to 20% compact stall parking and certain possible financial assistance]__.*

__*[X Co.]*__ ("Optionor") is willing to re-assign its rights as buyer under the escrow (the "Rights") to ____________ ("Optionee") and Optionee is willing to acquire an option to purchase the Rights under the following terms and conditions:

1. Option. In consideration of the payment by Optionee to Optionor of the sum of $__________ cash (the "Initial Option Payment"), the receipt of which is hereby acknowledged by Optionor, Optionor hereby grants to Optionee the exclusive right and option at any time prior to 4:00 p.m., __*[e.g., July 23, 2014—but see Optionee's right to extend closing in Paragraph 4]*__, 20__ ("Scheduled Closing Date"), to purchase the Rights on the terms and conditions hereinafter contained. *[To accommodate Optionee's "free look" window:]* If for any reason Optionee elects to terminate the option prior to the original Scheduled Closing Date, Optionee's Initial Option Payment shall be refunded to Optionee.

2. Optionee's Due Diligence. Optionee represents that it intends to purchase the Rights and the site subject to its completion of a due diligence investigation of the site, the escrow, and applicable regulatory agencies prior to closing. __*[Name of president of X Co.]*__, President and owner of __*[X Co.]*__ represents that he will assist Optionee without charge in meetings with regulatory agencies, consultants of Optionee's choosing and the like and will make his development files open for review, copying and questioning by Optionee during the option period. Both Optionor and Optionee will diligently work and cooperate with one another during the term of this option. Optionee agrees to pay for any consultants' costs or fees incurred as a result of its due diligence study.

3. Document Review. To assist Optionee in its due diligence, upon execution of this letter agreement, Optionor will hand Optionee the following documents:

3.1 Escrow Instructions. Escrow instructions for the escrow certified by __*[name of bank]*__ escrow department as of ___________, 20__, including an attached, approved preliminary title report and copies of exceptions, plotted easements and related correspondence (collectively, "Escrow Instructions"), a copy of which is attached hereto as Exhibit "D" and labeled "Escrow Instructions". Optionor represents that the Escrow Instructions fully and accurately describe the Rights.

3.2 Other Documents. *[Insert a comprehensive list of other documents, including but not limited to executed and proposed leases, city guidelines, approval forms, on- and off-site improvement cost breakdowns and plans, any engineering studies, proposed but unrecorded easements and the like, and each other material document in Optionor's files. After itemizing list, state that a copy of each such document is attached hereto as Exhibit "E" and labeled "Other Documents".]*

FORM 6-2

4. Option Extension Fees. Optionee may unilaterally elect to extend the Scheduled Closing Date of Optionee's purchase of the Rights by paying Optionor, in advance, the following "Option Extension Fee(s)" listed in column "(1)" on or before the due date described in column "(2)" in order to extend the Scheduled Closing Date to the date set forth in column "(3)":

Note: *Numbers and dates are merely examples.*

"(1)" Option Extension Fee	"(2)" Due Date/Time	"(3)" To Extend Closing To
$4000	4 p.m. Sat. 7/23/2014	4 p.m. 7/30/2014
$5000	4 p.m. Sat. 7/30/2014	4 p.m. 8/8/2014
$7000	4 p.m. Sat. 8/06/2014	4 p.m. 8/13/2014
$8000	4 p.m. Sat. 8/13/2014	4 p.m. 8/20/2014

If for any reason Optionee fails to exercise the option on or before the Scheduled Closing Date and fails to close, the Initial Option Payment and any Option Extension Fee(s) advanced to Optionor may be retained by Optionor as consideration for the granting of the option. In addition, in such event, Optionee will promptly return all documents received and will give Optionor copies of all site plans, engineering, studies and other consultant work generated by Optionee during the option period.

5. **Assignment Consideration.** On or before the closing, Optionee will deliver to Optionor, at the escrow department of __*[bank or escrow]*__, __*[city]*__, __*[state]*__, but outside of and not through escrow, a cashier's check for $__________, less the Initial Option Payment and any Option Extension Fee(s) paid Optionor, __*[and Optionee's promissory note for $________ ("Option Note"),]*__ in consideration for which Optionor will assign all Optionor's right, title, and interest in the escrow to Optionee, by concurrently depositing into escrow an assignment instrument substantially in the form of the Amendment to and Assignment of Purchase Escrow attached hereto as Exhibit "F". __*[The Option Note shall be prepared and executed in the format of the Promissory Note attached hereto as Exhibit "G"]*__.

6. **Additional Documents.** Optionor and Optionee will sign such additional documentation as may be necessary and reasonable by the escrow holder to accomplish the assignment, including a quitclaim deed from Optionor to Optionee.

7. **Commissions.** Optionee and Optionor each represent to the other that they have not entered into any agreement or incurred any obligation which might result in the obligation to pay a sales or brokerage commission based upon the consummation of the assignment contemplated herein __*[except as follows:]* __*[describe, as appropriate]*__

8. **Non-assignability Prior to Exercise of Option.** This option is personal to Optionee and unless and until Optionee exercises this option, Optionee shall have no right to assign any of its rights under this option.

9. **Confidentiality.** Optionee acknowledges that Optionor and __*[name of president of X Co.]*__ have undertaken extensive efforts in development of the site, particularly with respect to pending negotiations with various prospective tenants. Optionee understands that if this option is not exercised by Optionee, Optionor will continue to develop the site. Optionee represents that it will conduct its due diligence investigation with the highest degree of professionalism and confidentiality so as not to damage Optionor's relationships and position as developer. In particular, Optionee warrants it will be discrete in discussing the site and Optionor's project with the city and any consultants and will at all times introduce itself as a "potential investor" or that it is "arranging a transaction with __*[X Co. and/or its president]*__" or like terminology and will maintain the privacy of this option except with respect to the permitted disclosure to Optionee's legal counsel, Optionee's prospective lenders and equity partners, and Optionee's consultants. No contact will be made with tenants under current negotiation with Optionor except with the

prior notice to and approval of __*[name of president of X Co.]*__. If Optionee desires to discuss the project with any prospective tenant with whom __*[name of president of X Co.]*__ has conducted discussions, __*[name of president of X Co.]*__ will arrange a meeting or telephone conversation in which he will be present with Optionee. Optionee will have no discussions whatsoever with __*[name of seller of the site]*__, the current owner of the site, without __*[name of president of X Co.]*__'s prior approval __*[and concurrent attendance]*__.

10. No Changes to Escrow. __*[Name of president of X Co.]*__ warrants that so long as this option is in effect neither __*[he/she]*__ nor Optionor will alter or modify the terms or conditions of the escrow without Optionee's prior written approval and will timely make the __*[name of following month, i.e., next]*__ option payment.

FORM 6-2

11. Optionor's Representations and Warranties. *[Although various representations and warranties appear throughout this document, the attorney representing the party acquiring the Rights will want the opportunity to carefully prepare comprehensive representations and warranties provisions, particularly where potential mechanics' lien rights exist. For example:]* Optionor __*[and __________, its President]*__ hereby represent and warrant that (i) Optionor has the right to purchase the site as set forth in the Escrow Instructions; (ii) Optionor has not previously assigned the Rights to any other party; (iii) the escrow is in full force and effect in accordance with the terms of the Escrow Instructions and there are no amendments or modifications thereto except as set forth in the Escrow Instructions; __(iv) neither Optionor nor __*[name of president of X Co.]*__ have entered into any binding agreements with any governmental authority or any potential tenant of the site __*[except as disclosed above]*__; (v) to the actual present knowledge of Optionor and __*[name of president of X Co.]*__, no other party has any rights in or to the site or the escrow except as specifically set forth in the title report and the Escrow Instructions; and (vi) until the closing, __*[neither Optionor nor its president]*__ shall undertake any material act affecting the site or enter into any agreement regarding the site without Optionee's written consent. __*[Name of president of X Co.]*__ and Optionor shall indemnify and hold Optionee harmless from any liability, loss, cost or expense incurred by Optionee because any representation or warranty contained in this agreement is false or misleading.

These representations and warranties shall survive the closing and the close of escrow.

12. Time of Essence. Time is of the essence hereof and of the option granted Optionee.

Optionor's obligation to fully pay outstanding obligations to site architects, engineers and other consultants:

13. Optionor's Payments to Third Parties at Closing; Optionee's Right to Cure and Offset. Optionor shall, as of the close of Optionee's acquisition of the Rights, pay the following parties all amounts due them based on invoices provided by each such party. Optionee may, at its option, pay such invoices directly and reduce the $__*[insert cash assignment consideration amount]*__ payment by the amount thereof if Optionor has failed to arrange for satisfactory payment on or before the close:

> *[Listing of all outstanding architectural, engineering, and other consulting fees and costs and respective amounts of each, concluding with following statement:]*

Optionor is not aware of any other architect, soils engineer, surveyor, civil engineer, city agency or the like that is owed any sum regarding the site that is not accounted for in this agreement.

If Optionee's promissory note (the "Option Note") constitutes part of the assignment consideration, the following provision gives Optionee an offset right against the principal balance of the Option Note for Optionor's unpaid claims:

14. Optionee's Cure and Offset Rights Against Option Note. If any of the parties set forth in the preceding Paragraph __*[e.g. 13]*__ makes a claim for any additional sum due regarding the site, or if any other party asserts a right to receive payment, which party has, or would be entitled to place a lien against the site, and which claims are based solely on the actions of Optionor or its predecessors in interest in the escrow, and which claims are valid in the reasonable judgment of Optionee, Optionee may pay such claims and reduce the principal balance of the Option Note, by the amount of any such payment.

15. Cooperation. Upon exercise of this option by Optionee, Optionor's interest in the escrow and site shall terminate. However, __*[President of X Co.]*__, at Optionee's reasonable request, will make __*[himself/herself]*__ available to answer questions which Optionee may have with respect to the escrow or the site. *[Consider appropriately limiting scope of obligation or providing for consulting arrangement after closing.]*

16. Attorneys' Fees. If either party commences an action against the other to enforce any of the terms hereof or because of the breach by either party of the terms hereof, the losing or defaulting party shall pay to the prevailing party reasonable attorneys' fees, costs and expenses incurred in connection with the prosecution or defense of such action.

As a seller of option rights, try to avoid recourse against the escrow or the site in any Optionor-Optionee disputes:

17. No Right to Encumber Escrow or Site. Until the closing of this option is consummated, Optionee's rights herein and to the site shall for all purposes be deemed to be personal property and Optionee shall be deemed to have no interest in the site nor any right to file a lis pendens or notice of pendancy of action against the site or the escrow for any reason whatsoever. A fully negotiated and mutually-approved, material provision of this agreement is that any asserted breach of this agreement by Optionor shall be resolved by legal action against Optionor and/or __*[name of president of X Co.]*__ without encumbering the site or the escrow.

FORM 6-2

Insert the following paragraph, assuming this document is not intended to be binding:

18. Non-binding Letter of Intent. The parties do not intend this letter to be a binding contract. A contract between the parties will not exist unless and until the parties have executed a definitive escrow assignment agreement approved by legal counsel for each of the parties. The parties acknowledge that they have not set forth herein nor agreed upon all essential terms of the escrow purchase agreement and assignment, including without limitation, __*[e.g., mutually acceptable representations and warranties]*__. *[**Note:** As a checklist for additional issues that may not have been considered, consider rereading the purchase contingencies listed in Paragraph 6 of Form 4-1.]* Upon my timely receipt of a signed copy of this letter not later than _______, 20__, our respective lawyers will prepare formal documentation for our signatures.

OR

Use the following paragraph with caution: Once all legal and accounting refinements to the agreement have been made, the following paragraph, for use only with advice of legal counsel, provides that the modified letter agreement is intended to be a final contract between the parties.

18. Binding Agreement. This option letter agreement and its attached exhibits, having been reviewed and approved by legal counsel for each of the parties, is intended to be a binding, conclusive agreement concerning all terms and conditions of the assignment of the Rights.

19. Time For Acceptance. This option letter agreement shall expire unless accepted in writing and returned to Optionor on or before 4:00 p.m. _________, 20__. *[Add the following sentence only if letter is prepared in* *non-binding format:]* Assuming this non-binding letter agreement is timely accepted, Optionor and Optionee agree that full, final documentation shall be promptly negotiated and signed by the parties not later than *__[e.g., 4:00 p.m.]__ __[insert later date]__*, 20__ and that if the parties fail to sign final binding agreements on or before such time, neither party shall have any obligation to the other relative to the Rights.

> *When others not present in negotiations will have major decision-making power, take the opportunity to be persuasive in a proposal they will review. Do not rely upon the party with whom you are negotiating to make your characterization of the transaction clear to his or her constituents.*

20. Essence of the Bargain. Although it is understandable you may feel pressured by the extension fee schedule in Paragraph 4, the schedule is really very appropriate and reasonable under the circumstances. *[Substantiate reasonableness of structure, if necessary, for example:] __[Including today, Optionee is allowed the first __[e.g., 10]__ days, including an initial "free look," at a daily rate equivalent to the sum payable each day under the current $_______ monthly option rate which Optionor is paying. You are aware of the pending very substantial escalation in the monthly option payments due the seller and that effectively, risk-adjusted, Optionor is obligated substantially in excess of any extension payments payable through your first two extension payment periods. Thereafter, the extension payments increase but your risk should be substantially reduced as your due diligence is completed. The payment schedule allows Optionee to drop the option without paying for a full 30 days, assures Optionor of Optionee's continuing commitment, and all Optionee's extension payments are fully applicable to the total assignment consideration]__.*

Furthermore, you have my commitment that I will assist you in quickly and efficiently completing your due diligence. Accordingly, I have prepared this agreement to assist you so that we may proceed immediately.

Would you kindly give me your decision *__[e.g., promptly after your in-house development conference today]__*.

Very truly yours,

[Name of X Co.—"Optionor"]

[Name]
[Title]

UNDERSTOOD AND AGREED:
This __ day of __________, 20__.

[Name of developer—"Optionee"]

By: ______________

Its: ______________

[Attachments]

Exhibit "A"
[Map of Site]

Exhibit "B"
[Copy of escrow assignment from X Co.'s assignor to X Co. ("Optionor")]

Exhibit "C"
Summary of Buyer's Closing Costs
Estimated By Escrow Officer to
__*[President of X Co.]*__ ______, 20__

[Insert Schedule]

Exhibit "D"
[Certified copy of existing "Escrow Instructions", per Paragraph 3.1]

Exhibit "E"
[Copy of "Other Documents", per Paragraph 3.2]

Exhibit "F"
[Proposed assignment of Optionor's interest in the escrow to Optionee:]

Amendment to and Assignment of Purchase Escrow

1. Parties; Contemplated Assignment. For value received, __*[X Co. (name of "Optionor" in text of Form 6-2 letter agreement)]*__, a __*[name of state]*__ __*[type of entity, e.g., corporation/partnership]*__ ("Assignor"), as as-

FORM 6-2

signee from __*[insert name of original land purchaser that previously assigned to X Co.]*__ ("Buyer"), hereby transfers and assigns to __*[insert name of "Optionee" referenced in text of Form 6-2 letter agreement]*__ ("Assignee"), its heirs, legal representatives and assigns, all __*[X Co.]*__'s rights and interest in that certain escrow between __*[insert name of underlying land seller]*__ ("Seller") as seller, and Buyer as purchaser, subject to the covenants, conditions, and payments therein contained, all of which are hereby assumed by Assignee, for the sale of the unimproved land (the "site") described in the attached _________ Title Insurance Company Preliminary Report Number ________ dated ______, 20__, subject to exceptions __*[e.g., 1]*__ through __*[e.g., 10]*__ stated therein (a copy of which report and exceptions are attached hereto as Exhibit "A-1"). *[In addition, describe (i) additional supplemental exceptions and (ii) exceptions to which title will be taken that are not currently of record, for example:]* __*[In addition, title to the site is subject to a separate, supplementary recorded street dedication Item No. __(Exhibit "A-2") and a to-be-recorded "Irrevocable Offer to Dedicate (For Street Purposes)" (Exhibit "A-3") concerning a __ foot strip of land for __[Y Road]__, which road is currently under construction. The site will also be subject to that certain "Owner Participation Agreement" with the City of ____ Redevelopment Agency dated _______, 20__, affecting the site and certain other properties]*__.

2. Assignor's Deposits; Title. All funds presently on deposit for credit of or use of Assignor are to be herewith used for credit of Assignee. Title the site shall be vested as follows: _________________. In accepting such assignment, Assignee has independently satisfied itself with __*[name of title company]*__ or otherwise that satisfactory title insurance subject only to the above exceptions will be issued in favor of Assignee.

3. Assignee's Escrow Approval. Assignee's execution of this amendment constitutes Assignee's full approval of the terms and conditions set forth in the original escrow instructions dated _______, 20__ and any amendments and/or addendums thereto. Upon escrow holder's receipt of this fully-executed escrow amendment and assignment, Assignor will no longer be a party to the escrow. This document supersedes any contrary provision in and constitutes a part of the original instructions and any prior amendments.

4. Assignment Consideration. As a condition precedent to the authority granted Assignee by this assignment but for which escrow need not be concerned, Assignee shall pay by cashier's check, outside of escrow but concurrently herewith, a sum of money to Assignor __*[and deliver an "Option Note" drawn by Optionee]*__ as consideration for the assignment by Assignor. Execution of this assignment by Assignor in the presence of escrow shall constitute Assignor's receipt of such consideration.

5. Assignee's Right to Assign Concurrent with Assignor's Receipt of Full Payment. Assignee may assign all or any portion of its right, title or interest in and to the escrow and/or the site by additional written instructions from Assignee and Seller prior to close of escrow, but may not make any such assignment prior to Assignor's receipt of the cash sum __*[and Option Note]*__ due Optionor. *[Although the option letter agreement provides that the option is not assignable, this provision allows Optionee to assign the Rights as of the closing with Optionor, i.e., when the executed assignment instrument is deposited into escrow and Optionor has concurrently received the cashier's check and the Option Note.]*

FORM 6-2

6. Representations and Warranties. As a matter with which escrow holder need not be concerned but which constitutes a warranty to Assignee, __*[name of president of X Co.]*__ promises that within __ days following receipt of such payment, __*[he /she]*__ will pay or otherwise provide for payment of the outstanding expenses known by __*[him/her]*__ and confirmed by __*[name of X Co.'s previous financial partner]*__ with respect to development of the site by __*[XYZ Partnership]*__, a __*[partnership]*__ comprised of __*[e.g., name of president of X Co.]*__ and __*[e.g., name of X Co.'s previous financial partner]*__ which have not been previously paid pursuant to the Letter (as defined below) and Asssignor shall provide written evidence of the payment of any sum due pursuant to the Letter which is shown as a lien on title as of the date hereof or which could result in the imposition of such lien against the site. Furthermore, __*[name of president of X Co.]*__ warrants that __*[he/she]*__ owns and controls __*[X Co.]*__ and that there are no liens, encumbrances or other claims against __*[X Co.]*__ which would impair this assignment in any way and that Assignee's rights upon this assignment are no less than those which Assignee would have obtained had Assignee been substituted in place of __*[X Co.]*__ in its assignment from Buyer. Assignee has conducted its own review of the escrow and the site and this assignment is otherwise without warranty except for the specific warranties contained in that certain letter agreement ("Letter") by and among Assignee, Assignor and __*[name of president of X Co.]*__ dated _______, 20__. *[Refer to parties and date of specific letter agreement prepared pursuant to Form 6-2.]*

7. Assignee's Right to Receive Deed. Subject to the above conditions and promises, the undersigned authorizes and empowers Assignee in its performance of all of the above-mentioned covenants, conditions and payments, to demand and receive of Seller the deed covenanted to be given in the escrow contract hereby assigned in the same manner and with the same effect as Assignor could so demand and receive had the assignment not been made.

Date: ___________, 20__ __*[Name of Assignor, e.g., X Co.]*__
("Assignor")

By: _________________
[name]
[title]

Assignee accepts the above assignment of the subject escrow and agrees to perform all obligations to be performed by Assignor under the purchase escrow, according to the terms and conditions therein stated, and to indemnify Assignor against any liability arising from the performance or non-performance of such obligations.

Date: ___________, 20__ __*[Name of Assignee]*__
("Assignee")

By: _________________
[name]
[title]

UNDERSTOOD AND AGREED:

____
__*[Name of President of X Co. (signing individually)]*__

Date: _____________, 20__

____
__*[Name of underlying land "Seller"]*__
("Seller")

Date: _____________, 20__

FORM 6-2

Exhibit "G"

[Sample "Option Note" used as partial consideration for assignment of Rights in purchase escrow]

Promissory Note

$____________ ____________, 20__

__*[city]*__, __*[state]*__

For value received, the undersigned promises to pay to the order of __*[X Co.]*__ at __*[city]*__, __*[state]*__, the sum of __________ dollars ($__________) on or before the close of escrow No. __________ at __*[title company/bank]*__ ("escrow") or on the date which is __*[e.g., 60]*__ days after the date hereof, whichever shall first occur.

If the close of escrow is delayed for any reason outside the reasonable control of the undersigned or its assignees, __*[which shall not include the undersigned's or its assignee's delay or inability to obtain financing,]*__ the due date of this note may be extended for a reasonable period of time until ____________, 20__, on which date the entire principal amount plus accrued interest, if any, shall be due and payable notwithstanding anything in this paragraph to the contrary.

Should default be made in payment of principal, interest shall thereafter accrue thereon at the rate of ___ % per annum until paid and, in addition, the undersigned shall pay a late charge of __*[e.g., 3]*__ % of the amount due. Principal and interest is payable in lawful money of the United States.

If either party commences an action against the other to enforce any of the terms hereof or because of the breach by either party of the terms hereof, the losing or defaulting party shall pay to the prevailing party reasonable attorney's fees, costs and expenses incurred in connection with the prosecution or defense of such action.

[Optionee]

By: ____________________

Its: ____________________

END OF FORM 6-2

Form 6-3 was adapted from an offer received just before a center groundbreaking after an equity venture partner had funded a development partnership. Although the proposal was declined in this instance, it has been said that one's strength in the marketplace is directly related to the number of requests one makes. It can be overdone, but do not hesitate to make such proposals, particularly when you have some special knowledge or relationship with the transaction or its principals.

Form 6-3

Short-Form Offer to Purchase the Shops and Pads Portion of an Entitled, Supermarket-Anchored Neighborhood Center before Groundbreaking

[Buyer developer's letterhead]

[Date]

[Developer owner's
name and address
____
____
________________*]*

Re: ____________ Shopping Center
__*[city]*__, __*[state]*__

Dear ________:

This letter shall serve as our offer to __*[insert name of developer owner]*__ ("Seller") to purchase the land upon which to build the shops and __*[pads]*__ OR __*[outparcels]*__ portion of the above-referenced entitled shopping center project. If the terms and conditions are acceptable, Seller and __*[insert name of buyer developer's entity]*__ ("Buyer") would open a purchase escrow at __*[name of escrow company]*__, in __*[city]*__, __*[state]*__ consistent with the following terms:

1. The Sites. The land area upon which the shops and __*[pads]*__ OR __*[outparcels]*__ shall be built (the "sites") aggregate approximately _________ square feet of land ("sites land area"). The sites land area is calculated by taking the entire ___ -acre project area and subtracting therefrom the land area of the __*[e.g., name of supermarket]*__ parcel and the __*[e.g., name of other co-tenant parcel purchaser]*__ parcel, which __*[e.g., name of supermarket]*__ and __*[name of other co-tenant parcel purchaser]*__ are each purchasing from Seller concurrent with the closing of Seller's purchase of the total project land area.

2. Purchase Price. The purchase price for the sites shall be $_______________, or $_____ per square foot multiplied by the sites land area. The purchase price for the sites shall be payable in cash at the closing of the sites purchase escrow.

3. Closing. The sites purchase escrow closing date shall be the date the purchase escrows of __*[name of supermarket]*__ and __*[name of other major co-tenant parcel purchaser]*__ have each closed or fifteen (15) days after satisfaction of the contingencies set forth below, whichever shall last occur.

4. Contingencies. Close of the sites purchase escrow shall be contingent upon the following:

4.1 Title. Buyer's approval of a major title company Preliminary Title Report __*[,covering the entire project land area and the sites,]*__ within fifteen (15) days of receipt from escrow holder, which report shall be accompanied by copies of all documents that appear as exceptions together with a map depicting each easement, right of way, license or right capable of being plotted in accordance with normal title company practices.

4.2 Other Documents. Buyer's review and approval within 30 days of receipt of copies of all agreements, plans, permits and approvals applicable to the project and the sites, including but not limited to, all existing and pending leases and parcel sale agreements, building plans, engineering and soils reports, building permits, working drawings, development and operating agreements with __*[name of supermarket]*__, __*[name of other major co-tenant parcel purchaser]*__ and other tenants, reciprocal easement agreements, and conditions of development imposed by the __*[city/county]*__ of ______________ relative to the project and the sites.

5. Title and Escrow Fees. Seller shall provide at its expense a __*[See Appendix A, Form A-1]*__ policy of title insurance with liability equal to the purchase price. Escrow fees shall be divided equally and other closing costs and charges shall be paid in the manner customary in __*[county]*__, __*[state]*__.

6. Commissions. Seller shall be responsible for payment of (i) any sale commission due __*[name of broker]*__ regarding this proposed purchase and (ii) all leasing and sale commissions earned by __*[name of broker]*__ as owner's marketing agent in conducting owner's leasing and pad sale marketing program relative to the sites.

7. Non-binding. When signed by Buyer and Seller, this proposal shall constitute a non-binding letter of intent subject to mutual approval and execution of __*[e.g., a final Purchase Agreement]*__ OR __*[e.g., a final version of this agreement and applicable escrow instructions]*__. The parties do not intend this letter to be a binding agreement and no contract will exist, based upon this writing or the verbal communications of the parties. No contract between the parties shall exist unless or until such comprehensive formal __*[agreement]*__ OR __*[agreements]*__ covering all terms of the proposed transaction are signed by the parties and approved by legal counsel for each.

8. Time Limit. This proposal shall terminate at __*[e.g., 5:00]*__ p.m. on _________, 20__ unless written acceptance is received by Buyer on or before such date __*[and is contingent upon Buyer and Seller executing final documentation not later than _________, 20__]*__.

9. Action. If the above is acceptable, please sign and return a copy of this letter and we will immediately prepare final documentation in accordance with this non-binding letter of intent.

Very truly yours,

[Name of developer-purchaser]

[Name]
[Title]

UNDERSTOOD AND AGREED:
This __ day of ___________, 20__.

[Name of Seller]

By: ________________

Its: ________________

END OF FORM 6-3

PURCHASING A RESIDUAL UNDEVELOPED LAND AREA WITHIN A COMPLETED CENTER

Occasionally, a major tenant will acquire an entire shopping center site and obtain entitlements for the entire site, yet build only its own "free-standing" store or its store and some shops. Similarly, a developer's initial construction on a site may leave room for future buildout of additional leaseable space. A large national discount chain recently adopted an expansion strategy in certain regions whereby it will acquire an entire unentitled shopping center site, obtain development entitlements for the entire site, and then sell to a selected developer the land area outside the land parcel required for the chain's store and its attributable parking and common area. In other cases, older free-standing major chain stores are located on substantial land parcels owned by the chain. Residual parcels or "incomplete" project sites can often accommodate substantial additional development.

Form 6-4 is derived from an offer made to "complete" a California center where a major chain, also a developer, had recently built and opened one of its stores and some speculative shops on a shopping center site it owned. To make the form more understandable and readable, the specific deal economics are reproduced. The proposal may serve as a skeletal outline and method of organizing key issues involved in structuring such an acquisition. Consider Form 6-4 as a starting point in creating a proposal to acquire and develop the residual developable land area in a partially completed center subject to satisfaction of anchor tenant, site planning, and entitlement contingencies.

Form 6-4

Proposal to an Anchor Retailer That Has Constructed an Initial "Free-Standing" Store and Limited Shops on a Portion of a Land Parcel Owned by the Retailer. Developer Proposes to Purchase the Entire Parcel, Less the Land Area Attributable to the Anchor's Retail Operations, Subject to Developer's Ability to (i) Add a Second Anchor Tenant and (ii) Build Additional Shops and Pads, Consistent with Specified Amendments to an Existing, Approved Site Plan

[Date]

[Name and address of owner of center and existing major tenant store
____
____
____________________*]*

Re: __*[name of shopping center]*__
__*[city]*__, __*[state]*__

Dear __________:

I appreciate the time you have spent with me discussing the status of your __*[name]*__ Shopping Center development. I have reviewed the project with my proposed financial joint venture partner, __*[name of developer's financial partner]*__, and after giving the matter much thought, __*[name of financial partner]*__ has authorized me to pursue the purchase of a portion of your property, as outlined below. __*[I trust you are familiar with __[name of financial partner]__'s financial capabilities, as contained in its public Annual Report which I recently gave you]*__.

A. General Approach and Proposed Additional Major Tenant.

I understand that the total land area of your project is approximately __*[e.g., 380,237]*__ square feet and that __*[name of existing major tenant operated by seller ("major tenant #1")]*__ is willing to agree to absorb and retain __*[e.g., 130,000]*__ square feet of the total land area. Therefore, this letter will confirm the terms and conditions by which a joint venture of __*[name of developer's financial partner]*__ and myself ("Buyer") proposes to acquire from your company ("Seller") the remaining __*[e.g., 250,237]*__ net square feet of residual site area (the "site").

FORM 6-4

Senior management of _*[name of major tenant #2]*_ has informed me that _*[name of major tenant #2]*_ has a very strong desire to locate within the center and, subject to final review of demographic data, will probably have an affirmative answer in not more than 30 days. _*[Name of major tenant #2]*_ has expressed a willingness to pay _*[e.g., $4.00 to $6.00]*_ per square foot for an unimproved building pad, including its prorata parking area. At _*[e.g., $4.00]*_ per square foot, the total allocable _*[name of major tenant #2]*_ land area and such tenant's acquisition price may be calculated as follows:

[Calculation outlining economics of proposed land purchase by major tenant #2:]

35,000 sq. ft. building area + 10,000 sq. ft. for garden/nursery sales (According to the _*[City]*_ Planning Department, the garden/nursery area has the same parking requirements as the building.)
Thus, 45,000 sq. ft. x 4 [assumes building coverage is 25% of site] = 180,000 sq. ft. total allocable land area
180,000 sq. ft. x $4/s.f. = $720,000 land purchase price

We have carefully reviewed the site, and in light of current economic conditions and the site's location within growing but currently immature housing growth, we are not willing to purchase the site without a commitment from _*[name of major tenant #2]*_ or a comparable major co-tenant. However, once the major co-tenant is obtained, the joint venture would be willing to close the purchase of the site for cash.

We are prepared, at our expense, to revise the existing site plan, obtain amended site plan approvals, negotiate a parcel sale to _*[name of major tenant #2]*_ (or other major co-tenant), and develop and build out the remainder of the site on the following terms and conditions:

B. Outline of Site Purchase Specifics.

1. The Site. The land are which is the subject of this proposed purchase and sale transaction is the approximately _*[e.g., 250,237]*_ net square feet of residual land area (the "site") in your _*[name]*_ shopping center, as described above.

2. Closing. The closing date for Buyer's purchase of the site shall occur on or before _*[e.g., 120]*_ days from opening of escrow subject to the _*[e.g., two]*_ escrow extensions, as provided below.

3. Purchase Price. The total purchase price payable Seller shall be __*[e.g., $920,000]*__, all cash as provided herein.

4. Title Insurance and Escrow Costs. At close of escrow Seller, at Seller's expense, shall provide Buyer, and any of its assignee purchasers, with a __*[See Appendix A, Form A-1]*__ policy of title insurance, subject only to the title exceptions previously approved in writing by Buyer. However, the cumulative liability of all such policies shall equal Buyer's total purchase price for the site; and in no event shall Seller be obligated to pay a total title premium charge greater than the charge that would be incurred if Buyer alone (and no other assignee) were to purchase Seller's entire interest in the site in a single conveyance. Buyer and Seller shall each pay one-half the escrow fee and all other escrow costs and charges shall be paid in the manner customary in __*[county]*__, __*[state]*__.

5. Contingencies. Close of escrow shall be contingent upon:

5.1 Co-anchor Parcel Sale; Escrow Extension Payments. Concurrent sale through escrow of __*[e.g., 180,000]*__ square feet of land (in its current state of improvement) at not less than __*[e.g., $4.00]*__ per square foot, or __*[e.g., $720,000]*__ to __*[name of major tenant #2]*__. In addition, __*[name of major tenant #2]*__ shall agree to pay its prorata share of site improvement costs encountered by virtue of amending the site plan to incorporate a __*[name of major tenant #2]*__ building pad and garden supply area. If such sale does not close within __*[e.g., 120]*__ days after opening of escrow, Buyer may elect to release __*[e.g., $25,000]*__ to Seller through escrow for a __*[e.g., 90-day]*__ right to extend the closing. If such sale does not close within such __*[e.g., 90-day]*__ extension of the closing, Buyer may elect to release an additional __*[e.g., $25,000]*__ to Seller through escrow for a second and final __*[e.g., 90-day]*__ right to extend the closing. Both such closing extension payments shall be non-refundable but applicable to the purchase price for the site.

If __*[name of major tenant #2]*__ elects not to enter into the major tenant land sale described herein, close of escrow shall be contingent upon Buyer's ability to obtain an alternative satisfactory major tenant commitment within __*[e.g., 120]*__ days following the opening of escrow, with a similar right to extend the closing in accordance with the two aforementioned __*[e.g., 90-day]*__ extensions.

FORM 6-4

5.2 Title Approval. Buyer's approval of a preliminary title report and copies of all referenced exceptions with easements plotted by the title company within __*[e.g., 30]*__ days after receipt from the escrow holder.

5.3 Economic Feasibility. Buyer's investigation and approval, within __*[e.g., 60]*__ days after opening of escrow, of economic feasibility necessitated by required revisions to the site plan, site work, re-engineering, site utility alterations, and anticipated city conditions necessitated by revising the site plan in a manner acceptable to Buyer and Seller in accordance with this proposal.

5.4 Amended Site Plan Approval. Prior to closing, Buyer and Seller will jointly approve an amended site plan which is acceptable to and approved by the City of __*[name]*__. An acceptable site plan shall have the following characteristics:

5.4.1 Additional Major Tenant. It shall depict a __*[e.g., 35,000]*__ square foot __*[major tenant #2]*__ store with a __*[e.g., 10,000 square foot garden/nursery sales area]*__ (or a comparable major co-tenant in terms of size, financial condition and typical operating volumes);

5.4.2 Corner Pad. The area at the immediate corner of __*[e.g., _____ Street]*__ and __*[e.g., _______ Boulevard]*__ shall be approved for __*[e.g., 5,000]*__ square feet of buildable area which may include one conventional, sit-down restaurant, one fast food restaurant, or a combination of such uses;

5.4.3 11,000 S.F. Shops Building. A "phase __" shop building area which, although it may be contained in two buildings, shall not be less than a total of __*[e.g., 11,000]*__ square feet of shops which are not more than __*[e.g., 60]*__ linear feet in depth, located __*[describe]*__; and

5.4.4 5000 S.F. Shops Building. A "phase __" shop space building area containing not less than __*[e.g., 5,000]*__ square feet of shops which are not more than __*[e.g., 60]*__ feet in depth, located __*[describe]*__.

5.5 Parcel Map Recordation. The recordation of a parcel map on the site establishing each of the following land areas as a separate legal parcel: (i) your store and its attributable parking area, (ii) the __*[name of major tenant #2]*__ store, garden/nursery sales area and attributable parking area for __*[name of major tenant #2]*__'s use and (iii) the shops/free-standing building pad areas comprising the balance of the site (which may be further parcelized).

6. Brokers and Finders. Although Buyer represents it has not dealt with any finder or broker in initiating or negotiating this transaction, upon close of escrow, Seller will pay any finder's fee or brokerage commission due, if any, arising out of the subject transaction.

7. Entry License and Cooperation; Marketing Signs. __*[Upon execution of a final Purchase Agreement]*__ OR __*[Upon execution of a final version of this agreement and applicable escrow instructions]*__ Buyer shall have an immediate license to enter upon the site __*[and Seller's adjacent parcel(s) included within Seller's shopping center]*__ for the purpose of conducting feasibility, engineering, soil and other tests at Buyer's sole cost and expense. Buyer will indemnify Seller and hold Seller harmless from any and all loss or liability resulting from the acts of Buyer or its agents or employees upon the subject property and from all or any mechanics liens or other liens resulting from Buyer's conduct or the conduct of its agents or employees on the subject property. All expenses for tests, surveys, applications and approvals shall be born by Buyer but Seller agrees to cooperate with Buyer in attempting to obtain site plan amendments and all other related approvals, including executing such documents as may be required. Furthermore, upon execution of such final documentation, Seller will grant to Buyer, or Buyer's nominee or agent, the right to immediately erect a sign or signs offering retail space for sale or lease on the site. *[Possible additional clause:]* __*[Buyer and Seller, however, will negotiate a signage agreement which preserves Seller's need to market its existing speculative shop space while at the same time gives Buyer effective signage for its proposed development on the site]*__.

8. Non-binding. When signed by Buyer and Seller, this proposal shall constitute a non-binding letter of intent subject to mutual approval and execution of __*[a final Purchase Agreement]*__ OR __*[a final version of this agreement and applicable escrow instructions]*__. The parties do not intend this letter to be a binding agreement between them and no contract will exist, based upon this writing or the verbal communications of the parties. No contract between the parties shall exist unless or until such comprehensive formal __*[agreement]*__ OR __*[agreements]*__ covering all terms of the proposed transaction are signed by the parties and approved by legal counsel for each.

9. Time Limit. This proposal shall terminate at __*[e.g., 5:00]*__ p.m. on __________, 20__ unless written acceptance is received by Buyer on or before such date __*[and is contingent upon Buyer and Seller executing final documentation not later than _________, 20__]*__.

FORM 6-4

10. Action. If the above is acceptable, please sign and return a copy of this letter and we will immediately prepare final documentation in accordance with this non-binding letter of intent and begin our work with the __*[City]*__ Planning Department and __*[name of major tenant #2]*__.

Very truly yours,

[Developer Entity]

[name]
[title]

UNDERSTOOD AND AGREED:
This __ day of __________, 20__.

[Name of Seller's entity]

By: ________________

Its: ________________

END OF FORM 6-4

OVERVIEW

Chapter 7 considers the untapped opportunities and benefits of major retail chains and shopping center developers working cooperatively in an organized program of recycling or redeveloping outmoded chain store space.

FORM

7-1 Proposal to Purchase Retailer's Outmoded Stores. Developer Proposal to Major Food Retailer to Form Relationship Whereby Developer Will Acquire and Recycle Retailer's Outmoded Stores.

Chapter 7

Recycling Major Tenant Store Space: Purchasing Outmoded Space from Retailers

In order to compose, all you need to do is remember a tune that no one else has thought of.
–Robert Schumann

In early 1987 I had lunch with Tom Gregg, a seasoned real estate professional and friend who previously had served a productive career as real estate manager for a major supermarket chain. In the early 1980s I negotiated a build-to-suit lease with him for a new 42,000-square-foot combination food-drug store—the first of what was to become the largest prototype store in his chain at the time. Since then, dramatically larger new concepts have become commonplace. By 1991, nearly one-third of all U.S. supermarkets were operating under superstore or food-drug combinations. Such formats then accounted for more than half of all supermarket sales.

After our luncheon, Tom took me through a new mega-sized food store, described its enlarged trade area, and then predicted what the new store would do to the old, smaller, uncompetitive stores within the trade area. I credit him with what I believe to be a valuable notion: What opportunities are presented by the chain store's need to recycle out of its outmoded stores that are no longer workable in our large store environment?

Most retailers and developers have responded to changing times and the major tenant's continuing need for leasehold assignments and store dispositions on an ad hoc rather than from a broad, strategic perspective. Consequently, a visionary development company (or a division of it) could seize this opportunity by focusing specifically on acquisitions of older supermarket (and other) chain store real estate that is no longer competitive in its existing format. A prearranged, aggressive group of tenants could be selected to occupy the to-be-renovated space, many of whom could create a greater draw for a center than a marginally performing supermarket. The existing chain tenant's lease rates are typically very low in such centers, yet surrounding population counts are generally very high. Consider contacting the major chains with whom you have a relationship and implementing a major, structured acquisition and redevelopment plan.

I had relationships with a number of good "replacement" tenants, a financial partner, and the construction department of a major development company with whom I was a partner at the time. Frankly, however, I continued to occupy myself with other matters and never strongly pursued such a plan. Therefore, I cannot offer insights based upon my experience.

Nevertheless, I would like to share the following letter, reproduced as Form 7-1, which I wrote to the real estate manager of a major southern California supermarket chain. As an astute developer, use this as a springboard to contemplate: Is there untapped value you could create in your particular geographical area by "recycling" major chain stores or other undervalued space? What could you create—what need could you meet—that has not yet been addressed? Compared to new space, in most cases, existing building space can be converted at less cost, with less risk, with less governmental resistance, and within a shorter development cycle. Often, a new tenant mix will rejuvenate a mature or declining shopping center, creating renewed competitive viability.

Form 7-1

FORM 7-1

Developer Proposal to Major Food Retailer to Form Relationship Whereby Developer Will Acquire and Recycle Retailer's Outmoded Stores

[Developer Letterhead]
[Date]

[Name and address of
real estate manager for
major supermarket chain
____
____________________*]*

Dear __*[name of real estate manager]*__:

We are aware that as a result of your pending acquisition and development of larger supermarket stores encompassing greater trade areas, closure of certain existing __*[name of major supermarket chain]*__ stores may be imperative. Please be advised that __*[name of development company]*__ and __*[e.g., name of pension fund or REIT]*__, as an expansion of our continuing joint shopping center development activities, have made a commitment to aggressively acquire, rehabilitate, and re-lease supermarket space which is not competitive within today's growing, mega-sized supermarket environment.

In addition to our combined financial strength and in-house construction capabilities, we have relationships with a select group of quality, high-volume retailers that will enable us to purchase all-cash or accept leasehold assignments on a bulk basis free of pre-leasing or other cumbersome contingencies. Furthermore, the customer drawing power and high sales volumes of our tenants can dramatically offset attendant losses typically experienced when a major supermarket vacates its space in a shopping center. Finally, we have the capability and desire to pursue acquisitions of entire __*[name of major supermarket chain]*__ -anchored centers where __*[name of major supermarket chain]*__ has or intends to vacate.

We invite you to consider the mutual benefits of working together to facilitate your cycling to larger store formats. __*[Include appropriate closing: e.g., I will call you next week to discuss our proposal and to determine the appropriate action we can take together]*__.

Very truly yours,

[name of development company]

____
[name] [title]

cc: *[To above referenced real estate friend.]*

END OF FORM 7-1

OVERVIEW

Chapter 8 introduces a project marketing letter agreement by which a commercial brokerage firm will undertake a leasing and parcel sale program for a developer's shopping center project.

FORM

8-1 Project Marketing Letter Agreement. Marketing Letter Agreement between Developer and Exclusive Leasing/Marketing Broker Providing Leasing and Parcel Sale Services for a Strip Shopping Center.

Chapter 8

The Project Marketing Brokerage Contract

It is not enough to conquer;
one must know how to seduce.
—Voltaire

Many shopping center developers negotiate a marketing or brokerage contract with a third party to effectuate a shopping center's leasing and pad sale program. Form 8-1 is a basic marketing letter agreement that can be modified to satisfy most marketing needs.

PROJECT MARKETING AGREEMENT

To begin, recall that in the section describing the genesis of Form 6-2 (the option to acquire another developer's purchase escrow) the importance of ethics and diligence in one's relations with others in the industry was stressed.

Several months after consummating the sale of my company's purchase escrow rights to the other developer (as outlined in the explanatory text to Form 6-2), I received a call from the developer. I learned that the developer had intended to close his acquisition of the site with a particular insurance company financial partner. However, when the insurance company venture did not materialize, the developer formed an equity partnership composed of certain in-house personnel and an affiliated group. There was a special need to expedite the marketing effort. Since I had extensive experience and had commenced negotiations with a number of tenants, the developer requested that I undertake a focused marketing effort for the site.

The partnership requested that I concentrate on pad marketing, rather than major tenant and shop marketing, which were of less strategic importance to the equity partnership at the time. Since most developers would pursue pad transactions only after major tenancies were established, this request was very unusual. However, the developer wanted to acquire and integrate a much larger, surrounding, L-shaped adjacent property into the proposed development. This adjacent property was ideally suited for large anchor tenants. Yet the developer did not want to lose continuity in any negotiations I had commenced. The developer's intention, therefore, was to retain my company to negotiate primarily with an existing group of smaller pad tenants that I had identified for the corner site and concurrently engage a local brokerage firm to procure anchor tenants for location on the larger adjacent parcel. The equity sources apparently required that potential pad transactions and the specific economics of each be readily identified as a condition to funding the purchase of this corner site.

Being offered this marketing contract shows that, if one is habitually diligent, skillful, listens intently, and works honestly from a position of integrity, deals will come forth. This second opportunity was the direct result of how I performed for the developer when he purchased my escrow position. Although I did not particularly want this contract and it was somewhat outside my company's normal business, having sold the escrow rights to the developer, I felt a sense of responsibility in seeing that my successor was successful. Avoid expediency and operate from a long-term perspective to preserve your relationships. Specifically, when selling rights to a site under development, provide full and complete information regarding all matters that would be material to a prudent buyer. Go so far as to answer the material questions that are not even asked. Simply and without exception treat the buyer as you would want to be treated as a buyer, and never sacrifice your reputation by giving anything less.

As a corollary—whether you are a broker or a developer—do not take on a project unless you can give it your full effort and attention. If that is the case, communicate that you have other commitments and that, unfortunately, you cannot currently evaluate a certain site or take on a particular project. An otherwise sound reputation can be tarnished by being inattentive and not diligently carrying through with a project or leasing effort. Be aware that others are dependent upon your word and keep your word. Such a practice is fundamentally important in the quasi-partnership relationship between a competent developer and the developer's broker.

A marketing letter agreement (Form 8-1) was prepared to address the specific transaction mandated by the rather unique circumstances outlined above. "Alternative 'A'—'Case Study' Illustrative Introduction" is inserted to demonstrate its use in the preceding factual situation. This italicized language should not be reused. It is reproduced merely as a stylistic example. You should insert entirely new language replacing the italicized text or use the "Alternative 'B'—Standard Introduction.")

Notice how the "Alternative 'A'—'Case Study' Illustrative Introduction" and the first numbered paragraph of the letter set forth the underlying reasons for the articulated agreements between the parties. This brings to bear an important negotiating and drafting principle: Take the initiative and use this opportunity to put your agreements in context. Take the time to set forth the facts and underlying reasons (referred to by lawyers as "recitals") for which the agreement is being made. If a disagreement later arises as to an ambiguity or disputed interpretation of a specific provision, you will have the benefit of having the parties' underlying intentions in the body of the document itself. If a particular provision of an agreement is subject to varying interpretations, courts will generally attempt to interpret the provision consistent with the manifested intentions of the parties.

Note also the case study introduction's use of an Exhibit "B", a listing of specific tenants with whom there were previous negotiations and for which the broker's rights are confirmed. By analogy, a novel marketing strategy—particularly in larger projects—could be considered: A marketing program for a major project might be structured as a bifurcated effort whereby restaurant tenants and food court tenants, for example, could be approached by a specialized restaurant brokerage firm; concurrently, an exclusive marketing contract might be given to another firm, subject only to such restaurant tenant exclusions. In most cases, however, Form 8-1 would be prepared without any reference to such a specific tenant list (Exhibit "B") and you would start with and edit the "Alternative 'B'—Standard Introduction" provision beginning immediately after the case study illustrative insert.

Although Form 8-1 is not an example of a heavily negotiated, detailed marketing contract written by a skilled real estate lawyer, its outline format supports creative additions and amendments to meet most marketing requirements. Furthermore, the various commission formulas contained within it can be easily edited to meet prevailing local custom.

Form 8-1

Marketing Letter Agreement between Developer and Exclusive Leasing/Marketing Broker Providing Leasing and Parcel Sale Services for a Strip Shopping Center

[Broker letterhead—(could be amended to be addressed to broker from developer)]

[Date]

[name and address of developer ________
____
____________________*]*

Ref: __*[name]*__ Shopping Center
__*[location]*__,
__*[city]*__, __*[state]*__

Dear __________:

Alternative "A"
"Case Study" Illustrative Introduction (not for re-use)

The following introductory paragraphs are, in effect, "recitals" setting forth the underlying reasons for the specific agreements reached between the parties. This example, following the preceding discussion, is set forth merely to give you a flavor of the customizing possible. This example assumes that the parties agree at the inception of the transaction that the broker will be paid if a transaction is entered into with any of the agreed list of potential tenants listed on Exhibit "B". Go directly to "Alternative 'B'—Standard Introduction," below, for typical, generally applicable introductory language.

This letter will serve to confirm our discussions concerning your development plans and our proposed marketing contract for the above-referenced property (the "site") described on Exhibit "A". In summary, you stated that __*[name of development company (i.e., the purchaser of the purchase escrow rights in Form 6-2)]*__ had originally intended to close your acquisition of the site in joint venture with an insurance company financial partner.

However, when the proposed venture did not materialize, it became necessary for __*[name of development company]*__ to form an in-house equity partnership and to expedite the consummation of viable retail transactions on the above site, ideally within a 120-day time frame. You expressed interest in forming a consulting arrangement with my company due to my relationship with tenants I had identified for the site and my substantial retail leasing and development experience. You have considered retaining a local third-party marketing agent to effect a comprehensive marketing effort with respect to large anchor tenants to be located on the large __*[describe]*__ adjacent parcel surrounding the site.

With your present workload and desire to concentrate on city-processing strategy, financing, and other non-marketing development issues, you have requested that I take responsibility, subject to your direction, for negotiating any applicable transaction through the letter of intent stage covering all major issues, thereby facilitating subsequent documentation by your legal counsel. Specifically, this proposal assumes that I negotiate transactions in scope and format similar to my ________, 20__ letter agreement with ________ Corporation.

> ***Note:*** *A deal I had previously done created a standard that the developer was familiar with.*
>
> ***Note:*** *Always try to create some "standard" of skill or expectation, even if it is only something like "as a material condition of this agreement, broker will continuously perform throughout the term of this contract consistent with the highest standards and performance of shopping center real estate marketing professionals in __[city/region, etc.]__." The broker and developer should discuss this issue before the contract goes into effect. The developer needs to be able to make a clean, fair separation if the broker is not performing. Although this can be addressed by extensive, technical termination rights, it is often of greater practical importance to have a true business understanding between the parties as to what is expected. Part of that understanding can come from a careful discussion and drafting of the "Marketing Objective" section (Paragraph 1) of Form 8-1.*

As a consequence of your revised partnership structure, your primary objective is to subdivide the site and sell pads on the street frontages to reduce your land basis. You have requested and I have agreed, therefore, that I give my priority to such pad marketing as opposed to major tenant and shop marketing, which are presently of less strategic importance to you since you intend to enter into an agreement with a third party brokerage firm to procure anchor tenants for the adjacent parcel.

Therefore, __*[name of developer]*__ ("Developer") hereby agrees to retain and pay __*[name of brokerage entity]*__ ("Broker"), a licensed __*[state]*__ real estate broker, concerning the active negotiation of parcel sale and leasing transactions with Broker's prospective tenants listed on Exhibit "B" (the "List") and any other unregistered prospective tenants which Broker hereafter registers with Developer during the term of this agreement, as follows:

> ***Note:*** *Substantive alternative provisions to the agreement consistent with this introduction are not included below.*

OR

Alternative "B"
Standard Introduction

The following is a more generic introduction and assumes there is no specific group of tenants for which the broker is being protected, thus eliminating the need for the Exhibit "B" referred to in Alternative "A".

FORM 8-1

This letter will serve to confirm our discussions concerning your development plans and our proposed marketing contract for the above-referenced property (the "site") described on Exhibit "A". You presently contemplate developing a __*[e.g., "power" center]*__ with approximately ______ square feet of G.L.A., ______ pads and ______ square feet of shops with an overall layout __*[e.g., generally consistent with the conceptual site plan dated ________, 20__, a copy of which is attached as Exhibit "__."]*

You have requested and my company has agreed that we will diligently work to achieve the marketing objective described below.

Therefore, __*[name of developer]*__ ("Developer") hereby agrees to retain and pay __*[name of brokerage firm]*__ ("Broker"), a licensed __*[state]*__ real estate broker, concerning the active negotiation of parcel sale and leasing transactions, *[unusual but possible addition:]* __*[with the prospective tenants listed on Exhibit "B" (the "List") and any other unregistered prospective tenants which Broker hereafter registers with Developer during the term of this agreement,]*__ as follows:

End of Alternative "A" and "B" Introductions

Continue with body of text

__Note:__ Developer and Broker should spend the time to carefully consider, pragmatically plan and reduce to writing what they need and expect to accomplish.

1. Marketing Objective. Developer and Broker have fully discussed both the positive and negative attributes of the site from a shopping center development and marketing perspective. In particular, Broker and Developer have reviewed Developer's preliminary site plan dated _________, 20__, and preliminary development pro forma dated _______, 20__. Developer and Broker believe that the projected rental rates, parcel sale revenues and projected contributions granted occupants are appropriate and reasonably achievable in today's development environment.

Insert specific tenant mix or threshold that must be established:
Example #1:
__[Broker will give priority to quickly identifying and negotiating viable purchase or lease transactions with __[e.g., not less than __[e.g., 3]__ anchor tenants having a cumulative building square footage of not less than __[165,000]__ square feet]__. [The parties should go on to specify the desired tenant mix and retailing attributes that will be the focus of the marketing effort.]

OR

Example #2:
__[The site is 50 acres and only two "box" users over __[e.g., 90,000]__ square feet each have already been identified— ___________, a "category killer" discounter and _____________, a discount home improvement retailer. Because a "power" center development appears to be the only feasible retail development concept currently appropriate for the site, it will be necessary for Broker to obtain additional anchor tenants before a feasible site plan can be put together. Furthermore, the parties understand that Developer and Broker believe that not more than __[e.g., 15]__ % of total GLA __[(excluding pads/outparcels)]__ should be allocated to speculative shop space and that if anchor tenants (national or prominent regional tenants each exceeding ______ square feet of GLA) aggregating not less than ______ square feet cannot be identified, the project will not be feasible. If major tenant commitments establishing an appropriate tenant mix of __[describe]__ are not obtained within __[describe time period]__, Developer may elect to suspend development and terminate this agreement __[without obligation to Broker]__. Once this initial marketing objective is accomplished, Broker will complete the marketing of the project consistent with the site plan and the

*pro forma, as amended from time to time by Developer and Broker]*__.

2. Compensation. Broker shall be compensated in accordance with the following commission schedule:

2.1 Shops. For in-line shop space of less than __*[e.g., 12,000]*__ square feet, $__*[e.g., 4.00]*__ per square foot shall be paid without regard to the term of the lease. Broker shall attempt, however, to negotiate shop lease terms of not less than __*[e.g., 5]*__ years.

2.2 Ground Leases. A commission equal to __*[e.g., 5]*__ % of the "fee value" of a building pad which is ground leased shall be paid. The "fee value" shall be established for purposes of this letter agreement by capitalizing the fixed minimum annual ground rent payable for the first full year of the lease at the rate of __*[e.g., 10]*__ % per annum.

2.3 Pad Build-to-Suits. Commissions for pad build-to-suit transactions shall be __*[e.g., the sum of __ % of the fixed minimum annual rental for the first __ years of the lease term, __ % of the fixed minimum annual rental for the next __ years of the lease term and __ % of the fixed minimum annual rental for the next __ years of the lease term]*__ OR *[another example:]* __*[the sum of 30% of the first $100,000 of fixed minimum annual rental plus 20% of the fixed minimum annual rental in excess of $100,000 payable for the first year of the lease]*__.

2.4 Major Tenant Leases and Build-to-Suits. For major tenant leases of in-line space, $______ per square foot of gross building area shall be paid for space from __*[e.g., 12,000 to 20,000]*__ square feet and $__*[smaller number]*__ per square foot shall be paid for such space from __*[e.g., 20,000 to 35,000]*__ square feet. Commissions for space leases in excess of __*[e.g., 35,000]*__ square feet shall be __*[fixed number]*__ per square foot. *[Separate rates could be negotiated for sizes from, for example, 35,000 square feet to 60,000 square feet, and another percentage for space exceeding of 60,000 square feet. Alternatively, since very large tenant transactions should probably be negotiated, an alternative final, concluding sentence could provide:]* __*[Commissions for space leases in excess of 35,000 square feet shall be negotiated, it being the intention of Developer to reasonably compensate Broker for the value or contribution created by any such lease consistent with current commercial real estate practice in __[County]__, __[state]__, after consideration of the financial strength and financeability of the tenant, the magnitude of the Developer contribution (and subsidy, if any), a realistic projection of the tenant's gross sales, and the overall financial impact of such tenant to the center. However, an absolute minimum for*

FORM 8-1

any such commission shall be $________ per square foot and an absolute maximum shall be $__________ per square foot. The parties will promptly negotiate the amount of any such commission when the economics of the proposed transaction are known]__.

2.5 Pad Sales. A commission in the amount of __*[e.g., 5%]*__ of the "net purchase price" shall be payable upon the close of the sale of any building pad. In the event the purchase price for the pad includes (i) site mapping or processing costs payable third parties (prorata engineering, city fees, traffic engineering, or other consultant charges, etc., but excluding development or other overhead reimbursement chargeable by Developer) or (ii) other "hard" site improvement costs specifically advanced by Developer to accommodate such tenant, such costs and no other costs shall be deducted from the gross purchase price to establish the net purchase price for purposes of this paragraph.

Optional (covers adjacent land):

2.6 Adjacent Land Acquisition and Joint Venture. If during the term of this agreement Broker arranges a purchase, lease or joint venture between Developer and __*[name of adjacent property owner]*__ (or __*[e.g., his trust]*__, nominee or successor) concerning all or a portion of the __*[e.g., adjacent parcel currently beneficially owned by him and under lease to __________ (as depicted on Exhibit "__")]*__, Developer will pay Broker a fee of __*[e.g., 5%]*__ of the land value conveyed or ventured payable at close of escrow, or if there is no escrow, upon closing of the transaction. As of such date, __*[e.g., such adjacent property]*__ shall be subject to and included within the scope of this marketing agreement.

2.7 Site Sale or Venture. If Broker arranges a sale, lease or joint venture between Developer and any third party concerning all or a portion of the site, Developer will pay Broker a fee of __*[e.g., 5% of the land value conveyed or ventured]*__ OR __*[e.g., the lesser of 5% of the equity provided by the joint venture investor or 2% of the value obtained by multiplying total estimated project costs by the percentage ownership interest in the project acquired by the joint venture investor]*__ payable at close of escrow, or if there is no escrow, upon closing of the transaction.

Broker-oriented optional clause (Extends scope of leasing and parcel sale marketing agreement to cover sales of completed buildings):

2.8 Sale of Completed Buildings. Broker shall have an __*[open OR exclusive]*__ listing for the sale of any building located in the shopping center. In the event of such a sale the total sales commission will be __*[e.g., 6]*__ %

of the first $ __*[e.g., 500,000]*__ and __*[e.g., 5]*__ % of the gross sales price in excess thereof __*[; provided, however, in no event shall the sales commission exceed $ __[e.g., 250,000]__ in any one sale]*__. Sales commission(s) will be paid upon the close of escrow, or, if there is no escrow, then upon recordation of the deed.

3. Leasing Commission Payment Schedule. The above leasing commissions shall be paid as follows:

3.1 Ground Leases, Build-to-Suit Leases, and Major Tenant Leases. __*[E.g., One-half]*__ the commission for each such lease shall be paid upon the commencement of construction of tenant's building and __*[e.g., one-half]*__ shall be paid within __*[e.g., 30]*__ days following commencement of fixed minimum rent by tenant and tenant opens for business to the public.

3.2 Shop Leases. The commission for each shop lease shall be paid as follows: __*[e.g., One-third]*__ within __*[e.g., 30]*__ days of lease execution by both parties, all lease contingencies have been satisfied, and Developer has funded Developer's construction loan; __*[e.g., one-third]*__ upon commencement of construction; and __*[e.g., one-third]*__ shall be paid within __*[e.g., 30]*__ days following the date tenant begins paying fixed minimum rent (and not interim rent) and tenant opens for business to the public.

FORM 8-1

4. Other Brokers. In no event will Developer be obligated to pay more than a full commission in accordance with the compensation and payment schedules set forth above. Broker will cooperate with third party brokers representing specific tenants, it being the objective of this marketing agreement to expose the largest number of viable tenants to Developer. Any third party broker claims for all or a portion of a commission must be resolved by Broker.

Broker oriented (Developer's consent required if situation arises wherein Broker's licensee represents conflicting interests (i.e., as an agent for both landlord and tenant or both buyer and seller), such as if prospective tenant or buyer is not represented by an independent third party or is represented by another licensee employed by Broker):

__. Dual Agency. Developer authorizes Broker to represent and serve as agent for any prospective tenant or purchaser of the site ("interested party"). Broker may disclose to each interested party and Developer information concerning the transaction disclosed to Broker by either principal. However, Broker shall not disclose to either principal whether interested party or Developer would consider terms or conditions other than those terms and conditions that each such party has directed Broker to offer to the other party. Broker will not disclose any confidential information provided by Developer without Developer's prior written consent.

> ***Note:*** *The preceding paragraph raises a host of ethical and legal problems but does not solve them. Do not use or negotiate such a clause without the advice of legal counsel. See "dual agency" comments following this form. The rules regarding disclosure or non-disclosure of confidential information received by a broker in a dual agency capacity may differ by state. Brokers using this form should consult their attorneys for advice about specific rules in your state.*
>
> *Developers may want to prohibit the brokerage firm from acting in a dual agency capacity. If so, Paragraph 5 should be written to require the broker to represent the developer on an exclusive basis, thereby encouraging tenants to retain separate representation. This provision will not be popular with brokers seeking to collect full commissions. In a weak market, however, developers may have no choice but to agree to a dual agency relationship. Even if the developer or owner agrees to the dual agency, the broker must obtain the consent of the broker's client.*

5. Term. Subject to Developer's duty to pay commissions earned for transactions entered into during the term of this agreement, this agreement shall terminate __*[e.g., 6]*__ months after execution by all parties hereto. However, if within __*[e.g., 120 days]*__ after the termination of this agreement or any extension of it, Developer or its nominees or assignees enter into a lease or sale agreement with anyone with whom Broker negotiated concerning a possible lease or sale on the site during the term of this agreement or any extension of it, Broker shall be entitled to be compensated in the amount and on the terms specified herein. However, except with respect to tenants who have signed a letter of intent which has been delivered to Developer during the term hereof, Developer shall have no obligation to pay Broker under this provision unless, not later than 15 days after the expiration of this agreement or any extension of it, Broker provides Developer with a written list of all prospective tenants with whom Broker has negotiated for a possible sale or lease.

> ***Note:*** *It is important to be able to list such specific tenants so that such tenants can be excluded from any exclusive marketing contract the developer may enter into with a third party during the "run-off" period.*

6. Exclusions. Developer has __*[obtained commitments from]*__ OR __*[entered into transactions with]*__ the following prospective tenants relative to the site which are excluded from the operation of this agreement: __*[list any specific tenants]*__.

7. Miscellaneous. This agreement is subject to the following additional provisions:

7.1 Limitations on Fee Calculations. __*[Except as set forth above,]*__ [N]o lease extension terms, option to extend the lease term, option to enlarge the tenant's premises, right of first refusal, percentage rent, taxes, insurance or other charges, dues, or assessments shall be taken into account in calculating commissions payable Broker.

7.2 Authority. Broker shall not purport to have the authority to execute lease commitments or sales agreements or to bind Developer as to any matters whatsoever. However, the party signing this letter agreement on behalf of Broker individually represents and warrants that he is authorized to enter into this contract on behalf of Broker and that Broker has full power and authority to enter into and fully perform this agreement.

FORM 8-1

7.3 Diligence. As a material condition of this agreement, Broker will continuously perform throughout the term of this contract consistent with the highest standards and performance of shopping center real estate marketing professionals in __*[describe city/region, etc.]*__. Among other things, Broker will __*[describe, e.g., place appropriate signage on the site in compliance with local sign ordinances and codes, meet with Developer each __[describe frequency of weekly/monthly meetings]*__, as Developer may from time to time require, and keep Developer fully aware of Broker's progress.

Broker-oriented addition to paragraph 7.3:
__*[Although Broker will diligently attempt to enter into viable transactions with prospective tenants and will keep Developer advised of such progress, no representation or warranty is given that a closing will occur with any specific tenant]*__.

Broker oriented:

7.4 Developer Cooperation. In order to assist Broker in marketing the site, Developer will promptly provide Broker with copies of full-sized and reduced tentative site plans, copies of demographic materials and marketing studies, Developer's proposed construction schedule, Developer's proposed form shop lease, Developer's guidelines in negotiating build-to-suit and other leases where a non-standard contribution is being made by Developer __*[and* *anything else necessary, e.g., a draft reciprocal easement agreement]*__, and such other documents as may from time to time be reasonably required to enable Broker to diligently pursue its marketing obligations under this agreement.

7.5 Binding Effect. The obligations herein contained shall be binding upon and inure to the benefit of the parties hereto and their respective successors, heirs and assigns. Broker, however, may not assign its marketing rights or duties to any third party.

7.6 Amendment. Any amendment or extension of this agreement must be in writing.

Optional:

7.__ Authorization Letter. Upon execution of this agreement Developer will deliver Broker the letter in the format attached hereto as Exhibit "__."

Insert the following paragraph assuming this document is intended to be a non-binding letter of intent:

8. Non-binding Letter of Intent. While they have attempted to reach agreement on all key issues, Broker and Developer do not intend this letter to be a contract or to be bound by this letter. A contract between the parties will not exist unless and until the parties have executed a final, definitive marketing agreement approved by legal counsel for each of the parties. Upon my receipt of a signed copy of this letter, our respective lawyers will prepare a final agreement for our signatures. However, if for any reason we fail to agree upon and execute a final, binding agreement within _______ days of the signing of this non-binding letter of intent, neither party shall be under any obligation whatsoever to the other.

OR

Use the following paragraph with caution: Once all legal refinements to the agreement have been made, the following paragraph, for use only with advice of legal counsel, provides that the modified letter agreement is intended to be a final contract between the parties:

8. Binding Agreement. This letter, having been reviewed and approved by legal counsel for each of the parties, is intended to be a binding, conclusive agreement concerning all terms and conditions of the marketing contract between Developer and Broker concerning the site referenced on Exhibit "A".

Please sign and return a copy of this letter confirming our agreement.

Very truly yours,

[Name of brokerage company]

[Name]
[Title]
__*[State]*__ Broker's License #____

UNDERSTOOD AND AGREED:
This __ day of ___________, 20__.

[Name of development company]

By: _______________

Its: _______________

Exhibit "A"
[Description of the "site"]

Exhibit "B"
[Per "Alternative 'A'—'Case Study' Illustrative Introduction"
(generally not for reuse)

[Broker list of specific prospective tenants]

[Optional:]
Exhibit " "
[Attached preliminary site plan and/or preliminary pro forma]

[Optional:]
Exhibit " "
[Description of adjacent property]

FORM 8-1

[Optional:]
Exhibit " "

[This following letter may or may not be necessary but, in any event, it is not intended for general distribution. When necessary, it can be selectively given to a prospective tenant and/or the tenant's broker to quickly confirm Broker's authority and relationship with Developer.]

[Developer Letterhead]

________, 20__

TO WHOM IT MAY CONCERN:

This letter will confirm that effective __*[date of letter agreement]*__ __*[name of developer]*__ entered into an agreement with __*[name of brokerage company]*__ ("Broker"), a licensed __*[insert state]*__ real estate broker, under which Broker has been engaged to provide retail leasing and pad sale marketing services for a site consistent of approximately ______ acres of undeveloped land at the intersection of ______________ and ______________ in the city of __________, _________ County, __*[state]*__, for an initial period beginning with the effective date of the agreement __*[and ending __________ 20__]*__.

Very truly yours,

[Name of development company]

[Name]
[Capacity]

END OF FORM 8-1

BROKERS: BE MINDFUL OF "DUAL AGENCY" RISKS

"Dual agency" has become the subject of considerable controversy in recent years. As an agent, a real estate licensee owes a fiduciary duty to serve the interests of the principal. Examples of this duty include the duty to negotiate the best price (or rent) and terms on behalf of the principal and a duty of full disclosure. Essentially, a dual agency is created when a real estate licensee, through agreement or conduct, becomes the agent of parties having conflicting interests with inconsistent fiduciary obligations running to each of them. Examples of dual agencies include representing both buyer and seller or both landlord and tenant in the same transaction.

A dual agency can inadvertently be created in the common situation wherein a licensee becomes the agent of a developer or owner by signing a listing agreement; i.e., a so-called "listing" broker. While providing services to the developer/owner, the listing broker will often also assist or perform various services for a buyer or tenant. Ultimately, the listing broker might, for example, advise and assist the prospective buyer or tenant in preparing an offer to the developer/owner. The buyer or tenant may believe the listing broker represents the interests of the buyer or tenant. (In practice, rarely does the broker disclaim any fiduciary duty to such buyer or tenant.) In short, there is a very real danger that the listing broker, as agent for the developer or owner, may inadvertently also become an agent for the buyer or tenant concerning the listed property.

Dual agency also arises in the "in-house" brokerage situation wherein one licensee has negotiated a listing contract with a developer or owner and another licensee within the firm maintains a representation agreement with a specific tenant potentially interested in the listing agent's property. Each of the licensees are engaged by the same broker, which in this case, becomes a dual agent owing fiduciary duties to clients having conflicting interests relative to the subject property.

The dual agency must be fully disclosed to both principals and both principals must knowingly consent to the dual agency before negotiations may proceed. So long as both principals are given complete disclosure of all material information and knowingly consent, generally a licensee may serve as a dual agent. Yet in most commercial real estate transactions, notice and fully informed consent is rarely obtained. The consequences of failing to obtain the informed consent of both principals include disciplinary action against the licensee, the licensee's exposure to damages, and rescission of the transaction by the unaware or non-consenting principal.

How a broker (including a salesperson) effectively deals with problems of dual agency is beyond the scope of this book. However, a few comments are in order as the issue has some bearing upon a broker's prudent use of deal-making documents. First, study available resources concerning dual agency, including statutory and regulatory requirements, which are becoming increasingly common.[1] Once thoroughly considered, a broker will most likely reach the conclusion that it is extremely difficult to meet legal standards and at the same time maintain a dual agency since the fiduciary duties owed to the principals are so contradictory. Second, be aware that the broker's tendency to characterize the broker's valuable role as "facilitator" is really not consistent with legal standards demanding "advocacy" of the principal's interests at all times by the agent.

If you are a broker, before proceeding, carefully consider who you represent. Consider always who might also reasonably believe that you represent them. Provide full information, including your motivations, and obtain the prior written consent of both principals before proceeding in a situation wherein a dual agency would be created. Consequently, before preparing and presenting a proposal (such as a deal-making document in this book) in a situation where a dual agency would be created, obtain the informed written consent of both principals to the dual agency.

Brokers should consider including a clause in the listing contract granting the listing developer's or owner's advance approval of certain predetermined, permissible form(s) of dual agency. Such a clause should include, among other issues, how confidential information provided the broker by each of the principals will be appropriately handled so as to comply with local law. Concurrently, develop a consistent, systematic approach to obtaining the written consent of the buyer or tenant (and confirming the listing principal's knowledge and consent) as the need arises.

On the other hand, in a situation in which a dual agency relationship might otherwise be implied, also consider formally disavowing the potential agency relationship to one party to the transaction before proceeding so as to avoid acting as a dual agent. In other words, the leasing agent for a shopping center could tell potential tenants that he or she is representing solely the interests of the landlord. Query whether the landlord's leasing agent should then tell the tenant to seek representation by a separate licensee. Clearly, there is a strong financial disincentive to do so.

[1] For example, California Civil Code Sections 2373-2382 extensively regulate dual agency in residential real estate practice.

OVERVIEW

Chapter 9 addresses the negotiation of a build-to-suit lease letter of intent with an anchor tenant. Form 9-1 is a letter of intent confirming a traditional structure in which the landlord (developer) constructs both the tenant's building and all on- and off-site improvements. Form 9-2 provides that the tenant build its own store, which the landlord purchases after completion.

FORMS

9-1 Build-to-Suit Lease with Landlord Doing All Construction. Basic Major Tenant [Supermarket] Build-to-Suit Lease Letter of Intent; Landlord Constructs Tenant's Building and On- and Off-Site Improvements.

9-2 Build-to-Suit Lease with Shared Construction Responsibilities. Major Tenant [Supermarket] Build-to-Suit Lease Letter of Intent; Tenant Builds Tenant's Building; Landlord Constructs On- and Off-Site Improvements and Purchases Building after Tenant's Completion.

Chapter 9

Major Tenant Leases

Before you run in double harness,
look well at the other horse.
—Ovid

Attracting and consummating a transaction with a major tenant is the single most critical step in developing most shopping centers. Assuming the developer's site meets the major's "strategic" criteria, the developer's key initial focus is supplying the proposed tenant with sufficient data concerning existing and projected trade area demographics, actual and potential retailer competition, quantity and quality of customer and service access, land cost/value, anticipated on- and off-site improvement costs, and a general understanding of the entitlement process and applicable governmental fee structure applicable to the site. Typically, with substantial interaction between developer and the proposed tenant on these initial issues and developer's costs and financing objectives, a deal structure and appropriate economics naturally tend to evolve.

With the documentation format usually dictated by the major tenant, once the tenant's real estate committee has approved the economics of the proposed transaction, the focus shifts to negotiating and signing the tenant's form documentation. The frequency of personal interaction between the developer and the major tenant, the overriding importance of the major tenant transaction to the developer, and the tendency of developers to work often with the same majors probably leads to fewer formal letters of intent than would be expected in this area of deal-making. However, making a habit of promptly preparing a letter of intent confirming all business issues can substantially facilitate the tenant's real estate committee approval and expedite document production by the tenant's legal department once committee approvals are in place.

The key to making repeat deals with any tenant is consistently satisfying the tenant's needs and thereby solidifying a long-term relationship. Major tenant real estate representatives are inundated by requests and proposals from competing developers. Be the deal maker who clearly, concisely, and comprehensively summarizes the proposed transaction so the major tenant's real estate representative can quickly review and adopt your proposal. If materials submitted to the real estate representative are clear and comprehensive, chances are dramatically improved that the tenant's real estate committee will understand and similarly endorse the proposed transaction. Finally, never maneuver after real estate committee approval—if something is unique or novel or there is some deal point critical to you, be up front about it. This is the time to put it forth in a written pre-approval proposal—not afterward.

The major tenant letters of intent in this section are designed to be edited to cover the business issues for tenant's real estate committee approval. Although these forms were developed to create a flexible format that addresses most recurring deal points, including optional provisions, they are necessarily lengthy. Please do not be intimidated by length alone. The numerous alternative and optional clauses add length but will not be used in every case. The forms help you focus on and resolve recurring issues in major lease negotiations. Time spent carefully structuring and refining the transaction using a letter of intent will often eliminate avoidable problems and result in overall time efficiency.

For example, the forms encourage the reader to distinguish and clarify the specific costs that are to be included and excluded in the calculation of the tenant's building cost and the tenant's prorata share of on- and off-site costs. Similarly, the forms allow rent to be confirmed as a function of both the amount of land, building cost, and on- and off-site improvements attributable to the tenant's premises, as well as the specific discreet "return" values (e.g., 10%, 11%, 12%, etc.) to the landlord for each of these separate components from which rent is derived.

Using such a "definitional" and outline format invites the experienced developer to carefully consider, evaluate, and articulate the underlying bases upon which a particular deal structure is negotiated. For example, the forms prescribe in an easily editable format those specific costs that are to be included in (and excluded from) the "building cost." Similarly, a list of inclusions and exclusions is applied to on- and off-site improvement costs or "site costs." This format supports you in focusing on intelligent amendments to the form to satisfy the needs of a specific transaction. Seize the opportunity to precisely refine these definitions relative to your specific transaction by addressing those specific or unique contemplated project costs that might otherwise fall into uncertain categorization. Of course, in those cases where, by agreement of the parties, the land area attributable to the tenant's use and/or attributable on- and off-site improvement costs are fixed, subsequent paragraphs providing for rental adjustments because of changes in land area or on- and off-site costs could be eliminated.

Rental adjustments resulting from unexpected increases (and decreases) in the building cost and on- and off-site costs, alternative rent commencement provisions, choice in selecting common area reimbursement formulas, and a variety of additional and optional paragraphs are addressed both from the landlord's and the tenant's perspective. With underlying assumptions and deal components broken out and editable in a logical outline, editing the forms to confirm specific transactions should be relatively easy for the experienced deal maker or the deal maker's legal counsel.

Form 9-1 is a classic build-to-suit format wherein the landlord is responsible for constructing the tenant's building and all on- and off-sites for the shopping center, including on- and off-site improvements applicable to the tenant's use. Form 9-2, although similar in style and content, is a "reverse" build-to-suit wherein the landlord constructs on- and off-site improvements, the tenant builds the tenant's store, and the landlord purchases the tenant's store at completion. Annual rent is reduced commensurate with the landlord's threshold investment pending the landlord's purchase of the tenant's building. Forms 9-1 and 9-2 document a supermarket transaction, but they may readily be amended to apply to most other major tenant transactions within an integrated shopping center development.[1] However, the forms are not designed to cover the detailed co-tenancy, operation and reciprocal easement agreements expected in a multi-anchor major tenant mall transaction such as with a major department store.

(For readers not knowledgeable in the use of personal computers, most word processors facilitate "global" word changes within a document file. For example, in seconds, a copy of the form can be revised to change the word "supermarket" to "drugstore," "junior department store," "discounter," or other descriptive word choice. Likewise, the term "Supermarket Parcel" can be globally changed to "Drugstore Parcel," "Junior Department Store Parcel," "Discounter Parcel," or whatever.)

---

[1] I use the term "integrated" shopping center as a shorthand reference to the modern shopping center's unifying legal and operating structure wherein the various land, building, and leasehold interests are developed and governed subject to an overall, overriding plan with unifying operating covenants and reciprocal easements, including, e.g., shared parking and common area maintenance rights and obligations. In essence, such an "integrated" center operates as a unit and may be contrasted with certain older centers that were developed on contiguous parcels but without such unifying elements.

Form 9-1

Basic Major Tenant [Supermarket] Build-to-Suit Lease Letter of Intent; Landlord Constructs Tenant's Building and On- and Off-Site Improvements

[Developer Letterhead]
OR
[Supermarket Chain Letterhead]

__*[Date]*__

[Name and address
of developer OR
chain real estate representative
____
______________________*]*

Re: __*[Name of Shopping Center]*__
Corner of ______ and _______
__*[city]*__, __*[state]*__

Dear __________:

Introductory sentence—letter from developer:

In response to our recent discussions concerning the above-referenced project, the following sets forth the general terms and conditions of a proposed lease agreement for which __*[we]*__ request approval by __*[name of supermarket]*__'s Real Estate Committee:

Introductory sentence—letter from chain real estate representative:

With respect to the above-referenced project and pursuant to your _______, 20__ letter, the following sets forth the general terms and conditions of a proposed lease agreement which I would be willing to recommend to __*[name of supermarket]*__'s Real Estate Committee:

1. Tenant. __*[Name of supermarket]*__ ("Tenant").

2. Lease Term. __*[e.g., 25]*__ years with __*[e.g., 4]*__ five-year options.

3. Supermarket Parcel and Leased Premises. The developer-owner of the proposed shopping center ("Landlord") shall lease to Tenant a

FORM 9-1

_______ square foot __*[e.g., supermarket]*__ building (the "Building") on approximately _______ square feet of land (the "Supermarket Parcel"), as depicted on the preliminary site plan dated ________, 20__, attached hereto as Exhibit "A". The proposed Building and the Supermarket Parcel are collectively referred to as the "Leased Premises".

> ***Note:*** *This form could be altered to provide for other major tenants by amending the word "supermarket" to, for example, "drugstore" in this paragraph and globally changing "Supermarket Parcel" throughout the form to "Drugstore Parcel".*

4. Area of Supermarket Parcel. The square footage of the Supermarket Parcel shall be calculated by dividing the square footage of the Building by the total building square footage of the proposed shopping center, and then multiplying the resulting fraction by the total land area of the shopping center. *[Give specific numeric formula based upon a particular site plan. For example:]* __*[(The preceding 159,600 square foot figure for the Supermarket Parcel was determined by dividing the 42,000 square foot Building by the 100,000 square foot total* __*[approved/entitled]*__ *building area in the shopping center, i.e., 42%, and then multiplying this fraction by 380,000, the total land area of the entire shopping center, resulting in a Supermarket Parcel of 159,600 square feet.)]*__

> ***Note:*** *In an original major tenant transaction for an undeveloped center, achievable site coverage and possibly even the size of the major tenant's building may be uncertain. Paragraphs 4 and 4.1 reflect this developer concern by providing some flexibility in the land area deemed attributable to the Tenant's use. However, in the more typical situation—where the center is entitled (or partially completed) and site building coverage and the tenant's building size is certain—definition of the major's parcel can be much more specific.*

4.1 Area Adjustment. If the Building size or the total __*[planned]*__ OR __*[approved/entitled]*__ building square footage of the shopping center changes before __*[e.g., final governmental approval of the center's site plan]*__ OR *[conceivably]* __*[initial construction]*__, the size of the Supermarket Parcel, i.e., the area attributable to Tenant's proportionate use, shall be increased or reduced according to the preceding formula. *[Optional:]* __*[In no event, however, shall more than ______ square feet nor less than _______ square feet of land be attributable to the Supermarket Parcel for purposes of calculating* __*[Tenant's rent]*__ OR __*[Tenant's Site Costs Rent or Land Rent, as such terms are used in Paragraph* __*[9]*__*]*__.

Recommended but optional:

4.2 Parcelization. To facilitate the potential future financing or transfer of the Supermarket Parcel and the Building separate from the remainder of the shopping center, Landlord shall, concurrent with obtaining entitlements for the shopping center, cause the Supermarket Parcel to become a separate legal parcel. The area of the Supermarket Parcel shall be consistent with the above formula and its specific configuration shall be subject to approval by Tenant. The costs attributable to separately parcelizing the Supermarket Parcel shall be paid by ___________.

5. Landlord's Construction of Building and Site Work. Landlord shall be responsible for constructing the Building and all on- and off-site improvements ("Site Work" or "Site Costs"–defined below) for the Supermarket Parcel and the shopping center in accordance with plans and specifications approved by Tenant. Within __*[e.g., 30]*__ days after __*[e.g., execution of the lease]*__, Tenant shall provide Landlord with a Building layout and fixture plan together with a set of typical elevations for the selected store size. After __*[Landlord]*__'s preparation and __*[Tenant]*__'s approval of conceptual Building elevations consistent with the design and materials criteria for the shopping center, __*[Tenant]*__ shall prepare building plans and specifications for __*[Landlord]*__'s review and approval. After Landlord's approval of such plans and specifications, Landlord shall bid the Building to a group of contractors approved by Tenant. Landlord shall select the low bid contractor to complete the Building.

FORM 9-1

6. Specific Items Included Within the "Building Cost". In addition to the cost of the Building itself, the following specific cost items shall be aggregated and included within the cost advanced by Landlord for the Building and collectively referred to herein as the "Building Cost":

6.1 Building Design/Construction. All engineering, architectural, and consultant fees for design and construction of the Building (other than such engineering, architectural and consultant fees required by Landlord to fulfill Landlord's obligation to __*[rough/finish]*__ grade __*[and compact]*__ the Supermarket Parcel); *[**Note:** The cost of such services relative to the site are included in "Site Costs", below.]*

6.2 Building Studies. Environmental impact report(s) or other studies required to obtain entitlements (if required for the Building and not required for the entire shopping center);

6.3 Permits. Governmental processing fees, conditional use permits, applications, permits, plan check fees and other specific costs to obtain building permits for Tenant's intended use of the Leased Premises; and

Landlord oriented:

6.4 Financing Expense. Landlord's interest and financing fee expense reasonably allocated to construction of the Building.

6.5 Other. Any other direct costs for construction of the Building.

Analyze your specific, proposed transaction and consider including any additional contemplated costs that should be included within the cost of the Building.

Note that in this form governmental impact fees or assessments are not included in the Building Cost but are included in "Site Costs", Paragraph 8.2, below.)

7. Specific Items Not Included Within the Building Cost. The following specific cost items shall not be included within the Building Cost advanced by Landlord:

7.1 Center Grading Plan. Engineering, architectural and related consultant costs to obtain an approved grading plan for the entire shopping center, including grading within the Supermarket Parcel;

7.2 Center Processing Fees. Governmental processing fees for site plan review, environmental review, and any environmental impact report costs imposed for the entire shopping center development; and

7.3 On- and Off-Sites. The construction cost of on- and off-site improvements outside the Building __*[including Landlord's obligation to bring sewer and water laterals and sweeps of electricity and telephone conduit ("utilities") to a mutually-approved location __ feet from the proposed Building]*__.

8. Specific Items Included Within "Site Work" or "Site Costs". The construction cost of on- and off-site improvements for the proposed shopping center ("Site Work" or "Site Costs") shall include all direct construction costs required for development of the proposed shopping center (which includes the Supermarket Parcel) other than construction of its buildings and, in addition, shall include the following:

8.1 Site A & E. All site architectural, engineering and related consultant expenses incurred by Landlord *__[for work incurred on or after __[insert date]__ OR __[after obtaining final site plan approval for the shopping center]__*;

8.2 Impact Fees; Permits. All fees and charges levied by governmental authority as a prerequisite to commencing the Site Work including, without limitation, all plan check and construction permit fees (excluding the building permit for the Building or any other building within the shopping center), payment of all associated development impact fees assessed against the shopping center and payment of other governmental fees or assessments or performance of other required conditions not included within the Building Cost;

Landlord oriented:

8.3 Financing Expense. Landlord's interest and financing fee expense reasonably allocated to construction of such improvements; *__[and]__*

The sign structure cost could be deleted here as a portion of Site Costs (the proportionate cost for which Tenant is responsible based upon Tenant's prorata land area) and addressed in Paragraph 20, "Signs".

8.4 Major Signage. Landlord's cost to build the base and structural components for and supply utilities to *__[e.g., two]__* major shopping center *__[pylon or monument]__* signs *__[each of]__* which will have an acceptable position for Tenant's sign display. (Tenant shall cause Tenant's sign display to be manufactured and installed on such signs at Tenant's expense.)

Optional:

8.5 Other. *[Analyze the specific requirements of the proposed development. If, for example, an expensive fight over an impact fee or entitlements is expected, should Tenant be expected to share such pre-development risk by advance cash up front? Or, for example, should this risk be accounted for in an increased charge to Site Costs? Add any additional items unique to the project which should be included within Site Costs.]*

9. Rent. Tenant's fixed minimum annual rent ("Annual Rent") shall be the sum of annual Building Cost Rent, Site Costs Rent, and Land Rent (all as defined below), estimated at $*__[insert Annual Rent, i.e., the sum of Paragraphs 9.1, 9.2 and 9.3, e.g., $414,813]__*, calculated as follows:

9.1 Building Cost Rent. Building Cost Rent is a[n] *__[e.g., 11]__*

FORM 9-1

% return on the Building Cost advanced by Landlord. The parties currently estimate the Building Cost to be $__*[insert total estimated aggregate amount, i.e., $1,932,000]*__ (e.g., $__*[46]*__ per square foot) ("Building Base Price"). Assuming a Building Base Price of $__*[e.g., $1,932,000]*__, annual Building Cost Rent is approximately $__*[e.g., $212,520]*__ subject to adjustment __*[upward and downward OR upward]*__ by operation of Paragraph __*[10, below]*__ based upon the actual, final Building Cost.

9.2 Site Costs Rent. Site Costs Rent is a __*[e.g., 10.5]*__ % return on Site Costs (expressed on a per square foot basis) attributable to Tenant's use. The parties believe the approximate cost to construct the Site Work for the entire shopping center is $__*[e.g., $3.50]*__ per square foot of land area ("Site Costs Base Price"). Tenant's attributable share of Site Costs shall be determined by dividing the total square footage of the Supermarket Parcel by the square footage of the entire shopping center land area, and then multiplying such resulting fraction by the total of all Site Costs for the shopping center.

Alternative "A"—Continuation of Paragraph 9.2
Add the following italicized phrase if the square footage of the Supermarket Parcel has been limited, such as by use of the "optional" insert in Paragraph 4.1, above, and continue:

__*[Subject to any limitation on maximum or minimum Supermarket Parcel size for purposes of rent calculation, as contained in Paragraph 4.1, "Area Adjustment",]*__ Site Costs Rent shall be adjusted, up or down, based upon the ultimate Building size and final total land square footage of the Supermarket Parcel, as determined by the formula in Paragraph 4, above. Assuming a Building of __*[e.g., 42,000]*__ square feet, a Supermarket Parcel of __*[e.g., 159,600]*__ square feet, Site Costs Base Price of __*[e.g., $3.50]*__ per square foot, and return of __*[e.g., 10.5]*__ %, annual Site Costs Rent is $__*[e.g., $58,653]*__.

OR

Alternative "B"—Continuation of Paragraph 9.2
The following clause fixes the per-square-foot cost of Site Costs for calculation of rent. Delete Paragraph 11 if the following alternative is selected:

In calculating Annual Rent, Tenant's share of Site Costs shall be fixed at $_____ per square foot. Assuming a Building of __*[e.g., 42,000]*__ square feet, a Supermarket Parcel of __*[e.g., 159,600]*__ square feet, fixed Site Costs of __*[e.g., $3.50]*__ per square foot, and return of __*[e.g., 10.5]*__ %, annual Site Costs Rent is $__*[e.g., $58,653]*__.

9.3 Land Rent. Land Rent is a __*[e.g., 10]*__ % return on an agreed land value of $__*[e.g., $9.00—(arbitrarily selected for example)]*__ per square foot, multiplied by the land area of the Supermarket Parcel (__*[e.g., 159,600]*__ square feet), or $__*[e.g., $143,640]*__. Land Rent is to be adjusted, up or down, based upon the ultimate total land square footage of the Supermarket Parcel, as determined by the formula in Paragraph 4, above.

Edit paragraph title wording consistent with text options selected:

10. Increase (or Decrease) in Building Rent Based Upon Unexpected Increase (or Decrease) in Building Cost. If the actual Building Cost is less than the Building Base Price, then the Building Cost Rent set forth in Paragraph __*[9.1, above,]*__ shall __*[e.g., remain unchanged, and Landlord need not account to Tenant in any manner for the amount by which the Building Base Price exceeds the actual Building Cost]*__ OR __*[be reduced by __[e.g., 11]__ % of the amount by which the Building Base Price exceeds the actual Building Cost]*__.

If the actual Building Cost is more than the Building Base Price*__*[but not greater than __[e.g., $50 per square foot,]*__ Landlord shall have the option, by providing written notice to Tenant (within thirty (30) days after the date of such cost determination), to cause Tenant to either (i) pay the difference between the actual Building Cost and the Building Base Price with no adjustment in Building Cost Rent or (ii) increase the Building Cost Rent as set forth in Paragraph __*[9.1, above,]*__ by __*[e.g., 11]*__ % of the amount by which the actual Building Cost exceeds the Building Base Price.

Optional (but necessary if "*" insert used in preceding paragraph):

__. Mutual Lease Cancellation Right Upon Increase in Building Cost Above Agreed Maximum. Notwithstanding any other provision, the lease shall provide that if Landlord is unable to secure a bona fide Building Cost bid from an approved contractor for an amount such that the Building Cost is equal to or less than $__*[insert not-to-exceed amount, e.g., $50 from preceding paragraph]*__ per square foot ("Building Cost Maximum") and neither Landlord nor Tenant is willing to be responsible for the amount in excess of the Building Cost Maximum, Landlord and Tenant shall each have the right to cancel the proposed transaction.

Note: *The preceding clause provides that developer is at risk for various soft costs and plans and specifications expense if Building*

FORM 9-1

Cost bid exceeds the Building Cost Maximum.

Edit paragraph title wording consistent with text options selected

11. Increase (or Decrease) in Site Costs Rent Based Upon Unexpected Increase (or Decrease) in Site Costs. If the actual cost for Site Costs is less than the Site Costs Base Price, then the Site Costs Rent set forth in Paragraph __*[9.2, above,]*__ shall __*[e.g., remain unchanged, and Landlord need not account to Tenant in any manner for the amount by which the Site Costs Base Price exceeds the actual Site Costs]*__ *OR* __*[shall be reduced by* __*[e.g., 10.5]*__ *% of the difference between the Site Costs Base Price and the actual Site Costs multiplied by the square footage of the Supermarket Parcel]*__.

If the actual cost for Site Costs is more than the Site Costs Base Price *__*[but not greater than]*__ __*[e.g., $4.50 per square foot,]*__ Landlord shall have the option, by providing written notice to Tenant (within thirty (30) days after the date of such cost determination), to cause Tenant to either (i) pay the difference between the actual Site Costs and the Site Costs Base Price, multiplied by the square footage of the Supermarket Parcel, with no adjustment in Site Costs Rent or (ii) increase the Site Costs Rent as set forth in Paragraph __*[9.2, above,]*__ by __*[e.g., 10.5]*__ % of the amount by which the actual cost for Site Costs exceeds the Site Costs Base Price, multiplied by the square footage of the Supermarket Parcel.

Optional (but necessary if "*" insert used in preceding paragraph):

__. Mutual Lease Cancellation Right Upon Increase in Site Costs Above Agreed Maximum. Notwithstanding any other provision, the lease shall provide that if Landlord is unable to secure a bona fide Site Work bid from an approved contractor for an amount such that the Site Costs are equal to or less than $__*[insert not-to-exceed amount, e.g., $4.50 from previous paragraph]*__ per square foot of total land area of the shopping center ("Site Costs Maximum") and neither Landlord nor Tenant is willing to be responsible for the amount __*[attributable to the Supermarket Parcel]*__ in excess of the Site Costs Maximum, Landlord and Tenant shall each have the right to cancel the proposed transaction.

> ***Note:*** *The preceding clause assumes that developer is at risk for various soft costs and plans and specifications expense if Site Work bid exceeds the Site Costs Maximum.*

12. Increases to Annual Rent Based Upon Increases in Consumer Price Index. Beginning on the first day of the __*[e.g., 6th]*__ year following rent commencement and on each successive Adjustment Date (hereinafter defined), Annual Rent shall be increased by the increase in the Consumer Price Index ("CPI") on each Adjustment Date. Such increase shall be calculated by multiplying the then current Annual Rent by a fraction, the numerator of which shall be the CPI for the Adjustment Date and the denominator of which shall be the CPI for the previous Adjustment Date (or the CPI for the rent commencement date in the case of the adjustment for the first Adjustment Date). However, in no event shall any increase in the Annual Rent on the Adjustment Date exceed a cumulative __*[e.g., 1.25]*__ % per annum over the period of time in question for the first adjustment period and shall not exceed a cumulative __*[e.g., 2]*__ % per annum over the time in question for the remaining adjustment periods. ("Adjustment Date" means the date which is the first day of the __*[e.g., 6th, 16th, 21st, 26th, 31st, 36th, and 41st]*__ lease years.) __*[In addition, the cumulative percentage CPI increase over the entire lease term, including options, shall not exceed __[e.g., 50]__%]*__.

> ***Note:*** *As an additional precaution to avoid any potential implied covenant to operate, some major tenants have begun to use the term "bonus payment" or "bonus rent" in place of "percentage rent."*

FORM 9-1

13. Percentage Rent. In addition to Annual Rent, Tenant shall pay percentage rent equal to the excess by which __*[e.g., 1.0, 1.25 or 1.5]*__ % of Tenant's gross sales on the Leased Premises during each calendar year of the lease term exceeds Tenant's Annual Rent.

> ***Note:*** *Tenant may attempt to recapture the following from percentage rent: Real estate taxes applicable to the Leased Premises, Tenant's common area maintenance, insurance and/or Tenant's remodeling costs. (See Forms 18-2 and 18-3 in Chapter 18 for sample recapture clauses.) Percentage rent payable by supermarkets will differ slightly by geographic area. Customary percentage rent formulas applicable to non-supermarket major tenants will differ considerably.*

Alternative "A"—Paragraph 14
Traditional rent commencement provision

14. Rent Commencement. Tenant shall commence paying rent when Tenant opens for business to the public but not later than __ days after Landlord completes construction of the Building and that portion of the Site Work required for Tenant's operations.

Note: *Landlord should refine this language to describe the specific on- and off-site improvements that Landlord must complete as a pre-condition for Tenant to be obligated to commence payment of rent. For example, certain drive aisles and parking and common areas could be hatch-marked or shaded on the preliminary site plan (Exhibit "A") and referenced to indicate only those specific site improvements that must be completed before Tenant's rent obligation commences. Developers should consider the possibility that an intended co-tenancy transaction might not come together on a timely basis. Avoid being obligated to construct more site improvements than is necessary for Tenant's operations. A more refined example specifying required site improvements follows.*

OR

Alternative "B"—Paragraph 14
Landlord need only complete specific, agreed portion of total site work as a condition to Tenant being obligated to commence paying rent

14. Rent Commencement. Tenant shall commence paying rent when Tenant opens for business to the public but not later than __ days after Landlord completes construction of the Building and that portion of the Site Work necessary for Tenant's operations. All parking areas, roadways, walkways, landscaped areas, and service areas shown on Exhibit "A" and designated in __*[green]*__ (which are subject to future approved modifications to the site plan) are referred to herein as the "Total Site Work" and shall be fully completed by Landlord not later than __________, 20__. However, prior to the opening of Tenant's store and rent commencement by Tenant, only that portion of the Total Site Work which is necessary for Tenant's operations and which is __*[hatch-marked]*__ on Exhibit "A" must be graded, paved, drained, lighted, striped, and landscaped for vehicular and pedestrian ingress, egress, and parking purposes as a condition to Tenant's obligation to commence payment of rent.

Note: *In some cases the parties will need to designate certain specific site improvements which must be completed before construction of the Building can commence.*

OR

Alternative "C"—Paragraph 14

Tenant oriented

14. <u>Rent Commencement</u>. Tenant's obligation to pay rent shall commence on whichever date shall first occur: (i) The date when Tenant opens for business on the Leased Premises; or (ii) the __*[e.g., 90th]*__ day following the date when Tenant is required to enter the Building to commence fixturization; provided that if the Building and the Site Work are not fully completed in exact accordance with the agreed final plans and specifications within said __*[e.g., 90]*__ days, then Tenant's obligation to pay rent shall not commence until the Building and Site Work are so completed, and Tenant has thereafter completed the installation of its fixtures and the stocking of its store.

Alternative "A"—Paragraph 15
Landlord oriented

15. <u>Building Repair and Maintenance</u>. Consistent with the NNN nature of the lease, Tenant shall be responsible for all Building repair and maintenance, including structural repair and maintenance of the foundations, bearing and exterior walls and roof repair and replacement.

OR

Alternative "B"—Paragraph 15
Less Landlord oriented

15. <u>Building Repair and Maintenance</u>. Tenant shall be responsible for all Building repair and maintenance except structural repairs. Structural portions of the Building shall include only the foundations, bearing and exterior walls (excluding glass and doors) and the roof.

16. <u>Real Estate Taxes and Assessments</u>. Tenant will __*[e.g., pay]*__ *<u>OR</u>* __*[reimburse Landlord]*__ for all real estate taxes and assessments levied against the Leased Premises.

17. <u>Common Area Maintenance</u>. Tenant will __*[e.g., pay]*__ *<u>OR</u>* __*[reimburse]*__ Landlord for its prorata share of all costs for operating and maintaining the parking lot and common areas of the shopping center, including a __*[e.g., 10]*__ % administrative fee to Landlord ("CAM"). Tenant's liability for its prorata share of such CAM expense shall be computed on the basis of the relationship to the whole of such expenses as the square footage of the...

Alternative "A"

FORM 9-1

The following Landlord-oriented provision provides for Tenant to pay based upon Tenant's land area as a percentage of total shopping center land area without regard to whether other buildings are completed and occupied.

...Supermarket Parcel bears to the square footage of the total land area of the shopping center as shown on Exhibit "A".

Alternative "B"

The following Tenant-oriented provision provides for Tenant payment based upon Tenant's Building area relative to total building area even if all buildings are not concurrently constructed, i.e. Tenant is, in effect, subsidized through completion of final center buildout.

...floor area of the Building bears to the square footage of the floor area of all buildings in the shopping center as shown on Exhibit "A", whether actually built or not.

Alternative "C"

The following Landlord-oriented adjustment to the preceding Alternative "B" provides that Tenant's share of CAM is based upon Tenant's share of Building floor area relative to the floor area of completed [and leased/occupied] buildings in the center when such CAM expense is incurred.

...floor area of the Building bears to the square footage of the floor area of those buildings in the shopping center as shown on Exhibit "A" which are completed __*[and leased/occupied]*__ at the time such CAM costs are incurred.

Final sentence following selected Alternative "A", "B" or "C":
The exact square footages to be used in the above calculation shall be determined prior to lease execution and the lease will incorporate Tenant's proportionate share expressed as a percentage.

18. Insurance. Tenant shall carry all risk property insurance with an insurance company admitted in the state of __________ in an amount not less than the full replacement cost of the Building, naming Landlord as additional insured. The lease will contain additional insurance requirements. Landlord will provide public liability and property damage insurance on the parking areas and common facilities. Tenant will pay its prorata share of all such public liability and property damage insurance costs __*[including a 10% administrative fee to Landlord]*__ __*[e.g., using the same formula selected to allocate CAM costs]*__ OR __*[(by the ratio of the Supermarket Parcel to the total land area of the shopping center)]*__ OR __*[(by the ratio of Tenant's building area to total __[allowable]__ building area)]*__.

19. Utilities. Tenant shall pay for all utilities and utility fees applicable to the Leased Premises.

20. Signs. __*[Subject to size and materials limitations contained in the XYZ sign criteria and/or governmental approvals,]*__ Tenant may install its standard logo and signage on the exterior of the Building. Tenant shall also have the right to place its trade name and logo in the __*[top]*__ tenant position on each of __*[two]*__ shopping center __*[pylon or monument]*__ signs on the two major street frontages. Only those tenants exceeding __*[e.g., 20,000]*__ square feet will be allowed space on said shopping center __*[pylon or monument]*__ signs. Tenant will pay for the cost of its individual display placed thereon.

Note: *The construction cost of two major shopping center pylon or monument signs is included in Site Work (see Paragraph 8.4, above), the cost for which Tenant is responsible based upon its prorata land area. However, if the cost of such signs is not included in Site Work, language such as the following should be added here:*

__*[Tenant will pay its prorata share (based upon the area of the Building to the total allowable building area of tenant sign users) of the costs of such __[pylon or monument]__ sign structures]*__.

Ideally, attach a sketch of the proposed signs showing total sign area and sign area allocated to Tenant's display, which sketch is ultimately attached as an exhibit to the lease. Prepare and get Tenant's approval of the sketch early in negotiations to avoid ambiguity or "subject to" approval in lease documentation. (See example attached as Exhibit "B".)

21. Assignment and Subletting. *[Considerable give and take will be required in negotiating the anchor's typical assignment and subletting clauses. Anchor tenant assignment and subletting clauses are not discussed here. See Chapter 18, Form 18-10, "Selected Assignment and Subletting Clauses," for general discussion and alternative assignment and subletting clauses. Note, however, Paragraph 24, below.]*

FORM 9-1

The following Landlord-oriented provisions appearing as Paragraphs 22, 23 and 24 would have been "optional" in the recent past. However, with increasing scrutiny and adversity to risk manifested by lenders and investors, current trends indicate that at least some protection against a major tenant's cessation of operations is becoming a necessity. Working out a solution to these sensitive issues will require substantial discussion and understanding with the anchor tenant. Paragraphs 22, 23 and 24 are examples of minimal provisions to stimulate reader thought.

Developer oriented:

22. Initial Opening and Operations. In accordance with the planning, construction and fixturing time frames granted in the lease but subject to force majeure, Tenant will open for business in the Leased Premises and will operate a __*[e.g., name of chain]*__ supermarket store therein continuously for not less than __*[e.g., 3]*__ years thereafter.

Most anchor chain stores will covenant to open but virtually none will grant a continuous operating covenant. This provision is really not adequate, but better than nothing. Be familiar with your lender's requirements, if any, before negotiating this issue.

Developer oriented (with minimum expected Tenant response in italics):

23. Limited Right to Reacquire Leased Premises Upon Cessation of Operations. If Tenant ceases to operate its retail business on the Leased Premises (which cessation is not the result of force majeure) for a period greater than __*[e.g., 180 days]*__, Landlord shall have the option to provide Tenant with written notice of Landlord's election to cancel the lease. The effective cancellation date shall be not earlier than ___ days nor later than ___ days from the date of such Landlord notice. __*[As a condition to Landlord's right to cancel the lease in such event, Landlord shall reimburse Tenant for the unamortized cost of Tenant's leasehold improvements as of the effective cancellation date]*__.

Developer oriented (with minimum expected Tenant response in italics):

24. Limited Right to Reacquire Leased Premises Upon Tenant's Proposed Assignment or Subletting. If Tenant desires to assign or sublet the Leased Premises and the proposed assignee or subtenant meets the net worth and operating criteria established in the lease for a permitted assignment or subletting, Tenant shall first give Landlord notice of its intention to so assign or sublease. During the ___ days following said notice, Landlord may elect to cancel the lease by written notice to Tenant. Such notice shall specify the effective date of cancellation, which date shall be not earlier than __ days nor later than __ days from the date of Landlord's cancellation notice to Tenant. __*[As a condition to Landlord's right to cancel the lease in such event, Landlord shall reimburse Tenant for the unamortized cost of Tenant's leasehold improvements as of the effective cancellation date]*__.

Major-tenant-oriented optional:

__. **Co-tenancy.** Landlord represents that it has signed a letter of intent to enter into a major tenant lease with ____________ ("Co-tenant") for premises of the size and in the location shown on Exhibit "A" requiring Landlord to construct a store building for Co-tenant and Co-tenant to open a retail __*[describe type of operation]*__ on its premises for a lease term not less than __*[e.g., 20]*__ years commencing not later than __________, 20__. Tenant's execution of Tenant's proposed lease with Landlord shall be contingent upon Landlord's prior execution of a final lease agreement with Co-tenant not later than _______, 20__, consistent with such letter of intent. Landlord's lease with Co-tenant shall be non-cancelable except for customary and usual causes with respect to default, casualty, or condemnation.

Major-tenant-oriented optional:

__. **Concurrent Shops Construction.** Landlord will be obligated to commence and complete, concurrently with the construction of the Building, __*[an initial first-phase of]*__ ______ square feet of shell retail store space, at the locations designated on Exhibit "A." Said space shall be used only for sales and service businesses of the kind customarily found in quality __*[neighborhood]*__ shopping centers in __*[describe geographic area]*__ __*[and which shall be subject to the use and specific location restrictions described below]*__.

Example of "exclusive" required by anchor supermarket:

__. **Food and Drug Restrictions.** The reciprocal easement agreement ("REA") *[or CC & R's]* recorded against all parcels comprising the shopping center shall provide that no part of any parcel other than the Leased Premises shall be used as a supermarket (defined as any store or department containing at least __*[5000]*__ square feet of floor area primarily devoted to the retail sale of food for off-premises consumption); __*[as a bakery or delicatessen; for the sale of fresh or frozen meat, fish, poultry or produce for off-premises consumption; or for the sale of alcoholic beverages for off-premises consumption; or for the sale of any ethical pharmaceutical products requiring the services of a registered pharmacist]*__.

Developer "use it or lose it" addition to preceding paragraph:

However, if a supermarket is not operated on __*[the Leased*

FORM 9-1

*Premises]*__ for a continuous period of __*[e.g., 8]*__ months or more at any time after the date __*[name of supermarket]*__ first opens for business on __*[the Supermarket Parcel]*__ for any reason (other than __*[e.g., (i) a strike, lockout, casualty or other temporary closure beyond the reasonable control of Tenant or (ii) a temporary closure due to restoration, reconstruction, expansion, alteration or remodeling of the shopping center),]*__ then the restriction prohibiting a supermarket; __*[a bakery; a delicatessen; and such sale of meat, fish, poultry, produce, alcoholic beverages or ethical pharmaceutical products]*__ shall thereafter be void and of no effect.

Major-tenant-oriented optional (example):

__. **Use Restrictions.** Among other things, the reciprocal easement agreement ("REA") recorded against all parcels comprising the shopping center shall provide that no part of the shopping center shall be used as a bar, tavern, cocktail lounge, automotive maintenance or repair facility, warehouse, entertainment or recreational facility or training or educational facility. __*["Entertainment or recreational facility" shall include, without limitation, a theater, bowling alley, skating rink, gym, health spa or studio, dance hall, billiard or pool hall, massage parlor, game parlor or video arcade. The phrase "training or educational facility" shall include, without limitation, a beauty school, barber college, reading room, place of instruction or any other operation catering primarily to students or trainees as opposed to retail customers]*__.

Notwithstanding the limitations contained in the preceding paragraph, Parcels __ and __ may be used for the following: __*[e.g., (i) a TBA facility as is typically operated by _______ or ________, (ii) an auto lubrication facility as typically operated by ________ and/or (iii) a muffler or brake replacement store as is typically operated by __________. These uses shall be allowed only so long as the services provided by such businesses do not normally require that customers leave their vehicles at the shopping center overnight]*__. *[Continue describing other parcels and specific use exceptions.]*

Major-tenant-oriented optional (example):

__. **Location Restrictions.** No part of Parcels __, __, __, or __ shall be used as a restaurant or as medical, dental, professional or business offices ("office use") except as follows:

__.1 **Restaurant Use.** Up to ______ square feet of floor area on Parcel __ may be used as a restaurant; up to ____ square feet of floor area on Parcel __ may be used as a restaurant provided, however, no single restaurant business may exceed ______ square feet of floor area on said Parcel __ and only _____ square feet of said Parcel __ restaurant use may be within __*[e.g., 150]*__ feet of the __*[e.g., supermarket Building]*__ *OR* __*[Supermarket Parcel designated building area]*__; and Parcels __ and __ may be used as restaurants provided __*[describe]*__.

__**.2 Office Use.** Up to _____ square feet of floor area each on Parcels __ and __ may be used for office use provided that no more than __*[e.g., 1500]*__ square feet of floor area in each said Parcel may be located within __*[e.g., 150]*__ feet of the __*[e.g., supermarket Building]*__ *OR* __*[Supermarket Parcel designated building area]*__. Office use shall be allowed on Parcels __, and __ subject to the limitation than not more than a total of ____ square feet of floor area in the shopping center may be devoted to office use and no single office use building may exceed __*[e.g., 2000]*__ square feet of floor area.

***Note:** Consider possible additional deal points relative to the specific transaction; e.g., a radius clause prohibiting Tenant from opening a new store within a limited radius for a limited time period, Tenant's right of first refusal or option to purchase the Supermarket Parcel or the shopping center, etc. See Chapter 18, "Optional and Alternative Clauses for Lease Proposals," for ideas. If additional paragraphs are inserted, renumber the following paragraphs accordingly.*

FORM 9-1

25. Real Estate Commission. Developer will be responsible for a real estate commission payable to __________ upon the close of the contemplated transaction. The parties represent there are no other commissions payable with respect to the subject transaction.

26. Conditions. If the business terms of this letter are approved by Tenant's Real Estate Committee, consummating a lease would be subject to the following:

26.1 Site Plan. Agreeing upon a final site plan;

26.2 Access. Securing satisfactory ingress and egress to both ________ __*[Street]*__ and __________ __*[Avenue]*__;

26.3 Investigation. Tenant's investigation and approval of zoning, title, survey, soils and absence of hazardous materials or other environmental constraints; and

26.4 Documentation. Agreeing upon a mutually satisfactory Lease, Development Agreement, Reciprocal Easement Agreement and Common Area Maintenance Agreement.

26.5 [Other]. *[Add additional conditions as necessary:] __[E.g., Approval of the Board of Directors of ____________, Landlord's joint venture financial partner]__.*

Developer oriented:

27. Intermediate Approvals. If, prior to the review and approval by Tenant's Real Estate Committee, the approval by any specific executive of Tenant is required and any such required executive approval is not granted, Tenant will within __*[e.g., 4 business days]*__ of such event telephone and inform Landlord that such required executive approval was not obtained and that, therefore, the proposed transaction will not be reviewed by Tenant's Real Estate Committee.

Developer oriented:

28. Financing Contingency. Landlord shall have until ________, 20__ in which to obtain a binding __*[e.g., construction/permanent]*__ loan to construct __*[the Building]*__ OR __*[the Building and the remainder of the shopping center]*__. If Landlord is unable to obtain financing in form satisfactory to Landlord by _______, 20__, Landlord shall have the right to terminate the proposed lease by giving written notice of termination to Tenant.

29. Non-binding Letter. When signed by the parties, this letter shall constitute a non-binding letter of intent. The parties understand that this letter does not attempt to address all issues to be negotiated by the parties. __*[Although most of the business terms for the lease are set forth above, other terms and conditions will require further negotiation and agreement]*__. OR *[for lawyer readers:]* __*[The parties acknowledge that they have not set forth nor agreed upon all essential terms of the transaction described herein, including without limitation, representations and warranties, conditions precedent, indemnities and many other essential terms which will be the subject of further negotiations]*__.

This letter is subject to the approval of __*[Name of supermarket]*__ 's Real Estate Committee. No contract will exist unless or until __*[Name of supermarket]*__ 's Real Estate Committee has approved the business issues contained herein and the parties have executed formal agreements containing all terms as may be mutually acceptable to the parties.

Alternative "A"—Paragraph 30

Landlord-oriented optional

30. <u>Landlord's Limited Exclusive Right</u>. Notwithstanding our agreement that this letter is otherwise not binding, Landlord may rely upon Tenant's promise that during the __*[e.g., 60-day]*__ period following execution of this letter by the parties (during which period the real estate representative signing this letter on behalf of Tenant promises to make a good faith effort to obtain Real Estate Committee approval of the transaction), Tenant will not __ *[e.g., initiate negotiations and will suspend any existing negotiations to purchase or lease any other property for Tenant's potential operation of a __[e.g., supermarket]__ store within a radius of __[e.g., 3]__ miles of the site.*

OR

Alternative "B"—Paragraph 30
Tenant-oriented optional

30. <u>Tenant's Limited Exclusive Right</u>. Notwithstanding our agreement that this letter is otherwise not binding, Tenant may rely upon Landlord's promise that during the __*[e.g., 60-day]*__ period following acceptance of this letter by Landlord (during which period the real estate representative signing this letter on behalf of Tenant promises to make a good faith effort to obtain Real Estate Committee approval of the transaction), Landlord will not __*[e.g., offer the Supermarket Parcel for sale]*__ <u>AND/OR</u> __*[will not accept any offer to sell the Supermarket Parcel]*__ to any other __*[supermarket]*__ chain.

We anticipate that a mutually acceptable lease can be quickly finalized. Please acknowledge that you wish to proceed under the above general terms and conditions by signing and returning a copy of this letter to me. Contact me concerning any further questions you may have.

Very truly yours,

[Developer]

____

[capacity]

<u>*OR*</u>

[Name of Supermarket}

FORM 9-1

____
[e.g., Real Estate Manager]

UNDERSTOOD AND AGREED:
This __ day of __________, 20__.

[Name of Developer]
OR
[Name of Supermarket Chain]

By: _______________

Its: _______________

Exhibit "A"
[Attach copy of preliminary site plan marked as indicated above]

Exhibit "B"

[Optional: Sketch or diagram of pylon or monument identification signs, for example:]

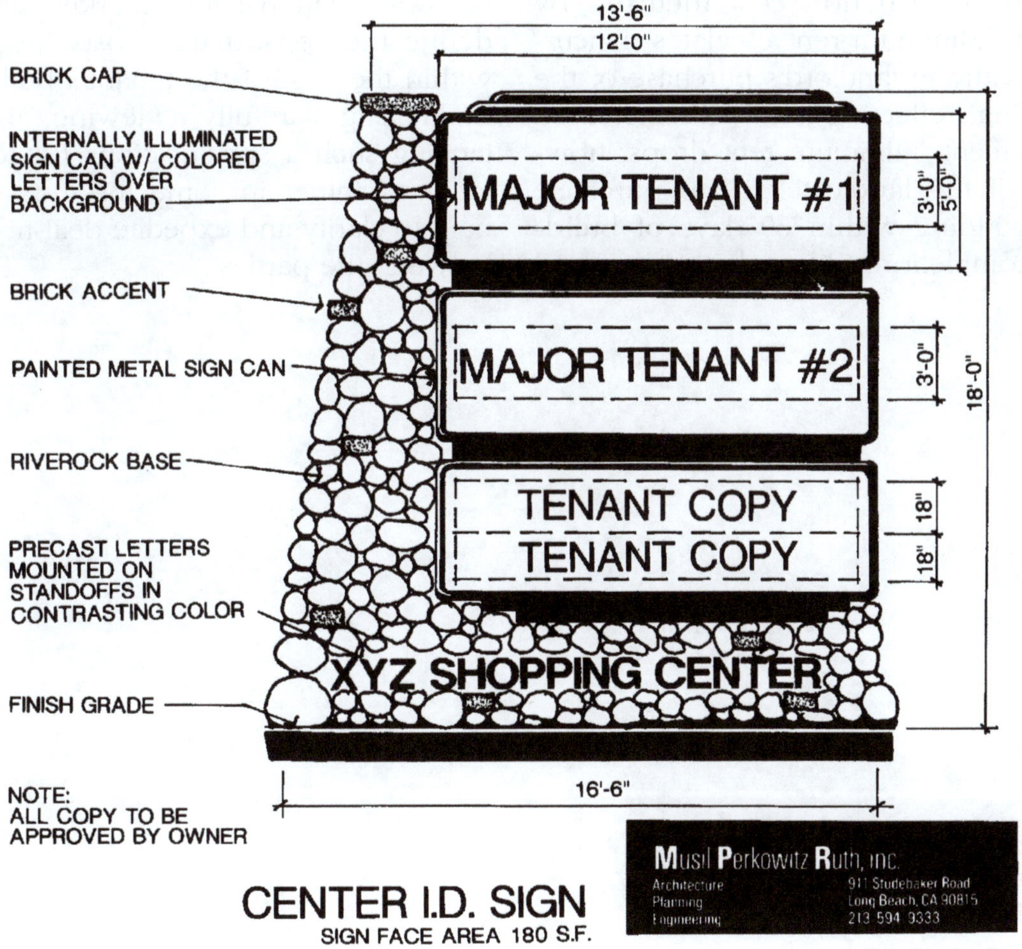

END OF FORM 9-1

FORM 9-1

Although otherwise similar to the preceding build-to-suit major tenant lease letter of intent, Form 9-2 provides for the tenant's construction of its own building at the tenant's cost. The form anticipates that shortly after building completion, however, the landlord will purchase the tenant's building at the actual construction cost incurred by tenant. Minimum rent escalates concurrent with the landlord's purchase of the building, reflecting landlord's increased investment. Minimum rent drops, however, if the landlord fails to purchase the building within 60 days of building completion, although the landlord has the right to complete the purchase within one year.

Adjustments to minimum rent are also provided to account for unanticipated increases in building costs and on- and off-site improvement costs. Exhibit "B" is a specifications list similar to one used by a national supermarket chain to define the construction costs included within the cost of the tenant's building. Requesting, carefully reviewing, and attaching such a specifications list to the letter of intent in some instances may help to clarify and expedite deal-making between the parties.

Form 9-2

Major Tenant [Supermarket] Build-to-Suit Lease Letter of Intent; Tenant Builds Tenant's Building; Landlord Constructs On- and Off-Site Improvements and Purchases Building after Tenant's Completion

[Developer Letterhead]
OR
[Supermarket Chain Letterhead]

__*[Date]*__

[Name and address
of developer OR
chain real estate representative
____
______________________*]*

Re: __*[Name of Shopping Center]*__
Corner of _____ and _____
__*[city]*__, __*[state]*__

Dear __________:

Introductory sentence—letter from developer:

In response to our recent discussions concerning the above-referenced project, the following sets forth the general terms and conditions of a proposed lease agreement for which __*[we]*__ request approval by __*[name of supermarket]*__ 's Real Estate Committee:

Introductory sentence—letter from chain real estate representative:

With respect to the above-referenced project and pursuant to your _______, 20__ letter, the following sets forth the general terms and conditions of a proposed lease agreement which I would be willing to recommend to __*[name of supermarket]*__'s Real Estate Committee:

1. Tenant. __*[Name of supermarket]*__("Tenant").

2. Lease Term. __*[e.g., 25]*__ years with __*[e.g., 4]*__ five-year options.

3. Supermarket Parcel and Leased Premises. The developer-owner of the proposed shopping center ("Landlord") shall lease to Tenant a

FORM 9-2

_________ square foot __*[supermarket]*__ building (the "Building") on approximately _______ square feet of land (the "Supermarket Parcel"), as depicted on the preliminary site plan dated _______, 20__, attached hereto as Exhibit "A". The proposed Building and the Supermarket Parcel are collectively referred to as the "Leased Premises".

> ***Note:*** *This form could be altered to provide for other major tenants by amending the word "supermarket" to, for example, "drugstore" in this paragraph and globally changing "Supermarket Parcel" throughout the form to "Drugstore Parcel".*

4. Area of Supermarket Parcel. The square footage of the Supermarket Parcel shall be calculated by dividing the square footage of the Building by the total building square footage of the proposed shopping center, and then multiplying the resulting fraction by the total land area of the shopping center. *[Give specific numeric formula based upon a particular site plan. For example:]* __*[(The preceding 159,600 square foot figure for the Supermarket Parcel was determined by dividing the 42,000 square foot Building by the 100,000 square foot total* __*[approved/entitled]*__ *building area in the shopping center, i.e., 42%, and then multiplying this fraction by 380,000, the total land area of the entire shopping center, resulting in a Supermarket Parcel of 159,600 square feet.)]*__

> ***Note:*** *In an original major tenant transaction for an undeveloped center, achievable site coverage and possibly even the size of the major tenant's building may be uncertain. Paragraphs 4 and 4.1 reflect this developer concern by providing some flexibility in the land area deemed attributable to the Tenant's use. However, in the more typical situation—where the center is entitled (or partially completed) and site building coverage and the tenant's building size is certain—definition of the major's parcel can be much more specific.*

4.1 Area Adjustment. If the Building size or the total __*[planned]*__ *OR* __*[approved/entitled]*__ building square footage of the shopping center changes before __*[e.g., final governmental approval of the center's site plan]*__ *OR [conceivably]* __*[initial construction]*__, the size of the Supermarket Parcel, i.e., the area attributable to Tenant's proportionate use, shall be increased or reduced according to the preceding formula. *[Optional:]* __*[In no event, however, shall more than ______ square feet nor less than _______ square feet of land be attributable to the Supermarket Parcel for purposes of calculating* __*[Tenant's rent]*__ *OR* __*[Tenant's Site Costs Rent or Land Rent, as these terms are used in*

Paragraph __[11]__]__.

Recommended but optional:

4.2 <u>Parcelization</u>. To facilitate the potential future financing or transfer of the Supermarket Parcel and the Building separate from the remainder of the shopping center, Landlord shall, concurrent with obtaining entitlements for the shopping center, cause the Supermarket Parcel to become a separate legal parcel. The area of the Supermarket Parcel shall be consistent with the above formula and its specific configuration shall be subject to approval by Tenant. The costs attributable to separately parcelizing the Supermarket Parcel shall be paid by __________.

5. <u>Landlord's Construction of On- and Off-Site Improvements ("Site Work" or "Site Costs")</u>. Landlord shall be responsible for constructing all on- and off-site improvements for the shopping center including the Supermarket Parcel ("Site Work" or "Site Costs") in accordance with plans and specifications approved by Tenant. The architect for said plans and specifications shall be determined by mutual agreement. Landlord will deliver a completed building pad to Tenant and will bring required utilities to within *__[e.g., five]__* feet of the Building.

6. <u>Specific Items Included within "Site Work" or "Site Costs"</u>. "Site Work" or "Site Costs" shall include all direct construction costs required for development of the proposed shopping center (which includes the Supermarket Parcel) other than construction of its buildings and, in addition, shall include the following:

6.1 <u>Site A & E</u>. All site architectural, engineering and related consultant expenses incurred by Landlord *__[for work incurred on or after _____, 20__]__ <u>OR</u> __[after obtaining final site plan approval for the shopping center]__*;

6.2 <u>Impact Fees; Permits</u>. All fees and charges levied by governmental authority as a prerequisite to commencing the Site Work including, without limitation, all plan check and construction permit fees (excluding the building permit for the Building or any other building within the shopping center), payment of all associated development impact fees assessed against the shopping center and payment of other governmental fees or assessments or performance of other required conditions not included within the Building Cost (defined below);

FORM 9-2

Landlord oriented:

6.3 Financing Expense. Landlord's interest and financing fee expense reasonably allocated to construction of such improvements; __*[and]*__

> ***Note:*** *If Site Work is defined to include Landlord's financing expense attributable to such work, Tenant may be more inclined to attempt to include Tenant's financing expense within the "Building Cost" (as defined below). Including Tenant's interest expense within the Building Cost will result in Landlord being obligated to pay Tenant a higher purchase price for the Building.*
>
> ***Note:*** *The sign structure cost could be deleted here as a portion of Site Costs (the proportionate cost for which Tenant is responsible based upon Tenant's prorata land area) and addressed in Paragraph 23, "Signs".*

6.4 Major Signage. Landlord's cost to build the base and structural components for and supply utilities to __*[e.g., two]*__ major shopping center __*[pylon or monument]*__ signs __*[each of]*__ which will have an acceptable position for Tenant's sign display. (Tenant shall cause Tenant's sign display to be manufactured and installed on such signs at Tenant's expense.)

Optional:

6.5 Other. *[Analyze the specific requirements of the proposed development. If, for example, an expensive fight over an impact fee or entitlements is expected, should Tenant be expected to share such pre-development risk by advance cash up front? Or, for example, should this risk be accounted for in an increased charge to Site Costs? Add any additional items unique to the project which should be included within Site Costs.]*

7. Tenant's Construction of Building. Tenant, at its own cost and expense, will construct the Building in the area shown as "__*[name of supermarket]*__" on Exhibit "A", in accordance with agreed plans and specifications. Within __*[e.g., 30]*__ days after execution of the lease, Tenant shall provide Landlord with a Building layout and fixture plan together with a set of typical elevations for the selected store size. After __*[Landlord]*__'s preparation and __*[Tenant]*__'s approval of conceptual Building elevations consistent with the design and materials criteria for the shopping center, __*[Tenant]*__ shall prepare building plans and specifications for __*[Landlord]*__'s review and approval. After Landlord's approval of such plans and specifications, Tenant shall bid the Building to a group of contractors approved by Tenant. Tenant shall select the low bid contractor to complete the Building. Landlord shall have the right to make periodic inspections of the Building during construction.

8. Specific Items Included Within the Cost of the Building. The following specific cost items shall be aggregated and included within the cost advanced by Tenant for the Building and collectively referred to herein as the "Building Cost":

8.1 Direct Construction. The direct construction cost of the Building __*[which shall include, without limitation, the specifications listed on the attached Exhibit "B"]*__.

Note: *Exhibit "B" is a reproduction of a typical list of specifications for a major chain supermarket. Reference to such a document is by no means mandatory. However, if a specifications list is available, it may serve to clarify the transaction and refine pricing and proposed rent.*

8.2 Building Design/Construction. All engineering, architectural, and consultant fees for design and construction of the Building (other than engineering required by Landlord to fulfill Landlord's obligation to __*[rough/finish]*__ grade __*[and compact]*__ the Supermarket Parcel);

FORM 9-2

8.3 Building Studies. Environmental impact report(s) or other studies required to obtain entitlements (if required for the Building and not required for the entire shopping center);

8.4 Permits. Governmental processing fees, conditional use permits, applications, permits, plan check fees and other specific costs to obtain building permits for Tenant's intended use of the Leased Premises; __*[and]*__

Tenant oriented:

8.5 Financing Expense. Tenant's interest and financing fee expense reasonably allocated to construction of the Building.

Note: *If Tenant's borrowing rate is lower, substantial cost savings may result from Tenant constructing the Building.*

8.6 Other. Any other direct costs for construction of the Building.

[Analyze your specific, proposed transaction and consider including any additional contemplated costs that should be included within the cost of the Building. (Note that in this form governmental impact fees or assessments are not included in the Building Cost but are included in "Site Costs", Paragraph

6.2, above.)]

9. Specific Items Not Included Within the "Building Cost". The following specific cost items shall not be included within the defined Building Cost advanced by Tenant:

9.1 Center Grading Plan. Engineering and architectural costs to obtain an approved grading plan for the entire shopping center including grading within the Supermarket Parcel;

9.2 Center Processing Fees. Governmental processing fees for site plan review, environmental review, and any environmental impact report costs imposed for the entire shopping center development; and

9.3 On- and Off-Sites. The construction cost of on- and off-site improvements outside the Building __*[including Landlord's obligation to bring sewer and water laterals and sweeps of electricity and telephone conduit ("utilities") to a mutually-approved location __ feet from the proposed Building]*__.

10. Landlord's Purchase of Completed Building. Following substantial completion of the Site Work and the Building, and upon Tenant providing Landlord a certified statement of the actual Building Cost to construct the Building in accordance with the agreed specifications (the "Completion Notice"), Landlord shall purchase the Building from Tenant. The purchase price for the Building __*[,which includes those specifications listed on Exhibit "B",]*__ shall be paid by Landlord to Tenant in cash within __*[e.g., 12]*__ months after Landlord's receipt of the Completion Notice. If Landlord fails to purchase the Building within __*[e.g., 12]*__ months from receipt of the Completion Notice, Landlord's purchase right shall terminate.

10.1 "Substantial Completion". "Substantial completion" is defined as the date Tenant furnishes Landlord (i) a Certificate of Substantial Completion from the architect for the Building, (ii) lien releases and as-built sepia drawings for the Building and (iii) copies of all required occupancy certificates for the Building. Tenant shall give Landlord __*[e.g., 60]*__ days prior written notice of the anticipated substantial completion date.

10.2 "Building Transfer Date". Upon payment of the purchase price ("Building Transfer Date"), Tenant's interest in the Building shall pass to and vest in Landlord subject to Tenant's leasehold estate.

11. Annual Rent (after Building Transfer Date). Tenant's fixed minimum annual rent ("Annual Rent") following the Building Transfer Date shall be the sum of annual Building Cost Rent, Site Costs Rent, and Land Rent (all as defined below), estimated at $__*[insert Annual Rent, i.e., the sum of Paragraphs 11.1, 11.2 and 11.3, e.g., $414,813]*__, calculated as follows:

11.1 Building Cost Rent. Building Cost Rent is a[n] __*[e.g., 11]*__ % return on the Building Cost advanced by Tenant. The parties currently estimate the Building Cost to be $__*[insert total estimated aggregate amount, i.e., $1,932,000]*__ (*e.g.*, $__*[46]*__ per square foot) ("Building Base Price"). Assuming a Building Base Price of $__*[e.g., $1,932,000]*__, annual Building Cost Rent is approximately $__*[e.g., $212,520]*__ subject to adjustment __*[upward and downward OR upward]*__ by operation of Paragraph __*[12, below]*__ based upon the actual, final Building Cost.

11.2 Site Costs Rent. Site Costs Rent is a __*[e.g., 10.5]*__ % return on Site Costs (expressed on a per square foot basis) attributable to Tenant's use. The parties believe the approximate cost to construct the Site Work for the entire shopping center is $__*[e.g., $3.50]*__ per square foot of land area ("Site Costs Base Price"). Tenant's attributable share of Site Costs shall be determined by dividing the total square footage of the Supermarket Parcel by the square footage of the entire shopping center land area, and then multiplying such resulting fraction by the total of all Site Costs for the shopping center.

FORM 9-2

Alternative "A"—Continuation of Paragraph 11.2
Add the following italicized phrase if the square footage of the Supermarket Parcel has been limited, such as by use of the "optional" insert in Paragraph 4.1, above

__*[Subject to any limitation on maximum or minimum Supermarket Parcel size for purposes of rent calculation, as contained in Paragraph 4.1, "Area Adjustment",]*__ Site Costs Rent shall be adjusted, up or down, based upon the ultimate Building size and final total land square footage of the Supermarket Parcel, as determined by the formula in Paragraph 4, above. Assuming a Building of __*[e.g., 42,000]*__ square feet, a Supermarket Parcel of __*[e.g., 159,600]*__ square feet, Site Costs Base Price of __*[e.g., $3.50]*__ per square foot, and return of __*[e.g., 10.5]*__ %, annual Site Costs Rent is $__*[e.g., $58,653]*__.

OR

Alternative "B"—Continuation of Paragraph 11.2
The following clause fixes the per-square-foot cost of Site Costs for calculation of rent. Delete Paragraph 13 if the following alternative is selected.

In calculating Annual Rent, Tenant's share of Site Costs shall be fixed at $_____ per square foot. Assuming a Building of __*[e.g., 42,000]*__ square feet, a Supermarket Parcel of __*[e.g., 159,600]*__ square feet, fixed Site Costs of __*[e.g., $3.50]*__ per square foot, and return of __*[e.g., 10.5]*__ %, annual Site Costs Rent is $__*[e.g., $58,653]*__.

11.3 Land Rent. Land Rent is a __*[e.g., 10]*__ % return on an agreed land value of $__*[e.g., $9.00—(arbitrarily selected for example)]*__ per square foot, multiplied by the land area of the Supermarket Parcel (__*[e.g., 159,600]*__ square feet), or $__*[e.g., $143,640]*__. Land Rent is to be adjusted, up or down, based upon the ultimate total land square footage of the Supermarket Parcel, as determined by the formula in Paragraph 4, above.

Edit paragraph title wording consistent with text options selected:

12. Increase (or Decrease) in Building Rent Based Upon Unexpected Increase (or Decrease) in Building Cost. If the actual Building Cost is less than the Building Base Price, then the Building Cost Rent set forth in Paragraph __*[11.1, above,]*__ shall __*[e.g., remain unchanged, and Tenant need not account to Landlord in any manner for the amount by which the Building Base Price exceeds the actual Building Cost]*__ *OR* __*[be reduced by __[e.g., 11]__ % of the amount by which the Building Base Price exceeds the actual Building Cost. In such event, the Completion Notice shall reflect such Building Cost decrease]*__.

If the actual Building Cost is more than the Building Base Price *__*[but not greater than __[e.g., $50 per square foot,]*__ Landlord shall have the option, by providing written notice to Tenant (within thirty (30) days after the date of such cost determination), to cause Tenant to either (i) pay the difference between the actual Building Cost and the Building Base Price with no adjustment in Building Cost Rent or (ii) increase the Building Cost Rent as set forth in Paragraph __*[11.1, above,]*__ by __*[e.g., 11]*__ % of the amount by which the actual Building Cost exceeds the Building Base Price. If Tenant chooses alternative (ii), the amount by which the actual Building Cost exceeds the Building Base Price shall be included in the Completion Notice.

Optional (but necessary if "*" insert used in preceding paragraph):

__. Mutual Lease Cancellation Right upon Increase in

Building Cost above Agreed Maximum. Notwithstanding any other provision, the lease shall provide that if Tenant is unable to secure a bona fide Building Cost bid from an approved contractor for an amount such that the Building Cost is equal to or less than $__*[insert not-to-exceed amount, e.g., $50 from preceding paragraph]*__ per square foot ("Building Cost Maximum") and neither Landlord nor Tenant is willing to be responsible for the amount in excess of the Building Cost Maximum, Landlord and Tenant shall each have the right to cancel the proposed transaction. *[The parties would be at risk for various soft costs and plans and specifications expense if Building Cost bid exceeds the Building Cost Maximum.]*

Edit paragraph title wording consistent with text options selected:

13. Increase (or Decrease) in Site Costs Rent Based Upon Unexpected Increase (or Decrease) in Site Costs. If the actual cost for Site Costs is less than the Site Costs Base Price, then the Site Costs Rent set forth in Paragraph __*[11.2, above,]*__ shall __*[e.g., remain unchanged, and Landlord need not account to Tenant in any manner for the amount by which the Site Costs Base Price exceeds the actual Site Costs]*__ *OR* __*[shall be reduced by __[e.g., 10.5]__ % of the difference between the Site Costs Base Price and the actual Site Costs multiplied by the square footage of the Supermarket Parcel]*__.

If the actual cost for Site Costs is more than the Site Costs Base Price *__*[but not greater than]*__ __*[e.g., $4.50 per square foot,]*__ Landlord shall have the option, by providing written notice to Tenant (within thirty (30) days after the date of such cost determination), to cause Tenant to either (i) pay the difference between the actual Site Costs and the Site Costs Base Price, multiplied by the square footage of the Supermarket Parcel, with no adjustment in Site Costs Rent or (ii) increase the Site Costs Rent as set forth in Paragraph __*[11.2, above,]*__ by __*[e.g., 10.5]*__ % of the amount by which the actual cost for Site Costs exceeds the Site Costs Base Price, multiplied by the square footage of the Supermarket Parcel.

Optional (but necessary if "*" insert used in preceding paragraph):

__. Mutual Lease Cancellation Right Upon Increase in Site Costs above Agreed Maximum. Notwithstanding any other provision, the lease shall provide that if Landlord is unable to secure a bona fide Site Work bid from an approved contractor for an amount such that the Site Costs are equal to or less than $__*[insert not-to-exceed amount, e.g., $4.50]*__ per square foot of total land area of the shopping center ("Site Costs Maximum") and neither Landlord nor Tenant is willing to be responsible for the amount __*[attributable to the Supermarket Parcel]*__ in excess of the Site Costs Maximum,

FORM 9-2

Landlord and Tenant shall each have the right to cancel the proposed transaction. *[The developer is at risk for various soft costs and site improvement plans and specifications expense if the Site Work bid exceeds the Site Costs Maximum.]*

14. Increases to Annual Rent Based Upon Increases in Consumer Price Index. Beginning on the first day of the __*[e.g., 6th]*__ year following rent commencement and on each successive Adjustment Date (hereinafter defined), Annual Rent shall be increased by the increase in the __*[insert, if desired, a specific regional abstract]*__ Consumer Price Index ("CPI") on each Adjustment Date. Such increase shall be calculated by multiplying the then current Annual Rent by a fraction, the numerator of which shall be the CPI for the Adjustment Date and the denominator of which shall be the CPI for the previous Adjustment Date (or the CPI for the rent commencement date in the case of the adjustment for the first Adjustment Date). However, in no event shall any increase in the Annual Rent on the Adjustment Date exceed a cumulative __*[e.g., 1.25]*__ % per annum over the period of time in question for the first adjustment period and shall not exceed a cumulative __*[e.g., 2]*__ % per annum over the time in question for the remaining adjustment periods. ("Adjustment Date" means the date which is the first day of the __*[e.g., 6th, 16th, 21st, 26th, 31st, 36th, and 41st]*__ lease years.) __*[In addition, the cumulative percentage CPI increase over the entire lease term, including options, shall not exceed __[e.g., 50]__ %]*__.

> ***Note:*** *As an additional precaution to avoid any potential implied covenant to operate, some major tenants have begun to use the term "bonus payment" or "bonus rent" in place of "percentage rent."*

15. Percentage Rent. In addition to Annual Rent, Tenant shall pay percentage rent equal to the excess by which __*[e.g., 1.0, 1.25 or 1.5]*__ % of Tenant's gross sales on the Leased Premises during each calendar year of the lease term exceeds Tenant's Annual Rent.

> ***Note:*** *Tenant may attempt to recapture the following from percentage rent: Real estate taxes applicable to the Leased Premises, Tenant's common area maintenance, insurance, and/or Tenant's remodeling costs. (See Forms 18-2 and 18-3 in Chapter 18 for sample recapture clauses.) Percentage rent payable by supermarkets will differ slightly by geographic area. Customary percentage rent formulas applicable to non-supermarket major tenants will differ considerably.*

Alternative "A"—Paragraph 16
Traditional rent commencement provision

16. Rent Commencement. Tenant shall commence paying rent when Tenant opens for business to the public but not later than __ days after Landlord completes construction of the Building and that portion of the Site Work required for Tenant's operations.

> ***Note:*** *Landlord should refine this language to describe the specific on- and off-site improvements that Landlord must complete as a pre-condition for Tenant to be obligated to commence payment of rent. For example, certain drive aisles and parking and common areas could be hatch-marked or shaded on the preliminary site plan (Exhibit "A") and referenced to indicate only those specific site improvements that must be completed before Tenant's rent obligation commences. Developers should consider the possibility that an intended co-tenancy transaction might not timely come together. Avoid being obligated to construct more site improvements than necessary for Tenant's operations. A more refined example specifying required site improvements follows.*

OR

FORM 9-2

Alternative "B"—Paragraph 16
Landlord need only complete specific, agreed portion of total site work as a condition to Tenant being obligated to commence paying rent

16. Rent Commencement. Tenant shall commence paying rent when Tenant opens for business to the public, but not later than the date which is (i) __*[e.g., 270]*__ days after Landlord has turned over the completed Building pad to Tenant for Tenant's construction of the Building and (ii) __*[e.g., 90]*__ days following Landlord's completion of that portion of the Site Work necessary for Tenant's operations. All parking areas, roadways, walkways, landscaped areas, and service areas shown on Exhibit "A" and designated in __*[green]*__ (which are subject to future approved modifications to the site plan) are referred to herein as the "Total Site Work" and shall be fully completed by Landlord not later than __________, 20__. However, prior to the opening of Tenant's store and rent commencement by Tenant, only that portion of the Total Site Work which is necessary for Tenant's operations and which is __*[hatch-marked]*__ on Exhibit "A" must be graded, paved, drained, lighted, striped, and landscaped for vehicular and pedestrian ingress, egress, and parking purposes as a condition to Tenant's obligation to commence payment of rent.

Note: *In some cases the parties will need to designate certain specific site improvements that must be completed before construction of the Building can commence.*

OR

Alternative "C"—Paragraph 16
Tenant oriented

16. Rent Commencement. Tenant's obligation to pay rent shall commence on whichever date shall first occur: (i) The date when Tenant opens for business on the Leased Premises; or (ii) the __*[e.g., 90th]*__ day following Tenant's substantial completion of the Building; provided that if the Site Work is not fully completed in exact accordance with the agreed final Site Work plans and specifications within said __*[e.g., 90]*__ days, then Tenant's obligation to pay rent shall not commence until the Site Work is so completed, and Tenant has thereafter completed the installation of its fixtures and the stocking of its store.

17. Preliminary Rent. From the rent commencement date but prior to the Building Transfer Date, Tenant shall pay adjusted Annual Rent in monthly installments, as follows:

17.1 Pre Building Transfer Rent. From the rent commencement date and ending the earlier of (i) __*[e.g., 60]*__ days after Landlord's receipt of the Completion Notice or (ii) the day immediately preceding the Building Transfer Date, Annual Rent shall be __*[the sum of the Land Rent and the Site Costs Rent, or $__[e.g., $202,293]__ OR __[insert an agreed, absolute sum]__.*

17.2 Rent If Landlord Fails to Purchase Building. If, following the rent commencement date, Landlord fails to purchase the Building within 60 days after receiving the Completion Notice, beginning 61 days after Landlord's receipt of the Completion Notice and ending the day preceding the Building Transfer Date, Annual Rent shall be __*[the sum of the Land Rent and the Site Costs Rent, __[e.g., $202,293]__, less $__[e.g., $25,000]__, or __[e.g., $177,293]__ OR __[insert an agreed, absolute sum]__.*

Note: *The transaction is structured assuming Landlord is obligated to purchase the supermarket building within 60 days following Tenant's substantial completion of the Building. Some rent reduction or penalty could be assessed against Landlord (here arbitrarily put at $25,000) if Landlord fails to timely purchase the Building.*

17.3 Post Building Transfer Rent. Following the rent commencement date and beginning on the Building Transfer Date, full fixed minimum Annual Rent shall be payable in accordance with Paragraph *__[11]__*, above.

Alternative "A"—Paragraph 18
Landlord oriented

18. Building Repair and Maintenance. Consistent with the NNN nature of the lease, throughout the lease term, Tenant shall be responsible for all Building repair and maintenance, including structural repair and maintenance of the foundations, bearing and exterior walls and roof repair and replacement.

OR

Alternative "B"—Paragraph 18
Tenant oriented

18. Building Repair and Maintenance. Until the Building Transfer Date Tenant shall be responsible for all Building repair and maintenance *__[including structural maintenance and roof repair and replacement]__*. Concurrent with the Building Transfer Date, (i) Tenant shall assign to Landlord all guarantees and warranties to which Tenant is entitled under any purchase, construction or installation contract relating to the Building components and (ii) Landlord shall be responsible for *__[insert Landlord's obligations, e.g., structural portions of the Building, which shall include only the foundations, bearing and exterior walls (excluding glass and doors) and the roof]__*.

19. Real Estate Taxes and Assessments. Tenant will *__[e.g., pay]__* OR *__[reimburse Landlord]__* for all real estate taxes and assessments levied against the Leased Premises.

20. Common Area Maintenance ("CAM"). Tenant will *__[e.g., pay]__* OR *__[reimburse]__* Landlord for its prorata share of all costs for operating and maintaining the parking lot and common areas of the shopping center, including a *__[e.g., 10]__* % administrative fee to Landlord ("CAM"). Tenant's liability for its prorata share of such CAM expense shall be computed on the basis of the relationship to the whole of such expenses as the square footage of the...

Alternative "A"
The following Landlord-oriented provision provides for Tenant to pay based upon Tenant's land area as a percentage of

FORM 9-2

total shopping center land area without regard to whether other buildings are completed and occupied.

...Supermarket Parcel bears to the square footage of the total land area of the shopping center as shown on Exhibit "A".

Alternative "B"
The following Tenant-oriented provision provides for Tenant payment based upon Tenant's Building area relative to total building area even if all buildings are not concurrently constructed, i.e. Tenant is, in effect, subsidized through completion of final center buildout.

...floor area of the Building bears to the square footage of the floor area of all buildings in the shopping center as shown on Exhibit "A", whether actually built or not.

Alternative "C"
The following Landlord-oriented adjustment to the preceding Alternative "B" provides that Tenant's share of CAM is based upon Tenant's share of Building floor area relative to the floor area of completed [and leased/occupied] buildings in the center when such CAM expense is incurred.

...floor area of the Building bears to the square footage of the floor area of those buildings in the shopping center as shown on Exhibit "A" which are completed __*[and leased/occupied]*__ at the time such CAM costs are incurred.

Final sentence following selected Alternative "A", "B", or "C":
The exact square footages to be used in the above calculation shall be determined prior to lease execution and the lease will incorporate Tenant's proportionate share expressed as a percentage.

21. Insurance. Tenant shall carry all risk property insurance with an insurance company admitted in the state of __________ in an amount not less than the full replacement cost of the Building, naming Landlord as additional insured. The lease will contain additional insurance requirements. Landlord will provide public liability and property damage insurance on the parking areas and common facilities. Tenant will pay its prorata share of all such public liability and property damage insurance costs __*[including a 10 % administrative fee to Landlord]*__ __*[e.g., using the same formula selected to allocate CAM costs]*__ OR __*[(by the ratio of the Supermarket Parcel to the total* *land area of the shopping center)]__ OR __[(by the ratio of Tenant's building area to total __[allowable]__ building area)]__.*

22. Utilities. Tenant shall pay for all utilities applicable to the Leased Premises.

23. Signs. *__[Subject to size and materials limitations contained in the XYZ sign criteria and/or governmental approvals,]__* Tenant may install its standard logo and signage on the exterior of the Building. Tenant shall also have the right to place its trade name and logo in the *__[top]__* tenant position on each of *__[two]__* shopping center *__[pylon or monument]__* signs on the two major street frontages. Only those tenants exceeding *__[e.g., 20,000]__* square feet will be allowed space on said shopping center *__[pylon or monument]__* signs. Tenant will pay for the cost of its individual display placed thereon.

***Note:** The construction cost of two major shopping center pylon or monument signs is included in Site Work (see Paragraph 6.4, above), the cost for which Tenant is responsible based upon its prorata land area. However, if the cost of such signs is not included in Site Work, language such as the following should be added here:*

__[Tenant will pay its prorata share (based upon the area of the Building to the total allowable building area of tenant sign users) of the costs of such __[pylon or monument]__sign structures]__.

Ideally, attach a sketch of the proposed signs as Exhibit "C" showing total sign area and sign area allocated to Tenant's display, which sketch is ultimately attached as an exhibit to the lease. Prepare and get Tenant's approval of the sketch early in negotiations to avoid ambiguity or "subject to" approval in lease documentation. (See example attached to Form 9-1 as Exhibit "B".)

24. Assignment and Subletting. *[Considerable give and take will be required in negotiating the anchor's typical assignment and subletting clauses. Anchor tenant assignment and subletting clauses are not discussed here. See Chapter 18, Form 18-10, "Selected Assignment and Subletting Clauses," for general discussion and alternative assignment and subletting clauses. Note, however, Paragraph 27, below.]*

The following Landlord-oriented provisions appearing as Paragraphs 25, 26, and 27 would have been "optional" in the recent

FORM 9-2

past. However, with increasing scrutiny and adversity to risk manifested by lenders and investors, current trends indicate that at least some protection against a major tenant's cessation of operations is becoming a necessity. Working out a solution to these sensitive issues will require substantial discussion and understanding with the anchor tenant. Paragraphs 25, 26 and 27 are examples of minimal provisions to stimulate reader thought.

Developer oriented:

25. Initial Opening and Operations. In accordance with the planning, construction and fixturing time frames granted in the lease but subject to force majeure, Tenant will open for business in the Leased Premises and will operate a __*[e.g., name of chain]*__ supermarket store therein continuously for not less than __*[e.g., 3]*__ years thereafter. *[Most anchor chain stores will covenant to open but virtually none will grant a continuous operating covenant. This provision is really not adequate, but better than nothing. Be familiar with your lender's requirements, if any, before negotiating this issue.]*

Developer oriented (with minimum expected Tenant response in italics):

26. Limited Right to Reacquire Leased Premises Upon Cessation of Operations. If Tenant ceases to operate its retail business on the Leased Premises (which cessation is not the result of force majeure) for a period greater than __*[e.g., 180 days]*__, Landlord shall have the option to provide Tenant with written notice of Landlord's election to cancel the lease. The effective cancellation date shall be not earlier than ___ days nor later than ___ days from the date of such Landlord notice. __*[As a condition to Landlord's right to cancel the lease in such event, Landlord shall reimburse Tenant for the unamortized cost of Tenant's leasehold improvements as of the effective cancellation date]*__.

Developer oriented (with minimum expected Tenant response in italics):

27. Limited Right to Reacquire Leased Premises Upon Tenant's Proposed Assignment or Subletting. If Tenant desires to assign or sublet the Leased Premises and the proposed assignee or subtenant meets the net worth and operating criteria established in the lease for a permitted assignment or subletting, Tenant shall first give Landlord notice of its intention to so assign or sublease. During the ___ days following said notice, Landlord may elect to cancel the lease by written notice to Tenant. Such notice shall specify the effective date of cancellation, which date shall be not earlier than __ days nor later than __ days from the date of Landlord's cancellation notice to Tenant. __*[As a condition to Landlord's right to cancel the lease in such event, Landlord shall reimburse Tenant for the unamortized cost of Ten-*

ant's leasehold improvements as of the effective cancellation date]__.

Major-tenant-oriented optional:

__. **Co-tenancy.** Landlord represents that it has signed a letter of intent to enter into a major tenant lease with ______________ ("Co-tenant") for premises of the size and in the location shown on Exhibit "A" requiring Landlord to construct a store building for Co-tenant and Co-tenant to open a retail *__[describe type of operation]__* on its premises for a lease term not less than *__[e.g., 20]__* years commencing not later than ________, 20__. Tenant's execution of Tenant's proposed lease with Landlord shall be contingent upon Landlord's prior execution of a final lease agreement with Co-tenant not later than ________, 20__, consistent with such letter of intent. Landlord's lease with Co-tenant shall be non-cancelable except for customary and usual causes with respect to default, casualty, or condemnation.

Major-tenant-oriented optional:

__. **Concurrent Shops Construction.** Landlord will be obligated to commence and complete, concurrently with the construction of the Building, *__[an initial first-phase of]__* ________ square feet of shell retail store space, at the locations designated on Exhibit "A." Said space shall be used only for sales and service businesses of the kind customarily found in quality *__[neighborhood]__* shopping centers in *__[describe geographic area]__* *__[and which shall be subject to the use and specific location restrictions described below]__*.

Example of "exclusive" required by anchor supermarket:

__. **Food and Drug Restrictions.** The reciprocal easement agreement ("REA") *[or CC & R's]* recorded against all parcels comprising the shopping center shall provide that no part of any parcel other than the Leased Premises shall be used as a supermarket (defined as any store or department containing at least *__[5000]__* square feet of floor area primarily devoted to the retail sale of food for off-premises consumption); *__[as a bakery or delicatessen; for the sale of fresh or frozen meat, fish, poultry or produce for off-premises consumption; or for the sale of alcoholic beverages for off-premises consumption; or for the sale of any ethical pharmaceutical products requiring the services of a registered pharmacist]__*.

Developer "use it or lose it" addition to preceding paragraph:

However, if a supermarket is not operated on *__[the Leased Premises]__* for a continuous period of *__[e.g., 8]__* months or more at any time after the date *__[name of supermarket]__* first opens for business on *__[the Supermarket Parcel]__* for any reason (other than *__[e.g., (i) a strike, lockout, casualty or other temporary closure beyond the reasonable control of Tenant or*

FORM 9-2

*(ii) a temporary closure due to restoration, reconstruction, expansion, alteration or remodeling of the shopping center),]*__ then the restriction prohibiting a supermarket; __*[a bakery; a delicatessen; and such sale of meat, fish, poultry, produce, alcoholic beverages or ethical pharmaceutical products]*__ shall thereafter be void and of no effect.

Major-tenant-oriented optional (example):

__. **Use Restrictions.** Among other things, the reciprocal easement agreement ("REA") recorded against all parcels comprising the shopping center shall provide that no part of the shopping center shall be used as a bar, tavern, cocktail lounge, automotive maintenance or repair facility, warehouse, entertainment or recreational facility or training or educational facility. __*["Entertainment or recreational facility" shall include, without limitation, a theater, bowling alley, skating rink, gym, health spa or studio, dance hall, billiard or pool hall, massage parlor, game parlor or video arcade. The phrase "training or educational facility" shall include, without limitation, a beauty school, barber college, reading room, place of instruction or any other operation catering primarily to students or trainees as opposed to retail customers]*__.

Notwithstanding the limitations contained in the preceding paragraph, Parcels __ and __ may be used for the following: __*[e.g., (i) a TBA facility as is typically operated by _______ or ________, (ii) an auto lubrication facility as typically operated by ________ and/or (iii) a muffler or brake replacement store as is typically operated by __________. These uses shall be allowed only so long as the services provided by such businesses do not normally require that customers leave their vehicles at the shopping center overnight]*__. *[Continue describing other parcels and specific use exceptions.]*

Major-tenant-oriented optional (example):

__. **Location Restrictions.** No part of Parcels __, __, __, or __ shall be used as a restaurant or as medical, dental, professional or business offices ("office use") except as follows:

__.1 **Restaurant Use.** Up to ______ square feet of floor area on Parcel __ may be used as a restaurant; up to ____ square feet of floor area on Parcel __ may be used as a restaurant provided, however, no single restaurant business may exceed ______ square feet of floor area on said Parcel __ and only _____ square feet of said Parcel __ restaurant use may be within __*[e.g., 150]*__ feet of the __*[e.g., supermarket Building]*__ *OR* __*[Supermarket Parcel designated building area]*__; and Parcels __ and __ may be used as restaurants provided __*[describe]*__.

__.2 **Office Use.** Up to ____ square feet of floor area each on Parcels __ and __ may be used for office use provided that no more than __*[e.g., 1500]*__ square feet of floor area in each said Parcel may be located within __*[e.g., 150]*__ feet of the __*[e.g., supermarket Building]*__ OR __*[Supermarket Parcel designated building area]*__. Office use shall be allowed on Parcels __, and __ subject to the limitation than not more than a total of ____ square feet of floor area in the shopping center may be devoted to office use and no single office use building may exceed __*[e.g., 2000]*__ square feet of floor area.

> ***Note:*** *Consider possible additional deal points relative to the specific transaction such as a radius clause prohibiting Tenant from opening a new store within a limited radius for a limited time period, Tenant's right of first refusal, or option to purchase the Supermarket Parcel or the shopping center, etc. See Chapter 18, "Optional and Alternative Clauses for Lease Proposals," for ideas. If additional paragraphs are inserted, renumber the following paragraphs accordingly.*

28. Real Estate Commission. Landlord will be responsible for a real estate commission payable to ________ upon the close of the contemplated transaction. The parties represent there are no other commissions payable with respect to the subject transaction.

29. Conditions. If the business terms of this letter are approved by Tenant's Real Estate Committee, consummating a lease would be subject to the following:

29.1 Site Plan. Agreeing upon a final site plan;

29.2 Access. Securing satisfactory ingress and egress to both ________ __*[Street]*__ and ________ __*[Avenue]*__;

29.3 Investigation. Tenant's investigation and approval of zoning, title, survey, soils and absence of hazardous materials or other environmental constraints; and

29.4 Documentation. Agreeing upon a mutually satisfactory Lease, Development Agreement, Reciprocal Easement Agreement, and Common Area Maintenance Agreement.

FORM 9-2

29.5 [Other]. *[Add additional conditions as necessary:] __[E.g., Approval of the Board of Directors of ____________, Landlord's joint venture financial partner]__.*

Developer oriented:

30. Intermediate Approvals. If, prior to the review and approval by Tenant's Real Estate Committee, the approval by any specific executive of Tenant is required and any such required executive approval is not granted, Tenant will within *__[e.g., 4 business days]__* of such event telephone and inform Landlord that such required executive approval was not obtained and that, therefore, the proposed transaction will not be reviewed by Tenant's Real Estate Committee.

Developer oriented:

31. Financing Contingency. Landlord shall have until ________, 20__ in which to obtain a binding *__[e.g., construction/permanent]__* loan to *__[e.g. construct the shopping center and acquire the Building upon receipt of the Completion Notice]__*. If Landlord is unable to obtain financing in form satisfactory to Landlord by _______, 20__, Landlord shall have the right to terminate the proposed lease by giving written notice of termination to Tenant.

32. Non-binding Letter. When signed by the parties, this letter shall constitute a non-binding letter of intent. The parties understand that this letter does not attempt to address all issues to be negotiated by the parties. *__[Although most of the business terms for the lease are set forth above, other terms and conditions will require further negotiation and agreement]__. OR [for lawyer readers:] __[The parties acknowledge that they have not set forth nor agreed upon all essential terms of the transaction described herein, including without limitation, representations and warranties, conditions precedent, indemnities and many other essential terms which will be the subject of further negotiations]__.*

This letter is subject to the approval of *__[Name of supermarket]__* 's Real Estate Committee. No contract will exist unless or until *__[Name of supermarket]__* 's Real Estate Committee has approved the business issues contained herein and the parties have executed formal agreements containing all terms as may be mutually acceptable to the parties.

Alternative "A"—Paragraph 33
Developer-oriented optional

33. Landlord's Limited Exclusive Right. Notwithstanding our agreement that this letter is otherwise not binding, Landlord may rely upon Tenant's promise that during the __*[e.g., 60-day]*__ period following execution of this letter by the parties (during which period the real estate representative signing this letter on behalf of Tenant promises to make a good faith effort to obtain Real Estate Committee approval of the transaction), Tenant will not __ *[e.g., initiate negotiations and will suspend any existing negotiations to purchase or lease any other property for Tenant's potential operation of a __[e.g., supermarket]__ store within a radius of __[e.g., 3]__ miles of the site.*

OR

Alternative "B"—Paragraph 33
Tenant-oriented optional

33. Tenant's Limited Exclusive Right. Notwithstanding our agreement that this letter is otherwise not binding, Tenant may rely upon Landlord's promise that during the __*[e.g., 60-day]*__ period following acceptance of this letter by Landlord (during which period the real estate representative signing this letter on behalf of Tenant promises to make a good faith effort to obtain Real Estate Committee approval of the transaction), Landlord will not __*[e.g., offer the Supermarket Parcel for sale or lease]*__ AND/OR __*[will not accept any offer to sell or lease the Supermarket Parcel]*__ to any other __ *[supermarket]*__ chain.

FORM 9-2

We anticipate that a mutually acceptable lease can be quickly finalized. Please acknowledge that you wish to proceed under the above general terms and conditions by signing and returning a copy of this letter to me. Contact me concerning any further questions you may have.

Very truly yours,

[Developer]

____

[capacity]

OR

[Name of Supermarket}

____

[e.g., Real Estate Manager]

UNDERSTOOD AND AGREED:
This __ day of _________, 20__.

[Name of Developer]
OR
[Name of Supermarket Chain]

By: _______________

Its: _______________

Exhibit "A"
[Attach copy of preliminary site plan]

Exhibit "B"
The following are building specifications similar to those used by a major supermarket chain to define the construction items to be included in the cost of tenant's building. This list is included as an example of typical building specifications for a supermarket.

Building Specifications

The construction cost of the Building, as adjusted by change orders approved by Tenant, shall include, without limitation, the following:

1. The cost of all insurance and performance and labor and material payment bonds, together with all sales, use or other taxes attributable to the construction contract or contracts.

2. The cost of a built-up twenty (20) year bondable roof if required by Tenant.

3. A reinforced dock and ramps at the delivery doors of Tenant's building complete with such walls, slabs, drainage facilities and other site improvements as may be required by Tenant which are not otherwise required to be constructed by Landlord __*[pursuant to the Development Agreement]*__.

4. The installation and connection of all utility lines and facilities (including fire sprinkler lines).

5. An automatic fire sprinkler and fire protection system with a water supply adequate to service said system and Tenant's other requirements. Said system shall be installed so there will be no insurance deficiency charge related thereto and shall be designed and installed in accordance with the requirements of Tenant's insurance carrier.

6. Final connection of any building or pylon sign or signage furnished

by Tenant.

7. A complete 120/280 volt (minimum) three (3) phase, four (4) wire electrical distribution system including main panels, branch circuits, control panels, switches and convenience outlets.

8. Store lighting complete with fixtures and lamps, wiring and controls for mechanical equipment, air conditioning motor control centers and refrigeration compressors and wiring and final connection for all trade fixtures and equipment furnished by Tenant.

9. A complete buzzer system at delivery doors according to Tenant's standards and empty conduit to cabinets and outlets for telephones and Tenant's intercommunication and music system.

10. Intercommunication and music system in accordance with Tenant's standard requirements.

11. Fly fans or other equivalent devices at all exterior doors.

12. Electric time clocks for automatic control of signs and equipment.

13. Power to Tenant's building signs.

14. A sanitary sewage system complete with line from Tenant's building to a public sewer.

15. All necessary water piping, venting, drains and fixtures including final plumbing connection to refrigerated cases, coolers, coils, equipment and fixtures and water to and connection of hose reels on produce cases.

16. Refrigerated air conditioning and heating of the sales area, rest room areas, and service areas by a ducted system and refrigerated air conditioning and heating of the office by a separate ducted system, both of which shall be adequate for local climatic conditions and designed according to Tenant's standards.

17. Electric drinking fountains, store clock, telephone counter, security mirrors and stainless steel sinks for all service food departments complete with garbage disposals according to Tenant's standard requirements.

18. Restroom facilities with wall hung fixtures and ceiling supported urinal partitions.

19. Construction materials installed per Tenant's standards, but not limited to, tile with rubber, wood, ceramic and concrete bases, quarry tile, ceramic tile, pre-finished plastic laminated panels in colored and wood-grained plank and panels designed according to Tenant's standards.

20. Automatic door operators and accessories, per Tenant's requirements.

21. Construction of all canopies and sidewalks in front of Tenant's building.

22. All surveys, soils tests and engineering studies incurred in connection with the design or construction of Tenant's building.

23. All architectural, engineering and other design or consulting fees,

together with all roof inspection costs or fees incurred in connection with the design or construction of Tenant's building.

24. The cost of all fees, permits, licenses, inspections, certificates and other items of like kind or nature relating to the design or construction of Tenant's building including, without limitation, construction permits, development impact fees, connection fees, flood control fees and government assessments. *[Note: Various development impact fees could be allocated between the Building Cost and Site Costs, but be careful not to charge any particular fee to both the Building Cost and Site Costs.]*

25. All capitalizable costs not specifically referenced herein associated with the acquisition, design, construction or sale to Landlord of Tenant's building.

26. Tenant's proportionate share of the cost of construction and installation of the center pylon sign structure(s) and Tenant's display thereon. *[Again, such structure(s) could be included in Site Costs.]*

Exhibit "C"

[Optional: Sketch or diagram of pylon or monument identification signs (Refer to Exhibit "B" to Form 9-1 for an example)]

END OF FORM 9-2

OVERVIEW

Chapter 10 discusses using a letter of intent as a tool with which to generate a parcel sale to an anchor tenant for the anchor tenant's construction of a store within an integrated, parcelized shopping center.

FORMS

10-1 Parcel Sale of Unimproved Site to Major Tenant. Letter of Intent with Major [Supermarket] Tenant for Parcel Purchase within Proposed Center; Tenant to Pay Pro Rata On- and Off-Site Expense and Construct Tenant's Building on Tenant's Parcel.

10-2 Site "Marketing" Letter to Major Tenant. Comprehensive "Marketing" Letter to Major [Supermarket] Chain to Initiate Parcel Purchase by Chain.

10-3 Tenant Right to Cancel under Certain Circumstances. Letter Agreement Granting Major Tenant Right to Cancel Major Tenant Parcel Purchase Escrow If Developer Is Unable to Record Parcel Map or Commence Grading within Specified Time Periods; Developer May Cancel If On- and Off-Site Costs Exceed an Agreed Sum.

Chapter 10

Parcel Sales to Major Tenants

Make not the sauce till you have caught the fish.
—English Proverb

In an effort to lower long-term occupancy costs and to be free of restrictions and complexities in negotiating and operating under a lease, many major retailers prefer to purchase sites. Although a developer may be compelled to make a parcel sale in order to secure a particular tenant's occupancy, the developer must be acutely aware of the benefits versus the true cost. For example, can the center be adequately financed in the absence of a lease for such anchor occupancy? What is the effect upon the center's overall value from a potential future financing and investment sale perspective? Although such decisions must be made case-by-case, developers will continue to selectively make parcel sales to major tenants. The prudent developer, however, will attempt to carefully negotiate the sale documentation and operating agreements with the purchasing retailer so that, practically speaking, the relative rights and obligations between the parties over time will be much the same as though the parties had structured a lease rather than a sale.

The following form covers the major business issues and some of the possible operating restrictions and obligations that might be imposed in a major tenant parcel sale within a shopping center under development. Form 10-1 is prepared for a supermarket tenant, but it could be amended to cover virtually any major tenant purchasing a site and constructing its building within an integrated shopping center. (For convenience, to facilitate your conceivable use of selected parcel sale clauses in lease proposals (and vice versa), the major tenant "purchaser" is referred to herein as "Tenant".)

Form 10-1

Letter of Intent with Major [Supermarket] Tenant for Parcel Purchase within Proposed Center; Tenant to Pay Prorata On- and Off-Site Expense and Construct Tenant's Building on Tenant's Parcel

[Developer Letterhead]
OR
[Supermarket Chain Letterhead]

[Date]

[Name and address
of developer OR
chain real estate representative
____
________________*]*

Re: __*[Name of Shopping Center]*__
Corner of ______ and ______
__*[city]*__, __*[state]*__

Dear __________:

Introductory sentence—letter from developer:

In response to our recent discussions concerning the above-referenced project, the following sets forth the general terms and conditions of a proposed parcel purchase and sale agreement for which the developer requests approval by __*[name of supermarket]*__'s Real Estate Committee:

Introductory sentence—letter from chain real estate representative:

With respect to the above-referenced project and pursuant to your ________, 20__ letter, the following sets forth the general terms and conditions of a proposed parcel purchase and sale agreement which I would be willing to recommend to __*[name of supermarket]*__'s Real Estate Committee:

1. Purchaser/"Tenant". __*[Name of supermarket]*__ ("Tenant").

2. Purchase and Sale of Supermarket Parcel; Supermarket Premises and Use. The developer-owner of the proposed shopping center ("Developer") shall sell Tenant approximately ______ square feet of land (the "Supermarket Parcel"), as depicted on the preliminary site plan dated ________, 20__ attached hereto as Exhibit "A". In addition, Developer shall

FORM 10-1

construct the "Site Work" (as defined below) applicable to the Supermarket Parcel for which Developer shall be reimbursed by Tenant, as provided below.

Tenant shall construct a ______ square foot __*[e.g., supermarket]*__ building (the "Building") on the Supermarket Parcel __*[e.g., concurrent with Developer's development and first-phase construction of a __[e.g., neighborhood]__ shopping center on ___ acres of which the proposed Supermarket Parcel is a part]*__. The Supermarket Parcel and the Building are collectively referred to as the "Supermarket Premises". Tenant shall use the Supermarket Premises for the purpose of conducting thereon the retail operation of its major __*[supermarket]*__ business.

Optional:

__. **Adjustments to Building Size and Location.** The final location of the Building and the configuration and dimensions of the remainder of the buildings in the shopping center are subject to future agreement, but will generally follow the __*[name of architect]*__ preliminary site plan dated ________, 20__. *[Renumber below if this paragraph is selected.]*

Parcel size based upon Tenant's prorata impact area:

3. Area of Supermarket Parcel. The square footage of the Supermarket Parcel shall be calculated by dividing the square footage of the Building by the total building square footage of the proposed shopping center, and then multiplying the resulting fraction by the total land area of the shopping center. *[Give specific numeric formula based upon a particular site plan. For example:]* __*[(The preceding 159,600 square foot figure for the Supermarket Parcel was determined by dividing the 42,000 square foot Building by the 100,000 square foot total __[approved/entitled]__ building area in the shopping center, i.e., 42%, and then multiplying this fraction by 380,000, the total land area of the entire shopping center, resulting in a Supermarket Parcel of 159,600 square feet.)]*__

> ***Note:*** *In an original major tenant transaction for an undeveloped center, achievable site coverage and possibly even the size of the major tenant's building may be uncertain. Paragraphs 3 and 3.1 reflect this developer concern by providing some flexibility in the land area deemed attributable to the Tenant's use. However, in the more typical situation—where the center is entitled (or partially completed) and site building coverage and the tenant's building size is certain—definition of the major's parcel can be much more specific.*

3.1 Area Adjustment. If the Building size or the total __*[planned]*__ OR __*[approved/entitled]*__ building square footage of the shopping center changes before __*[e.g., final governmental approval of the center's site plan]*__ OR __*[e.g., close of escrow]*__, the size of the Supermarket Parcel, i.e., the area attributable to Tenant's proportionate use, shall be increased or reduced according to this formula. *[Optional:]* __*[However, assuming a Building not greater than _______ square feet, in no event shall more than ______ square feet nor less than _______ square feet of land be attributable to the Supermarket Parcel for purposes of calculating the parcel purchase price]*__ __*[and Tenant's attributable share of Site Costs (as defined below)]*__.

3.2 Parcelization. Developer shall, concurrent with obtaining entitlements for the shopping center, cause the Supermarket Parcel to become a legal parcel separate from the remainder of the shopping center. The area of the Supermarket Parcel shall be consistent with the above formula and its specific configuration shall be subject to approval by Tenant. The costs attributable to separately parcelizing the Supermarket Parcel shall be paid by ________.

4. Parcel Purchase Price. The Supermarket Parcel purchase price shall be $__*[insert calculated price, e.g., $1,436,400]*__, payable all cash. The purchase price was determined by multiplying the total __*[estimated]*__ square footage of the Supermarket Parcel (__*[e.g., 159,600]*__ square feet) by an agreed unimproved land value of __*[e.g., $9.00—(arbitrarily selected for example)]*__ per square foot. __*[The final purchase price shall be determined by multiplying the final square footage of the Supermarket Parcel by such land value, but subject to an agreed minimum parcel purchase price of $_________ and a maximum purchase price of $___________.*

> ***Note:*** *This provision parallels Paragraph 3.1, above. Assuming a fixed land value, the final purchase price range could be determined by multiplying the agreed minimum and maximum parcel size by the agreed land value per square foot.*

In addition to the parcel purchase price, Tenant shall pay for the costs of the Site Work attributable to the Supermarket Parcel, as described below.

5. Purchase Escrow. The parcel sale shall be accomplished through an escrow at _____________ in accordance with a parcel purchase and sale agreement and escrow instructions ("Purchase Agreement") to be negotiated in accordance with the general terms and conditions outlined in this letter of intent.

FORM 10-1

5.1 Closing. The close of escrow (the "closing") shall take place, subject to satisfaction of all of the conditions contained in the Purchase Agreement, not later than __*[e.g., ten business days]*__ after the recordation of a __*[e.g., parcel map]*__ conforming with the requirements of the Supermarket Parcel and the approved site plan and all governmental approvals have been issued so as to construct the Site Work and the Building, but in no event later than ________, 20__ (the "Scheduled Closing Date").

If, after a date certain, as a condition to keeping the escrow or transaction open, (i) funds are to be released by Tenant to Developer or (ii) the purchase price of the Supermarket Parcel is to escalate, the following paragraph may be edited to provide for periodic cash advances by Tenant or a price escalation from the Scheduled Closing Date through the actual, extended closing.

5.2 Financial Adjustments for Extended Closing. If required approvals are delayed beyond the Scheduled Closing Date by more than __ days for reasons other than Developer's failure to timely process and cooperate in the processing of such matters, __*[and all other contingencies to closing have been satisfied or waived by Tenant,]*__ in order to compensate Developer for Developer's costs in controlling the site,

Alternative "A"
Tenant cash advance

Tenant shall pay Developer $______ per __*[month]*__ __*[from the end of said __ -day period]*__ OR __*[from the Scheduled Closing Date]*__ until the actual closing, which in no event shall be later than ________, 20__. Such __*[monthly]*__ payments __*[shall/shall not]*__ be applicable to the purchase price and shall be forfeited by Tenant if Tenant fails to close.

OR

Alternative "B"
Purchase price escalation

the parcel purchase price shall increase at the rate of __ % per month __*[from the end of said __ -day period]*__ OR __*[from the Scheduled Closing Date]*__ until the actual closing, which in no event shall be later than ________, 20__.

5.3 Title Insurance. Developer will provide Tenant a __*[See Appendix A, Form A-1]*__ of title insurance. __*[Any additional premium for __[e.g., an ALTA Extended Owner's Policy]__, if required by Tenant, will be paid by Tenant]*__.

5.4 Escrow Fees and Closing Costs. All escrow charges shall be shared equally by Developer and Tenant and all other closing costs not specifically provided for in other provisions of this letter shall be shared in the manner customary in ___________ county, __*[state]*__.

> ***Note:*** *Refer to Form 17-4, "Allocation of Specific Purchase and Sale Transaction Costs", for an alternative, more comprehensive clause.*

6. Elevations and Building Plans. Within __*[e.g., 30]*__ days after execution of the __*[Purchase Agreement]*__, Tenant will provide Developer with a Building layout and fixture plan together with a set of typical elevations for the selected store size. After __*[Developer]*__'s preparation and __*[Tenant]*__'s approval of conceptual Building elevations consistent with the design and materials criteria for the shopping center, __*[Tenant]*__ shall prepare and complete Building plans and specifications not later than _______, 20__, subject to __*[Developer]*__'s reasonable review and approval.

7. Developer to Construct On- and Off-Site Improvements ("Site Work" or "Site Costs"). Developer shall be responsible for constructing all on- and off-site improvements ("Site Work" or "Site Costs") for the Supermarket Parcel and the shopping center in accordance with plans and specifications approved by Tenant. __*[Site Work shall generally include all improvements other than the center's buildings, including without limitation, all parking areas, landscaped areas, curbs, gutters, sewers, sidewalks, roads, water mains, irrigation systems, street lights, and the like required for operation of the shopping center]*__. The architect for said plans and specifications shall be determined by mutual agreement. Developer will deliver a completed building pad to Tenant and will bring the required utilities within __*[e.g., five]*__ feet of the Building. The technical standards and obligations concerning preparation of the Building pad shall be subject to negotiation and agreement by the parties after review and approval of Developer's soils report and the engineering recommendations made by Developer's engineers and contractors.

> ***Note:*** *Although the letter of intent may not be the place to initiate the point, be very careful in agreeing to provide Tenant a buildable site. Obligations or representations concerning the specifics of the grading and compaction should be subject to confirmation by Developer's engineers and contractors. Developer's documentation of*

FORM 10-1

the transaction should attempt to insulate Developer from liability if a problem with Tenant's building site should later occur. Engineering design and construction involved in the preparation of Tenant's building site is rarely an area of Developer expertise, but certain chain tenants will vigorously attempt to preserve Developer as an additional defendant if for any reason a site-preparation defect arises. Although Tenant should have the right to pursue a remedy against Developer's engineers and contractors, the typical Developer should not be liable for any deficiency in the finished Tenant pad short of gross negligence or truly tortious conduct (e.g., wrongfully concealing material information or committing fraud upon which Tenant detrimentally relies). The appropriate standard might be significantly higher relative to a Developer that is also acting in the role of general contractor or engineer or is similarly actively involved in the design and construction of the pad. Consult your attorney, your engineer, and your contractor before committing to provide Tenant a finished building pad.

8. Tenant's Payment for Site Costs Applicable to the Supermarket Parcel. __*[As of the closing]*__ OR __*[Upon satisfaction of the various conditions precedent to closing,]*__ Tenant shall pay or reimburse Developer for the portion of the Site Work applicable to the Supermarket Parcel as such costs are incurred by Developer. The parties believe the approximate cost to construct the Site Work for the entire shopping center is $__*[e.g., $3.50]*__ per square foot of entire land area ("Site Costs Base Price"). Tenant's attributable share of Site Costs shall be determined by dividing the total square footage of the Supermarket Parcel by the total square footage of the entire shopping center site land area, and then multiplying such resulting fraction by the total of all Site Costs for the shopping center.

Alternative "A"—Continuation
Tenant's share variable—dependent upon final parcel size;
Optional per-square-foot cost cap

Add the following italicized phrase if the square footage of the Supermarket Parcel has been limited, such as by use of the "optional" insert in Paragraph 3.1, above, then continue; final sentence includes optional per-square-foot cap:

__*[Subject to any limitation on maximum or minimum Supermarket Parcel size for purposes of calculating the purchase price for the Supermarket Parcel, as contained in Paragraph 3.1, "Area Adjustment",]*__ Tenant's share of Site

Costs shall be adjusted, up or down, based upon the ultimate Building size and the final total land square footage of the Supermarket Parcel, as determined by the formula in Paragraph 3, above. Assuming a Building of _*[e.g., 42,000]*_ square feet, a Supermarket Parcel of _*[e.g., 159,600]*_ square feet and a Site Costs Base Price of _*[e.g., $3.50]*_ per square foot, Tenant's share of Site Costs is projected to be _*[e.g., $558,600]*_. *[Optional cap:]* _*[In no event, however, shall Tenant's share of Site Costs exceed _[e.g., $4.50]_ per square foot multiplied by the square footage of the Supermarket Parcel]*_.

OR

Alternative "B"—Continuation
Per-square-foot fixed cost

The following clause fixes the per square foot cost of Site Costs; however, the total amount payable by Tenant for Site Costs is subject to variation if the land area of the Supermarket Parcel changes (per Paragraph 3 area formula):

Tenant's share of Site Costs shall be fixed at $____ per square foot of land area included within the Supermarket Parcel. Assuming a Building of _*[e.g., 42,000]*_ square feet, a Supermarket Parcel of _*[e.g., 159,600]*_ square feet, and fixed Site Costs of _*[e.g., $4.00]*_ per square foot, Tenant's share of Site Costs is _*[e.g., $638,400]*_.

OR

Alternative "C"—Continuation
Absolute, fixed total amount

The following clause provides an absolute Site Cost amount:

Provided Tenant's Building does not exceed _*[e.g., 42,000]*_ square feet, Tenant's share of Site Costs shall be fixed at the sum of $_*[insert total sum, e.g., $638,400]*_.

End of Paragraph 8—Proceed to Paragraph 9

The parties can avoid misunderstandings by negotiating and confirming the particular components of Site Costs likely to be controversial:

9. <u>Specific Items Included within "Site Work" or "Site Costs"</u>. As described above, "Site Work" or "Site Costs" shall include all

FORM 10-1

direct on- and off-site construction costs required for development of the proposed shopping center (which includes the Supermarket Parcel) other than construction of its buildings and, in addition, shall include the following:

9.1 Impact Fees, Permits. All fees and charges levied by governmental authority as a prerequisite to commencing the Site Work including, without limitation, governmental processing fees for site plan review, environmental review, any environmental impact report costs imposed for the processing of the shopping center development, payment of all associated development impact fees assessed against the shopping center, all plan check and construction permit fees (excluding the building permit for the Building or any other building within the shopping center), and payment of other governmental fees or assessments or performance of other required conditions not included within the Building Cost (defined below);

9.2 Site A & E. All site architectural and engineering expenses incurred by Developer _*[for work charged on or after ________, 20__ OR __[after obtaining final site plan approval for the shopping center]*__;

The sign structure cost could be deleted here as a portion of Site Costs (the proportionate cost for which Tenant is responsible based upon Tenant's prorata land area) and addressed in Paragraph 14, "Signs."

9.3 Major Signage. Developer's cost to build the base and structural components for and supply utilities to _*[e.g., two]*_ major shopping center _*[pylon or monument]*_ signs _*[each of]*_ which will have an acceptable position for Tenant's sign display. (Tenant shall cause Tenant's sign display to be manufactured and installed on such signs at Tenant's expense.); _*[and]*_

Developer oriented:

9.4 Financing Expense. *[Developer's interest and financing fee expense reasonably allocated to construction of such improvements.]*

Optional:

9.5 Other. *[Analyze the specific requirements of the proposed development. If, for example, an expensive fight over an impact fee or entitlements is expected, should Tenant be expected to share such pre-development risk by advance cash up front? Or, for example, should this risk be accounted for in an increased charge to Site Costs? Add any additional items unique to the project that should be included within Site Costs.]*

10. Tenant's Construction of Building. Tenant, at its own cost and expense, will construct the Building consisting of approximately __*[e.g., 42,000]*__ square feet in the area shown as " __*[name of supermarket]*__ " on Exhibit "A", in accordance with agreed plans and specifications. Tenant shall select the contractor to complete the Building. __*[Developer shall have the right to make periodic inspections of the Building during construction]*__.

> *Although Tenant is solely responsible for the cost of constructing the Building, carefully defining what is included within the "Building" will assist the parties in defining what is and what is not includable in "Site Costs."*

11. Specific Items Included within the Cost of the Building. The following specific cost items shall be aggregated and included within the cost advanced by Tenant for the Building and collectively referred to herein as the "Building Cost":

11.1 Direct Construction. The direct construction cost of the Building __*[which shall include, without limitation, the specifications listed on the attached Exhibit "B" (Consider Exhibit "B" to Form 9-2, a typical list of specifications for a major chain supermarket, for a specific example)]*__ *OR* __*[which shall include, without limitation, sidewalks and curbs within* __*[e.g., 10]*__ *feet of the Building (and extending to and including the parking lot curb in front of the Building), loading dock, truck loading ramp, and fees and costs to connect utilities to the Building]*__;

11.2 Building Design/Construction. All engineering, architectural, and consultant fees for design and construction of the Building (other than engineering required by Developer to fulfill Developer's obligation to __*[rough/finish]*__ grade __*[and compact]*__ the Supermarket Parcel);

11.3 Permits. Governmental processing fees, conditional use permits, applications, permits, plan check fees and other specific costs to obtain building permits for Tenant's Building;

11.4 Building Studies. Environmental impact report(s) or other studies required to obtain entitlements (if required for the Building and not required for the entire shopping center); __*[and]*__

11.5 Financing Expense. *Tenant's interest and financing fee expense reasonably allocated to construction of the Building.*

Note: *Although Tenant's interest expense is generally not Developer's concern in a parcel sale transaction, Tenant's cost basis in the Building could be relevant if Developer is able to negotiate a preferential right to reacquire the Building at a formula tied to "book" value upon, for example, Tenant's proposed assignment of its purchase rights, cessation of operations on the Supermarket Parcel or election to sell the Building to a third party.*

11.6 <u>Other</u>. Any other direct costs for construction of the Building. *Carefully analyze your specific, proposed transaction and consider including any additional specific contemplated costs that should be included within the cost of the Building. (Note that in this form governmental impact fees or assessments are not included in the Building Cost but are included above in "Site Costs" (Paragraph 9.1). Depending upon the methodology by which impact fees are assessed, in certain circumstances such fees should be paid directly by the parcel purchaser and not included within Site Costs.*

Note: *See Chapter 4, Form 4-1, Paragraph 6 for additional contingencies that may be considered for inclusion.*

12. <u>Contingencies</u>. While the Purchase Agreement will ultimately contain negotiated conditions precedent for the benefit of both Tenant and Developer, the following contingencies are the major conditions precedent to Tenant's obligation to complete the purchase of the Supermarket Parcel __*[and shall be satisfied within the times set forth below]*__:

12.1 <u>Title</u>. Approval by Tenant of a current preliminary title report and legal description complete with copies of each document referenced in said title report together with a map prepared by ___________ Title Company depicting each easement, right of way, license, right, etc. which is capable of being plotted in accordance with normal title company practices. *[Tenant will have __[e.g., 21 working]__ days from receipt to approve such documents]__.*

12.2 <u>Real Estate Committee Approval</u>. Approval of the business terms of this letter of intent by Tenant's Real Estate Committee __*[within __[e.g., 45]__ days following execution of this letter]*__.

12.3 <u>Document Execution</u>. Agreeing upon a mutually satisfactory Purchase Agreement and related documentation __*[including, e.g., a Development Agreement, Reciprocal Easement Agreement ("REA"), Common Area Maintenance Agreement and any supplemental agreement(s) required to document* *the proposed transaction]__. __[Tenant will have __[e.g., 90]__ days following execution of this letter of intent in which to negotiate and sign all required documentation with Developer]__.*

12.4 Feasibility. Tenant's completion of a formal feasibility study forecasting Tenant's operating results within the proposed center and Tenant's investigation and determination that there are no governmental, physical or economic constraints *__[(including zoning, survey, soils conditions, absence of hazardous materials or other environmental constraints)]__* which would render construction of Tenant's Building unfeasible or uneconomic. *__[Tenant will have __[e.g., 90]__ days from execution of the Purchase Agreement in which to complete Tenant's feasibility analysis, including review of Developer's soils test results and Developer's Phase 1 environmental investigation report]__. If Tenant elects to conduct additional testing of the Supermarket Parcel, Tenant will have an additional __[30 days]__ in which to conduct and evaluate such tests]__.*

Optional Inserts

If soils and hazardous materials investigation of the site is not covered within the preceding "Feasibility" contingency, the following "Soils Tests" and "Hazardous Materials" contingencies could be added. Both provisions could be modified to reflect a common practice whereby the developer provides the major tenant with the right to review the developer's specific, existing tests and investigations and the tenant undertakes additional investigation or testing only if warranted.

12.__ Soils Tests. Tenant's approval of soils tests conducted by Tenant on the Supermarket Parcel at Tenant's cost. *__[Such testing and review by Tenant shall be completed within __[e.g., 60]__ days following execution of the Purchase Agreement]__.*

12.__ Hazardous Materials Investigation. Tenant's approval of a *__[Phase 1 environmental investigation]__* conducted by *__[a reputable third party selected by Tenant]__* at Tenant's cost. (Tenant may elect to but is under no obligation to conduct physical testing of the Supermarket Parcel *__[and Developer's adjacent parcel(s).)]__*

Note: *See Paragraph 19, below. In the event the site contains hazardous materials, refer to Form 17-3, "Hazardous Materials: Example of Expanded Site Purchase Offer Provisions for Use in Acquiring a Site Where Significant Investigation and Cleanup Is Expected."*

End of preceding optional inserts—renumber Paragraphs 12.5 et seq., if preceding "Optional inserts" are used.

Optional Paragraph 12.5
Tenant-oriented co-tenancy contingency

12.5 Co-tenancy. Developer securing ________ __*[and/or]*__ ____________ as __*[a]*__ major co-tenant*[s]* which will open __*[a]*__ store*[s]* not less than ______ __*[and]*__ ________ *square feet,* __*[respectively,]*__ __*[in the building(s) designated on Exhibit "A"]*__ substantially concurrent with the opening of Tenant's Building. __*[Landlord will have* ___ *days from* __*[e.g., signing this letter of intent]*__ *in which to negotiate a binding lease or parcel sale agreement with such co-tenant(s) in satisfaction of this co-tenancy contingency]*__.

OR

Optional Paragraph 12.5
Another tenant-oriented co-tenancy contingency

12.5 Co-tenancy. Developer represents that it has signed a letter of intent to enter into a __*[major tenant]*__ lease with __________ ("Co-tenant") for premises of the size and in the location shown on Exhibit "A" requiring Developer to construct a store building for Co-tenant and Co-tenant to open a retail __*[describe type of operation]*__ on its premises for a lease term not less than __*[e.g., 20]*__ years __*[with occupancy]*__ commencing not later than ________, 20__. __*[Tenant's execution]*__ *OR* __*[The closing]*__ of Tenant's Purchase Agreement with Developer shall be contingent upon Developer's prior execution of a final lease agreement with Co-tenant consistent with such letter of intent. __*[Developer's lease with Co-tenant shall be non-contingent and non-cancelable except for customary and usual causes with respect to default, casualty, or condemnation]*__.

End of Paragraph 12.5 optional clauses

12.6 Final Site Plan. Agreeing upon a final site plan __*[which includes satisfactory ingress and egress to both* ________ __*[Street]*__ *and* ________ __*[Avenue]*__*]*__. __*[Tenant will have* __*[e.g., 90]*__ *days from opening of escrow in which to negotiate an acceptable final site plan with Developer]*__.

12.7 Parcel Map Recording. Recordation, following approval by all required governmental entities, of a __*[parcel]*__ *OR* __*[subdivision]*__ map permitting the conveyance of the Supermarket Parcel (in its finally negotiated configuration) separate from the remaining land area of the shopping center. __*[The REA will be recorded against all parcels comprising the shopping center not later than recordation of the Supermarket Parcel deed to Tenant]*__.

12.8 Entitlements. Obtaining all required permits, approvals and agreements, and final issuance of all other required entitlements from all required agencies or bodies for the development of the subject property and the shopping center in accordance with the site plan attached hereto as Exhibit "A" ("Governmental Approvals") __*[,all of which shall be obtained prior to close of escrow]*__. Such Governmental Approvals shall include but not be limited to, all required environmental clearances, acceptable development fee agreements, on- and off-site building permits, conditional use permits (if required), and any required utility agreements. In particular, Governmental Approvals shall include all permits to construct __*[e.g., the Site Work, Developer's]*__ __*[first phase of]*__ __*[building improvements consisting of]*__ __*[describe]*__, __*[and Tenant's Building]*__.

> ***Note:*** *If closing is to be conditioned on issuance of Tenant's building permit, Tenant should be obligated to timely submit required building plans and other documentation to required agencies so as not to delay issuance of Tenant's building permit and any operating licenses.*

FORM 10-1

12.9 Operating Permits. Issuance of any necessary operating permits required by Tenant's operation, including __*[e.g., a liquor license for operation of a package liquor store and the sale of alcoholic beverages for off-premises consumption]*__. __*[Tenant will have until]*__ __*[e.g., close of escrow]*__ *in which to approve, disapprove or waive this contingency]*__.

Five examples of cancellation rights:

Cancellation if Site Costs excessive:

12.__ Mutual Right to Cancel Purchase Agreement If Site Costs Exceed Agreed Maximum. Notwithstanding any other provision, the Purchase Agreement shall provide that if Developer __*[, within __ days following execution of the Purchase Agreement,]*__ is unable to secure a bona fide Site Work bid from an approved contractor for an amount such that the Site Costs are equal to or less than $__*[insert not-to-exceed amount, e.g., $4.50]*__ per square foot of total land area of the shopping center ("Site Costs Maximum") and neither Developer nor Tenant is willing to be responsible for the amount __*[attributable to the Supermarket Parcel]*__ in excess of the Site

Costs Maximum, Developer and Tenant shall each have the right to cancel the proposed transaction. *[The developer is at risk for various soft costs and site improvement plans and specifications expense if not-to-exceed cost figure cannot be achieved.]*

Cancellation if Building Cost excessive:

12.__ Mutual Right to Cancel Purchase Agreement If Building Cost Exceeds Agreed Maximum. Notwithstanding any other provision, the Purchase Agreement shall provide that if Tenant *__[, within __ days following execution of the Purchase Agreement,]__* is unable to secure a bona fide Building Cost bid from an approved contractor for an amount such that the Building Cost is equal to or less than $*__[insert not-to-exceed amount, e.g., $50]__* per square foot ("Building Cost Maximum") and neither Developer nor Tenant is willing to be responsible for the amount in excess of the Building Cost Maximum, Developer and Tenant shall each have the right to cancel the proposed transaction. *[The parties would be at risk for various soft costs and plans and specifications expense if not-to-exceed cost figure cannot be achieved.]*

Tenant-oriented fee cap:

12.__ Cap on Governmental Fees and Permit Costs. The Purchase Agreement shall provide that the sum of all applicable governmental development fees, assessments and permits ("fees") leviable against Tenant shall not exceed $_____ per square foot of *__[Tenant's proposed Building]__ OR __[the Supermarket Parcel]__ [Possible Developer response:] __[excluding any such fees included within Site Costs payable by Tenant to Developer]__*. If fees leviable against Tenant exceed $_________ and neither Developer nor Tenant is willing to be responsible for the amount in excess of such sum, Developer and Tenant shall each have the right to cancel the proposed transaction.

Tenant-oriented provision requiring Developer to provide assurance that sufficient funds exist to complete the Site Work (expandable to also include Developer's first phase of building improvements):

12.__ Assurance of Developer's Financial Capability. The Purchase Agreement shall provide that by __________, 20__ Developer will provide Tenant reasonable assurance that Developer or Developer's lender holds sufficient funds *__[e.g., in an escrow account]__* to complete and pay for the Site Work *__[and Developer's first phase of the center's building improvements]__* (subject to payment or reimbursement in part by Tenant in the manner described herein). If Developer fails to provide such assurance to Tenant by such date, Tenant shall have the right to cancel the proposed transaction.

The developer needs an ability to terminate the transaction if the project cannot be financed:

12.__ Developer's Financing Contingency. The Purchase Agreement shall provide that Developer shall have until _________, 20__ in which to obtain a binding __*[e.g., construction/permanent]*__ loan to __*[e.g. construct the shopping center, including the Site Work described in this letter]*__. If Developer is unable to obtain financing in form satisfactory to Developer by such date, Developer shall have the right to cancel the proposed transaction.

End of contingencies and cancellation right examples

Think: *Have you carefully considered the specific factual situation and included the major contingencies critical to the particular deal? As noted above, examples of other contingencies to consider are set forth in Chapter 4, Form 4-1, Paragraph 6 of the comprehensive site purchase proposal. If additional contingencies are added, the time allowed for the satisfaction of each such additional contingency should be considered. Although the above listing includes routinely negotiated major contingencies, it is by no means comprehensive.*

Although Paragraph 12.4 (and the "optional inserts" following Paragraph 12.4) touch upon soils and hazardous materials issues, this form, being a deal-making document, stops short of providing detailed provisions regarding environmental investigation, inspection and testing, soils investigation and remediation, site survey rights, and a host of other technical matters left for later refinement. While technical issues are often reserved for final, instead of deal-making, documents, make a special effort to articulate contingencies appropriate to the particular factual context at hand. What may be a trivial issue in one transaction may be a critical deal point in another.

13. Tenant's Diligence and Cooperation. During the contingency period Tenant will exercise reasonable diligence to investigate all aspects of the site and attempt to timely satisfy such contingencies. __*[Upon satisfaction of such contingencies,]*__ Tenant and Developer will work cooperatively to expeditiously develop the proposed center __*[including an assurance to concurrently submit working drawings for the Site Work, Tenant's Building and Developer's first phase of building improvements. Similarly, the parties will attempt to obtain concurrent issuance of building permits for the Site Work, the Building, and Developer's first phase of building improvements]*__.

Optional: Extraordinary conditions causing termination:

Optional provision for specific events, unique to the transaction, that would cause its termination:

__. **Extraordinary Conditions.** On or before the closing, none of the following shall have occurred:

Illustrative examples:

__.1 **Imposition of City/County Surcharge.** The __*[e.g., City/County]*__ of __*[name of jurisdiction]*__ shall have imposed after the date hereof further material site conditions, parcel map conditions, declarations, reservations, an increase in the __*[name]*__ fee __*[(imposed by ordinance XYZ)]*__ in excess of __ % of the present amount thereof or the imposition of any fees for additional items or matters which are not also imposed upon all other __*[commercial]*__ property owners within the __*[planning area, e.g., __[name]__ Specific Plan]*__.

__.2 **Building Moratorium.** The __*[e.g., City/County]*__ of __*[name of jurisdiction]*__ shall have imposed any building moratorium or, after the date hereof, amended any material rules, regulations, ordinances, policies or restrictions (except health and safety matters) which would limit __*[Developer's/Tenant's]*__ ability to obtain __*[e.g., building permits]*__ and/or proceed with the construction of the __*[e.g., Site Work, Building and the remainder of the shopping center]*__.

End of optional provision—Proceed to next paragraph.

14. Signs. __*[Subject to size and materials limitations contained in the XYZ sign criteria and/or governmental approvals,]*__ Tenant may install its standard logo and signage on the exterior of the Building. Tenant shall also have the right to place its trade name and logo in the __*[top]*__ tenant position on each of __*[two]*__ shopping center __*[pylon or monument]*__ signs on the two major street frontages. Only those tenants exceeding __*[e.g., 20,000]*__ square feet will be allowed space on said shopping center __*[pylon or monument]*__ signs. Tenant will pay for the cost of its individual display placed thereon.

> ***Note:*** *The construction cost of two major shopping center pylon or monument signs is included in Site Work (see Paragraph 9.3, above), the cost for which Tenant reimburses based upon its prorata land area. However, if the cost of such signs is not included in Site Work, language such as the following should be added here:]*

__[Tenant will pay its prorata share (based upon the area of the Building to the total allowable building area of tenant sign users) of the costs of such sign structures]__.

Ideally, reference and attach a sketch of the proposed signs showing total sign area and sign area allocated to Tenant's display, which sketch is ultimately attached as an exhibit to parcel sale documentation. Prepare and get Tenant's approval of the sketch early in negotiations to avoid ambiguity or "subject to" approval in purchase documentation. (See example attached as optional exhibit.)

***Note:** The following Developer-oriented provisions appearing as Paragraphs 15 and 16 would have been "optional" in the recent past. However, with increasing scrutiny and risk adversity by lenders and investors, current trends indicate that at least some protection against a major tenant's cessation of operations are becoming a necessity. Working out a solution to these sensitive issues will require substantial discussion and understanding with the anchor tenant. Paragraphs 15 and 16 are examples of provisions designed to stimulate reader analysis.*

Developer oriented:

15. Initial Opening and Operations. In accordance with the planning, construction and fixturing time frames negotiated and contained in the Purchase Agreement (but subject to force majeure), Tenant will open for business in the Building and will operate a *__[e.g., name of chain]__ __[supermarket]__* store therein continuously for *__[e.g., 3]__* years thereafter.

Nearly all anchor chain stores will covenant to open and virtually none will grant a continuous operating covenant. This provision is really not adequate, but better than nothing. Unfortunately, it may not be achievable. Be familiar with your lender's requirements, if any, before negotiating this issue.

Developer oriented:

16. Developer's Preferred Right to Purchase or Lease. *__[For the period ending __ years after Tenant's purchase of the Supermarket Parcel,]__* Developer (and any successor to Developer's interest in the shopping center), shall have a preferred right to purchase the Supermarket Parcel with all Site Work and other improvements constructed thereon (including the Building but excluding trade fixtures and equipment) (the "Supermarket Premises") or acquire a leasehold interest in the Supermarket Premises on the following terms

FORM 10-1

and conditions:

16.1 Purchase Rights If Tenant Goes Dark. If, after completion of the Building and Site Work on the Supermarket Parcel, Tenant ceases to operate its retail business out of the Supermarket Premises (which cessation is not the result of force majeure) for a period greater than *__[e.g., 180 days]__*, Developer may elect to exercise a preferred right to (a) purchase Tenant's fee interest in the Supermarket Premises or (b) if Tenant has previously leased the Supermarket Premises to a third party, Developer shall have the right to purchase Tenant's fee interest subject to such leasehold.

The purchase price payable for Tenant's fee interest in the Supermarket Premises or Tenant's fee interest subject to such leasehold interest shall be the greater of (i) Tenant's current book value or (ii) fair market value established by fair market appraisal *__[but in any case not more than Tenant's cost of the Supermarket Parcel, the Building and the Site Work plus an imputed escalation of __[e.g., 8%]__ per annum from the date Tenant incurred such costs through the closing of any such purchase by Developer]__. __[Such purchase price for the Supermarket Premises shall in each case be reduced by the total subsidy, if any, granted by Developer to Tenant in Developer's initial transaction with Developer relative to the Supermarket Premises, compounded at a rate of __[e.g., 8%]__ per annum from the date of the advance of such subsidy by Developer through closing of the preferred purchase]__.*

16.2 First Right of Refusal to Purchase or Lease. If Tenant or any successor of Tenant elects to sell or lease all or any portion of the Supermarket Premises, Developer shall have the prior and first right of refusal by which to so acquire by fee or lease such property. *__[However, Tenant's consummation of a typical long-term sale-leaseback transaction with a third party for Tenant's financing of the Supermarket Premises __[within the first ___ years of the closing of the Purchase Agreement]__ shall be exempt from Developer's first right of refusal right]__.*

Major tenant oriented optional:

__. Concurrent Shops Construction. Developer will be obligated to commence and complete, concurrently with the construction of the Building, *__[an initial first-phase of]__* ________ square feet of shell retail shop space, at the locations designated on Exhibit "A." Said space shall be used only for sales and service businesses of the kind customarily found in quality *__[neighborhood]__* shopping centers in *__[describe geographic area]__ __[and which shall be subject to the use and specific location restrictions described below]__.*

Example of "exclusive" required by an anchor supermarket:

__. **Food and Drug Restrictions.** The reciprocal easement agreement ("REA") *[or CC & R's]* recorded against all parcels comprising the shopping center shall provide that no part of Parcels __, __ and __ *[i.e., all except anchor's parcel]* shall be used as a supermarket (defined as any store or department containing at least __*[5000]*__ square feet of floor area primarily devoted to the retail sale of food for off-premises consumption); __*[as a bakery or delicatessen; for the sale of fresh or frozen meat, fish, poultry or produce for off-premises consumption; or for the sale of alcoholic beverages for off-premises consumption; or for the sale of any ethical pharmaceutical products requiring the services of a registered pharmacist]*__.

Developer "use it or lose it" addition to preceding paragraph:

However, if a supermarket is not operated on __*[the Supermarket Parcel]*__ for a continuous period of __*[e.g., 8]*__ months or more at any time after the date __*[name of supermarket]*__ first opens for business on __*[the Supermarket Parcel]*__ for any reason (other than __*[e.g., (i) a strike, lockout, casualty or other temporary closure beyond the reasonable control of Tenant or (ii) a temporary closure due to restoration, reconstruction, expansion, alteration or remodeling of the shopping center),]*__ then the restriction prohibiting a supermarket; __*[a bakery; a delicatessen; and such sale of meat, fish, poultry, produce, alcoholic beverages or ethical pharmaceutical products]*__ shall thereafter be void and of no effect.

FORM 10-1

Major tenant oriented illustrative optional (example):

__. **Use Restrictions.** The reciprocal easement agreement ("REA") recorded against all parcels comprising the shopping center shall provide that no part of the shopping center shall be used as a bar, tavern, cocktail lounge, automotive maintenance or repair facility, warehouse, entertainment or recreational facility or training or educational facility. __*["Entertainment or recreational facility" shall include, without limitation, a theater, bowling alley, skating rink, gym, health spa or studio, dance hall, billiard or pool hall, massage parlor, game parlor or video arcade. The phrase "training or educational facility" shall include, without limitation, a beauty school, barber college, reading room, place of instruction or any other operation catering primarily to students or trainees as opposed to retail customers]*__.

Notwithstanding the limitations contained in the preceding paragraph, Parcels __ and __ may be used for the following: __*[e.g., (i) a TBA facility as is typically operated by _______ or ________, (ii) an auto lubrication facility as typically operated by ________ and/or (iii) a muffler or brake replacement store as is typically operated by __________. These uses shall be allowed only so long as* *the services provided by such businesses do not normally require that customers leave their vehicles at the shopping center overnight]__. [Continue describing other parcels and specific use exceptions.]*

Major tenant oriented optional (example):

__. **Location Restrictions.** No part of Parcels __, __, __, or __ shall be used as a restaurant or as medical, dental, professional or business offices ("office use") except as follows:

__.1 **Restaurant Use.** Up to ______ square feet of floor area on Parcel __ may be used as a restaurant; up to ____ square feet of floor area of Parcel __ may be used as a restaurant provided, however, no single restaurant business may exceed ______ square feet of floor area on said Parcel __ and only _____ square feet of said Parcel __ restaurant use may be within __*[e.g., 150]*__ feet of the __*[e.g., supermarket Building]*__ OR __*[e.g., the Supermarket Parcel designated building area]*__; and Parcels __ and __ may be used as restaurants provided ____________.

__.2 **Office Use.** Up to _____ square feet of floor area each on Parcels __ and __ may be used for office use provided that no more than __*[e.g., 1500]*__ square feet of floor area in each said Parcel may be located within __*[e.g., 150]*__ feet of the __*[e.g., supermarket Building]*__ OR __*[e.g., the Supermarket Parcel designated building area]*__; office use shall be allowed on Parcels ___ and ___ subject to the limitation than not more than a total of ____ square feet of floor area in the shopping center may be devoted to office use and no single office use building may exceed __*[e.g., 2000]*__ square feet of floor area.

> ***Note:*** *Consider possible additional deal points relative to the specific transaction. For example, a radius clause could be inserted into the REA prohibiting Tenant from opening a new store within a limited radius for a limited time period. Such a clause could be adapted from Form 18-8 in Chapter 18, "Optional and Alternative Clauses for Lease Proposals". Refer also to Chapter 17, "Optional and Alternative Clauses for Purchase and Sale Proposals" for ideas. If any insertions are made, renumber the following paragraphs accordingly.*

17. Common Area Maintenance. Tenant will __*[e.g., pay]*__ OR __*[reimburse]*__ Developer for its prorata share of all costs for operating and maintaining the parking lot and common areas of the shopping center, including a __*[e.g., 10]*__ % administrative fee to Developer ("CAM"). Tenant's liability for its prorata share of such CAM expense shall be computed on the basis of the relationship to the whole of such expenses as the square footage of the...

Alternative "A"

The following Developer-oriented provision provides for Tenant to pay based upon Tenant's land area as a percentage of total shopping center land area without regard to whether other buildings are completed and occupied.

...Supermarket Parcel bears to the square footage of the total land area of the shopping center as shown on Exhibit "A".

OR

Alternative "B"

The following Tenant-oriented provision provides for Tenant payment based upon Tenant's Building area relative to total building area even if all buildings are not concurrently constructed, i.e. Tenant is, in effect, subsidized through completion of final center buildout.

...floor area of the Building bears to the square footage of the floor area of all buildings in the shopping center as shown on Exhibit "A", whether actually built or not.

OR

Alternative "C"

The following Developer-oriented adjustment to the preceding Alternative "B" provides that Tenant's share of CAM is based upon Tenant's share of Building floor area relative to the floor area of completed [and leased/occupied] buildings in the center when such CAM expense is incurred.

...floor area of the Building bears to the square footage of the floor area of those buildings in the shopping center as shown on Exhibit "A" which are completed __*[and leased/occupied]*__ at the time such CAM costs are incurred.

FORM 10-1

Final sentence following selected Alternative "A", "B", or "C":
The exact square footages to be used in the above calculation shall be determined prior to signing the Purchase Agreement and the Purchase Agreement will incorporate Tenant's proportionate share expressed as a percentage.

18. Insurance. __*[Optional: Tenant shall carry fire and extended coverage insurance with a rated insurance company in an amount not less than 90% of full replacement costs, naming Developer as additional insured.]*__ Developer will provide public liability and property damage insurance on the parking areas and common facilities in accordance with the REA. Tenant will pay its prorata share of all such public liability and property damage insurance costs __*[including a 10% administrative fee to Developer]*__ __*[e.g., using the same formula selected to allocate CAM costs]*__ *OR* __*[(by the ratio of the Supermarket Parcel to total land area of shopping center)]*__ *OR* __*[(by the ratio of Tenant's Building area to the total* __*[allowable]*__ *building area)]*__.

Mutual right to terminate if hazardous materials discovered during investigatory period:

19. Hazardous Materials. If, within __*[e.g., 120 days]*__ following execution of the Purchase Agreement, the report(s) of any environmental investigation, inspection and testing of the Supermarket Parcel conducted by reputable third party consultants indicate that any toxic waste, contamination or hazardous substance is discovered or is likely to exist, either party may elect to terminate the transaction. If the parties elect to proceed with the transaction, Developer shall pay for any corrective work required and complete any such work prior to close of escrow. Developer's obligation to pay for corrective work shall include the cost to obtain environmental clearance certificate(s) satisfactory to all appropriate governmental agencies showing the Supermarket Parcel __*[and Developer's adjacent parcel(s)]*__ free and clear of any toxic waste, contamination or hazardous substance.

For a more comprehensive, alternative format where hazardous materials are contemplated, see Chapter 17, Form 17-3: "Hazardous Materials: Example of Expanded Site Purchase Offer Provisions for Use in Acquiring a Site Where Significant Investigation and Cleanup Is Expected." For additional perspectives, refer to Paragraph 13 (Alternatives "A" and "B") and comments, Form 4-1.

20. Utilities. Tenant shall pay for all utilities applicable to the Supermarket Premises.

21. Real Estate Taxes and Assessments. Tenant will pay all real estate taxes and assessments levied against the Supermarket Premises.

22. Real Estate Commission. With appropriate representations from Tenant, Developer will be responsible for any real estate commissions resulting from the contemplated transaction.

Developer oriented:

23. Intermediate Approvals. If, prior to the review and approval by Tenant's Real Estate Committee, the approval by any specific executive of Tenant is required and any such required executive approval is not granted, Tenant will within __*[e.g., 4 business days]*__ of such event telephone and inform Developer that such required executive approval was not obtained and that, therefore, the proposed transaction will not be reviewed by Tenant's Real Estate Committee.

24. Non-binding Letter of Intent. While this proposal sets forth the very basic terms of Developer's proposed sale and Tenant's interest in purchasing and occupying the Supermarket Parcel in the proposed shopping center, the parties do not intend this letter to be a contract or to be bound by this letter.

FORM 10-1

The proposed transaction is subject to the approval of Tenant's Real Estate Committee. A contract between the parties will not exist unless and until Tenant's Real Estate Committee has approved this transaction and the parties have executed __*[final, definitive agreements approved by their respective lawyers regarding the subject matter of this letter and containing all other essential terms of an agreed upon transaction]*__ *OR [Alternatively, refer to specific documents, if known:]* __*[e.g., the Purchase Agreement, the Development Agreement, the Reciprocal Easement Agreement, the Common Area Maintenance Agreement and the Supplemental Agreement]*__. *[Optional:]* __*[The parties acknowledge that they have not set forth nor agreed upon all essential terms of the transaction described herein, including without limitation, representations and warranties, conditions precedent, indemnities and many other essential terms which will be the subject of further negotiation]*__.

Alternative "A"—Paragraph 25
Developer-oriented optional

25. Developer's Limited Exclusive Right. Notwithstanding our agreement that this letter is otherwise not binding, Developer may rely upon Tenant's promise that during the __*[e.g., 60-day]*__ period following execution of this letter by the parties (during which period the real estate representative signing this letter on behalf of Tenant promises to make a good faith effort to obtain Real Estate Committee approval of the transaction), Tenant will not __ *[e.g., initiate negotiations and will suspend any existing negotiations to purchase or lease any other property for Tenant's potential operation of a __[e.g., supermarket]__ store within a radius of __[e.g., 3]__ miles of the site.*

OR

Alternative "B"—Paragraph 25
Tenant-oriented optional

25. <u>Tenant's Limited Exclusive Right</u>. Notwithstanding our agreement that this letter is otherwise not binding, Tenant may rely upon Developer's promise that during the *__[e.g., 60-day]__* period following acceptance of this letter by Developer (during which period the real estate representative signing this letter on behalf of Tenant promises to make a good faith effort to obtain Real Estate Committee approval of the transaction), Developer will not *__[e.g., offer the Supermarket Parcel for sale or lease]__ <u>AND/OR</u> __[will not accept any offer to sell or lease the Supermarket Parcel]__* to any other __ *[supermarket]__* chain.

End of Paragraph 25—Proceed to closing paragraph

If you wish to proceed under the above terms and conditions, please so indicate by signing a copy of this letter and returning it to me no later than _____, 20__. Following my receipt of a fully executed counterpart of this letter *__[and Real Estate Committee approval of the transaction]__*, we will begin to prepare final agreements.

Very truly yours,

[Developer]

____

[capacity]

<u>OR</u>

[Name of Supermarket}

____

[e.g., Real Estate Manager]

UNDERSTOOD AND AGREED:
This __ day of __________, 20__.

[Name of Developer]
OR
[Name of Supermarket Chain]

By: ________________

Its: ________________

Exhibit "A"
[Attach copy of preliminary site plan]

Exhibit "B"
[Optional: Attach Building specifications—
Refer to Exhibit "B" to Form 9-2 for an example]

FORM 10-1

Exhibit " "

[Optional: Attach sketch or diagram of pylon or monument identification signs, for example:]

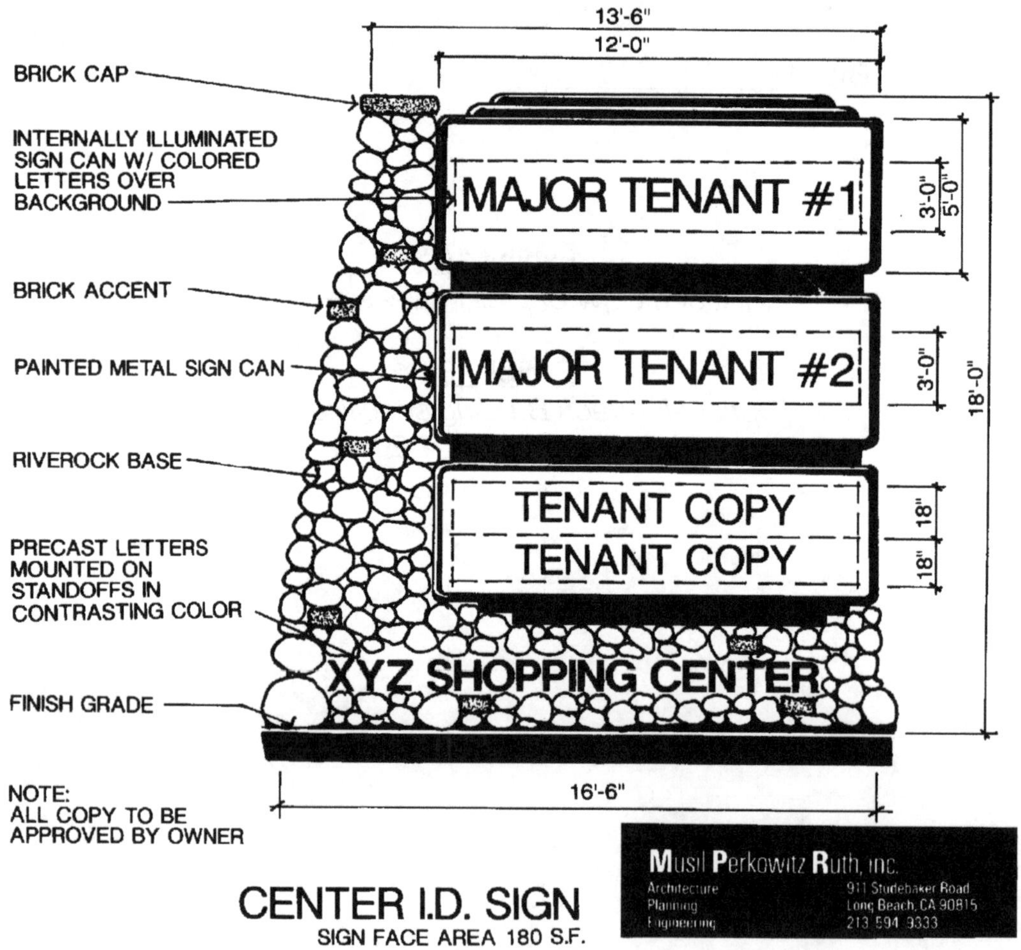

END OF FORM 10-1

Each of the preceding major tenant letters of intent (Forms 9-1, 9-2, and 10-1) serves as a vehicle to confirm the parties' prior discussions. Form 10-2, however, illustrates the use of a letter to introduce a parcel sale opportunity to a major chain tenant. The letter—in this unusual instance the first communication between the developer and the tenant—summarizes key site attributes and also outlines the deal structure proposed by the developer. Illustrating an approach to generate a tenant response, Form 10-2 is included to stimulate creative thinking about marketing possibilities rather than as a reusable form.

Form 10-2 was derived relative to a 16-acre site for which a fully-executed build-to-suit lease had been signed with a major supermarket chain. However, the chain's corporate parent abruptly sold all of its operating units in the state and decided not to occupy stores under development. Although the center was substantially pre-leased and the physical attributes of the site were outstanding, all other potential supermarket chains already had stores within the trade area.

However, one of the brokers on the marketing team had just begun to establish a rapport with an out-of-state supermarket retailer that was beginning to secure sites in the region. This "new" retailer appeared to have significant interest in the site and its real estate committee was scheduled to meet four days hence; an extensive in-house review of the site had been planned. It was believed that this prospective retailer was probably the only possible supermarket candidate, at least for the near term. With entitlements in place, making a deal with a new anchor tenant was critical to maintaining the project's momentum.

The developer enjoyed a close relationship with the broker and it was assumed in this context that the tenant's real estate representative would more likely "open up" to the broker than to the developer. Given the relationship between the developer and the broker on the one hand, and the broker's relationship with the tenant on the other, in this unusual instance a draft of the letter was written by the developer for submission on the broker's letterhead to the tenant. The letter summarizes the site's physical attributes, site demographics, the development entity, and the terms of the proposed deal. The objective was to generate a response from the retailer and quickly determine whether an acceptable deal could be negotiated to preserve the approved development plan and proceed to construction.

Within the letter are some requests not typically granted by supermarket chains. However, laying out all these issues in one document serves to facilitate and accelerate negotiation of these points. In this case, it appeared that, to secure the tenant's commitment, the tenant would only purchase (rather than lease) and that a slight tenant subsidy would be required to make this deal (although site improvement costs were not clearly known). The letter, in effect, attempts to trade off such subsidy in return for developer "control" rights relative to the prospective tenant's proposed parcel.

As a conceptual illustration, Form 10-2 may stimulate your thinking on initiating or confirming proposals with major tenants in general. Note, for example, that key demographic attributes and site characteristics are conveniently summarized for the chain together with the proposed economics. In this case, the one document served as a complete summary of the opportunity for the scheduled real estate committee meeting.

Do not take for granted that busy tenant real estate representatives or members of the real estate committee will skillfully summarize or organize submitted materials into an executive summary format. Real estate representatives appreciate having materials summarized so it is easy for them to review and present up the line. Furthermore, if one document summarizes all major issues, the developer is subjected to less risk that the tenant's real estate representative's submittal to senior management will be found deficient for the reason that he or she neglected to include an important fact or document in the submittal. Providing organized summaries of materials also helps the real estate representative focus on the critical qualifying elements of the site and its trade area.

Form 10-2

Comprehensive "Marketing" Letter to Major [Supermarket] Chain to Initiate Parcel Purchase by Chain

Illustration of a marketing example—not a reusable format

[Project Marketing Broker's Letterhead]

[Date]

[Name and address
of chain supermarket
real estate representative
____
__________________*]*

Re: Community shopping center site
__*[describe location]*__;
__*[city]*__, __*[state]*__

Dear ___________:

I am writing to advise you of our developer's interest in locating a __*[name of supermarket chain]*__ __*[combination food and drug store]*__ in the community shopping center to be constructed at the above-referenced site. It is my understanding that a formal in-house review of the site will be conducted under your direction on _________, 20__. *[In example, 4 days away.]* Consequently, this letter details critical background data concerning the site, the developer partnership, and the terms and conditions by which __*[name of supermarket]*__ 's acquisition of a major supermarket site may be accomplished.

1. The Site. Enclosed herewith you will find a tentative site plan depicting a __*[name of supermarket]*__ 's ______ square foot combination food and drug store. I believe it depicts an excellent conceptual layout for __*[name of supermarket]*__. Economics, however, will require some modification of the overall plan to increase site coverage (site coverage on the enclosed approximately 16-acre preliminary plan is only 23%).

The subject property appears to be the last parcel in which __*[name of supermarket chain]*__ could locate in this dynamic marketplace. Developer has received signed letters of intent from _____________, _____________, _____________, _____________, and ________________ and has signed leases

FORM 10-2

with ____________, ____________, and ____________. We are in final lease negotiations with ___________, a major regional theater chain. Strong interest has been expressed by a major electronics outlet, __*[name of tenant]*__, __*[name of another tenant]*__, a __*[10,000 square foot]*__ __*[type of use]*__, __ *[name of tenant]*__*[(10,000–12,000 square feet)]*__ and other dominant retailers and restaurant chains. __*[Name of Insurance Company]*__ plans the immediate construction of an attractive one-story 22,500 square foot health management out-patient clinic ("HMO") on the 3-acre parcel at the westerly border of the subject site. The HMO site has been integrated into the center through a recorded reciprocal easement agreement which provides permanent ingress and egress through the HMO site yet permanently insures that the HMO parcel will have more than sufficient parking for its use.

Sixteen acres within the designated site were acquired by the developer joint venture partnership at an all cash acquisition cost of $____ per square foot. A land loan well in excess of 100% of the land purchase price was obtained to close the 16-acre land purchase escrow as a result of (i) a MAI appraisal dated _______, 20__ of $_______ per square foot and (ii) the financial strength of the venture financial partner. *[**Author's note:** Remember the good old days?]*

2. Demographics. Area demographics are particularly strong. A __*[name of major demographic research company]*__ site demographic study completed _______, 20__, indicates a designated, specific trade area population of _________ people with an average family income in excess of $_______ and a median family income in excess of $_________. More than _______ persons live within a 1-mile ring of the site, _______ live within a 2-mile ring, and ______ live within a 3-mile ring of the site.

As of _______, 20__, the total traffic count within a 24 hour period at the intersection is __*[insert combined count]*__ (_______ Boulevard's count is _________ and ________ Avenue has a count of ________ vehicles). Furthermore, the ___________ Community Hospital is located on ___________ Road approximately 2 blocks west of the parcel and to the rear of the subject site. __________ Community Hospital is the largest acute care institution within the west end of __________ County. Statistics furnished by the hospital indicate it is licensed for ____ beds and has a medical staff of ____ members as of _________, 20__. With nearly _______ employees, the hospital is the city's largest employer. It appears likely that medical office condominiums and other general office buildings or apartment buildings will be developed on the parcel behind the site (under option by the financial partner). All such potential uses are consistent with existing zoning.

Finally, you should be aware that the installation of a new traffic signal at the intersection of ________ and ________ (the western edge of the site) is permitted and planned to be completed by the City of ______ at city expense by _______, 20__. When this work is completed, the site will have the benefit of traffic signals at three corners of the site. The relatively large roadway entrance to the site and the frontage road depicted on the site plan conform with existing, fully plan-checked city street improvement plans processed by the developer.

3. The Developer. The developer entity is a joint venture partnership between ____________ (as the developer partner and "Managing Venturer") and ____________, a subsidiary of __________ (the "financial partner"). __*[The financial partner]*__ is the U.S. operating arm of ___________ a publicly-owned building and diversified land development company. Enclosed herewith you will find a photocopy of a Statement of Joint Venture of ___________ recorded ___________, 20__ in _________ County, __*[state]*__, depicting _________ as the Managing Venturer under the terms of the joint venture agreement. Also enclosed is an original copy of the financial partner's Annual Report for 20__.

4. Tenant Subsidy and Special Terms. The developer would prefer to ground lease or build-to-suit but is aware of your expressed preference to purchase at a total finished cost not to exceed $_____ per square foot of total required land area. Obviously, to sell you a finished __ acre parcel at $____ per square foot would require a cash subsidy from the developer.

It is the developer's position, with which I agree, that if the developer is required to pay out of pocket to obtain __*[name of supermarket chain]*__'s commitment, your company should be willing to provide reasonable protections assuring the developer of your company's continued occupancy on the site.

Specifically, the developer is willing to sell __*[name of supermarket chain]*__ an agreed unimproved _____ square foot (__ acre) land parcel for $___ per square foot for your construction of a combination unit. (If possible, the developer would prefer to narrow the proposed ____ foot frontage on your store and increase its depth proportionately to produce a more efficient overall site plan.)

__*[Name of project architectural firm]*__ of __*[city]*__, __*[state]*__, prominent shopping center architects and project architects for this development, and project contractors have estimated that on- and off-site work should not exceed $_____ per square foot. __*[We]*__ propose that __*[name of supermarket*

FORM 10-2

*chain]*__ and developer share in the costs of the on- and off-site work attributable to the __ -acre supermarket parcel as follows: __*[describe]*__

Such a plan would give __*[name of supermarket chain]*__ the dominant anchor location within an approved, major center at a price about $________ per square foot or approximately $_____ *below* developer's actual costs.

5. Developer Protections. The developer reasons that the consideration for the developer's investment in the __*[name of supermarket chain]*__ ___ -acre parcel and the center's spatial dependency upon the extremely large combination supermarket store warrants __*[name of supermarket chain]*__ 's reasonable assurance to the developer of a period of continued operations and other reasonable protections. In a sense, the developer is merely asking for certain protections which would be included within a comprehensive ground lease or build-to-suit transaction that pragmatically addresses the parties' economic positions from a long term perspective. Such safeguards may be summarized as follows:

5.1 Operating Protections. __*[Name of supermarket chain]*__'s agreement to continue to operate the store on the site in its typical first class fashion for an agreed time period. Such an agreement may be critical to developer's financing arrangement.

5.2 No Trade Area Openings. __*[Name of supermarket chain]*__'s agreement that it will not open another store within the trade area or __*[3]*__ miles from the site for an agreed period of time.

5.3 Preferential Repurchase Right. Certain __*[name of supermarket chain]*__'s parcel sale restrictions will have to be negotiated. If a sale of the __*[supermarket]*__ parcel were to be allowed, the developer believes that a control mechanism should be established whereby the __*[supermarket]*__ site could be reacquired by the center owner in light of developer's cash investment in the parcel and the parcel's critical importance to the continuing success of the commercial complex.

The developer's Managing Venturer is resourceful and reasonable. I am confident that an acceptable agreement could be reached which would be sensible to both your company and the developer.

6. Standard Parcel Sale Terms. To be complete, the developer's standard parcel sale provisions may be summarized as follows:

6.1 Escrow. An escrow would be opened for __*[name of supermarket chain]*__ 's purchase of the proposed parcel;

6.2 Architectural, Engineering and Fees. __*[Supermarket]*__ would pay the architectural and engineering costs and all governmental fees and assessments attributable to its ___ -acre development relative to the entire 16-acre shopping center, i.e., any governmental fees or assessments charged on an acreage basis to the entire project would be chargeable to __*[name of supermarket chain]*__ in proportion by which the acreage of the supermarket site bears to the total acreage of the shopping center;

6.3 Concurrent Construction. __*[Name of supermarket chain]*__ would commence construction of its improvements along with the developer's improvements immediately after issuance of building permits by the City of ______;

6.4 On- and Off-Site Reimbursement. __*[Name of supermarket chain]*__ would pay its prorata share of on- and off-site improvement costs, in the amount described above, as such construction costs are incurred;

6.5 CAM. Common area maintenance ("CAM") costs payable by __*[name of supermarket chain]*__ would be __*[that portion of the total CAM costs that the total number of square feet in the __[supermarket]__'s building bears to the total number of leaseable square feet in the shopping center]*__ OR __*[that portion of the total CAM costs that the total number of square feet of land in the __[supermarket]__ parcel bears to the total number of square feet of land in the entire shopping center site]*__. CAM charges would be paid monthly with __*[quarterly]*__ adjustments;

6.6 Real Property Taxes and Insurance. __*[Supermarket]*__ would pay all of the real property taxes and insurance applicable to its ownership of the __*[supermarket]*__ parcel;

6.7 REA. An acceptable reciprocal easement agreement would be negotiated for the entire center. (The City of ______ has indicated that its approval of such an agreement will be required); and

6.8 Development Agreement. A development agreement would be negotiated to carry out development of the site by __*[name of supermarket chain]*__ and the developer.

7. Non-binding Agreement; Proposed Action. The developer joint venture agreement requires that a tenant letter of intent be signed and

FORM 10-2

submitted by each proposed tenant for approval by the venture's Management Committee before formal documentation of any agreement.

Accordingly, it would be appreciated if you would sign and return a copy of this letter indicating your approval of the deal points outlined in this letter. This conceptual outline, however, is not intended to be legally binding on either party, it being our intention that neither party would be bound unless or until formal legal documentation has been signed by __*[name of supermarket chain]*__ and the developer.

We look forward to working with you in what we feel will be a very successful center.

Very truly yours,

[Name of Broker's Company]

By: ____________________

Its: ____________________

Enclosures: (1) Site Plan;
(2) Statement of Joint venture of
_____________________; and
(3) _______________ Annual Report
for fiscal year ending ______, 20__.

<u>UNDERSTOOD AND AGREED</u>:
This __ day of _______, 20__.

[Name of chain supermarket]

By: _______________

Its: _______________

END OF FORM 10-2

Form 10-3 is derived from a letter agreement generated with a proposed co-tenant that anxiously wanted to purchase a site and build a store within the center described in the introduction to Form 10-2. (The developer had signed a lease with a credit anchor tenant but, because of a corporate restructuring, the anchor would not occupy the space; there was a period of uncertainty as to whether a substitute anchor could be found for the non-performing anchor's space.) Nevertheless, the proposed co-tenant did not care whether or not the center had any other anchor tenants. Having successfully consummated difficult initial entitlement issues and obtained site plan approval, negotiations progressed prior to issuance of final approvals.

Needing to open a store within a precise time frame because of a lease termination at another location, the co-tenant was extremely averse to becoming locked into a purchase if there was a significant possibility that issuance of final entitlements and groundbreaking could be substantially delayed. In essence, although more than willing to pay an excellent price for its site, the prospective tenant—mindful of the rigorous entitlement process—did not want to become entrenched in a prolonged entitlement battle. If final entitlements could not be secured within a certain time, the co-tenant needed to be able to cancel its purchase agreement and find an alternative site. With entitlement availability and timing issues constantly affecting transactions, this example is included for your consideration.

Briefly, Form 10-2 provides that on the day the shopping center parcel map creating the tenant's parcel is recorded, the tenant deposits into a purchase and sale escrow an amount equal to the on- and off-site improvement costs attributable to the tenant's parcel. Subject to the developer's right to terminate escrow if final on- and off-site costs exceed an agreed sum and the tenant's right to terminate escrow if recordation of the parcel map or commencement of grading is delayed, escrow closes when the developer has commenced grading the tenant's parcel.

Form 10-3

Letter Agreement Granting Major Tenant Right to Cancel Major Tenant Parcel Purchase Escrow If Developer Is Unable to Record Parcel Map or Commence Grading within Specified Time Periods; Developer May Cancel If On- and Off-Site Costs Exceed an Agreed Sum

[Date]

[Name and address of major tenant ____
____
____________*]*

Re: __*[name]*__ Shopping Center
__*[location]*__, __*[state]*__

Dear __________:

The purpose of this letter is to confirm our understanding of the revised business terms and conditions of the purchase and sale of the __*[insert name of major tenant]*__ ("Tenant") parcel in __________ Shopping Center. __*[Based upon our meeting with you and* __________ *on* __________*, 20*__*, Developer understands that Tenant will revise its purchase offer as follows:]*__

1. <u>Total Consideration</u>. Tenant will pay Developer $__________, the sum of the "Parcel Purchase Price" and the "Site Costs", as follows:

1.1 <u>Parcel Purchase Price</u>. The purchase price for Tenant's unimproved parcel is $__________.

1.2 <u>Site Costs</u>. The on- and off-site improvement cost of improving Tenant's parcel ("Site Costs") shall be fixed at $__________ and paid by Tenant in addition to the Parcel Purchase Price. (While this amount will not change if the size of Tenant's parcel changes, the parties currently estimate that Tenant's unimproved parcel will be approximately __________ square feet and that Site Costs will be $______ per square foot.)

2. <u>Payment Procedure</u>. Tenant shall pay for its parcel and the Site Costs as follows:

2.1 <u>Deposit</u>. Tenant will deposit $__*[insert aggregate "Site Costs"*

FORM 10-3

*amount from Paragraph "1.2", above]*__ into escrow on the day the final parcel map (the "Parcel Map") for __*[name]*__ Shopping Center is recorded. These funds will be deposited into a money market fund or certificates of deposit. Developer will give Tenant __*[insert number]*__ days prior written notice of the anticipated date on which the Parcel Map will be recorded.

2.2 Interest. Interest accrued on the funds deposited into escrow will be credited as provided below.

2.3 Payment of Site Costs. The total of $__*[amount in "1.2", above]*__ Site Costs will be paid in monthly installments as __*[Developer]*__ completes the site improvement work, provided escrow has previously closed.

2.4 Escrow Closing; Cancellation If Start of Grading Delayed. The parcel purchase price, plus accrued interest, if any, and any portion of the Site Costs incurred before the close of escrow will be paid to Developer when escrow closes. Escrow will close when Developer has started to grade Tenant's site. (We need to define what event will constitute the start of grading.) If escrow has not closed on or before __*[e.g., 210]*__ days after recordation of the Parcel Map, escrow will be automatically canceled.

2.5 Tenant's Cancellation Right; Parcel Map. If the Parcel Map has not been recorded on or before ____________, 20__, Tenant shall have the right to cancel escrow without penalty.

If Developer is able to effectuate an early closing, Developer gets an interest "bonus":

3. Payment of Interest. If escrow closes within __*[e.g., 120]*__ days after the Parcel Map is recorded, interest accrued on the funds deposited into escrow will be paid to Developer. If escrow closes after the end of said __*[e.g., 120]*__ -day period, all interest accrued on such funds from the date of deposit to the close of escrow will be paid to Tenant.

4. Miscellaneous Provisions.

4.1 Bond. Developer will purchase before the close of escrow a completion bond in the actual estimated cost of __*[grading]*__ Tenant's parcel, subject, however, to subparagraph "__*[4.2]*__" below.

4.2 Developer's Cancellation Right; On- and Off-Site Costs. If the final estimated cost of on- and off-site costs attributable to Tenant's parcel (as determined with respect to the final approved grading and on- and off-site improvement plans for the shopping center) exceeds $____ per square foot, Developer shall have the right to cancel escrow without penalty by sending Tenant written notice to such effect. Tenant shall have *__[e.g., 15]__* days after receipt of such notice in which to elect to pay the actual Tenant parcel improvement costs in excess of the Site Costs set forth in Paragraph *__[1.2]__*, above, or to agree to cancel escrow. If Tenant elects to pay the increased sum, escrow will continue.

4.3 Tenant's Approval Right; Parcel Map. Before recording the Parcel Map, Developer will submit it to Tenant for its reasonable review and approval. Tenant will have *__[e.g., 15]__* days after receipt of the Parcel Map in which to approve or disapprove it. Failure to timely disapprove the Parcel Map in writing will constitute approval of it.

4.4 Contingency Approval Deadline. Tenant shall satisfy all other contingencies to the close of escrow no later than *__[e.g., 60]__* days after *__[City Council]__* approval or opening of escrow, whichever occurs last.

4.5 Force Majeure. The time for performance of the parties' obligations under the purchase agreement will be extended during the occurrence of events of force majeure.

I believe our meeting was quite productive and I am confident that we will soon be in a position to close escrow. Please sign and return by FAX a copy of this non-binding, unenforceable letter, indicating your approval of this conceptual revision to your purchase offer and your request to have our respective attorneys proceed to amend your purchase offer accordingly.

FORM 10-3

Very truly yours,

[Developer]

[Name]
[Title]

UNDERSTOOD AND AGREED:
This __ day of ___________, 20__.

[Name of major tenant]

By: ________________

Its: ________________

END OF FORM 10-3

OVERVIEW

Chapter 11 provides a letter of intent for confirming a proposed transaction between a developer (or landlord) and a satellite or shop tenant.

FORMS

11-1 Satellite or Shop Tenant Letter of Intent. General Letter of Intent to Enter into Space Lease in Shopping Center.

Chapter 11

Satellite Tenant or Shop Leases

If you would have your hen lay,
you must bear the cackling.
—Edward J. Clode

A form letter of intent and its systematic use by the developer and the developer's leasing team can help in carrying out a successful leasing program. Form 11-1 is a generic letter of intent adapted from a format used in a shopping center development venture with a publicly held company that was the financial partner in a venture for which I was the developer partner. Pursuant to the venture agreement, a signed letter of intent consistent with an agreed form was generally required prior to finally documenting each tenant transaction.

Although Form 11-1 now only barely resembles its original format, this form letter of intent could be further edited to generally outline the terms of virtually any space lease—including the very basic terms of a major tenant transaction—in addition to the standard shop lease for which it is intended.

For additional deal points that you could incorporate into this deal-making document, refer to Chapter 18, "Optional and Alternative Clauses for Lease Proposals."

Form 11-1

General Letter of Intent to Enter into Space Lease in Shopping Center

[Leasing agent or developer stationery]

*[Address to
prospective tenant
____
____
_________________]*

Re: __*[name]*__ Shopping Center
__*[location]*__, __*[state]*__

Dear ______________:

__*[In response to your recent proposal on the above-referenced project,]*__ the owner, ________________ ("Landlord"), desires to indicate its interest in negotiating a lease with __*[you]*__ OR __*[your company]*__ ("Tenant"), on the following general terms and conditions:

1. Premises. Approximately __*[e.g.,* ________ *square foot proposed building XYZ]*__ *OR* __*[*________ *square feet within the XYZ building]*__ (the "premises") located as shown on the attached Exhibit "A".

2. Term. The lease term shall commence __*[*__________, *20*__*]*__ *OR* __*[the earlier of (i)* ___ *days after Landlord tenders the premises to Tenant for commencement of Tenant's tenant improvements or (ii) the date on which Tenant opens for business to the public]*__. The lease term shall be __ years.

3. Minimum Rent. Minimum rent shall be $_____ per rentable square foot ("s.f.") per year __*[for the first year of the lease term, $*_____ *per s.f. per year for the second year of the lease term, $*_____ *per s.f. per year for the* __*[and so forth]*__ *year of the lease term]*__, absolutely net.

Although the following clause is optional, some adjustment to minimum rent is customary. This clause provides for a CPI adjustment and assumes the italicized portion of the preceding paragraph is not used (unless Paragraph 4 is edited to accommodate such fixed-rent years preceding application of the CPI adjustment.)

4. Adjustments to Minimum Rent. Annual minimum rent shall be increased __*[annually]*__ OR __*[every __ years]*__ of the __*[initial]*__ term __*[and any option term]*__ (collectively, the "rental adjustment dates") based upon __ *[e.g., 100% of]*__ any increase in the __*[describe specific consumer price index, e.g., "Consumer Price Index for all Urban Consumers (Los Angeles/Anaheim/ Riverside area)" ("CPI")]*__ occurring from the commencement of the lease term to the lease __*[or option period]*__ rental adjustment date in question. *[Optional cap and floor (between adjustments):]* __*[; provided, however, that in no event shall any increase in the minimum rent on any rental adjustment date exceed an annualized cumulative increase greater than __[e.g., 5]__ % per year or less than __[e.g., 2]__ % per year over the period of years since the preceding rental adjustment date (or, with respect to the first rental adjustment date, over the period of year(s) since the commencement of the lease term)]*__.

> ***Note:*** *The preceding paragraph is designed to allow the user to describe any escalation floors, caps, and other limitations on adjustments. Consider also an adjustment by appraisal toward the end of the lease term; i.e., with "the then current fair market rental value to be determined by independent appraisal." For a sampling of minimum rent adjustment models, refer to Form 18-14, "Tenant Option to Extend Lease Term."*

5. Rent Commencent. Rent shall commence __*[on]*__ OR __*[___ days following]*__ commencement of the lease term.

6. Percentage Rent. In addition to the minimum rent, Tenant shall pay as percentage rent the amount by which __ % of Tenant's gross annual sales made from or upon the premises during each calendar year exceeds the minimum rent.

Optional:

7. Option(s) to Extend Lease Term. __*[Provided Tenant __[shall not have been sent more than two notices of lease non-compliance during Tenant's occupancy and]__ is not in __[material]__ default under the lease from the time of the exercise of any option to extend the term until the commencement of any option term,]*__ Tenant shall have the right to extend the lease term for __*[e.g., two]*__ consecutive periods of __*[e.g., two]*__ years each by giving Landlord written notice of Tenant's election to extend the lease at least __*[e.g., 180]*__ days __*[but not more than 365 days]*__ prior to expiration of the initial term and each extension thereof. Minimum rent during __*[each]*__ option period shall be payable as follows: __*[Describe adjustments—For examples, refer to Chapter 18, Form 18-14, "Tenant Option to Extend Lease Term"]*__.

8. Use. During the lease term, the premises shall be used solely for the purpose of conducting the retail business of __*[narrowly defined use]*__ and for no other use or purpose.

Note: *To control tenant mix and potential assignment and subletting, the developer should attempt to narrowly define the permitted use. Tenant, on the other hand, should attempt to negotiate as broad a use clause as possible.*

9. Trade Name. The business conducted on the premises shall be operated under the trade name ______________.

Note: *Similar to the effect of the use clause, a restrictive trade name provision effectively operates as a "hidden" anti-assignment provision.*

10. Tenant Finish Work. Prior to tendering the premises to Tenant, Landlord shall complete the standard tenant finish work as set forth in Landlord's standard Exhibit "C" Work Letter __*[, a copy of which is attached hereto as Exhibit "B"]*__. Landlord's work shall include a standard storefront; one rear entry door (where applicable); demising party walls that are dry walled, taped, sanded and ready for paint; one toilet facility enclosed by interior partitioned walls; troweled concrete floor; acoustical ceiling; roof mounted heating and air conditioning system; and a separate electric meter. __*[In addition to the Exhibit "C" work, Landlord shall make the following additional specific improvements to the premises: __[describe]__.*

All other work required to make the premises suitable for Tenant's occupancy and operation of its business shall be completed by Tenant at Tenant's sole cost and expense. Tenant's space planning and working drawings shall be submitted to Landlord for review and approval __*[within __ days of lease execution]*__. __*[Tenant will diligently process and obtain building permits for all other required entitlements for Tenant's work not later than ________, 20__]*__.

For additional clauses covering construction and improvement allowances and Tenant's right to recapture construction and fixturing costs from percentage rent, see Chapter 18, "Optional and Alternative Clauses for Lease Proposals," Forms 18-1 and 18-2.

FORM 11-1

11. Parking. Undesignated parking spaces shall not exceed an allocation of one for each __*[e.g., 200]*__ square feet of rentable area.

Be mindful of the tenant's use and the applicable jurisdiction's parking requirement for that use. For example, parking codes governing restaurant tenants—often based upon formulas which consider the total dining area, the number of fixed and moveable seats and the number of employees—may impose a much greater parking burden than a conventional retailing use. In such a case, it may be prudent for the landlord to condition the lease upon governmental approval of a specific required parking count. Not being cautious with respect to this issue may result in the landlord not being able to make a subsequent deal because the parking code cannot be satisfied—even when there is a reciprocal parking agreement. In addition, consider mitigation of potential long-term parking conflicts and the possibility of designating a specific area for tenant employee parking.

12. Signage. Tenant shall have the right, subject to approval by the City of ____________ and Landlord, to construct, at Tenant's cost and expense, mutually-acceptable building identification and parapet elevation signs on the ground floor of Tenant's premises __*[and identification on one free-standing monument sign designated by Landlord]*__. Landlord shall have a right to review and approve Tenant's proposed sign location(s), design and materials for required consistency with the __*[Name]*__ Shopping Center Sign Criteria.

13. Permits for Tenant's Operations. Tenant shall be responsible for obtaining, at Tenant's cost and expense, all permits and authorizations necessary to conduct Tenant's business on the premises, including any permits necessary to install or operate Tenant's signs.

Alternative "A"—Paragraph 14
Right to object to assignment based upon reasonableness standard

14. Assignment and Subletting. Tenant shall neither assign the lease nor sublet all or any portion of the leased premises without obtaining Landlord's prior written consent __*[which consent shall not be unreasonably withheld]*__. *[Be wary of changing case law in this area, and before using, refer to Chapter 18, Form 18-10, "Selected Assignment and Subletting Clauses."]*

OR

Alternative "B"—Paragraph 14
Absolute prohibition

14. No Assignment or Subletting. Tenant shall neither assign the lease nor sublet all or any portion of the leased premises.

Optional:
__. **Limited Right to Sublease.** Notwithstanding the prohibition on assignment and subletting contained in Paragraph __*[e.g., 14]*__, Tenant shall have the right to sublease up to __ % of its space to __*[give specific reasons/ circumstances]*__ subject to precise standards to be negotiated and incorporated into the lease.

End of Paragraph 14—Proceed to Paragraph 15

15. Repairs and Maintenance. The premises and the common areas shall be maintained as follows:

15.1 Premises. In general, Landlord shall repair the roof, exterior walls and structural portions of the shopping center. Tenant shall pay to Landlord Tenant's prorata share __*[insert formula]*__ of the costs of such repairs. Tenant, at Tenant's expense, shall maintain and repair the interior of the premises and the store front, including the plate glass.

15.2 Parking and Common Areas. Landlord shall maintain and repair the shopping center's parking and common areas. Tenant shall pay to Landlord __*[e.g., on a quarterly basis]*__ Tenant's prorata share __*[insert formula]*__ of the cost of maintenance and upkeep of the parking and common areas, including but not limited to repairs, taxes and assessments, public liability and property damage insurance and other appropriate expenses.

15.3 Property Insurance. Property insurance shall be maintained by Landlord and paid for by Tenant on a prorata basis __*[insert formula]*__.

16. Utilities. Tenant shall pay for all water, heat, light, power, telephone and __*[snow and/or trash]*__ removal services and all other services and utilities supplied to the premises.

17. Property Taxes. Tenant shall pay Landlord Tenant's prorata share __*[insert formula]*__ of all real property taxes levied upon and assessed against the shopping center. Tenant shall also pay all taxes on its trade fixtures, leasehold improvements, merchandise and other personal property.

18. Security Deposit. Tenant shall pay Landlord a security deposit of $ ___________ upon execution of the lease.

19. REA. Any lease negotiated between Landlord and Tenant shall be subject to the specific reciprocal easement agreement ("REA") for _____________ Shopping Center and any amendments and supplements to the REA which may be executed from time to time.

20. Financial Statements. Concurrent with the signing of this proposal, Tenant __*[and each of Tenant's guarantor(s)]*__ shall provide Landlord with a current financial statement (prepared and dated within ninety (90) days of the date of the signing of this letter) and financial statements for each of the two (2) years prior to the current fiscal statement year. The lease shall provide that Tenant shall submit to Landlord monthly and annual statements of Tenant's gross receipts. In addition, Tenant shall, at any time during the lease term, upon Landlord's request, provide updated financial statements to Landlord and any actual or potential lender or financial partner then negotiating with Landlord for equity or debt financing. Landlord shall hold such information in confidence, except Landlord may provide any lender, equity partner, or prospective purchaser with the information contained in such statements.

Optional:

__. **Guarantor(s).** __*[Insert name]*__ *("Guarantor") shall]*__ OR __*[name]*__ *and* __*[name]*__ *("Guarantors") shall jointly and severally]*__ guarantee all Tenant's obligations to Landlord under the lease __*[together with interest accrued thereon and costs of collection thereof, including reasonable attorney's fees,]*__ in accordance with a specific, commercial form guaranty agreement to be entered into between Landlord and Guarantor(s) concurrent with execution of the lease.

Optional:

__. **Release of Guarantee.** __*[Guarantor(s)]*__ shall be released from liability under the guaranty when (i) the net worth of Tenant, as shown on audited financial statements of Tenant prepared by an independent certified public accountant, is greater than $________ for __*[e.g., 2]*__ consecutive fiscal years of Tenant's operations and (ii) Tenant's net after tax profits for each of the same two fiscal years, as shown on such financial statements, is greater than $____________. __*[Guarantor(s)]*__, however, shall remain liable under the guaranty for breaches of the lease occurring before the guaranty release date.

__. **[Other].** *[Include any other key deal points, e.g., brokerage commission(s), co-tenancy clause, radius clause, expansion, relocation or termination rights, exclusives, recapture of certain operating costs from percentage rent, special CAM or property tax allocations or issues, payment of annual environmental monitoring costs such as for a dry cleaner, or other provisions unique to the transaction. See Chapter 18, "Optional and Alternative Clauses for Lease Proposals," for examples.]*

21. Non-binding Letter; Rights Contingent Upon Signed Lease. This letter constitutes merely an invitation to Tenant to negotiate a lease of the premises described above on the general terms and conditions herein. No contract between the parties will exist unless or until the parties have signed a complete, final lease agreement and any other required documentation containing all essential terms of the proposed transaction. The parties acknowledge that they have not set forth herein nor agreed upon all essential lease terms.

22. Time Limit. This proposal shall remain open until 5:00 p.m. _______, 20__ (the "deadline"). If this letter has not been accepted in writing by Tenant and returned to Landlord by the deadline, this proposal shall be deemed automatically revoked and Landlord may continue to offer the premises for lease to other parties without any obligation to Tenant, even if the parties are engaged in good faith negotiations for the lease of the premises as of the deadline. If this letter is accepted in writing by Tenant on or before the deadline, Landlord and Tenant shall have until __*[insert a later date]*__, 20__ in which to negotiate and sign a binding lease agreement and all other required documentation.

23. Contingency. The lease will be contingent upon the groundbreaking of _____________ Shopping Center within __ months from commencement of the lease term.

24. Conditions. This non-binding proposal is subject to the following approvals:

24.__ Senior Officers. Approval by the senior officers of Landlord by __________, 20__;

24.__ Board of Directors. Approval of the Board of Directors of __*[e.g., XYZ Corp., Landlord's financial partner,]*__ by __________, 20__; and

24.__ Final Lease Documentation. Landlord and Tenant's execution of all final lease documentation by ___________, 20__.

If the foregoing meets with your approval, please so indicate by executing a copy and returning it to me within the time period provided above. Upon its timely receipt, we will begin to prepare the lease and other necessary documentation.

Very truly yours,

[Leasing Agent or Developer]

UNDERSTOOD AND AGREED BY "TENANT"
This __ day of ___________, 20__.

[Name of Tenant]

By: ________________

Its: ________________

[Include Developer's signature block if letter is prepared on Leasing Agent stationery and signed by Leasing Agent]
UNDERSTOOD AND AGREED BY "LANDLORD"
This __ day of ___________, 20__.

[Name of Landlord]

By: ________________

Its: ________________

Exhibit "A"
[Attach plan showing location of leased premises]

Exhibit "B"
[Consider attaching Landlord's standard Exhibit "C" work letter]

END OF FORM 11-1

OVERVIEW

Chapter 12 addresses the use of a deal-making document to confirm the proposed sale of an outparcel or "pad" to a retailer for the retailer's construction of a free-standing building. Form 12-1 is a letter of intent to sell a pad to a conventional fast-food restaurant with a drive-through. Form 12-2 provides for the creation and sale of a land parcel to a quasi-retail "office" user perceived to be a significant customer draw to a community center. In this instance, while providing customer visibility from the main street, the parcel is configured to locate the user's building and parking within a low-rise office component behind the center's retail core.

FORMS

12-1 Sale of Unimproved Building Pad to Typical Retailer. Letter of Intent to Sell Proposed Outparcel to Fast-Food Chain for Chain's Construction of Free-Standing Fast-Food Restaurant and Drive-Through.

12-2 Sale of Unimproved Building Pad to Desirable "Non-Retailer." Letter of Intent to Create and Sell 1.5 Acre "Office" Site for Service Tenant Building and Parking behind Retail Core of Shopping Center; Development Approvals and Construction to Occur Concurrent with Shopping Center.

Chapter 12

Pad or Outparcel Sales to a Proposed Tenant

Listen to the river and you'll catch a trout.
–Irish proverb

Form 12-1 confirms the major business points of a proposed outparcel or "pad" sale to a major fast-food chain for the chain's construction of a fast-food restaurant with a drive-through. The land sale price is fixed and provides that the developer complete all site improvements up to an agreed "work of improvement" line with utility lines provided to a point in the drive-through footprint. The "tenant" is obligated to complete construction of all site improvements and the building within the "work of improvement" line (which encompasses the drive-through)

The letter of intent stage of an outparcel sale demands deliberate, pragmatic thinking. Carefully consider what on- and off-site improvements need to be completed on and surrounding the subject outparcel and which party should be responsible for which particular improvements. Anticipate the timing and effect of adjacent construction and how possible changes in the timing of such construction could affect the transaction under negotiation. Be thoughtful and creative in resolving these issues. Many of the problems that arise in outparcel sales can be readily avoided if, at the beginning of the transaction, the parties deliberate and creatively work out solutions to potential problems. Try to segregate the developer's and the tenant purchaser's construction responsibilities in a way that practically takes into account the physical aspects of the required improvements.

For example, why should the developer pave only to a midpoint of a driveway entrance (e.g., stopping at the tenant's legal parcel line)—requiring tenant's asphalt contractor to feather into it—when the paving responsibility could end with a specified curb or gutter? Similarly, it rarely makes sense to have the outparcel tenant responsible for installing a single parking lot light standard or two when an agreement could be made for the developer's contractor to install

all parking lot lighting and an appropriate reimbursement or other cooperative economic arrangement worked out with the tenant.

Develop skill in identifying and accommodating all potential construction and coordination problems at the outset of the transaction. Be able to recognize elements of the dialogue with the tenant that are workable and those that are not and then be able to piece together and integrate all such issues in a single letter of intent. For example, Form 12-1 confirms the acceptability of the tenant's revision of the site plan, yet also identifies particular provisions of the tenant's form purchase agreement requiring changes. It is helpful to the deal makers, senior management and their attorneys if the letter of intent covers all significant matters under negotiation. The astute deal maker is consistently able to identify and weave diverse economic, construction, entitlement, and human factors into a comprehensive, practical solution that works.

In addition, because the outparcel is being purchased by the tenant, consideration must be given to the proposed transaction's effect on the center's reciprocal easement agreement ("REA"). In most cases, the tenant's operation will be subject to the common area assessment, management and other reciprocal easement obligations and rights that govern other tenants in the shopping center. Unfortunately, some major fast-food and dinner-house chains operate from the premise that, because they are purchasing an outparcel lot, their operation is separate from the center and consequently need not be subject to such controls and charges. At least in California, many jurisdictions will require that all free-standing pad operators be subject to an REA and its perceived operating and maintenance benefits to the overall center. Consider addressing from the outset the purchaser's obligation to be subject to the REA and any other reasonable operating and management rules and obligations designed to benefit the entire center.

Particularly for the more complex outparcel sale, provisions within the anchor tenant parcel sale Form 10-1 could be considered. Review the topics in Chapter 17, "Optional and Alternative Clauses for Purchase and Sale Proposals," for additional clauses.

Form 12-1

Letter of Intent to Sell Proposed Outparcel to Fast-Food Chain for Chain's Construction of Free-Standing Fast-Food Restaurant and Drive-Through

[Date]

[Name and address of fast food chain real estate representative _
____
___________________*]*

Ref: __*[Name of shopping center]*__
Re: __*[Name of fast food tenant]*__ Proposed Parcel Purchase

Dear ________:

This letter will serve to confirm the conceptual approval of __*[name of development company]*__ ("Developer") to the recent offer of __*[name of fast food tenant]*__ ("Tenant") to purchase Parcel No. __*[e.g., 4]*__ (the "parcel") on the following terms and conditions:

1. Parcel Description. *[Note: Technically, the term "lot" would be inserted in place of the term "parcel" if a "tract" map were being processed rather than a "parcel" map.]* Parcel ___ on the proposed, unrecorded final __*[Parcel]*__ OR __*[Tract]*__ Map, No. _____, as shown on the photocopy attached hereto as Exhibit "A", which generally conforms to the __*[insert name of architect]*__ city-approved shopping center site plan dated _______, 20__ bearing a last revision date of _________, 20__ (the "tentative site plan"), a copy of which is attached hereto as Exhibit "__*[B]*__". The parcel contains approximately ______ square feet __*[e.g., but may be reduced to approximately ________ square feet after the anticipated required dedication for road and highway uses]*__.

> ***Note:*** *The parcel size will generally be configured based upon the purchasing tenant's impact area. Most developer's would initiate negotiations applying the land area required by tenant to operate in a free-standing location; i.e., not within an integrated shopping center.*

FORM 12-1

Optional:

The dimensions of the parcel may be changed in the course of obtaining governmental approvals for development of the parcel. Tenant hereby approves and consents to such changes, provided no such change materially or adversely affects Tenant's ability to conduct its business on the premises.

Although center parking will generally be on a reciprocal basis, be certain that Developer and Tenant are both operating under the same assumptions regarding building size and the governmentally imposed parking burden.

2. Building Description. Tenant shall build its standard __*[describe prototype]*__ fast food restaurant building on the parcel. The building shall not be larger than _______ square feet __*[e.g., with not more than _____ square feet of interior dining area and, in accordance with applicable parking codes, require not more than ____ total parking stalls]*__. *[Ideally, attach a copy of the building's floor plan:]* __*[A copy of the building's floor plan is attached hereto as Exhibit "__[C]__"]*__.

One example of a defined use:

3. Use. Tenant shall operate a ________ restaurant on the parcel. The restaurant shall be run in a first-class manner for restaurants engaged in a similar type of business in __________ County, __*[state]*__.

In this example, Developer, at Developer's expense, completes all on-site improvements up to a negotiated "work of improvement line" on the subject parcel and the purchasing Tenant completes all other improvements on the parcel:

4. Price. The parcel purchase price shall be *[absolute price:]* __*[insert price ($_______)]*__ *OR [per square foot price:]* __*[$____ per square foot multiplied by the final net land area of the parcel, subject to a maximum price of $_________ and a minimum price of $_________]*__ payable in cash at time of closing.

Alternative "A"—Paragraph 5
Limited parcel improvements contributed by Developer

In a conventional approach, Developer, at Developer's expense, completes all off-site improvements and all on-site improvements up to a negotiated "work of improvement line" on the subject parcel. The purchasing Tenant completes all other improvements on the parcel. The sale price economics take into account Developer's ob-

ligation to make limited improvements to the parcel (i.e., improvements to the area inside the parcel lines but outside the parcel's negotiated "work of improvement" line).

5. Parcel Improvements. The parcel purchase price shall include Developer's completion of the on- and off-site construction improvements finished up to the "work of improvement line" (as shown on the copy of the tentative site plan which has been enlarged and cropped to show only the parcel and its proposed improvements, attached hereto as Exhibit "__*[D]*__") together with required utility lines provided to a point in the drive-through footprint acceptable to Developer and Tenant. Tenant will pay for the construction of its building and drive-through lane, patio area, trash enclosure and all other on-site improvements on the parcel required for Tenant's use, including, but not limited to, paving, curbs and gutters, landscaping and signage. *[Any exceptions? For example:]* __*[The trash enclosure shall be located in the city-required location indicated on Exhibit "__[e.g., E]__"]__ and paid for and maintained by Tenant even though such location is not within the "work of improvement" line]__.*

OR

Alternative "B"—Paragraph 5
Only nominal parcel improvements are made by Developer without reimbursement; bulk of parcel improvements are paid for by Tenant—payable as costs are incurred by Developer's contractor

In this example, Developer is responsible only for the cost of rough grading the parcel and providing limited utility work. Although Developer's contractor constructs all on- and off-site improvements outside the "work of improvement line", Tenant is obligated to pay Developer's contractor the cost of Tenant's share of on- and off-site improvements. Also, like the preceding Alternative "A", Tenant is obligated to construct and pay for all parcel improvements within the "work of improvement line". Unlike Alternative "A", however, Alternative "B" specifically requires Tenant to pay a prorata share of governmental development fees. (If Alternative "A" is used, Paragraph 6, below, could be edited to include this obligation.) Alternatives "A" and "B" illustrate only some of the many ways improvement costs and governmental fees could be allocated between a developer and a parcel purchaser.

FORM 12-1

5. Parcel Improvements. __*[Tenant]*__ will pay all costs and expenses attributable to improvement of the parcel, including on- and off-site improvements, development fees, bonds and permits, with the exception that (a) the parcel will be rough graded by Developer at Developer's expense concurrent with the rough grading of the shopping center and (b) Developer will provide __*[e.g., sweeps of electrical and telephone conduit to the site parcel line and sewer and water laterals five feet inside the parcel line]*__.

5.1 On-site Improvement Costs. __*[Tenant]*__ will construct its own building and drive-through lane, patio area __*[, trash enclosure]*__ and all other on-site improvements within the "work of improvement line" shown on Exhibit "__*[D]*__". On-site improvements outside the "work of improvement line" but within the parcel will be constructed by Developer's contractor and paid for by __*[Tenant]*__. Tenant shall pay for such on-site improvements at Developer's cost. Where such costs are not precisely known, Tenant shall pay a reasonable allocation of the prorata cost of each specific applicable on-site improvement relative to the total square footage of like on-site work for the entire project. For example, Tenant shall be charged for paving, curb and gutter, parking lot lighting, landscaping, and the like, based upon rationally and objectively applied linear or square footage apportionment.

5.2 Off-Site Improvement Costs. __*[Off-site improvements will be constructed by Developer's contractor and]*__ __*[Tenant]*__ shall pay its prorata share of applicable street improvements, street lights, utility connection charges, fire hydrants, and other off-site assessments and infrastructure charges applicable to the development of the shopping center ("off-site improvement costs"). Tenant's prorata share of off-site improvement costs shall be that percentage of total off-site improvement costs __*[which the land area of the site (_______square feet) bears to the net land area of the entire shopping center (________square feet)*__ __*[, which portion is approximately __ % of total off-site costs]*__ OR __*[which the total linear street frontage of the site (________ feet) bears to the total linear street frontage of the entire shopping center (________ feet)*__ __*[, which portion is approximately __ % of total off-site costs]*__ OR __*[devise an equitable combination of both such factors or another formula]*__.

Allocating an equitable off-site burden to a tenant is much easier if cost estimates are known. Unfortunately, such land sale transactions are often negotiated before reliable construction cost information is known. But it usually helps to convey what is known. For example:

__[Developer has been informed by its project architect and received an informal estimate from its proposed general contractor that the total of all on- and off-site work (including landscaping and asphalt parking areas) should not exceed $__________ per square foot of land area of the shopping center. Tentative street and utility improvement plans are now at the City of __[city]__ in final plan check]__.

5.3 Governmental Development Fees. *__[Tenant]__* shall pay a prorata share of all *__[e.g., county]__* development fees (gross fees less credits) applicable to the development of the shopping center. Tenant's prorata share of such development fees shall be determined in the same manner (resulting in the same percentage share) as Tenant's prorata share of off-site improvement costs *__[, as described in the preceding paragraph]__*.

End of Alternatives "A" and "B" to Paragraph 5
—Continue to Paragraph 6

6. Building Fees and Permits. Tenant will independently pay for all of its own governmental processing fees and entitlement costs required to obtain governmental approvals and building permits for Tenant's intended use of the parcel.

Often the conceptual agreement is based upon a revision to an original site plan, for example:

7. Building Location on the Parcel. Your proposed revision to the tentative site plan, as contained in your conceptual site plan prepared by *__[name of architect or other description]__* dated ______, 20__ and forwarded along with your offer dated ________, 20__ is attached hereto as Exhibit "*__[D-1]__*" and is acceptable to Developer subject to *__[City]__* approval.

8. Purchase Agreement. Tenant's purchase of the parcel shall be accomplished *__[through an escrow at ______________]__* in accordance with a parcel purchase and sale agreement *__[and escrow instructions]__* ("Purchase Agreement") to be negotiated in accordance with the general terms and conditions outlined in this letter of intent.

8.1 Closing. The *__[closing]__ OR __[close of escrow (the "closing")]__* shall take place, subject to satisfaction of all of the conditions contained in the Purchase Agreement, not later than *__[e.g., ten business days]__* after (i) recordation of the final *__[e.g., parcel map]__*, (ii) issuance of all governmental approvals required to allow Developer to construct all required on- and off-site improvements, (iii) issuance of permits for construction of Tenant's

FORM 12-1

building and Tenant's parcel improvements, and (iv) __*[describe any other events]*__, but in no event later than ________, 20__ (the "Scheduled Closing Date"). Each party will be obligated to diligently complete its duties required to timely close the transaction.

If, after a date certain, as a condition to keeping the escrow or transaction open, (i) funds are to be released by Tenant to Developer or (ii) the purchase price of the parcel is to escalate, the following paragraph can be edited to provide for periodic cash advances by Tenant or a price escalation from the Scheduled Closing Date through the actual, extended closing.

8.2 Financial Adjustments for Extended Closing. If required approvals are delayed beyond the Scheduled Closing Date by more than __ days for reasons other than Developer's failure to timely process and cooperate in the processing of such matters, __*[and all other contingencies to closing have been satisfied or waived by Tenant,]*__ in order to compensate Developer for Developer's costs in controlling the parcel,

Alternative "A"
Tenant cash advance

Tenant shall pay Developer $______ per __*[month]*__ __*[from the end of said __ -day period]*__ OR __*[from the Scheduled Closing Date]*__ until the actual closing, which in no event shall be later than ______, 20__. Such __*[monthly]*__ payments __*[shall/shall not]*__ be applicable to the parcel purchase price and shall be forfeited by Tenant if Tenant fails to close.

OR

Alternative "B"
Purchase price escalation

the parcel purchase price shall increase at the rate of __ % per month __*[from the end of said __ -day period]*__ OR __*[from the Scheduled Closing Date]*__ until the actual closing, which in no event shall be later than ______, 20__.

Occasionally a tenant will be willing to close its site purchase before entitlements are issued, provided the developer agrees to repurchase the subject parcel it the tenant is ultimately unable to obtain required entitlements. The following optional tenant-oriented provision gives the tenant purchaser a limited right to re-sell the subject parcel back to Developer if Tenant is unable to obtain required entitlements.

Optional provision used by developer to accelerate sale closing (prior to issuance of Tenant's entitlements):

__. **Repurchase Agreement.** In the event Tenant closes its purchase of the parcel before all required building and other permits necessary to construct Tenant's improvements are issued and Tenant is diligent but unable to obtain all such required permits within __*[e.g., one]*__ year after closing, Tenant may in such event elect to require Developer to repurchase the parcel on the same terms and conditions relating to price and title as when Developer sold the parcel to Tenant. __*[Similarly, during the __[e.g., one]__ year period following Tenant's closing of the parcel purchase, if Developer is unable to provide Tenant with reasonable assurance that the remainder of the center will be constructed substantially concurrent with Tenant's improvement of Tenant's parcel, Tenant may elect to require Developer to repurchase Tenant's parcel under like terms and conditions]*__.

9. Title Insurance. At closing, Developer will provide Tenant a __*[See Appendix A, Form A-1]*__ of title insurance. __*[Any additional premium for __[e.g., an ALTA Extended Owner's Policy]__, if required by Tenant, will be paid by Tenant]*__.

10. Closing Costs. __*[All escrow charges shall be shared equally by Developer and Tenant and]*__ [A]ll __*[other]*__ closing costs not specifically provided for in other provisions of this letter of intent shall be shared in the manner customary in ___________ county, __*[state]*__.

FORM 12-1

__Note:__ Refer to Form 17-4, "Allocation of Specific Purchase and Sale Transaction Costs", for an alternative, more comprehensive example.

11. Signage and Elevations. *[Sign rights and color and material coordination can be major, time-consuming issues. Why not specify at the outset for Tenant's benefit what will be required? Such an approach may take a bit more time at the outset but may save substantial time, money and aggravation overall. For example:]* Tenant will comply with the __*[name of center]*__ sign criteria, including the colors and materials schedule approved for the center by the __*[e.g., name of city]*__ __*[e.g., Architectural Commission]*__, a copy of which is attached as Exhibit "__*[F]*__". In addition, no Tenant identification on either of the __*[e.g., two]*__ major center identification signs will be allowed. *[Note any other unique issues, for example:]* __*[Further, the City of ________* *has required that the "Center Identification Sign" located in the northwest corner of Parcel __ must be constructed and maintained on the subject parcel (and not in the adjacent right of way), as indicated in the drawing attached hereto as Exhibit "__[G]__". Tenant agrees to such relocation of the Center Identification Sign]__.*

12. Taxes and Common Area Expense. The reciprocal easement agreement ("REA") will require that Tenant pay all real property taxes levied against Tenant's parcel. In addition, Tenant will pay its prorata share of common area insurance and maintenance expense, plus a *__[e.g., 10% or 15% (varies regionally)]__* administrative fee. Tenant's prorata share of common area charges will be determined by multiplying the total of such common area charges by the ratio by which Tenant's building square footage bears to the overall square footage of the center *__[(excluding the __[supermarket]__ mezzanine)]__. __[(However, because Tenant will be directly paying all real property taxes levied against the parcel, Tenant will not be obligated to pay common area real property taxes.)]__*

13. Documentation. This transaction is subject to approval of the various documents to be negotiated and signed by the parties. *[Make reference to any unacceptable provisions in Tenant's proposal. For example:] __[Among other things, please note that the ________ clause and the ______ provision contained in Tenant's standard __[e.g., Purchase and Sale Agreement]__ are not acceptable because __[describe reasoning]__.*

14. Non-binding Letter; Rights Contingent Upon Signed Purchase Agreement. This letter constitutes merely an invitation to Tenant to negotiate a comprehensive Purchase Agreement on the general terms and conditions described herein. No contract between the parties will exist unless or until the parties have signed the Purchase Agreement containing all essential terms of the proposed transaction. The parties acknowledge that they have not set forth herein nor agreed upon all essential terms of the Purchase Agreement. This proposal, however, shall remain open until 5:00 p.m. _______, 20__. If this letter has not been accepted in writing by Tenant by such date, this proposal shall be deemed automatically revoked. If this letter is accepted in writing by Tenant on or before such date, Developer and Tenant shall have until ______, 20__ in which to negotiate and sign a binding Purchase and Agreement.

15. Contingencies. The Purchase Agreement will be contingent upon the following:

15.1 Map Recordation; Entitlements. Recordation of the __*[parcel]*__ OR __*[tract]*__ map and issuance of all entitlements to construct all on- and off-site improvements and the initial shop building phase of __*[name]*__ Shopping Center within __ months following execution of the Purchase Agreement.

15.2 Financing. Developer shall have until _______, 20__ in which to obtain a binding __*[e.g., construction/permanent]*__ loan to __*[e.g. construct the shopping center, including Developer's share of the on- and off-site improvements described in this letter]*__. If Developer is unable to obtain financing in form satisfactory to Developer by _______, 20__, Developer shall have the right to terminate the proposed parcel sale by giving written notice of termination to Tenant.

16. Conditions. This non-binding proposal is subject to the following approvals:

16.__ Senior Officers. Approval by the senior officers of Developer by _________, 20__;

16.__ Board of Directors. Approval of the Board of Directors of __*[e.g., Developer's financial partner,]*__ by _______, 20__; and

16.__ Final Purchase Agreement. Developer and Tenant's execution of all final purchase documentation not later than _______, 20__.

FORM 12-1

Consider making any additional comments indicating progress to date to build Tenant's confidence that the transaction will be consummated. For example:

__[City Council approval for the development has been obtained, including a conditional use permit approval allowing a drive-through restaurant on __[e.g., the subject fast food parcel]__. The final grading plan is scheduled to be deposited for city plan check by ________, 20__]__.

Please sign and return a copy of this non-binding letter not later than ________, 20__, indicating your approval of the above-referenced revisions. Assuming these points are approved, our legal counsel will then proceed to amend your purchase offer consistent with this letter.

Very truly yours,

[Developer]
By: ____________________

Its: ____________________

UNDERSTOOD AND AGREED:
This __ day of __________, 20__.

[Name of Tenant]

By: ________________

Its: ________________

Exhibit "A"
[Copy of proposed parcel or subdivision map depicting Tenant's proposed parcel (the "parcel")]

Exhibit "B"
[Copy of tentative site plan depicting entire shopping center and Tenant's proposed parcel with proposed building and site improvements]

Exhibit "C"
[Ideally, attach a copy of the building's floor plan (showing seating and dining area for evaluation of parking requirement)]

Exhibit "D"
[Copy of tentative site plan enlarged to depict parcel and "work of improvement" line showing limits of Developer's improvement obligation (and in this case, Tenant's revised site plan drawing as Exhibit "D-1")]

Exhibit "E"
[Example: Drawing of city-required trash location]

Exhibit "F"
[Optional: Copy of __[name of center]__ sign criteria]

Exhibit "G"
[Example: Revised location of "Center Identification Sign"]

END OF FORM 12-1

Form 12.2 was derived from a proposed parcel sale to a well-known, financially strong service tenant that became interested in locating within a project just as the site plan was being "solidified" for final submittal to the city. The tenant wanted to purchase 1.5 acres for construction of a 12,000 square foot two-story building. Although technically an office user, the potential tenant's service facility would have created a substantial draw for the community center and its master-planned adjacent office component.

To make such a deal work, the developer must overcome long-term parking conflicts, resistance by anchor tenants, and other site-planning problems. In this case, although the tenant demanded visibility from the main street, the key to making the deal work was the tenant's willingness to locate "behind" the center, with frontage and access off a third street running just behind the center. A proposed six-plex theater was similarly physically segregated from the retail core but actually a synergistic part of the overall community complex. This solution also benefitted the remaining five adjacent acres behind the center, which were owned by the joint venture financial partner and zoned for office use and master-planned concurrently with the retail center. The premise was that this popular service facility would serve as a sort of "quasi-anchor" to both the retail and the office component of the project.

Consent by the supermarket and other major tenants will typically be required to approve reconfiguration of the center's site plan and to allow development of a two-story building within the land area described in the supermarket lease and/or the reciprocal easement agreement as "the shopping center." In this case, however, consent and lease modifications were obtained from controlling majors because the proposed tenant's building location and attributable parking area were really not functionally within the "center." Paragraph 3, "Development Coordination and Preconstruction Costs," attempts to create a cooperative work effort and outlines the tenant's duties to revise or prepare applicable on- and off-site plans. Paragraph 4, "Construction Coordination," provides a rational approach to allocating on- and off-site costs attributable to the tenant's parcel for payment by the tenant.

This form is included to assist your in making a transaction with an atypical or "non-retailing" tenant, the inclusion of which—subject to prudent site planning—may serve as a beneficial customer draw to a suburban center or mixed-use project.

Form 12-2

Letter of Intent to Create and Sell 1.5 Acre "Office" Site for Service Tenant Building and Parking behind Retail Core of Shopping Center; Development Approvals and Construction to Occur Concurrent with Shopping Center

[Date]

[Name and address of
"retail-compatible" office
user ______________
____
______________*]*

Ref: __*[name]*__ Shopping Center
__*[location]*__
__*[city]*__, __*[state]*__

Dear ________:

__*[At our last meeting you requested an outline of the terms by which* __*[name of tenant]*__ *could acquire a building site within* __*[name]*__ *Shopping Center (the "center") now under development]*__. This letter will confirm the terms and conditions whereby __*[name of joint venture partnership]*__, a joint venture development partnership comprised of ______________ as the financial partner and ______________, as the developer or "Managing Venturer" (which partnership is referred to as "Developer") proposes to sell approximately __*[e.g., 1.5]*__ acres within the center to __*[name of tenant]*__ ("Tenant").

As a result of our discussions, Developer is prepared to reduce the sales price to $_____ per square foot, all cash at close of escrow, provided a purchase escrow is promptly opened on the following summarized terms and conditions:

1. Site Configuration; Building Location. The unimproved land parcel (the "site") to be purchased by Tenant shall consist of approximately __*[e.g., 1.5]*__ acres. The general location of the site is designated on the preliminary site plan of the center prepared by ______________, architects, last revised ________, 20__ (the "site plan") and attached hereto as Exhibit "A". The parties will attempt to alter the site plan to provide the site with __*[e.g., visibility from* __________ *Boulevard [the main street] and approximately* ___ *feet*

FORM 12-2

of frontage on ____________ Road to accommodate Tenant's __[e.g., 12,000]__ square foot two-story building and __[approximately __[e.g., 110]__ parking stalls]__ OR __[sufficient parking as required by local codes]__. __[The overall objective in designing a mutually-acceptable site shall be to secure Tenant a window of visibility from ________ Boulevard yet, at the same time, design Tenant's street access, landscaping and parking so that parking for Tenant's patrons and employees will occur on site and not conflict with or burden adjacent retailers' parking]__.

The exact location and dimensions of the site shall be subject to the approval of Tenant and Developer *__[during escrow]__ OR __[before opening of escrow]__*. As a further condition, the written approval of *__[insert name(s) of any anchor tenant(s) having a right to approve such a modification to the site plan, e.g., name of supermarket chain]__* in the form of *__[e.g., a final executed lease amendment]__* signed by *__[e.g., name of supermarket chain]__* and Developer "incorporating" the configuration of the proposed site into the shopping center site plan previously approved by *__[e.g., name of supermarket tenant]__* shall be required. *__[(Please note, however, that the regional real estate representative of __[e.g., name of supermarket tenant]__ has verbally approved the attached tentative site plan.)]__*

2. Price. The purchase price shall be $_____ per square foot of unimproved land area actually purchased payable all cash at closing. Assuming the approved site consists of exactly *__[e.g., 1.5]__* acres, the purchase price would be $____________, i.e., $_____ per square foot times *__[e.g., 63,340]__* square feet.

3. Development Coordination and Pre-construction Costs. Assuming timely agreement among Tenant, Developer and *__[name of supermarket anchor]__* concerning the configuration of the site (and the building location, parking layout, curb cuts, and other proposed improvements), Developer will use its best efforts to obtain those entitlements for development of the site which can be obtained concurrent with Developer's processing of governmental approvals for the entire shopping center.

3.1 Developer's Pre-construction Submittals and Work Product. It is anticipated that Developer will file, at Developer's cost, for the entire shopping center, *__[e.g., the required environmental documentation to obtain a negative declaration, an application for site plan review, an application for Architectural Commission Review (Tenant to timely supply, at its own expense, elevations and preliminary plans for its proposed building) and the required Parcel Map]__*.

Developer has completed certain soils tests, topographic surveys, tentative grading plans, street improvement and sewer plans, all of which will be made available without charge to Tenant upon Tenant's request.

3.2 Tenant's Pre-construction Work. Tenant will promptly prepare, at Tenant's own cost and expense, all engineering and architectural plans necessary to modify Developer's existing plans and to provide for Tenant's improvements to and occupancy of the site. In particular, Tenant shall pay the cost of any modifications to __*[e.g., existing street improvement plans and utility plans]*__ necessitated by specifically locating Tenant's building within the project. Except for the above-referenced processing steps in which Developer will accommodate Tenant by submitting Tenant's plans for the site concurrent with Developer's governmental submittal for the entire shopping center, Tenant shall pay for all other development costs concerning the development of Tenant's site __*[e.g., including, but not limited to, Tenant's grading plan, building plans and permits, landscape plan and the like]*__.

Nevertheless, Developer will cooperate with Tenant to provide Tenant with names of consultants and documentation within Developer's files to aid Tenant in completing Tenant's work efficiently and economically.

4. Construction Coordination. As set forth above, it is anticipated that the site will be developed and constructed in conjunction with Developer's development of the center. Tenant and Developer will reasonably cooperate with one another to concurrently bid and construct on- and off-site improvements.

FORM 12-2

4.1 On-site Improvement Costs. __*[Tenant]*__ will construct its own building and all other on-site improvements within the "work of improvement line" shown on the sketched, preliminary plan for the site, Exhibit "__*[B]*__". On-site improvements outside the "work of improvement line" but within the parcel will be constructed by Developer's contractor and paid for by __*[Tenant]*__. Tenant shall pay for such on-site improvements at Developer's cost. Where such costs are not precisely known, Tenant shall pay a reasonable allocation of the prorata cost of each specific applicable on-site improvement relative to the total square footage of like on-site work for the entire project. For example, Tenant shall be charged for paving, curb and gutter, parking lot lighting, landscaping, and the like, based upon rationally and objectively applied linear or square footage apportionment.

4.2 Off-site Improvement Costs. __*[Tenant]*__ shall pay its prorata share of applicable street improvements, street lights, utility connection charges, fire hydrants, and other off-site assessments and infrastructure charges applicable to the development of the shopping center ("off-site improvement costs"). Tenant's prorata share of off-site improvement costs shall be that percentage of total off-site improvement costs __*[which the land area of the site (_______square feet) bears to the net land area of the entire shopping center (________square feet)* __*[, which portion is approximately* __ *% of total off-site costs]*__ OR __*[which the total linear street frontage of the site (________ feet) bears to the total linear street frontage of the entire shopping center (________ feet)* __*[, which portion is approximately* __ *% of total off-site costs]*__ OR __*[devise an equitable combination of both such factors or another formula]*__.

4.3 Governmental Development Fees. __*[Tenant]*__ shall pay a prorata share of all __*[e.g., county]*__ development fees (gross fees less credits) applicable to the development of the shopping center. Tenant's prorata share of such development fees shall be determined in the same manner (resulting in the same percentage share) as Tenant's prorata share of off-site improvement costs __*[, as described in the preceding paragraph]*__.

4.4 Building Fees and Permits. __*[Tenant]*__, however, will independently pay for all of its own governmental processing fees, applications, plan check fees, building permits and other governmental costs to obtain building permits for Tenant's intended use of the site.

5. Reciprocal Easement Agreement. The City of __________ requires that the site and the contiguous acreage shown on the tentative site plan be developed as an "integrated commercial center."

A reciprocal easement agreement ("REA") prepared in a form acceptable to __*[e.g., the City Attorney, Planning Director, Developer]*__ __*[and Tenant]*__ will be recorded against the site and the center to ensure reciprocal vehicular and pedestrian access and circulation, vehicular parking, and maintenance of all parking and landscaped areas. The REA will

Alternative "A"—Continuation
Developer provides site CAM and charges Tenant

require that Tenant pay its prorata cost of common area maintenance charges plus an administrative fee of __*[10]*__ % of such costs ("CAM"). Tenant's CAM charge shall be calculated by dividing the land area of the site by the entire land area of the shopping center and then multiplying such percentage by the total CAM for the entire shopping center. __*[However, because the site* *will become a separate legal parcel owned by Tenant (containing Tenant's building and all Tenant's required parking) for which Tenant is wholly responsible for its real estate taxes, Tenant shall not be allocated real property taxes within Tenant's CAM charges]*__.

OR

Alternative "B"—Continuation
Tenant maintains site independently (generally not recommended)

allow Tenant, however, to elect to maintain and insure the site at its own cost and expense rather than reimbursing Developer for Tenant's prorata share of such costs. In return for Tenant's right to independently maintain its site, the REA will require tenant to continuously meet the management quality standards applicable to the entire center.

AND

Optional continuation: Will the REA include architectural controls?

In addition, the REA will require Tenant to develop and maintain the site in conformity with the general architectural theme of the center. Accordingly, Developer will have the right to approve preliminary architectural and landscape plans. The REA will avoid strict "architectural control" approval rights but will assure initial and future development of the site in conformity with the overall general architectural theme of the center.

6. Purchase Agreement. Tenant's purchase of the site shall be accomplished __*[through an escrow at ____________]*__ in accordance with a parcel purchase and sale agreement __*[and escrow instructions]*__ ("Purchase Agreement") to be negotiated in accordance with the general terms and conditions outlined in this letter of intent.

6.1 Closing. The __*[closing]*__ OR __*[close of escrow (the "closing")]*__ shall take place, subject to satisfaction of all of the conditions contained in the Purchase Agreement, not later than __*[e.g., ten business days]*__ after (i) recordation of the final __*[e.g., parcel map]*__ legally creating the site, (ii) issuance of all governmental approvals and permits required to allow construction of all required on- and off-site improvements and Tenant's building, and (iii) __*[describe any other events]*__, but in no event later than _______, 20__ (the "Scheduled Closing Date"). Each party will be obligated to diligently complete its duties required to timely close the transaction. __*[We anticipate that construction of the center and your improvements could commence in about ___ months]*__.

If, after a certain date, as a condition to keeping the escrow or transaction open, (i) funds are to be released by Tenant to Developer or (ii) the purchase price of Tenant's site is to escalate, the following paragraph can be edited to provide for periodic cash advances by Tenant or a price escalation from the Scheduled Closing Date through the actual, extended closing.

6.2 Financial Adjustments for Extended Closing. If required approvals are delayed beyond the Scheduled Closing Date by more than __ days for reasons other than Developer's failure to timely process and cooperate in the processing of such matters, __*[and all other contingencies to closing have been satisfied or waived by Tenant,]*__ in order to compensate Developer for Developer's costs in controlling the site,

Alternative "A"
Tenant cash advance

Tenant shall pay developer $______ per __*[month]*__ __*[from the end of said __ -day period]*__ *OR* __*[from the Scheduled Closing Date]*__ until the actual closing, which in no event shall be later than ______, 20__. Such __*[monthly]*__ payments __*[shall/shall not]*__ be applicable to the site purchase price and shall be forfeited by Tenant if Tenant fails to close.

OR

Alternative "B"
Purchase price escalation

the site purchase price shall increase at the rate of __ % per month __*[from the end of said __ -day period]*__ *OR* __*[from the Scheduled Closing Date]*__ until the actual closing, which in no event shall be later than ______, 20__.

6.3 Title Insurance. At closing, Developer will provide Tenant a __*[See Appendix A, Form A-1]*__ of title insurance. __*[Any additional premium for __[e.g., an ALTA Extended Owner's Policy]__, if required by Tenant, will be paid by Tenant]*__.

6.4 Closing Costs. __*[All escrow charges shall be shared equally by Developer and Tenant and]*__ [A]ll __*[other]*__ closing costs not specifically provided for in other provisions of this letter of intent shall be shared in the manner customary in __________ county, __*[state]*__.

Note: *Refer to Form 17-4, "Allocation of Specific Purchase and Sale Transaction Costs," for an alternative, more comprehensive example.*

7. Non-binding Letter; Rights Contingent Upon Signed Purchase Agreement. This letter constitutes merely an invitation to Tenant to negotiate a comprehensive Purchase Agreement relative to the site on the general terms and conditions described herein. No contract between the parties will exist unless or until the parties have signed a final Purchase Agreement containing all essential terms of the proposed transaction. The parties acknowledge that they have not set forth herein nor agreed upon all essential terms of the Purchase Agreement. This proposal, however, shall remain open until 5:00 p.m. _______, 20__. If this letter has not been accepted in writing by Tenant by such date, this proposal shall be deemed automatically revoked. If this letter is accepted in writing by Tenant on or before such date, Developer and Tenant shall have until ______, 20__ in which to negotiate and sign a binding Purchase Agreement.

Optional:

__. **Tenant's Board Approval and Action.** It is my understanding that Tenant's Board of Directors will either accept or reject this proposal on or before ________, 20__. This proposal shall remain open until 5:00 p.m. _______, 20__ to allow Tenant's Board approval within the above due date of the executed letter of intent.

FORM 12-2

Optional:

__. **Purchase Agreement Subject to Final Approval by Financial Partner's Board of Directors.** Although __*[e.g., name of venture financial partner's key executive]*__ has authorized and approved the general terms of this proposal, __*[name of venture financial partner]*__ requires that final approval of the sale documentation be subject to the approval of __*[name of venture financial partner]*__'s Board of Directors.

8. Contingencies. The Purchase Agreement will be contingent upon the following:

8.1 Map Recordation; Entitlements. Recordation of the __*[par-*

*cel]*__ OR __*[tract]*__ map and issuance of all entitlements to construct all on- and off-site improvements and the initial shop building phase of __*[name]*__ Shopping Center within __ months following execution of the Purchase Agreement.

8.2 Financing. Developer shall have until ________, 20__ in which to obtain a binding __*[e.g., construction/permanent]*__ loan to __*[e.g. construct the shopping center, including Developer's share of the on- and off-site improvements described in this letter]*__. If Developer is unable to obtain financing in form satisfactory to Developer by _______, 20__, Developer shall have the right to terminate the proposed parcel sale by giving written notice of termination to Tenant.

I would be pleased to answer any questions you and your board may have and would be willing to provide you with copies of architectural, engineering and other consultants' work product or documentation within my files.

We look forward to working with you and your company.

Very truly yours,

[Name of developer]

[Name]
[Title, e.g., Managing Venturer
XYZ Investors,
a joint venture]

UNDERSTOOD AND AGREED:
This __ day of __________, 20__.

[Name of tenant]

By: _______________

Its: _______________

Exhibit "A"

[Attach copy of tentative site plan depicting entire shopping center and Tenant's proposed parcel (the "site") with Tenant's building and parking

located on it]

<u>Exhibit "B"</u>

[Sketched preliminary plan for the "site" showing tentative "work of improvement" line]

END OF FORM 12-2

FORM 12-2

OVERVIEW

Chapter 13 provides letters of intent for use in negotiating an outparcel or "pad" build-to-suit lease.

FORMS

13-1 Build-to-Suit Proposal for Free-Standing Building. Key Provisions Contained in a Typical Build-to-Suit Lease Proposal for a Free-Standing Restaurant in a Neighborhood Shopping Center.

13-2 Build-to-Suit Letter of Intent Where Certain Terms Are Subject to Future Negotiation. Letter of Intent with Major Theater Operator for Build-to-Suit Lease of Free-Standing Multiplex Theater; Minimum Annual Rent Conditioned upon Negotiating (i) Acceptable Revisions to Community Shopping Center Site Plan and (ii) Land Area/Value Attributable to Tenant's Use.

Chapter 13

Pad or Outparcel Build-to-Suit Leases

Every time history repeats itself
the price goes up.
—The Developer's Creed

Negotiating the sale of a free-standing building pad (Chapter 12) and negotiating a build-to-suit lease for a free-standing building have some fundamental similarities. In both, you typically begin by defining the subject land area or "site." In the usual development context, both the pad sale and the build-to-suit lease require an agreement relative to a "work of improvement" line—a line demarcating improvement allocations or responsibilities of the parties. In both the parcel sale and the build-to-suit lease, improvements outside the work of improvement line are typically provided by the developer. Improvements constructed inside the work of improvement line, in both cases, are expended more or less exclusively for the tenant's use and benefit; however, in the case of the parcel sale, the tenant routinely advances such costs. In the build-to-suit, such costs are advanced by the developer in return for the receipt of rent payable under a lease.

Thus, it is critically important in negotiating letters of intent for both parcel sales and build-to-suit leases to carefully ascertain all of the various costs to be encountered in completing this "mini-project" and addressing and allocating them by agreement between the parties.

The developer will typically grant the build-to-suit tenant a specific dollar allowance for specified improvements. It is critical to have an absolutely clear understanding as to which costs are and which costs are not to be paid out of the allowance. With the rent structure based upon an agreed allowance advanced by the developer, it is also essential to agree in advance what will happen if the allowance proves insufficient to meet anticipated costs. For instance, will the tenant be required to fund all or a portion of any deficit? Alternatively, will the developer be required to advance additional capital (usually subject to an agreed maximum) for which the developer will receive additional rent? If the developer is obligated to advance additional capital, how will the developer's return on such incremental capital be calculated?

With these issues in mind, Form 13-1 is a letter that can be used to succinctly outline a build-to-suit proposal. One could extract additional applicable clauses from other forms such as the major tenant build-to-suit lease letters of intent in Forms 9-1 and 9-2, the fast-food parcel sale Form 12-1, or the optional and alternative clauses for lease proposals contained in Chapter 18. Moreover, this abbreviated restaurant build-to-suit format is designed to be easily editable to provide for a build-to-suit transaction with another tenant type.

As a final note, a shopping center developer should be absolutely certain of applicable regulatory requirements—particularly parking regulations—before committing to a specific transaction. It is especially important to be mindful of the complexity of modern parking regulations relative to the development and operation of restaurants. The number of required parking stalls per square foot for restaurant space is often substantially more than that required for normal retail space. Substantial variation in required parking may turn on how much of the space is "dining" area as differentiated from space dedicated to supporting uses, whether the dining area contains fixed or moveable seating, whether there is a drive-through, and the number of restaurant employees.

Knowledge of regulatory requirements applicable to the particular site can be learned by visiting appropriate municipal agencies such as planning departments, building departments, fire departments, and other agencies having jurisdictional control. Know the rules and get a floor plan from the prospective tenant before entering into a real estate transaction with a proposed restaurant tenant.

Form 13-1

Key Provisions Contained in a Typical Build-to-Suit Lease Proposal for a Free-Standing Restaurant in a Neighborhood Shopping Center

[Date]

[Name and address of Tenant's real estate representative ______
____
____________________*]*

Ref: __*[Name of shopping center]*__
Re: __*[Name of fast food tenant]*__ Proposed Build-to-Suit Lease

Dear ________:

This letter will serve to confirm the conceptual approval of __*[name of development company]*__ ("Landlord") to the recent proposal of __*[name of restaurant tenant]*__ ("Tenant") to enter into a build-to-suit lease on the following terms and conditions:

1. <u>The Site and Leased Premises</u>. Landlord shall lease Tenant a ________ square foot __*[describe restaurant]*__ building (the "building") on __*[approximately]*__ _______ square feet of land consisting of __*[e.g., Parcel __ on Final Parcel Map No. __]*__ (the "site"), as depicted on the photocopy attached hereto as Exhibit "__*[e.g., A]*__". The proposed building and the site are collectively referred to herein as the "leased premises". The site is a portion of an integrated shopping center and the building and other improvements to be constructed on the site generally conform with the shopping center site plan prepared by __*[name of architectural firm]*__ dated ______, 20__, bearing a last revision date of ________, 20__, a copy of which is attached hereto as Exhibit "__*[e.g., B]*__." *[Optional: Ideally, attach a copy of the building's floor plan:] __[A copy of the building's floor plan is attached hereto as Exhibit "__[D]__"]__.*

2. <u>Use</u>. During the lease term, the leased premises shall be used solely for the purpose of conducting the retail business of __*[narrowly defined use]*__ and for no other use or purpose.

Note: *To control tenant mix and potential assignment and sublet-*

FORM 13-1

ting, the developer should attempt to narrowly define the permitted use. Tenant, on the other hand, should attempt to negotiate as broad a use clause as possible.

3. Trade Name. The business conducted on the premises shall be operated under the trade name ________________.

Note: *Similar to the effect of the use clause, a restrictive trade name provision effectively operates as a "hidden" anti-assignment provision.*

4. Work Letter. The lease to be negotiated between Landlord and Tenant shall contain a "work letter" describing the specific responsibilities of Landlord and Tenant to complete the building and other improvements on the site. The drawing attached hereto as Exhibit "__*[e.g., C]*__" is an enlarged drawing of those improvements shown on the shopping center site plan (Exhibit "__*[e.g., B]*__") which are located within the site. Landlord, at landlord's expense, shall complete all on- and off-site improvements located on the site outside of the "work of improvement" line designated on Exhibit "__*[e.g., C]*__". In addition, Landlord shall *[describe Landlord's work inside the "work of improvement" line:]* __*[e.g., grade the entire site to one finished flat level across the site]*__ __*[including compaction of the approved building area on the site to mutually acceptable specifications, provided Tenant timely obtains all required governmental entitlements for and Landlord's approval of same so that such compaction specifications can be incorporated into the planning, entitlement and execution of Landlord's overall grading of the shopping center]*__.

All other improvements located within the work of improvement line ("Tenant's work") shall be the responsibility of Tenant.

Note: *Landlords should be very careful in making representations concerning the specifics of the grading and compaction Landlord will provide. Make any such representation subject to confirmation by Landlord's engineer and contractor and try to structure the transaction so as to avoid Landlord liability to Tenant if a site preparation defect is subsequently discovered. Most likely, the engineering and construction aspects of site preparation is not an area of Landlord's expertise. Prudently structure the deal so that Tenant must look to Landlord's consultants and general contractor (and not Landlord) for a remedy if a grading/engineering problem arises. Consult with your attorney, your engineer, and your contractor before making representations concerning specifics of grading and compaction.*

5. Construction Allowance; Cost Overruns. __*[Tenant]*__ shall construct the building on the site and shall complete all Tenant's work in consideration for which Landlord shall provide a construction allowance of $__*[e.g., $300,000]*__ (the "construction allowance"). __*[Tenant shall pay any and all amounts in excess of the construction allowance to complete Tenant's work]*__. OR __*[If the actual cost to complete Tenant's work exceeds the construction allowance, Landlord shall advance such excess, but not to exceed a total of $__[e.g., $325,000]__. The advance by Landlord of improvement costs in excess of the construction allowance shall result in an increase in the minimum annual rent by a factor of __[e.g., 13]__ % multiplied by the amount of Landlord's contribution in excess of the construction allowance]*__.

Alternative "A"—Paragraph 6

Pragmatically think about the specific transaction and itemize costs to be specifically excluded or included within the construction allowance. For example:

6. Specific Cost Items Payable by Tenant. The following specific cost items shall be payable directly by Tenant and not included within the construction cost allowance or any cost overrun advanced by Landlord:

OR

Alternative "B"—Paragraph 6

6. Specific Cost Items Included within the Improvement Allowance. The following specific cost items shall be included within the construction cost allowance or any cost overrun advanced by Landlord:

Alternatives "A" and "B"—Paragraph 6 (Continuation)

6.1 A & E. Engineering and architectural fees *[consider the following insert if Alternative "B" (above) is selected:]* __*[not to exceed a total of $____________]*__;

6.2 Studies. Environmental impact report(s) or any other studies required to obtain entitlements for Tenant's work *[consider the following insert if Alternative "B" (above) is selected:]* __*[not to exceed a total of $____________]*__;

FORM 13-1

6.3 Fees/Permits. City processing fees, CUP applications/permits, and other governmental costs to obtain building permits for Tenant's intended use;

6.4 Plan Check. Plan check fees applicable to Tenant's building and improvements within the work of improvement line; and

6.5 Other. __*[describe]*__.

7. Specific Cost Items Payable by Landlord. Landlord shall, at Landlord's expense, over and above the $__________ construction cost allowance, pay for the following: *[Itemize]*

7.1 A & E for Center. Engineering and architectural costs to obtain an approved grading plan __*[and on- and off-site improvement plans]*__ for the entire shopping center, including the grading and site preparation to be performed by Landlord within the site, as specified above;

7.2 Fees and Studies for Center. City processing fees for site plan review for the shopping center, environmental review, and any environmental impact report costs imposed by the city of _______ for the entire shopping center development; and

7.3 Construction Outside Work of Improvement Line. The construction cost required to improve all areas on the site outside the work of improvement line __*[including Landlord's obligation to bring sewer and water laterals and sweeps of electricity and telephone conduit ("utilities") to a point 5 feet inside the site]*__.

> ***Note:*** *Although this form provides for Landlord to complete the on-site improvements outside the defined "work of improvement" line, the transaction need not be so structured. Clearly, Tenant's on-site improvement obligations and/or application of the allowance could extend to all improvements on the site, wherever situated. Of course, so altering the deal structure in this paragraph would require amendment of preceding paragraphs.*

8. Rent Commencement; Lease Term. The parties will negotiate a reasonable time period in which to coordinate and complete Landlord's and Tenant's work. The lease term shall commence and rent shall commence ___ days following substantial completion of Landlord's and Tenant's work or when Tenant opens for business, whichever first occurs. The lease term shall be __ years.

Note: *Consider preliminary or stepped rent, attributable land carry cost, or payment of property taxes beginning at an earlier date, such as the date Landlord obtains site plan approval or accomplishes a specific entitlement milestone for the center. See the following paragraph for but one example.*

Also, for more precise allocation of entitlement and construction responsibilities, see Form 18-16, "Detailed Construction Responsibilities and Coordination Between Landlord and Tenant."

Optional:

__. **Financial Adjustments for Delay in Issuance of Entitlements.** If issuance of all required entitlements is delayed beyond ________, 20__ for reasons other than Landlord's failure to timely process and cooperate in the processing of such matters, __*[and all other contingencies to the lease have been satisfied or waived by Tenant,]*__ in order to compensate Landlord for Landlord's costs in controlling the site, Tenant shall pay Landlord $______ per __*[month]*__ from such date until the lease has commenced and rent is payable under the lease, which in no event shall be later than ______, 20__. Such __*[monthly]*__ payments shall not be applicable to rent and shall be forfeited by Tenant if, through no fault of Landlord, the lease is not consummated or Tenant defaults under the lease.

9. Minimum Rent. Annual minimum rent shall be $________ per year for the first ____ years of the lease term and shall be absolutely net throughout the lease term.

10. Adjustments to Minimum Rent. Annual minimum rent shall be increased __*[annually]*__ OR __*[every __ years]*__ of the __*[initial]*__ term __*[and any option term]*__ (collectively, the "rental adjustment dates") based upon __ *[e.g., 100% of]*__ any increase in the __*[describe specific consumer price index, e.g., "Consumer Price Index for all Urban Consumers (Los Angeles/Anaheim/Riverside area)" ("CPI")]*__ occurring from the commencement of the lease term to the lease __*[or option period]*__ rental adjustment date in question. *[Optional cap and floor (between adjustments):]* __*[; provided, however, that in no event shall any increase in the minimum rent on any rental adjustment date exceed an annualized cumulative increase greater than __[e.g., 5]__ % per year or less than __[e.g., 2]__ % per year over the period of years since the preceding rental adjustment date (or, with respect to the first rental adjustment date, over the period of years since the commencement of the lease term)]*__.

FORM 13-1

Note: For a sampling of minimum rent adjustment structures, refer to Form 18-14, "Tenant Option to Extend Lease Term."

11. Percentage Rent. In addition to the minimum annual rent, Tenant shall pay as percentage rent the amount by which __*[the sum of]*__ __*[e.g., 5]*__ % of Tenant's gross annual __*[food]*__ sales __*[and 7% of liquor sales]*__ made from or upon the premises during each calendar year exceeds the minimum annual rent. *[Tenant oriented optional:]* __*[Tenant, however, shall have the right to recapture from percentage rent __[on a cumulative/non-cumulative basis]__ __[e.g., one-half]__ the __[e.g., real property taxes]__ levied against the site]*__.

Optional:

12. Option to Extend Lease Term. Tenant shall have the right to extend the lease term for __*[e.g., two]*__ consecutive option periods of __*[e.g., five]*__ years each. Minimum rent and percentage rent during the option periods shall be the same as set forth above, adjusted as follows: __*[describe adjustments]*__

Note: Refer to Form 18-14, "Tenant Option to Extend Lease Term," for a variety of option period rental structures.

13. Assignment and Subletting. *[Be wary of changing case law in this area. Refer to Chapter 18, Form 18-10, "Selected Assignment and Subletting Clauses," for discussion and a variety of forms.]*

Optional:

__. Limited Right to Sublease. Notwithstanding the prohibition on assignment and subletting contained in Paragraph __*[13]*__, Tenant shall have the right to sublease up to __ % of its space to __*[give specific reasons/circumstances]*__ subject to precise standards to be negotiated and incorporated into the lease.

14. Signage. Tenant shall have the right, subject to approval by the City of ______________ and Landlord, to construct, at Tenant's cost and expense, mutually-acceptable signage on the building __*[and identification on one free-standing monument sign designated by Landlord]*__. Landlord shall have a right to review and approve Tenant's proposed sign location(s), design and materials for required consistency with the __*[Name]*__ Shopping Center Sign Criteria.

15. Real Property Taxes and Common Area Expense. During

the term of the lease Tenant will pay all real property taxes and assessments levied against the leased premises. In addition, Tenant will pay its prorata share of common area insurance and maintenance expense, plus a __*[e.g., 10% or 15% (varies regionally)]*__ administrative fee. Tenant's prorata share of common area charges will be determined by multiplying the total of such common area charges by the ratio by which Tenant's building square footage bears to the overall square footage of the center __*[(excluding the __[super-market]__ mezzanine)]*__. __*[(However, because Tenant will be directly paying all real property taxes levied against the site, Tenant will not be obligated to pay common area real property taxes.)]*__

Note: *Free-standing buildings are generally more expensive and assessed at a higher tax rate than an equivalently-sized portion of an "in-line" shop building. It is suggested that the developer create a legal or tax parcel that truly represents Tenant's impact area and require Tenant to pay all real property taxes and assessments applicable thereto. If such a parcel is created, Tenant may then be excused from real property taxes included within CAM charges (except if there is some other identifiable real property for which Tenant should equitably share the tax burden).*

It can be argued that, in a free-standing build-to-suit lease context, basing Tenant's real property tax burden on that portion of total shopping center real property taxes that the Tenant's building square footage bears to all buildings in the shopping center gives the Tenant in a free-standing pad a windfall and unfairly burdens tenants occupying in-line shops. A more equitable approach would be to separately parcelize (at least for property tax purposes) each free-standing building based upon its impact area and require the tenant to pay all property taxes levied against such parcel; in-line tenants would then pay that portion of the total in-line shops parcels' tax bill that the square footage of the tenant's space bears to the total square footage of in-line shops.

16. REA. Any lease negotiated between Landlord and Tenant shall be subject to the specific reciprocal easement agreement ("REA") for ______________ Shopping Center and any amendments and supplements to the REA which may be executed from time to time.

17. Financial Statements. Concurrent with the signing of this letter of intent, Tenant __*[and each of Tenant's Guarantor(s)—(see next optional paragraph)]*__ shall provide Landlord with a current financial statement (prepared

FORM 13-1

and dated within __*[e.g., 90]*__ days of the date of the signing of this letter of intent) and financial statements for each of the __*[e.g., 2]*__ years prior to the current fiscal statement year. The lease shall provide that Tenant shall submit to Landlord monthly and annual statements of Tenant's gross receipts. In addition, Tenant shall, at any time during the lease term, upon Landlord's request, provide updated financial statements to Landlord and any actual or potential lender or financial partner then negotiating with Landlord for equity or debt financing. Landlord shall hold such information in confidence, except Landlord may provide any lender, equity partner, or prospective purchaser with the information contained in such statements.

Optional:

__. **Guarantor(s).** __*[Insert name]*__ *("Guarantor")]*__ OR __*[name]*__ *and* __*[name]*__ *("Guarantors")]*__ shall __*["jointly and severally" (in the case of multiple guarantors)]*__ guarantee all Tenant's obligations to Landlord under the lease __*[together with interest accrued thereon and costs of collection thereof, including reasonable attorney's fees]*__ in accordance with a specific, commercial form guaranty agreement to be entered into between Landlord and Guarantor(s) concurrent with execution of the lease.

Optional:

__. **Release of Guarantee.** __*[Guarantor(s)]*__ shall be released from liability under the guaranty when (i) the net worth of Tenant, as shown on audited financial statements of Tenant prepared by an independent certified public accountant, is greater than $________ for __*[e.g., 2]*__ consecutive fiscal years of Tenant's operations on the leased premises and (ii) Tenant's net after tax profits for each of the same __*[e.g., 2]*__ fiscal years, as shown on such financial statements, is greater than $_________. __*[Guarantor(s)]*__, however, shall remain liable under the guaranty for breaches of the lease occurring before the guaranty release date.

__. **[Other].** *[Include any other key deal points, e.g., co-tenancy clause, radius clause, expansion, relocation or termination rights, exclusives, special CAM or property tax allocations or issues, payment of annual environmental monitoring costs, restaurant pest and sanitation control clauses, or other provisions unique to the transaction. For examples, see Chapter 18, "Optional and Alternative Clauses for Lease Proposals," as well as the major tenant build-to-suit forms in Chapter 9. Consider, also, any specific REA provisions (including any special parking arrangements or limitations on future build-out configuration on the site), specific easement(s) affecting the site, and payment of brokerage commissions or finders' fees.]*

18. Contingencies. The lease will be contingent upon the following:

18.1 Map Recordation; Entitlements. Recordation of the __*[parcel]*__ OR __*[tract]*__ map for the site and issuance of all entitlements to construct all on- and off-site improvements and the first building phase of __*[name]*__ Shopping Center, including the leased premises, within __ months following execution of the lease.

18.2 Financing. Landlord shall have until ________, 20__ in which to obtain a binding __*[e.g., construction/permanent]*__ loan to __*[e.g. construct the shopping center, including Landlord's funding of the construction allowance and construction work outside the work of improvement line, as described in this letter]*__. If Landlord is unable to obtain financing in form satisfactory to Landlord by _______, 20__, Landlord shall have the right to terminate the proposed lease by giving written notice of termination to Tenant.

19. Conditions. This non-binding proposal is subject to the following approvals:

19.__ Senior Officers. Approval by the senior officers of Landlord by __________, 20__;

19.__ Board of Directors. Approval of the Board of Directors of __*[e.g., XYZ Corp., Landlord's financial partner,]*__ by __________, 20__; and

19.__ Final Lease. Landlord and Tenant's execution of the final lease documentation by ____________, 20__.

FORM 13-1

20. Non-binding Letter; Rights Contingent Upon Signed Lease. This letter constitutes merely an invitation to Tenant to negotiate a lease on the general terms and conditions described above. No contract between the parties will exist unless or until the parties have signed a final lease agreement containing all essential terms of the proposed transaction. The parties acknowledge that they have not set forth herein nor agreed upon all essential terms of the lease.

21. Time Limit. This proposal shall remain open until 5:00 p.m. _______, 20__ (the "deadline"). If this letter has not been accepted in writing by Tenant and returned to Landlord by the deadline, this proposal shall be deemed automatically revoked and Landlord may continue to offer the premises for lease to other parties without any obligation to Tenant, even if the parties are engaged in good faith negotiations for the lease of the premises as of the deadline. If this letter is accepted in writing by Tenant on or before the deadline, Landlord and Tenant shall have until __*[insert a later date]*__, 20__ in which to negotiate and sign a binding lease agreement.

If the foregoing is acceptable, please so indicate by executing a copy and returning it to me within the time period provided above. Upon its timely receipt, we will begin to prepare the lease.

Very truly yours

[Name of developer]

[Name]
[Title]

UNDERSTOOD AND AGREED:
This __ day of __________, 20__.

[Name of tenant]

By: ______________

Its: ______________

Exhibit "A"
[Attach copy of parcel or tract map depicting the "site"]

Exhibit "B"
[Attach copy of shopping center site plan]

Exhibit "C"
[Attach drawing showing improvements within the "site" and "work of improvement" line. (In this example, Landlord, at Landlord's expense (and not included within the allowance), completes all improvements outside of the "work of improvement" line.)]

<u>Exhibit "D"</u> *[et seq.]*

[Optional: Attach diagram of Tenant's signage, floor plan, seating plan (fixed vs. moveable seating and total seat count may be critical for jurisdiction's parking allocation relative to intended restaurant use), or other attachments unique to the transaction. Often a key deal point can be clearly and easily confirmed by attaching an appropriate exhibit.]

END OF FORM 13-1

Most of the preceding forms presume the parties have had extensive dialogue and are relatively close to reaching a specific agreement. Occasionally, however, because of insufficient information, it may not be possible to agree upon a key deal point, such as a specific rent figure; yet the developer may want to demonstrate a good faith intention to work to make a mutually acceptable lease with a particular tenant. Nevertheless, until an architect has prepared a site-planning study amending the existing site plan, you really cannot fully appreciate how the proposed tenant's building will functionally integrate into the existing, overall center site plan, nor can you fully assess the land-use impact or parking burden caused by the tenant.

Of course, it may be possible to suspend negotiations until a revised site plan is prepared and analyzed. Nevertheless, circumstances may dictate that the developer quickly demonstrate a preliminary commitment or the tenant may make a deal at a competitive site. In such event, while awaiting architectural or other consultant analysis, the developer could prepare a letter that confirms all issues that can be agreed upon currently and that provides an approach or "formula" to negotiating critical unresolved issues such as rent once the site plan has been conceptually "fine-tuned" to accommodate the tenant's proposed use.

Form 13-2 is an example of such a preliminary letter. It proposes a build-to-suit lease with a major theater chain for development of a multiplex theater. In the factual scenario that gave rise to the creation of Form 13-2, the tenant became available shortly before the final site plan for the center was to be submitted for city approvals. The developer's financial partner owned some land parcels immediately behind the center with uniquely excellent access but less-than-ideal visibility. The theater use was an ideal use for a portion of these parcels but, since the land had not been contributed to the venture, this additional land area had not been seriously studied for such potential use. Wanting to proceed and to demonstrate the seriousness of the developer's interest, however, the following proposal was prepared and submitted for discussion with the prospective tenant.

Form 13-2 is included because it demonstrates that the parties can come very close to making a deal even if they lack sufficient information from which to agree upon an issue so basic as a precise rent figure. In this case, site-planning studies needed to be conducted to ascertain the land area attributable to the proposed tenant's use. Yet by agreeing upon a methodology or formula by which land rent would ultimately be calculated, each party was able to obtain a level of assurance or commitment from the other that the deal was worth pursuing and would ultimately be made.

Form 13-2

Letter of Intent with Major Theater Operator for Build-to-Suit Lease of Free-Standing Multiplex Theater; Minimum Annual Rent Conditioned upon Negotiating (i) Acceptable Revisions to Community Shopping Center Site Plan and (ii) Land Area/Value Attributable to Tenant's Use

[Date]

[Name and address of theater chain real estate representative ______

____

____________________*]*

Ref: __*[name]*__ Shopping Center
__*[location]*__
__*[city]*__, __*[state]*__

Dear __________:

It was a pleasure discussing your expansion plans with you last _________. As we discussed, I would like __*[name of major theater chain]*__ ("Tenant") to become a major tenant in __*[name]*__ Shopping Center under development by ___________ ("Landlord").

Give summary of other committed tenants, key demographic and competitive reasons the proposed tenant should negotiate a lease for this particular site, and other salient points, in an effort to get tenant's early interest and commitment to be part of this development instead of competitive sites.

__*[The existing joint venture with my financial partner requires that a letter of intent be signed and submitted by each proposed tenant for approval by the venture's Management Committee before preparation and execution of the final lease agreement]*__.

A build-to-suit lease may be negotiated on the following terms and conditions:

1. <u>Site and Building; Leased Premises.</u> Landlord shall lease Tenant an approximately __*[e.g., 75,000]*__ square foot multiplex theater building (the "building") on a land parcel the size of which shall be negotiated based upon Tenant's impact area (the "site"). The site shall have reciprocal parking rights with adjacent occupants and shall conform with a reconfiguration of the *__[XYZ Shopping Center]__* tentative site plan to be negotiated and approved by Landlord and Tenant. The site will be created to form an integral part of *__[XYZ Shopping Center]__* and the building and other improvements to be constructed on the site will generally conform with the shopping center site plan *__[and elevations]__* prepared by *__[name of architectural firm]__* dated ______, 20__, bearing a last revision date of ________, 20__, a copy of which is attached hereto as Exhibit "*__[e.g., A]__*." *[Optional: Ideally, attach a copy of the building's floor plan:] __[A copy of the building's floor plan (and typical elevations) __[is/are]__ attached hereto as Exhibit "__[B]__"]__*. The proposed building and the site are collectively referred to herein as the "leased premises".

__[I understand that a __[e.g., 75,000]__ square foot building will accommodate your typical __[e.g., six-plex]__ theater. Given our discussions, we feel it would be appropriate that, if you elected to build only a six-plex or eight-plex theater now, that a sufficient land area should, nevertheless, be set aside and planned for later expansion of the building into a ten-plex complex]__.

2. Landlord's Improvement Contribution. We anticipate that Landlord will provide an improvement contribution of $_____ per square foot of building area, or approximately $*__[insert total, absolute amount]__*. Subject to refinement of preliminary cost figures, Landlord will, within this sum, provide Tenant with Tenant's prorata site improvement work and finished building shell, including special footings and subfloor, complete with HVAC, plumbing, and electrical. The extent of any tenant improvements provided by Landlord shall be the subject of further negotiation.

> ***Note:*** *In such a case, where the land area attributable to Tenant's use is not yet determined, the cost component for site improvement work is merely a "guesstimate."*

3. Minimum Annual Rent Formula. The "minimum annual rent" shall be the sum of land rent and improvements rent, calculated as follows:

3.1 Land Rent. An agreed land area shall be negotiated which will accommodate Tenant's required parking and building area. The land area, multiplied by $____ per square foot (unimproved land value) shall be multiplied by *__[e.g., 10]__* % per annum to determine Tenant's annual land rent.

In this case no differential rate of return is applied to the building cost as distinguished from on- and off-site improvements, all of which are lumped together.

3.2 Improvements Rent. Tenant shall pay as "improvements rent" the sum of the improvement costs allocable to the leased premises (including prorata on- and off-site costs and governmental development fees and assessments) multiplied by a rent factor which exceeds by __*[e.g., 1]*__ % the permanent loan constant on Landlord's permanent takeout loan. The rent factor, however, shall be not less than __*[e.g., 6]*__ % nor more than __*[e.g., 10]*__ %. For example, assuming a 10% takeout constant, a 75,000 square foot structure, and __*[e.g., $140.00]*__ per square foot building improvement costs, plus on- and off-site costs and fees of $_____, the improvements rent would be calculated as follows:

(a) 75,000 sq. ft. x $140.00 /sq. ft. = $__________ building improvement costs plus on- and off-site costs and fees for a total of $__________ total improvement costs.

(b) $____________ total improvement costs x 10% = $__________ improvements rent.

Thus, the total "minimum annual rent", consisting of the sum of "land rent" and "improvements rent" (immediately above), will be negotiated after our project architect has completed an acceptable tentative site plan which incorporates the proposed theater complex into the development and thereby allows us to agree upon the land area attributable to your company's use.

4. Percentage Rent. In addition to the payment of the minimum annual rent, Tenant shall pay to Landlord as percentage rent an amount equal to __*[e.g., 8%]*__ on all sales made upon the leased premises including concessions, less the aggregate payments of minimum annual rent made during each calendar year.

5. Additional Rent. As additional rent, Tenant will pay typical prorata costs or assessments such that the lease is NNN, including insurance, common area maintenance, and real estate taxes applicable to the leased premises.

6. Use. The leased premises shall be used as a __*[name of tenant]*__ multi-screen theater complex.

7. Term; Options and Rental Adjustments. The lease term will commence (i) __*[e.g., 60]*__ days after completion of Landlord's work and tender of the premises to Tenant for commencement of Tenant's tenant improvements or (ii) when Tenant opens for business, whichever first occurs. The lease term shall be __*[e.g., 25]*__ years plus __*[e.g., 3]*__ successive __*[e.g., 5]*__ -year options. The lease will provide for periodic increases to the minimum annual rent during the initial lease term. The minimum annual rent during each successive __*[e.g., 5]*__ -year option period shall be adjusted upward __*[e.g., based upon the then fair market rental value to be determined by independent appraisal]*__. However, the adjusted minimum annual rent during each successive option period shall never be lower than the preceding minimum annual rent.

8. Parking. As set forth in Paragraph __*[3.1]*__ above, the minimum annual rent will include a return to Landlord for parking area attributable to Tenant's prorata use. It is our understanding that Tenant's use typically requires approximately one parking stall for each 3 or 4 seats. An acceptable parking configuration will be determined by your reasonable requirements and the requirements of the City of ________ on a reciprocal basis.

The following security provision is unique to a theater tenant:

9. Security. Tenant at Tenant's expense throughout the term of the lease shall provide sufficient security to prevent unruly behavior, vandalism and malicious conduct on and around Tenant's premises. If Tenant fails to provide adequate security, the lease will provide that Landlord may provide such security and add such additional cost to Tenant's common area maintenance charges.

10. Architectural and Signage Control. Landlord shall have reasonable architectural control over Tenant's proposed building so that Tenant's building will reasonably conform with the architectural theme of the center. In addition, Tenant shall have the right, subject to approval of the City of ________, to have identification on a free-standing sign (together with the name of the center and any other major co-tenant(s) granted such identification). Landlord shall have the right to approve the design and location of all Tenant's signage. Parapet elevation sign(s) shall be available as allowed by the City of ___________ and the __*[XYZ Shopping Center]*__ sign criteria. __*[Landlord will allow construction of a theme tower over the theater complex to provide Tenant identity so long as such design is compatible with the center architecture and the City of __________'s design and building requirements]*__.

11. Construction. Upon execution of the subject lease and related documentation, Landlord and Tenant will cooperate to promptly schedule the construction of the theater complex. Landlord and Tenant will cooperate to obtain the lowest overall improvement costs commensurate with good workmanship.

12. Lease Contingencies. The lease will be contingent upon the following:

12.1 Map Recordation; Entitlements. Recordation of a __*[parcel]*__ OR __*[tract]*__ map defining the site and issuance of all entitlements to construct all on- and off-site improvements and the first building phase of __*[XYZ Shopping Center]*__, including the leased premises, within __ months following execution of the lease.

12.2 Financing. Landlord shall have until __________, 20__ in which to obtain a binding __*[e.g., construction/permanent]*__ loan to __*[e.g. construct the shopping center, including all on- and off-site improvements and the first phase of buildings, including the leased premises, as described in this letter]*__. If Landlord is unable to obtain financing in form satisfactory to Landlord by _______, 20__, Landlord shall have the right to terminate the proposed lease by giving written notice of termination to Tenant.

13. Conditions. This non-binding proposal is subject to the following approvals:

13.__ Site Plan and Rent. Negotiation of a mutually-acceptable site plan, agreed land area attributable to Tenant's use and an agreed rent structure not later than ___________, 20__.

13.__ Board of Directors. Approval of Tenant's financial statement and the proposed economic terms of the transaction by __*[e.g., XYZ Corp., Landlord's financial partner,]*__ by _______, 20__; and

13.__ Final Lease Execution. Landlord and Tenant's execution of final lease documentation not later than _______, 20__.

14. Non-binding Letter; Rights Contingent Upon Signed Lease. This letter constitutes merely an invitation to Tenant to negotiate a comprehensive lease agreement on the general terms and conditions described herein. No contract between the parties will exist unless or until the parties have signed a final lease and related documentation containing all essential terms of the proposed transaction. The parties acknowledge that they have not set forth herein nor agreed upon all essential terms of the lease.

FORM 13-2

This proposal, however, shall remain open until 5:00 p.m. ______, 20__. If this letter has not been accepted in writing by Tenant by such date, this proposal shall be deemed automatically revoked. If this letter is accepted in writing by Tenant on or before such date, Landlord and Tenant shall have until _________, 20__ in which to negotiate and sign binding documentation. Unless or until formal lease documentation is signed by the parties, neither party will have any duty, right, claim or obligation to the other.

If you agree with these general terms, please sign below and return a copy to me not later than _________, 20__. Upon receipt, we shall revise the site plan to accommodate your operation in the manner we discussed. If the revised tentative site plan is mutually acceptable and we can promptly negotiate the minimum annual rent, we will then proceed to lease documentation.

We look forward to working with you in what we feel will be a very successful center.

Very truly yours,

[Name of Landlord]

[Name]
[Title]

<u>UNDERSTOOD AND AGREED BY TENANT</u>:
This __ day of _________, 20__.

[Name of tenant]

By: _____________

Its: _____________

<u>UNDERSTOOD AND AGREED BY LANDLORD</u>:
This __ day of _________, 20__.

[Name of developer joint venture partnership]

[Name of developer partner]

By: _______________

Its: _______________

[Optional: Name of joint venture financial partner]

By: _______________

Its: _______________

<u>Exhibit "A"</u>
[Attach copy of existing tentative site plan (and elevations) for the shopping center]

<u>Exhibit "B"</u>
[Attach copy of the building's floor plan (and elevations, if available)]

END OF FORM 13-2

OVERVIEW

Chapter 14 provides deal-making documents for use in negotiating ground leases of outparcels or "pads" for free-standing buildings.

FORMS

14-1 Developer's Detailed Ground Lease Proposal. Developer Letter of Intent to Major Oil Company for Ground Lease of Corner Service Station Pad to Be Developed Concurrent with Shopping Center; Includes (i) Allocation of On- and Off-Site Costs and Development Fees and (ii) REA Restrictions.

14-2 Tenant's Generic Ground Lease Proposal with Developer-Oriented Comments. Letter of Intent From Bank to Ground Lease Free-Standing Bank Pad in Neighborhood Center with Selected Developer-Oriented Comments Addressing How Refinements Could Be Made to Cooperatively Expedite the Transaction.

Chapter 14

Pad or Outparcel Ground Leases

In the long run men [and women] *hit only what they aim at. Therefore, though they should fail immediately, they had better aim at something high.*
—Henry David Thoreau

Well-negotiated and professionally documented ground leases of key pad or outparcel locations to major oil companies, selected financial institutions, and other credit tenants can give a major boost to the yield and stability of a center's income stream, thereby incrementally lowering the market capitalization rate at which the center would sell to a prudent buyer.

Provided the site is attractively developed, a ground lease to a major oil company has the advantage of minimally effecting the view corridor into the center. Of course, the developer must be extremely mindful of potential hazardous materials and environmental liabilities. Therefore, such transactions require skilled legal counsel and advisory services from a qualified environmental consultant. At the outset of the transaction, the developer should undertake site studies to confirm site conditions, creating a baseline from which any future alterations to site conditions can be compared. Be sure that construction is in compliance with federal and state requirements and includes state-of-the-art double-walled storage tanks. Ground-lease documentation should require regular and frequent environmental monitoring and protect the developer from potential liabilities.

Form 14-1 is a relatively detailed letter of intent for use in negotiating a ground lease of an undeveloped site to a major oil company. Legal documentation can be more efficiently undertaken and the developer's overall work effort can be substantially reduced by using a signed letter of intent as a guide through final documentation and consummation of the transaction.

A difficult and increasingly common issue is the negotiation of an operative agreement relative to the parties' sharing of increasingly large site development fees. In some cases, the governmental fees to be charged the developer and the credits and reimbursements the developer is to receive (and, similarly, the credits and reimbursements allocable to the tenant) are uncertain or subject to unpredictable increases during the development cycle. If fee caps have to be negotiated, consider increasing them from month to month or year to year if a lengthy transaction is a possibility.

Note Form 14-1's method for allocating costs to the tenant for on-site improvements outside the "building envelope" and the tenant's obligation to pay for off-site improvements and net development fees and assessments based upon the tenant's prorata land area relative to the land area of the entire shopping center. (There are many other ways to structure such cost-sharing arrangements. Carefully consider alternatives and select a method that produces the best, unambiguous method in the particular factual context. For example, where the tenant's corner pad has substantial street frontage relative to its size, the developer may prefer to structure tenant's off-site reimbursement obligation based upon the linear street frontage of the tenant's parcel relative to the entire street frontage of the center.)

Although a letter of intent may require substantial effort to negotiate and prepare, in the majority of cases it is nevertheless a very efficient use of a deal maker's time. There is no substitute for careful, deliberate, objective, comprehensive thinking translated into a written plan. Professionally tailoring such a letter to the particular transaction at hand assures the parties that major issues have been covered to the best of the parties' abilities.

Personally, I like to create a deal once and give it to my lawyer in a comprehensive letter of intent format. From then on, I am only minimally interrupted from other matters during the documentation process and have my letter agreement to refer to. If a letter of intent is bypassed and from the outset intricate changes to a credit tenant's standard ground-lease form are attempted, however, you can spend countless frustrating hours being distracted from other matters to recall what had been agreed to and to "manage" the final document production. Preparing a thorough letter of intent in a complex transaction encourages the application of comprehensive thinking early in the transaction, saves time overall, increases one's productivity, and probably increases the likelihood that the transaction will be successfully concluded.

Form 14-1

Developer Letter of Intent to Major Oil Company for Ground Lease of Corner Service Station Pad to Be Developed Concurrent with Shopping Center; Includes (i) Allocation of On- and Off-Site Costs and Development Fees and (ii) REA Restrictions

[Date]

[Name and address of
real estate representative for
major oil company ("Oil Company")
____
____
______________________*]*

Ref: __*[Oil Company]*__ Ground Lease
________ Shopping Center
__*[city]*__, __*[state]*__

Dear ________:

Thank you for your draft ground lease on your company's form dated __________, 20__ (the "lease draft"). Due to the complexity of this transaction, I am outlining the basic terms of our proposed transaction in this letter. If this outline is acceptable to you, our attorney will modify the lease draft accordingly. Would you please sign and return a signed copy of this letter confirming your agreement with the terms as outlined herein, understanding, however, that neither __*[name of developer]*__ ("Landlord") nor __*[name of oil company]*__ ("Tenant") will be bound in any manner unless or until a final ground lease and any required additional final documentation has been signed by the parties.

1. Site. Assuming the parties consummate present negotiations, the ________ square foot corner parcel (the "site") identified as __*[describe]*__ on the attached site plan dated _________, 20__, (Exhibit "A") will be leased to Tenant. The site plan conforms with Tenant's proposed preliminary layout __*[with the exception that...]*__ *[describe any differences between the preliminary layout and the layout actually intended].* A __*[parcel]*__ OR __*[tract]*__ map will be processed to create the site as a separate legal parcel.

2. Use. Construction and operation of a __*[name of Tenant]*__ retail service station engaged in the retail sale of gasoline and related petroleum products. Tenant shall also have the right, subject to governmental approval __*[and the terms of the REA]*__, to sell snack food items incidental to the primary use of a service station. *[Optional:]* __*[The sale of alcoholic beverages*

FORM 14-1

of any kind from the site is specifically prohibited]__. [Alternative last sentence:] __[The sale of beer and wine from the site shall be permitted so long as all required local, state and federal permits are obtained and maintained in force by Tenant]__.

Optional: Continuous operations and recapture right:

__. Continuous Operations and Recapture Right. Tenant will be obligated to continuously operate the business consistent with the preceding use clause. If Tenant fails to continuously operate such business for a period of __*[e.g., 6]*__ consecutive months of the lease term, except during any period constituting force majeure (excluding Tenant's financial condition), Landlord shall have the right but not the obligation to recapture the premises.

3. Initial and Option Term. An unimproved NNN ground lease with a __*[e.g., 5]*__ -year fixed term and __*[e.g., five, 5]*__ -year options.

4. Fixed Term Rent. Rent during the __*[e.g., 5]*__ -year fixed term shall be __*[e.g., $71,928]*__ per year. The initial fixed term rent was negotiated on the basis of __*[e.g., 10]*__ % return on the agreed land value of the site.

5. Option Period Rent. Rent during each of the __*[e.g., 5]*__ -year option periods shall be payable as follows:

Option Period	Rent or Escalation Formula
1	$__*[e.g., 87,756]*__
2	The greater of $__*[e.g., 107,064]*__ or __*[e.g.,10]*__ % of appraised fair market value ("FMV")
3	$__*[e.g, 130,608]*__ or __*[e.g., 1.22]*__ times Option Period #2 rent if FMV is used in Option Period #2
4	The greater of $__*[e.g., 159,336]*__ or __*[e.g., 10]*__ % FMV
5	$__*[194,388]*__ or __*[e.g., 1.22]*__ times Option Period #4 rent if FMV used in Option Period #4

***Note:** Absolute rent figures of an actual transaction are shown in Paragraphs 4 and 5 to illustrate an overall rent structure and rent escalation formulation. In this example, Option Periods "2" and "4" provide for adjustments to fair market value (if the fair market value exceeds specified increased minimum rent levels). A comparison of absolute rent figures will demonstrate that the rental increase* *in each option period exceeds the rent payable in each prior period by not less than 22% (rounded).*

6. Initial "Feasibility" Option Payment. In consideration of an initial $__*[nominal amount]*__ option payment, Tenant will have a __*[e.g., 90]*__ -day period in which to conduct a study of the site and to sign an agreed lease form, which period can be extended __*[e.g., 30]*__ days upon timely payment of an additional $_______ advance option payment. If such $__*[insert additional advance amount]*__ is timely paid, it will be credited against improvements to the site reimbursable to Landlord under Paragraph __*[11]*__, below.

7. Tenant's Lease Execution and Deposit. At the end of the above __*[e.g., 90]*__ -day option period (extendible to __*[e.g., 120]*__ days, at Tenant's option, as above), Tenant must (i) give notice that Tenant has elected not to sign the lease or (ii) return the signed lease to Landlord accompanied by a $__*[substantial amount]*__ check payable to Landlord (the "deposit"). The entire deposit will be applicable to fixed term rent if approvals are obtained and fixed rent is payable.)

8. "Preliminary Term" Rent. The "preliminary term" __*[(as defined in Tenant's lease draft)]*__ will commence upon Tenant's execution and delivery of the final, agreed lease form and the deposit to Landlord. The lease shall provide that preliminary term rent is $________ per month for the first __*[e.g., three]*__ months of the preliminary term, $________ per month for the next __*[e.g., six]*__ months and $_________ per month thereafter until commencement of the fixed term.

9. "Fixed Term." The preliminary term shall end and the "fixed term" shall commence (and payment of fixed term rent shall commence) __*[e.g., 4]*__ months after Tenant's permits are received or when Tenant opens for business, whichever first occurs, but in no event later than __*[e.g., 18]*__ months after the commencement of the preliminary term. If Tenant is unable to obtain all required entitlements on or before the scheduled commencement of the fixed term, Tenant may elect to terminate the lease and __*[all option, deposit and rent payments to date thereof shall remain the property of Landlord]*__ OR __*[, ___ % of the deposit will be returned to Tenant and all other sums paid Landlord by Tenant may be retained by Landlord]*__.

10. Tenant Diligence. The lease will require Tenant's diligence at all times, including obtaining necessary internal management approvals for the site during the option period, preparing and processing plans, permits and licenses for required approvals.

11. Improvement Costs. Tenant will pay all costs and expenses attributable to improvement of the site, including on- and off-site improve-

FORM 14-1

ments, development fees, bonds and permits __*[, with the exception that]*__ __*[e.g., (a) Landlord will rough grade the site at Landlord's expense concurrent with the rough grading of the shopping center and (b) Landlord will provide the utility work described in Paragraph* __*[13]*__*, below]*__.

11.1 Improvements Inside the Building Envelope. Tenant, at Tenant's expense, will construct the __*[e.g., building, service pumps and all other improvements]*__ located within the "building envelope" shown on Exhibit "__*[B]*__".

11.2 On-site Improvements Outside the Building Envelope. Improvements outside the building envelope but within the site will be constructed by Landlord's contractor and paid for by Tenant. Tenant shall pay for such on-site improvements at Landlord's cost. Where such costs are not precisely known, Tenant shall pay a reasonable allocation of the prorata cost of each specific applicable on-site improvement relative to the total square footage of like on-site work for the entire project. For example, Tenant shall be charged for paving, curb and gutter, parking lot lighting, landscaping, and the like, based upon rationally and objectively applied linear or square footage apportionment. In other words, Tenant will pay the same per square foot cost for paving that Landlord's contractor charges Landlord for like work.

11.3 Off-Site Improvement Costs. Tenant shall pay Tenant's prorata share of all off-site improvements. Off-site improvements will be constructed by Landlord __*[e.g., and the County of* ____________*]*__. Tenant will pay or reimburse Landlord that portion of total off-site improvement costs which the site's square footage (_______ square feet) bears to the entire shopping center site (_______ square feet), or __ %.

12. Governmental Development Fees. Similarly, net applicable __*[e.g., county]*__ development fees __*[(gross fees less credits, if any)]*__ will be payable by Tenant in the same manner as off-site costs, i.e., Tenant will pay __*[same % as in previous paragraph]*__ % of the total development fees payable with respect to the total shopping center development. Tenant, however, will independently pay for all of its own plan check, inspection, building permit and other typical governmental processing fees. *[Add any other details regarding government fees, assessments or processing, for example:]* __*[The County represents that it will pay for certain* _______ *Boulevard and* ________ *Road off-sites out of the development fees]*__.

Optional: Often there are uncertainties in the governmental fee structure applicable to the site, for example:

12.__ Adjustment to Cap On Governmental Development Fees. The __*[e.g., County of* ___________*]*__ is presently unable to enter into a development agreement with Landlord as a result of pending changes in the development fee structure applicable to the subject shopping center project and the site. Notwithstanding such uncertainty, however, the parties understand that substantial scheduled increases in applicable __*[county]*__ fees will be payable if building permits for the entire shopping center, including the site, are issued in 20__*[e.g., the next year]*__ instead of 20__*[e.g., insert the present year]*__. The parties believe that all required entitlements for the shopping center and the site will be issued in 20__*[e.g., insert the present year]*__.

Provided full entitlements for the shopping center and the site are issued by __*[e.g., a date within present year]*__, Tenant's __*[e.g., insert same % as in Paragraph 12, above]*__ % portion of __*[e.g., county]*__ development fees shall not exceed $________. If a building permit for the site is not issued until 20__*[the next year]*__, Tenant will pay __*[e.g., insert same % as in Paragraph 12, above]*__ % of the total shopping center development fees payable, but Tenant's cap shall be raised to $__*[increased absolute cap]*__.

Optional: If the tenant demands a cap on governmental fees and such fees are subject to material increase, Landlord should consider the right to back out of the transaction in the event the transaction becomes uneconomic, for example:

12.__ Landlord's Limited Right to Terminate Based Upon Unacceptable Fee Agreement. In the unlikely event that Landlord in good faith is unable to negotiate an acceptable project development fee and reimbursement agreement with the __*[e.g., County of _____]*__ __*[such that the transaction becomes uneconomic from Landlord's perspective]*__, Landlord may elect to terminate the lease, provided Landlord refunds all moneys previously advanced to Landlord by Tenant pursuant to the lease __*[, excluding the initial $________ option payment referenced in Paragraph __[6]__, which Landlord, in such event, may retain]*__.

13. Utilities. Landlord's engineers and general contractor will provide for the following utility planning and construction, suitable for Tenant's use, at no additional cost to Tenant:

13.1 Electricity and Telephone. Sweeps of empty conduit to the site parcel line; and

13.2 Sewer and Water. Laterals provided to five feet inside the site parcel line.

Note: *Add any specific additional utility improvements Landlord will provide.*

14. Connection and Metering Charges. Notwithstanding Paragraphs __*[13.1]*__ and __*[13.2]*__, Tenant will pay all utility connection and metering costs and all costs to bring such utilities to Tenant's improvements within the site.

Because it is assumed Tenant pays all real property taxes assessed against Tenant's site, Tenant is excused from payment of the real property tax portion of CAM:

15. Property Taxes and CAM. Tenant will pay all real estate taxes levied against the site and __*[e.g., same % as in Paragraph 11.2 or 12, above]*__ % of all common area maintenance ("CAM") charges. Such CAM charges include common area insurance, parking lot maintenance, sweeping, parking lot lighting, etc. Because Tenant will directly pay all real property taxes assessed against the site (which will become a separate parcel under the parcel map being processed by Landlord), Tenant's CAM charges will not include an assessment for real property tax __*[except]*__ __*[provide for any exception(s) such as property taxes relative to a particular common area parcel which benefits Tenant]*__.

16. Reciprocal Easement Agreement. All parcel owners within the center will sign and Landlord will record a reciprocal easement agreement ("REA") providing for continued ingress and egress, establishment of common and building areas, architectural harmony consistent with the center's __*[name]*__ architectural theme __*[e.g., (river rock and "clinker" brick bulkhead/ column detail, eased detail on heavy beams, and pitched roof)]*__, approval of signage plan, payment of common area expenses, and other matters.

Optional: An example of use restrictions (contained in CC & R's or the REA) to insure visibility into center and provide for purchase and sale rights of Tenant and the center's owner:

16.1 Use Controls and Rights of First Refusal. During the term of the proposed lease, the site shall be used only in accordance with the use clause above. To insure perpetual street visibility for owners and tenants to the rear of the site, future construction on the site shall be limited to one-story buildings not to exceed a total of __*[e.g., 5000]*__ square feet within an agreed, designated building area contiguous to the building setback line on the corner. The required parking count for any future building use on the site will be confined to the site. If Landlord elects to sell Tenant's site in a sale separate from the sale of all or a portion of the remainder of the center, Tenant may exercise a right of first refusal to purchase the site. Prior to any subsequent resale of Tenant's site, any subsequent owner of Tenant's site shall be required to first offer the site to the then-existing owner of the shops parcel.

Optional: Set criteria in the REA so that any major tenant or others holding approval rights are held to specific, articulated standards.

16.2 Elevations and Future Building Use Controls. __*[Major supermarket tenant and]*__ Landlord shall have the right to approve Tenant's proposed elevations. (The REA will also provide that upon termination of Tenant's lease, __*[e.g., names of specific anchor tenant(s)]*__ will approve any future building use on the site so long as it meets the size and location criteria established in the REA __*[, as generally described above,]*__ and complies with the established architectural criteria.)

Landlord shall supply Tenant with a draft of the REA by _______, 20__.

17. Underground Tank Specifications, Environmental Monitoring and Insurance. No above ground tanks may be installed and the lease shall provide that all underground tanks and pressurized piping shall be made of state of the art materials and comply with all applicable federal, state and local laws and regulations. Underground tanks shall be __*[e.g., double-walled fiberglass with fiberglass piping]*__, all of which shall be installed subject to certified leak detection testing. Each underground tank and all pressurized piping shall continuously be served by leak detectors and shall be regularly monitored and tested by approved, independent third parties. A daily inventory control and reconciliation shall be made and Tenant's inventory and environmental records shall be available for Landlord's review at all times.

At the end of the term, prior to vacating, Tenant shall remove and dispose of all underground tanks and containers. Concurrent with such removal, Tenant shall fully test the site and fill and compact the resulting holes in compliance with all applicable laws and regulatory requirements. If a leak or contamination is detected, Tenant shall clean up the site and all other affected areas to the satisfaction of federal, state and local authorities. Tenant shall provide insurance in coverages and amounts satisfactory to Landlord. Required insurance coverage shall contain specific wording to cover hazardous spill clean-up efforts. The lease shall contain a provision indemnifying Landlord for any loss or cost resulting from any underground storage tank leak or discharge of hazardous materials.

> ***Note:*** *Be certain to keep up with rapidly changing technology. The second sentence (italicized insert) over time may no longer be state-of-the-art. Removal of underground tanks followed by soils testing after tank removal is to be preferred to insure that no hazardous materials exist below or around the tanks in an area that otherwise might remain undetected. Before using, review contents of this paragraph with appropriate consultants knowledgeable about the*

transaction under negotiation.

18. Contingencies. The lease will be contingent upon the following:

18.1 Map Recordation; Entitlements. Recordation of the __*[parcel]*__ OR __*[tract]*__ map for the site and issuance of all entitlements to construct all on- and off-site improvements and the first building phase of __*[name]*__ Shopping Center, including all proposed improvements to the site, within __ months following execution of the lease.

18.2 Financing. Landlord shall have until ________, 20__ in which to obtain a binding __*[e.g., construction/permanent]*__ loan to __*[e.g. construct the shopping center in which the site is a part]*__. If Landlord is unable to obtain financing in form satisfactory to Landlord by _______, 20__, Landlord shall have the right to terminate the proposed lease by giving written notice of termination to Tenant.

19. Miscellaneous.

19.1 Notice. Tenant will give Landlord __*[e.g., 180]*__ days notice of each election to exercise an option to extend the lease term.

Optional: An example to show Tenant that entitlement progress is being made. Such information is important for the Tenant's planning.

19.2 Existing Approvals. Tenant is aware that Landlord has obtained __*[e.g., County Development Review Committee]*__ and __*[e.g., Planning Commission]*__ approvals for the attached tentative site plan, which includes Tenant's proposed schematic layout. No further site planning approvals are required. Conceptual elevations have been approved by the __*[jurisdictional agency]*__. A mass grading permit has also been issued. Mass grading is scheduled to commence approximately ________, 20__.

Optional example:

19.3 Liquor. Tenant's proposed sale of beer and wine will not be objected to by Landlord but shall be subject to approval by __*[e.g., name of major supermarket tenant]*__ __*[e.g., and the County of ______]*__. The County Planning Director has indicated that such sales incidental to retail gasoline sales will not be permitted in __*[name of jurisdiction]*__.

19.4 Lender Modifications. Tenant will agree to reasonable lease modifications required by Landlord's lender provided that such changes do not modify the economic terms of the proposed transaction.

20. Non-binding Letter; Rights Contingent Upon Signed Lease. This letter constitutes merely an invitation to negotiate a lease on the general terms and conditions described above. Neither party shall be bound by this letter and no contract between the parties will exist unless or until the parties have signed a final lease agreement containing all essential terms of the proposed transaction. The parties acknowledge that they have not set forth herein nor agreed upon all essential terms of the lease. Landlord's interest in entering into the contemplated ground lease is expressly conditioned upon Landlord's receipt of a signed copy of this letter on or before __*[date #1]*__, 20__.

21. Time Limit. This proposal shall automatically expire as of 5:00 p.m. on __*[date #1]*__, 20__, unless Tenant's acceptance is communicated in writing to Landlord before that time. If the parties do not execute a final ground lease on or before 5:00 p.m. on __*[date #2]*__, 20__, Landlord shall have the right to offer the site to other parties without any obligation to Tenant to hold the site off the market, even if the parties are engaged in good faith negotiations for the ground lease of the site on __*[date #2]*__, 20__.

If the foregoing outline meets with your approval, would you please so indicate on the space provided below and return a copy to me. We look forward to working with you in development of __*[Name]*__ Shopping Center.

Very truly yours,

[development company]

[name]
[capacity]

UNDERSTOOD AND AGREED:
This __ day of ___________, 20__.

[Major Oil Company]

By: ________________

Its: ________________

Exhibit "A"

[Attach copy of shopping center site plan showing Tenant's parcel (the "site")]

FORM 14-1

Exhibit "B"

[Attach plan of "site" showing "building envelope" within which Tenant is responsible for the cost of all improvements. (In this example, Tenant reimburses Landlord for site improvements Landlord constructs within the "site" but located outside the "building envelope".) The following "Service Station Parcel" plan depicts the "site" and the "building envelope" referenced in the preceding example.]

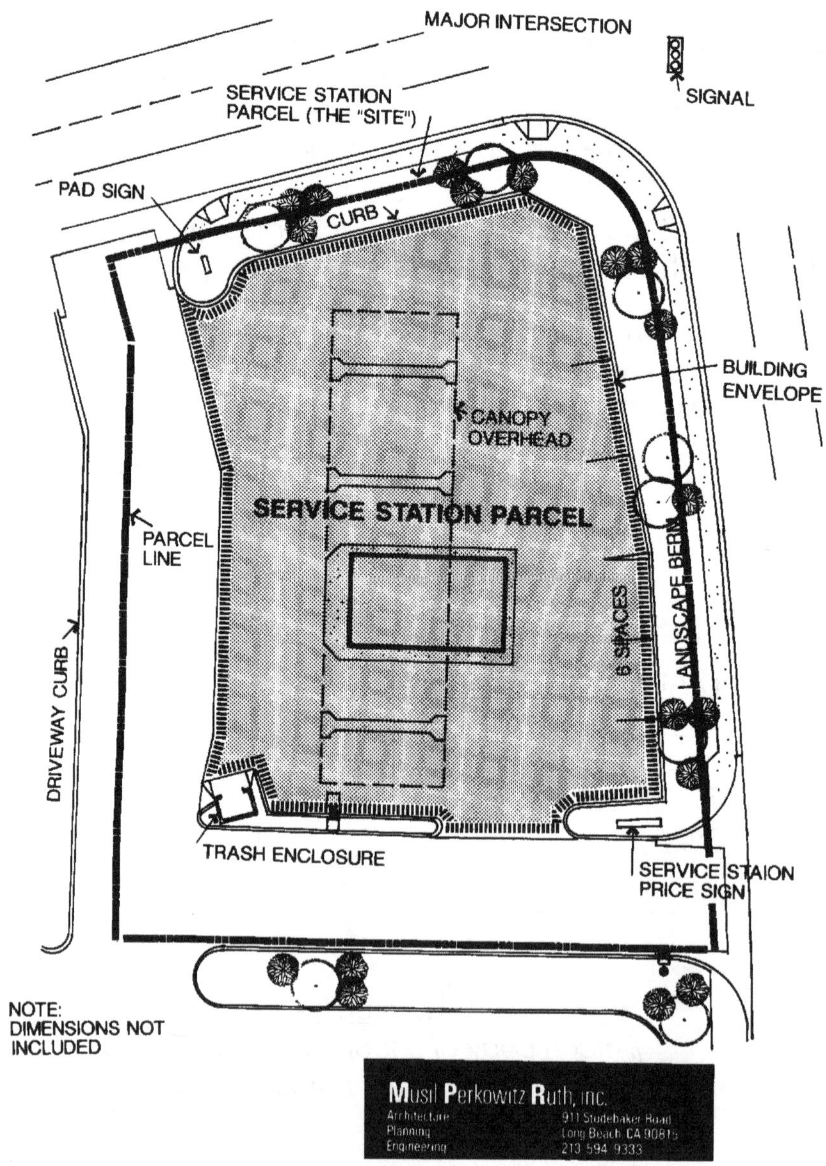

END OF FORM 14-1

The preceding forms in this book are generally designed for use in the format presented. Often, however, rather than generating an initial proposal, a deal maker will be obligated to respond to a proposal prepared by someone else. Form 14-2 is a hypothetical tenant proposal included for review to consider how the transaction might be restructured or refined, rather than another reusable form. The purpose is not to review legal aspects, but rather, to create a better deal; i.e., improve the economics or relative obligations of the parties to create a more efficient or cooperative structure. If you started at the beginning of the book, Form 14-2 gives you an opportunity to consider and apply materials previously covered.

Form 14-2 is a typical "generic" offer derived from an actual proposal from a bank desiring to ground lease a pad in a neighborhood shopping center under development. Following a simple outline format, Form 14-2 is easy to read and covers the major issues in the ground lease of a free-standing bank site. Note, however, this document does not creatively deal with specific governmental, architectural, construction, or timing issues—issues with which the professional developer should be well versed. How could the tenant's generic proposal be customized to cover all pertinent issues and streamline consummation of the deal? Annotations to the form and cross-references to other sections of this book are included to stimulate creative thinking.

For the developer, the letter of intent stage is an opportunity to anticipate and deal with any unique or special problems that may arise relative to the particular project and the proposed tenant's specific site. From the outset, mental energies should be applied to articulating a structure to make, expedite, and complete the transaction. In other words, considering a time line from first tenant contact through tenant occupancy, what specifically can be done to create a context in which the parties, their attorneys, consultants, contractors, and governmental representatives can all be orchestrated to cooperatively, efficiently and quickly complete what needs to be done?

A tenant's proposal to the developer usually reflects the tenant's standard deal structure and does not address important development issues unique to the proposed transaction. The developer, however, generally has a much greater knowledge of site and development issues relative to the developer's project. Unfortunately, faced with such a tenant proposal, many developers fail to take advantage of the opportunity to refine the document except with respect to the barest economic essentials such as the rent, adjustments to minimum rent, term, option rights, and developer contribution, if any.

It has been said that experience is what you get when you get what you don't want. Cultivate an attitude of applying to each new deal lessons learned in each past project. Each project has unique site, entitlement, construction, and financial problems that can be anticipated. In reviewing a tenant's proposal, consider how refinements to the transaction as proposed could be made to get the deal consummated faster (with greater cooperation), with reduced risk, and with less energy merely by carefully considering the broadest possible range of solutions and the most rational choices among such alternatives.

Although Form 14-2 addresses the key business issues, the comments suggest "pro-developer" refinements or revisions. These are merely examples of some of the possible amendments to the deal-making document to improve the deal, prevent avoidable problems, and get the deal done more efficiently.

This is the last complete developer-tenant letter of intent form in this book. For those of you who have read the text to this point, use this opportunity to see how much has been learned and to further consider how a tenant's proposal might be fine-tuned. For those of you disgruntled by such an approach (particularly if you started at this chapter), consider editing Form 14-1 and using only those sections from Form 14-2 that are unique to a financial institution ground lease. (Note that unlike the preceding oil company ground lease (Form 14-1), the bank transaction included as Form 14-2 does not assume the tenant's involvement in complicated governmental fee exactions, credits, and reimbursements.)

Form 14-2

Letter of Intent from Bank to Ground Lease Free-Standing Bank Pad in Neighborhood Center with Selected, Developer-Oriented Comments Addressing How Refinements Could Be Made to Cooperatively Expedite the Transaction

[Bank's Broker's Letterhead]

[Date]

[Name and address
of proposed developer-
Landlord ___________
____
___________________*]*

Dear ___________:

__*[Name]*__, __*[e.g., Real Estate Manager]*__ for __*[name of bank]*__ ("Tenant") has, pursuant to our joint discussions, authorized me to make the following ground lease proposal to __*[name of developer/owner]*__ ("Landlord") relative to __*[name]*__ Shopping Center (the "center") in __*[city]*__, __*[state]*__:

1. Site. Parcel __, designated as the __*[e.g., "Financial Pad"]*__ on the center site plan, when finally parcelized, will contain approximately __________ square feet of land (the "site"). The site will be ground leased to Tenant for Tenant's construction of a __*[e.g., name]*__ bank building not to exceed __________ square feet __*[plus a drive-through]*__.

Is a separate legal parcel or lot to be created? If so, who processes lot split and who pays related costs? Does the site's size encompass Tenant's entire impact area? If so, will the land area attributed to the site define Tenant's real property tax/assessment obligations (or will such obligations be based upon Tenant's building square footage relative to other buildings in the center)? Consider describing the location of specific building improvements on the site by referencing attached exhibit(s). Consider restrictions upon future relocation, remodeling or rebuilding on the site, a key issue being the ability to preserve the intended view corridor into the center. In provisions that follow, what is the fundamental "deal"—can Tenant build whatever Tenant wants, or is building use, location, size, and/or design to be restricted?

2. <u>Use</u>. Any lawful business purpose not in conflict with any exclusive use rights currently granted to any other tenant in the center.

Obviously, for a host of reasons, developer will attempt to require that the premises be used solely for conducting a retail bank business.

3. <u>Initial Term</u>. __*[e.g., 20]*__ years.

4. <u>Options to Extend Lease Term</u>. Tenant shall have the right to extend the term of the ground lease for __*[e.g., 2]*__ additional periods of __*[e.g., 5]*__ years each. Tenant shall give the Landlord not less than __*[e.g., 6]*__ months notice of Tenant's intention to extend prior to the expiration of the then existing term.

See Chapter 18, Form 18-14, for alternative language.

5. <u>Tenant's Right to Terminate</u>. __*[E.g., Ten]*__ years after rent commencement, Tenant shall have the right to terminate. Notice of intention to terminate shall be given to Landlord at least __*[e.g., 6]*__ months prior to end of said __*[e.g., 10]*__ -year period.

What is the effect upon Landlord's financing if this provision is accepted?

6. <u>Minimum Annual Rent</u>. Tenant shall pay Landlord a minimum annual rent of $________ payable monthly __*[in advance]*__ for years __*[1]*__ through __*[5]*__.

[Ideally, add: __[and $_______ per month for years __[6]__ through __[10]__; $_______ per month for years __[11]__ through __[15]__; and $_______ per month for years __[16]__ through __[20]__. [Of course, Landlord will attempt to negotiate successively higher minimum rent floors, particularly where the COL adjustment (below) has no minimum increase per adjustment period. Although it is assumed minimum rent continues through year 20, Tenant's proposal is not literally so written.]

7. <u>[Adjustments to] Minimum Annual Rent</u>. Beginning with the __*[e.g., 5th]*__ year of the lease term, minimum rent shall be __*[adjusted]*__ every __*[e.g., 5]*__ years (*) based upon any __*[change]*__ in the Consumer Price Index. The Consumer Price Index __*[change]*__ shall be computed based upon a maximum __*[change]*__ of __*[4]*__ % for each year with a maximum __[change]__ of __[20]__ % for each five year period.

Do not inadvertently allow the rental adjustment formula to reduce minimum rent based upon a potential decrease in the C.P.I.: Change "[Adjustments to]" in the caption to "Increases in", change the word "adjusted" (where noted) to "increased" and replace the word "change" (where noted) with the word "increase".

If intended, make certain the CPI adjustments apply to option periods as well as the initial lease term. Accordingly, add one of the following inserts where the "(*)" appears: __[of the initial lease term]__ OR __[of the lease term and any option term]__. If the second alternative clause is inserted, delete Paragraph 8.

See Chapter 18, Form 18-14, "Tenant Option To Extend Lease Term".

8. Option Period Rent. Minimum rent for each option period shall be __[e.g., 90]__ % of the fair market value for branch bank facilities of a similar size in __[various selected cities]__.

Consider the option period rent structure in Paragraph 5 of Form 14-1, which combines fixed rent, appraised market value and capitalization concepts to create an option period rent schedule. See also, Form 18-14, "Tenant Option To Extend Lease Term".

9. Rent Commencement. Rent shall commence upon the Tenant's opening for business.

Attempt to obtain preliminary or reduced rent, particularly where the approval process is long or if the tenant's particular use requires an extended approval period. Tie rent commencement into governmental permitting date, with an absolute pay or terminate date. See, for example, Paragraphs 8 and 9, Form 14-1.

10. Pad Delivery. Landlord shall provide a building pad to grade, compacted and ready to receive Tenant's building to be constructed on spread footings. All underground utilities, including but not limited to, electrical power, water, natural gas, sewer, storm drainage and telephone conduit, shall be delivered by Landlord to within five (5) feet of tenant's building.

Try to persuade Tenant to accept the pad as already prepared (per available grading specifications to be provided Tenant) to avoid creating a duty to recompact, i.e., try to get Tenant to accept pad as certified by engineer without potential liability to developer. Similarly, by this point in the development process the developer should know where utilities are located. Having properly planned the pad for future tenant development, utilities will be available or prudently planned. Get Tenant to specifically accept utility placement at the location(s) where they are already stubbed out or where they are already planned to be stubbed out per developer's plans. Why agree to deliver utilities to an uncertain new location when usually, after informed discussion, the originally contemplated location is sufficient? The point is to have the discussion.

Landlord shall pay for all costs for site work for areas adjacent to Tenant's building pad including but not limited to, grading, paving, landscaping and striping.

This sentence is ambiguous. Use and analyze your specific site plan. Thoughtfully (and not mechanically) negotiate and prepare a "building envelope" or "work of improvement line" within Tenant's site. Specifically segregate Landlord's and Tenant's construction responsibilities inside and outside the line. Paragraph 11, "Improvement Costs", of Form 14-1, for example, could be modified to provide for Landlord to complete all on-site improvements outside the building envelope. As in Form 14-1, Tenant could reimburse Landlord for such costs. (Customarily, Tenant will reimburse Landlord for on-site improvement costs to improve the area within Tenant's site that fall outside the building envelope.)

11. Site Plan. Prior to lease execution, Landlord's and Tenant's construction representatives shall agree to a mutually acceptable site plan which shall include, but not be limited to, both building and parking layouts.

Start with the existing site plan and specifically address what amendments Landlord and Tenant will attempt to make, and set a schedule to resolve such changes. If conceptual agreement cannot be reached immediately as to the general size, configuration, and location of the building and required parking, should negotiations stop pending preparation of new site studies?

12. Local Government Agencies. Tenant's obligations under the lease shall be expressly conditioned upon Tenant obtaining approval from the city of __*[name]*__ and other governmental agencies having jurisdiction over the center to build a branch bank building substantially similar to exhibits to be attached to the lease.

Within what time frame? Do the parties know what entitlement steps are required? Reach agreements on appropriate time frames, termination rights, extension rights, and consideration therefor. Look at renderings and plans of similar buildings: Are there any problems that can be identified and resolved now? Review plans, elevations, and rendering now and attach to letter of intent, particularly to demonstrate or confirm a specific agreement.

13. Architectural Criteria. Landlord shall provide Tenant with a copy of the center's architectural design standards, specifications and color and materials board.

Consider attaching an exhibit demonstrating the criteria for Tenant's management approval concurrent with execution of the letter of intent. Do not run the risk that Tenant's management might quash the deal later when it is belatedly realized that Tenant's standard building must be modified to meet required architectural standards for the site.

14. Signage. Tenant shall have the right to install the maximum exterior signage available __*[consistent with local codes and ordinances and Landlord's signage criteria for the center]*__ and in no event shall be allowed less than two exterior building parapet signs. One monument sign shall be allowed on _______ Avenue, plus door signage consistent with Tenant's corporate signage standards __*[all of which shall be consistent with the center sign criteria and applicable governmental requirements]*__.

Self-explanatory changes are noted in italics.

15. Restricted Parking. While Tenant shall have reciprocal parking rights throughout the center, Tenant shall have the right to designate all parking spaces on the site as "___________ Bank Customer Parking Only" (or similar language).

Developer would typically want to retain the reciprocal nature of all parking throughout the center. Be careful that any such language does not violate your REA, CC&R's or any leases or other agreements made with major or other tenants. At most, such restricted parking

FORM 14-2

rights are probably necessary only for ATM access.

16. Subletting and Assignment. Tenant shall have full, unrestricted right to sublease or assign the site.

With unrestricted-use clause and such unrestricted subletting and assignment rights, developer loses control of the disposition and use of this prominent, free-standing pad for a very long potential lease term. See Chapter 18, Form 18-10, "Selected Assignment and Subletting Clauses," for alternative structures.

17. Completion of On-site Improvements. Tenant shall construct its building and all on-site improvements per plans and specifications to be reasonably approved by Landlord prior to Tenant applying for a building permit.

As referenced above, promptly reach a conceptual understanding of who pays for which on-site improvements. Set a procedure and deadline requiring Tenant to produce plans for Landlord's review as quickly as possible. For ideas, consider construction coordination language in Form 18-16 of Chapter 18.

18. Completion of Off-site Improvements. Prior to Tenant opening for business or being obligated to pay rent for the site, Landlord shall provide all off-site common area improvements up to the outside of the Tenant's sidewalk surrounding its building. Off-Site improvements shall include, but not be limited to, paving, curbing, lighting and landscaping.

Had the scope of the parties' work been concisely defined above, this paragraph would not have been necessary (except for the introduction of requested rent abatement if Landlord fails to timely perform). Again, usually it is more productive to work from the specific site plan graphically depicting the specific improvement responsibilities of Landlord and Tenant relative to an agreed building envelope and/or work of improvement line. The parties should be careful in how each is using customary language. The meaning attributed to "off-site" in this context would not be universally understood.

19. On-site Maintenance and Expense. Tenant shall provide, at Tenant's expense, all on-site building and landscape maintenance within the sidewalks surrounding the building.

The developer should be concerned that the "harmony" of landscape and property care is consistent throughout center. Aesthetic concerns usually result in Landlord exercising control over all of the center's common area landscaping and maintenance.

20. <u>Off-Site Maintenance and Expense (CAM)</u>. Landlord shall provide, through CAM assessment based upon the ratio of the Tenant's building size (approximately __*[e.g., 4,500]*__ square feet) to the total building square footage of the center, all maintenance and expense attributable to areas in the center outside of the sidewalks surrounding Tenant's building used in common by Tenant and other tenants of the center.

Should Landlord credit (not charge) Tenant for CAM expense attributable to areas inside the sidewalks, which in this case are maintained by Tenant? For aesthetic consistency, should Landlord also manage the area inside the sidewalks and charge Tenant under the CAM formula? Is it more appropriate to allocate CAM based upon the relative land area of the site relative to the overall land area of the center (rather than relative building areas)? Note that Tenant in this paragraph is unconventionally using "off-site" to mean the area "outside of the sidewalks surrounding Tenant's building". Again, by defining on- and off-site improvements and how they will be shared, ambiguity and confusion can be avoided.

21. <u>Title Report and C.C.&R. Approval</u>. Landlord shall provide Tenant a preliminary title report and a copy of any C.C. & R.'s and any reciprocal parking agreements together with all documentation governing the rights of __*[names of anchor tenants]*__ and other tenants in the center to the extent the rights of such other occupants affect the rights of Tenant. At lease signing Landlord shall provide Tenant with a policy of leasehold title insurance.

Why let the preliminary title report review linger? Get documents to Tenant as soon as possible and set a reasonable but limited review period. Do not leave Tenant and Tenant's attorneys in the dark relative to facts that may be important to complete the lease documentation—or in quickly determining that the proposed transaction is not workable. For example, a public right-of-way easement might encroach upon a proposed drive-through location; if the site plan cannot be adequately revised and having a drive-through is a key deal point, it would be to the parties' advantage to know this immediately rather than to incur further time and expense.

22. Exclusive Financial Institution and ATM Rights. Tenant shall have exclusive financial institution and ATM rights for the center.

As always, be prudent in considering the grant of an exclusive right. If such a right is to be granted, however, provide for its termination if the right is not used for a given time period ("use it or lose it"). For example, see Form 18-7, "Tenant's Limited Exclusive Merchandising Right", for limiting language.

23. Commission. _*[Name of broker]*_ is a licensed California real estate broker representing Tenant. Landlord agrees to pay _*[name of broker]*_ a commission equal to _*[e.g., 3]*_ % of the first _*[e.g., 5]*_ years minimum rent, _*[e.g., 2]*_ % of the second _*[e.g., 5]*_ years minimum rent and _*[e.g., 1.5]*_ % of the next _*[10]*_ years minimum rent. Said commission shall be payable in full when Tenant commences payment of rent in accordance with the terms of the lease.

Landlord should state clearly that any obligation to pay is contingent upon lease execution and satisfaction of all contingencies. Many landlords would also hold back a substantial portion of the commission pending the Tenant's opening for business on the site.

24. Contingencies. Tenant's interest is subject to the following contingencies:

24.1 Internal Approvals. This letter is specifically subject to approval by the Bank's (i) Senior Management and (ii) either the Board of Directors or the Bank's Executive Committee.

Within how many days from the signing of the letter? What is the substance of the approval—the economics, the letter, or is it actually the lease itself?

24.2 Comptroller of the Currency Approval. Landlord acknowledges that Tenant's obligations under any lease will be contingent upon Tenant obtaining approval from the Comptroller of the Currency to establish a branch bank in the center. Tenant agrees to use its best efforts to obtain all necessary governmental approvals.

How long is the normal Comptroller of the Currency approval? What are Landlord's true costs of holding this site and how long is Landlord willing to keep this outparcel off the market? Should Ten-

ant be required to pay for its "option" and any additional period required to obtain additional approvals? Consider preliminary or "stepped" rent similar to the preliminary rent structure in Form 14-1. Preliminary rent payments could be structured consistent with Tenant's approval/entitlement schedule; i.e., as Tenant's risk decreases over time (as entitlements are issued), preliminary rent payments could increase and perhaps be applicable, at least in part, to permanent rent.

Contingencies benefitting Landlord should also be considered, notably Landlord's entitlements for the center (including map recordation) and acceptable financing. See, for example, Chapter 13, Form 13-1, Paragraph 18.

25. Not Binding. This counter-proposal is an invitation to negotiate. It is neither an offer nor a contract. No party shall have any legal rights or obligations with respect to any other party, and no party should take any action or fail to take any action in detrimental reliance on this document until definitive, formal legal agreements have been prepared and signed by all parties involved.

Provide for a date by which the letter must be signed and a subsequent date when final documentation must be executed. Landlord should have the documented freedom to negotiate with substitute tenants if negotiations break down. See, for example, Form 14-1, Paragraphs 20 and 21.

If the terms set forth are acceptable, please sign below and return a copy of this letter to the undersigned within __*[e.g., 10]*__ days.

We look forward to receiving your response.

Very truly yours,

[Brokerage firm representing bank]

[Name]
[Title]

UNDERSTOOD AND AGREED:
This __ day of __________, 20__.

[Name of developer]

By: _______________

Its: _______________

Exhibits

Note: *No exhibits are included in this hypothetical presentation. Usually, marked-up portions of site plans and other materials can be prepared, with very little effort, to effectively articulate the parties' intentions.*

END OF FORM 14-2

OVERVIEW

Chapter 15 discusses the major deal points in negotiating an agreement to enter into a joint venture to develop a new shopping center. The financial partner contributes substantially all of the capital required for the venture's operation in return for an equity interest in the venture. The developer receives fee income and a project equity interest.

FORMS

15-1 Preliminary Venture Agreement between Developer and Proposed Financial Partner. Letter of Intent to Enter into Joint Venture to Develop a Shopping Center.

Chapter 15

Joint Venturing with a Financial Partner

Brains, wits and creative ability will beat money 10 times out of 10. So if you're short of money, start using your head.

— H. Ross Perot

For many developers, forming a joint venture with an equity partner is an essential step to obtain third-party debt financing. However, even the well-capitalized developer may form a venture relationship with a deep-pocket equity partner to reduce developmental risk and achieve a relatively assured fee income. From the financial partner's perspective, investing equity in a venture provides an opportunity to participate in future profits on a wholesale basis and to receive a risk-adjusted return higher than market alternatives. In short, the essence of the venture relationship is a sharing of skills and capital, profits and losses, and balancing of risks and rewards.

Although the rationale for joint venture structuring may be relatively intuitive to the experienced retail developer, the complex business, legal, and tax issues perplex even the most skilled legal and accounting professionals. Ample books and articles have been written on the subject of joint ventures and fully addressing these issues is beyond the scope of this text. Unfortunately, however, many developers have no practical deal-making form to aid them in verbalizing their intentions in forming a joint venture and are consistently frustrated in creating new venture partnerships and formats. Understandably, they attempt to hold on to proven financial partners and habitual practices.

Mindful that the issue cannot be fully addressed in the space allotted, this chapter contains one editable deal-making document that covers the major economic terms of a "front end" venture wherein the venture is formed at the inception of a project and serves as the project developer and borrower. The form assumes the financial partner contributes substantially all of the venture's required capital. Form 15-1 in most cases will serve merely as a preliminary discussion memorandum from which to begin to negotiate the terms of a formal joint venture agreement.

Given the complexities, the numerous possible entities and deal structures characteristic of joint ventures, and the impossibility of preparing a single letter of intent format that reasonably accommodates them all, a format was designed to emphasize the financial requirements for the venture in a way that could be easily completed by the developer. Accordingly, Form 15-1 references an attached business plan prepared by the developer. Although developers routinely prepare pro formas, the "Business Plan" is essentially an expanded pro forma. If the developer applies sound thinking and carefully prepares the business plan, the business plan will, in effect, define the equity, working capital, and debt requirements of the venture.

Once the financial requirements are determined, the intention is that the letter can then be prepared in a format that outlines a business structure that appropriately satisfies the financial requirements. The most fundamental step, therefore, is to apply sound reasoning and judgment in the preparation of the business plan. In preparing the business plan, be particularly attentive to risk (e.g., construction risk, long term financing risk, and leaseup/value risk) and how elements of risk can be appropriately reduced by a careful refinement of venture provisions. Be alert to the potential for cost overruns and shortfalls in anticipated revenues. Careful preparation of the business plan and the deal letter should provide for possible contingencies and availability of additional capital if needed.

Form 15-1 assumes the prevailing general partnership format. Many institutional investors prefer the role of general partner within a general partnership structure because a limited partnership interest does not provide the degree of control they seek. Unfortunately, space does not allow discussion of various alternative entities and their relative advantages and disadvantages. Alternative formats include use of the limited partnership, participating or convertible mortgage, land sale and leaseback with a participating leasehold mortgage, and, less frequently, a corporate format.

Frequently, ventures are structured with a site's landowner whereby the site is contributed to the venture. The landowner could be referenced as the "Financial Partner" and contribute the site as the Financial Partner's capital contribution (in addition to other capital, such as cash). Many refinements to the venture structure may satisfy the particular needs of the landowner as venture partner (e.g., right to extract cash from a land or construction loan, option right to purchase venture improvements, and provisions protecting the landowner's income or estate tax planning), but these issues are not addressed in Form 15-1.

Form 15-1 also ignores critical refinements found in many venture agreements such as special allocations and guaranteed payments for tax purposes, specific management criteria, appointment of a third-party contractor or construction manager, developer's obligation to adhere to an agreed construction schedule, obligation for cost overruns, equity dilution or "squeeze down," and other consequences of the failure of the developer or the financial partner to contribute agreed capital, transfers of interests and buy-sell procedures, dissolution and liquidation, and many other important but less fundamental or more "legal" provisions. The attorney representing a financial partner will probably want to add selected additional provisions to this basic letter form.

It is crucial that the developer obtain qualified legal and accounting help to properly plan and structure the venture. Be aware that there are significant tax and accounting issues inherent in the formation of development ventures that this chapter does not address. The developer should be aware that when a developer receives an interest in capital or profits disproportionate to the developer's contributed capital, an income tax issue is raised as to whether the developer's participation is received in return for past or future services and thus subject to income tax on a current basis. Skilled legal and accounting professionals can provide a host of refinements, including structuring the transaction to insulate the developer from current recognition of income tax.

Form 15-1 has been prepared to allow the letter to be directed either from the developer to the prospective financial partner or from the financial partner to the developer.

Form 15-1

Letter of Intent to Enter into Joint Venture to Develop a Shopping Center

[Developer Letterhead]

OR

[Financial Joint Venture Partner Letterhead]

__*[Date]*__

[Name and address of developer OR *financial partner* ______________
____
______________________*]*

Re: __*[Name of Shopping Center]*__
__*[describe location]*__
__*[city]*__, __*[state]*__

Dear __________:

This letter sets forth the general terms and conditions upon which __*[insert name of potential joint venture partner]*__ *("Financial Partner")]*__ OR __*[name of developer's entity]*__ *("Developer")]*__ is willing to form a joint venture __*[organized as a general partnership]*__ (the "venture") with *[select preceding name* not *selected:]* __*[name of developer's entity]*__ *("Developer")]*__ OR __*[name of potential joint venture partner]*__ *("Financial Partner")]*__ to develop the "project" described below. The joint venture agreement shall be acceptable in form and substance to Financial Partner and Developer and consistent with the following general provisions:

1. Purpose of Venture. The venture will be formed to acquire approximately ___ acres of undeveloped land (the "site") located in __*[city, state]*__, described on the attached Exhibit "__*[A]*__", and to develop and construct on the site a __*[e.g., power center consisting of approximately* _______ *square feet of anchor tenant stores,* ____ *square feet of small tenant shops, and* ___ *free-standing outparcels/pads comprising a total building space of approxi-*

FORM 15-1

mately ______ square feet]__ (the "project").

2. Parties. The venture will be comprised of the two joint venturers, *__[Financial Partner and Developer]__ OR __[Developer and Financial Partner]__*. No other parties will be admitted to the venture without the consent of *__[both parties]__*.

3. Formation. The venture will be formed after Financial Partner has completed its due diligence review of the site and the various conditions precedent to formation of the venture (described below) have been satisfied or waived. Title to the site will be conveyed to the venture at the time the venture is formed. The transfer of the site to the venture will be effected through an escrow.

4. Term of Venture. The term of the venture shall commence upon the date of the "closing" (defined below), and shall continue until ____________, 20__ unless sooner terminated.

5. Definitions. The following definitions shall apply:

This letter of intent format assumes Developer has carefully prepared a "Business Plan" (defined below) projecting the sources and uses of required funds and the forecasted financial results. If the Business Plan depicts the capital required at each phase of the project, cash flow after given debt service and the various specific fees payable to Developer and/or Developer's affiliates (e.g., overhead reimbursement fee, leasing and parcel sale fee, construction fee, and post-completion management fee), the proposed Financial Partner will be more inclined to favorably consider the project and the letter of intent to enter into the venture will be easier to prepare since it will largely "incorporate by reference" such Business Plan. One cannot escape the careful, reasoned, objective thinking that is required to professionally complete the Business Plan.

5.1 Business Plan. The project will be developed in accordance with an agreed "Business Plan", which shall mean a document prepared by Developer containing (a) pro forma projections of anticipated net operating revenues and sale proceeds for the project, (b) the related equity capital requirements and costs and expenses *__[by project phase]__*, (c) *__[committed]__* required debt financing and its cost and terms *__[by project phase]__* and (d) the resulting *__[after tax]__* profits and losses of the venture *__[for X annual operating periods]__*. A preliminary Business Plan prepared by Developer is attached hereto as Exhibit "__*[B]*__".

5.2 Capital. The term "capital" means the agreed value of all "property" (including, but not limited to, cash, real property, personal property, and contract rights), and all Pre-development Expenses incurred on behalf of the project contributed to the venture by the venturers.

5.3 Net Cash Flow. The term "Net Cash Flow" means that portion of the cash revenues or receipts of the venture (other than "Proceeds of Capital Transactions") remaining to the venture after (a) the payment of all expenses and other current commitments of the venture with respect to the project, including interest and principal payments currently due on any venture loans payable to third parties or any lending venturer and (b) the creation of reasonable cash contingency reserves for the venture.

5.4 Proceeds of Capital Transactions. The term "Proceeds of Capital Transactions" means all proceeds resulting from the refinancing or sale of the project.

5.5 Financial Partner Preference. __*[With reference to Financial Partner]*__ [t]he term "Preference" means a preferred, but not a guaranteed distribution, payable to Financial Partner equal to __*[e.g., 9]*__ % on an annual basis on Financial Partner's "Unrecovered Capital", as defined below. The Preference shall be cumulative, so that to the extent Financial Partner has not received a full __*[e.g., 9]*__ % annual amount in any prior period, Financial Partner shall be entitled to receive additional amounts under the Preference until there has been a cumulative __*[e.g., 9]*__ % annual amount actually distributed. (As the Preference shall be payable only on Financial Partner's capital for so long as it is contributed, no Preference shall be paid after Financial Partner has received the full amount of Financial Partner's Unrecovered Capital.)

FORM 15-1

Optional: Although the Developer's investment has traditionally been reimbursed concurrent with the venture closing and capital infusion by the financial partner, current financial partners may require a significant equity investment by the Developer. The following paragraph provides for a preferential return on Developer's capital. If used, add as Paragraph 5.6 and renumber subparagraphs 5.6 and 5.7.

5.__ Developer Preference. With reference to Developer the term "Preference" means a preferred, but not a guaranteed distribution, payable to Developer equal to __*[e.g., 9]*__ % on an annual basis on Developer's "Unrecovered Capital", as defined below. The Preference shall be cumulative, so that to the extent Developer has not received a full __*[e.g., 9]*__ % annual amount in any prior period, Developer shall be entitled to receive additional amounts under the Preference until there has been a cumulative __*[e.g., 9]*__ % annual amount actually distributed. (As the Preference shall be payable only on Developer's capital for so long as it is contributed, no Preference shall be paid after Developer has received the full amount of Developer's Unrecovered Capital.)

5.6 Unrecovered Capital. The term "Unrecovered Capital" means the sum of any original and additional contributions of capital made by a venturer, less any cash distributed to such venturer (in excess of the Preference, if any, allocable to such venturer).

5.7 Pre-development Expenses. The term "Pre-development Expenses" means the total out-of-pocket expenses advanced by Developer in furtherance of the project (excluding Developer's overhead expense) made prior to the venture's acquisition of the site. The total Pre-development Expenses incurred through the date of this letter and the total Pre-development Expenses projected through the venture's acquisition of the site are set forth in Exhibit "__*[C]*__".

6. Profit and Loss Sharing Interests. Financial Partner will own a __*[e.g., 50]*__ % interest and Developer will own a __*[50]*__ % interest in the profits and losses of the venture ("Profit and Loss Sharing Interests").

7. Initial Capital Contributions. Developer and Financial Partner shall make the following initial capital contributions to the venture:

7.1 Developer. At the closing (as defined below), Developer shall contribute the following to the venture:

(a) All developer's interest in the site, together with all easements, licenses, appurtenances, entitlements and all other rights of Developer relating to the site at an agreed value of __*[$__________, Developer's cost basis in the site, plus all Developer's actual Pre-development Expenses, as estimated in Exhibit "__[C]__". Such Pre-development Expenses include __[e.g., option/interest]__ payments of $_______ per __[e.g., month/quarter]__ payable to _______ through the closing]__ OR __[alternatively, insert another valuation methodology for Developer's contribution]__*.

(b) *[List all other property or assets to be contributed to the venture by Developer, such as personal property, plans, developmental approvals, contract rights, leases, accrued leasing commissions, etc., not included above.]*

7.2 Financial Partner. At the closing, Financial Partner shall contribute the following to the venture:

(a) Cash in the amount of $ __________ _*[e.g., being the difference between the total project costs set forth in the Business Plan and third party loan commitments _[arranged OR to be arranged]_ by Developer]*_; _*[and]*_

(b) *[List any other property to be contributed to the venture by Financial Partner.]*

Alternative "A"—Paragraph 8

A developer will typically be obligated to prepare and live by the developer's budget. Unfortunately, the developer can become "trapped" in the budget when an excellent high-rent paying tenant (necessitating an additional unanticipated capital contribution) becomes available after formation of the venture and the financial partner's approval of the budget. There may be very sound economic reasons to build for such a tenant, but the financial partner may be unwilling to advance additional capital solely because such additional construction cost exceeds the developer's budget. Having no legal obligation to advance additional capital, the financial partner may attempt to extract concessions from the developer as a condition to amending the budget. The following clause, although loose, addresses this issue (and also assumes an additional specific capital contribution is required to fund a second phase of the project). Carefully consider the underlying financial assumptions of the Business Plan before drafting such a paragraph, paying close attention to potential project events that could trigger a need for additional capital and the estimated amount of such capital.

FORM 15-1

8. Additional and Contingent Capital Contributions. As set forth in the Business Plan, Financial Partner will make an additional capital contribution of $________ at _*[describe event when required, e.g., at the commencement of phase two of the project]*_*(the "Phase Two Capital Contribution")]*_. Furthermore, while the Pro Forma demonstrates the need for the initial capital contribution and the $_*[same as preceding number, e.g., Phase Two Capital Contribution]*_, the parties also understand that from time to time tenant prospects may become available such that it is in the venture's best interests for the Financial Partner to advance more capital to the project in return for increased rental revenues and incremental project yield.

For example, although the Business Plan projects an outparcel/parcel sale to a free-standing tenant, as a result of the project's marketing results, it may instead be prudent to enter into a build-to-suit transaction with such a tenant. Consequently, the joint venture agreement will provide specific standards by which Financial Partner will agree to contribute capital (in excess of Financial Partner's initial capital contribution and the __*[e.g., Phase Two Capital Contribution]*__) in a total additional amount not to exceed $________ ("Contingency Capital"). Such standards will provide that such Contingency Capital __*[e.g., (i) will be advanced to effectuate transactions with creditworthy tenants, (ii) will return an annual capitalized yield to the venture of not less than __ % at the time any such transaction is entered into; and (iii) such capital is used only for such costs not previously included within the Business Plan and not for cost overruns or expenses which Developer failed to control]*__. *[Financial Partner may request the following:]* Nevertheless, if it is necessary to contribute additional capital to the venture in excess of the preceding amounts, the parties shall contribute the additional capital in proportion to their respective interests in the profits and losses of the venture.

OR

Alternative "B"—Paragraph 8

The following is a typical, traditional approach to the thorny issue of additional capital contributions.

8. Additional Capital Contributions. If it is necessary to contribute additional capital to the venture, the parties shall contribute the additional capital in proportion to their respective interests in the profits and losses of the venture.

End of Alternatives "A" and "B" to Paragraph 8 —Continue to Paragraph 9.

9. Project Loans. This letter of intent assumes __*[Developer]*__ will procure, on behalf of the venture, the project loan(s) described in the Business Plan subject to the following terms and conditions: __*[describe]*__

If applicable:

10. Assumption of Liabilities. As of the closing, each of the venturers shall be deemed to have assumed that percentage of the obligations and liabilities set forth on Exhibit "__*[D]*__" as is consistent with each of the venturer's Profit and Loss Sharing Interest. __*[Upon such assumption of such liabilities, the venturers' liability therefor (as among the venturers) shall be several and not joint]*__. *[Renumber subsequent paragraphs if this paragraph is not applicable.]*

11. Profits and Losses; Adjustments. Initially, all net profits, losses, income, credits and deductions shall be allocated among the venturers proportionate to the venturers' Profit and Loss Sharing Interests set forth above. Notwithstanding this principle, income realized by the venture, whether from the leasing of the project, the sale of any capital asset of the venture, or upon termination of the venture, shall be allocated first to Financial Partner to the extent that it has or should have received any distributions of the Preference *[if applicable:]*__*[and then to Developer to the extent it has or should have received the amount described in Paragraph* __*[12(d)]*__*]*__.

> ***Note:*** *The priority of distributions could always change based upon the amount of the developer's money actually invested. The following example assumes the developer is obligated to make a nominal cash contribution repayable only after the financial partner's capital is repaid.*

12. Distributions of Net Cash Flow. Upon completion of construction and substantial occupancy, the venture's Net Cash Flow shall be distributed to the venturers in the following order of priority:

(a) Repayment of interest on __*[, and then principal of,]*__ loans made by any venturer to the venture;

> ***Note:*** *If the preceding italicized phrase is not included in this clause (i.e., repayment of principal is subordinated to other items given higher priority of payment), be certain to provide for repayment of principal elsewhere within this Paragraph 12.*

(b) Payment of the Preference to Financial Partner;

(c) Repayment of Financial Partner's Unrecovered Capital;

Alternative "A"—Paragraph 12(d)

__*[(d) Payment to Developer of an amount equal to the Preference paid Financial Partner;]*__

FORM 15-1

OR

Alternative "B"—Paragraph 12(d)

__*[(d) Payment of the Preference to Developer;]*__

Note: *This reference is to the optional payment of a Preference to Developer, as described in Paragraph 5.__ "Developer Preference," above.*

OR

Alternative "C"—Paragraph 12(d)

Leave blank—Insert neither Alternative "A" nor Alternative "B" Paragraph 12 "(d)" choices. Change the following Paragraphs "(e)" and "(f)" to "(d)" and "(e)", respectively. (If Alternative "C" is selected, also delete the italicized phrase at the end of Paragraph 11, above.)

End of Alternatives "A", "B" and "C" to Paragraph 12(d) —Continue to Paragraph 12(e)

(e) Repayment of Developer's Unrecovered Capital; and

(f) Thereafter, to the venturers in proportion to their respective interests in the profits of the venture.

13. <u>Distributions of Proceeds from Capital Transactions</u>. Proceeds of capital transactions shall be distributed or applied in the following order of priority:

(a) Repayment of any indebtedness of the venture to third parties (and the creation of adequate, reasonable reserves therefor);

(b) For so long as the venture continues to operate the project, the creation of or addition to reasonable reserves in amounts necessary to provide for contingent liabilities in a manner consistent with customary practices in the shopping center industry;

(c) Repayment of interest on, and then principal of, loans made by any venturer to the venture;

(d) Repayment to Financial Partner of its Unrecovered Capital together with any Preference to which Financial Partner is entitled;

__*[(e) Payment to Developer of the amount described in subparagraph 12(d);]*__

> ***Note:*** *If neither Alternative "A" nor Alternative "B" were selected as Paragraph 12 "(d)" above, do not insert this Paragraph 13 "(e)" and change the following Paragraphs "(f)" and "(g)" to "(e)" and "(f)", respectively:*

(f) Repayment of Developer's Unrecovered Capital; and

(g) Pro rata to the venturers in accordance with their respective Profit and Loss Sharing Interests.

When negotiating the final joint venture agreement, the venturer's accountants and attorneys will refine the parties' description of profits and losses, allocation of cash flow and capital structure (as outlined in the preceding Paragraphs __*[e.g., 11, 12 and 13]*__) so that the business arrangement conforms with standard legal and accounting principles.

> ***Note:*** *Paragraphs 11, 12 and 13 raise complex accounting and legal issues beyond the scope of this text. The preceding paragraph is included as a reminder that although the parties may do their best, accountants and lawyers may necessarily make substantial changes to the parties' articulation of the business agreement.*

14. Escrow and Closing. The formation of the venture shall be consummated through an escrow with __*[e.g., ________ Title Insurance Company]*__ at __*[describe location]*__, __*[state]*__ ("escrow"). The escrow will close (the "closing") after all conditions of the close of escrow have been waived or satisfied and title to the site has been conveyed to the venture. The parties plan the closing to occur on or about ________, 20__ (the "Scheduled Closing Date").

FORM 15-1

"Optimistic" Developer-oriented optional:

14.1 Reimbursement of Developer's Pre-development Expenses. Given the risks assumed by Developer in advancing and carrying the Pre-development Expenses to date, Developer's accommodation to Financial Partner in providing a lengthy escrow prior to the closing and the parties' acknowledgment that Financial Partner will have substantial knowledge of the site and the project prior to the actual venture closing, __*[all]*__ OR __ *[$______]*__ OR __*[__ %]*__ of Developer's Pre-development Expenses shall be reimbursed to Developer by Financial Partner __ days prior to the Scheduled Closing Date. __*[The remaining balance]*__ OR __*[__ %]*__ of Developer's Pre-development Expenses accumulated through the closing shall be reimbursed to Developer by Financial Partner at the closing.

15. Contingencies. Financial Partner's obligation to form the venture is contingent upon Financial Partner's approval of the following matters before the Scheduled Closing Date __*[and within the specific time periods set forth below]*__:

15.1 Title. Financial Partner's review and approval of a current ALTA survey of the site and condition of title to the site, including, without limitation, all covenants, encumbrances, encroachments and other matters affecting title to the site. Developer shall furnish Financial Partner with an ALTA survey and preliminary title report, including legible copies of all exceptions referenced therein within __*[e.g., 21]*__ days following full execution of this letter of intent. __*[Within __[e.g., 21 working]__ days of its receipt, Financial Partner will approve such documents]*__.

15.2 Title Policy. Issuance of a __*[See Appendix A, Form A-1]*__ policy of title insurance adequately insuring Financial Partner's interest in the venture at closing, subject only to the title matters approved by Financial Partner.

15.3 Review of Existing and Proposed Agreements, Leases and Approvals. Financial Partner's review and approval of all agreements, contracts and records which relate to, concern or affect the site, including without limitation, any and all current or prospective leases, brokerage contracts, management agreements, maintenance contracts, governmental agreements, governmental permits and approvals, and any other documents and instruments pertaining to the leasing and tenancy, management, operation or development of the site, including any correspondence with governmental entities. __*[Financial Partner will have ___ days from __[e.g., receipt of all such documentation]__ in which to approve this contingency]*__.

15.4 Environmental Investigation. Not later than ______, 20__ Developer shall provide Financial Partner, at Developer's cost and expense, with a __*[e.g., Phase I]*__ environmental assessment report of the site. The environmental assessment report shall be furnished by an experienced engineering firm approved by Financial Partner and be satisfactory in form and substance to Financial Partner. __*[Financial Partner will have ___ days from receipt of the* *report (and any subsequent report recommended and issued by such firm) in which to approve this contingency]__.*

15.5 Additional Investigations. Financial Partner's receipt and approval of such financial, physical, engineering, geological, hazardous substance and other audits, studies, reports, inspections and investigations of the site which it requires. *__[Financial Partner shall identify and request that Developer provide any such specific additional matters within __ days after execution of this letter of intent. Financial Partner shall have __ days to review any such responsive materials supplied by Developer in response to such a request by Financial Partner]__.*

If applicable:

15.6 Project Loan Commitment. Within __ days following execution of this letter of intent, *__[Developer]__* shall have procured from an institutional lender a commitment to fund the project loan(s) presumed by the Business Plan. *__[The loan commitment shall provide for the funding of a $________ venture loan, on or before the closing, with an interest rate not greater than __ % amortized over not less than __ years with the following additional terms: __[describe]__ __[Financial Partner]__ will have __ days from receipt of each such commitment in which to approve the terms of any such proposed venture loan]__.*

> ***Note:*** *Generally, the required debt structure will be the difference between total project costs and the anticipated equity contributions of the parties.*

If applicable:

15.__ Tenant Estoppel Certificates. Financial Partner shall have received and approved a tenant estoppel certificate, duly executed by each tenant of the site (if any) in form and substance satisfactory to Financial Partner.

15.__ Miscellaneous. *[List all other conditions to closing specific to this transaction such as receipt of specific governmental approvals, acceptance of contract assignments, etc.]*

Financial-Partner oriented:

If Financial Partner is not satisfied, in Financial Partner's sole discretion, as to all contingencies set forth in this Paragraph *__[e.g., 15]__* and fails to delivered to Developer a written notice to proceed to closing on or before the Scheduled Closing Date, Financial Partner shall be deemed to have ter-

FORM 15-1

minated this letter of intent and neither party shall have any further rights or obligations hereunder.

To appease the Financial Partner going into the deal:

16. Developer's Representations and Warranties Regarding Condition of Site and Project. While the parties will negotiate various representations and warranties during negotiation of the joint venture agreement, Developer will, among other things, represent and warrant that Developer has no knowledge of any undisclosed condition (including without limitation, toxic or hazardous substances, geological conditions, governmental restrictions, required governmental approvals, and pending or threatened governmental action) concerning the site which could adversely affect the venture's intended use and development of the site.

> ***Note:*** *Developer should fully disclose any potential problems and the steps being taken to alleviate or remedy them.*
>
> ***Note:*** *The parties will need to determine the circumstances in which the managing venturer can act unilaterally on behalf of the venture and when the managing venturer's actions will require unanimous consent.*

17. Major Decisions. No act shall be taken or sum expended or obligation incurred by the venture or any venturer with respect to a matter within the scope of any of the strategic decisions ("Major Decisions") affecting the venture, without the unanimous approval of the venturers. A listing of such Major Decisions shall be negotiated and included within the joint venture agreement and shall include such matters as acquiring additional property, financing or rearranging the financing of venture property, selling the project or leasing the project on terms other than as set forth in guidelines previously approved by the venturers, and further matters of fundamental or strategic importance.

18. Managing Venturer. Developer shall be the managing venturer and shall have full power and authority to manage, subject to the restrictions and other terms set forth in the joint venture agreement, the day-to-day operations and administration of the venture and its business consistent with the Business Plan.

19. Developer's Fees. __*[As depicted in the Business Plan,]*__ Developer shall receive the following fees payable by the venture during the term of the venture:

Some developers have attempted to structure the development overhead fee as a distribution or withdrawal of capital from the venture rather than as fee income currently taxable, thereby attempting to defer income tax recognition, possibly until sale or disposition of the project. However, if the financial partner desires to participate in tax losses, it will prefer that any such fee payable to the developer be structured as a conventional venture expense so as to be deductible by the venture in the year paid. If the financial partner does not seek tax losses, it may allow payment in the form of capital withdrawals provided future distributions of profits reflect such capital withdrawals.

19.1 Developer Overhead Fee. Developer shall receive a Developer overhead fee to reimburse Developer for salaries and administrative overhead expense incurred in connection with the management of the project and the venture. The Developer overhead fee shall be *__[$________]__ OR __[e.g., 3%]__ of the sum of __[e.g., the gross site purchase cost and the cost of all on- and off-site improvements and buildings constructed by Developer]__ OR __[e.g., $2.50 per square foot of total gross building area proposed for development on Developer's proposed site plan]__*. The Developer overhead fee shall be payable from *__[capital advanced by Financial Partner]__ OR __[loans obtained by the venture]__* and paid in *__[e.g., 24 equal monthly]__* installments in advance beginning on *__[the date of the closing]__ OR __[______, 20__]__* and ending *__[e.g., 24 months thereafter]__ OR __[_______, 20__]__*.

Optional:

If at any time additional land is acquired for additional development and construction by the venture, the monthly installment of the Developer overhead fee payable shall be adjusted upward consistent with the preceding formula.

Alternative "A"—Paragraph 19.2
One idea (Marketing contract with Developer or Developer's affiliate)

19.2 Leasing and Parcel Sale Fees. *__[XYZ Brokerage Co., an affiliate of Developer]__ OR __[Developer]__* shall earn leasing and parcel sale fees in accordance with the proposed Site Marketing Agreement attached hereto as Exhibit "*__[E]__*".

To prepare this agreement, complete and attach an appropriately edited version of the marketing letter agreement included in Chapter 8 as Form 8-1. The parties to this edited version of the marketing letter agreement would be the venture as the payor of such fees and the Developer as the retained "Broker" payee.

OR

Alternative "B"—Paragraph 19.2
Another idea (Marketing contract with independent brokerage firm with optional override to Developer)

19.2 Leasing and Parcel Sale Fees. The venture shall enter into a site marketing contract with __*[XYZ Brokerage Co., an independent brokerage firm]*__ which shall earn leasing and parcel sale fees in accordance with the proposed Site Marketing Agreement attached hereto as Exhibit "__*[E]*__".

To prepare this agreement, complete and attach an appropriately edited version of the marketing letter agreement included in Chapter 8 as Form 8-1. The parties to this edited version of the marketing letter agreement would be the venture as the payor of such fees and the independent, third-party brokerage firm as the retained "Broker" payee. Continue with the following optional deal point:

To compensate Developer for Developer's skill and administrative efforts in overseeing such parcel sale and leasing effort, Developer shall be paid an override of __ % on each such fee payable to __*[XYZ Brokerage Co.]*__.

End of Alternatives "A" and "B" to Paragraph 19.2
—Continue to Paragraph 19.3.

Optional (Developer general contractor fee):

19.3 Construction Fee. Developer shall act as the project's general contractor on behalf of the venture and shall receive as its general contractor's fee an amount not to exceed __ % of the venture's agreed base construction cost set forth in the Business Plan, as adjusted by agreement of the parties.

19.4 Management Fees after Development and Construction. Upon completion of construction, the venture shall retain Developer as property manager for the shopping center. The annual fee payable by the venture for such services shall be not less than __*[e.g., 4]*__ % of the NNN income received by the venture before debt service. __*[A typical "arm's length" property management agreement shall be entered into by and between the venture and Developer as the property manager]*__.

Not common but possible optional:

__. **Financial Partner's Fee.** Financial Partner shall receive a fee of $__________ to reimburse it for salaries of representatives employed in connection with the venture and related overhead, payable in equal monthly installments of __*[amount]*__ from __*[capital advanced by Financial Partner]*__ OR __*[loans obtained by the venture]*__. *[Note: If this paragraph is inserted, renumber the following paragraphs:]*

20. Other. *[List any other special provisions to be included in the joint venture agreement, such as special allocations and guaranteed payments for tax purposes, restrictions on transfers, buy-sell rights and procedures, consequences of the failure to contribute agreed capital, appointment of third-party contractor/construction manager, Developer's obligation to adhere to an agreed upon construction schedule, buy-sell rights, and any other material deal points.]*

21. Costs and Prorations.

21.1 Closing Costs. __*[Developer]*__ OR __*[The venture]*__ shall pay all real estate commissions and finders' fees payable in connection with the transaction, including a real estate commission of __*[amount]*__ to _______, which __*[Developer agrees to pay]*__ OR __*[the venture shall pay]*__ through escrow upon recordation of the deed to the venture.

Continue with one of the following:

Alternative "A"
Developer oriented

The venture shall pay through escrow all title company charges for ALTA Title Insurance, survey costs, documentation and transfer fees, recording costs, all escrow fees and other normal closing costs for the transaction.

OR

Alternative "B"
Financial-Partner oriented

Developer shall pay through escrow all title company charges for ALTA Title

Insurance, documentation and transfer fees and one-half the escrow fee. The venture shall pay all recording costs, survey costs, and one-half the escrow fee. Other normal closing costs for the transaction, if any, and only if escrow successfully closes as provided for herein, shall be paid by the venture.

21.2 Prorations. Real estate taxes and assessments, personal property taxes, rent and operating expenses and all other income and expenses of the site shall be prorated as of the closing date.

Alternative "A"—Paragraph 22
Developer oriented

22. Non-assignment. Developer has bargained for the continued involvement and participation of Financial Partner. Consequently, Financial Partner shall have no right to independently assign Financial Partner's interest in the venture to any third party except with the consent of Developer or by operation of law.

OR

Alternative "B"—Paragraph 22
Financial Partner oriented

22. Assignment. Financial Partner shall be entitled to assign this letter of intent or Financial Partner's interest in the venture to ____________, or to an affiliate of Financial Partner.

End of Alternatives "A" and "B" to Paragraph 22
—Continue to Paragraph 23

23. Duration of Offer. This offer shall remain open, unless withdrawn or extended, until 5:00 p.m., Pacific Standard Time, ____________, 20__. If this offer is not accepted by that time, it shall become null and void.

Optional:

__. Financial Partner Parent Approval. In addition to other contingencies set forth herein, this letter of intent and Financial Partner's obligations hereunder shall be specifically subject to approval of Financial Partner's parent company. If Financial Partner has not, for any reason, notified Developer in writing on or before ______, 20__ that Financial Partner has obtained its parent company approval, Financial Partner shall be deemed to have terminated this letter of intent and neither party shall have any further rights or obligations hereunder.

24. Non-binding Letter of Intent. This conceptual letter of intent is not intended to constitute an agreement which will legally bind either party.

24.1 Further Negotiation. A contract between the parties will not exist unless and until the parties have executed a definitive joint venture agreement, approved by legal counsel for each of the parties, containing all essential terms of an agreed upon transaction. The parties acknowledge that they have not set forth herein nor agreed upon all essential terms of the transaction described herein, including without limitation, required refinements to the conceptual understandings of the parties, representations and warranties, conditions precedent, indemnities and financing matters, and that such essential terms will be the subject of further negotiations.

Further exculpatory language generally protecting Financial Partner:

24.2 No Reliance. The parties acknowledge that it would be imprudent and unreasonable to rely upon the expectation of entering into the joint venture agreement. Efforts by either party to complete due diligence, negotiate and obtain financing, or prepare the joint venture agreement shall not be considered as evidence of intent by either party to be bound by this letter. The performance by either party prior to execution of the joint venture agreement of any obligations which may ultimately be included in such agreement when negotiations are completed shall not be considered as evidence by either party to be bound by this letter.

Financial-Partner-oriented optional:

25. Exclusivity. Notwithstanding the otherwise non-binding nature of this letter, from and after joint execution of this letter and until ________, 20__ or until such time as (a) the parties cannot in good faith, agree upon the terms and conditions of the joint venture agreement or (b) Financial Partner does not proceed with this transaction pursuant to the terms of this letter, Developer will not (i) offer the site for sale, (ii) accept any offer to sell the site, (iii) seek or accept any other financial partner with which to own or develop the site or (iv) lease, transfer, hypothecate, mortgage or otherwise convey any interest in the site without the prior written consent of Financial Partner.

If you are in agreement with the foregoing, please indicate your approval by executing a copy of this letter and returning it to me no later than ________, 20__. Following my receipt of a fully executed counterpart of this letter, Financial Partner will begin to satisfy the contingencies and commence its investigations set forth above and our attorneys shall be instructed to be-

FORM 15-1

gin to prepare the definitive joint venture agreement.

Very truly yours,

[Name of developer]
OR
[Name of financial partner]

[Name][Title]

UNDERSTOOD AND AGREED:
This __ day of __________, 20__.

[The following sentence would sometimes be required if the letter is written by Financial Partner for execution by Developer:]

The undersigned hereby approves and accepts the foregoing provisions and conditions, and represents and warrants that the person executing this document on behalf of Developer is fully authorized to do so.

[Name of developer]
OR
[Name of financial partner]

By: _______________

Its: _______________

Exhibit "A"
[Description of the "site"]

Exhibit "B"
[Copy of preliminary Business Plan prepared by Developer]

Exhibit "C"
[Breakdown showing Developer's total Pre-development Expenses incurred through the date of this letter and total Pre-development Expenses projected through the venture's acquisition of the site]

[If applicable:]
Exhibit "D"
[List of obligations and liabilities assumed by each of the venturers]

<u>Exhibit "E"</u>

[Proposed Site Marketing Agreement showing proposed leasing and parcel sale fees]

END OF FORM 15-1

FORM 15-1

OVERVIEW

Chapter 16 considers the purchase of a closely held corporation's stock as a means to acquire the corporation's real estate. Corporate acquisitions yield opportunities for developers and retailers.

FORMS

16-1 Stock Purchase of Company Owning Real Estate. Letter of Intent to Enter into Stock Purchase Agreement for 100% of Stock of Privately Held Operating Business; Cash Base Price at Closing Plus Incentive Price Payable in Installments Based upon Earnout Formula.

Chapter 16

Purchasing the Stock of a Company to Control Its Real Estate

As long as you're going to be thinking anyway, think big.
—Donald Trump

Many of the major corporate mergers, acquisitions, and leveraged buyouts arranged by Wall Street investment bankers represent an attempt to exploit the untapped, unrecognized value of underlying real estate assets of the acquired company. Prevailing U.S. accounting standards require that real estate assets be carried on a company's financial statements at book value rather than at current market value. Although current market value of real estate assets can be shown in supplementary footnotes to the financial statements (a focal point of the financially astute), in keeping with a conservative accounting tradition, the accountant's historical cost valuation of net book value per share may dramatically understate the true intrinsic value of the company's assets.

Although public security market stock prices may be viewed as a theoretical approximation of true intrinsic value, arbitrators, raiders, leveraged buyout artists, and others make a business of acquiring securities of companies under-valued by the market. Although the market in effect gives an overall "cap" rate to a company's income stream, these buyers, in effect, are saying that the overall value of the discrete parts of the target company are greater than the market's valuation of the whole. In other words, by applying the old "salami" theory of buying in bulk, fractionating and selling in pieces, the maximum value (at least short term) can be realized; rather than accepting the company's overall yield, a higher yield can be achieved by segregating the various parts or divisions and/or selectively liquidating all or portions of the company.

Occasionally, the astute, entrepreneurial shopping center developer will run across an operating business having one or more valuable potential development sites or operating properties. Obvious examples would be an old independent drive-in theater chain, a sleepy retailer, or a manufacturing company having a plant in the path of growth or redevelopment. It might also make sense to buy the company merely on its own merits notwithstanding its real estate potential. Certainly, if one could buy the company and receive current income pending future development planning and entitlements, there may be strong business and tax justification for acquiring the company's stock or a controlling interest therein, rather than a traditional land-purchase or ground-lease transaction.

Retailers should also consider the potential benefits of growth through merger or acquisition. With many chain stores lacking the financial backing and sales volumes to compete effectively, acquisition opportunities will become available to strong retailers with a well-conceived strategic plan. With careful market analysis, cautious due diligence, and the help of experts, growth by merger or acquisition may prove an excellent way for a retailer to increase market share and long-term profitability.

Form 16-1 is a letter of intent to enter into a Stock Purchase Agreement whereby the buyer will purchase 100% of the stock of a closely held manufacturing company for a base price consisting of cash and installment payments. In addition, the selling shareholders receive an "earnout" in the form of additional installments that are contingent upon the company reaching certain specified revenue targets.

If you find a company that appears to have the intrinsic value you seek, retain skilled corporate legal counsel and accounting assistance from the outset. Do not use Form 16-1 without expert advice. Among other issues, there may be compelling reasons to structure the deal as a purchase of assets rather than a stock purchase transaction. Although the form should stimulate creative thinking about new opportunities, it also highlights many major issues encountered in a corporate stock purchase acquisition.

Form 16-1

Letter of Intent to Enter into Stock Purchase Agreement for 100% of Stock of Privately Held Operating Business; Cash Base Price at Closing Plus Incentive Price Payable in Installments Based upon Earnout Formula

[Purchaser's Letterhead]
[Date]

To the Shareholders of
__*[Holding Company]*_
__*[Address]*________
____________________]

Dear Shareholders:

This letter of intent sets forth the terms upon which we have agreed in principle to acquire not less than one hundred percent (100%) of the outstanding stock (the "Holding Company Stock") of __*[name of holding company]*__, a __*[state]*__ corporation (the "Holding Company"). It is understood that the Holding Company owns all the outstanding stock (hereafter, the "Subsidiary Stock") of __*[name of wholly-owned company]*__, a __*[state]*__ corporation (the "Subsidiary"), and that you (the "Shareholders") in turn own all of the outstanding stock of the Holding Company. The Holding Company and the Subsidiary are sometimes collectively referred to as the "Companies." The Holding Company Stock and the Subsidiary Stock may sometimes be collectively referred to as the "Stock."

1. Scheduled Closing Date. At a closing to be held at a mutually agreeable time and place within __*[e.g., 90]*__ days after the date of execution by all parties of a definitive Stock Purchase Agreement (as described below), but in no event later than ______, 20__, __*[name of purchaser]*__ or its nominee (hereafter, "Buyer") will purchase all of the Stock for the consideration described in this letter, subject, however, to satisfaction of the contingencies set forth below.

2. Purchase Price. The purchase price (the "Purchase Price") for the Stock will consist of two components: (a) a base price (the "Base Price") of __*[$ amount]*__ and (b) an incentive price (the "Incentive Price") of __*[$ amount]*__. The Purchase Price shall be payable as provided below.

2.1 Base Price. The Base Price shall be paid as follows:

2.1.1 Cash at Closing. __*[$ amount]*__ will be paid in cash at the closing.

2.1.2 Installments. __*[Insert number, e.g., Four]*__ installments of $_______ each (the "Base Price Installments") will be paid in cash on or before __*[e.g., January 15, 2014, April 15, 2014, July 15, 2014 and October 15, 2014, respectively]*__, subject to adjustment as provided in subparagraph __*[2.3]*__, below.

2.2 Incentive Price. The Incentive Price shall be paid as follows:

2.2.1 Installments Contingent Upon Subsidiary's Revenues. Subject to adjustment as provided in subparagraph __*[2.2.2]*__, the Incentive Price shall be paid in installments in the amounts and at the times specified in the following table, provided the Subsidiary's gross annual revenues (as shown on its annual financial statements prepared in accordance with generally accepted accounting principles and practices consistently applied) for the fiscal years indicated equal or exceed the amounts indicated:

Numeric values and dates below have been inserted merely to illustrate concept.

Fiscal Year Ending	Minimum Gross Annual Revenues ("Revenue Targets")	Amount of Installments	Dates Payable
6/30/2014	*$6,600,000*	*$90,000*	*10/15/2014*
		$90,000	*4/15/2015*
6/30/2015	*$7,800,000*	*$90,000*	*10/15/2015*
		$90,000	*4/15/2016*

2.2.2 If Revenue Targets Not Met. Buyer shall not be obligated to pay the installments of the Incentive Price unless the Revenue Targets are met; provided, however, that, with respect to the fiscal year ending __*[June 30, 2014]*__, if the Revenue Target for that fiscal year is not met, but the Revenue Target for the fiscal year ending __*[June 30, 2015]*__ is met, Buyer shall pay the installment of the Incentive Price due for the fiscal year ending __*[June 30, 2015]*__, plus __*[e.g., 50]*__ % of the installment of the Incentive Price due for the fiscal year for which the Revenue Target was not met.

2.3 Uncollectible Accounts Receivable Credited Against Base Price. Notwithstanding anything in this Paragraph 2 to the contrary, it is agreed that, with respect to the Base Price Installments payable under subparagraph __*[2.1.2]*__ of this Paragraph 2, if any portion of the Subsidiary's accounts receivable, net of reserves, as shown on the Companies' books and records on the closing date, proves to be uncollectible within __*[e.g., 6]*__ months after the closing, after reasonable collection efforts by Buyer (which shall not include the filing of legal action), then such uncollectible portion shall be offset and credited against the Base Price Installments.

2.4 Security; Pledge of Subsidiary Stock. The obligation to pay the Base Price Installments and the Incentive Price shall be secured by a pledge of the Subsidiary Stock. The pledge holder of the Subsidiary Stock shall be __*[e.g., name of law firm]*__. The pledge holder shall cooperate in any reorganization or merger of the Holding Company and the Subsidiary by Buyer.

3. Indemnity. Shareholders will indemnify Buyer against any loss or liability arising from events or circumstances occurring before the closing which are not disclosed to Buyer. Buyer shall have the right to offset against any unpaid portion of the Purchase Price any amounts due Buyer by reason of the above indemnity.

4. Treatment of Certain Assets. Buyer will agree to sell any life insurance policies on the lives of any Shareholder to the insureds for a price equal to the cash surrender value of such policies as of the date of purchase.

5. Representations and Warranties. In connection with the purchase of the Stock, in addition to standard representations, warranties and conditions reasonably requested by Buyer's counsel in the Stock Purchase Agreement, the Shareholders and/or the Companies are making the following representations in connection with this letter:

5.1 Shareholders' Ownership. The Shareholders own all of the Holding Company Stock free of any encumbrance, lien or interest of any third party;

5.2 Holding Company Ownership. The Holding Company owns all of the Subsidiary Stock free of any encumbrance, lien or interest of any third party;

5.3 Subsidiary Ownership. The Subsidiary owns all of its capital equipment and other assets, whether or not reflected on its balance sheet, free and clear of any liens or encumbrances of any nature __*[except as shown on the balance sheet]*__;

5.4 No Undisclosed Liabilities. The Subsidiary has no liabilities, contingent or otherwise, not previously disclosed in the financial statements previously furnished to Buyer;

5.5 No Default. The Companies are not in default or anticipate default under any contract or agreement to which they are a party;

5.6 No Material Litigation. There is no material litigation pending or threatened against, the Shareholders, the Subsidiary or the Holding Company;

5.7 Accuracy of Financial Statements. The financial statements of the Companies already made available to Buyer, including the __________, 20__ quarterly statement to be prepared by the Companies, are accurate, complete and in conformity with generally accepted accounting principles and practices consistently applied;

5.8 Pension Plan. There is no unfunded past service liability with respect to any pension plan of the Companies;

5.9 Legal Compliance. To the best knowledge of the Shareholders, the Companies are in compliance in all material respects with all laws, governmental regulations and orders affecting their business, including without limitation OSHA, EPA, EEOC, land use laws, governmental regulations and orders, and no notice of any violation of any such laws, regulations, and/or orders has been received by the Companies or the Shareholders; and

5.10 No Unionization. The Companies are not a party to any labor union contract or agreement, and, to the best knowledge of the Shareholders, no union organization campaign is presently being conducted or planned to be conducted among any of the Companies' employees.

6. Stock Purchase Agreement. As soon as possible after the complete execution of this letter, the parties will proceed with the negotiation of a definitive Stock Purchase Agreement mutually satisfactory to the parties. These negotiations shall be conducted in good faith, and in a manner consistent with the understanding expressed in this letter. It is understood that the Stock Purchase Agreement will contain usual and customary representations and warranties concerning the Subsidiary's organization, capitalization, properties, assets, business, financial condition and future prospects and the legal, tax and accounting matters related to or affecting the Subsidiary, as well as the ownership of all the issued and outstanding Stock.

7. Contingencies. After execution of the Stock Purchase Agreement, Buyer's obligation to purchase the Stock will be contingent upon the fulfillment of the following conditions:

7.1 Due Diligence. Completion, with results satisfactory to Buyer, of a thorough investigation of the Companies' properties, assets, business and financial condition. This investigation will include an independent audit, at Buyer's expense, of the accounting and financial records of the Companies, title review of the Subsidiary's real properties, due diligence review of the Subsidiary's real properties and facilities, including investigation of potential hazardous materials and environmental contamination, and review of all contracts and agreements to which the Companies are a party;

7.2 Legal and Accounting Review. Completion, with results satisfactory to Buyer, of a thorough investigation of legal, tax and accounting matters related to or affecting the Subsidiary; and

7.3 No Adverse Changes. Buyer's determination that no material adverse changes have occurred in the net worth, business or goodwill of the Subsidiary between _________, 20__ and the date of closing.

Note: *State securities regulations will differ from state to state.*

8. Compliance with Securities Laws. It is understood that the Stock is "legend" stock for purposes of the __*[e.g., California]*__ Corporations Code and that the sale of the Stock contemplated by the parties has not been qualified with the Commissioner of Corporations of the State of __*[e.g., California]*__. As a result, the issuance of the Stock or the payment or receipt of any part of the consideration therefor prior to such qualification is unlawful. The rights of all parties to this letter are expressly conditioned upon such qualification being obtained.

9. Covenants Not to Compete. Upon the signing of the definitive Stock Purchase Agreement, it is agreed that the Subsidiary will obtain customary covenants not to compete from each of the Shareholders for a period of __*[e.g., 3]*__ years after the effective date of the purchase of the Stock; provided, however, that __*[insert specific exceptions or refinements. As an illustration of the issues involved, the following specific covenants were negotiated in the purchase of a decal manufacturing business:]*

9.1 SAM JONES. Sam Jones ("Jones") may compete with the Subsidiary in the business (the "decal business") of selling decals for various commercial

FORM 16-1

and industrial applications on the following terms and conditions:

9.1.1 Jones may not establish a business which competes with the Subsidiary in the manufacturing, printing or production of silkscreen vinyl decals or acquire or own (directly or indirectly) an interest in any such business;

9.1.2 Jones may not be employed by or represent in any capacity, whether as an independent contractor or manufacturer's representative or otherwise, a business entity in the silkscreen vinyl decal business which has a principal place of business in the Excluded Counties (as hereafter defined) or which has a printing, manufacturing or production facility in the Excluded Counties;

9.1.3 The Excluded Counties are Santa Barbara, Ventura, Orange, Los Angeles, San Bernardino, Riverside and San Diego Counties;

9.1.4 During the __[e.g., 12]__ month period following the closing, Jones shall not contact or solicit orders for silkscreen vinyl decals from any of the customers or potential customers (the "Protected Customers") of the Subsidiary listed on Exhibit "A," whether located in the Excluded Counties or elsewhere in the United States;

9.1.5 Except as provided in subparagraph 9.1.4, the above restrictions on Jones shall expire __[e.g., 2]__ years after the closing.

9.2 JOHN SMITH. John Smith ("Smith") shall have the right to compete with the Subsidiary in the decal business if his business relationship as a sales representative with the Subsidiary is involuntarily terminated during the __[e.g., 3]__ year period provided for above.

> ***Note:** Many courts now often refuse to enforce these so-called "non-compete" clauses. For example, the U.S. Court of Appeals overturned such an agreement in the case of a scientist who defected to a direct competitor to take a similar job—even though he had signed an agreement not to work for his company's rivals for one year after leaving. (Baxter International Inc. v. Morris. Eighth U.S. Circuit Court of Appeals, St. Louis, No. 92-2079, October 9, 1992.) Although the form language example was extracted from an actual but dated transaction, experienced legal counsel should be consulted in negotiating non-compete agreements. The legal issues involving non-compete clauses are beyond the scope of this book.*

10. Companies' Covenants. After the date of this letter, the Shareholders and the Companies will provide Buyer and its agents and representatives full access to all documents, books, records, financial records and operations of the Companies. The shareholders and the Companies agree that they:

10.1 Continued Normal Operations. Will continue to operate the business of the Companies in the ordinary course as it has been operated previously;

10.2 No Dividend or Asset Transfer. Will not allow the Companies to declare, pay or distribute any dividends whatsoever, nor to increase compensation of any employee, nor to dispose, transfer or encumber any of their respective assets; and

10.3 No Stock Transfer. Will not authorize, approve or ratify (in any capacity) the granting of any stock option nor the sale, issuance or transfer (for consideration or otherwise) of any stock or other securities by either the Holding Company or the Subsidiary.

11. No Third Party Solicitations. Except with respect to an acquisition of the Stock by Buyer, neither the Companies nor any Shareholder shall, without the prior written consent of Buyer, directly or indirectly, solicit, contact or have any discussion with, any person or entity with a view to, nor shall any Shareholder or the Holding Company (acting in any capacity) authorize, approve or ratify (a) the acquisition of more than one percent (1%) of the gross assets of the Subsidiary as reflected on its books; (b) the acquisition of any of the Stock; (c) the merger of consolidation of the Subsidiary (or the Holding Company) with any other person or entity; or (d) the acquisition by the Subsidiary of the stock or assets of any other person or entity. Upon receiving notice of any contact or inquiry relating to any such event, the party receiving notice thereof shall forthwith notify Buyer, giving all relevant details of such contact or inquiry.

12. Liquidated Damages. THE SHAREHOLDERS AND THE COMPANIES ACKNOWLEDGE AND AGREE THAT IN CONNECTION WITH THE TRANSACTIONS CONTEMPLATED IN THIS LETTER, BUYER HAS INCURRED, AND WILL INCUR IN THE FUTURE, SUBSTANTIAL COSTS AND EXPENSES, INCLUDING BUT NOT LIMITED TO LEGAL AND ACCOUNTING SERVICES AND COSTS ATTRIBUTABLE TO THE TIME OF BUYER, AND THAT IF THE TRANSACTIONS CONTEMPLATED BY THIS LETTER ARE NOT CONSUMMATED DUE TO A BREACH BY THE SHAREHOLDERS OF THE

TERMS OF PARAGRAPH 11 OF THIS LETTER, BUYER WILL BE SUBSTANTIALLY DAMAGED. THE SHAREHOLDERS AND THE COMPANIES FURTHER ACKNOWLEDGE AND AGREE THAT SUCH COSTS, EXPENSES AND DAMAGES ARE NOT, AND WILL NOT BE READILY SUSCEPTIBLE TO MEASUREMENT. TO AVOID DISPUTE WITH RESPECT THERETO, THE SHAREHOLDERS, THE COMPANIES AND BUYER DESIRE TO SPECIFY A SUM AS LIQUIDATED DAMAGES TO BE PAID TO BUYER IN THE EVENT THAT THE SHAREHOLDERS AND/OR EITHER OF THE COMPANIES SHALL BREACH PARAGRAPH 11 OF THIS LETTER. ACCORDINGLY, THE SHAREHOLDERS AND THE COMPANIES HEREBY AGREE THAT BUYER WILL BE ENTITLED TO RECEIVE THE SUM OF __*[insert dollar amount]*__AS LIQUIDATED DAMAGES TO COMPENSATE BUYER FOR THE ITEMS REFERRED TO ABOVE IN THE EVENT OF A BREACH OF THE PROVISIONS OF PARAGRAPH 11.

______________ Buyer's Initials ______________ Shareholders' Initials

13. Fees. Each party will be responsible for paying any broker or brokers retained by it and its own legal and accounting fees. The Shareholders shall pay their own legal and accounting fees and such fees shall not be paid by the Companies.

Optional clause allowing specific individual selected by Buyer to become President and CEO upon acceptance of offer:

14. Employment of New CEO. The parties acknowledge and agree that the Companies are currently operating at a loss. In order to insure the survival of the Companies until the closing, it is agreed that, upon acceptance of this offer by all parties, __*[name]*__ shall be named as President and the Chief Executive Officer of the Holding Company and the Subsidiary, with full right and authority to manage and control the business of the Companies until the first to occur of: (i) the closing, or (ii) other termination of the negotiations contemplated in this letter. Any costs or obligations to third parties incurred as a result of __*[new president's name]*__'s assumption of the duties provided for in this Paragraph __*[14]*__ shall not be used as a ground for terminating Buyer's obligation to purchase the Stock under Paragraph __*[7.3]*__, nor shall any such costs or obligations be considered in the determination provided for in Paragraph __*[7.3]*__.

If you are in agreement with the foregoing, please sign and return the enclosed copy of this letter in the space provided below not later than ________, 20__.

Very truly yours,

[Name of Purchaser]

By: ________________

Title: ________________

UNDERSTOOD AND AGREED:
This __ day of ___________, 20__.

[Name of Holding Company]

By: ________________

Its: ________________

UNDERSTOOD AND AGREED:
This __ day of ___________, 20__.

[Name of Subsidiary Company]

By: ________________

Its: ________________

SHAREHOLDER APPROVAL: *[Both husband and wife sign where co-owners]*

1. _________________________ _________________________
No. of shares ________ *[e.g., spouse of Shareholder #1]*

2. _________________________ _________________________
No. of shares ________ *[e.g., spouse of Shareholder #2]*

3. _________________________ _________________________
No of shares ________ *[e.g., spouse of Shareholder #3]*

[continue shareholder signature lines as necessary]

Exhibit "A"

[Attach list of "Protected Customers" of the Subsidiary per Illustrative Covenant Not to Compete in Paragraph 9.1 (italicized insert)]

END OF FORM 16-1

OVERVIEW

Chapter 17 contains numerous optional and alternative deal-making clauses for selective incorporation into the preceding purchase and sale forms. Generally, these clauses cover more specialized or complex issues. Selections include the right to "repurchase" a tenant parcel and appurtenant improvements, use of a letter of credit as a purchase deposit, hazardous materials investigation and remediation, allocation of specific transaction costs, a site entry license, selected representations and warranties, and a provision for use by attorney readers confirming the amendment of a non-binding letter of intent into a final, binding agreement. ("Optional and Alternative Clauses for Lease Proposals" is the topic of Chapter 18.)

These clauses are not designed for insertion into operative purchase and sale agreements. They merely conceptualize legal and economic rights and relationships for purposes of structuring preliminary agreements among the parties and their attorneys.

FORMS

17-1 Repurchase Right Due to Tenant Actions. Developer's Right to Purchase Tenant's Premises If Tenant Goes Dark or Elects to Sell or Lease.

17-2 Developer's Use of Letters of Credit as Escrow Deposits. Buyer's Initial Cash Escrow Deposit Replaced by Successively Larger Letters of Credit upon Satisfaction of Escrow Contingencies and Other Event(s).

17-3 Expanded Hazardous Material Provisions. Hazardous Materials: Example of Expanded Site Purchase Offer Provisions for Use in Acquiring a Site Where Significant Investigation and Cleanup Is Expected.

17-4 Cost Allocation. Allocation of Specific Purchase and Sale Transaction Costs.

17-5 Pre-Closing Site Entry. Provision for Entry upon the Site and Indemnification.

17-6 Developer-Oriented Representations and Warranties. Selected Seller Representations and Warranties for a Developer's Site Purchase Agreement.

17-7 Binding Agreement (For Use Only with Advice of Legal Counsel). Letter Is to Be a Binding, Conclusive Agreement.

Chapter 17

Optional and Alternative Clauses for Purchase and Sale Proposals

Give a man a fish and you feed him for a day.
Teach a man to fish and you feed him for a lifetime.
—Chinese proverb

Each purchase or lease transaction tends to have unique deal points. The forms in the preceding chapters generally contain deal-making provisions that address the commonly encountered business issues in shopping center site acquisition and leasing transactions. This chapter contains a variety of optional and alternative provisions designed for selective insertion into the site purchase and parcel sale proposals included in earlier chapters. (Chapter 18 contains optional and alternative provisions for lease deal-making documents.)

Use the utmost care in considering these provisions, as many require significant legal expertise to professionally integrate them into a functional document. For example, acquisition of a site where known hazardous materials exists invites a host of liability issues beyond the business issues of coordinating the investigation and clean-up effort. Similarly, use of an overly-broad radius clause in a lease or deed restriction may invoke a restraint of trade issue. At a minimum, however, a reading and understanding of the various alternative and optional letter of intent provisions in this chapter (and Chapter 18) should improve your deal-making skills and competence in lawyer-client interactions.

Although this chapter contains "purchase and sale" provisions and Chapter 18 contains "lease" provisions, some principles are applicable to both purchase and sale transactions and leases. For example, although a radius clause will typically be found in a lease (and is therefore covered in Chapter 18), a reciprocal easement agreement or deed restriction governing a tenant's operations on a parcel within a center could also be drafted to contain a limited radius restriction. Space does not allow an exhaustive summary, but an attempt has been made to provide a variety of useful alternative deal-making provisions.

REPURCHASE RIGHT

In considering whether to make a parcel sale to a proposed tenant, the developer must weigh the economic advantages of making the parcel sale against the "loss of control" usually accompanying such a parcel sale. Ideally, the developer should try to preserve a right to reacquire the tenant's parcel if the tenant "goes dark" or desires to re-sell or lease the tenant's premises to a third party. Obviously, the tenant will oppose such infringement of the tenant purchaser's "property" rights. The following structure offers a solution somewhere between the idealized perspectives of the developer and the purchasing tenant. Although rights to acquire the tenant's premises are a major deal point in major tenant parcel sale negotiations, the issue should also be considered in pad or outparcel sale negotiations.

Be aware that although the following principle is rather simple, final documentation would require extensive, sophisticated drafting. Developer's repurchase rights would normally be contained within an instrument recorded against the tenant's parcel.

(The essence of Form 17-1 is included within the body of the major tenant parcel purchase and sale Form 10-1.)

Form 17-1

Developer's Right to Purchase Tenant's Premises If Tenant Goes Dark or Elects to Sell or Lease

__. **Developer's Preferred Right to Purchase or Lease.** __*[For the period ending __ years after Tenant's purchase the subject parcel to be acquired by Tenant]*__ Developer (and any successor to Developer's interest in the shopping center), shall have a preferred right to purchase Tenant's parcel with all Site Work and other improvements constructed thereon (including the Building but excluding trade fixtures and equipment) (the "Tenant Premises") or acquire a leasehold interest in the Tenant Premises on the following terms and conditions:

__.1__ **Purchase Rights If Tenant Goes Dark.** If, after completion of the Building and Site Work on the Tenant Parcel, Tenant ceases to operate its retail business out of the Tenant Premises (which cessation is not the result of force majeure) for a period greater than __*[e.g., 180 days]*__, Developer may elect to exercise a preferred right to (a) purchase Tenant's fee interest in the Tenant Premises or (b) if Tenant has previously leased the Tenant Premises to a third party, Developer shall have the right to purchase Tenant's fee interest subject to such leasehold.

The purchase price payable for Tenant's fee interest in the Tenant Premises or Tenant's fee interest subject to such leasehold interest shall be the greater of (i) Tenant's current book value or (ii) fair market value established by fair market appraisal __*[but in any case not more than Tenant's cost of the Tenant Parcel, the Building and the Site Work plus an imputed escalation of __[e.g., 8]__ % per annum from the date Tenant incurred such costs through the closing of any such purchase by Developer]*__. __*[Such purchase price for the Tenant Premises shall in each case be reduced by the total subsidy, if any, granted by Developer to Tenant in Developer's initial transaction with Developer relative to the Tenant Premises, compounded at a rate of __[e.g., 8]__ % per annum from the date of the advance of such subsidy by Developer through closing of the preferred purchase]*__.

__.2__ **First Right of Refusal to Purchase or Lease.** If Tenant or any successor of Tenant elects to sell or lease all or any portion of the Tenant Premises, Developer shall have the prior and first right of refusal by which to so acquire by fee or lease such property. __*[However, Tenant's consummation of a typical long term sale-leaseback transaction with a third party for Tenant's financing of the Tenant Premises __[within the first ___ years of the closing of the Purchase Agreement]__ shall be exempt from Developer's first right of refusal right]*__.

END OF FORM 17-1

LETTERS OF CREDIT AS ESCROW DEPOSITS

Form 17-2 revises Paragraph 9 ("Escrow and Initial Deposit") and other affected paragraphs (i.e., Paragraphs 10, 11, 12, and 23) of purchase offer Form 4-1 to provide for the substitution of an initial cash escrow deposit by two successively larger letters of credit. Specifically, upon the last to occur of the expiration of contingencies ("Contingency Expiration Date") and/or another selected date or described event, the escrow holder is instructed to return buyer's initial cash deposit concurrent with the buyer's deposit of an "initial" letter of credit. Thereafter, the escrow holder returns buyer's initial letter of credit when the buyer makes a "final" deposit consisting of an irrevocable letter of credit in an amount equal to 100% of the purchase price (subject to adjustment). The proceeds of the final deposit are used to close the site purchase escrow.

Although accommodating the use of a letter of credit as an escrow deposit and at the same time preserving the buyer's right to extend the closing by making monthly cash deposits for release to the seller, this alternative format is quite complex. Nevertheless, it provides a starting point for the preparation of specific proposals using letters of credit. The deal structure could be simplified by providing for an extended period in which to close after buyer deposits the initial letter of credit, thereby eliminating any discussion of buyer's obligation to incrementally deposit additional cash sums to extend the closing date.

In general, letters of credit should be considered as escrow deposits only when protracted escrows are contemplated because of anticipated delays in obtaining development entitlements or in accommodating the seller's preference to effect a tax-deferred exchange. The reasons for avoiding the use of letters of credit include their lack of flexibility, problems that could arise from their expiration or non-renewal, the risks of the insolvency or governmental seizure of the issuing bank, and problems that could arise from the buyer's insolvency or default in the buyer's obligations to the issuing bank. Also, the buyer needs to consider whether obtaining a letter of credit in lieu of making a cash deposit is cost effective. The cost of obtaining a letter of credit is not insignificant.

Form 17-2

Buyer's Initial Cash Escrow Deposit Replaced by Successively Larger Letters of Credit upon Satisfaction of Escrow Contingencies and Other Event(s)

9. Escrow. __*[Upon deposit into escrow of a mutually approved and executed final Purchase Agreement between the parties, but not later than ______, 20__]*__ OR __*[Within __ business days after acceptance of this proposal by Seller,]*__ Buyer and Seller will open escrow at _________ Title Company in __*[city]*__, __*[state]*__ ("escrow holder"). Escrow holder shall notify Buyer and Seller of the date on which escrow instructions signed by Buyer and all parties required to sign on behalf of Seller have been deposited into escrow ("opening of escrow"). The escrow instructions shall incorporate all terms and conditions of __*[the Purchase Agreement]*__ OR __*[this agreement]*__.

9.1 Escrow Fees and Closing Costs. All escrow charges shall be shared equally by Buyer and Seller and all other closing costs not specifically provided for in other provisions of this agreement shall be shared in the manner customary in __________ county, __*[state]*__. *[Refer to Form 17-4, "Allocation of Specific Purchase and Sale Transaction Costs," for an alternative, more comprehensive clause.]*

9.2 Initial Deposit. Upon opening of escrow, Buyer shall deposit $__*[$25,000 in this example]*__ cash into escrow as a good faith "Initial Deposit". *[Seller oriented optional insert:]* __*[Until the Initial Deposit has been made,* __*[the Purchase Agreement]*__ OR __*[this agreement]*__ __*[shall not be binding upon Buyer and Seller]*__. At the direction of Buyer, the Initial Deposit shall be deposited into an interest bearing account, with all interest accruing to the benefit of Buyer. The scheduled closing shall occur ___ days after satisfaction of all contingencies ("Contingency Expiration Date"), but not later than __*[e.g., 5]*__ months from opening of escrow (as defined above) or __*[insert specific date]*__, whichever occurs later (the "scheduled closing date"). In the event any of the escrow contingencies described above are not satisfied during the __*[e.g., 5]*__ -month period following opening of escrow, Buyer's Initial Deposit shall be returned in full, less any applicable escrow cancellation charge.

9.3 Initial Letter of Credit. Upon the last to occur of: (i) the Contingency Expiration Date or (ii) ___ business days after the date on which Seller __*[describe event/performance]*__, Buyer shall deposit into escrow an irrevocable standby letter of credit (the "Initial Letter of Credit") in an amount equal to __*[e.g., 15]*__ % of the purchase price set forth in Paragraph __*[e.g.,*

FORM 17-2

*2, above]*__. The Initial Letter of Credit shall be __*[a nonnegotiable, nontransferable]*__ OR __*[an]*__ irrevocable letter of credit issued by __*[state requirements for issuing bank]*__ which serves as a guarantee of Buyer's financial obligations __*[under the Purchase Agreement]*__ OR __*[hereunder]*__ issued in favor of the escrow holder, in a form and from a bank approved by Seller. The Initial Letter of Credit shall provide that it may be drawn upon Seller's certification that: (i) __*[describe event]*__, or (ii) Buyer has, through no fault of Seller, failed or refused to close the purchase of the site in a timely fashion. Upon receipt of the Initial Letter of Credit, the escrow holder shall release the Initial Deposit to Buyer, together with any interest earned thereon.

9.4 Final Deposit. Within _____ days of __*[describe event]*__, Buyer shall deposit into escrow an irrevocable standby letter of credit (or the equivalent thereof) (the "Final Deposit") in an amount equal to __*[e.g., 100]*__ % of the purchase price set forth in Paragraph __*[e.g., 2, above]*__, less sums appropriately credited pursuant to Paragraph __*[9.5, below]*__. Upon receipt of the Final Deposit, the escrow holder shall return the Initial Letter of Credit to Buyer. The proceeds of the Final Deposit shall be used to close the purchase of the site.

9.5 Escrow Extension Deposit Credits. That portion of any Extension Deposit (defined below) which is applicable to the purchase price and deposited into escrow before Buyer's Final Deposit is made shall be credited to and proportionately reduce the amount of the required Final Deposit. Similarly, that portion of any Extension Deposit which is applicable to the purchase price but which is deposited into escrow after Buyer's Final Deposit is made shall be credited to Buyer through escrow.

> ***Note:*** *A portion of Extension Deposits made before the Final Deposit may be applicable to the purchase price. An appropriate credit is therefore given against the Final Deposit. However, to the extent Buyer elects to make such Extension Deposits after the Final Deposit is deposited, Buyer is "over-depositing" and the portion of "applicable" Extension Deposit payments made after the Final Deposit is made is credited to Buyer at closing. One way Buyer could avoid the need for this second credit would be to provide in Paragraph 9.4 that the Final Deposit be "an amount equal to 100% of the purchase price set forth in Paragraph __[2, above]__, less that portion of all allowable Extension Deposits which Buyer could elect to make which are applicable to the purchase price.*

On its own, the alternative Paragraph 9 is a relatively simple substitute for a traditional "cash" deposit escrow provision. However, its application and incorporation into Form 4-1 illustrates a drafting issue of which non-lawyers should be extremely cognizant. In short, be careful in amending a paragraph or inserting new provisions to be certain that ambiguities or inconsistencies are not created relative to other provisions in the document. In this example, if this alternative Paragraph 9 is used instead of the original Paragraph 9:

(i) Paragraph 10 ("Escrow Extensions") should be amended consistent with the modified escrow deposit provisions selected in alternative Paragraph 9. In the original Form 4-1 format, the Initial Deposit was released from escrow to Seller as a condition to Buyer's right to make Extension Deposits to extend the closing. How are extensions to be conditioned? Is Buyer's deposit of the Initial Letter of Credit to be in lieu of any obligation to make monthly escrow Extension Deposit payments? If Buyer's right to extend the closing is assumed to be conditioned upon the making of cash deposits out of which the Extension Deposit payments will be released to Seller, both cash and letter of credit deposits are required. Although complex, this example assumes Buyer is obligated to make such Extension Deposits in cash to extend the closing.

(ii) Paragraph 11 ("Buyer's Termination Right") must be reconsidered. Assuming Extension Deposits are required to extend the closing notwithstanding deposit of the Initial Letter of Credit, if Buyer terminates after the Initial Letter of Credit is deposited and Extension Deposit(s) are made, can Seller retain all such consideration? This example assumes Seller can.

(iii) Paragraph 12 ("Seller's Termination Right") should be amended to confirm escrow holder's duty to return any deposited letter of credit to Buyer if Seller makes a timely election to terminate.

(iv) Paragraph 23 ("Remedies") must be addressed to consider the liquidated damages payable upon Buyer's default.

(v) Other paragraphs in Form 4-1 should be reviewed for internal consistency with such revisions.

Although tedious, this exercise raises several important points. First, do not assume a legal drafting role if you are not qualified. This ex-

ample raises difficult drafting issues even for an experienced lawyer. A wise person is one who knows what he or she knows and knows what he or she does not know. Know your limitations. Second, even highly skilled lawyers make drafting errors. The owner, developer, tenant, broker, or asset manager, as a negotiator and consumer of legal services, should be intimately involved in deal creation and documentation review. The non-lawyer deal maker should carefully create the deal structure with a skilled attorney's advice and review all documents and his or her attorney's documents for internal logic and consistency. The diligent, committed client deal maker can often make a major contribution to an initial draft of an attorney's documentation. Such attorney-client involvement is particularly important in form documentation designed for repetitive use.

Subject to such precautions, Paragraphs 10,11,12, and 23 of Form 4-1 are revised below to conform with the underlying assumptions of this generic, alternative Paragraph 9. Text revisions to these paragraphs are italicized to highlight changes from Form 4-1. This example illustrates that a relatively minor change in a deal point may sometimes require many revisions throughout a document.

10. Escrow Extensions. So long as Buyer is actively proceeding to develop the site as a shopping center, Buyer may elect to extend, in monthly increments, the scheduled closing by up to _*[e.g., eight]*_ monthly periods by authorizing escrow holder to disburse from escrow directly to Seller, a sum payable in advance for each such monthly extension ("Extension Deposit"). Each Extension Deposit so made shall extend by one month the then scheduled or extended closing date and be applicable or not applicable to the purchase price, as follows:

The *Initial Letter of Credit shall be timely received by the escrow holder* as a condition to Buyer's right to elect to extend the scheduled closing date by depositing the first Extension Deposit.

Monthly Escrow Extension	Extension Deposit Amount	Applicable ("A") or Not Applicable ("N.A.") To Purchase Price
1st	$10,000	A
2nd	10,000	A
3rd	20,000	A
4th	25,000	A
5th	25,000	N.A.
6th	30,000	N.A.
7th	30,000	N.A.
8th	30,000	N.A.
	[and so forth]	

Buyer shall redeposit an additional __*[$25,000]*__ within 10 days of *Buyer's deposit of the Initial Letter of Credit with the escrow holder.* If Buyer fails either to close escrow or give notice to terminate escrow on the scheduled closing or any extended escrow closing date, escrow holder shall be deemed to be irrevocably instructed to release from escrow to the account of Seller, from Buyer's *cash* escrow *deposits*, the monthly Extension Deposit payable for the following monthly extension period until Buyer either closes or terminates escrow. Buyer shall deposit sufficient additional cash funds to provide for such releases.

11. Buyer's Termination Right. Buyer may terminate escrow at any time during the contingency period by providing written notice to escrow holder. If any of the escrow contingencies described above are not satisfied and Buyer terminates during the first __*[e.g., 5]*__ months of the escrow period, *the Initial Letter of Credit* shall be returned to Buyer, *provided Buyer pays its share of* any escrow cancellation charges. If Buyer terminates after the first monthly escrow Extension Deposit has been released to Seller, Seller may retain the *Initial Letter of Credit (or if the Final Deposit has been made, that portion of the Final Deposit which the Initial Deposit bears to the Final Deposit)* and each Extension Deposit released to Seller through termination.

Upon such termination, Buyer shall promptly assign and deliver to seller, lien free and without charge, copies of all tentative site plans, engineering, and soils and environmental studies concerning the site that Buyer generated prior to termination and, thereupon, Seller shall have the right to use the work and various studies (limited only by such copyright and other limitations placed upon such work product in the normal course of business by the third party consultants or producers of such work product. In other words, Buyer shall assign all Buyer's rights to such work product to Seller but Seller shall have no greater rights to such work product than the rights enjoyed by Buyer.) *Buyer's retention of the Initial Letter of Credit (or the portion of the Final Deposit equal thereto)* shall constitute liquidated damages pursuant to Paragraph __*[e.g., 23]*__ below, and release Buyer from any further claims of Seller concerning the escrow. *Once Seller obtains possession of the Initial Letter of Credit, Seller shall be entitled to demand payment thereunder.*

12. Seller's Termination Right. Buyer shall have until __*[date certain—ideally before any escrow release to Seller is required and substantially before Final Deposit would be deposited]*__ in which to form a venture with an equity financial partner, obtain a binding financing commitment from an institutional lender, or otherwise show sufficient resources to close the escrow. If by the end of this period Buyer has not presented Seller with the name, net

FORM 17-2

worth, and general financial condition of Buyer's financial partner or other financial resources reasonably demonstrating Buyer's ability to close the subject escrow, Seller may, upon ___ days written notice to Buyer and escrow holder, elect to terminate the escrow. *If escrow is terminated pursuant to this paragraph, the Initial Deposit (or the Initial Letter of Credit if escrow holder is holding same) and any Extension Deposits released to Seller shall be concurrently refunded to Buyer.*

> ***Note:*** *Should developer's soft costs such as preliminary architectural and engineering fees or marketing costs be reimbursed by Seller?*

> ***Note:*** *Most buyers desire to limit their liability to the seller in the event of a breach of the purchase agreement by agreeing to pay the seller a specified sum as liquidated damages. The amount of liquidated damages can be the subject of extensive negotiations. Please note that the following form is based on California law. The requirements for an enforceable liquidated damages provision may differ from state to state. Before using this form, non-lawyers should consult a real estate attorney in the state in which the real property to be purchased is located to be sure that the liquidated damages provision complies with local law.*

23. Remedies. __*[The final contract between the parties shall contain the following provision:]*__ Buyer shall, in addition to all other rights provided herein or as may be provided by law, be entitled to specific performance and injunctive relief to enforce Buyer's rights hereunder in the event of a breach by Seller, it being understood hereby because of the special and unique character of the site and the proposed project thereon, a remedy at law would be inadequate to compensate Buyer for any default of Seller under this agreement.

> IN THE EVENT BUYER IS IN MATERIAL DEFAULT IN THE PERFORMANCE OR OBSERVANCE OF ANY COVENANT, CONDITION OR AGREEMENT OF BUYER CONTAINED IN THIS OFFER, THE SOLE AND EXCLUSIVE REMEDY OF SELLER AGAINST BUYER SHALL BE SELLER'S RETENTION OF*(1) THE INITIAL LETTER OF CREDIT, IF HELD BY THE ESCROW HOLDER AT THE TIME OF BUYER'S DEFAULT, OR, (2) IF THE FINAL DEPOSIT IS HELD BY THE ESCROW HOLDER AT THE TIME OF BUYER'S DEFAULT, THAT PORTION OF THE FINAL DEPOSIT WHICH THE INITIAL LETTER OF CREDIT BEARS TO THE FINAL DEPOSIT AND (3)* THE EXTENSION DEPOSITS THERETOFORE DEPOSITED WITH OR PAID TO THE ESCROW HOLDER AND RELEASED TO SELLER PURSUANT TO THE TERMS AND PROVISIONS HEREOF.

BECAUSE IT WOULD BE IMPRACTICAL OR EXTREMELY DIFFICULT TO FIX ACTUAL DAMAGE, SUCH SUM IS THE AMOUNT OF DAMAGE PRESUMED THAT SELLER WOULD SUSTAIN BY REASON OF ANY SUCH DEFAULT BY BUYER, AND BUYER DESIRES TO LIMIT ITS LIABILITY HEREUNDER TO SUCH SUM. SELLER AGREES TO LOOK SOLELY TO SUCH SUM FOR SATISFACTION OF ANY OF SELLER'S REMEDIES FOR THE COLLECTION OF A JUDGMENT OR OTHER JUDICIAL PROCESS REQUIRING THE PAYMENT OF MONEY BY BUYER TO SELLER IN THE EVENT OF DEFAULT BY BUYER HEREUNDER.

______________ ______________

Seller's Initials Buyer's Initials

Note: *Seller's claim against the Final Deposit (100% of the purchase price) is tempered by the preceding liquidated damages provision. Although it is unlikely that a Buyer default would occur after Buyer makes the Final Deposit, the Initial Letter of Credit is returned to Buyer and thus not under the control of the escrow holder once the Final Deposit is made. The above language is a "compromise" drafting approach designed to subject only a portion of the Final Deposit to liquidated damages.*

END OF FORM 17-2

HAZARDOUS MATERIALS INVESTIGATION AND REMEDIATION

As stated in the site purchase proposal (Form 4-1), expert legal and technical advice should be obtained at the outset if one is aware of any potential hazardous materials issues. Form 17-3 is included as an example to illustrate how a site purchaser's letter of intent might be restructured, after appropriate legal and technical advice, to provide for the necessary investigation (and cost allocation between buyer and seller) in an instance where toxic substances have been identified but their scope is not fully known at the time the transaction is being negotiated. Form 17-3 would replace Paragraph 13, "Hazardous Materials," in Form 4-1 (requiring the renumbering of subsequent paragraphs). Although drafting skills required to incorporate the form may be beyond the capabilities of some readers, the form, nevertheless, should help to elucidate a deal structure or methodology to cope with an increasingly common problem.

Form 17-3

Hazardous Materials: Example of Expanded Site Purchase Offer Provisions for Use in Acquiring a Site Where Significant Investigation and Cleanup Is Expected

13. Hazardous Materials Due Diligence Period. Environmental investigation, inspection, testing and any necessary remedial work shall be accomplished as follows:

13.1 Inspections. The "Hazardous Materials Due Diligence Period" shall be defined as the period of time between the execution of __*[this agreement]*__ OR __*[the Purchase Agreement]*__ and the "Hazardous Materials Due Diligence Period Expiration Date." During the Hazardous Materials Due Diligence Period, Buyer shall have the right to conduct various environmental, soils compaction and engineering investigations on the site to ascertain the feasibility and development potential regarding the construction of an approximately ________ square foot shopping center on the site. Buyer and Buyer's agents may enter onto the site for the purpose of inspection and for the purpose of conducting such tests, surveys and other studies, provided that Buyer (i) keeps the site free of liens, (ii) repairs all damage to the site, and (iii) indemnifies and holds Seller harmless from all claims, damages or liabilities arising from or connected with the tests, surveys and studies. No later than __*[e.g., 10]*__ days after execution of this __*[this agreement]*__ OR __*[the Purchase Agreement]*__, Seller shall provide Buyer with a map showing the location of all underground utilities located on the site. Buyer shall conduct its tests and surveys and studies in a manner not to cause damage to underground utilities identified by Seller.

13.2 Environmental and Soils Investigation. __*[E.g., Seller]*__, at __*[e.g., Seller's]*__ sole cost and expense, has commissioned an environmental consultant, __*[e.g., name of environmental consultant]*__, to conduct a preliminary environmental investigation (the "Phase I Investigation") of the site to determine whether certain materials (the "Hazardous Materials") considered to be "hazardous" to human health or the environment under federal, state or local laws, statutes, ordinances, rules or regulations are located on or under the site, and to develop a scope of further investigation to confirm or deny the existence of hazardous waste contamination on the site. Buyer and Seller acknowledge that Hazardous Materials probably exist on the site as evidenced by __*[e.g., a letter dated _______, 20__, from __[name of environmental consultant]__ , a copy of which is attached hereto as Exhibit "__."]*

FORM 17-3

Alternative "A"

Upon execution of __*[this agreement]*__ OR __*[the Purchase Agreement]*__

OR

Alternative "B"

After execution of __*[this agreement]*__ OR __*[the Purchase Agreement]*__ and Buyer's approval or satisfaction of the __*[e.g., title, feasibility and major tenant contingencies, which are listed above as contingencies 6.1, 6.2 and 6.3, respectively,]*__

After selection Alternative "A" or "B", continue:

Buyer will request __*[name of same environmental consultant]*__ to conduct a further environmental investigation (the "Phase II Investigation") to perform the work described in the __*[name of environmental consultant]*__ __*[e.g., letter dated ______, 20__, a copy of which is attached hereto as Exhibit "__"]*__. The cost of the Phase II Investigation shall be shared __*[e.g., equally]*__ by the parties, unless the parties otherwise agree in writing. If the Phase II Investigation confirms the presence of Hazardous Materials on the site, __*[name of environmental consultant]*__ may recommend a scope of Phase III investigation to more fully characterize and develop recommended remedial action (the "Remedial Action"). The cost of the Phase III Investigation shall be shared __*[e.g., equally]*__ by Buyer and Seller, unless the parties otherwise agree in writing.

13.3 Hazardous Materials Due Diligence Period Expiration Date. The Hazardous Materials Due Diligence Period shall expire on the date (the "Hazardous Materials Due Diligence Period Expiration Date") which is __*[e.g., 10]*__ days after the date on which __*[name of environmental consultant]*__ delivers written notice to Buyer, Seller and escrow holder that the Phase III Investigation has been completed. If a Phase III Investigation is not recommended by __*[name of environmental consultant]*__, the Hazardous Materials Due Diligence Expiration Date shall be the date which is __*[e.g., 10]*__ days after the date on which __*[name of environmental consultant]*__ delivers written notice to Buyer, Seller and escrow holder that the Phase II Investigation has been completed.

13.4 Cancellation of Escrow During Hazardous Materials Due Diligence Period. At any time prior to the Hazardous Materials Due Diligence Expiration Date, Buyer may elect to terminate __*[this agreement]*__

OR __[the Purchase Agreement]__ without penalty, and receive a refund of all amounts Buyer has deposited in escrow (less any escrow cancellation fee), if (i) Buyer is not satisfied with either the materials delivered to it pursuant to Paragraph __[e.g., 5]__ or the results of the inspections conducted pursuant to this Paragraph __[13]__ or (ii) Buyer determines that its share of the cost of the "Additional Remedial Action" (as defined in Paragraph __[14.2]__) would be excessive.

14. Seller's Obligations Regarding Clean-up of Hazardous Materials.

14.1 Responsibility for Remedial Action. Seller shall be responsible for completing the Remedial Action __[before close of escrow]__ OR __[on or before ________, 20__]__. The Remedial Action is described in the __[name of environmental consultant]__ letter dated ______, 20__ attached hereto as Exhibit "__" __[and shall include without limitation the following items:

Illustrative example of scope of specific remedial work taken from a sample letter:

a. Remediation and disposal of the contaminated soils at the end of the concrete casting beds;

b. Remediation and disposal of the contaminated soils along the crane path;

c. Remediation and disposal of the contaminated soils in the chemical dispensing/work area;

d. Removal of the boiler and supporting diesel tanks and the remediation and disposal of the surrounding contaminated soils;

e. Removal of the above-ground gasoline tank and remediation and removal of the surrounding contaminated soils;

f. Remediation and removal of soils contaminated by waste oil used to kill vegetation on the site;

g. Removal of all 55-gallon drums located on the site and the remediation and removal of the surrounding contaminated soils;

h. Remediation of soils contaminated by metals used in sandblasting; and

i. Removal of any and all asbestos containing materials from the site __[and any building improvement thereon]__. [and so forth]

FORM 17-3

14.2 Additional Remedial Action. The cost of Remedial Action not listed in Paragraph __*[14.1(a)-(i)]*__ above ("Additional Remedial Action") shall be shared __*[e.g., equally]*__ by Buyer and Seller unless the parties otherwise agree in writing. In no event, however, shall Buyer's share of the cost of Additional Remedial Action exceed $____________. Seller shall be responsible for completing the Additional Remedial Action __*[before close of escrow]*__ OR __*[on or before ________, 20__]*__. *[Optional:]* __*[It is understood by the parties that Additional Remedial Action may include remediation and disposal of* __*[describe]*__.

> ***Note:*** *Negotiating a firm date for Seller's completion of the "Additional Remediation Action" may be very difficult when the scope of the work is not known at the time the deal is being negotiated.*

14.3 Completion of Remedial Action and Additional Remedial Action. The failure of Seller to fulfill its clean-up obligations shall constitute a material breach of __*[the Purchase Agreement]*__ OR __*[this agreement]*__.

14.4 Remediation Action Notice. __*[Name of environmental consultant]*__ shall deliver to Buyer and Seller written notice (the "Remediation Notice") of the completion of the Remedial Action and the Additional Remedial Action. Receipt of the Remediation Notice by Buyer and Seller shall be a condition to the close of escrow, unless the parties agree otherwise.

AND

> ***Note:*** *If the preceding Paragraphs 13 and 14 are inserted in place of Paragraph 13 in Form 4-1 (and subsequent paragraphs renumbered), Paragraph 6.6 of Form 4-1 (the "Hazardous Materials Investigation" contingency) should be revised, for example:*

6.6 Hazardous Materials Investigation. Buyer's approval and satisfaction of an environmental and soils investigation of the site, as provided in Paragraph __*[13]*__, "Hazardous Materials Due Diligence Period."

AND

> *In addition, the approval period contained in Paragraph 7.3 of Form 4-1, which describes the approval period for satisfaction of the soils and hazardous materials contingency, should be revised, for example:*

7.3 Soils and Hazardous Materials Investigation. Buyer will have until the "Hazardous Materials Due Diligence Period Expiration Date", as that term is defined in Paragraph __*[13]*__, below, in which to approve the contingencies contained in Paragraph __*[e.g., 6.5]*__ and __*[e.g., 6.6]*__.

Note: *This form assumes the geologic or bearing qualities of the soil is investigated concurrently with the hazardous materials aspect of the site's soil and that an equivalent approval period is allowed for each, which need not necessarily be the case.*

Exhibit(s) "__"

[Referenced letter(s), if any, from environmental consultant]

END OF FORM 17-3

ALLOCATION OF SPECIFIC TRANSACTION COSTS

Form 4-1 does not precisely allocate transaction costs between the parties. Particularly in a complex or large transaction where substantial costs will be incurred in a hazardous materials investigation of the site, a paragraph should be added to describe all anticipated transaction costs and the respective obligations of the parties relative to such costs.

Form 17-4 illustrates a style that could be used and assumes the hazardous materials investigation expense language from the preceding Form 17-3 has been incorporated into the site purchase offer. Carefully edit Form 17-4, making certain that the language comprehensively and accurately covers all costs and that the language selected is consistent with all other provisions of the final proposal. Be mindful of local custom in allocating closing costs. Custom in the reader's geographic area may differ from the allocation shown here.

If a paragraph similar to the one included as Form 17-4, below, is added to Form 4-1, do not use Paragraph 9.1 ("Escrow Fees and Closing Costs") of Form 4-1. The Form 17-4 paragraph, after appropriate editing, should usually be inserted toward the end of the document, after defined terms within it have been introduced.

Form 17-4

Allocation of Specific Purchase and Sale Transaction Costs

__. **Transaction Costs.** Each party shall pay costs incurred on its own behalf, including without limitation, attorneys' fees incurred to prepare and review required documentation. Other transaction costs shall be allocated as follows:

__.__ **Seller's Costs.** Seller shall be responsible for paying *__[e.g., one-half]__ the cost of the survey, __[e.g., the brokerage commission of $__________ payable to ____________, the documentary transfer tax, the cost of the __[See Appendix A, Form A-1]__ policy of title insurance with a liability limit of $__________, __[e.g., one-half]__ the cost of the Phase II and Phase III Investigations, the cost of the Remedial Action as defined in Paragraph __, the cost of the Additional Remedial Action as defined in Paragraph __ __[e.g., (less Buyer's one-half share which shall not to exceed $________)]__ and __[e.g., one-half]__ the escrow fees]__.*

__.__ **Buyer's Costs.** Buyer shall pay *__[e.g., one-half]__ the cost of the survey, __[e.g., one-half]__ the cost of the Phase II and Phase III Investigations, __[e.g., one-half]__ the cost of the Additional Remedial Action as defined in Paragraph ___ but not to exceed $__________, __[e.g., one-half]__ of the escrow fees and the cost of recording the deed conveying title to Buyer]__*. The escrow holder shall make any necessary adjustments to account for all of the foregoing on or before the closing date.

END OF FORM 17-4

FORM 17-4

RIGHT OF ENTRY TO INSPECT AND INVESTIGATE THE SITE

Many of the purchase and lease transactions covered in this book will require substantial inspection, investigation and testing of the subject property by the prospective purchaser or tenant. Although such rights, given appropriate indemnities, would typically be included in final documentation, the following is a short paragraph confirming such rights. (Form 4-1 includes an abbreviated entry-right clause as Paragraph 14 and a marketing-sign-right clause at Paragraph 15.)

Form 17-5

Provision for Entry upon the Site and Indemnification

__. **Entry Upon the Site.** After the __*[e.g., execution date of __[the Purchase Agreement]__ OR __[this agreement]__ __[enter name of party acquiring rights, e.g., purchaser, optionee, tenant (such as a retailer purchasing a parcel)—hereafter "Developer/Tenant" [select one] in this paragraph]__* shall have the right to enter upon the site, at __*[Developer/Tenant]*__ 's sole cost and expense, in order to inspect and investigate the site, and to perform all soil, drainage, utilities and other tests that __*[Developer/Tenant]*__ may deem necessary. __*[The Purchase Agreement]*__ *OR* __*[this agreement]*__ shall provide that __*[Developer/Tenant]*__ will indemnify and hold __*[insert name of appropriate party, e.g., the site owner and Developer where Developer is negotiating with Tenant and Developer does not yet own the site]*__ and the site free and harmless from and against all liabilities, claims, expenses and liens arising out of any such entry by __*[Developer/Tenant]*__ or its representatives, agents or designees, except any claims or damages arising from __*[Developer/Tenant]*__ 's negligence or willful misconduct. *[Where Developer is acquiring rights to the site:]* As of the __*[e.g., execution date of the Purchase Agreement]*__ *OR* __*[this agreement]*__ __*[name of owner of the site]*__ grants to __*[Developer]*__ the right to erect a sign or signs offering retail space for lease on the site.

END OF FORM 17-5

FORM 17-5

REPRESENTATIONS AND WARRANTIES

Representations and warranties can provide additional remedies to a site purchaser. At the deal-making document stage, use them very sparingly, if at all, and for specific reasons. It typically irritates one who is selling or ground leasing his or her land to receive an initial offer with a seemingly endless stream of requested representations and warranties. Appropriate representations and warranties do have their place, however, especially where equal knowledge will not be available to the buyer or ground lessee. A proposed representation or warranty may serve to "flush out" information in the seller's or ground lessor's control that would otherwise be difficult to obtain. The following are some examples of representations and warranties that address issues of concern to shopping center developers.

The deal maker's attorney should be responsible for refining and inserting appropriate protections into the final, operative agreements between the parties. Nevertheless, by re-reading these provisions before meeting with a land seller or concurrent with the preparation of a purchase proposal, lines of inquiry, additional areas of risk, and appropriate refinements to the transaction may come to mind. (The site purchaser will similarly benefit by re-reading the various "contingencies" listed in Paragraph 6 of the comprehensive purchase proposal Form 4-1.)

Note that, for the most part, the representations and warranties included as Form 17-6 were prepared from the perspective of a developer purchasing a site for development and, therefore, are generally contrary to the landowner's interests. (Refer to Chapter 18, Form 18-20 for representations and warranties for use by a developer in making a ground lease proposal.)

Paragraph 21 ("Representations and Warranties") of Form 4-1 merely includes broad, general language describing customary representations and warranties to be negotiated and included in a final agreement between the parties. Although portions of Form 17-6 could be selectively inserted into Paragraph 21 of Form 4-1, Form 17-6 is not designed to replace Paragraph 21 of Form 4-1. Form 17-6 is merely a sampling of representations and warranties—appropriate as factual circumstances warrant—applicable to recurring site acquisition issues from the developer's perspective. These clauses are intended to stimulate thinking in a comprehensive and broadened perspective rather than serve as a source of reusable deal points.

Form 17-6

Selected Seller Representations and Warranties for a Developer's Site Purchase Agreement

Typical introductory clause:

__. **Express Warranties of Seller.** Seller and each individual signing on Seller's behalf, in addition to the representations and warranties set forth herein, specifically represents and warrants to Buyer the following, all of which are true as of the date of this agreement and shall be true as of the close of escrow, except as specified otherwise, and each shall survive the close of escrow:

[a. General, limited listing:]

__.__ **Authority.** Seller has full power and authority to enter into and fully perform and comply with this agreement and has full power and authority to transfer the site to Buyer.

__.__ **No Pending or Threatened Actions.** To the best of Seller's knowledge and belief, __*[but without any duty of inquiry or investigation by Seller,]*__ there are no actions, suits or proceedings pending or threatened against the site or any portion thereof in any court or before any federal, state, county or municipal department, commission, board, bureau or agency or other governmental instrumentality, nor are there any such actions, suits or proceedings pending or threatened which could or would affect Seller's ability to perform its obligations under __*[this agreement]*__ *OR* __*[the Purchase Agreement]*__.

OR

Another version of preceding paragraph:

__.__ **No Pending or Threatened Action.** Seller has received no notice of, nor does it have any knowledge of __*[(but without any duty of inquiry or investigation by Seller)]*__, any pending or threatened action or governmental proceeding in eminent domain, zoning change, rent control, or otherwise, which would directly affect the site.

__.__ **No Contemplated Street or Highway Modification.** Seller is not aware of any existing, proposed, or contemplated plan to widen, modify or realign any street or highway or any existing, proposed or contemplated eminent domain proceedings which would affect the site in any way whatsoever.

FORM 17-6

__.__ **No Third-Party Rights to Site Not Disclosed in Preliminary Title Report.** There are not and will not be any leases, contracts, agreements, written or oral, or other understandings entered into by Seller with respect to the ownership, maintenance or operation of the site which are not disclosed in the preliminary title report to be delivered to Buyer for review and approval during the contingency approval period and which will be binding upon or in any way affect, impair, or diminish any of Buyer's rights, title and interest in the site or any improvements thereon.

__.__ **Seller to Make Site Information Available to Buyer.** Within __ days following the signing of __*[this agreement,]*__ OR __*[the Purchase Agreement]*__ Seller shall make available to Buyer for copying at Buyer's expense, in connection with the acquisition of the site, a copy of whatever surveys, engineering reports, technical information and other similar matters that Seller and Seller's agents and consultants may have covering the site or any portion thereof __*[and any contiguous property]*__.

__.__ **Seller Cooperation.** Seller will cooperate fully with Buyer and with federal, state and local governmental and quasi-governmental agencies, to the extent such cooperation relates to timely securing approvals and permits for the development of the site, __*[provided such actions by Buyer do not adversely impact the value of the site nor restrict or reduce the marketability of the site]*__. In furtherance of the foregoing and after a reasonable period not to exceed ten (10) business days for review, Seller will execute any and all conforming instruments necessary or appropriate for the development of the site, including but not limited to, maps, dedications, easements and rights of way and off-site improvement agreements with governmental and quasi-governmental authorities and adjacent property owners.

__.__ **No Governmental Violations.** Seller has no knowledge or reason to believe that Seller is presently in violation of any building code, license, or business statute or any other law of a governmental authority exercising jurisdiction over the site.

Seller oriented:

__.__ **No Warranty of Suitability; Buyer to Conduct Own Investigation.** *[A sophisticated Seller will typically request the insertion of a provision similar to the following:]* Except as otherwise expressly set forth in this agreement, Seller has not made and is not making to Buyer any other representation or warranty whether express or implied, in law or in fact, concerning the physical condition of the site or its suitability for Buyer's intended use. Buyer's proceeding to closing shall constitute confirmation that Buyer will have conducted whatever tests, studies and investigations Buyer shall have deemed necessary with respect to the site.

[b. Example of sample abbreviated clauses concerning hazardous materials and environmental matters:]

__.__ **No Hazardous Substance.** To Seller's best knowledge and belief, __*[but without any duty of inquiry or investigation by Seller,]*__ there is no contamination, hazardous waste or toxic substance in existence on or below the surface of the site including, without limitation, asbestos in any buildings or any contamination of the soil, subsoil or ground water, which constitutes a violation of any law or regulation of any government entity having jurisdiction thereof or which exposes Buyer to liability to third parties.

OR

An abbreviated version of preceding paragraph:

__.__ **No Hazardous Substance.** To Seller's best knowledge and belief, __*[but without any duty of inquiry or investigation by Seller,]*__ no substance identified as a hazardous or toxic material under any federal, state, or local law has been generated, stored, released, or otherwise deposited in or on the site.

Continue:

__.__ **No Hazardous Substances On or In Contiguous Lands.** To Seller's best knowledge and belief, __*[but without any duty of inquiry or investigation by Seller,]*__ no substance identified as a hazardous or toxic material under any federal, state, or local law has been generated, stored, released, or otherwise deposited in or on any parcel of land contiguous to the site.

__.__ **Water.** To Seller's best knowledge and belief, __*[but without any duty of inquiry or investigation by Seller,]*__ the site's ground water and surface water do not contain any hazardous substance.

__.__ **Asbestos.** To Seller's best knowledge and belief, __*[but without any inquiry or investigation by Seller,]*__ no portion of any building or other improvement on the site, including the walls, ceilings, structural steel, flooring, pipes, boilers or equipment is wrapped, insulated, fireproofed or surfaced with any asbestos-containing material.

__.__ **No Underground Storage Tanks.** To Seller's best knowledge and belief, __*[but without any duty of inquiry or investigation by Seller,]*__ there are no underground storage tanks within the site.

OR
(alternative to preceding sentence)

__.__ **Specified Underground Storage Tanks.** To Seller's best knowledge and belief, __*[but without any inquiry or investigation by Seller,]*__ the site contains only __*[e.g., 3]*__ underground storage tanks, all of which fully comply with federal, state and local regulation and none of which currently leak or have ever leaked, and the location, age, contents, size, and material composition of each is described on the attached Exhibit __ .

__.__ **No Wetland.** To Seller's best knowledge and belief, __*[but without any inquiry or investigation by Seller,]*__ neither the site nor any portion thereof constitutes a "wetland" under federal, state or local regulation.

__.__ **No Environmental Violations.** Seller has not received any notice of any possible violation of any environmental law concerning the site, and Seller neither knows of nor suspects any such violation.

__.__ **Environmental Compliance.** To Seller's best knowledge and belief, __*[but without any inquiry or investigation by Seller,]*__ the site fully complies with all environmental laws and Seller has obtained and maintained all permits, licenses, and approvals, if any, required under all environmental laws.

END OF FORM 17-6

BINDING AGREEMENT (FOR USE ONLY WITH ADVICE OF LEGAL COUNSEL)

The site purchase proposal Form 4-1 is designed to be used in its non-binding format. With an attorney's advice the form could be amended to create a binding contract when signed by the parties. In California, the resulting contract would typically be incorporated by reference into attached, pre-printed "boilerplate" title company escrow instructions.

Form 17-7, for use only with advice of legal counsel, modifies the "non-binding" language of Paragraph 24 of Form 4-1 to provide that the parties intend the document to be a binding, conclusive agreement. Such a provision should be implemented only when all agreements covering the transaction (including all final escrow provisions) have been comprehensively drafted and agreed upon by the parties. Although a single letter of intent could contain both binding and non-binding provisions, such specialized drafting is beyond the scope of this book.

Form 17-7

Letter Is to Be a Binding, Conclusive Agreement

24. Binding Agreement. The parties intend this document to be a binding, conclusive agreement __*[subject only to execution of escrow instructions incorporating the terms and conditions of this agreement]*__. This Agreement and its exhibits contain the entire agreement between the parties hereto with respect to the __*[e.g., purchase of the site]*__ by Buyer from Seller and supersede any and all prior agreements, negotiations or understandings of __*[e.g., Buyer and Seller]*__. No addition to or modification of any term or provision shall be effective unless set forth in a writing, signed by both __*[e.g., Buyer and Seller]*__.

END OF FORM 17-7

OVERVIEW

Chapter 18 contains a sampling of various additional and alternative clauses for selective consideration and incorporation into the lease deal-making documents in preceding chapters. ("Optional and Alternative Clauses for Purchase and Sale Proposals" is the topic of Chapter 17.)

The first section, "Controversial Business Provisions," covers special business issues likely to be hotly negotiated between sophisticated landlords and tenants. A variety of forms and deal structures may be drawn upon to reconcile conflicting interests of landlords and tenants. In some instances, forms include alternative provisions advocating the disparate perspectives of landlord and tenant. Controversial lease clauses addressed in this chapter include tenant construction allowances, tenant's rights of recapture from percentage rent, defining the scope of real property taxes payable by tenant, continuous operating covenants, co-tenancy clauses, exclusive rights, radius restrictions, assignment and subletting, kickout clauses, and tenant options to renew and to purchase.

The second section, "Technical and Special-Purpose Provisions," includes a rather detailed provision outlining the duties and obligations of the parties in coordinating the construction of a proposed build-to-suit transaction, plumbing and cleanliness standards geared primarily to "greasy" fast-food tenants, an expanded hazardous materials due diligence provision, and selected representations and warranties applicable to lease transactions.

These clauses are not designed for insertion into operative leases. They merely show legal and economic rights and relationships for purposes of structuring preliminary agreements among the parties and their attorneys.

FORMS

Controversial Business Provisions

18-1 Special Improvements or Construction Allowance. Landlord to Provide Non-Standard Improvement(s) or Construction/Improvement Allowance to Tenant.

18-2 Tenant Recapture of Improvement Costs. Tenant's Recapture of Construction and Fixturing Costs or Construction Interest Expense from Percentage Rent.

18-3 Tenant Recapture of Operating Costs. Tenant's Recapture of Certain Operating Costs from Percentage Rent.

18-4 Separately Parcelizing Tenant's Site for Property Tax Purposes. Real Property Taxes Payable by Tenant Assume Tenant's Site Is Separately Parcelized.

18-5 Continuous Operations. Tenant's Obligation to Continuously Operate.

18-6 Co-Tenancy. Initial (Not Ongoing) Co-Tenancy Clause.

18-7 Tenant Exclusive. Tenant's Limited Exclusive Merchandising Right.

18-8 Radius Restriction (Favors Landlord). Radius Restriction.

18-9 "Reverse" Radius Restriction (Favors Tenant). "Reverse" Radius Restriction.

18-10 Various Alternative Assignment and Subletting Provisions. Selected Assignment and Subletting Clauses.

18-11 Right to Terminate If Inadequate Sales. Landlord's and/or Tenant's Right to Terminate Lease If Gross Sales Target Not Met.

18-12 Right of First Offer. Tenant Right of First Offer.

18-13 Right of First Refusal. Tenant Right of First Refusal.

18-14 Option to Extend. Tenant Option to Extend Lease Term.

18-15 Purchase Option. Tenant Option to Purchase Premises.

Technical and Special-Purpose Provisions

18-16 Build-to-Suit Construction Coordination. Detailed Construction Responsibilities and Coordination between Landlord and Tenant.

18-17 Restaurant Cleanliness. Restaurant Pest and Sanitation Control.

18-18 Hazardous Materials. Sample Ground-Lease Letter of Intent Hazardous Materials Provision Where Significant Investigation and Remedial Work Is Contemplated.

18-19 Allocation of Specific Lease Costs. Allocation of Specific [Ground] Lease Transaction Costs.

18-20 Landlord-Oriented Representations and Warranties. Selected Representations and Warranties for Lease Transactions.

Chapter 18

Optional and Alternative Clauses for Lease Proposals

Be careful to leave your sons [and daughters] *well instructed rather than rich, for the hopes of the instructed are better than the wealth of the ignorant.*
—Epictetus

Each lease transaction tends to have unique deal points. This chapter contains optional and alternative clauses designed for selective insertion into the leasing proposals included in earlier chapters. (Chapter 17 contains optional and alternative clauses for site purchase and sale proposals.)

Use the utmost care in applying these provisions, as many require significant legal expertise to professionally integrate them into a functional document. At a minimum, however, a reading and understanding of the various optional and alternative forms contained in this chapter and in Chapter 17 should help improve your deal-making skills and competence in attorney-client interactions.

Space does not allow an exhaustive summary of possible deal structures, but a variety of useful alternative provisions have been selected. In many instances, alternative "landlord-" or "tenant-oriented" clauses manifest the disparate perspectives of landlord and tenant.

CONTROVERSIAL BUSINESS PROVISIONS

Tenant Construction Allowances

The first clause in Form 18-1 confirms a landlord agreement to make specific improvements to the premises beyond the typical finish. The succeeding clauses confirm a tenant finish or construction allowance granted either as a lump sum or based upon a fixed sum per square foot with variable payout terms.

Form 18-1

Landlord to Provide Non-Standard Improvement(s) or Construction/Improvement Allowance to Tenant

Limited but specific, non-standard improvements provided by Landlord:

__. Specific Improvements to Premises Provided by Landlord. Landlord shall complete the leased premises in accordance with the attached __*[e.g., Exhibit "C" work letter]*__. In addition to the standard __*[e.g., Exhibit "C" work]*__, Landlord shall make the following additional specific improvements to the premises at Landlord's expense: __*[describe specific improvements]*__. All other work required to make the premises suitable for Tenant's occupancy and operation of Tenant's business shall be completed by Tenant at Tenant's sole cost and expense.

OR

Finish allowance with indefinite disbursement procedure:

__. Tenant Finish Allowance. __*[Conditioned upon timely store opening,]*__ Tenant shall be entitled to a Tenant Finish Allowance of $______ per square foot of the leased premises. Assuming ______ square feet of leased premises, this amounts to a total allowance of $_______. Landlord shall pay the Tenant Finish Allowance to Tenant in accordance with Landlord's disbursement procedures __*[upon Landlord's receipt from Tenant of invoices for Tenant's work from Tenant's contractors and such other documentation as Landlord may reasonably require, including, without limitation, lien waivers, certificate of occupancy, and approved, as-built plans and specifications]*__.

OR

Flat sum or fixed amount per square foot disbursed in installments:

__. Construction Allowance. As an incentive for Tenant to enter into the lease and provided Tenant is not in default, Landlord shall pay Tenant a construction allowance of *[Flat sum:]* __*[$__________]*__ *OR [Fixed amount per square foot:]* __*[$_________ per square foot of the leased premises]*__ for improvements acceptable to Landlord. The allowance shall be paid __*[e.g., 1/3]*__ upon submission to Landlord of invoices, lien releases and evidence of completion of __*[e.g., 1/3]*__ of Tenant's work, __*[e.g., 1/3]*__ upon submission to Landlord of invoices, lien releases and evidence of completion of __*[e.g., 2/3]*__ of Tenant's work, and the balance upon Tenant's final completion as accepted by Landlord in accordance with the lease __*[and Tenant has opened for business at the premises]*__.

END OF FORM 18-1

FORM 18-1

Tenant Recapture of Tenant's Construction and Fixturization Costs or Construction Interest Expense from Percentage Rent

When capital is limited, as an alternative to a landlord cash advance (or in addition to a reduced landlord advance), the lease could provide that specified construction and fixturing costs advanced by the tenant could be recaptured as a credit against the tenant's percentage rent. Alternatively, the tenant could finance such construction and fixturing costs and negotiate a right to recapture from percentage rent the resulting interest expense attributable to such improvements. Such alternative but unconventional deal-making provisions are set forth below.

Form 18-2

Tenant's Recapture of Construction and Fixturing Costs or Construction Interest Expense from Percentage Rent

If Tenant is advancing construction and fixturing costs, the following provision gives Tenant the right to recapture Tenant's initial construction and fixturing costs from percentage rent subject to (i) an annual limitation and (ii) an obligation to repay all sums so recaptured from percentage rent upon lease assignment, termination, or Tenant default prior to Tenant's full recapture of such costs.

__. **Tenant's Recapture of Tenant's Construction and Fixturing Costs From Percentage Rent.** Tenant may recapture as a credit against annual percentage rent payable under the lease, an amount (the "Tenant Construction Advance") not to exceed $________ of Tenant's actual cost to initially construct and fixturize the leasehold premises. __*[The available credit shall be based upon legitimate, paid third-party invoices provided Landlord together with all appropriate lien releases]*__. However, the amount Tenant may recapture in any lease year shall not exceed __*[e.g., 60]*__ % of the annual percentage rent otherwise payable during such lease year. In calculating the credit, annual percentage rent __*[shall not]*__ *OR* __*[shall]*__ be carried over or aggregated from lease year to lease year. The credit shall terminate when Tenant has recaptured the Tenant Construction Advance (as provided above), the lease is assigned, transferred or terminated, or Tenant materially defaults, whichever first occurs.

Tough, landlord-oriented final paragraph (which could be eliminated) requiring restitution of Tenant's recapture benefits:

If Tenant's recapture right terminates because the lease is assigned, transferred or terminated, or Tenant materially defaults, for any reason, before Tenant's full recapture of the $__________ Tenant Construction Advance, Tenant shall forfeit any credit for any portion of the Tenant Construction Advance not yet recaptured by Tenant, and Tenant shall within __*[e.g., 60]*__ days reimburse Landlord in cash (payable as additional rent) for any portion of the Tenant Construction Advance previously credited against annual percentage rent. *[Refer to the note at the end of the next page.]*

OR

Alternatively, the following provision grants Tenant a right to recapture from percentage rent Tenant's interest expense attributable Tenant's initial construction and fixturing costs, subject to (i) a

FORM 18-2

term limitation, (ii) an annual cap and (iii) an obligation to repay all sums so recaptured from percentage rent upon lease assignment, transfer, termination, or Tenant default prior to the expiration of Tenant's recapture right.

__. **Tenant's Recapture of Construction Interest Expense From Percentage Rent.** For the first __*[e.g., 5]*__ full accounting periods for which annual percentage rent is calculated (the "Recapture Period"), Tenant may recapture as a credit against annual percentage rent payable under the lease, an amount (the "Tenant Construction Interest Expense") not to exceed $_________ per lease year for the actual cost of interest paid by Tenant to an institutional lender (during the lease year for which such percentage rent is payable) for agreed initial construction improvements to the leased premises made by Tenant. __*[The actual cost of such improvements shall be substantiated by legitimate, paid third-party invoices provided Landlord together with all appropriate lien releases]*__. The Tenant Construction Interest Expense so credited shall not exceed the actual rate paid by Tenant or the prime rate of interest chargeable by __*[insert name]*__ bank as of __*[e.g., the date of Tenant's first draw under Tenant's loan]*__ plus __*[e.g., 2]*__ %. In addition, the amount Tenant may recapture in any lease year shall not exceed __*[e.g., 60]*__ % of the annual percentage rent otherwise payable during such lease year. In calculating the credit, annual percentage rent __*[shall not]*__ OR __*[shall]*__ be carried over or aggregated from lease year to lease year. The credit shall terminate when the Recapture Period has expired, the lease is assigned, transferred or terminated, or Tenant materially defaults, whichever first occurs.

Tough, landlord-oriented final paragraph (which could be eliminated) requiring restitution of Tenant's recapture benefits:

If Tenant's recapture right terminates because the lease is assigned, transferred or terminated, or Tenant materially defaults, for any reason, before expiration of the Recapture Period, Tenant shall forfeit any credit for any portion of the Tenant Construction Interest Expense not yet recaptured by Tenant, and Tenant shall within __*[e.g., 60]*__ days reimburse Landlord in cash (payable as additional rent) for any portion of the Tenant Construction Interest Expense previously credited against annual percentage rent.

Note: *The harshness of the preceding final paragraph could be reduced by revising its introductory clause to read: "If Tenant's recapture right terminates because Tenant materially defaults, for any reason, __[during the first three years of the lease term]__, ...".*

END OF FORM 18-2

Tenant Recapture of Tenant's Real Property Taxes, Insurance and CAM Charges from Percentage Rent

A tenant with a strong bargaining position may attempt to recapture various occupancy costs from percentage rent. Form 18-3 is designed to allow the form user to set forth the basic business issues of such a credit. Such a recapture clause would normally be inserted immediately following the percentage rent clause.

Form 18-3

Tenant's Recapture of Certain Operating Costs from Percentage Rent

Broad, tenant-oriented recapture right:

__. **Tenant's Recapture of Certain Occupancy Costs From Percentage Rent.** During each accounting year in which percentage rent is payable under the lease, Tenant may recover as a credit against annual percentage rent payable under the lease __*[e.g., 50]*__ % of the sum of __*[all real property taxes, insurance premiums paid by Tenant to insure its building and improvements, and all other common area maintenance expenses]*__ paid by Tenant with respect to Tenant's operations on the premises during such year.

AND
Add Alternative "A" or "B"

Alternative "A"
Landlord oriented: Credit not cumulative.

If the sum of such creditable items paid by Tenant in any such accounting year exceeds the amount of percentage rent payable by Tenant to Landlord for such accounting year, the remaining balance may not be credited against any percentage rent due for any subsequent accounting period. *[A similar but less precise result could be achieved by inserting the words "non-cumulative credit" in place of the word "credit" in the preceding paragraph describing Tenant's recapture right.]*

OR

Alternative "B"
Tenant oriented: Credit cumulative.

If the sum of such creditable items paid by Tenant in any such accounting year exceeds the amount of percentage rent payable by Tenant to Landlord for such accounting year, the remaining balance thereof shall be credited against any percentage rent thereafter due and payable by Tenant to Landlord during the remainder of the lease term or any extension or renewal of it.

END OF FORM 18-3

Real Property Taxes Payable by Tenant Based upon Tenant's Impact Area

Free-standing pad or out-parcel buildings are generally more expensive to construct, are often built on higher-valued land than "in-line" shop space and, consequently, on a per-square-foot of building basis, customarily receive higher real property tax assessments. In addition, retailers occupying free-standing pad or out-parcel buildings usually have a greater "impact area" or effectively use a greater land area relative to their building square footage than do "in-line" shop tenants. Similarly, major tenant buildings are often more highly improved and have a higher assessed value than do "in-line" shop buildings. Consequently, allocating all real property taxes among the shopping center's tenants based solely upon relative building square footage tends to subsidize the free-standing and major tenant buildings at the expense of the small "in-line" shop tenants.

Form 18-4 assumes the parties will attempt to separately parcelize the tenant's premises or "site" (as defined in a preceding section of the letter of intent) and provides that if the tenant's building and land area attributable to tenant's use is, in fact, separately assessed for property tax purposes, the tenant will pay all such assessed taxes. Such tax obligation is in lieu of the tenant's "traditional" obligation to pay its prorata share of taxes levied against its premises based upon the tenant's building area relative to the total building area covered by the tax bill. Note, however, that as a protective measure Form 18-4 provides that if the separate parcelization is not accomplished, the tenant will pay its prorata share of taxes levied against its premises based upon the tenant's building area relative to the total building area covered by the tax bill. (Defining the scope of what is and is not to be considered real property taxes could be the subject matter of an additional paragraph but is usually not negotiated until final lease documentation.)

Consider this alternative real property tax structuring in each free-standing "pad" or major tenant transaction.

Form 18-4

Property Taxes Payable by Tenant Assume Tenant's Site Is Separately Parcelized

__. **Real Property Taxes Payable by Tenant Assume Tenant's Site Is Separately Parcelized.** Real property taxes payable by Tenant shall include all real estate taxes, levies and assessments with respect to (1) Tenant's building and any improvements and equipment located therein or adjacent thereto __*[e.g., such as the trash area shown on Exhibit "__" used by Tenant]*__, and (2), in the event Tenant's site is made a separate legal __*[or tax]*__ parcel, the site. If Tenant's site is made a separate legal __*[or tax]*__ parcel, the size of such parcel shall not exceed _______ sq. ft., which the parties agree is a reasonable estimate of the land area required for Tenant's building, vehicular access, parking area and ancillary improvements. Landlord shall have the right, but not the obligation, to parcelize the site at any time during the term of the lease. Tenant shall cooperate with Landlord in parcelizing the site.

__.__ **If Tenant's Site Is Separately Parcelized.** If the site is made a separate legal __*[or tax]*__ parcel, Tenant shall pay the real property taxes referenced in the first sentence of the preceding paragraph and, in consideration of such payment, Tenant shall not be obligated to pay the portion of common and parking area expenses allocable to real estate taxes. The parcelization of the site, however, shall not expand Tenant's maintenance obligations, it being understood that Landlord will continue to maintain all common areas, including those portions of the site not required to be maintained by Tenant.

__.__ **If Tenant's Site Is Not Separately Parcelized.** If for any reason the site is not separately assessed for tax purposes, then Tenant's obligation to pay the real property taxes applicable to the site, including the building, shall be apportioned according to the floor area of Tenant's building, as it relates to the total ground floor area (excluding mezzanines) of all buildings (including Tenant's building) which are covered by the tax bill levying such taxes.

END OF FORM 18-4

Continuous Operating Covenants

An obligation to continuously operate for the term of the lease is commonplace in satellite tenancies in regional malls and strip retail centers. With increasing frequency, however, tenants with strong bargaining power will insist on tempering such obligation to remain open with a co-tenancy requirement that certain major tenant(s) and a certain percentage of satellite space remain open. Form 18-5 provides an example of operating obligations together with an illustrative tenant response. The developer loses significant control over the operation of the center in acceding to the tenant's request. Although the developer's lease documentation can create an "obligation" for other tenants to remain open, the developer cannot control whether such tenants are "actually" open. Of course, the tenant's real concern is that such other tenants are "actually" open.

(Author's comment: *Although anchor tenants in strip centers have been notoriously unwilling and have in the past not been required to give operating covenants, operating covenants have long been a fact of life in regional malls. In strip center development, there is a prevailing "all-or-nothing" stereotypical thinking or response that the tenant either will or will not grant an operating covenant. Possible middle grounds are seldom discussed.*

I speculate that some creative, evolutionary changes may be forced upon the parties by equity and debt markets. A mandate for some form of operating covenant may become a major issue between major tenants and the developer's lender. If so, this becomes a critical deal point for the developer and may effect which major tenant is selected by the developer. To get deals done in the future, there will be growing pressure to be more creative and sophisticated in accommodating the interests of the developer, tenant, and the lender.

To illustrate, one major department chain will grant a 15-year operating covenant—five years as a department store and thereafter as a retailing use—with the covenant terminating if certain other majors cease operations for 12 months. Such a covenant is less than ideal from each of the perspectives of the tenant, the developer, or the lender. Yet, rather than uncritically follow past practices, tomorrow's successful developers and tenants will create deal structures that rationally balance the requirements of the developer, tenant and lender in the particular factual context. Perhaps future strip center anchor transactions will evolve into a blend of operating rights and obligations starting with a covenant to open, a short covenant to operate in a precise format, and a final period of rights and obligations that appropriately blends the interests of the developer, tenant, and lender. Perhaps, as the major's operating covenant tapers off, the developer's recapture rights could become more potent and minimum rent could be increased to the percentage rent payable preceding the tenant's going dark.)

Form 18-5

Tenant's Obligation to Continuously Operate

__. **Continuous Operations.** Tenant will open for business in the premises and, after its initial opening for business, Tenant shall continuously (i) operate Tenant's business in the premises for the entire lease term so as to maximize net sales and (ii) maintain adequate stock and inventory together with adequate merchandise, sufficient personnel, and personal property to service customers, so as to produce the maximum return to Landlord and Tenant and maximize the percentage rent payable Landlord. *[Tenant oriented insert:] __[Notwithstanding such duty, however, Tenant shall only be required to open for business during those hours that the _____ square foot building __[currently OR to be]__ occupied by __[name of major tenant]__ is __[actually]__ OR __[obligated to be]__ open and operating as a __[e.g., supermarket]__ AND __ [e.g., 60]__ % of total G.L.A. of the in-line shop tenant space is leased and such shop tenants are __[actually]__ OR __[obligated to be]__ open for business]__.*

END OF FORM 18-5

FORM 18-5

Co-Tenancy Clauses

Tenants want to be certain that the center will be a viable, dynamic one, anchored with appropriate chain stores. The co-tenancy clause gives the tenant the right to terminate its parcel purchase or lease agreement, or otherwise not be obligated to open or pay rent, if certain minimum leaseup fails to occur. Of course, it signifies a significant loss of control to the developer.

A major distinction should be made between co-tenancy clauses that prescribe "initial" or "opening" criteria (that either will or will not be satisfied within a relatively short time period) and those with "ongoing" requirements. An opening requirement may not be a major risk to a developer, but an ongoing clause that would allow a tenant to leave a center if certain co-tenants ceased to operate is a serious risk to the developer and developer's lender. Developers argue that if a tenant is a retailer, why should the landlord bear the risk of the retailer's ineffective management? If an ongoing co-tenancy provision is imposed, the developer should negotiate a cure period so the tenant cannot terminate if the co-tenancy condition is not met for a short period.

The following clause allows a major tenant to condition its transaction upon the requirement that the developer enter into a transaction with a specified co-tenant. The risk of not being able to secure the co-tenant is usually relatively quantifiable and if the contingency is not satisfied, the transaction is terminated. However, if a co-tenancy condition must be granted, the developer should try to negotiate a clause whereby a particular tenant category and/or floor area (e.g., a "drugstore" co-tenant) will satisfy the condition instead of being obligated to enter into transaction(s) with specific named tenants.

(Because this issue arises most often during negotiation of major tenant transactions, paragraphs similar to Form 18-2 are included as optional provisions within the body of the major tenant lease Forms 9-1 and 9-2 and the major tenant parcel purchase and sale Form 10-1.)

Form 18-6

Initial (Not Ongoing) Co-Tenancy Clause

Co-tenancy clause allowing Tenant to terminate its lease if transaction(s) not executed with selected co-tenant(s):

__. **Co-tenancy Contingency.** As of the date of this letter of intent, Landlord is in the process of negotiating a __*[lease OR parcel sale escrow]*__ with ________ and a __*[lease OR parcel sale escrow]*__ with ________. If __*[lease(s)/parcel sale escrow(s)]*__ for space in the shopping center by both __________ and ____________ have not been executed by _________, 20__, Tenant shall have the right to terminate Tenant's lease with Landlord on or before _________, 20__. If Tenant elects to so terminate due to the failure of such co-tenancy condition, the lease shall terminate and neither Landlord nor Tenant shall have any further rights or obligations under the lease and neither party shall be responsible for any costs incurred by the other.

Note: *A more tenant-oriented approach would require that a co-tenant's lease become uncontingent by a given date (rather than merely executed) or that a co-tenant's parcel purchase escrow actually close by a prescribed date.*

END OF FORM 18-6

FORM 18-6

Exclusive Rights

Exclusive-use provisions give a tenant the exclusive right to conduct a certain business or sell specific types or lines of merchandise. Given resulting management, marketing, leasing, and operating problems, a developer should avoid granting an exclusive whenever possible. Exclusives are generally not given to small tenants and, if an exclusive is granted, it should be carefully and narrowly defined, limited in scope and duration, provide for exceptions, and, ideally, include some form of buyout right. For example, if the developer is not careful, the granting of an "apparel" exclusive to a 2,000-square-foot shop could block the developer's subsequent ability to lease to a department store.

Any exclusive granted should be so precisely defined that the exclusive will not put a "chilling effect" on future marketing opportunities from uncertainty about whether a potential new tenant's use would conflict with the granted exclusive. In addition, it should have a "use it or lose it" provision—the exclusive right should lapse if the tenant ceases to use it. Be particularly mindful of the evolving nature of retailing and that a reasonable definition of a protected interest for a lease signed today could become uncertain, overly broad, and unreasonable or inappropriate in the future.

Form 18-7

Tenant's Limited Exclusive Merchandising Right

__. **Exclusive Right.** __*[For the first __ years of the initial lease term,]*__ Tenant shall have the exclusive right to sell __*[e.g., insert Tenant's narrowly defined primary line of business]*__ within __*[a radius of ____ feet of Tenant's store]*__ *OR* __*[the XYZ shopping center]*__ and Landlord shall not grant any other tenant the right to operate a business within __*[such area of]*__ the shopping center which interferes with such exclusive right*[.]* __*[, provided:]*__

Selectively consider the following limitations and renumber subparagraphs accordingly:

__.1 **Continuous Primary Use.** __*[At all times the sale of such __ [e.g., insert Tenant's narrowly defined primary line of business]__ continues to be the primary use of Tenant's space;]*__

__.2 **Certain Tenants Excluded.** __*[Any tenant over ______ square feet]*__ *AND/OR* __*[Tenant(s) A, B and C shall not be bound by the exclusive granted Tenant;]*__

__.3 **Limited Exceptions.** __*[Any other tenant in XYZ shopping center may sell* __*[e.g., insert Tenant's narrowly defined primary line of business]*__ provided any such tenant's __*[total selling square footage devoted to such item does not exceed ______ square feet]*__ *OR* __*[gross sales of such item are not greater than __ % of such tenant's average total gross sales over any ___ -month period]*__.

__.4 **Excluded Lands.** __*[The exclusive shall not extend to any land contiguous to the land area currently improved and known as XYZ shopping center;]*__ __*[and]*__

__.5 **Termination.** __*[The exclusive right shall automatically terminate if]*__ __*[Tenant stops selling]*__ __*[describe protected primary line]*__ *for __ months]*__ *OR* __*[Tenant's total average gross sales for Tenant's store for any consecutive __ -month period is less than $______ per square foot]*__ *OR* __ *[Tenant ceases to operate on the premises for a __ -month period]*__.

END OF FORM 18-7

FORM 18-7

Radius Restrictions

The radius clause is a developer-oriented clause designed to prevent the tenant from draining sales from the subject center to another location and thereby inhibiting the developer's receipt of percentage rent. The clause also has the intended effect of protecting the volumes of other tenants in the center by preserving the customer base and vitality of the center. Even if there is no percentage rent and the tenant is not bound by an operating covenant, the radius clause protects the developer from the tenant picking up the next best lease opportunity. The negotiation of a radius clause is a business negotiation that intertwines a host of business issues (demographic assumptions, volume projections, competition analysis) and legal issues (operating covenants, tenant's right, if any, to assign or sublease, kick-out rights, etc.). Often a developer will grant an exclusive only if the tenant agrees to a radius restriction.

Issues include defining a narrowly prescribed protective area, specifying the limited duration of the restriction, defining an offending business enterprise, and creating appropriate exclusions. Most, but not all, courts will uphold "reasonable" restrictions (i.e., reasonable in duration, distance, and purpose) but legal counsel should review the factual context and consult applicable antitrust statutes and local case law before drafting an operative radius restriction.

Form 18-8

Radius Restriction (Favors Landlord)

__. **Limited Operating Restriction.** The lease shall provide that, during the first __*[e.g., 3]*__ years of the lease term, neither Tenant nor any person, enterprise, or corporation directly or indirectly controlling, controlled, or under common control with Tenant ("Restricted Parties") shall, without the prior written consent of Landlord, operate, manage, franchise, license, or otherwise have any interest in any other business within a radius of __*[e.g., 2]*__ miles from the outside boundary of __*[name]*__ shopping center, which business is engaged in the same or similar use as Tenant's proposed use.

__.1 **Landlord's Remedies If Tenant Violates Restriction.** If, during such period, any Restricted Party operates, manages, franchises, licenses or otherwise has any interest in any such business without Landlord's prior written consent, Landlord may elect to: (i) increase the minimum rent to an amount equal to __*[e.g., 90]*__ % of the total minimum annual rent and percentage rent payable to Landlord by Tenant for the preceding __*[e.g., 12]*__ month period; or (ii) require that __*[e.g., 70]*__ % of the sales resulting from any such businesses shall be included in the amount of the gross receipts from which percentage rent is calculated under the lease. __*[If no percentage rent is chargeable Tenant and Tenant violates this provision, commencing with Tenant's breach Tenant shall pay __[e.g., 140]__ % of the minimum rent otherwise payable under the lease]*__.

EXCEPTIONS
One or more could be added, numbering consecutively after preceding paragraph

Limited exception for an existing business within radius:

__.__ **Existing Business Exception.** Tenant represents that Tenant (i) has an interest in __*[describe name of existing enterprise within restricted radius]*__ that operates a __*[describe nature of business]*__ at __*[describe specific location]*__ and (ii) that no Restricted Party has any interest in any other commercial establishment within the radius. Such establishment __*[and no other within the radius]*__ may continue to be operated and owned in the same manner as of the date of this letter of intent __*[e.g., free of the inclusion of such enterprise's gross sales in the calculation of Tenant's rent]*__ OR __*[e.g., without any impact upon the proposed lease between Landlord and Tenant]*__.

FORM 18-8

Limited exception for additional store(s) within radius resulting from substantial merger, acquisition, or sale:

__.__ **Corporate Transaction Exception.** This restriction shall not include or apply to any business which might result by means of (i) a merger or consolidation of Tenant with another business entity or (ii) Tenant's purchase of a controlling interest in another business entity, or (iii) the sale of a controlling interest in Tenant to another business entity, provided, in each such case, __*[e.g., the other business entity has not less than __[Landlords: insert large number]__ total retail stores immediately prior to such merger, consolidation or change in control]*__.

Limited exclusion of a store relocation within radius:

__.__ **Store Relocation Within Radius Exception.** This restriction shall not include or apply to any permitted Restricted Party business existing as of the date of this letter of intent which is subsequently relocated within the radius __*[e.g., provided the floor area of such business' store in the new location does not exceed the floor area of its existing store by more than]*__ __*[e.g., 10%]*__ *OR* __*[e.g., provided such business is relocated to a new location within the current boundaries of the shopping center in which it is currently located]*__.

END OF FORM 18-8

Reverse Radius Restrictions

A "reverse" radius clause is a tenant-oriented restrictive covenant that restricts the landlord in making leases or conveyances to competitors of the tenant on landlord's other properties within a narrowly prescribed radius. Like conventional radius clauses, such clauses have been upheld notwithstanding antitrust issues so long as they are deemed "reasonable" in duration, distance, and purpose. (See, e.g., *Vermont National Bank* v. *Chittenden Trust Company* (1983) 465 A. 2d 284.) However, such a provision may run afoul of the law if the radius is significant enough to allow the benefited business to operate free of competitive pressures or if there is no other space in the trade area in which a competitor of the benefited business could locate. Legal counsel should review the factual context and consult applicable antitrust statutes and local case law before drafting and implementing an operative "reverse" radius restriction. Such clauses are infrequently used.

Form 18-9

"Reverse" Radius Restriction (Favors Tenant)

__. **Limited Leasing or Sale Competition.** The lease shall provide that Landlord __*[or an affiliate of Landlord]*__ shall not, during the first __*[e.g., 3]*__ years of the lease term, without the prior written consent of Tenant, enter into a lease or sale transaction or have any business interest with __*[e.g., any bank or savings and loan institution]*__ concerning any real property within a radius of __*[e.g., 2]*__ miles from the outside boundary of __*[name]*__ shopping center for any retail or service use including a __*[e.g., bank or savings and loan business]*__.

Note: *Tenant, with the help of Tenant's counsel, should consider an appropriate remedy in the event of Landlord's breach of the preceding deal point.*

EXCEPTIONS:
One or more could be added, numbering consecutively after preceding paragraph

Limited Landlord exception for an existing business within radius:

__.__ **Existing Business Exception.** Landlord represents that Landlord (i) has a __*[e.g., lease]*__ with __*[describe name of existing tenant within restricted radius]*__ that operates a __*[describe nature of business]*__ at __*[describe specific location]*__ and (ii) that Landlord has no business interest with any other tenant so restricted within such radius. The lease with such tenant __*[and no other specified tenant within the radius]*__ may continue in the same manner as of the date __*[of this letter of intent]*__ free of any such restriction on Landlord.

Limited Landlord exception for additional store(s) within radius resulting from acquisition by Landlord of another center within the radius:

__.__ **Center Acquisition Exception.** This restriction shall not include or apply to any business which might result by means of an acquisition by Landlord of an entire shopping center within the radius (even if all parcels within the center are not purchased) __*[e.g., provided any such shopping center purchased contains not less than __ total retail stores and encompasses not less than ___ acres of gross land area immediately prior to such acquisition]*__ *AND* __*[e.g., a bank or savings and loan business]*__ __*[is a tenant or occupant of such center as of the date of such acquisition]*__.

FORM 18-9

Limited Landlord exclusion of a store relocation within radius:

__.__ **Store Relocation Within Radius Exception.** This restriction shall not include or apply to any tenant of Landlord existing as of the date of this letter of intent which is subsequently relocated to another property of Landlord within the radius __*[e.g., provided the floor area of the tenant's store in the new location does not exceed the floor area of the tenant's existing store by more than]*__ __*[e.g., 10%]*__ *OR* __*[e.g., provided such tenant's business is relocated to a new location within the current boundaries of the shopping center in which it is currently located]*__.

END OF FORM 18-9

Assignment and Subletting

In the absence of a contractual provision to the contrary, leases can be freely assigned and leasehold space can be sublet. With substantial economic value at stake, unavoidable conflict exists between knowledgeable landlords and tenants relative to negotiating the transferability of the tenant's leasehold interest. While tenants want free assignability to allow a sale or transfer of tenant's interest prior to the end of the lease term, landlords have a legitimate need to be assured that a proposed transferee of tenant's leasehold will not only be capable of fulfilling tenant's obligations under the lease but will also be a compatible occupant, no less likely to pay percentage rent than the tenant.

In essence, the issue is, "Who controls the real estate?" In a majority of states, if a lease requires that the landlord consent to an assignment or subletting (and the lease contains no express standards or conditions for giving or withholding consent), a landlord can be arbitrary and unreasonable in denying consent. However, in a growing number of minority jurisdictions, a landlord's consent to an assignment or subletting cannot be "unreasonably" withheld. Developers should be particularly mindful of developer conduct that might subsequently be deemed unreasonable or overreaching under future legal standards or interpretations. The prudent developer's final lease document should confirm why the landlord is relying on the specific tenant's performance, what the tenant is bringing to the center, and show that the assignment and subletting standards agreed upon were freely negotiated.

In recent years courts have struggled to resolve assignment and subletting conflicts and the reader should be wary of changing case law in this area. It is beyond the scope of this text to provide a definitive analysis of leasehold assignment and subletting options. Although the purpose of this section is to outline various prevailing approaches, you should develop an integrated policy and format grounded upon sound legal advice and applicable state law. Such counsel is critical, as recent statutory changes and case law can significantly affect rational decision making in drafting appropriate assignment provisions.

For example, relaxing a reasonableness standard imposed by prior case law, effective January 1, 1990, California Civil Code Sections 1995.010 through 1995.270 permits parties to commercial leases to adopt "any express standard or condition" to an assignment or subletting, including ". . . a provision that the landlord is entitled to some or all of any consideration the tenant receives from a transferee in excess of the rent under the lease." (Cal. Civ. Code Section 1995.240.) In fact, "A restriction on transfer of a tenant's interest in a lease may absolutely prohibit transfer." (Cal. Civ. Code Section 1995.230.) However, under California's statutory scheme, a commercial reasonableness standard will be implied if a lease requires landlord's consent to a transfer but does not provide standards or conditions governing the landlord's right to grant or withhold consent.

In California, the landlord's remedies upon the tenant's breach are even affected by the "reasonability" of tenant's transfer rights. A properly drafted lease may allow a California landlord to unreasonably withhold consent to a proposed transfer, but there is a cost to retaining such a right. If a lease unreasonably restricts or prohibits the tenant from assigning or subletting, the landlord loses the "lock-in" remedy or right to treat the lease as remaining in effect and to continue to collect rents for the remaining lease term following the tenant's breach and abandonment. (Cal. Civ. Code Section 1951.4.) In such a case, the landlord's only practical remedy may be to terminate the lease and sue for damages.

Determine an approach appropriate for your own management style after careful consideration of applicable legal consequences. Landlords should be certain not to be silent on the issue of tenant transferability. In California and in a majority of states, if a lease contains no restriction on transfer, the tenant may freely transfer its interest in the lease.

Landlords and tenants frequently accommodate their conflicting interests by carefully crafting mutually acceptable standards or conditions by which the landlord will be obligated to consent to an assignment or subletting. In many cases, the deal structure will include a landlord "recapture right" whereby the landlord may first elect to recapture the premises (or a portion thereof, as is applicable) upon tenant's requested assignment or subletting. If the landlord does not recapture, the tenant may then sublease or assign to a qualified party.

The relative bargaining strength of landlord and tenant will determine how "bonus value" (any excess by which the present value of market rent exceeds the present value of the rent provided for in the lease) will be allocated or shared in a proposed assignment or subletting. The parties must be able to separate profits resulting from the assignment or subletting of the leasehold and profits or revenues generated from the sale or disposition of non-real estate business assets such as goodwill. The parties must also negotiate which actual or imputed costs incurred to effectuate the transfer will be accounted for before such profits are split. (Usually, by agreement, a corporate transaction such as a merger, consolidation, or transfer involving the tenant as a going concern would be exempted from any recapture right or bonus value consideration.)

Contemporary assignment and subletting provisions may generally be categorized into the following types:

1. Absolute prohibition on assignment or subletting;

2. Tenant may not assign or sublet without first obtaining landlord's consent, yet the lease contains no specific standard by which landlord may withhold consent;

3. Tenant may not assign or sublet without first obtaining landlord's consent, but the lease provides that landlord's consent cannot be unreasonably withheld;

4. The parties negotiate express, contractual standards or conditions by

which the tenant may assign or sublet, typically providing that excess or "bonus" rents are allocated between landlord and tenant in a pre-arranged fashion; or

5. The parties negotiate express, contractual standards (like the preceding paragraph "4") that are subject to landlord's recapture rights under a "recapture clause." Upon landlord's receipt of tenant's notice of a proposed transfer, landlord has the option to (i) recapture the premises (or such portion as is applicable) and directly enter into a transaction with the proposed transferee or a new third-party tenant or (ii) consent or not consent to the tenant's proposed transfer.

Specific examples (and hybrids) of these approaches are contained within Form 18-10.

Form 18-10

Selected Assignment and Subletting Clauses

Example 1: Absolute prohibition:

__. **No Assignment or Subletting.** Tenant shall neither assign the lease nor sublet all or any portion of the leased premises. __*[Landlord and Tenant have negotiated with the understanding and intention that Landlord shall have no obligation to consider a proposed assignment or sublease]*__.

OR

Example 2: Assignment or subletting requires Landlord's consent—with no standard governing Landlord's giving or withholding consent:

__. **Assignment and Subletting.** Tenant shall neither assign the lease nor sublet all or any portion of the leased premises without obtaining Landlord's prior written consent.

OR

The following basic assignment and subletting clause requires that landlord's consent may not be unreasonably withheld. At a minimum, a tenant should insist that the landlord agree not to unreasonably withhold consent to a proposed transfer. In the absence of such language, in many states a landlord could arbitrarily withhold consent to a proposed transfer or demand conditions to landlord's granting of consent.

Example 3: Assignment or subletting requires Landlord's consent, which shall not be unreasonably withheld or delayed:

__. **Assignment and Subletting.** Tenant shall neither assign the lease nor sublet all or any portion of the leased premises without obtaining Landlord's prior written consent, which consent shall not be unreasonably withheld or delayed.

OR

In leases between sophisticated parties, specific transfer standards will often be negotiated. The following is an example of a negotiated, extensive letter of intent provision with express contractual conditions providing standards by which the tenant may assign or sublet but which nevertheless highly restrict the tenant's transfer rights. In addition, three alternative provisions are included to

FORM 18-10

describe the landlord's participation in the tenant's assignment or subletting receipts. The form allows minimum rent to be increased concurrent with the transfer. This is an unusually extensive form for a letter of intent. Nevertheless, promptly negotiating an acceptable assignment and subletting provision may be the critical deal point in determining whether a transaction will proceed. If such is the case, the following provides a starting point.

Example 4: Extensively negotiated provision in which assignment and subletting are highly restricted but subject to express conditions or standards:

__. **Assignment and Subletting.** Tenant shall neither assign the lease nor sublet all or any portion of the leased premises without obtaining Landlord's prior written consent.

__.1 **Standards Required for Landlord's Consent.** Landlord's consent shall not be unreasonably withheld or delayed. Landlord and Tenant agree that Landlord may withhold consent to any proposed transfer for any commercially reasonable reason, including, but not limited to the following freely negotiated standards:

__.1.1 **Use Conflict.** The proposed transferee, assignee, or sublessee ("Transferee") proposes to change the use of the premises from the permitted and required use in __*[insert reference to "use" clause, e.g., Paragraph __]*__ of this letter of intent __*[,which change in use is absolutely prohibited by such use clause]*__;

__.1.2 **Insufficient Net Worth or Working Capital.** The net worth or working capital of the Transferee __*[e.g., as evidenced by a current financial statement audited by a certified public accountant]*__ is not sufficient in Landlord's __*[sole discretion]*__ *OR* __*[business judgment]*__ to assure the future performance by Transferee of Tenant's obligations under the lease for the full lease term, and in no event shall Transferee's net worth and working capital be less than that of Tenant __*[at the commencement of the lease term]*__ *OR* __*[as of the date of the proposed transfer]*__;

__.1.3 **Adverse Reputation.** Transferee's reputation or proposed use of the premises would have an adverse effect upon the reputation of the shopping center and/or other businesses located within it;

__.1.4 **Potential Decrease in Percentage Rent.** Based upon Landlord's assessment of the anticipated volume of Transferee's gross receipts, percentage rent following the proposed transfer could reasonably be expected to be less than that of Tenant;

__.1.5 **Additional Vacant Space.** There is vacant or unleased space in the shopping center at time of the requested assignment __*[which could accommodate Transferee]*__;

__.1.6 **Violation of Agreement.** The transfer would breach any covenant of or affecting Landlord concerning radius, location, use, exclusivity or other obligation in any other lease, financing provision, reciprocal easement agreement or other agreement relating to the shopping center or would violate any applicable law, code, or ordinance;

__.1.7 **Lease Amendment Required.** The proposed transfer would __*[in Landlord's sole and exclusive discretion]*__ require an amendment to a material term of the lease;

__.1.8 **Hazardous Materials.** Transferee's anticipated use of the leasehold premises involves the generation, storage, use, treatment or disposal of a hazardous material;

__.1.9 **Additional Burden.** Transferee's proposed use of the premises would cause increased wear and tear on the premises or require extra or more costly services from Landlord or common area assessments;

__.1.10 **Insufficient Retailing Experience.** Transferee fails to submit written evidence satisfactory to Landlord of substantial retailing experience and operating proficiency in shopping centers comparable in nature and size to the subject shopping center and in the sale of merchandise and services pursuant to the permitted use described in __*[insert reference to "use" clause, e.g., Paragraph __, of this letter of intent]*__; __*[or]*__

Concept here is to allow Landlord to be able to maintain a desired "high end," "fashion," "discount," or "factory outlet" tenant mix:

__.1.11 **Adverse Impact Upon Tenant Mix and Operating Style.** While Transferee's line of business may not be inconsistent with the permitted use described in __*[insert reference to "use" clause, e.g., Paragraph __ of this letter of intent]*__, Transferee's merchandising methodology is inconsistent with the merchandising methodology of Tenant. Thus, a transfer would have an adverse impact upon the center's tenant mix or impair Landlord's attempt to preserve a __*[insert description]*__ operating character within the center.

FORM 18-10

__.2 **Tenant's Transfer Notice.** If Tenant at any time desires to assign the lease or to sublet the premises or any portion thereof, Tenant will give Landlord written notice of Tenant's intention to do so not less than __ *[e.g., 75]*__ days prior to the effective date of such proposed transfer, specifying in such notice (a) whether Tenant proposes to assign or sublet; (b) the name of the proposed subtenant or assignee; (c) the nature of the proposed subtenant's or assignee's business to be carried on in the premises; (d) the terms and provisions of the proposed sublease or assignment; and (e) such financial information and operating history as Landlord may reasonably request concerning the proposed subtenant or assignee.

Note: *Substantial additional material could be required of Tenant but is not included for letter of intent purposes. Consider, however, the following:*

__*[Such notice shall be accompanied by a copy of the proposed assignment, sublease, license or concession agreement, or, if no such document is available at the time of the notice, by a letter of commitment, or a letter of intent]*__.

__.2.1 **Landlord's Response.** Landlord shall, within __*[e.g., 30]*__ days after Landlord's receipt of all information required of Tenant, as generally specified in __*[subparagraph __.2 (preceding paragraph)]*__, elect to (a) recapture the premises or the portion thereof specified in Tenant's notice, or (b) consent to the proposed assignment or subletting, or (c) refuse to consent to the proposed assignment or subletting.

__.2.1.1 **Landlord's Election to Recapture Premises.** Landlord may recapture the premises (or such portion thereof as is applicable) in order to market the premises or a portion thereof to any third party selected by Landlord, including Transferee, for the period of time, in the case of a sublease, offered by Tenant. The effective date of Landlord's recapture shall be __*[e.g., the effective date of Tenant's proposed transfer]*__ OR __*[e.g., 75 days following Tenant's notice of proposed transfer]*__. __*[Upon Landlord's recapture of the premises any tenant improvements shall become Landlord's property]*__.

Note: *Should Tenant be reimbursed for anything of value such as the depreciated value of tenant improvements advanced by Tenant? What about disposition of fixtures? To improve the odds that a California court will find a recapture clause enforceable in a specific instance, California landlords should provide that any tenant improvements become the landlord's property upon recapture of the premises. [See Carma Developers (California), Inc.,* *v. Marathon Development California, Inc., 2 Cal.4th 342, 826 P.2d 710, (1992).]*

Note also that Landlord's recapture right could be drafted even stronger to enable Landlord to terminate the entire lease upon any request by Tenant to assign or sublet a portion of the premises. Many landlords would attempt to characterize an assignment or a sublease of most of the remaining lease term as a tenant offer to terminate the lease. Similarly, this provision could be edited to limit the percentage of the space that Tenant can sublease and to provide that, effective upon any sublease, Landlord could have the right to terminate the lease with respect to the remaining portion of the premises.

__.2.1.2 Landlord's Consent to Assignment or Subletting. If Landlord consents to the proposed assignment or subletting, Tenant may within __*[e.g., 45]*__ days after the expiration of Landlord's __*[e.g., 30]*__ -day response period enter into a valid assignment or sublease of the premises or portion thereof, upon the terms and conditions set forth in the information furnished Landlord by Tenant. Unless Landlord notifies Tenant otherwise in writing within Landlord's __*[e.g., 30]*__ -day response period, Landlord shall be deemed to have consented to the proposed assignment or subletting. Any permitted assignment or subletting shall be subject to all the provisions of the original lease. *[Tenants—be mindful of "hidden" assignment provisions; i.e., other lease clauses that effectively inhibit assignment, as referenced below.]*

Alternative "A"—Paragraph __.3

Given the depressed real estate market of the early 1990s, the following provisions relating to the allocation of lease bonus value could assume greater importance in the next few years—if the real estate market recovers. Current rents may be near market lows. Therefore, there may be a reasonable expectation that bonus values will actually occur in the future.

The relative bargaining strength and skill of Landlord and Tenant will determine how "bonus value" (any excess by which the present value of market rent exceeds the present value of the rent provided for in the lease) will be allocated or shared in a proposed assignment or subletting. In the following Landlord-oriented Alternative "A", Landlord retains all assignment consideration and is even reimbursed for initial improvements to Tenant's space.

FORM 18-10

Tough, Landlord-oriented allocation of assignment consideration:

__**.3 Allocation of Transfer Consideration.** If Landlord consents to a proposed assignment or subletting, Tenant shall cause Landlord to be paid all rent and other consideration received by Tenant from any such Transferee either initially or over the term of the assignment, sublease or transfer, in excess of the rent called for under the lease. __*[In addition, if Landlord consents to a proposed transfer, Tenant shall repay to Landlord the unamortized portion of the tenant improvement allowance received by Tenant from Landlord for the initial construction and/or remodeling of the premises]*__.

OR

Alternative "B"—Paragraph __.3

The following abbreviated, more Tenant-oriented Alternative "B" provides that Landlord and Tenant share gross consideration in excess of rent payable by Tenant under the lease.

Assignment consideration shared by Landlord and Tenant:

__**.3 Allocation of Transfer Consideration.** If Landlord consents to a proposed assignment or subletting, Tenant shall cause Landlord to be paid __*[e.g., 50]*__ % of any consideration received by Tenant with respect thereto (whether denominated as rent or otherwise at the time Tenant receives same) in excess of the rent payable by Tenant under the lease.

OR

Alternative "C"—Paragraph __.3
(includes Sub-paragraphs __.3.1 and __.3.2)

More comprehensive Tenant-oriented Alternative "C": Landlord and Tenant share assignment and subletting consideration net of negotiated costs incurred by Tenant. (Tenant's assignment and subleasing costs may be amortized over sublease or assignment term.)

__**.3 Allocation of Transfer Consideration.** If Landlord consents to a proposed assignment or subletting and Tenant assigns the lease or sublets any portion of the premises in accordance with the lease, Tenant shall cause Landlord to be paid ___ % of Tenant's "net assignment profits" or ___ % of Tenant's "net sublease profits" attributable during each calendar year to any assignment or sublease.

__**.3.1 Net Assignment Profits.** "Net assignment profits" shall mean the amount by which all consideration paid to Tenant by the assignee for or by reason of such assignment exceeds the sum of customary and reasonable costs incurred by Tenant relative to the assignment, including __*[brokerage commissions, any tenant improvement allowance, alteration costs, attorneys' fees, architects and engineering costs, the cost of any free rent period provided assignee and direct costs resulting from any default by the assignee]*__ __*[, prorated over the remaining initial term plus exercised renewals thereof on a straight-line basis]*__.

__.3.2 **Net Sublease Profits.** "Net sublease profits" shall mean the amount by which all minimum rent, additional rent and other consideration paid by the sublessee to Tenant for the applicable calendar year exceeds the sum of (a) all items of rent payable by Tenant under the lease during the applicable calendar year attributable to the subleased space, and (b) customary and reasonable out-of-pocket costs incurred by Tenant in connection with the subleasing, including __*[brokerage commissions, any tenant improvement allowance, alteration costs, attorneys' fees and engineering costs, the cost of any free rent period provided sublessee, direct costs resulting from a default by a subtenant under a sublease and the customary and reasonable cost of services provided by Tenant to the sublessee (to the extent not deducted under "(a)" above)]*__ __*[, prorated on a straight-line basis over the initial term of the sublease, attributable to the applicable year]*__ *OR* __*[paid during the applicable year]*__.

After selecting Alternative "A", "B", or "C" to Paragraph __.3, above, proceed to Paragraph __.4

Landlord-oriented increase in minimum rent effective upon transfer:

__.4 **Transfer Rent Adjustment.** If Tenant makes a permitted transfer, the minimum rent shall be increased, effective as of the date of such transfer, to the highest of (a) if the transfer is in the form of a sublease, the total __*[minimum]*__ rent payable by the Transferee pursuant to such transfer; or (b) an amount equal to the total of the minimum rent, plus percentage rent, required to be paid by Tenant under the lease during the __*[e.g., 12]*__ month period immediately preceding such transfer, or (c) the minimum rent as adjusted in accordance with the cost of living provisions of the lease.

The following would allow Tenant to assign Tenant's interest to a controlled partnership or corporation:

__.5 **Assignment to Partnership or Corporation.** Tenant shall have a __*[one-time]*__ right to assign the lease to a partnership or corporation, provided, in the case of a partnership that Tenant is a general partner

FORM 18-10

__*[owning not less than 51]*__ % of the partnership and, in the case of a corporation, that tenant owns and controls not less than __*[e.g., 51]*__ % of the corporation's stock.

Alternative "A"—Paragraph __.6

The following could be added if Landlord specifically wants to limit a corporate Tenant's ability to undergo a change in control or corporate restructuring free of the assignment clause and its restrictions. Most corporate tenants would not accept such a provision.

__.6 Merger and Consolidation. If Tenant or any guarantor of the lease is a corporation the stock of which is not traded on any national securities exchange, the following shall constitute an assignment under the lease: (a) the merger, consolidation or reorganization of such corporation and/or (b) the sale, issuance, or transfer, cumulatively or in one transaction, of any voting stock, by Tenant or the guarantor or the stockholders of record of either as of the date of the lease, which results in a change in the voting control of Tenant or the guarantor. If Tenant or any guarantor of the lease is a joint venture, partnership or other association, then the sale, issuance or transfer, cumulatively or in one transaction, of either voting control or of __*[e.g., twenty-five percent (25%) interest]*__, or the termination of any joint venture, partnership or other association, shall constitute an assignment, except any such transfer by inheritance or testamentary disposition.

OR

Alternative "B"—Paragraph __.6

Tenant-oriented "corporate transaction" exception to Landlord consent requirement:

__.6 Merger and Consolidation. No merger, consolidation, reorganization of Tenant, nor any sale of Tenant's stock (including a stock sale which results in a change of voting control of Tenant), __*[nor ________]*__ whether involving an assignment of the lease or a sublease of the premises, shall be considered an assignment or subletting requiring Landlord's consent.

After selecting or editing Alternative "A" or "B" to Paragraph __.6, above, proceed to Paragraph __.7

__.7 Reimbursement of Landlord's Costs. Tenant shall reimburse Landlord for Landlord's reasonable costs and attorneys' fees incurred in conjunction with the processing and documentation of any such requested assignment, subletting or transfer of the lease.

__.8 **Continuing Tenant Responsibility.** No permitted assignment, subletting or other transfer of Tenant's interest in the lease shall relieve Tenant of Tenant's obligation to pay rent and to perform all other obligations to be performed by Tenant under the lease *[Optional:] __[except as provided in the Paragraph 9, below]__.*

Optional: Tenant should consider a negotiated novation whereby Tenant is discharged from future lease liability effective upon lease assignment to the third party. Tenant may be willing to trade off some percentage of "bonus value" to secure this right.

__.9 **Tenant's Release From Future Lease Obligations.** In consideration of Tenant's agreement to share the assignment and sublease transfer consideration in the manner described in *__[e.g., Paragraph __.3, above]__*, upon consummation of any proposed lease assignment approved by Landlord, Tenant will be formally released from any future liability arising under the lease. *[Possible Landlord addition:] __[provided, at the time of the proposed assignment, the assignee (a) has a net worth not less than $________, (b) operates not less than __ total retail stores, and (c) has a demonstrated average per square foot sales volume among all assignee's other stores of not less than $________ per square foot. Furthermore, no such requested assignment and release of Tenant shall take place before the beginning of the __[e.g., 4th]__ year of the lease term and any such request shall be conditioned upon Tenant not having been in default during the lease term]__.*

Note: *Tenants should consider requesting to alter assignment standards after an initial period, such as:*

__[After the expiration of the first __[number]__ years of the lease term, Tenant may assign the lease and/or sublet the leased premises __[insert reduced, less onerous standards, such as, in the extreme "without Landlord's prior consent"]__.

Again, negotiate assignment and subletting provisions with great caution and with an awareness of applicable local legal standards. With substantial economic values at stake, this has been a hotly litigated area of the law, resulting in statutory and case law that differs substantially from state to state.

As a final comment, the lease negotiator should be mindful of the interplay of "hidden" anti-assignment clauses. Specifically, the trade name, continuous occupancy, use, signage, alterations, non-disturbance, expansion, and renewal option clauses may all serve to inhibit the ability of the tenant to effectively transfer its leasehold interest. For example, the trade name clause could be drafted so narrowly as to effectively not allow an assignee to operate except under the original tenant's trade name; the continuous occupancy clause may not allow the time needed for the transferee to remodel the premises; or lease expansion or extension options may be negotiated to apply to only the original tenant, etc. Both landlord and tenant lease negotiators must be mindful that other lease clauses may seriously affect the operation of the assignment and subletting provisions negotiated by the parties.

The developer and the developer's legal counsel have much to gain by thoughtfully devising a standard, objective set of universally applied procedures in dealing with the assignment and subletting issue. With so many recent cases seeded with "reasonableness" considerations, if a developer carefully formulates and applies a standard, consistent methodology in dealing with the assignment/subletting issue, a court may be more willing to conclude that the developer was commercially reasonable in a given instance.

END OF FORM 18-10

Kickout or Cancellation Clauses

Often, tenants fail to achieve the gross sales volumes expected when the lease was negotiated. Should the tenant, landlord or both landlord and tenant have the right to terminate the lease if gross sales targets are not met? The following three alternative kickout provisions grant a termination right to (i) landlord, (ii) tenant, and (iii) both landlord and tenant.

Form 18-11

Landlord's and/or Tenant's Right to Terminate Lease If Gross Sales Target Not Met

Landlord oriented:

__. **Landlord's Right to Terminate Lease If Tenant Fails to Meet Gross Sales Target.** If Tenant does not achieve gross sales of $_____ per square foot per year during any of the first __*[e.g., 3]*__ full lease years, Landlord may elect to terminate the lease by written notice to Tenant within *[Alternative "A":]* __*[e.g., 90]*__ *days following the first* __*[e.g., 3]*__ *full lease years]*__ *[OR, Alternative "B":]* __*[the* __*[e.g., 90]*__ *day period following the end of any such full lease year for which the gross sales target was not met]*__. Any such termination shall be effective on the __*[e.g., 90th]*__ day following Landlord's notice to Tenant. *[Optional:]* __*[Upon lease termination based upon Tenant's failure to achieve such gross sales target, Tenant shall pay Landlord the unamortized cost of any construction or tenant finish allowance granted Tenant by Landlord, after amortizing the amount of such allowance on a straight-line basis over the lease term]*__.

OR

Tenant oriented:

__. **Tenant's Right to Terminate Lease If Gross Sales Target Not Met.** If Tenant does not achieve gross sales of $_____ per square foot per year during any of the first __*[e.g., 3]*__ full lease years, Tenant may elect to terminate the lease by written notice to Landlord within *[Alternative "A":]* __*[e.g., 90]*__ *days following the first* __*[e.g., 3]*__ *full lease years]*__ *[OR, Alternative "B":]* __*[the* __*[e.g., 90]*__ *day period following the end of any such full lease year for which the gross sales target was not met]*__. Any such termination shall be effective *[if Alternative "A" selected:]* __*[upon expiration of the* __*[e.g., 6th]*__ *full month following the* __*[e.g., 3rd]*__ *full lease year]*__ *[OR, if Alternative "B" selected:]* __*[on the* __*[e.g., 90th]*__ *day after such notice is given by Tenant]*__.

OR

Mutual right to terminate by both Landlord and Tenant:

__. **Mutual Right to Terminate Lease If Gross Sales Target Not Met.** If Tenant does not achieve gross sales of $_____ per square foot per year during any of the first __*[e.g., 3]*__ full lease years, either Landlord or Tenant may elect to terminate the lease by written notice to the other. Notice of termination must be given, if at all, within the __*[e.g., 90]*__ day period following the end of any such full lease year for which the gross sales target was not met. Lease termination shall be effective on the __*[e.g., 90th]*__ day following such notice.

END OF FORM 18-11

FORM 18-11

Tenant Right of First Offer and Right of First Refusal to Lease Additional Space

A landlord may be required to grant a tenant a right to acquire additional (usually contiguous) space in the center when such space becomes available for lease. Form 18-12 provides a right of first offer and Form 18-13 confirms a right of first refusal to lease additional space. Obviously, Form 18-13 confirms much greater rights to the tenant and may significantly burden the landlord in efforts to market the affected space. In each case, optional additional language illustrates how the tenant's rights might be pared.

Form 18-12

Tenant Right of First Offer

__. **Right of First Offer to Lease.** Provided Tenant __*[shall not have been sent more than two prior notices of lease non-compliance during Tenant's occupancy and]*__ is not in __*[material]*__ default under the lease, during the first __ years of the lease term Tenant shall have the right of first offer to lease the approximately _______ square foot space located __*[e.g., immediately north of]*__ the leasehold premises __*[e.g., at fair market terms and conditions as reasonably determined by Landlord]*__ when such space becomes available for releasing. *[Optional:]* Such right of first offer shall be personal to __*[insert name of original tenant]*__ and may be exercised solely by __*[insert name of original tenant]*__ while actually occupying not less than __*[80]*__ % of Tenant's premises.

END OF FORM 18-12

FORM 18-12

Form 18-13

Tenant Right of First Refusal

__. **Right of First Refusal to Lease.** Provided Tenant __*[shall not have been sent more than two prior notices of lease non-compliance during Tenant's occupancy and]*__ is not in __*[material]*__ default under the lease, during the first __ years of the lease Term Tenant shall have a first right of refusal to lease the approximately _______ square foot space located __*[e.g., immediately north of]*__ the leasehold premises (the "expansion space"). During such period each time the expansion space becomes available and Landlord has finalized terms and conditions by which Landlord and a third party tenant are prepared to enter into a lease of the expansion space, Tenant shall have a first and prior right to enter into a lease for such space on the terms and conditions accepted by Landlord. *[Optional:]* Such right of first refusal shall be personal to __*[insert name of original tenant]*__ and may be exercised solely by __*[insert name of original tenant]*__ while actually occupying not less than __*[80]*__ % of Tenant's premises.

END OF FORM 18-13

Tenant Option to Extend Lease Term

Many tenants secure appropriate option rights to fully realize the benefits of goodwill created in a location. Options also allow the tenant to amortize the tenant's investment over an extended period. Although options to renew or extend are generally thought to benefit only the tenant, they are a fact of life for the developer. The following forms provide some examples of renewal-right provisions appropriate for deal-making documents. Each five-year period is structured differently merely to illustrate a sampling of various rent escalation mechanisms. You may abstract and amend the various provisions to meet your circumstances.

Form 18-14

Tenant Option to Extend Lease Term

__. **Option(s) to Extend Lease Term.** __*[Provided Tenant* __*[shall not have been sent more than two notices of lease non-compliance during Tenant's occupancy and]*__ *is not in* __*[material]*__ *default under the lease from the time of the exercise of any option to extend the term until the commencement of any option term,]*__ Tenant shall have the right to extend the lease term for __*[e.g., three]*__ consecutive periods of __*[e.g., five]*__ years each by giving Landlord written notice of Tenant's election to extend the lease at least __*[e.g., 180]*__ days __*[but not more than 365 days]*__ prior to expiration of the initial term and each extension thereof. Minimum rent during each option period shall be payable as follows:

Fixed rental:

__. **First Option Period.** Rent during the first option period shall be $________ for the first year, $________ for the second year, $________ for the third year, $________ for the fourth year and $________ for the fifth year.

Formula CPI adjustment:

__. **Second Option Period.** Rent during the first year of the __*[second]*__ option period shall be the rent during the first year of the __*[first]*__ option period increased by __*[e.g., 100% of]*__ any increase in the __*[describe specific consumer price index, e.g., "Consumer Price Index for all Urban Consumers (Los Angeles/Anaheim/Riverside area)" ("CPI")]*__ occurring from the beginning of the first year of the __*[first]*__ option period to the beginning of the first year of the __*[second]*__ option period. Rent in each subsequent year of the __*[second]*__ option period shall be __*[the rent payable during the preceding year of the* __*[second]*__ *option period increased by* __*[e.g., 100% of]*__ *any increase in the CPI occurring during the year preceding the* __*[second]*__ *option period lease year in question]*__ OR __*[calculated as follows:]* __*[describe]*__.

OR

Formula CPI adjustment with a floor and a "cap" for first year of second option period. Each subsequent year of the second option period is subject to a full annual CPI increase.

__. **Second Option Period.** Rent during the first year of the __*[second]*__ option period shall be the greater of:

(a) __*[e.g., 112]*__ % of the rent payable during the first year of the __*[first]*__ option period, or

FORM 18-14

(b) the lesser of (i) the rent payable during the first year of the __*[first]*__ option period plus the following: __*[e.g., 70]*__ % of the increase in the __*[describe specific consumer price index, e.g., "Consumer Price Index for all Urban Consumers (Los Angeles/Anaheim/Riverside area)" ("CPI")]*__ occurring from the beginning of the first year of the __*[first]*__ option period to the beginning of the first year of the __*[second]*__ option period, multiplied by the rent payable during the first year of the __*[first]*__ option period, <u>or</u> (ii) __*[e.g., 123]*__ % of the rent payable during the first year of the __*[first]*__ option period.

Rent in each subsequent year of the __*[second]*__ option period shall be __*[the rent payable during the preceding year of the __[second]__ option period increased by __[e.g., 100% of]__ any increase in the CPI occurring during the year preceding the __[second]__ option period lease year in question]*__ <u>OR</u> __*[calculated as follows:]* __*[describe]*__.

> ***Note:*** *The following example illustrates the interplay of Paragraphs "(a)" and "(b)", above. Assume the following: (i) The first option period is 5 years, (ii) annual rent payable during the first year of the first option period is $1000 and (iii) the CPI index increases 18% from the first year of the first option period to the first year of the second option period. Rent payable for the first year of the second option period, the greater of "(a)" or "(b)", would be calculated as follows:*
>
> *(a) 112% of $1000 = $1120*
>
> *(b)*
> *(i) $1000 + [(70% x 18%, or 12.6%) x $1000)] = $1126*
> *(ii) 123% of $1000 = $1230*
> *(Thus, the lesser of (b)(i) and (b)(ii) is $1126)*
>
> *Rent payable for the first year of the second option period would be $1126, i.e., "less" than (b)(ii)'s $1230 and "greater" than (a)'s $1120.*

Fair market appraisal:

__. **<u>Third Option Period</u>.** Rent during the first year of the __*[third]*__ option period shall be the fair market rental value of Tenant's premises __*[including <u>OR</u> excluding]*__ the value of any tenant improvements installed and paid for by __*[Landlord <u>AND/OR</u> Tenant]*__ as determined by independent fair market appraisal __*[assuming the highest and best retailing use for the premises <u>OR</u> assuming Tenant's existing use]*__. Rent in each subsequent year of the __*[third]*__ option period shall be calculated as follows: __*[describe]*__.

OR

Landlord's then-prevailing lease rate for comparable space:

__. **Third Option Period.** Rent during the __*[third]*__ option period shall be the rate which Landlord would quote to third parties for space comparable to the premises, if the premises were to become available for lease, for a lease term coinciding with the __*[third]*__ option term. In no event, however, shall the rental rate be less than Tenant's rent payable immediately prior to the commencement of the option term. __*[Furthermore, during the __ [third]__ option term the lease may be subject to Landlord's then prevailing terms and conditions including, among other provisions, escalations, passthroughs, and other matters then included in Landlord's standard lease form for the shopping center which it then uses for leasing space to third parties]*__.

OR

Another alternative: General CPI language for use where annual CPI increase follows established initial and subsequent option period rents.

__. **Option Period Rent.** The minimum rent for the first year of any option period shall be equal to the minimum rent for the first year of the initial lease term (or in the case of subsequent option periods, the minimum rent for the first lease year of the immediately preceding option period) ("base period rent") as increased annually by that percentage by which the __*[describe specific consumer price index, e.g., "Consumer Price Index for all Urban Consumers (Los Angeles/Anaheim/Riverside area)" ("CPI")]*__ has increased from the base period rent to the year in question. Rent in the second and each subsequent year of any option period shall be __*[the rent payable during the preceding year increased by __[e.g., 100% of]__ any increase in the CPI occurring during the preceding lease year]*__ OR __*[calculated as follows:]* __*[describe]*__.

AND

Optional restriction on right to exercise option:

__. **Option to Extend Exercisable Solely by Original Tenant.** Any option granted Tenant to extend the lease term shall be personal to __*[insert name of original tenant]*__ and may be exercised solely by __*[insert name of original tenant]*__ __*[while actually occupying not less than __[e.g., 80]__ % of the premises]*__.

END OF FORM 18-14

FORM 18-14

Tenant Option to Purchase

Sometimes a tenant will be granted an option to purchase the premises. The following form may be edited to articulate such a deal point.

Form 18-15

Tenant Option to Purchase Premises

__. **Option to Purchase.** __*[Provided Tenant __[shall not have been sent more than two notices of lease non-compliance during Tenant's occupancy and]__ is not in __[material]__ default under the lease after giving notice of Tenant's election to exercise Tenant's purchase option,]__* Tenant shall have the right beginning with __*[e.g., the fourth year of the lease term and ending ________, 20__]__ OR __[describe event]__* to purchase the building constituting Tenant's premises under the lease *[add if land included:] __[and the roughly _______ square foot land parcel upon which the building and Tenant's appurtenant parking is situated]__ OR __[if subject to leasehold:] __[subject to the existing underlying ground lease in favor of ___________]__*.

Fixed price:

The purchase price for the __*[building]__ OR __[building, land and site improvements]__* shall be $___________ if the purchase closes not later than _______, 20__ and $__________ if the purchase closes after _________, 20__ but not later than _______, 20__ and __*[continue as necessary]__*.

OR

Fixed price, adjusted by CPI:

The purchase price for the __*[building]__ OR __[building, land and site improvements]__* shall be $___________ if the purchase closes not later than _______, 20__ and $__________ if the purchase closes after _________, 20__ but not later than _______, 20__ (the "final fixed price date"). Thereafter, the purchase price shall escalate by a factor equal to __*[e.g., 100]__* % of the increase in the __*[describe specific consumer price index, e.g., "Consumer Price Index for all Urban Consumers (Los Angeles/Anaheim/Riverside area)"]__* occurring from the final fixed price date through the actual closing date of Tenant's purchase.

AND

The purchase price shall be payable __*[in cash]__ OR __[with a down payment of __[$________ OR ___ % of the purchase price]__* and the balance payable in the form of a purchase money note bearing an interest rate of __ % all due and payable ____ months after the closing. The note shall be secured by a __*[e.g., first]__ __[mortgage/deed of trust]__* on the subject property.

FORM 18-15

AND

Optional: Restriction on Tenant's right to exercise option:

__. **Option to Purchase Exercisable Solely by Original Tenant.** Any option granted Tenant to purchase Tenant's premises shall be personal to *__[insert name of original tenant]__* and may be exercised solely by *__[insert name of original tenant]__ __[while actually occupying not less than __[e.g., 80]__ % of the premises]__*.

END OF FORM 18-15

TECHNICAL AND SPECIAL-PURPOSE PROVISIONS

Detailed Construction Coordination Provision for Proposed Build-to-Suit Lease

From time to time a developer needs a more detailed, step-by-step business letter to coordinate construction with a tenant. The following construction coordination form is designed to help the parties articulate the sequential pre-construction and construction responsibilities of the parties and their consultants. Certain definitions are included to clarify the agreement. These definitions could be amended to alter the deal structure and could possibly be used in other contexts.

In Form 18-16, Landlord is responsible for constructing, at its own expense, all site improvements and advances funds to construct the "Building Shell" and "Interior Improvements" up to an agreed maximum. Tenant is responsible for installing, at its own cost, Tenant's "Trade Fixtures". The form addresses plan preparation, plan modification, the permitting and approval process, bidding, and construction with a substantial degree of detail for a letter of intent. The form is broken down into relatively short subheading paragraphs to assist you in using the form as an outline or checklist. Reading this form may serve as a helpful checklist to prepare for a negotiation or to mentally refine the appropriate agreements necessary to complete a given transaction.

To aid in integrating Form 18-16 into other forms in the book, Form 18-16 is designed to be numbered as but a single numbered paragraph with numerous numbered subparagraphs.

Form 18-16

Detailed Construction Responsibilities and Coordination between Landlord and Tenant

__. **Construction.** The construction of the subject __*[describe, e.g., restaurant]*__ building shall be accomplished as described in this paragraph.

__.1 **Responsibilities.** Landlord and Tenant shall have the following responsibilities relative to the construction work:

> ***Note:*** *The following paragraph establishes "Landlord's Maximum Contribution", the absolute maximum sum that Landlord may be obligated to contribute for the "Building Construction Costs." However, Paragraph __.7 (at the end of the form) provides for insertion of the estimated or anticipated Building Construction Cost, a sum less than the maximum. If the estimated or anticipated cost is exceeded, Paragraph __.7 provides that either Tenant pays such excess or Landlord pays the excess in return for increased rent.*

__.1.1 **Building Shell.** Landlord shall construct the Building Shell (as defined below) and the Interior Improvements (as defined below) according to plans and specification prepared by Tenant's architect. Subject to the following Paragraph __*[__.7]*__, "Adjustment to Minimum Rent", below, Landlord shall pay all costs of such construction (the "Building Construction Costs"), provided the Building Construction Costs do not exceed $__*[e.g., 300,000]*__. The specific items of expense to be included in the Building Construction Costs are specified below. Said sum of $__*[same amount as above]*__ is hereafter referred to as "Landlord's Maximum Contribution." Tenant shall pay all Building Construction Costs in excess of Landlord's Maximum Contribution, regardless of whether such excess is the result of change orders requested by Tenant or otherwise.

__.1.2 **Site Improvements.** Landlord shall also be responsible for constructing at its own cost and expense, all Site Improvements (as defined below). Unless expressly provided otherwise, the cost of the Site Improvements shall not be included as part of the Building Construction Costs.

__.1.3 **Tenant's Trade Fixtures.** Tenant shall be responsible for installing, at its own cost and expense, all Tenant's Trade Fixtures (as hereafter defined) in accordance with plans and specifications approved as provided below.

__.2 **Construction Timetable.** The construction work contemplated under this paragraph shall be accomplished according to the following timetable:

__.2.1 **Tenant's Plans.** Tenant shall provide Landlord with Tenant's standard plans and specifications for the Building Shell and the Interior Improvements no later than __*[e.g., 60 days after Landlord has received final site plan approval for the shopping center from applicable governmental agencies]*__;

__.2.2 **Plan Modifications.** Tenant shall, at its own cost and expense, have these plans and specifications modified as necessary to have the Building constructed on the site in accordance with applicable local governmental codes and ordinances;

__.2.3 **Modified Plans Set to Landlord.** Tenant shall provide Landlord with one complete set of the modified plans and specifications for Landlord's review and approval as provided in the following subparagraph;

__.2.4 **Landlord's Approval of Modified Plans.** Landlord shall have __*[e.g., 15]*__ business days after receipt of the modified plans and specifications in which to approve or disapprove of same. If Landlord disapproves of the modified plans and specifications, Landlord shall deliver Tenant a written notice within said __*[e.g., 15]*__ -day period, specifying in reasonable detail the reasons for such disapproval;

__.2.5 **Bidding.** After the modified plans and specifications are approved, Tenant shall solicit at least __*[e.g., 3]*__ bids to construct the Building, it being understood that Tenant shall accept the lowest responsible bid, subject to Landlord's reasonable approval;

__.2.6 **Letting Contract.** Landlord shall enter into a construction contract with the contractor whose bid is accepted, but before entering into any construction contract, Landlord shall submit the same to Tenant for its review and approval, which shall not be unreasonably withheld or delayed, it being understood that, if Tenant disapproves of same, it shall so notify Landlord in writing no later than __*[e.g., 10]*__ business days after receipt of same;

__.2.7 **Commencement of Building Construction.** Landlord shall commence construction of the Building Shell and the Interior Improvements promptly after the construction bid is accepted, but not later than _________, 20__;

__.2.8 **Substantial Completion.** Construction of the Building Shell and the Interior Improvements shall be "substantially completed" (as defined below) no later than __*[e.g., 150]*__ days after commencement of construction; and

__.2.9 **Installation of Tenant's Trade Fixtures.** Tenant shall have __*[e.g., 30/45]*__ days after Landlord substantially completes construction of the Building Shell and the Interior Improvements in which to complete installation of Tenant's Trade Fixtures. It is understood that __*[Landlord's]*__ contractor will complete the connection of any Tenant's Trade Fixtures that require connection to utility lines, as specified in Tenant's plans and specifications.

__.3 **Performance of Construction Work.**

__.3.1 **Permits and Approvals.** Except as specified in the following sentence, Landlord shall use its best efforts to cause to be obtained all necessary approvals and permits from all state and local governmental agencies having authority over the construction of the Building Shell and the Interior Improvements. Tenant shall, however, submit the approved plans and specifications for construction of the Building Shell and the Interior Improvements for plan check, obtain all building permits and pay all fees therefor. Tenant shall also assist Landlord in obtaining all approvals and permits to be obtained by Landlord for the leased premises, including but not limited to __ *[itemize if possible, e.g. zoning approval, site plan approval, etc.]*__. The cost of all such approvals and permits obtained by Landlord shall be included in the Building Construction Costs.

__.3.2 **Workmanship.** All work performed by either party shall be done in a good and workmanlike manner with first class materials and in accordance with the modified plans and specifications as approved by Landlord and Tenant.

__.3.3 **Supervising Architect.** Landlord's architect shall be the supervising architect in charge of construction of the Site Improvements, the Building Shell and the Interior Improvements.

__.3.4 **Tenant Inspection.** Tenant, or its designated agent, shall have the right at all reasonable times to inspect the progress of the construction work to be performed by Landlord. If Tenant, or its designated agent, notifies Landlord of any defects or deficiencies in such construction, Landlord shall cause its contractor or subcontractors to promptly make appropriate corrections.

__.3.5 **Fixturization by Tenant.** Subject to the provisions of Landlord's construction contract, Tenant shall be entitled to enter the leased premises during construction of the Building Shell and the Interior Improvements for the purpose of installing Tenant's Trade Fixtures and stocking merchandise therein; provided, however, that Tenant shall do so only in such manner as will not interfere with the work of Landlord's general contractor and its subcontractors and shall be at Tenant's own risk.

__.4 **Acceptance of Construction.** After construction of the Building Shell and the Interior Improvements is substantially completed, Tenant shall promptly inspect the same and shall accept possession of the leased premises, subject, however, to Landlord's correcting any so-called "punch-list" items noted by Tenant in the course of its inspection. Tenant shall be entitled to refuse to accept the premises only if the Building Shell and the Interior Improvements as constructed deviate materially from the modified plans and specifications as approved by Tenant. Tenant's taking possession of the leased premises for any purpose, including fixturization, shall constitute acceptance thereof. Tenant shall confirm its acceptance of the leased premises in writing upon demand of any lender or purchaser of Landlord's interest in the lease.

__.5 **Guarantees and Warranties.** Landlord shall assign to Tenant all guarantees and warranties of its general contractor, and its subcontractors and suppliers of material and equipment installed on or furnished to the leased premises. Both Landlord and Tenant shall have the right to proceed against the parties obligated on such guarantees and warranties. Tenant, nonetheless, shall, on behalf of itself and Landlord, diligently enforce all such guarantees or warranties unless Landlord requests otherwise in writing.

__.6 **Definitions.**

__.6.1 **Building Shell.** The "Building Shell" shall consist of (a) a completed shell, including roofing, fascia, exterior walls and windows, for the Building, (b) the Building's footings and concrete floor, (c) the Building's sprinkler system (if installation is required by the City of __*[insert name of city or applicable jurisdictional body]*__), (d) the Building's heating, ventilation and air conditioning systems, exclusive of distribution wiring, connections, etc., millwork items, interior finishes and the like for such systems and (e) plumbing, conduit and wiring for distribution of utilities throughout the premises, as shown in Tenant's plans and specifications.

__.6.2 **Building Construction Costs.** The terms "Building Construction Costs" shall mean and include (a) the cost and expense of constructing the Building Shell and the Interior Improvements, (b) the cost and expense of any other work performed by Landlord in accordance with the approved plans and specifications for the Building, and (c) all other construction costs and expenses (exclusive of land acquisition costs and the cost and expense of the Site Improvements) directly related to the construction of the Building, including, without limitation, any cost incurred by Landlord to modify Tenant's standard plans and specifications, other architectural and engineering fees incurred with respect to construction of the Building Shell and the Interior Improvements, the premiums on any construction-related insurance policies or bonds, the cost of any governmental fees or permits obtained by Landlord, the cost of any change orders, and __*[anything else? e.g., the cost of the trash enclosure referenced in subparagraph __ below]*__. *[**Note:** Are there any other specific items to be excluded from the defined Building Construction Costs?]* __*[E.g., Interim interest, loan points and loan fees shall not be included in the Building Construction Costs]*__.

__.6.3 Interior Improvements. The "Interior Improvements" shall consist of all interior improvements constructed in the Building which are not part of the Building Shell, e.g., interior walls, wiring, plumbing, etc., as shown in Tenant's plans and specifications. The Interior Improvements do not include any of Tenant's Trade Fixtures.

__.6.4 Site Improvements. The "Site Improvements" shall consist of all improvements to be constructed on the site which are not part of or contained in the Building, including without limitation, paving, striping, landscaping __*[(which, with the exception of trees planted in locations approved by Landlord, shall not exceed __[e.g., 24]__ inches in height)]*__, exterior lighting for the site, __*[and, e.g., an enclosed trash enclosure with gates]*__. The Site Improvements shall also include bringing all utilities required for the operation of the leased premises to the point of connection with the Building and grading and compacting the site __*[to specifications subject to agreement after review by Landlord's and Tenant's engineers and contractors]*__.

__.6.5 Substantial Completion. The term "substantial completion" or "substantially completed" shall mean the completion of the work to be performed by Landlord to the extent that such work has been inspected and approved by local building inspectors and that the general contractor performing such work has notified Landlord of such completion and has removed the general contractor's personnel and equipment from the leased premises, except to the extent that some such personnel and equipment may be required to correct punch list items and to make equipment connections required to be installed by Landlord.

__**.6.6 <u>Tenant's Trade Fixtures</u>.** "Tenant's Trade Fixtures" shall consist of all trade fixtures, equipment and personal property installed in the Building, __*[including,]*__ *[for a restaurant building, for example:]* __*[e.g., kitchen appliances, counters, decorations, chairs, tables, etc.,]*__ and all signs erected or installed in or about the interior or exterior of the Building, except as shown in Tenant's plans and specifications.

Using the defined terms above, although "Landlord's Maximum Contribution" is a not-to-exceed amount, typically rent is negotiated based upon a budgeted sum. If the budgeted sum is exceeded, either Tenant contributes such "Excess Cost" (in which event rent remains unchanged) or Landlord contributes such "Excess Cost", in which event rent is incrementally increased based upon an agreed formula.

__**.7 <u>Adjustment to Minimum Rent</u>.** While Paragraph __*[__.1.1]*__, above, establishes Landlord's Maximum Contribution, if the Building Construction Costs exceed $__*[e.g., 275,000]*__, Tenant shall have the right to elect to either (a) pay the amount of such excess (the "Excess Cost") or (b) require Landlord to pay the amount of the Excess Cost; provided, however, that in no event shall the aggregate amount of the Building Construction Costs payable by Landlord exceed Landlord's Maximum Contribution. If Tenant elects to require Landlord to pay the Excess Cost, the guaranteed minimum monthly rent payable under the lease shall be increased by an amount equal to one-twelfth of __*[e.g., 13.5]*__ % of the Excess Cost paid by Landlord.

END OF FORM 18-16

Restaurant Plumbing and Cleanliness Standards

The following clauses are designed to contend with the potentially messy fast-food or other restaurant tenant creating large quantities of trash and grease. Unchecked grease disposal into the center's sewer lines can increase common area maintenance costs and cause management problems with aggrieved co-tenants. Review these ideas with a property manager to consider what additional "property management" problems can be addressed and avoided relative to a particular proposed tenant.

Form 18-17

Restaurant Pest and Sanitation Control

__. **Pest Control and Plumbing.** In an effort to ensure that Tenant's use of the leased premises remains clean and does not interfere with adjacent uses, the lease shall include the following cleanliness standards.

__.1 **Pest and Sanitation Control.** Tenant shall, at its own cost and expense, keep the premises and any trash collection area used exclusively by Tenant, free and clear of insects, rodents and other vermin. If Tenant fails to do so, Landlord shall notify Tenant in writing of such failure. If Landlord sends Tenant more than __*[e.g., 2]*__ such notices in any one calendar year, Landlord shall have the right to require Tenant, for the __*[e.g., 12]*__ month period immediately following the date of the second notice, to retain a licensed, bonded professional pest and sanitation control service to perform inspections of the premises not less frequently than once each __*[e.g., 30]*__ days for the purpose of controlling infestation by insects, rodents and other vermin and to cause any corrective or extermination work recommended by such service to be performed. If Tenant fails to perform such obligations, Landlord may, at its option and after __*[e.g., 5]*__ days written notice to Tenant, cause such inspection to be performed and any necessary corrective or extermination work which is recommended to be done and the cost of such inspection and corrective or extermination work shall be additional rent payable by Tenant to Landlord upon demand.

__.2 **Grease/Disposal.** Tenant shall not dispose of any grease down the drains of the Building, but shall, instead, contract with a disposal service to collect and remove the same from the leased premises. If Tenant shall, nonetheless, dispose of grease down the drains of the Building and the sewer line between the Building and any trunk sewer line located in the public right-of-way becomes clogged or plugged at any point, whether or not within the boundary of the premises, by reason of such disposal, __*[and no other cause]*__, Tenant shall promptly, at its own cost and expense, clean the sewer line between the premises and its terminus in the public right-of-way. If Tenant fails to do so within __*[e.g., 24]*__ hours after oral request by Landlord, Landlord shall have the right to have the sewer line cleared at Tenant's cost and expense. If the cause of the clogged or plugged sewer line is not clearly the fault of Tenant, the cost to clear sewer line shall be borne as part of the shopping center common area maintenance cost as per Paragraph __. __*[It shall be landlord's responsibility to clearly substantiate Tenant's fault in creating said clogged or plugged sewer line condition]*__.

FORM 18-17

__.3 **Grease Trap.** __*[If required at any time by the City of __________,]*__ Tenant shall install a grease trap in the floor drain of the kitchen of the premises. Tenant acknowledges that it shall install such grease trap and shall, during the term of the lease, clean and maintain such grease trap in such manner as may be required by the Health Department of the City of _______ or other governmental authorities having jurisdiction. Failure to clean and maintain such grease trap in such manner shall, upon notice, be deemed an event of default by Tenant.

END OF FORM 18-17

Hazardous Materials Investigation and Remediation

Expert legal and technical advice should be obtained at the outset if one is aware of any potential environmental or hazardous materials issues. Form 18-18 is included to illustrate in principle how a developer's site acquisition ground-lease proposal or letter of intent might be revised, after appropriate legal and technical advice, to provide for the necessary investigation and cost allocation between landlord (the landowner) and tenant (the developer) if toxic substances are known to exist on the site but the scope is not known at the time the transaction is being negotiated.

Form 18-18, as prepared, replaces Paragraph 13, "Hazardous Materials," in the "Long-Form Letter of Intent to Enter into Site Ground Lease" included as Form B-1 in Appendix B. (Insertion of Form 18-18 into Form B-1 in Appendix B will require renumbering of subsequent paragraphs.) Note also the required changes to Paragraphs 6.6 (the more conventional "Hazardous Materials Investigation" contingency) and Paragraph 7.3, the approval period for this contingency.

With appropriate amendments, substantive deal points within this provision could also be considered for incorporation into a non-binding space lease letter of intent. The drafting sophistication required to use the form may be beyond the capabilities of many readers. Nevertheless, the form should help to elucidate a deal structure or methodology to cope with potential hazardous waste contamination.

The optional references to an "escrow holder" are for consideration in a major ground-lease transaction. In some areas of the country, an escrow may be opened—particularly in the case of a developer ground leasing a substantial site—prior to the consummation of such a transaction.

Form 18-18

Sample Ground Lease Letter of Intent Hazardous Materials Provision Where Significant Investigation and Remedial Work Is Contemplated

13. Hazardous Materials Due Diligence Period. Environmental investigation, inspection, testing and any necessary remedial work shall be accomplished as follows:

13.1 Inspections. The "Hazardous Materials Due Diligence Period" shall be defined as the period of time between the execution of __*[this letter of intent]*__ *OR* __*[the final ground lease]*__ and the "Hazardous Materials Due Diligence Period Expiration Date" contained in the ground lease. During the Hazardous Materials Due Diligence Period, Tenant shall have the right to conduct various environmental, soils compaction and engineering investigations __*[of the site]*__ *OR* __*[of the site and adjacent land area]*__ to ascertain __*[e.g., the feasibility of constructing an approximately ________ square foot]*__ __*[e.g., shopping center]*__ *OR* __*[e.g., Tenant building]*__ *on the site]*__. Tenant and Tenant's agents may enter onto the site for the purpose of inspection and for the purpose of conducting such tests, surveys and other studies, provided that Tenant (i) keeps the site free of liens, (ii) repairs all damage to the site, and (iii) indemnifies and holds Landlord harmless from all claims, damages or liabilities arising from or connected with the tests, surveys and studies. No later than __*[e.g., 10]*__ days after execution of this __*[this letter of intent]*__ *OR* __*[the ground lease]*__, Landlord shall provide Tenant with a map showing the location of all underground utilities located on the site. Tenant shall conduct its tests and surveys and studies in a manner not to cause damage to underground utilities identified by Landlord.

13.2 Environmental and Soils Investigation. __*[E.g., Landlord]*__, at __*[e.g., Landlord's]*__ sole cost and expense, has commissioned an environmental consultant, __*[e.g., name of environmental consultant,]*__ to conduct a preliminary environmental investigation (the "Phase I Investigation") of the site to determine whether certain materials (the "Hazardous Materials") considered to be "hazardous" to human health or the environment under federal, state or local laws, statutes, ordinances, rules or regulations are located on or under the site, and to develop a scope of further investigation to confirm or deny the existence of hazardous waste contamination on the site. Landlord and Tenant acknowledge that Hazardous Materials probably exist on the site as evidenced by __*[e.g., a letter dated _______, 20__, from __[e.g., name of environmental consultant]__ __[, a copy of which is attached hereto as Exhibit "__"]__.*

FORM 18-18

Upon execution of the ground lease __*[and Tenant's approval or satisfaction of the]*__ __*[e.g., title, feasibility and major tenant contingencies, which are listed above as contingencies 6.1, 6.2 and 6.3, respectively]*__, Tenant will request __*[e.g., name of same environmental consultant]*__ to conduct a further environmental investigation (the "Phase II Investigation") to perform the work described in the __*[e.g., name of environmental consultant]*__ __*[e.g., letter dated ______, 20__, a copy of which is attached hereto as Exhibit "__"]*__. The cost of the Phase II Investigation shall be shared __*[e.g., equally]*__ by the parties, unless the parties otherwise agree in writing. If the Phase II Investigation confirms the presence of Hazardous Materials on the site, __*[e.g., name of environmental consultant]*__ may recommend a scope of Phase III Investigation to more fully characterize and develop recommended remedial action (the "Remedial Action"). The cost of the Phase III Investigation shall be shared __*[e.g., equally]*__ by Landlord and Tenant, unless the parties otherwise agree in writing.

13.3 Hazardous Materials Due Diligence Period Expiration Date. The Hazardous Materials Due Diligence Period shall expire on the date (the "Hazardous Materials Due Diligence Period Expiration Date") which is __*[e.g., 10]*__ days after the date on which __*[e.g., name of environmental consultant]*__ delivers written notice to Landlord and Tenant __*[and escrow holder]*__ that the Phase III Investigation has been completed. If a Phase III Investigation is not recommended by __*[e.g., name of environmental consultant]*__, the Hazardous Materials Due Diligence Expiration Date shall be the date which is __*[e.g., 10]*__ days after the date on which __*[e.g., name of environmental consultant]*__ delivers written notice to Landlord and Tenant __*[and escrow holder]*__ that the Phase II Investigation has been completed.

13.4 Cancellation of Ground Lease During Hazardous Materials Due Diligence Period. At any time prior to the Hazardous Materials Due Diligence Period Expiration Date, Tenant may elect to terminate the ground lease without penalty if (i) Tenant is not satisfied with either the materials delivered to Tenant pursuant to Paragraph __*[e.g., 5]*__ or the results of the inspections conducted Pursuant to this Paragraph __*[e.g., 13]*__ or (ii) Tenant determines that its share of the cost of the "Additional Remedial Action" (as defined in Paragraph __*[14.2]*__) would be excessive.

14. Landlord's Obligations Regarding Clean-up of Hazardous Materials.

14.1 Responsibility for Remedial Action. Landlord shall be responsible for completing the Remedial Action __*[before close of escrow]*__

<u>OR</u> __*[on or before ________, 20__]*__. The Remedial Action is described in the __*[e.g., name of environmental consultant]*__ letter dated ______, 20__ attached hereto as Exhibit "__" __*[and shall include without limitation the following items:*

Illustrative example of scope of specific remedial work:

a. Remediation and disposal of the contaminated soils at the end of the concrete casting beds;

b. Removal of all 55-gallon drums located on the site and the remediation and removal of the surrounding contaminated soils; and

c. Removal of any and all asbestos containing materials from the site __ [and any building improvements thereon]__.

[and so forth]

14.2 <u>Additional Remedial Action</u>. The cost of Remedial Action not listed in Paragraph __*[14.1(a)-(c)]*__ above ("Additional Remedial Action") shall be shared __*[e.g., equally]*__ by Landlord and Tenant unless the parties otherwise agree in writing. In no event, however, shall Tenant's share of the cost of Additional Remedial Action exceed $________. Landlord shall be responsible for completing the Additional Remedial Action __*[before close of escrow]*__ <u>OR</u> __*[on or before ________, 20__]*__. *[Optional:]* __*[It is understood by the parties that Additional Remedial Action may include remediation and disposal of __[describe particular problem to be remedied]__.*

Note: *Negotiating a firm date for Landlord's completion of the "Additional Remediation Action" may be very difficult when the scope of the work is not known at the time the deal is being negotiated.*

14.3 <u>Completion of Remedial Action and Additional Remedial Action</u>. The failure of Landlord to fulfill its clean-up obligations shall constitute a material breach of the __*[escrow and the ground lease]*__.

14.4 <u>Remediation Action Notice</u>. __*[E.g., Name of environmental consultant]*__ shall deliver to Landlord and Tenant written notice (the "Remediation Notice") of the completion of the Remedial Action and the Additional Remedial Action. Receipt of the Remediation Notice by Landlord and Tenant shall be a condition to __*[the close of escrow]*__ <u>OR</u> __*[Tenant's obligation to pay rent under the ground lease]*__, unless the parties agree otherwise.

FORM 18-18

AND

Note: *If the preceding Paragraphs 13 and 14 are inserted in place of Paragraph 13, "Hazardous Materials," in the "Long-Form Letter of Intent to Enter into Site Ground Lease" included as Appendix B, Form B-1 (and subsequent paragraphs renumbered), Paragraph 6.6 of Appendix B, Form B-1 (the "Hazardous Materials Investigation" contingency), should be revised, for example:*

6.6 <u>Hazardous Materials Investigation</u>. Tenant's approval and satisfaction of an environmental and soils investigation of the site, as provided in Paragraph __*[13]*__, "Hazardous Materials Due Diligence Period."

AND

In addition, the approval period contained in Paragraph 7.3 of Appendix B, Form B-1, which describes the approval period for satisfaction of the soils and hazardous materials contingency, should be revised, for example:

7.3 <u>Soils and Hazardous Materials Investigation</u>. Tenant will have until the "Hazardous Materials Due Diligence Period Expiration Date", as that term is defined in Paragraph __*[e.g., 13]*__, below, in which to approve the contingencies contained in Paragraphs __*[e.g., 6.5]*__ and __*[e.g., 6.6]*__.

Note: *This form assumes the geologic or bearing qualities of the soil is investigated concurrently with the hazardous materials aspect of the site's soil and that an equivalent approval period is allowed for each, which need not necessarily be the case.*

Exhibit(s) "__"
[Referenced letter(s), if any, from environmental consultant]

END OF FORM 18-18

Allocation of Specific Transaction Costs

Particularly in a ground-lease transaction or other large or complex lease transaction where substantial costs will be incurred in a hazardous materials investigation of the site, a paragraph should be added to describe all anticipated transaction costs and the obligations of the parties relative to such costs.

Form 18-19 illustrates a style that could be used and assumes the hazardous materials investigation expense language from the preceding Form 18-18 has been inserted into Appendix B, Form B-1, "Long-Form Letter of Intent to Enter Into Site Ground Lease." Do not use the form without very careful editing, making certain that the language comprehensively and accurately covers all costs and that the language selected is consistent with all other provisions of the final proposal. For example, although the form includes an allocation of survey costs, survey costs may not be an issue. Be mindful of local custom in allocating closing costs. Custom in your geographic area may differ substantially from the allocation shown here.

If a paragraph similar to the one included as Form 18-19, below, is added to Appendix B, Form B-1, do not use Paragraph 9.1 ("Escrow Fees and Closing Costs") of Appendix B, Form B-1. The Form 18-19 paragraph, after appropriate editing, should usually be inserted toward the end of the document, after defined terms within it have been introduced.

As a final caution (repeated in the introduction to Chapter 5 and in Appendix B), note that Form B-1 is designed to serve as a proposal confirming a developer's intention to ground lease a site from a landowner for developing a shopping center. It is *not* intended to serve as a deal-making document between a developer and one of the developer's tenants in the center. Observe, also, that in Form B-1 the developer is referred to as "Tenant" (i.e., "tenant" under the long-term ground lease) and the landowner is referred to as "Landlord" (i.e., "landlord" under the ground lease). Form 18-19 is consistent with such terminology.

Form 18-19

Allocation of Specific [Ground] Lease Transaction Costs

__. **Transaction Costs.** Each party shall pay costs incurred on its own behalf, including without limitation, attorneys' fees incurred to prepare and review required documentation. Other transaction costs shall be allocated as follows:

__.__ **Landlord's Costs.** Landlord shall be responsible for paying *__[e.g., one-half]__ the cost of the survey, __[e.g., the brokerage commission of $__________ payable to __________, the cost of the __[See Appendix A, Form A-1]__ leasehold policy of title insurance with a liability limit of $__________, __[e.g., one-half]__ the cost of the Phase II and Phase III Investigations, the cost of the Remedial Action as defined in Paragraph __, the cost of the Additional Remedial Action as defined in Paragraph ___ __[e.g., (less Tenant's one-half share which shall not to exceed $________)]__ and one-half the escrow fees]__.*

__.__ **Tenant's Costs.** Tenant shall pay *__[e.g., one-half]__ the cost of the survey, __[e.g., one-half]__ the cost of the Phase II and Phase III Investigations, __[e.g., one-half]__ the cost of the Additional Remedial Action as defined in Paragraph __ but not to exceed $__________ and __[e.g., one-half]__ the escrow fees]__.* The escrow holder shall make any necessary adjustments to account for all of the foregoing on or before the closing date.

END OF FORM 18-19

FORM 18-19

Representations and Warranties

Representations and warranties can provide a landlord or a tenant with additional remedies. At the deal-making document stage, however, use them sparingly, if at all, and for specific reasons. A lease negotiator is typically irritated by receipt of an initial proposal with a seemingly endless stream of requested representations and warranties. Appropriate representations and warranties do have their place, however, especially where equal knowledge will not be available to the non-owner. A proposed representation or warranty may serve to "flush out" information in the other party's control that would otherwise be difficult to obtain. The following are some examples addressing shopping center leasing transactions.

The deal maker's attorney should be responsible for refining and inserting appropriate protections into the final, operative lease agreements between the parties. Nevertheless, by re-reading these examples prior to negotiations or concurrent with the preparation of a proposal, lines of inquiry, additional areas of risk, and appropriate refinements to the transaction may come to mind.

The following selected representations and warranties generally favor the developer "tenant" under a long-term ground lease. For the most part these are statements intended to be made by the landowner "landlord" for the benefit of the developer "tenant" to confirm specific aspects of the site. However, a developer "tenant" will also encounter requests for similar representations and warranties in the context of the negotiation of sublease to a major tenant. Where the name of the party has been italicized in brackets, party names could possibly be reversed (accompanied often by additional editing).

Because the ground lessee's perspective relative to site warranties parallels that of a buyer, readers considering representations and warranties from a ground lessee's perspective could also start with the fee purchase representations and warranties Form 17-6 ("Selected Seller Representations and Warranties for a Developer's Site Purchase Agreement"). As suggested in the introduction to Form 17-6, one could globally change "Seller" to "Ground Lessor" and "Buyer" to "Ground Lessee" and edit as appropriate. Space lease tenants considering editing the selected representations and warranties in Form 18-20 should start by changing the word "site" to a term such as "premises" or "leasehold premises."

Form 18-20 is not designed to replace any particular paragraph or section in preceding forms; it is merely a sampling of representations and warranties—appropriate as factual circumstances warrant—applicable to recurring lease issues. (Again, however, in their present form they would typically be intended for a developer's site acquisition by ground lease transaction.) These clauses are included to stimulate thinking in a comprehensive and broadened perspective rather than serve as a source of reusable deal points.

Form 18-20

Selected Representations and Warranties for Lease Transactions

Typical introductory clause:

__. **Express Warranties of Landlord.** The ground lease shall provide that __*[Landlord]*__ shall specifically represent and warrant __*[Tenant]*__ that:

> ***Note:*** *Again, in a ground lease context, this book uses the term "Landlord" to refer to the landowner. The "Tenant" under the ground lease is assumed to be a developer or its functional equivalent.*

[a. General, limited listing:]

__.__ **Authority.** __*[Landlord/Tenant]*__ has full power and authority to enter into and fully perform and comply with the proposed lease.

__.__ **No Pending or Threatened Actions.** To Landlord's best knowledge and belief, __*[but without any duty of inquiry or investigation by Landlord,]*__ there are no actions, suits or proceedings pending or threatened against the site or any portion thereof in any court or before any federal, state, county or municipal department, commission, board, bureau or agency or other governmental instrumentality, nor are there any such actions, suits or proceedings pending or threatened which could or would affect Landlord's ability to perform its obligations under the __*[ground]*__ lease.

OR

Another version of preceding paragraph:

__.__ **No Pending or Threatened Action.** Landlord has received no notice of, nor does it have any knowledge of (but without any duty of inquiry or investigation by Landlord), any pending or threatened action or governmental proceeding in eminent domain, zoning change, rent control, or otherwise, which would directly affect the site.

More narrowly:

__.__ **No Contemplated Street or Highway Modification.** Landlord is not aware of any existing, proposed, or contemplated plan to widen, modify or realign any street or highway or any existing, proposed or contemplated eminent domain proceedings which would affect the site in any way whatsoever.

__.__ **No Third-Party Rights to Leasehold Premises Not Disclosed in Preliminary Title Report.** There are not and will not be any leases, contracts, agreements, written or oral, or other understandings entered into by Landlord with respect to the ownership, maintenance or operation of the site which are not disclosed in the __*[describe unrecorded agreement(s)]*__ AND/OR __*[preliminary title report]*__ to be delivered to Tenant for review and approval during __*[e.g., the contingency approval period]*__ and which will be binding upon or in any way affect, impair, or diminish any of Tenant's rights, title and interest in the site __*[or any appurtenances or facilities thereof]*__.

__.__ **Landlord to Make Site Information Available to Tenant.** Within ____ days following the signing of __*[this letter of intent,]*__ Landlord shall make available to Tenant for copying at Tenant's expense, in connection with Tenant's proposed lease of the site, a copy of whatever building plans, surveys, engineering reports, technical information and other similar matters that Landlord or Landlord's agents and consultants may have covering the site or any portion thereof.

__.__ **Cooperation.** __*[When final lease documentation has been signed by Landlord and Tenant]*__, __*[Landlord]*__ will cooperate with __*[Tenant]*__ and with federal, state and local governmental and quasi-governmental agencies, to the extent such cooperation relates to timely securing approvals and permits for Tenant's use of the site, provided such actions by __*[Tenant]*__ do not create risk or liability to __*[Landlord]*__ or adversely impact the value of the site nor restrict or reduce the marketability of the site from Landlord's perspective in Landlord's subjective opinion. In furtherance of the foregoing and after a reasonable period not to exceed ten (10) business days for review, __*[Landlord]*__ will execute any and all conforming instruments necessary or appropriate for the __*[construction/remodeling]*__ of the site.

__.__ **No Governmental Violations.** Landlord has no knowledge or reason to believe that Landlord is presently in violation of any building code, license, or business statute or any other law of a governmental authority exercising jurisdiction over the site.

A sophisticated Landlord may request the insertion of a provision similar to the following:

__.__ **No Warranty of Suitability; Tenant to Conduct Own Investigation.** Except as otherwise expressly set forth in __*[e.g., the ground lease]*__, Landlord has not made and is not making to Tenant any other representation or warranty whether express or implied, in law or in fact, concerning the physical condition of the site, or its suitability for Tenant's intended use; and, __*[upon commencement of the]*__ __*[lease term OR obligation to pay minimum rent under the lease]*__, Tenant will implicitly acknowledge to Landlord that Tenant will have conducted whatever tests, studies and investigations Tenant shall have deemed necessary with respect to the site.

[b. Example of sample abbreviated clauses concerning hazardous materials and environmental matters:]

__.__ **No Hazardous Substance.** To Landlord's best knowledge and belief, __*[but without any duty of inquiry or investigation by Landlord,]*__ there is no contamination, hazardous waste or toxic substance in existence on or below the surface of the site including, without limitation, asbestos in any buildings or any contamination of the soil, subsoil or ground water, which constitutes a violation of any law or regulation of any government entity having jurisdiction thereof or which exposes Tenant to liability to third parties.

OR

An abbreviated version of preceding paragraph:

__.__ **No Hazardous Substance.** To Landlord's best knowledge and belief, __*[but without any duty of inquiry or investigation by Landlord,]*__ no substance identified as a hazardous or toxic material under any federal, state, or local law has been generated, stored, released, or otherwise deposited in or on the site.

Continue:

__.__ **No Hazardous Substance On or In Contiguous Lands.** To Landlord's best knowledge and belief, __*[but without any duty of inquiry or investigation by Landlord,]*__ no substance identified as a hazardous or toxic material under any federal, state, or local law has been generated, stored, released, or otherwise deposited in or on any parcel of land contiguous to the site.

__.__ **Water.** To Landlord's best knowledge and belief, __*[but without any duty of inquiry or investigation by Landlord,]*__ the site's ground water and surface water do not contain any hazardous substance.

__.__ **Asbestos.** To Landlord's best knowledge and belief, __*[but without any inquiry or investigation by Landlord,]*__ no portion of any building or other improvement on the site, including the walls, ceilings, structural steel, flooring, pipes, boilers or equipment is wrapped, insulated, fireproofed or surfaced with any asbestos-containing material.

__.__ **No Underground Storage Tanks.** To Landlord's best knowledge and belief, __*[but without any duty of inquiry or investigation by Landlord,]*__ there are no underground storage tanks within the site.

OR
(alternative to preceding sentence)

__.__ **Specified Underground Storage Tanks.** To Landlord's best knowledge and belief, __*[but without any duty of inquiry or investigation by Landlord,]*__ there are only __ underground storage tanks on the site, all of which are in full compliance with all laws (including, without limitation, any registration requirements), none of which have ever leaked or are currently leaking, and the precise location, age, contents, size, and material of construction of each is described on Exhibit __ attached hereto.

__.__ **No Wetland.** To Landlord's best knowledge and belief, __*[but without any duty of inquiry or investigation by Landlord,]*__ neither the site nor any portion thereof constitutes a "wetland" under any law.

__.__ **No Environmental Violations.** Landlord has not received any notice of any possible violation of any environmental law concerning the site, and Landlord neither knows of nor suspects any such violation.

__.__ **Environmental Compliance.** To Landlord's best knowledge and belief, __*[but without any duty of inquiry or investigation by Landlord,]*__ the site fully complies with all environmental laws and Landlord has obtained and maintained all permits, licenses, and approvals, if any, required under all environmental laws.

END OF FORM 18-20

OVERVIEW

Chapter 19 provides instruction in creating your own computerized form file system to store and retrieve past work product. Such a system uses the deal-making document forms in this book as a starting point. Efficiency and productivity gains will result by systematically creating, storing, re-editing, and re-using your deal-making work product.

Since this chapter was included in the first edition there have been major technological changes to PC computers and software. While technologically out of date, this chapter is included for its broad discussion of the powerful benefits of creating and using your own personalized form file system.

Chapter 19

How to Create and Maintain a Deal-Making Document Form File System

Observe always that everything is the result of change, and get used to thinking that there is nothing Nature loves so well as to change existing forms and make new ones like them.
—Marcus Aurelius

This book has covered the basics of most site acquisition and tenant transactions encountered by a shopping center developer. The virtually limitless factual situations in real life, however, will demand thoughtful and creative amendments, additions, and refinements to the forms contained in this resource.

Were you to use this text as only an aid in making future proposals, the material would be a valuable resource in your everyday work. Yet there is a much more powerful way to use this resource, and that is to use the Forms Diskette as the basis for a computerized file system of your deal-making documents.

You may be asking yourself, "Why should I bother?" Consider for a moment certain inefficiencies that prevail in many development companies. Frequently, after identifying a site for acquisition, the deal maker will give the relevant names, property description, economic terms, and other deal points to the company's lawyer for preparation of a proposal. Even the most timely, responsive lawyer will usually take days producing an initial draft, which is then typically reviewed by the deal maker, then edited and recycled through the lawyer's word-processing system an additional time or two.

This prevailing practice is risky. During the period that the deal maker is in limbo awaiting a final document for delivery, the target property or tenant is not under contract and is open to being put under contract by a competitor. Furthermore, such a process can be unnecessarily wasteful of both the deal maker's time and legal resources. And finally, if the deal does not go together, the file is usually closed and the deal maker's resulting work product forever unused.

Some developers avoid using computers, believing computers are too complicated, that it will be difficult to find what they want, and that learning computer mastery is too time consuming. If this is your viewpoint, you may have already decided you don't want to have anything to do with managing electronic forms.

If this is true for you, you are not alone. My discussions with developers have confirmed that all too many of them believe document generation is the domain of their secretaries and that, with the possible exception of financial analysis, only their secretaries should have to deal with computerized text and the related "paper" work.

Furthermore, the typical deal maker has no committed plan nor systematic methodology for retaining work product that does not result in a consummated deal. Many have failed to address this issue from a management perspective. Perhaps part of the reason so many developers have no system of making past work product available for re-use is that they believe any such "filing" or indexing chore is a "secretary's" job, not the deal maker's responsibility. Sexism aside, this is a naive "smokestack-age" response inappropriate to the demands and opportunities of the Information Age.

These points of view ignore the power and opportunity that can be yours. You can avoid the process and not get involved; but if you stay on the sidelines, enlightened, aggressive competitors will be passing you by very soon.

> "[T]he truly strategic weapons today are knowledge-based. What counts ... in the long run are products of mind-work: scientific and technological research ... the education of the work force ... sophisticated software ... smarter management ... advanced communications ... electronic finance. These are key sources of tomorrow's power, and among these strategic weapons none is more important than superior organization—especially the organization of knowledge itself."[1]

The developer who organizes the knowledge at hand is in a position to respond quickly to opportunity. Today, the computer is indispensible for organizing that knowledge and reacting quickly.

Therefore, you should set up and maintain your own computerized work product storage and retrieval system so you can efficiently create, retain, re-edit, and re-use deal-making documents, constantly improving your competence and productivity.

Create a comprehensive deal-making document form file system (a work product database set up along the lines of the table of contents of this book) in which each past proposal and letter of intent can be quickly and conveniently accessed as a guide for future deal-making and drafting. You will be amazed at the resources you can create and control at your fingertips and at the speed with which you can react to the marketplace.

---

1 Toffler, *Powershift*, p. 165.

This is not a time-consuming process. It merely takes the commitment to create an organized, systematic method of saving your work and the discipline to insert a duplicate of each proposal you make into the appropriate location within your computerized form file system.

To illustrate how such a system can be created, here is what I have done, using an Apple Macintosh computer.[2]

When a Macintosh is turned on, a "desktop" appears on which one can, just like on a normal desktop, open one or a number of file "folders." With a click of the "mouse" button, a new file folder can be created and named appropriately. One or more folders (complete with the files contained in each) can be dragged into another folder with any other appropriate name. This is just like using paper files, in which a hanging file folder, for example, may contain one or more additional file folders. In a matter of minutes, a beginner can begin clicking and dragging files from folder to folder, which is about all it takes to start programs and manage files. It is easy and takes but a few minutes to learn.

The Macintosh interface provides a graphic "icon" (a small symbolic image or picture) for each file folder and each specific file within the folder. In an instant, folders and files can be named and renamed as desired. Of key importance, the Macintosh interface creates a graphic, hierarchical display of everything stored in the computer in the manner *you* decide is appropriate. And if you later see a better way, you can easily change folder names and folder/file organization at any time. The Macintosh Graphic User's Interface (GUI), therefore, provides a powerful, yet incredibly simple and efficient, method of organizing a deal-making documents form file system. Such a system should be found particularly attractive to the computer novice.

To illustrate, a "Deal-Making Documents Form File" folder has been set up and is reproduced on the next page as **Figure 1**. This "Deal Making Documents Form File" folder contains separate file folders for each of various deal-making document form types, generally following the table of contents of this book.

The Macintosh interface allows the option, with a mere click of the mouse, to view files and folders by "Icons," "Lists," "Columns," or "Album Covers. "Icons" can be dragged by the mouse to specific locations on the display where they will stay until moved. In **Figure 1**, various types of site "offer" folders have been grouped across the top, folders concerning major tenant transactions have been grouped to the left, pad transactions are clustered in the center and all other folders are located to the right. Unless or until they are moved, each time the "Deal-Making Documents Form File" folder is viewed by "Icon," the specific screen locations of file folders and the files contained therein will be unchanged. The ability to spatially group logically consistent folders is an advantage.

---

[2] Apple® and Macintosh® are registered trademarks of Apple Computer, Inc. Following this discussion I explain how my system can be adapted to users of IBM compatibles.

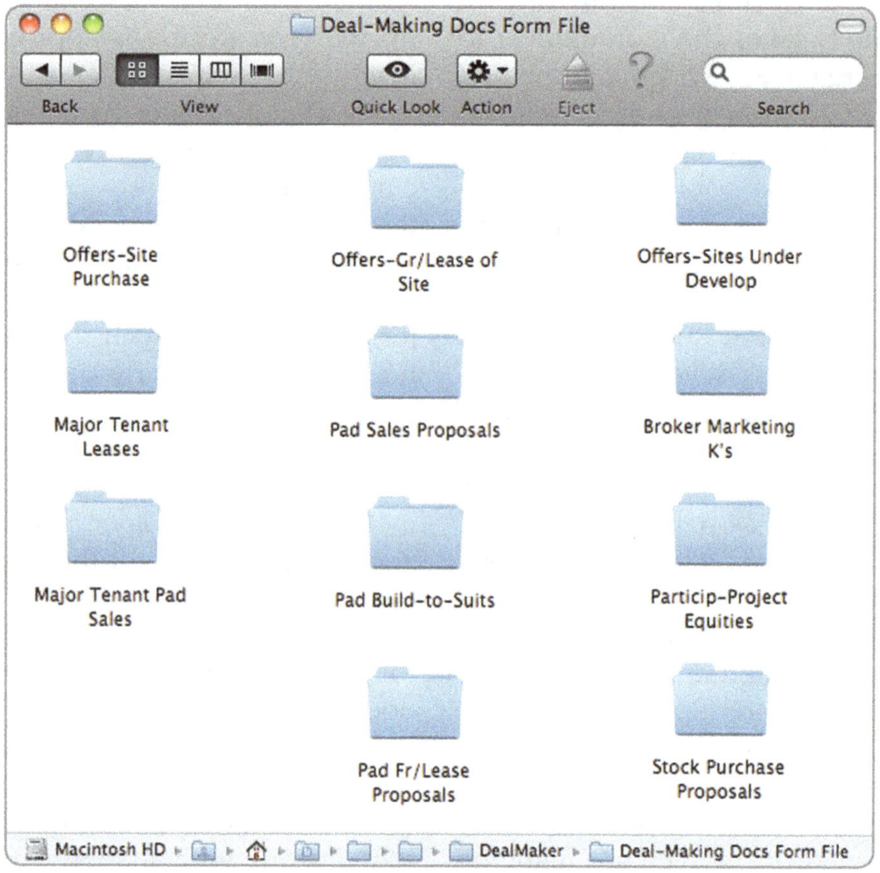

Figure 1

Figure 2 depicts the same Deal-Making Documents Form File viewed by "List" (files displayed by list automatically appear in alphabetical order) rather than by "Icon". Viewing the contents of a folder by "List" (see **Figure 2**) is usually preferable to viewing by "Icon" when the selected folder contains a large number of subfolders.

Setting up the basic form file illustrated in **Figure 1** takes only a few minutes. To create a new empty folder, merely point to the file menu and click on "New Folder," or type the "Command" "Shift" and "F" keys simultaneously), which results in an unnamed folder appearing on the desktop. Then type the name you wish for the folder and the name stays on the folder until you change it. Once this skeleton is established, additional folders can be created within any of these broad headings for further differentiation or organization of past work product.

For example, within the folder "Pad Build-to-Suits," separate folders for "Restaurants" and "Service Stations" could be inserted. Thus, when the "Pad Build-to-Suits" folder is double-clicked, the folder would open and two separate folders within it, one labeled "Restaurants"

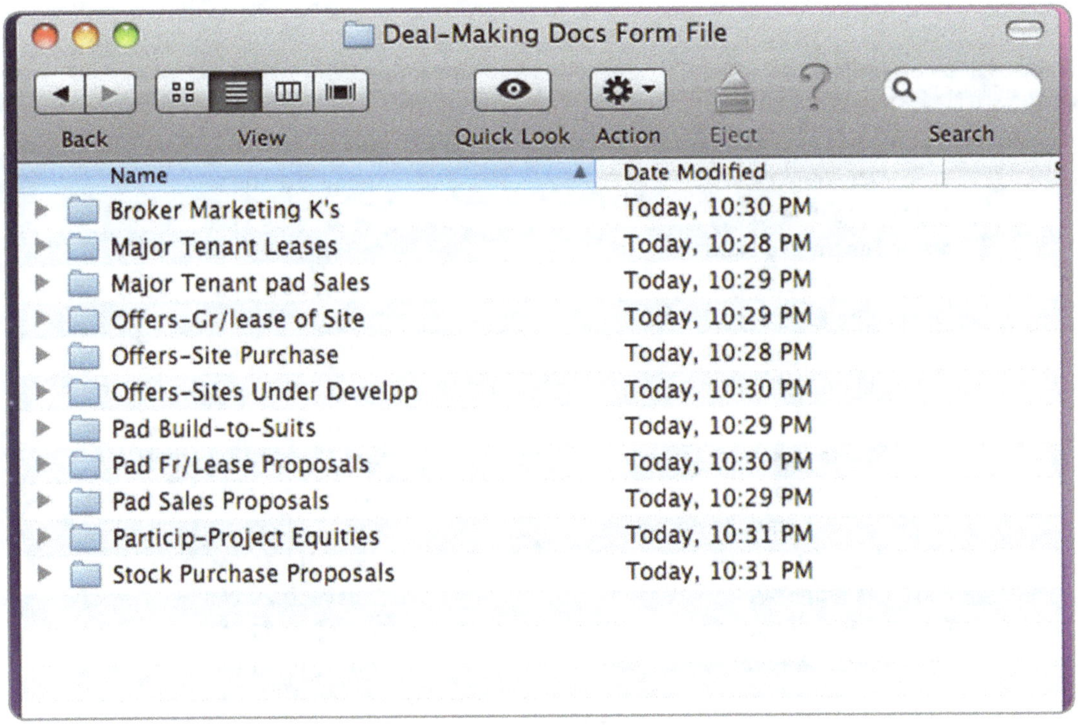

Figure 2

and the other labeled "Service Stations" would appear, as shown in **Figure 3** on the following page. Text files of prior deal-making documents for restaurants and service stations can be inserted into their respective folders merely by sliding each file into the appropriate folder and then letting go of the mouse. This process of creating a logical folder system for your form file system can yield an incredibly refined network of distinctions and folders and subfolders.

A detailed or complete system need not be devised at the beginning. For example, you could start with the "Pad Build-to-Suit" leases folder shown in **Figure 1**. Over time, as work product contained within the folder grows, separate subfolders within the folder can later be made. For example, these could be named "Service Stations," "Restaurants," "Financial Institutions," "Office Buildings," or other specific pad build-to-suit transaction type or any other distinguishing category, subcategory, or deal type deemed appropriate.

In other words, you can design and redesign your system based upon your ever-changing experiences and needs. If you no longer like an aspect of your system, merely rename inappropriate folders, drag all or certain files within the folder to a more appropriate folder, or any combination of the above. Once you create such a system and discover how easy it is to organize and reorganize your work and instantly retrieve it, you will become much more creative, efficient and productive.

This GUI filing system is a great advantage in organizing all company

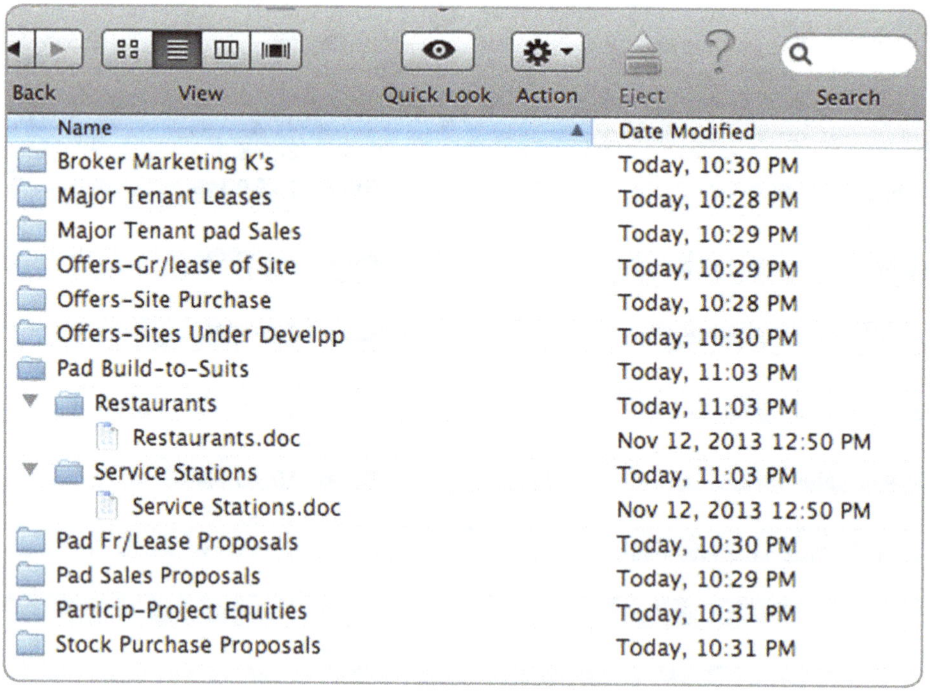

Figure 3

work product as well as personal matters. For example, when my company's Macintosh network is turned on, one first sees a dozen or so major folders, one of which is entitled "Projects." A click of the mouse on the "Projects" icon opens the "Projects" folder and displays a separate and distinct folder for each of the past and present development projects. A click on any project icon, such as "XYZ Shopping Center," will access the numerous folder icons contained within, typically broken down into folder names such as "Site Acquisition," "Pro Formas," "ABC Major Tenant Lease," "Entitlements," "Partnership Agreements," "Construction Contracts," "XYZ Lease," "Sale of Center," etc. (Again, separate additional folders can be created within any of these categories.)

Documents created more than 10 years ago can be accessed immediately, key provisions highlighted, and past work product copied into current proposals or documents in a matter of seconds. (In fact, the organization and grouping of project files within the user's paper file cabinets should usually be designed to follow the Macintosh folder hierarchy for the project. See, for example, Appendix D: "File Cabinet Project File Index.")

When an acquisition or lease proposal is generated, its file is typically kept in its appropriate project file; i.e., the general folder identified by the project's street or city. If the proposal is at all unique or potentially valuable as a form, at the time the file is created and saved within its project folder, a copy should be made for the form file. If the mouse is pointed on the file folder and "file-duplicate" is clicked from the menu, within seconds a separate identical "duplicate" file folder appears on the desktop. One need only point the mouse on the duplicate file and "drag" its icon across the desktop into the appropriate forms file folder for reference in making future proposals. Thus, with almost no extra time or effort, one can simultaneously create both a text file in the specific project file and a copy in the forms file, in the place most appropriate to find it the next time a similar proposal is needed.

This is an incredibly intuitive, fast and efficient method of creating your own system (organized to suit your own needs) whereby you can easily find and efficiently use your past work product in future transactions. But it is far better than that. I have found that since it is so easy to scan these folders and files, very often I will get new, creative ideas merely by looking at the array of file icons and selectively clicking on one or a group of them to review the contents. I often get good ideas because it is so easy to take a glance at a file after seeing an icon and thinking, "Oh, yes, in that deal I did x. Let's take a look." Deal structuring ideas and usable language are readily available because past work product is available in an organized, readily re-usable format.

A similar, organized system can be set up on IBM and IBM-compatible computers[3] running on any Microsoft Windows platform. To create a new folder right-click with the cursor somewhere on your Desktop. From the menu of options, which appear next to your cursor select "New," where then another pane of options appears and select "Folder." This "New Folder" will be named as such until edited and will fall in line with the other icons on your Desktop.

To re-name this "New Folder" "DEALFORM," fore example, one right-clicks after the cursor has clicked once on the "New Folder." A menu pane appears and near the bottom will be the option to "Rename." Name the folder "DEALFORM."

To create subfolders within the "DEALFORM" folder double-click the "DEALFORM" folder and then right-click with the cursor inside the parameters of the opened folder, from the menu pane that appears cursor down and select, "New," cursor down again to "Folder."A new folder will appear within the "DEALFORM" folder, and like its parent folder will be named, "New Folder" until edited.

To re-name this "New Folder" to "RAWFORM" one right-clicks after the cursor has clicked once on the "New Folder." A menu pane appears and near the bottom is "Rename." Name the folder "RAWFORM".

To create subfolders within the "RAWFORM" folder double-click the "RAWFORM" folder and then right-click with the cursor inside the parameters of the opened folder, from the menu pane that appears cursor down and select,

[3] IBM® is a registered trademark of International Business Machines Corporation. Microsoft®, and Windows® are registered trademarks of Microsoft Corporation. The author has no affiliation whatsoever with any computer manufacturer and has received no remuneration for any recommendations made in this chapter.

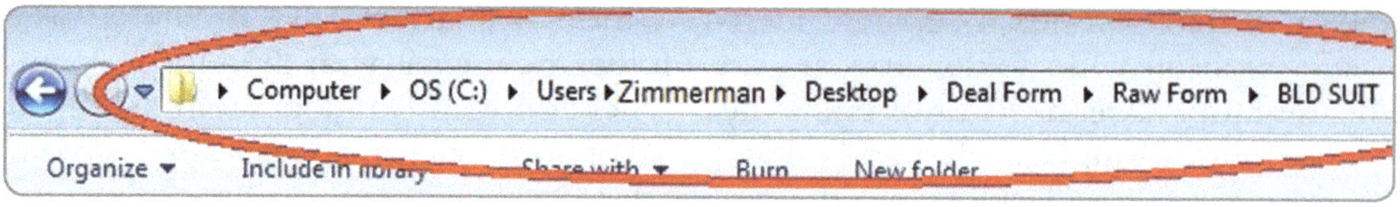

Figure 4

"New," cursor down again to "Folder." A new folder will appear within the "RAWFORM" folder.

To re-name this "New Folder" to "BLDSUIT" one right-clicks after the cursor has clicked once on the "New Folder," a menu pane appears and near the bottom is "Rename." Name the folder "BLDSUIT."

When complete, your folder structure will look something like **Figure 4**, above.

Please note, the computer from which this screen shot originated was named, "Zimmerman," therefore in place of "Zimmerman" one will see the name of the computer on which they are working.

Now, following the example used to describe my Macintosh file system, create other sub-directories inside the DEALFORM folder. Figure 5, below, gives some suggested names using two word documents. Of course, you may create additional sub-directories within each of these sub-directories, if necessary, for storing particular documents according to increasingly refined deal-type distinctions or any other grouping methodology that makes sense to you.

In **Figure 5** below the two word files within the sub-directory "BLDSUIT," called "Document_1" and "Document_2," respectively, are solely for educational purposes, wherein on your actual sub-directory, you would name each file with an appropriate and dynamic name.

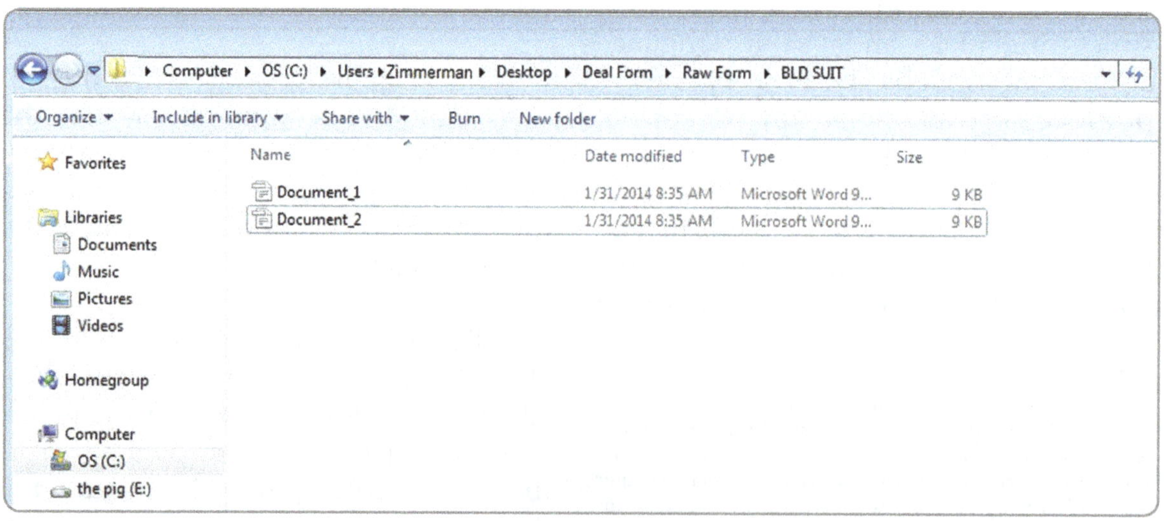

Figure 5

That's all there is to it. You now have an organized system that you can use to quickly find an editable document for almost any type of deal you might want to create.

In outlining this system, I am not suggesting that the deal maker's lawyer be left out of the forms system creation process. The deal maker and the deal maker's lawyer might start by jointly devising a standard land purchase proposal format (possibly using Form 4-1 as a starting point) and a systematic approach to using it. For example, the deal maker could be responsible for the initial draft, which ideally would be produced in a software format compatible with the lawyer's word processing program for speedy, cost-effective editing by the lawyer.

Cultivate a cooperative relationship with your lawyer. Your lawyer should be a member of your project team rather than just someone whom you need to contend with to get the job done. If you are open to being "coached" by your lawyer in preparing deal-making documents, in time you can become very adept in preparing and using them.

Set up and maintain your own computerized work-product storage and retrieval system so you can efficiently retain, re-edit, and re-use deal-making documents, constantly improving your competence and productivity. If, in general, you are compensated relative to your productivity and skill in mastering complex circumstances, at a minimum a basic ability to comprehensively articulate and revise proposals is demanded by the marketplace.

It is my goal that this reference book and the accompanying Forms CD serve you by assisting you in making yourself a more resourceful, responsive and productive deal maker.

OVERVIEW

Appendixes A, B, C, and D provide the following supplemental materials referenced in the text:

Appendix A: Form inserts describing title insurance coverage;

Appendix B: A long-form letter of intent to enter into a site ground lease for development of a shopping center;

Appendix C: An outline of various traditional approaches to structuring rent; and

Appendix D: A sample project file index to serve as a developer's guide to "paper" file cabinet organization consistent with the computerized deal-making document form file system introduced in Chapter 19.

FORMS

A-1 Inserts for Description of Title Insurance Coverage

A-2 Seller to Provide Survey and ALTA Title Commitment

B-1 Long-Form Letter of Intent to Enter into Site Ground Lease

D-1 Project File Index for File Cabinet Organization

Appendixes

Do not hover always on the surface of things nor take up suddenly, with mere appearances; but penetrate into the depth of matters, as far as your time and circumstances allow, especially in those things which relate to your own profession.

—Isaac Watts

Appendix A: Form Inserts Describing Title Insurance Coverage

Purchase and ground lease proposals in this sourcebook include clauses requiring one of the parties (e.g., a seller or ground lessor) to provide title insurance coverage. Unfortunately, local custom and language used to describe alternative title insurance coverages differs among geographical regions within the United States. Note also that in most instances major title companies, when insuring a leasehold rather than a fee interest, will use the same "owner's" policy of title insurance form—the difference merely being that instead of inserting a description of the fee interest insured, a description of the insured leasehold is inserted.

The fee purchase or ground lease proposal forms that contain a blank line for inserting a description of the proposed title insurance coverage may usually be completed by using one of the three alternative provisions contained in Form A-1. Although no precise, universal language is used in all regions, for purposes of a non-binding letter of intent, the descriptions in Form A-1 should be reasonable approximations of available coverages.

Local custom varies as to the responsibility for payment of the title insurance premium. In southern California it is customary for the seller to provide and pay for standard coverage afforded by a standard owner's policy. If the buyer desires the additional coverage afforded by an ALTA Extended Owner's Policy, local custom dictates that the buyer pay for the incremental additional premium.

In certain areas of the South, however, title companies do not customarily increase the title premium when providing ALTA extended coverage so long as the policy purchaser provides the title company with the required ALTA survey. In western states, in addition to the cost of the survey, title companies customarily charge an additional premium for ALTA extended coverage.

The ALTA Standard Owner's Policy with Regional Exceptions is a reasonably close approximation to the standard coverage contained in the former CLTA Owner's Policy, previously used in California, and both contain exclusions from coverage for matters not shown by public records. Examples of such exclusions include easements, liens or encumbrances or claims thereof which are not shown by public records; and discrepancies, conflicts in boundary lines, shortage in area, encroachments or other facts that a correct survey would disclose and are not shown by public records.

Occasionally, key business issues regarding the feasibility of developing a site will turn on the outcome of a survey and a seller may be willing to provide ALTA extended coverage. Form A-2 could be used to modify title provisions in the various acquisition forms to require the seller to provide an ALTA survey and an ALTA extended coverage title commitment at Seller's expense at the inception of the agreement.

Form A-1

Inserts for Description of Title Insurance Coverage

Alternative "A"
("ALTA" refers to American Land Title Association)

ALTA Standard Owner's Policy With Regional Exceptions

Alternative "B"
("ALTA" refers to American Land Title Association)

ALTA Extended Owner's Policy

Note:
California only
("CLTA" refers to California Land Title Association)

CLTA Owner's Policy *(This term is no longer used)*

END OF FORM A-1

Form A-2

APPENDIXES

Seller to Provide Survey and ALTA Title Commitment

__. **Survey and Title Commitment.** Within ___ days following execution of __*[this letter of intent]*__ *OR* __*[this agreement]*__ *OR* __*[the Purchase Agreement]*__, Seller shall provide to Buyer, at Seller's sole cost and expense, (a) a current ALTA survey of the site containing such information and detail as are sufficient to obtain extended title insurance coverage over survey exceptions, prepared by a land surveyor registered in the state where the site is located and confirming that no part of the site is situated in a flood plain, wetlands or other specially environmentally controlled, regulated or protected area, and (b) a commitment for an ALTA Extended Owner's Policy of title insurance (or the closest equivalent in the state where the site is located) in the full amount of the purchase price, providing for full extended coverage over all general exceptions and containing endorsements reasonably required by Buyer, which shall be updated at closing to cover the conveyance of title to Buyer.

END OF FORM A-2

Note: *As a final comment, particularly in situations where a building owner may be experiencing financial problems or foreclosure, even space lease tenants should consider obtaining title insurance, especially if the tenant is making a substantial investment in tenant improvements. Accurate title information could reveal that a proposed sublease term exceeds the term of the underlying lease or that the tenant is not dealing with the proper party.*

FORM A-2

Appendix B: Long-Form Letter of Intent to Enter into Site Ground Lease

Form B-1, a developer's long-form proposal to enter into a site ground lease, is described in the introduction to Form 5-1 in Chapter 5. Form B-1 is derived from and conceptually resembles the standard, long-form fee purchase offer Form 4-1. Form B-1 allows the convenient insertion of negotiated sums to be released from escrow to the landowner during the escrow period preceding lease commencement. The extensive key exhibit, "Summary of Ground Lease Terms," designed for attachment to this ground lease proposal, is printed in this book as an exhibit to Form 5-1. (Because Form B-1 is lengthy, Form B-1 is included in this appendix to provide better balance within Chapter 5.)

The ground lease term typically commences upon recordation of an abstract of the lease (or, infrequently, the lease itself). In California, recordation of a lease abstract will usually occur at the closing of an escrow. Given that a ground lease is a complex document requiring substantial time and expense to negotiate and that due diligence and marketing analysis in the early stages of the escrow could lead the developer to drop the project, the parties should carefully consider how the escrow and negotiation of the ground lease are to be coordinated.

One approach would be to commence due diligence and open escrow only after final documentation of both the escrow instructions and the ground lease. However, if any of the initial escrow steps (e.g., review of preliminary title report, survey, engineering analysis, securing major tenant interest, or the like) proves fatal, time and expense negotiating the full ground lease will have been in vain. Alternatively, the parties and their attorneys could initially exchange information informally, negotiating final documentation only after a certain "comfort" level and project feasibility is attained.

Another method would be to accomplish certain initial due diligence before opening escrow, but then promptly open escrow subject to an "agreement to agree" whereby the parties would commit to negotiate and deposit into escrow, by a certain date, a final ground lease having specified terms and conditions. The developer would proceed to develop the site and begin to arrange anchor transactions in reliance upon the general provisions of the ground lease conceptually agreed upon by the parties, incurring the risk, however, that an impasse could occur, potentially resulting in the landowner refusing to sign the ground lease.

No particular format is universally applicable and the appropriate structure for each situation will be affected by one's assessment of risk. Pragmatically, in many cases the developer's best approach will be to attempt to quickly control the site through an escrow providing that the particularized lease will be negotiated and deposited into escrow by a specified future date. For simplicity, however, the following form assumes that both the escrow instructions and the ground lease will be negotiated and signed by a certain date and that upon execution of such documents the escrow will be opened. You are advised, however, to customize the form for your particular transaction.

Before using this form, also review the many annotations to the long-form fee purchase offer Form 4-1. (For brevity, many of the annotated comments and some of the alternative provisions contained in Form 4-1 are not repeated here.)

As a final caution (repeated in the introduction to Chapter 5), note that Form B-1 is designed to serve as a proposal confirming a developer's intention to ground lease a site from a landowner for developing a shopping center. It is *not* intended to serve as a deal-making document between a developer and one of the developer's tenants in the center.

Observe, also, that in this form the developer is referred to as "Tenant" (i.e., "tenant" under the long-term ground lease) and the landowner is referred to as "Landlord" (i.e., "landlord" under the ground lease). The terms selected are consistent with this book's attempt to use the fewest possible party names and thereby facilitate incorporation of selected form language from one deal-making document to another. You could easily globally change the names of the parties to "Developer" and "Landowner".

Form B-1

Long-Form Letter of Intent to Enter into Site Ground Lease

[Date]

[Insert Name and
address of landowner
____
____
__________________*]*

Re: ___ -acre shopping center site located at the __*[e.g., southeast]*__ corner of __*[e.g., _______ Street]*__ and __*[Avenue]*__; __*[City]*__, __*[State]*__ (See attached maps, Exhibits "A", "B" and "C", and "Summary of Ground Lease Terms", Exhibit "D")

Dear __*[Name of landowner]*__:

Caveat: *Review the annotations at the beginning of Form 4-1 discussing the persuasive importance of your introduction. Insert appropriate introductory language based upon specific involvement and relationships relative to the particular site.*

Then, continue, for example:

__[I appreciated meeting you and discussing this site rather extensively with you. As I explained, my company will only proceed provided sufficient major tenant interest is established. A great deal of preliminary due diligence, research and marketing effort is required until we can be certain that our proposed development will be viable and that we can attract sufficient major tenant interest.

Accordingly, this proposal outlines the terms of an escrow period during which we will conduct our due diligence, complete demographic studies and undertake preliminary site planning, all in an effort to develop a viable, major-tenant anchored shopping center on your site. This proposal provides for certain releases of funds to you through escrow during the escrow period. As of the closing of the escrow, the proposed ground lease would go into effect in accordance with the terms of the "Summary of Ground Lease Terms" attached as Exhibit "__[D]__" to this proposal.

Although this proposal is not intended to address all terms, conditions and obligations of a final ground lease and escrow instructions, we believe we have addressed the major deal points. During negotiation of final documentation, either of us may raise additional issues and propose additional terms and conditions relating to your disposition of the site.

I look forward to the possibility of working together with you on this project and am pleased to submit the following proposal to you]__:

1. Parties. Upon satisfaction of the escrow contingencies contained herein, __*[name of shopping center developer]*__, or its nominee or assignee ("Tenant"), will ground lease the "site" (defined below) from the site's present owner, __*[name of landowner]*__ ("Landlord"). Upon execution of this letter by Landlord, Tenant's legal counsel will prepare a ground lease ("ground lease") and joint escrow instructions ("escrow instructions") consistent with the terms and conditions of this letter of intent.

2. Consideration. Tenant will pay Landlord, as and for the use of the site, the ground rent stated in the attached Exhibit "__*[D]*__", "Summary of Ground Lease Terms", on the terms and conditions stated therein.

3. Site. The "site" is an unimproved, roughly ___ -acre land parcel located at the __*[e.g., southeast]*__ corner of __________ and __________ in __*[city]*__, __*[state]*__ as shown on the attached __*[assessor's parcel map]*__ *OR* __*[plat map]*__ attached hereto as Exhibit "__*[A]*__". The parties understand the site is currently designated ___________ in __*[name of city]*__'s General Plan and is zoned ___________. Landlord represents that the net developable land area (as conceptually designated on the preliminary site plan attached hereto as Exhibit "__*[B]*__") is not less than ___ acres or ________ square feet of land area. *Describe any specific or unique adjustments to the site. (See, for example, Paragraph 3, Form 4-1). Note that the "optional" paragraph at the end of Paragraph 5 in the proposed exhibit, "Summary of Ground Lease Terms", provides that ground rent is to be adjusted in accordance with the total net square footage of the site, as surveyed.*

The exact legal description of the site shall be approved by Tenant and Landlord in escrow.

> ***Optional:*** *Use a paragraph or more if necessary to refine any unique aspects of the transaction, specific areas of Landlord-Tenant cooperation during the escrow, or development work in process prior to addressing title and customary specific contingencies. The fol-*

lowing is merely an example of a paragraph that could be inserted as Paragraph 4:

4. <u>Adjacent Property Escrow</u>. Not later than ____ days after opening of the site ground lease escrow, Tenant and __*[insert name of apparent adjacent owner]*__ (or the owner of record) of the approximately ___ (net) acres immediately __*[describe, e.g., southwest of the site as shown on Exhibit "__[C]__"]*__ shall have entered into a mutually acceptable purchase or ground lease agreement for the purchase or long term lease by Tenant of such adjacent property ("Adjacent Owner Escrow"). If the Adjacent Owner Escrow is not entered into before __________, 20__, Tenant may elect to terminate this letter and any escrow instructions or ground lease entered into between Tenant and Landlord concerning the site shall also terminate (except for continuing obligations, if any, agreed to by the parties).

5. <u>Title Search and Document Delivery</u>. Within __*[e.g., ten business]*__ days after "opening of escrow" (defined below), Landlord will provide Tenant with a preliminary title report __*[prepared as of a date after the date of this letter]*__, and all of the following:

5.1 <u>Leases and Agreements</u>. Copies of all leases, rental agreements, licenses or other agreements concerning the site which are presently in effect, whether recorded or not;

5.2 <u>Soils Reports and Investigations</u>. Copies of all soils reports and investigations relating to the site, which are in Landlord's possession or the possession of Landlord's agents or consultants; __*[and]*__

5.3 <u>Surveys, Studies and Plans</u>. Copies of all surveys, preliminary site plans, grading plans, improvement plans, engineering on- and off-site plans and other engineering studies and maps of the site __*[and adjacent parcels]*__ which are in Landlord's possession or the possession of Landlord's agents or consultants __*[.]*__ <u>*OR*</u> __*[; and...]*__

Optional: If a sepia is available, it will expedite preliminary site planning.

5.__ <u>Sepias</u>. One architect's or engineer's scaled full-sized sepia of Landlord's boundary survey. (Landlord will authorize, cooperate with or otherwise assist Tenant in obtaining required additional copies provided Tenant pays any necessary copying expense.)

To eliminate any doubt and if you are aware of specific work Land-

lord has performed, consider itemizing it and requiring delivery of a copy to Tenant. For example:

__*[To date, Landlord has caused to be conducted various tests and studies concerning the site, including, but not limited to, its archeology, geotechnical and hydrologic aspects relative to wetlands and the river frontage, environmental issues, biological characteristics, and fish and game aspects. An application is now pending with the Army Corps of Engineers for issuance of a "404 Permit" and other permits relating to proposed work in the flood plain. Within __ days from opening of escrow, Landlord will provide Tenant with copies of all such tests, studies, applications, and pending permits affecting the site. If Tenant terminates escrow, Tenant shall promptly return such copies to Landlord]*__.

6. Contingencies. The following contingencies are conditions precedent to Tenant's obligation to consummate the ground lease of the site. In the event any of the contingencies are not satisfied prior to the date set forth herein, Tenant may at its option waive such contingencies or terminate the escrow instructions and the ground lease by delivery of written notice to Landlord. If notice of approval of any contingency is not received by Landlord on or before the applicable deadline set forth in Paragraph __*[7]*__, such contingency shall be deemed __*[not approved]*__ *OR* __*[approved]*__.

6.1 Title. Approval by Tenant of a current preliminary title report and legal description as provided by Landlord at Landlord's cost. Such preliminary title report shall not be deemed received by Tenant until Tenant has been furnished from __*[insert name]*__ Title Company a preliminary title report complete with copies of each and every document referenced in said title report together with a map prepared by ___________ Title Company depicting each easement, right of way, license, right, etc. which is capable of being plotted in accordance with normal title company practices. Escrow will order and issue such documents upon opening of escrow.

Note: *To avoid the time and inconvenience of piecemeal review of title documents, this provision provides that Tenant's duty to review title matters does not commence until all backup copies and plotted easements have been delivered to Tenant.*

6.2 Feasibility. Tenant's preliminary investigation and determination that there are no governmental, physical or economic constraints which would render development of the site as a __*[e.g., community]*__ shopping center unfeasible or uneconomic.

6.3 Major Tenant Commitments. Obtaining major tenant commitments in form and substance acceptable to Tenant.

6.4 Entitlements. Obtaining building permits for all proposed improvements. (This assumes obtaining final site plan approval and required approvals from all required agencies for Tenant's proposed shopping center on the site. *__[Such approvals include, but are not limited to,]__ __[e.g., Army Corps of Engineers, U.S. Fish and Wildlife, assessment districts governing portions of on site and off-site improvements, acceptable development fee agreements, conditional use permits (if required), and utility agreements]__.*)

6.5 Soils Tests. Tenant's approval of soils tests provided by Tenant or Tenant's contractor at Tenant's cost.

6.6 Hazardous Materials Investigation. Tenant's approval of a Phase 1 environmental investigation of the site to be performed by Tenant at Tenant's cost. (Tenant may elect to but is under no obligation to conduct physical testing of the site.)

> ***Think:*** *Have you carefully considered the* specific *factual situation and tailored the contingencies to meet the factual context? Add other contingencies as necessary. Examples of other contingencies to consider are set forth below. (Some of these contingencies overlap or refine the preceding contingencies enumerated above.) If any additional contingencies are added, be certain to describe the time period allowed for the satisfaction of each such additional contingency under Paragraph 7.*

__.__ Zoning and Utilities. *Approval by Tenant that the site is zoned commercially for development of a ______________ shopping center consisting of __[describe type of center/tenant mix, etc.]__ and that sewer capacity, water service, and all other utilities are available for the development.*

__.__ Site Survey. *Tenant's approval of Landlord's ALTA survey of the site or, in the event Landlord does not have such a survey, Tenant's approval of Tenant's survey of the site conducted at Tenant's expense.*

__.__ Termination of Easement. *Termination or removal __[by close of escrow]__ of the apparent water easement running diagonally across the site, as set forth in __[e.g., the assessor's parcel map]__.*

__.__ **Site Plan Approval.** *Final approval by the _____ city planning department [or city council] of the proposed final site plan prepared by Landlord as __________ architectural firm job number _______ and last revised _________, 20__, depicting a shopping center complex of _________ square feet of buildings on _____________ square feet of land with parking for _______ cars __[with any governmentally-imposed changes thereto subject to Tenant's approval]__.*

__.__ **Approval of Landlord's Development Documentation.** *Landlord's delivery to Tenant and Tenant's approval of copies of all documents in Landlord's control relating to the project, including but not limited to: (a) existing and required city and other governmental approvals, (b) the status of a proposed _____________ lease for approximately __________ square feet of space in the proposed center, and (c) all conceptual and proposed site plans, building plans, topographic maps and engineering work.*

__.__ **Site Not in Flood Plain.** *Confirmation that the site is not located in a flood plain.*

__.__ **No Wetlands.** *That no portion of the site is designated or in the process of being designated or protected as a "wetlands" under any federal or state statute.*

__.__ **No Endangered Species.** *That no portion of the site contains a habitat for an "endangered species" or a "threatened species" as defined by the federal Endangered Species Act or any similar federal or state statute which prohibits or restricts development in order to preserve a habitat for the survival of any animal or plant species.*

__.__ **Cap on Governmental Fees and Permit Costs.** *That the sum of all applicable governmental development fees, assessments and permits leviable against the proposed project __[through construction of its initial phase]__ shall not exceed $____ per square foot of proposed building area.*

__.__ **General Plan, Zoning, Infrastructure Financing and Design and Environmental Approvals In Support of Project.** *Passage of _____ City Council resolutions approving a General Plan amendment of the site consistent with retail commercial use, a zoning amendment allowing retail commercial uses, [California:] formation of a Mello-Roos financing district for the construction of the freeway off-ramp and ______ Road improvements, [California:] CALTRANS approval for the interchange and off-ramp to the site, and environmental permits permitting the construction and operation of Tenant's proposed development of the site, all of which shall be approved by Tenant in its sole and* *absolute discretion and none of which shall have any conditions unacceptable to Tenant in Tenant's sole and absolute discretion.*

Consider adding this optional clause to the preceding paragraph:

__[If any of the approvals described in the preceding paragraph are delayed beyond the scheduled closing date by more than ___ days for reasons other than Landlord's failure to timely process and cooperate in the processing of such matters and all other contingencies to closing have been satisfied or waived by Tenant, (i) the purchase price shall increase at the rate of __ % annually from the end of said __ day period until the closing, which in no event shall be later than ________, 20__ and (ii) notwithstanding Tenant's escrow extension obligations contained in Paragraph __[e.g., 10]__, Tenant shall, under such circumstances, be under no obligation to make any monthly Extension Deposit for the period beginning from the end of said __ day period until the closing]__.

__.__ Bankruptcy Court and Lien Holder Approvals. *Landlord securing on or before ________, 20__, all necessary approvals from __[the U.S. Bankruptcy Court]__ and/or existing lien holders which will permit Landlord to deliver marketable leasehold title to the site free and clear of all monetary and other liens unacceptable to Tenant and otherwise permit Landlord to perform all its obligations under the ground lease and the escrow, provided, however, that such approvals shall be in a form and substance satisfactory to Tenant in Tenant's sole and absolute discretion.*

Some Landlords will resist a long list of contingencies. Major tenant and approval issues can be combined, as can other issues, to "shorten" the offer, for example:

__.__ Major Tenant Commitments and Entitlements. *Obtaining major tenant commitments acceptable in form and substance to Tenant and obtaining final site plan approval and issuance of appropriate building permits and all other required entitlements from all required agencies for Tenant's planned __[e.g., community]__ shopping center on the site, including but not limited to, all required environmental clearances, acceptable development fee agreements, off-site permits, conditional use permits (if required), and utility agreements.*

7. Contingency Approval Periods. Each of the contingencies listed above shall be approved, disapproved or waived prior to the dates specified below.

7.1 Title. Tenant will have *__[e.g., 21 working]__* days from the receipt of the title documents described in Paragraph *__[e.g., 6.1]__* to approve such documents.

7.2 Feasibility and Major Tenant Commitments. Tenant will have __*[e.g., 120]*__ days from the opening of escrow in which to satisfy the contingencies contained in Paragraphs __*[e.g., 6.2 and 6.3]*__.

7.3 Soils Tests and Hazardous Materials Investigation. Tenant will have __*[e.g., 150]*__ days from the opening of escrow in which to satisfy the contingencies contained in Paragraphs __*[e.g., 6.5 and 6.6]*__.

7.__ [List other contingencies by name]. *[After each, insert:]* Tenant will have __ days from the opening of escrow in which to satisfy the contingency contained in Paragraph __.

7.__ Entitlements. Tenant will have ___ months from the opening of escrow __*[but not later than ________, 20__]*__ in which to satisfy the contingency contained in Paragraph __*[e.g., 6.4]*__.

The prudent landlord should expect a diligence standard:

8. Tenant's Reasonable Diligence. During the contingency period Tenant will exercise reasonable diligence to investigate all aspects of the site and attempt to timely satisfy such contingencies. Upon satisfaction of such contingencies, Tenant will work diligently to develop the proposed center in an expeditious manner. *[Optional:]* __*[Once acceptable major tenant commitments are obtained, Tenant will proceed with reasonable diligence to attempt to obtain* __*[e.g., "Plot Plan Approval"]*__ *for the layout of a* __*[e.g., community]*__ *shopping center on the site in reasonable conformity to Tenant's and its prospective major tenants' requirements for ingress and egress, parking and building size, location, height and building elevations]*__. During the escrow period __*[name of experienced major leasing firm]*__ or persons of similar commercial retail leasing experience shall conduct a first-class marketing effort for the proposed center. Tenant will regularly advise Landlord __*[(not less than monthly)]*__ on the status of marketing efforts and negotiations with major tenants.

9. Escrow. Within __ business days after acceptance of this proposal by Landlord, Tenant and Landlord will negotiate, sign and deposit mutually-acceptable escrow instructions and the final ground lease at __________ Title Company in __*[city]*__, __*[state]*__ ("escrow"). Escrow shall notify Landlord and Tenant of the date on which escrow instructions and the ground lease, signed by all parties required to sign on behalf of Landlord and Tenant, have been deposited into escrow ("opening of escrow"). The escrow instructions and the ground lease shall be consistent with the terms and conditions of this letter of intent.

9.1 Escrow Fees and Closing Costs. All escrow charges shall be shared equally by Tenant and Landlord and all other closing costs not specifically provided for in other provisions of this agreement shall be shared in the manner customary in ___________ county, __*[state]*__.

> ***Note:*** *To prepare a clause that more precisely allocates costs, see Chapter 18, Form 18-19, "Allocation of Specific [Ground] Lease Transaction Costs".*

9.2 Initial Deposit. Upon opening of escrow, Tenant shall deposit $__*[$25,000 in this example]*__ cash into escrow as a good faith "Initial Deposit". At the direction of Tenant, the Initial Deposit shall be deposited into an interest bearing account, with all interest accruing to the benefit of Tenant. The scheduled closing shall occur ___ days after satisfaction of all contingencies, but not later than __*[e.g., 5]*__ months from opening of escrow (as defined above) or __*[specific date]*__, whichever occurs later (the "scheduled closing date"). If any of the escrow contingencies described above are not satisfied during the __*[e.g., 5]*__ -month period following opening of escrow and Tenant elects to terminate, Tenant's Initial Deposit shall be returned in full, less any applicable escrow cancellation charge.

10. Escrow Extensions. So long as Tenant is actively proceeding to develop the site as a shopping center, Tenant may elect to extend, in monthly increments, the scheduled closing date by up to __*[e.g., eight]*__ monthly periods by authorizing escrow to disburse from escrow directly to Landlord, a sum payable in advance for each such monthly extension ("Extension Deposit"). Each Extension Deposit so made shall extend by one month the then scheduled or extended closing date and be applicable or not applicable to the purchase price, as follows:

Monthly Escrow Extension	Amount	Applicable ("A") or Not Applicable ("N.A.") To Purchase Price
1st	$10,000	A
2nd	10,000	A
3rd	20,000	A
4th	25,000	A
5th	25,000	NA
6th	30,000	NA
7th	30,000	NA
8th	30,000	NA
	[and so forth]	

The __*[e.g., $25,000]*__ Initial Deposit shall be released to Landlord through escrow as a condition to Tenant's right to elect to extend the scheduled closing date by depositing the first Extension Deposit.

> ***Note:*** *Be mindful that this form provides that if Tenant fails to affirmatively terminate, Escrow will make the Extension Deposit payments from Tenant's escrow deposit until Tenant either closes or terminates escrow.*

Tenant shall redeposit an additional __*[e.g., $25,000]*__ within 10 days of escrow holder's release of the Initial Deposit to Landlord. If Tenant fails either to close escrow or give notice to terminate escrow on the scheduled closing or any extended escrow closing date, escrow holder shall be deemed to be irrevocably instructed to release from escrow to the account of Landlord, from Tenant's escrow deposit, the monthly Extension Deposit payable for the following monthly extension period until Tenant either closes or terminates escrow. Tenant shall deposit sufficient additional funds to provide for such releases.

11. Tenant's Termination Right. Tenant may terminate escrow at any time during the contingency period by providing written notice to escrow holder. If any of the escrow contingencies described above are not satisfied and Tenant terminates during the first __*[e.g., 5]*__ months of the escrow period, Tenant's deposit shall be returned to Tenant, less any escrow cancellation charges. If Tenant terminates after the first monthly escrow Extension Deposit has been released to Landlord, Landlord may retain the Initial Deposit and each Extension Deposit released to Landlord through termination. Upon such termination, Tenant shall promptly assign and deliver to Landlord, lien free and without charge, copies of all tentative site plans, engineering, and soils and environmental studies concerning the site that Tenant generated prior to termination. Thereupon, Landlord shall have the right to use the work and various studies (limited only by such contract, copyright and other legal limitations placed upon such work product in the normal course of business by the third party consultants or producers of such work product. In other words, Tenant shall assign all Tenant's rights to such work product to Landlord but Landlord shall have no greater rights to such work product than the rights enjoyed by Tenant.) Receipt of the Initial Deposit and any such Extension Deposits shall constitute liquidated damages pursuant to Paragraph __*[e.g., 22]*__ below, and release Tenant from any further claims of Landlord concerning the escrow.

Optional: In an economic climate of limited equity capital and debt financing, a sophisticated Landlord may negotiate for the insertion of the following Landlord oriented provision:

12. Landlord's Termination Right. Tenant shall have until __*[date certain, ideally before any Extension Deposit is required to be released to Landlord]*__, 20__, in which to form a venture with an equity financial partner, obtain a binding financing commitment from an institutional lender, or otherwise show sufficient resources to close the escrow and pay the negotiated ground rent. If by such date Tenant has not presented Landlord with the name, net worth, and general financial condition of Tenant's financial partner or other financial resources reasonably demonstrating Tenant's financial ability to perform, Landlord may, upon ___ days written notice to Tenant and escrow holder, elect to terminate the escrow. __*[If escrow is terminated pursuant to this paragraph, the Initial Deposit and any Extension Deposit(s) released to Landlord shall be concurrently refunded to Tenant]*__.

Note: *Should developer's soft costs such as preliminary architectural and engineering fees or marketing costs be reimbursed by Landlord?*

A prudent developer should require Landlord to complete any hazardous waste or contamination cleanup at Landlord's expense prior to closing. This conventional approach is outlined in the following Tenant-oriented Alternative "A" of Paragraph 13. Alternative "B" is a more risky and very unconventional approach to the subject and is an illustration of a negotiated compromise. If, for example, the Landlord is a limited partnership in which the general partner is unable to collect cleanup costs from the limited partners, language similar to Alternative "B" could be considered. The developer's lawyer should provide guidance in this area, which due to its complexity and potential liability is beyond the scope of this material.

Alternative "A"—Paragraph 13
Tenant investigates and Landlord completes any corrective work at Landlord's expense before closing.

13. Hazardous Materials. Assuming sufficient anchor tenant interest is established and Tenant elects to proceed to ground lease the site, before closing Tenant may conduct an environmental investigation, inspection and testing of the site by a reputable environmental consultant acceptable to Tenant. The results of such study will be set forth in the consultant's report. Landlord shall pay for any corrective work required and complete any such work prior to close of escrow and lease commencement. Landlord's obligation to pay for corrective work shall include the cost to obtain environmental clearance certificate(s) satisfactory to all appropriate governmental agencies showing the site free and clear of any toxic waste, contamination or hazardous substance.

OR

Alternative "B"—Paragraph 13
Example of negotiated compromise where cleanup appears minimal; Tenant pays limited cleanup cost and receives like credit as offset to ground rent.

13. Hazardous Materials. Landlord has disclosed to Tenant that the site is contaminated with __*[specify hazardous substance]*__. Assuming sufficient anchor tenant interest is established and Tenant elects to proceed to ground lease the site, before closing Tenant may conduct an environmental investigation, inspection and testing of the site by a reputable environmental consultant acceptable to Tenant. The results of such study will be set forth in the consultant's report. Tenant shall pay for any corrective work required in an amount not to exceed $__________ and receive a credit at close of escrow and an offset against ground rent for the full amount of such work up to the $__*[same amount]*__ maximum. The above-described work shall be completed prior to close of escrow and the creditable cost of the work shall include the cost to obtain environmental clearance certificate(s) satisfactory to all appropriate governmental agencies showing the site free and clear of any toxic waste, contamination or hazardous substance. In the event the projected cost to complete all such corrective work is more than $__*[same amount]*__ and Landlord is unwilling to credit the increased cost of such corrective work against ground rent (with interest to accrue at __*[e.g., 10]*__ % on such credited amount), Tenant may elect to terminate escrow and all funds theretofore released to Landlord shall be promptly returned to Tenant and escrow shall return any escrow deposit to Tenant. __*[Upon opening of escrow Landlord shall sign an agreement securing Landlord's obligations under this paragraph]*__.

Important Note: *There are very significant risks in relying upon Landlord's unsecured obligation to return escrow releases. Consider also the need in such a case for reimbursement of other costs incurred through escrow termination. If Tenant is willing to consider leasing a contaminated site, the ground lease and escrow instructions should be modified as follows:*

1. There should be no releases of cash to Landlord before the close of escrow;

2. Tenant should be able to cancel escrow without penalty if Tenant's lender will not finance a long term leasehold on contaminated property;

3. Tenant's obligation to expend money should be carefully limited to an amount the Tenant is prepared to lose; and

4. Tenant should attempt to have Landlord pay for all or a portion of the cleanup costs by delaying closing until work is completed and paid for or requiring a very significant "holdback" of the Initial Deposit, any Extension Deposits and ground rent to pay for the cleanup costs. The amount of the holdback should be equal to 150% of a written estimate of the cleanup cost prepared by a reputable environmental engineering firm.

For a more comprehensive, alternative format where hazardous materials are contemplated, see Chapter 18, Form 18-18: "Sample Ground Lease Letter of Intent Hazardous Materials Provision Where Significant Investigation and Remedial Work Is Contemplated".

Get expert advice at the outset if you are aware of any potential hazardous materials issues. The law is complex and potential liability risks so significant that a skilled lawyer's advice is crucial.

End of Alternatives "A" and "B" to Paragraph 13 —Continue to Paragraph 14

14. Entry. Tenant shall have an immediate license to enter upon the site for the purpose of conducting economic feasibility, engineering, soil and other tests at its sole cost and expense. Tenant will indemnify Landlord and hold Landlord harmless from any and all loss or liability resulting from the acts of Tenant or its agents, employees, or invitees upon the site and from all or any mechanics liens or other liens resulting from Tenant's conduct or the conduct of its agents or employees on the site.

15. Marketing Signs. Landlord grants to Tenant, and Tenant's nominee or agent, the right to erect a sign or signs offering retail space for lease during the term of the escrow.

Occasionally, additional detail is needed, such as illustrated by the following:

__[However, Landlord currently is a party to month-to-month agreements with X Corp and Y Corp ("home builders") which allow each of such home builders to place tract marketing signs on the site. Landlord shall use its best efforts to renegotiate such signage agreements so as to allow Tenant premier space for its retail marketing signs on the site within __ days after opening of escrow yet allow such home builders to continue to market their tracts so long as such signs do not interfere with Tenant's marketing signs. Landlord shall retain any sign right income from such home builders through close of escrow]__.

16. Landlord Cooperation. *[Start with specifying any specific or unique duties which should be required of Landlord relative to the site and its development and then continue:]* Landlord will fully cooperate in timely supplying the various documents, maps, plans and studies required to be delivered to Tenant pursuant to Paragraph *__[e.g., 5, above]__*. Landlord will continue to furnish copies of any such additional materials generated by Landlord or Landlord's consultants during the escrow period. *[Continue with following broad language:]* Landlord will cooperate fully with and assist Tenant in negotiating with private and public special interest groups, adjacent property owners, federal, state and local governmental and quasi-governmental agencies, as such negotiations relate to timely securing approvals and permits for the site. Landlord will also execute any and all instruments necessary or appropriate for the development of the site, including but not limited to, maps, dedications or easements and rights of way to governmental and quasi-governmental authorities and adjacent property owners provided such execution is consistent with normal practices.

> ***Note:*** *The following provides for one of Landlord's partners to provide entitlement consulting services to Tenant. Use of such a provision might arise if the partner had substantial expertise relative to the site or entitling authorities, Landlord lacked the necessary development capital to proceed or the partner sought continued involvement in the project and Tenant had the capital necessary to complete the project. (Of course, any partner receiving the benefits of such a consulting arrangement must fully disclose and obtain consent from his or her partners in accepting such a contract.)*

Under the following optional provision, Tenant retains one of Landlord's partners as a consultant for entitlement assistance.

__. Entitlement Assistance Consulting Services. Tenant and *__[name of one of Landlord's partners (for convenience, "John Slick" in this paragraph]__* shall enter into a mutually acceptable consulting agreement whereby *__[John Slick]__* shall provide processing and entitlement assistance to Tenant for Tenant's proposed shopping center development for a total fee of $________, $________ of which shall be deposited into escrow at the opening of escrow and shall be released to __*[John Slick]*__ upon Tenant's approval __*[in Tenant's sole and absolute discretion]*__ of __*[e.g., the title, feasibility, soils, and environmental contingencies described in Paragraphs 6.1, 6.2, 6.5 and 6.6, above]*__. *[(Conform language with specific contingencies contained in the proposal—See Paragraph 6, "Contingencies".)]* The remaining $________ shall be paid at the rate of $________ monthly thereafter. Tenant's obligation to make any such payment shall terminate if the escrow or the ground lease is terminated or canceled by Tenant. __*[Tenant shall approve or disapprove such contingencies within __[e.g., 120]__ days from the opening of escrow]*__.

17. Assignment. Tenant may assign all of Tenant's rights and duties under the ground lease or the escrow or nominate any entity to take title to the site, upon the giving of written notice to Landlord, which notice may not be given less than __*[e.g., three]*__ days prior to closing. Any such assignment is conditional upon such assignee agreeing to be bound by all consents and approvals theretofore given or deemed to have been given by Tenant, and such assignment or nomination shall not relieve Tenant of any of Tenant's obligations under the ground lease or the escrow.

18. Condemnation Prior to Closing. If prior to closing the site or any part thereof becomes the subject of a condemnation proceeding, Landlord agrees to immediately advise Tenant thereof. If such condemnation would make it impractical for Tenant to develop the site as contemplated, Tenant shall have the option to (i) take leasehold title in accordance with the terms and conditions of the applicable agreements between the parties and negotiate with the condemning authority for the condemnation award and receive the benefits thereof without affecting the ground rent, or (ii) terminate the agreements between Tenant and Landlord and declare Tenant's obligations under the escrow and the ground lease null and void and of no further effect, in which event all sums theretofore paid or released to Landlord or to escrow shall be returned to Tenant.

19. Title. At the close of escrow, the parties shall cause to be recorded an abstract confirming Tenant's right, title and interest as ground lessee under the ground lease, which shall be deposited into escrow by Tenant and approved by Landlord on or before ________, 20__. Tenant's title, as ground lessee, shall be a marketable leasehold interest subject only to those matters of record which have been disclosed to Tenant in the preliminary title report and approved in writing by Tenant. In addition, Landlord shall deliver to Tenant at close of escrow, at Landlord's expense, a __*[See Appendix A, Form*

*A-1]*__ policy of title insurance insuring marketable title in Tenant's leasehold interest for $__________, subject only to the reversionary interest of Landlord and the title items previously approved by Tenant.

20. Brokerage Commissions. Tenant and Landlord each separately represent and warrant that it did not incur any brokerage commission in connection with this transaction and that no commission or finder's fee is payable to Tenant or any third party upon consummation of this transaction __*[with the exception of ______]*__. *[Give details of parties to whom a brokerage or finder's fee is payable, the amounts thereof, and how such parties are to be paid.]*

21. Representations and Warranties. The escrow instructions and the ground lease shall give Tenant customary representations, warranties and indemnities concerning all information provided by Landlord, and other matters, such as but not limited to, environmental conditions, title, the absence of undisclosed liabilities or material facts regarding the site or Tenant's intended development, claims, litigation and financial matters.

Consider the judicious use of any representations or warranties necessary to protect Tenant. Typically, the negotiation of representations and warranties is resolved by the lawyers documenting the final agreement between the parties. [See, however, Chapter 18, Form 18-20, "Selected Representations and Warranties for Lease Transactions," for a listing of various representations and warranties clauses which could be negotiated and inserted. Reading such clauses and carefully thinking about the specific transaction at hand may encourage refinements to the draft proposal. Two basic representations are listed below.

21.1 Landlord's Authority. Landlord represents that the party listed under the heading "Landlord" on the signature page herein is the sole owner of the entire right, title and interest in and to the site and has the right to lease it to Tenant.

21.2 Site Protection. Landlord represents it will not allow the site to be used as a dump site and that no debris will be left on the site at close of escrow. Other than normal, minor modifications resulting from Tenant's soils, environmental or other consultants investigating the site on behalf of Tenant, Landlord will maintain the site in its current condition through close of escrow __*[e.g., subject to assessment district improvements or other permitted approvals or modifications to the site approved by Landlord and Tenant and made during escrow]*__.

Note: *Most developers desire to limit their liability to the landowner in the event of a breach of the escrow agreement by agreeing to pay the landowner a specified sum as liquidated damages. The amount of liquidated damages can be the subject of extensive negotiations. The requirements for an enforceable liquidated damages provision may vary from state to state.*

Alternative "A"—Paragraph 22

Final escrow instructions to contain a liquidated damages clause limiting damages recoverable by Landlord to amounts deposited and released to Landlord through escrow:

22. <u>Tenant's Default</u>. The escrow instructions shall contain a liquidated damages provision providing that if Tenant defaults under any Tenant obligation, Landlord's exclusive remedy shall be to retain amounts theretofore deposited with or paid to escrow holder and released to Landlord.

OR

Alternative "B"—Paragraph 22

The following provision is based on California law and attempts to preserve Tenant's right to specific performance in the event of Landlord's breach, yet limit damages recoverable by Landlord (upon Tenant's breach) to Tenant's deposit(s) released through escrow to Landlord. The large pitch type and separate initialing are required under California law. Before using this form, non-lawyers should consult a real estate attorney in the state in which the real property to be ground leased is located in order to insure that the liquidated damages provision complies with local law.

22. <u>Remedies</u>. The escrow instructions shall contain the following provision: Tenant shall, in addition to all other rights provided herein or as may be provided by law, be entitled to specific performance and injunctive relief to enforce its rights hereunder in the event of a breach by Landlord, it being understood hereby because of the special and unique character of the site and the proposed project thereon, a remedy at law would be inadequate to compensate Tenant for any default of Landlord under this agreement.

IN THE EVENT TENANT IS IN MATERIAL DEFAULT IN THE PERFORMANCE OR OBSERVANCE OF ANY COVENANT, CONDITION OR AGREEMENT OF TENANT CONTAINED IN THIS CONTRACT, THE SOLE AND EXCLUSIVE REMEDY OF LANDLORD AGAINST TENANT SHALL BE LANDLORD'S RETENTION OF THE INITIAL DEPOSIT AND THE EXTENSION DEPOSITS THERETOFORE DEPOSITED WITH OR PAID TO ESCROW HOLDER AND RELEASED TO LANDLORD PURSUANT TO THE TERMS AND PROVISIONS HEREOF. BECAUSE IT WOULD BE IMPRACTICAL OR EXTREMELY DIFFICULT TO FIX ACTUAL DAMAGE, SUCH SUM IS THE AMOUNT OF DAMAGE PRESUMED THAT LANDLORD WOULD SUSTAIN BY REASON OF ANY SUCH DEFAULT BY TENANT, AND TENANT DESIRES TO LIMIT ITS LIABILITY HEREUNDER TO SUCH SUM. LANDLORD AGREES TO LOOK SOLELY TO SUCH SUM FOR SATISFACTION OF ANY OF LANDLORD'S REMEDIES FOR THE COLLECTION OF A JUDGMENT OR OTHER JUDICIAL PROCESS REQUIRING THE PAYMENT OF MONEY BY TENANT TO LANDLORD IN THE EVENT OF DEFAULT BY TENANT HEREUNDER.

____________ Landlord's Initials   ____________ Tenant's Initials

End of Alternatives "A" and "B" to Paragraph 22
—Continue to Paragraph 23

23. Non-binding. When signed by Tenant and Landlord, this agreement shall constitute a non-binding letter of intent subject to mutual approval and execution of _*[final escrow instructions and the ground lease]*_. The parties do not intend this letter to be a binding agreement between them and no contract will exist based upon this writing or the verbal communications of the parties. No contract between the parties shall arise unless or until such comprehensive formal _*[agreements]*_ covering all terms of the proposed transaction are signed by the parties and approved by legal counsel for each.

The developer's lawyer will typically prepare final escrow instructions and the ground lease consistent with this letter. The developer's objective should be to reach a comprehensive business agreement on all major deal points.

A lawyer could revise this letter agreement to constitute a binding agreement for attachment to a title company's typical boilerplate escrow cover sheet and fine print standard conditions (in which

case the preceding "Non-binding" paragraph would be omitted and other modifications to the form would be made). (Form 17-7, in Chapter 17, is an example of a purchase agreement "Binding Agreement" clause (which must be amended for use in a lease proposal context.) Form 17-7 should only be used with advice of legal counsel.)

Caveat: *In this and each of the other deal-making documents in this sourcebook, state in your document and manifest by consistent conduct whether or not the document is intended to be a binding contract. Except for readers with legal training and in those cases where the proposal has been reviewed by the user's legal counsel, the document should specifically state that the writing is not intended to be a legally binding agreement. Avoid ambiguous writing and conduct and always act in good faith, whether or not the writing is a final agreement. While the prevailing view may be that letters of intent are not binding, parties' conduct at the time of and after execution of a letter of intent has been introduced to prove a binding contract, even though the parties stated in writing that there was no intention to be bound. Be careful and avoid being misunderstood. Consistently establish and maintain a reasonable but firm deadline for preparation and signing of formal documents.*

24. Miscellaneous.

Note: *Generally, an attorney's fees clause would not be included in a letter of intent.*

24.1 Attorney's Fees. __*[While each party shall be responsible for paying its own legal fees in the negotiation and documentation of the proposed transaction,]*__ in the event an action is brought by either party to enforce the terms of __*[the escrow or the ground lease]*__ or for damages resulting from a breach of __*[either]*__ agreement, the prevailing party in such action shall be entitled to reasonable attorney's fees, costs and expenses in connection with the prosecution or defense of such action.

24.2 Prorations. Real and personal property taxes and assessments (if any) shall be prorated between the parties as of the close of escrow.

24.3 Counterparts. The parties agree that this proposal and any r· vision of the escrow instructions relating hereto may be signed in counter- and that when signed by all parties, such counterparts shall constitute the signed agreement by all the parties.

Alternative "A"—Paragraph 25
Tenant (developer) oriented

25. Time Limit. This proposal shall terminate at __*[e.g., 5:00]*__ p.m. on _______, 20__ unless written acceptance is received by Tenant on or before such date __*[and is contingent upon Tenant and Landlord executing final escrow instructions* __*[and the ground lease]*__ __*[and opening escrow]*__ at __*[XYZ Title Company]*__ *not later than _______, 20__]*__.

OR

Alternative "B"—Paragraph 25
Landlord (landowner) oriented

25. Time Limit. This proposal shall terminate at __*[e.g., 5:00]*__ p.m. on ______, 20__ unless written acceptance is received by Tenant on or before such date __*[and is contingent upon Tenant and Landlord executing final escrow instructions* __*[and the ground lease]*__ __*[and opening escrow]*__ *not later than _____, 20__]*__. In the event the parties do not execute the escrow instructions and the ground lease and open escrow on or before 5:00 p.m. on _______, 20__, Landlord shall have the right to lease the site to other parties without any obligation to Tenant and the right to hold the site off the market, even if the parties are engaged in good faith negotiations for the site on __*[insert same, preceding date]*__, 20__.

End of Alternatives "A" and "B" to Paragraph 25
—Continue to Paragraph 26

26. Confidentiality and Good Faith. Beginning with the date this letter is signed by Landlord and continuing throughout the period ending ______, 20__, *[insert, for example, second date in preceding paragraph]* Landlord and Landlord's agents shall not disclose the terms of this proposed transaction to any third party (except Landlord's legal and accounting advisors, who, Landlord warrants, shall be obligated not to communicate such information to others) nor will Landlord negotiate with any third party for the sale, lease or joint development of the site.

If the foregoing is acceptable as to the terms and conditions upon which __*[you]*__ OR __*[name of entity]*__ will ground lease the site to Tenant, please so indicate on the signature line provided below and return a signed copy to me.

Very truly yours,

[Name of Tenant entity]

[name of individual signing]
[capacity]

Attachments (as referenced)
cc: __*[Tenant's broker/others]*__

<u>UNDERSTOOD AND AGREED BY "LANDLORD"</u>:

This __ day of ___________, 20__.

Alternative "A"

XYZ CORPORATION

By: _________________
[name]
[capacity]

Date: ________, 20__

Alternative "B"

XYZ PARTNERSHIP, a
__*[state]*__*[general/limited]*__ partnership,

By: _________________
[name]
General Partner

Date: ________, 20__

By: __________________
[name]
General Partner

Date: ________, 20__

Add when lawyer prepares as binding agreement:
Accepted for Escrow Purposes:

__*[Name]*__ Title Insurance Company

By: ________________
Escrow Officer

[Carefully review and attach exhibits, in this example, "A" through "D":]

Exhibit "A"
[Assessor's parcel map or plat map referenced in Paragraph 3]

Exhibit "B"
[Preliminary site plan referenced in Paragraph 3]

Exhibit "C"
[An exhibit could also be used to depict the adjacent land subject to the "Adjacent Owner Escrow" referenced in Paragraph 4. Make liberal use of exhibits to clarify your proposal.]

Exhibit "D"
Summary of Ground Lease Terms
[Edit and insert the "Summary of Ground Lease Terms" attached as an exhibit to Form 5-1]

END OF FORM B-1

Appendix C: Approaches to Rent

Typical Shopping Center Developer Approaches to Rent.

Historically, rental yields generally follow but do not coincide with prevailing long term interest rates. The following are various "rule of thumb" approaches to rent negotiation:

Margin—115% of total costs (land, building & soft) multiplied by loan constant = minimum rent payable. For example, if loan constant equals 11.8 (11.5%, 30 yr.), requested rent = .1357 multiplied by total costs. (1.15 x .118 = 13.57% times total costs). [Cf. "Cap Rate" approach, below.]

Cap Rate—Annual return on total costs = 6%-12% "capitalization rate".

Traditional Approach—10%-11% return on land value and 12%-14% return on building and soft costs.

Other Factors Affecting Developer's Final Decision

Anticipated Sales Volume—What sales volume can be reasonably expected and to what extent can this be translated into percentage rent?

Benefits to Center—Factors include: Perceived tenant operating skill and ability to create high volume occupancy contributing to vitality of the shopping center as a whole, creditworthiness of tenant and ability to pre-sell/finance build-to-suit or other form of tenant leasehold.

Tenant Mix/Site Planning—To what extent is tenant desired to satisfy a perceived need not easily duplicated by alternate tenant(s)? Consider also the physical "fit" of tenant within site plan or particular space configuration compared to alternative occupants.

Risk Assessment—Factors include: Extent to which building and interest costs are known (and likelihood that funds advanced by the developer for tenant building improvements will be of value to any successor tenant), relationship with and knowledge of tenant's line of business, general business conditions and forecast relative to tenant's line of business, tenant's operating condition relative to competition, and lease documentation (to whom is it favorable, e.g., how tight are use and assignment clauses—who gets "bonus value", if any, on assignment?), etc.

Intangible—Integrity, flexibility, and ability to obtain required approvals and cooperatively resolve problems quickly and cooperatively as they arise; perceived commitment to quickly consummate and complete the transaction.

Appendix D: Project File Index

The following is an example of a generic project's "paper" file organizatition which is consistent with the hierarchical, computerized deal-making document form file system discussed in Chapter 19.

Form D-1

Project File Index for File Cabinet Organization

Project File Index:
[Name] Shopping Center

1. Site Acquisition

1.1 Offers/Correspondence
1.2 Option/Purchase Contract
1.3 Title
1.4 Escrow
1.5 City/County Development Agreement

2. Pro Formas

3. Marketing

3.1 Marketing Info/Demographics
3.2 Broker/Listing Agreement(s)
3.3 Prospective Tenants

4. Major Tenant(s)

4.1 __*[XYZ Major Tenant]*__ Final Agreements
  4.1.1 __*[XYZ Major Tenant]*__ draft Agreements and Correspondence
4.2 __*[XYZ Major Co-Tenant]*__ Final Agreements
  4.2.1 __*[XYZ Major Co-Tenant]*__ draft Agreements and Correspondence

5. Partnerships *[Or Development Fee Agreements]*

5.1 Joint Venture Agreement
  5.1.1 __*[Name of Financial Partner]*__ Final Joint Venture Agreement
  5.1.2 __*[Name of Financial Partner]*__ Joint Venture Draft Agreements and Correspondence
5.2 Partnership Agreement *[For developer equity participants]*
  5.2.1 Final Partnership Agreement *[For developer equity participants]*
  5.2.2 Partnership Draft Agreements & Correspondence *[For developer equity participants]*

6. <u>Entitlements</u>

6.1 Site Approval
6.2 Parcel/Tract Map Approval
6.3 Signage
6.4 Other *[set up separate files, e.g., Army Corps of Engineers, Fish & Game, etc.]*

7. <u>Consultants</u>

7.1 Architect __*[name]*__
    7.1.1 Preliminary Site Planning
    7.1.2 Final A.I.A. Contract & Work
7.2 Civil Engineer __*[name]*__
    7.2.1 Preliminary T & M
    7.2.2 Grading Plan
    7.2.3 On/Off-Site Improvement Plans
    7.2.4 Parcel/Tract Map
    7.2.5 Construction Staking
7.3 Soils engineer __*[name]*__
7.4 Hazardous Materials/Environmental __*[name]*__
7.5 Paleontologist __*[name]*__
7.6 Traffic Engineer __*[name]*__
7.7 Landscape architect __*[name]*__

8. <u>Loans</u>

8.1 Purchase Money Note
8.2 Construction Loan With __*[name of lender]*__
8.3 Permanent Loan With __*[name of lender]*__

9. <u>Construction</u>

9.1 General Contractor
    9.1.1 __*[Name]*__ Construction Contract
    9.1.2 Budgets/Building & Site
9.2 Permits

10. <u>Insurance</u>

10.1 Course of Construction/Liability
10.2 Permanent

11. Project Lease Forms

11.1 Percentage Lease
11.2 Non-Percentage Lease
11.3 Option—C.P.I.
11.4 Option—Market Rate
11.5 Exhibit "A" (Site Plan)
11.6 Exhibit "B" (Legal Description)
11.7 Exhibit "C" (Work Letter)
11.8 Exhibit "D" (Sign Criteria)
11.9 Exhibit "E" (Rules and Regulations)
11.10 Exhibit "F" (Guarantee of Lease)

12. Tenant Files

12.1 __*[ABC Service Station]*__ Final Ground Lease
  12.1.1 __*[ABC Tenant]*__ Lease Drafts & Correspondence.
12.2 __*[Create separate files, as above, for each tenant]*__

13. Management *[break down as necessary]*

14. Accounting

14.1 Chart of Accounts
14.2 Project Invoices
14.3 Taxes & Assessments

END OF FORM D-1

A

B

C

M

O

-This Form May Be Photocopied-

QUICK ORDER FORM

SHOPPING CENTER DEALMAKER'S HANDBOOK® comes with "Forms CD" software, which will be sent to purchaser's email address upon proof of purchase.

3 Ways to Order

FAX **Complete this form and FAX to 24-hour fax line: (949) 852-1050.**

PHONE **Call (949) 275-5407. Have your credit card ready.**

MAIL **Mail this form with check payable in U.S. dollars to Business Source Publishing Co.®**
18201 Von Karman Ave., Suite 310, Irvine CA 92612; www.ShoppingCenterDealMakersHandbook.com

ORDER
Please send me _____ copies of SHOPPING CENTER DEALMAKER'S HANDBOOK® @ $140 each, including email of "Forms CD" software upon proof of purchase. "Forms CD" is not sold separately. Do not use Forms software separate from the Handbook®.

PAYMENT ❑ Check enclosed made payable in U.S. funds to Business Source Publishing Co. (address above)

Charge to my ❑ Visa ❑ MasterCard ❑ Am Express:*

No. _________-_________-_________-_________ __________ Exp. Date

________________________________ Name on Card

________________________________ Authorizing Signature (required for credit approval)

*Credit cards not charged until product is shipped

Daytime Phone: ____________________________

Email Address: ____________________________

SHIPPING

Size: One book: 9" x 12" x 2" (5 lbs.)

U.S Destinations: (fill in order form from chart below)

FedEx	Western U.S.*	Eastern U.S.*	Hawaii	Alaska
❑ 2 Day (no Sat. deliv.)	$25	$31	N/A	N/A
❑ Express Saver (4 bus. days)	$21	$22	$57	$48
❑ Ground (5 bus. days)	$17	$16	$41	$38

* West v. East of Mississippi River

International Destinations:
❑ Email bzimmerman@ClarionConsultsUSA.com the country and postal code for shipping quote.
FedEx Intl. Priority (2 days) USPS Priority Mail
FedEx Intl Economy (5 days) (6-10 days, most countries)
❑ Bill to Buyer's FedEx Account
Account Number: ____________________
Name of Account Holder: ____________________
International orders may be subject to additional customs and duty fees.

Books .... $ __________

Sales tax (8% on..................... $ __________
California deliveries)

Shipping and Handling
(from table below)
____ books x $______ per book = $ __________

TOTAL .... $__________

ORDERED BY

Name

Address (Sorry, we cannot ship to P.O. boxes)

City

State & ZIP

Daytime Phone

Email Address

SHIP TO (if different)

Name

Address (Sorry, we cannot ship to P.O. boxes)

City

State & ZIP

Daytime Phone

Email Address

❑ I am interested in receiving information about seminars by the author on this subject.

All prices subject to change. Call for current price and shipping information.

NOTE: Book's on-demand printer can not send "Forms CD" with the book. The "Forms CD" software will be emailed to purchaser's email address with proof of purchase. Email or mail a copy of your purchase receipt to Business Source Publishing Co. See address under "3 Ways to Order," above.

RETURN POLICY: This is a software package consisting of the Handbook® and its electronic "deal-making" Forms in Word®. This system has been extensively reviewed and endorsed by leading U.S. legal and real estate journals and no buyer has requested a return of the first edition. This second edition is printed on demand from five locations in the world, with the licensed software distributed separately from the publisher to the consumer upon purchase. Please purchase the system with confidence but system is not returnable. The very low purchase price is designed to get the system into the hands of every interested real estate professional.

Form Code: 2

www.ingramcontent.com/pod-product-compliance
Lightning Source LLC
LaVergne TN
LVHW062152200926
848484LV00007B/1902